THE DEMES OF ATTICA

THE DEMES OF ATTICA

508/7–CA. 250 B.C.

A POLITICAL AND
SOCIAL STUDY

by

David Whitehead

PRINCETON UNIVERSITY PRESS

Copyright © 1986 by Princeton University Press

Published by Princeton University Press, 41 William Street,
Princeton, New Jersey 08540
In the United Kingdom: Princeton University Press, Guildford, Surrey

Library of Congress Cataloging in Publication Data will be
found on the last printed page of this book

ISBN 0-691-09412-8

Publication of this book has been aided by grants from
the National Endowment for the Humanities and
the Whitney Darrow Fund of Princeton University Press

This book has been composed in Linotron Sabon

Clothbound editions of Princeton University Press books
are printed on acid-free paper, and binding materials are
chosen for strength and durability

Printed in the United States of America by Princeton University Press
Princeton, New Jersey

CONTENTS

LIST OF ILLUSTRATIONS

CONVENTIONS AND ABBREVIATIONS

1. The Sources: Literary Texts

The names of some ancient writers and/or their works are abbreviated to a degree not, I would hope, incompatible with their remaining self-explanatory. Recourse to the "Index of Passages Cited," where full versions are given, should resolve any problems of identification. I have used the Oxford or (failing that) the Teubner texts where they exist; otherwise the text cited is that of the most recent scholarly edition.

The fragments of historical writing follow the numeration (and text) of F. Jacoby, *Die Fragmente der griechischen Historiker [FGrH]*, Berlin and Leiden, 1923-1958.

The fragments of Attic Comedy follow, unless otherwise stated, the numeration (and text) of T. Kock, *Comicorum Atticorum Fragmenta [CAF]*, three volumes, Leipzig, 1880-1888. Only for later material have I used—with caution—J. M. Edmonds, *The Fragments of Attic Comedy after Meineke, Bergk, and Kock [FAC]*, three volumes in four, Leiden, 1957-1961.

2. The Sources: Epigraphic Texts

Inscriptions are normally cited by their number in *Inscriptiones Graecae* [IG] where such a number exists, but sometimes a superior text is to be found elsewhere, as indicated. For more recent discoveries a reference to the *Supplementum Epigraphicum Graecum* [SEG] will usually replace an original notice or *editio princeps*, even in *Hesperia* (which I foreshorten to *Hesp.*). The "key" reference to frequently cited inscriptions is given in Appendix 3. Both there and in general the following abbreviations are employed:

Agora 15   B. D. Meritt and J. S. Traill, *The Athenian Agora, XV, Inscriptions: The Athenian Councillors*, Princeton, 1974 (Occasional citation of other *Agora* volumes will take this same form.)

Dedications   A. E. Raubitschek (with L. H. Jeffery), *Dedications from the Athenian Akropolis*, Cambridge, Mass., 1949

Lois   F. Sokolowski, *Lois sacrées des cités grecques*, Paris, 1969

Lois, Suppl.   F. Sokolowski, *Lois sacrées des cités grecques: Supplément,* Paris, 1962

ML   R. Meiggs and D. M. Lewis, *A Selection of Greek Historical Inscriptions to the end of the fifth century B.C.*, Oxford, 1969

Pachturkunden   D. Behrend, *Attische Pachturkunden: ein Beitrag zur Beschreibung der μίσθωσις nach der griechischen Inschriften,* Vestigia 12, Munich, 1970

Syll.   W. Dittenberger, *Sylloge Inscriptionum Graecarum,* 3d ed., Leipzig, 1915-1924 (unchanged in the Hildesheim "edition" of 1960)

Tod   M. N. Tod, *A Selection of Greek Historical Inscriptions,* vol. 2, Oxford, 1948

Wünsch   R. Wünsch, *Inscriptiones Graecae* III, Appendix: *defixionum tabellae Atticae,* Berlin, 1897

3. Modern Works

Books and articles cited by author and short title are listed as the "Select Bibliography." Both there and in general the titles of periodical journals are abbreviated on the system of *L'Année philologique*, with two exceptions: for the *Mitteilungen des Deutschen Archäologischen Instituts, Athenische Abteilung,* I use *AM,* the abbreviation latterly sanctioned by that publication itself; and *Hesp.,* as already stated, stands for *Hesperia.*
    Note also the following:

LSJ   H. G. Liddell and R. Scott, *A Greek-English Lexicon,* 9th ed., revised H. S. Jones, Oxford, 1940

PA   J. Kirchner, *Prosopographia Attica,* two vols., Berlin, 1901 and 1903 (Note that PA numerals designate entries, not page numbers.)

RE   Pauly-Wissowa, *Real-Encyclopädie der classischen Altertumswissenschaft,* Stuttgart, 1893-

4. Numbers in Bold-face Type

These refer to the numbered entries (**1-368**) in the Prosopography.

PREFACE

The need has long been recognized for a modern counterpart to Bernard Haussoullier's classic study of the internal organization and activities of the Attic demes, *La Vie Municipale en Attique* (Paris, 1884). Its combination of complete mastery of the ancient source-material then available, an enviable Gallic felicity of expression, and a secure faith in the value of its subject made it one of the outstanding books about ancient Athenian society of its age; and the Arno Press reprint (New York, 1979) is thus a welcome one. Yet the more fundamental the subject—and Haussoullier's claims, for his, are amply justified—the more lamentable that in order to gain intimate acquaintance with it one must still resort to a treatise written a full century ago, with all that that implies for the extent of the evidence then in existence and for the questions which a scholar of that epoch thought to ask of it. If the terms of Alfred North Whitehead's famous exaggeration about Plato and the course of Western philosophy may be borrowed by a namesake (though no relation), I am tempted to maintain that modern work on "municipal life" in classical Attica has for a hundred years now amounted to little more than footnotes to Haussoullier.

The present book, as will be seen, is at times positively bottom-heavy with footnotes, literal or figurative, which aim to do justice not only to Haussoullier but to every scholar whose work I have read with profit. First and foremost, though, I have sought to make a fresh start: to set out *in extenso* old data as well as new, and to juxtapose new problems with old, in the conviction that one of the most important and all-pervading institutions of classical Athenian society ought again to be the subject of a full, synoptic treatment.

It could hardly be claimed that the present moment is a uniquely opportune one (except insofar as it may be taken to mark the Haussoullier centennial) for such a conflation of monograph and manual. All the same, the task of anyone who works on the Attic demes has become a lighter one during the decade since the publication of John Traill's *The Political Organization of Attica* (1975). Quibble as one may with some of the conclusions and hypotheses of Traill's magisterial tome, it is, for the matters with which it deals, a marvellous *vademecum*.

Through their writings or in less formal ways, other experts and friends too have helped to bring the present book into being, and it is the most pleasant of duties to record my thanks to them here—though in doing so I should not be understood to be inculpating others in a project for which the prime responsibility, of conception and execution alike, is wholly my own.

To the undergraduate lectures of Geoffrey Woodhead in Cambridge in 1971-1972 I owe an embryonic appreciation of the place of the demes in Athenian political and social life, and of the stature of Haussoullier's study of them. (I am also grateful to Mr. Woodhead for a service both more recent and more tangible, that of providing me with a text of the two fragmentary deme decrees which he will be including in *Agora 16*, and of discussion of various points arising from them. Epigraphic aid of other kinds has been rendered, from time to time, by David Lewis, Ronald Stroud, John Traill, and Michael Walbank). When plans for my own *Vie Municipale* began to crystallize, in 1980, valuable criticism and support came from Sir Moses Finley and, in particular, John Davies. I am acutely conscious that either of these scholars, had he cared to tackle my subject for himself, would have produced a book more innovative and challenging than mine, but it is some consolation to reflect that almost anyone seeking guidance from such quarters would (or should) be forced to a similar admission. At all events I hope that they will not feel their help and encouragement squandered.

In 1981-1982 I was privileged to go to Princeton as Visiting Member (and Herodotus Fellow) of the School of Historical Studies in the Institute for Advanced Study—financial support being provided by the Institute itself, together with the (American) National Endowment for the Humanities and the Fulbright-Hays Program—and there, in delightful surroundings and with unrivalled academic amenities, my real work began. There can be few richer prizes for the ancient historian than a year at the Institute, where scholarship and friendship alike are so freely exchanged, and for an abundance of both my warmest thanks must go to Christian Habicht (and his sometime assistant Steve Bradford), to Homer Thompson, to Glen Bowersock, to Martin Ostwald, fellow visitor and daily fund of wisdom and companionship, and to a host of others. At nearby Princeton University Professors Connor, Keaney, and Luce extended the hospitality and expertise of the Department of Classics; and the opportunity to present some "work in progress" to a Californian audience, at Stanford, was genially granted by Michael Jameson.

Since reluctantly leaving the New World and resuming old commitments I have inevitably proceeded more solitarily as well as more slowly, but various sources of assistance (of disparate kinds) should be mentioned. My Danish friends Mogens Herman Hansen of the University of Copenhagen and Signe Isager of Odense University have given timely encouragement as well as aid on particular points. Another friend, my former student Jane Laughton, has helped me to clarify some views about the working relationship between demes and tribes. And I must acknowledge a heavy debt of gratitude to Robin Osborne of King's College, Cambridge, who since 1982 has generously kept me in touch with the evolution of his work on classical Attica—to the extent, now, of allowing me (with the agreement of Cambridge University Press) to see and utilize a proof copy of his book *Demos: the discovery of classical Attika*, scheduled for publication in 1985. Dr. Osborne and I differ in the weight we attach to the institutional structure of the demes as a determinant of life in the classical Athenian polis, and insofar as he offers new theories about deme institutions *per se* I have found them largely unconvincing. We share many common interests nonetheless, and the validity of our conclusions about most of the broader aspects of the deme/polis relationship cannot but be vindicated by the fact that we have reached them independently of each other and from significantly different starting-points.

In writing the present book, a foolproof solution to the problem of how to treat Greek proper names has eluded me as it has others. The negligent approach advocated by T. E. Lawrence in his preface to *Seven Pillars of Wisdom* ("I spell my names anyhow, to show what rot the systems are") is less justifiable, however, with regard to Greek names than to his Arabic ones, and I can only point out here that my practice has been more systematic than might appear at first sight. I retain such English (e.g. Athens) and Latin (e.g. Attica) forms as are entrenched in common usage, but adopt direct transliteration from Greek for the great majority of place names, including the names of all demes. Most personal names too are in transliterated form; but I have preferred the traditional latinized (e.g. Thucydides) or even occasional anglicized (e.g. Aristotle) versions of the names of Greek *authors*—recognizing, to be sure, that such attempted categorization may in practice leave a small residue of anomalies.

Another practical problem is posed by the Greek language itself. While writing this book it seemed to me only prudent to contemplate who its readers might be, and to bear in mind that for some of them, perhaps these days the majority, an encounter with untranslated Greek would spell delay or even bafflement. I have therefore done my utmost—by means of translation, transliteration, and circumlocution—to make at least the text of the book fully accessible to those who did not, as I did, spend their adolescent years grappling with the language of Aristophanes, Demosthenes, and the Athenian stone-cutters. For the handful of occasions where this did not prove practicable I apologize in advance. The notes are another matter, however. There I have been unable, and indeed unwilling, to compromise my overall aim of producing a study pitched at the highest level of traditional classical scholarship of which I am capable. As such books appeal nowadays to an ever-diminishing minority of publishers in my own country, I count myself fortunate to have seen mine accepted by Princeton University Press, with its fine and continuing tradition in the fields of classics and ancient history. The prospect of my work's being published in Princeton, where so much of it took shape, has been the source of deeply pleasurable anticipation to me, and I am greatly beholden to Mrs. Joanna Hitchcock, the readers, and the staff of the Press for all their efforts in its realization. As I write, the burdens of proofreading still lie ahead, but they are to be shared with a master of the craft, Tony Birley.

I conclude on a personal note with grateful thanks to my wife Mary, who took the photograph of the Thorikos *fasti* inscription and who, together with our daughters Penelope and Harriet, has made sure that my long preoccupation with the demes only rarely exceeded reasonable bounds.

DAVID WHITEHEAD
Department of History, Manchester
October 1, 1984

INTRODUCTION

———————— ✳ ————————

"If the [Athenian] citizen, individually in office, and, more important, collectively in deliberation, played such a large part, how was his practical wisdom developed and brought out by experience, so that he was not at a loss in state affairs, and only occasionally not perpetually deluded? How was that travesty of good judgment, opinion without information, avoided as far as possible? Above all, how did the citizens get to know each other: an essential for those who take it in turns to rule and be ruled? [. . .] Here comes in something which I think has been too much neglected by ancient and modern students of the Athenian democracy, namely, the infra-structure (if I may be allowed to use that term) of the Athenian state organization [. . .] A man who knew his deme business would not be lost in state business. Above all a man would know his fellows."

In the interstices between these three quoted extracts, R. J. Hopper, newly appointed Professor of Ancient History at the University of Sheffield, sought to explain to his audience in 1957 what he perceived to be one fundamental element in *The Basis of the Athenian Democracy*.[1] It was the network of demes (δῆμοι, *dēmoi*), the local constituent wards within the city of Athens itself and the villages and hamlets of rural Attica. Created (he explained) by Kleisthenes in the late sixth century,[2] the system of the demes, together with the ten tribes (*phylai*) into which they were grouped, formed not only the political and demographic "infra-structure" of the classical Athenian polis but also one of the most obvious explanations, for us, of the success with which radical, participatory democracy functioned in fifth- and fourth-century Athens. After Kleisthenes, the Athenian citizen-body was precisely defined as the totality of adult males with registered membership of these demes, the smallest subdivisions of the polis; and, as Hopper observed, the operation of the Athenian democracy rested both structurally and actually upon a basis of activity and effort at the levels of deme and tribe. It was a structural basis, in that the mechanics of appointment to both the city council (the *boulē*) and the numerous boards of city magistrates, which together com-

[1] Hopper, *Basis*, pp. 13, 14, 17.
[2] All ancient dates in this book are B.C. unless otherwise indicated.

prised the constitutional executive, took account of the need to draw from all localities within Attica. And it was an actual basis, in that such a constitution, entailing as it did the active annual participation of large numbers of men willing and able to hold office, could hardly have been a working reality—or so Professor Hopper reasoned—without some opportunity for administrative and political apprenticeship at a lower, parochial level. For the demes were not only subdivisions of central government but self-contained and self-determining units of local government in their own right. A deme chose various officials, headed by a *dēmarchos*, to administer its affairs in accordance with resolutions passed by an assembly of all the demesmen. It owned property; it levied (and spent) income; it organized local cults and festivals. It was tantamount to a polis in microcosm.

Hopper's modest summary—less than a thousand words, all told—of the nature and significance of the Kleisthenic demes has achieved more in the way of both celebrity and longevity than its author can have anticipated; for it stands, at least in terms of English and English-speaking scholarship, in a remarkable academic vacuum. A generation on, there is still nothing else which can be cited so conveniently on the subject.[3] But more interesting and important is the matter of its antecedents. None were acknowledged, beyond the primary sources themselves; and (as we have seen) Hopper believed that this aspect of his chosen theme had been "too much neglected by ancient and modern students" alike. Half of this claim is true: no ancient commentator on the Athenian democratic system informs us that the demes played a crucial role therein. But the other half is false. In scholarship as in anything else the wheel can only be invented once; and whether Professor Hopper was aware of it or not, his subject had been set upon solid and durable foundations almost three quarters of a century earlier.

*

The course of serious scholarly interest in and knowledge of the Attic demes since the early decades of the nineteenth century—to regress no further than that—can be traced as two distinct strands.

The more continuous and substantial of the two is research into *the archaeology and topography of the demes*. Here clear progress has been made and continues to this day. Following in the footsteps of Pausanias and his periegetic predecessors, such scholar-travellers of the early nine-

---

[3] See for instance Ostwald, *Nomos*, p. 153 (and in his discussion of Kleisthenes in the second edition of the *Cambridge Ancient History*, part II, chap. 6, forthcoming); Rhodes, *Commentary*, p. 256.

teenth century as Dodwell, Fauvel, Niebuhr, and Pittakys[4] tested the ancient topographic and antiquarian accounts against the rural Attica of their own times, observing archaeological and onomastic relics and, where possible, suggesting identifications between the demes of antiquity and contemporary settlements. In addition they made copies of the local inscriptions which their excursions brought to light; and when the first volume of August Boeckh's *Corpus Inscriptionum Graecarum (CIG)* appeared, in 1828, it rightly found room for a handful of documents from the Attic demes and others pertaining to them. There followed half a century of steady increase both in archaeological and topographical work and in the epigraphical documentation which was its byproduct. Colonel Leake's *Demi of Attica* ran to two editions and a German translation.[5] Hermann Sauppe made an influential study of the demes of the city of Athens itself;[6] and the same year, 1846, saw a treatise on the demes "and their distribution amongst the tribes, according to inscriptions" by Ludwig Ross.[7]

With the work of Ross in particular, purely topographical investigation[8] into the location of demes had begun already, it is clear, to take on extra significance. The new epigraphical sources were by then revealing fuller details of Kleisthenes' three-tiered demographic and constitutional order—demes, trittyes, tribes; and the need to fit individual topographic identifications into a coherent overview of the system as a whole is plain to see in the labors of the two preeminent Attic topographers of the last quarter of the nineteenth century, Milchhöfer[9] and Löper.[10] It was Arthur Milchhöfer who was called upon to supply more than forty entries on individual demes for the early fascicles of the *Real-Encyclopädie*, and the relay of others who succeeded him in that task[11] were content for

[4] For their seventeenth- and eighteenth-century precursors, see C. Hanriot, *Recherches sur la topographie des dèmes de l'Attique*, Paris, 1853, pp. xxv-xxxi.

[5] W. M. Leake, *The Topography of Athens and the Demi, Volume II: The Demi of Attica*, 1st ed., London, 1829; German translation by A. Westermann, Braunschweig, 1840; 2d English ed., London, 1841.

[6] H. Sauppe, *De demis urbanis Athenarum*, Leipzig, 1846.

[7] L. Ross, *Die Demen von Attika und ihre Vertheilung unter die Phylen, nach Inschriften*, ed. and annotated M.H.E. Meier, Halle, 1846.

[8] Continued, for example, by Hanriot (see above, n. 4); cf. also the Rev. Christopher Wordsworth's *Athens and Attica: a journal of residence there*, London, 1836.

[9] A. Milchhöfer, "Über Standpunkt und Methode der attischen Demenforschung," *Sitzb. d. Königl. Preuss. Akad. d. Wiss.*, Berlin, 1887, 1 Halbband, pp. 41-56; "Untersuchungen über die Demenordnung des Kleisthenes," *Abh. d. Königl. Preuss. Akad. d. Wiss.*, Berlin, 1892, pp. 3-48; and articles in *AM* between 1887 and 1893. See also his "Erläuternder Text" to the *Karten von Attika* of E. Curtius and J. A. Kaupert, Berlin, 1881-1900.

[10] R. Löper, "Die Trittyen und Demen Attikas," *AM* 17, 1892, pp. 319-433.

[11] Chiefly W. Kolbe, E. Honigmann, W. Wrede, J. Wiesner, and E. Meyer. Note also

the most part to adhere to the methodological principles which he and Löper had been the first to formulate.

Much the most important and far-reaching of these principles was that of the compact geographical trittys. This was the presumption that in each of the thirty trittyes, three per tribe, into which Kleisthenes had grouped his demes (?Aristot. *Ath. Pol.* 21.4) those demes were with very few exceptions contiguous. Thus, given a definite or probable location for at least one deme in every trittys and the means of determining the other demes of that trittys (chiefly by reference to the bouleutic catalogs, Athenian public inscriptions which listed members of the city council in accordance with an *apparent* arrangement of demes in geographical trittys-groupings), one would have an indication of at least the general area in which to look for any particular deme, if no help was forthcoming from a direct appeal to literary, epigraphical, and archaeological evidence. In 1957 Ernst Kirsten, a scholar well versed in Attic cartography,[12] reported to the Third International Epigraphic Congress, in Rome, on "the current state of research into Attic demes."[13] Here the principle of compact geographical trittyes received fresh endorsement. It was vindicated also in the best modern study of the topography and archaeology of a particular group of demes, C.W.J. Eliot's *Coastal Demes of Attika*.[14] And it underpins many of the topographical identifications suggested in what is now the indispensable modern handbook of data about "the demes, trittyes, and phylai, and their representation in the Athenian council," J. S. Traill's *The Political Organization of Attica*.[15]

The principle *may*, however, have been something of a delusion. Apparent violations of it—the so-called "enclaves," where demes are found geographically sundered from what ought on the orthodox view to be their trittys context—have stubbornly refused to be explained away, and the adherents of the system have been driven to ever more Procrustean lengths in order to accommodate them. Furthermore, the methodological foundation of the principle itself, which takes the bouleutic lists as con-

---

H. Hommel's article on the trittyes in *RE* 7 A 1, 1939, cols. 330-370, and *Klio* 33, 1940, pp. 181-200.

[12] See his appendix and notes to A. Philippson, *Die griechischen Landschaften, I: Der Nordosten der griechischen Halbinsel, Teil III, Attika und Megaris*, Frankfurt, 1952; also his map of Attica in *Westermanns Atlas zur Weltgeschichte*, Braunschweig, 1956, p. 13.

[13] E. Kirsten, "Der gegenwärtige Stand der attischen Demenforschung," *Atti del terzo congresso internazionale di epigrafia greca e latina*, Rome, 1957 [1959], pp. 155-171.

[14] See Eliot, *Coastal Demes*, pp. 49, 140, and passim.

[15] Traill, *Organization*, pp. 37-55. He does however point out (ibid., pp. 54-55) that "although the compact trittys was obviously the general rule of the Kleisthenic political organization, there is now no question but that the divided trittys did exist"; see further below, with n. 18.

forming to geographical trittyes, is no longer secure. In 1966 Wesley Thompson offered a radically different explanation of the arrangement and purpose of these documents by reference to the trittyes "of the *prytaneis*" mentioned in ?Aristot. *Ath. Pol.* 44.1. On this basis the rationale behind the groupings of demes in the bouleutic lists was essentially not a topographical one at all, however much topographical relationships might be discerned therein. Its object was instead, Thompson argued, the collocation of groups of demes whose representatives on the council totalled one-third—sixteen or seventeen—of the fifty members drawn from all the demes of a particular tribe (who as the fifty *prytaneis* took on in turn primary responsibility for one-tenth of the administrative year).[16] Thompson's thesis found little favor for some time,[17] but during the last decade or so its attractions have grown more compelling; and the traditional, geographical trittys—and, with it, "the simplest interpretation of *Ath. Pol.* 21.4"—may have to be modified, even discarded.[18]

The *raison d'être* of the trittyes, beyond the self-evident one of linking demes with tribes, thus remains obscure;[19] and little more on the subject will be said in this book. How far the search for trittyes has misdirected the search for demes is a moot point, but in broad terms the controversies of recent years should be seen in the context of what has otherwise, to reiterate, been a tale of steady and encouraging progress for a hundred and fifty years and more.[20] As matters now stand, around two-thirds of

[16] W. E. Thompson, "Τριττὺς τῶν πρυτανέων," *Historia* 15, 1966, pp. 1-10; cf. his "Kleisthenes and Aigeis," *Mnemosyne* 22, 1969, pp. 137-152.

[17] Cf. P. J. Rhodes, "Τριττὺς τῶν πρυτανέων," *Historia* 20, 1971, pp. 385-404; and Traill, *Organization*, pp. 37-55, passim.

[18] J. S. Traill, "Diakris, the inland trittys of Leontis," *Hesp.* 47, 1978, pp. 89-109, at 109 ("Addendum").

[19] The best treatment is arguably still that of Lewis, "Cleisthenes," esp. pp. 27-36; note also D. W. Bradeen, *TAPhA* 86, 1955, pp. 22-30. A thoroughgoing reinterpretation of the whole trittys problem, taking Traill's most recent remarks (reference in the preceding note) as its starting-point and postulating an essentially *military* purpose for the trittyes, is P. Siewert, *Die Trittyen Attikas und die Heeresreform des Kleisthenes*, Vestigia 33, Munich, 1982; see the reviews by D. M. Lewis (*Gnomon* 55, 1983, pp. 431-436) and A. Andrewes (*CR* 33, 1983, pp. 346-347), and, for early absorption into a general account, S. Hornblower, *The Greek World 479-323 B.C.*, London and New York, 1983, p. 113.

[20] For the last half-century much of this progress can be credited to one man: Eugene Vanderpool, sometime Professor of Archaeology at the American School of Classical Studies at Athens, whose painstaking autopsy has made him the supreme Attic topographer of the modern era; witness not only his own published work (listed, up to 1981, in the recent *Festschrift*: *Hesp.* Suppl. 19, 1982, pp. vii-xii) but also the prefaces of numerous books and articles by others. My own book, I reiterate, does not aim to advance our knowledge of deme topography; nor have I made any consistent attempt to evoke the physical setting, archaeology, and monuments of the demes—a task which, given their enormous variety in these respects (cf. Osborne, *Demos*, p. 74), could not properly be couched in generalities

the Kleisthenic demes can be assigned an exact, or else an approximate, location. Map 2 from Traill's *Organization*, reproduced opposite, stands in need of some revision (which Traill himself plans to undertake), but it remains the best that we have at present.

The history of *the internal organization and activities of the demes*, however, is something else entirely; for there has been an almost negligible degree of interplay between this facet of deme studies and the developments summarized so far. A full bibliographical history would be otiose, but again it may be useful to sketch the general picture.

As in so many other areas of Greek, and particularly Athenian, history, the beginning of the modern epoch of research into the interior (so to speak) of the demes is marked out by the appearance and, in consequence, the ever-increasing exploitation of epigraphic evidence. True, there is valuable testimony of other and older kinds. The literary sources—especially the fourth-century orators—and the lexicographers and scholiasts who garnished them provide essential information and insight, and studies which relied exclusively upon literary data are not, even now, to be despised.[21] Nevertheless such work did not, one may now assert, become fully three-dimensional until it began to take account also of epigraphic evidence, whether documenting the internal life of the demes themselves or their relationship with the central government in Athens. Volume I of Boeckh's *CIG* had a relatively small impact in this respect.[22] However, during the ensuing half-century new epigraphical discoveries (and new work on stones already known) accumulated afresh, and so, piecemeal, did a substantial body of material both from and concerning the demes. By 1877, when the four volumes of *CIG* were finally rounded off with a set of indexes, the pressing need for another epigraphic corpus to supersede it had already long been recognized, at any rate as regards the Athenian material. This was the *Corpus Inscriptionum Atticarum (CIA)*, volumes I and II, subsequently redesignated *Inscriptiones Graecae* I and II, the work of Adolf Kirchhoff and Ulrich Köhler; and we need look no further than this, or its early volumes (*CIA* I in 1873; *CIA* II in 1877) for the catalyst of escalating interest in the demes and their doings

---

but would entail description of dozens of individual sites. For this I must refer readers to the scholars cited in the foregoing footnotes, and to others such as Sir James Frazer in his massive commentary on Pausanias. For deme sites, identifiable and unidentifiable by name, see Traill, *Organization*, pp. 37-54, and (selectively) Osborne, *Demos*, Appendix B.

[21] See for instance E. Platner, *Beiträge zur Kenntnis des attischen Rechts*, Marburg, 1820, chap. 6.

[22] Except insofar as it was consulted by, for example, George Grote for his *History of Greece*; see, for Kleisthenes and the demes, volume 3 of the ten-volume re-edition, London, 1888, pp. 346-354.

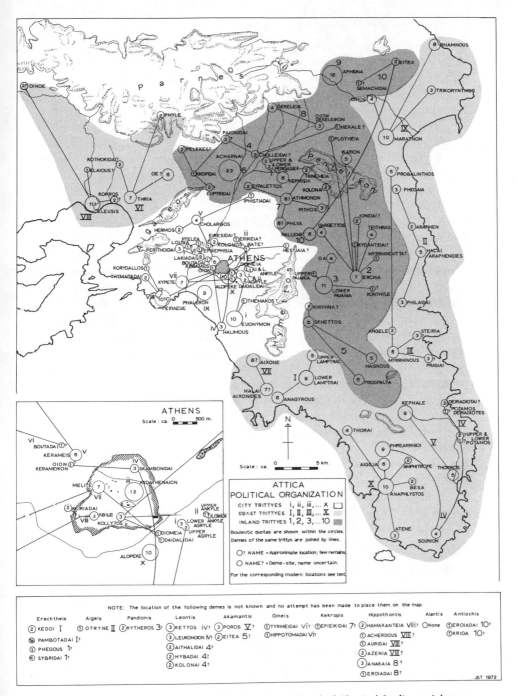

The Kleisthenic demes. Courtesy of the American School of Classical Studies at Athens.

which now followed.[23] For example, Emil Szanto gave full recognition to the central role of the demes in his pioneering treatise on the epigraphic evidence for Athenian citizenship (1881), and included seminal discussions of some deme documents.[24]

But already by then a work devoted exclusively to the demes, in and for themselves, had made its appearance. This was Otto Müller's *de demis atticis*, submitted as a dissertation to the University of Göttingen in 1880 and published in that same year at Nordhausen. In a mere sixty-four pages of scholars' Latin, Müller gave a concise and intelligent exposition of the main areas of his subject, deploying the full range of source material available to him, and showing especial awareness of what, as we shall see, is an all-pervasive methodological problem in deme studies, namely, the extent to which information and conclusions about particular demes can properly be held to apply to demes in general.

Unfortunately for Müller, however, a far more comprehensive study of the Attic demes, destined to eclipse his own efforts, was already in preparation in France. In 1876, Georges Perrot had reported on the work of the French Archaeological Schools in Athens and Rome during the previous year.[25] "La vie politique *de l'État athénien*," he declared, "commence à être assez bien connue; ne s'éclairerait-elle point d'un jour encore plus vif si l'on pouvait nous faire connaître, au moins par une rapide esquisse, *la vie municipale* en Attique?" By *la vie municipale*, as he proceeded to explain, Perrot meant that of the demes, and plainly his remarks were intended as a call for someone to investigate and evaluate the internal life of the demes on a scale commensurate with the accumulated evidence and the acknowledged importance of the topic. The challenge was met. A young French scholar and former student of the French School in Athens, Bernard Charles Louis Marie Haussoullier, began such a work—duly dedicating it to Perrot—and it was published in 1884 as the thirty-eighth volume of the *Bibliothèque* series of the French Schools. Its title was *La Vie Municipale en Attique: essai sur l'organisation des dèmes au quatrième siècle*.[26] A "grundlegendes Werk," pronounced von Schoef-

---

[23] What other contemporary or personal factors came into play is less clear, but a suggestion may be made in one instance: A. Hug's *Bezirke, Gemeinden und Bürgerrecht in Attika* (Freiburg and Tübingen, 1881) shows an insight into the character of the demes considerably sharpened by his familiarity with the cantons of his native Switzerland. Cf. Haussoullier, *Vie*, pp. 208-209.

[24] E. Szanto, *Untersuchungen über das attische Bürgerrecht*, Vienna, 1881.

[25] G. Perrot, *Rapport de la Commission des Écoles d'Athènes et de Rome sur les travaux de ces deux Écoles pendant l'année 1875*, Paris, 1876. I take this reference, and the quotation which now follows, from Haussoullier, *Vie*, p. i, but the emphasis in the quotation is my own.

[26] Its essence was later distilled into Haussoullier's "Demos" entry in C. Daremberg,

fer in 1903;[27] a "grundlegende und erschöpfende Behandlung des bis dahin vorliegenden Stoffes," opined Busolt and Swoboda in 1926[28]—the year of Haussoullier's death.

There was no hyperbole in these assessments: Haussoullier had indeed done the demes proud. Yet the greater the book, the harder it is to follow, and (in consequence) the greater the likelihood of its stifling further advance in the subject. Much of the evidence was cited anew by von Schoeffer, who made a contribution where he could. So, too, somewhat more independently, did Busolt and Swoboda. Ulrich Kahrstedt took a characteristically idiosyncratic view and found some new facets to examine.[29] Meanwhile—immediately before the First World War—at the suggestion and under the guidance of Gildersleeve, J. B. Edwards, a graduate student at the Johns Hopkins University, had completed a dissertation entitled *The Demesman in Attic Life*; and although distinctly "dated," even for its own day, in both conception and content—its use of epigraphic evidence was negligible—it is not lacking in insight.[30] But otherwise there is little to note beyond the *crambe repetita* of the late nineteenth century, and latterly (as Hopper unwittingly demonstrated) sometimes not even that.

So a new *Vie Municipale* is badly needed—self-evidently so, after a full century's accumulation of fresh evidence, both literary and epigraphic. Most of this material has not, to be sure, wanted for study *per se*, but it has not been integrated into another synoptic treatment of the whole subject. A trio of obvious examples come to mind. Haussoullier wrote before the rediscovery of the Aristotelian *Athenaion Politeia*, and thus in an era, for Athenian constitutional studies, almost literally antediluvian! The thirty-odd deme decrees on stone which were known to him have now grown in number, by degrees, threefold. And the excavations of only the last quarter-century have brought an augmentation of the data pertaining to religion and cult in the demes (sacrificial *fasti*, "*leges sacrae*," and the like) which is little short of spectacular.[31]

E. Saglio, and E. Pottier, *Dictionnaire des antiquités grecques et romaines d'après les textes et les monuments*, vol. 2, part 1, Paris 1892, at pp. 83-91. (By then, though not in 1884, he had heard of Müller's *de demis*: see his n. 152.)

[27] Schoeffer, "Demoi," col. 30.

[28] Busolt/Swoboda, *Staatskunde*, p. 979.

[29] Kahrstedt, *Staatsgebiet*, esp. pp. 44-48, on roads and their upkeep.

[30] Edwards, *Demesman*.

[31] A useful preliminary digestion of much of this new religious material, with guidelines for further work, is Mikalson, "Religion"; see further below, Chap. 7.

The enduring value of Haussoullier's *La Vie Municipale*, and the simplest explanation for why it has never yet been superseded, lies in its insistently clear conceptualization of the dual nature of the Kleisthenic deme, as simultaneously whole and part: a self-contained, self-administering local *"association"*[32] which served also as an administrative subdivision of (and contributor to) the polis as a whole—with the demarch as the main pivot between the two.[33] This formulation might be couched in modern jargon, according to taste, but it can scarcely be bettered in substance; and the aims and scope of Haussoullier's study seem quite as valid today as ever they were.[34] But if indeed they are, it becomes all the more necessary, in the light of the superior documentation now available, to pose again the questions which he posed and to see how our answers to them compare with his. In addition, ancient historians of the 1980s naturally think of issues to raise which would not have occurred to their counterparts of the 1880s; and these must be incorporated into the investigatory scheme.

An outline of the scheme adopted in this present book may be helpful here. The book falls into four unequal parts. After the preliminaries of establishing the context, historical (Chapter 1) and evidential (Chapter 2), for an examination of the demes on the lines adumbrated above, the second and third parts—reflecting the basic conceptual division of the subject established, as explained, by Müller and Haussoullier—then form the main substance of the study. In Part II we probe the interior of the demes themselves, identifying and classifying their inhabitants, observing their management of affairs sacred and secular, and attempting to recreate something of the character and quality of life that they provided. Part

---

[32] It is this role in *local* government which above all else gives the demes of Attica their unique interest and importance. A number of other poleis consisted, politically speaking, of demes (see Schoeffer, "Demoi," cols. 33-34, 121-131); and in the case of the example best known—the demes of Eretria (see W. P. Wallace, *Hesp.* 16, 1947, pp. 115-146)—there are some noteworthy parallels with Athens, particularly in the use of a *dēmotikon* as the official citizen nomenclature. Nothing, however, indicates that these Eretrian demes were units of local government. For the (five) demes of Miletos, see M. Piérart, *MH* 40, 1983, pp. 1-18, esp. 9-15; again there were demotics, of a sort, but deme membership was neither hereditary nor, as at Athens, a determinant of citizen status.

[33] This conceptual framework was to some extent anticipated, though not strongly emphasized, by Müller, *de demis*.

[34] I have heard the suggestion that its very title, *La Vie Municipale*, betrays its author as a man whose vision was distorted by his age, and thus an unreliable interpreter of a society distant in time and different in ethos. But it is no simple matter to demonstrate that the circumstances of the Third Republic (which has in any case been dubbed "one of the most confusing and paradoxical of political regimes": T. Zeldin, *France 1848-1945*, vol. 1, Oxford, 1973, p. 570) impaired Haussoullier's perspective on classical Athens; cf. *Vie*, pp. 209-210.

III then lengthens the perspective. Here we shall see the demes as parts of a greater whole, the Athenian polis, by scrutinizing the relationships between local and central government (Chapter 9) and between local and city politics (Chapter 10)—the latter by prosopographical examination, chiefly, of the individuals involved. In Chapter 11 a different means to a similar end takes the form of a discussion of the image of the demes, collective and individual, presented by one of the key genres of contemporary Athenian literature, comic drama. Finally, a brief Conspectus reflects upon "the demes and history" and pursues the possibility of detecting signs of change and development in the deme system during the classical and early Hellenistic periods.

The matter of the chronological limits of this book, embodied in its title, calls for a final word of explanation in this Introduction. The upper terminus is self-selecting, given the clear evidence (which we shall review in Chapter 1) that it was Kleisthenes who first gave the demes their formally organized role in both local and central government.[35] Thereafter, the contemporary literary and epigraphic testimony swells in volume throughout the classical period, attaining a peak during the last third of the fourth century and tailing off during the first half of the third. Admittedly, the system of regular quotas for deme representation in the city council persisted until the year 200,[36] and *irregular* deme representation in the council lasted as long as did that body itself, that is, until the mid third century A.D.[37] Again, insofar as the enactment of decrees by demes is an index of their internal vitality, that attribute can still be predicated of two demes, at any rate, in the first half of the second century;[38] and the deme-name (*dēmotikon*), devised by Kleisthenes as the standard nomenclature for every Athenian citizen, is still found in use as late as the fourth century A.D.[39] For a book of this kind, nonetheless, a lower terminus of ca. 250, in round terms, is effectively enforced both by the lapse of an adequacy of contemporary evidence and by general historical considerations.

[35] The establishment of the deme system by Kleisthenes is not explicitly discussed within the synchronic framework of *La Vie Municipale*, but it was planned, we are told, for a second volume (see *Vie*, pp. 201-202, cf. 154). No such volume was completed, however.

[36] Traill, *Organization*, pp. 1, 61-64.

[37] Traill, *Organization*, p. xviii; cf. *Agora* 15, p. 22.

[38] Eleusis: IG II²949, lines 30ff. Melite: *Hesp.* 11, 1942, pp. 265-274, no. 51.

[39] IG II²3716. Perhaps significantly, the deme is Melite again.

I

*

PROLEGOMENA

CHAPTER 1

BEFORE AND AFTER
KLEISTHENES

"So first he distributed everyone into ten tribes instead of the (previous) four, with the object of mixing them up so that more might share in the rights of a citizen. From this arose the saying 'No prying into tribes' as a retort to those wishing to enquire into ancestry . . . (4) And he divided the country, by demes, into thirty parts—ten in the city area, ten around the coast, ten inland. These he called trittyes, and he assigned three by lot into each tribe, so that each (tribe) should share in all the three regions. And he made (fellow-)demesmen of those living in each of the demes, in order that they would not, by using patronymics, expose the new citizens, but would call them after the demes; and hence Athenians do call each other after the demes. (5) He also established demarchs, with the same responsibility as that of the previous *naukraroi*; for he made the demes to replace the naukraries. Some of the demes he named after their localities, others after their founders, as (founders) no longer existed for all the places. (6) But he left everyone free to belong to clans and brotherhoods and to hold priesthoods as tradition dictated. He gave the tribes ten eponymous heroes, whom the priestess at Delphi chose from a pre-selected one hundred."[1]

---

[1] ?Aristot. *Ath. Pol.* 21.2 and 4-6: πρῶτον μὲν οὖν συνένειμε πάντας εἰς δέκα φυλὰς ἀντὶ τῶν τεττάρων, ἀναμεῖξαι βουλόμενος, ὅπως μετάσχωσι πλείους τῆς πολιτείας· ὅθεν ἐλέχθη καὶ τὸ μὴ φυλοκρινεῖν πρὸς τοὺς ἐξετάζειν τὰ γένη βουλομένους. . . . (4) διένειμε δὲ καὶ τὴν χώραν κατὰ δήμους τριάκοντα μέρη, δέκα μὲν τῶν περὶ τὸ ἄστυ, δέκα δὲ τῆς παραλίας, δέκα δὲ τῆς μεσογείου, καὶ ταύτας ἐπονομάσας τριττῦς ἐκλήρωσεν τρεῖς εἰς τὴν φυλὴν ἑκάστην, ὅπως ἑκάστη μετέχῃ πάντων τῶν τόπων. καὶ δημότας ἐποίησεν ἀλλήλων τοὺς οἰκοῦντας ἐν ἑκάστῳ τῶν δήμων, ἵνα μὴ πατρόθεν προσαγορεύοντες ἐξελέγχωσιν τοὺς νεοπολίτας, ἀλλὰ τῶν δήμων ἀναγορεύωσιν· ὅθεν καὶ καλοῦσιν Ἀθηναῖοι σφᾶς αὐτοὺς τῶν δήμων. κατέστησε δὲ καὶ δημάρχους τὴν αὐτὴν ἔχοντας ἐπιμέλειαν τοῖς πρότερον ναυκράροις· καὶ γὰρ τοὺς δήμους ἀντὶ τῶν ναυκραριῶν ἐποίησεν. προσηγόρευσε δὲ τῶν δήμων τοὺς μὲν ἀπὸ τῶν τόπων, τοὺς δὲ ἀπὸ τῶν κτισάντων· οὐ γὰρ ἅπαντες ὑπῆρχον ἔτι τοῖς τόποις. τὰ δὲ γένη καὶ τὰς φρατρίας καὶ τὰς ἱερωσύνας εἴασεν

Since the rediscovery of the work on papyrus at the end of the nineteenth century, the twenty-first chapter of the Aristotelian *Athenaion Politeia* has represented proof positive, for most scholars, that Kleisthenes was the legislator responsible for the formal creation of the Attic deme system. Prior to that rediscovery, the only fragment of the chapter preserved in the manuscript tradition merely reported Klcisthenes' creation of the demarchs,[2] and thus left open the possibility that the demes themselves were in official (that is, constitutional) as well as unofficial existence before Kleisthenes. The best-known version of such a view was Beloch's thesis that both the demes and the ten new *phylai* into which they were grouped were the brainchildren of the tyrant Peisistratos.[3] That it was, on the contrary, Kleisthenes who created the *phylai* is expressly stated by Herodotus (5.68-69), for whom they were virtually synonymous with Athenian democracy itself.[4] As regards the demes, however, Herodotus does not say in so many words that Kleisthenes created them, merely (in 5.69.2) that he "allocated the demes to the tribes." Other evidence is vaguer still. Isocrates, for example, alludes to the *progonoi* of the Athenians "dividing the polis by *kōmai* and the country by demes" (7.46, διελόμενοι τὴν μὲν πόλιν κατὰ κώμας, τὴν δὲ χώραν κατὰ δήμους). A. E. Raubitschek asserted that this gives "the substance of the Kleisthenian deme legislation."[5] But that begs a question: no explicit subject governs the intriguing participial phrase in the passage, and one has to retreat fully thirty chapters, to 7.16, to find there two names—Solon and Kleisthenes!

Should we then regard the Aristotelian testimony, ascribing sole responsibility to Kleisthenes, as decisive? Certainly the residue of the evidence, as we shall see, puts no obstacle in the way of accepting it. Yet equally demonstrable is the fact that Kleisthenes did not conjure his political and demographic infrastructure *ex nihilo*. On the contrary, almost all his raw materials were ready to hand,[6] awaiting only the new, official, systematized role in central and local government with which the reforms of the late sixth century were to invest them.

ἔχειν ἑκάστους κατὰ τὰ πάτρια. ταῖς δὲ φυλαῖς ἐποίησεν ἐπωνύμους ἐκ τῶν προκριθέντων ἑκατὸν ἀρχηγετῶν, οὓς ἀνεῖλεν ἡ Πυθία, δέκα. (A number of points of interpretation in my translation will be taken up, as they arise, later in the chapter.)

[2] Aristot. fr. 353 Rose (from Harpoc., δήμαρχος, and schol. Aristoph. *Clouds*, line 37).

[3] K. J. Beloch, *Griechische Geschichte*, vol. I (2d ed.), part 2, Strasburg, 1916, pp. 328ff. For rebuttals, see the references in Raubitschek, *Dedications*, p. 467. Beloch's main supporter was U. Kahrstedt, *RE* 9.1, 1921, col. 621 (and *Staatsgebiet*, p. 200); and note also the partial acceptance by Hignett, *Constitution*, pp. 119-122.

[4] See Herod. 6.131.1, with Ostwald, *Nomos*, p. 150.

[5] Raubitschek, *Dedications*, p. 467.

[6] Cf. Schoeffer, "Demoi," cols. 1-3; Raubitschek, *Dedications*, pp. 467ff.

A. The Demes before Kleisthenes

". . . a big area of irregular fertility, with her population here scattered, there clustered, like pebbles on a board . . ." Such is L. H. Jeffery's description of seventh-century Attica,[7] and it is borne out by both the literary and the archaeological record.

Of the size of the Attic peninsula, which came to form the polis of the Athenians, there is of course no room for doubt. Its extent of approximately a thousand square miles—modern Luxemburg would be a fair comparison—was unsurpassed amongst the poleis of mainland Greece, excepting only the special and anomalous case of Sparta.[8] In agricultural terms much of this area was indeed mediocre, as is pointed out by the ancient authorities from Thucydides (1.2.5) onwards, but that fact did not prevent archaic Athens from becoming an agriculturally oriented polis like all the rest; and such agricultural resources as Attica did boast could not have been adequately exploited without substantial numbers of "Athenians" living not, in fact, in Athens but out in the countryside (*chōra*). This was still true, furthermore, in the last third of the fifth century, on the eve of the Peloponnesian War. In another well-known passage (2.14-16) Thucydides describes the evacuation of Attica which that war made necessary, and he observes that the associated upheavals were all the more distressing because most Athenians had "always" been used to an independent existence in the country (2.14.2, cf. 16.1).

What Thucydides reveals here about the distribution of the Athenian citizen population in his own day is naturally of the greatest interest, but the word *always* (αἰεί) marks the important point on which he—and presumably his contemporaries—must now stand corrected by the evidence of archaeology.[9] It is now clear that, during the centuries which followed upon the destruction and collapse of Mycenaean Greece in the period ca. 1200-1150, the Attic countryside was very sparsely inhabited indeed; which is to say that numerous Mycenaean settlements outside Athens itself, many of them on or near the coast, had been abandoned. Athens itself was one of the very few Mycenaean cities to have survived the twelfth century unscathed, yet the chaos and disruption of that period and its aftermath was long-lived in its effects upon settlement patterns in Attica at large. "Two centuries after the fall of Mycenae, even though

---

[7] Jeffery, *Archaic Greece*, p. 87.

[8] Cf. V. Ehrenberg, *Der Staat der Griechen, I: der hellenische Staat*, Leipzig, 1957, p. 22.

[9] For what follows here I rely heavily, as will be seen, on the account of J. N. Coldstream in his two books *Geometric Pottery* (esp. pp. 335-362) and *Geometric Greece* (esp. pp. 35, 51, 70-71, 78-81, 109, 133-135).

the conditions of daily life were more settled . . . there was still a great concentration of people in Athens, while the Attic coasts and plains were extremely underpopulated. The men of Attica, so it seems, were still affected by a general feeling of insecurity, which deterred them from living in small villages."[10] This remained largely true, it would appear, of the second half of the tenth century and even of the first half of the ninth. The quasi-urban center (*asty*) of Athens itself—in fact little more than a cluster of villages[11]—to which the rural population had fled for refuge during the troubles, still housed the vast preponderance of the population. Otherwise there is evidence of habitation from a mere handful of the old Mycenaean sites, notably Eleusis, Haliki Glyphadas (ancient Aixone), Marathon, Menidi (Acharnai), Merenda (Myrrhinous), and Thorikos. Not surprisingly, all these outlying townships or villages survived to become incorporated, ultimately, into the Kleisthenic deme network.

During the next century (850-750), however, signs of change are increasingly plain. There begins at last a gradual repopulation of the countryside—specifically and particularly, a movement back to the coastal areas, where the old-established centers such as Eleusis and Marathon grew in size still further and others apparently sprang up to join them.[12] Nor was this a decentralization of population only; it was also a decentralization of wealth. The richest graves of the early eighth century come not from Athens itself but from Eleusis and Anavysos (ancient Anaphlystos).[13] To be sure, this (apparent) decline in the affluence of the denizens of "urban" Athens, when compared with the mid ninth century, was not a lasting one. There are graves from the mid eighth century which are no less wealthy than those of a hundred years earlier. More important, the sheer number of the inhabitants of the *asty* started to rise, during the second quarter of the eighth century, at a rate which at its full extent has been dubbed by one archaeologist a "population explosion."[14] Yet

[10] Coldstream, *Geometric Pottery*, p. 336. He added the *caveat* that "the apparent desertion of the coasts may be no more than an illusion, liable to be modified by future discoveries"; but no such discoveries have so far been made.

[11] Such is the description of *eighth*-century Athens which archaeologists now give (e.g. Coldstream, *Geometric Greece*, p. 303; Snodgrass, *Archaic Greece*, pp. 31-34), so it must apply *a fortiori* to the period 950-850. Whether it was still true of the late *sixth* century will be considered below, in sec. B.

[12] E.g. Palaia Kokkinia (in the Peiraieus area) and Anavysos (Anaphlystos): see Coldstream, *Geometric Pottery*, pp. 344, 348, and *Geometric Greece*, p. 78.

[13] Coldstream, *Geometric Greece*, pp. 78-81.

[14] Snodgrass, *Archaic Greece*, pp. 19-25, who uses datable burials for his conclusion (ibid., p. 23) "that in the space of two thirty-year generations, between about 780 and 720 B.C., the population [of Athens and Attica] may have multiplied itself by a factor of

the results of this are to be seen even more dramatically in the Attic countryside, where the surge in population over the same period was evidently more vertiginous still;[15] and although the unsystematic manner in which rural Attica has been excavated means that the basis for such generalizations is less firm than one would like, it does nonetheless look as though many sites, both on the coast and inland, which had remained unoccupied since Mycenaean times were resettled during the second half of the eighth century.

This then was the time, seemingly, when numerous centers of population which were later given official recognition as demes came into existence. No Iron Age pottery from an earlier period has come to light at, for example, Helleniko (ancient Halimous), Phaleron, Trachones (Euonymon), or Vari (Anagyrous), of the coastal demes; nor, for example, at Draphi (?Ionidai),[16] Kaki Thalassa (Kephale), Kalyvia Kouvaras (Prospalta), or Koropi (Sphettos), of the demes in the inland plains. This (re-) settlement of the plains is of course especially significant, as has properly been observed; for whereas the location of many of the coastal settlements is ambiguous in terms of the orientation of their inhabitants towards either sea or land, the same obviously could not be said of a site like Koropi/Sphettos, where arable farming must have been the overriding objective.[17] Moreover the decentralization of wealth was ever-increasing

---

approximately seven"; more details are given in his Cambridge Inaugural Lecture, *Archaeology and the rise of the Greek State*, Cambridge, 1977, pp. 10-13. See also Coldstream, *Geometric Pottery*, p. 360 with n. 1 (cf. *Geometric Greece*, p. 109), on the increasing number of wells in or near the Agora area as an index of a threefold population growth for that area during the course of the eighth century. Note, however, that at *Geometric Greece*, p. 221, this is described as a *two*fold increase during the eighth century, threefold during the Geometric period as a whole (i.e. 900-700). The statistics themselves clearly give rise to this confusion (see *Geometric Pottery*, p. 360, n. 1), as they necessarily make comparisons between periods rather than between fixed points. On the wells, see in full E.T.A. Brann, *Agora 8*, pp. 108, 125-131, and especially J. McK. Camp II, *Hesp.* 48, 1979, pp. 397-411, who in contrast to Coldstream and Snodgrass lays emphasis on the wells as indicators not of life but of death (during drought); cf. M. K. Langdon, *Hesp.* Suppl. 16, 1976, p. 89, n. 49; and (critical of Camp) T. W. Gallant, *ABSA* 77, 1982, p. 115, n. 36.

[15] Coldstream, *Geometric Pottery*, p. 360, and esp. Snodgrass, *Archaic Greece*, p. 23, where in fig. 4 the Athens/Attica figures are broken down into their two components, to reveal "a slight net emigration from the town to the country."

[16] On this identification, see Traill, *Organization*, p. 40, n. 12.

[17] See the map (fig. 43) in Coldstream, *Geometric Greece*, p. 134. (This is not necessarily to say, however, that arable farming was unknown in Attica before this period, as was argued by T. P. Howe, *TAPhA* 89, 1958, pp. 44-65, and is now maintained by Snodgrass in *The Dark Age of Greece*, Edinburgh, 1971, pp. 378-380, and (somewhat modified) in *Archaic Greece*, pp. 35-37. For a contrary view of the ninth century see E. L. Smithson, *Hesp.* 37, 1968, pp. 77-116, at 92-97, and M. K. Langdon, *Hesp.* Suppl. 16, 1976, pp. 87-91.)

as the eighth century ran its course. A veritable rural "gentry"[18] was taking shape, and the growth in the population as a whole was being successfully absorbed by the Attic countryside itself. The Athenians, it is regularly commented, took no part in the overseas colonization movements which began in the second half of the eighth century. We can now appreciate one important reason for this: they were busy "colonizing" their own *chōra*.[19]

As far as Athens and Attica are concerned, then, the population growth of eighth-century Greece led above all else to a dioecism, a centrifugal dispersal from *asty* to *chōra*. At first sight this seems paradoxical, since the ninth and (especially) eighth centuries comprise the period wherein the majority of scholars would set the very opposite process, the synoecism of Attica attributed by Athenians of the classical age (e.g. Thuc. 2.15) to Theseus. But the paradox may admit of a simple resolution. First, there were two kinds of Greek *synoikismos*. Sometimes the process did entail a literal, physical "settling together," a centripetal human migration; in other instances, however, a more accurate term might be *sympoliteia*, a centralization of political and religious institutions with little or no change of actual habitation—the result, often, of the pressure of *force majeure*; and it is plain that the synoecism of Attica belongs in the second of these categories.[20] Secondly, that very fact makes its date all the more difficult to determine. The principal reason for locating at least part of the Attic synoecism as late as the end of the eighth century has been the belief that Eleusis and the Marathonian Tetrapolis (Marathon, Oinoe, Probalinthos, and Trikorynthos) were still independent of Athenian control then. The evidence for this has been shown to be weak, however, and the case well argued for a synoecism in Mycenaean times.[21] The theory is by no means implausible *per se*, for the remains of Mycenaean Athens are those of a city which might well have dominated all or most of the Attic townships of its period.[22] On the other hand, such domination is unlikely, to say the least, to have survived the great twelfth-century collapse intact, so any Mycenaean synoecism will surely have

---

[18] Coldstream, *Geometric Pottery*, p. 362.

[19] Cf. Coldstream, *Geometric Greece*, p. 135.

[20] See for instance Snodgrass, *Archaic Greece*, p. 34; it is perverse of him, however, to favor the account in Livy (31.30.6) over that of Thucydides. For a full catalog of synoecisms, with *testimonia* and bibliographies, see M. Moggi, *I sinecismi interstatali greci, I: dalle origini al 338 a.C.*, Pisa, 1976; Attica is his no. 12.

[21] See most recently R. A. Padgug, *GRBS* 13, 1972, pp. 135-150, with references to the minority of scholars who have espoused this view in the past and to the majority who have rejected it. For a rebuttal, see now S. Diamant, *Hesp.* Suppl. 19, 1982, pp. 38-47.

[22] E. Vermeule, *Greece in the Bronze Age*, Chicago, 1964, pp. 267-268, gives a good brief description.

had to be repeated later;[23] and thus the problem of the date simply recurs in another form. Coldstream has recently suggested that Athenian control of Thorikos, at any rate, may go back to the mid ninth century. It seems that the silver mines at nearby Laurion were already in production then, yet there is no sign that the profits from them went to the men of Thorikos itself. Instead, the gold and other luxuries for which (the argument runs) the silver was traded turn up as grave-goods *in Athens*.[24] Whatever the truth, however, of this ingenious idea—and it does unfortunately rest upon a long concatenation of assumptions—it is not, as it is claimed to be, support for the hypothesis of a prior synoecism of the whole of Attica. The view of a piecemeal process, extending through most of the ninth and the eighth centuries, remains the one which best accommodates the bulk of the evidence and is therefore most likely to represent the historical reality.

Thus, "the process whereby the demes of Attica were fused into a general sympolity with Athens as the official capital and seat of government seems to have been mostly completed by c. 700."[25] To be more precise one should perhaps say "such of the demes as were by then in existence." Many were, as we have seen; and despite the indications that Athens and Attica now experienced a relative recession, both artistic and demographic, after the eighth-century peak,[26] it will be safe to assume that the process of "colonizing" the Attic *chōra* continued through the seventh and sixth centuries, with the establishment of more and more deme-centers as its (for us) most important manifestation.[27] Whether this

[23] Cf. Hignett, *Constitution*, p. 36.

[24] Coldstream, *Geometric Greece*, pp. 70-71.

[25] Jeffery, *Archaic Greece*, p. 84.

[26] Artistic decline from ca. 700 (or a little earlier) to ca. 650: see for example T. J. Dunbabin, *ABSA* 37, 1936-1937, p. 88; J. Boardman and D. C. Kurtz, *Greek Burial Customs*, London, 1971, p. 68, cf. Coldstream, *Geometric Greece*, pp. 132-133. The most satisfactory attempt to account for this and to set it in a broader context of archaeological evidence has been made by J. McK. Camp II, *Hesp.* 48, 1979, pp. 397-411. As noted above (n. 14), Camp takes issue with Coldstream and Snodgrass over the eighth-century "population explosion," but at p. 400, n. 10, offers the layman a chance of reconciling the two scenarios: "that the population of Athens increased in the eighth century is not questioned; it would appear, however, on the basis of present evidence as though the growth was not sustained but fell off sharply."

[27] Neither literary not archaeological evidence, it has been maintained, gives a simple answer to the question of whether rural settlement in Attica consisted of a mixture of village centers and isolated "homestead" farms or whether the latter were a rarity: see J. Pečírka in M. I. Finley, ed., *Problèmes de la terre en Grèce ancienne*, Paris and The Hague, 1973, pp. 113-147, at 133-137, with ample bibliography. Yet while the evidence is undeniably meagre it does strongly suggest, as Osborne (*Demos*, chap. 2, with Appendices A and B) has now shown, that nucleated settlement was the norm. See also J. E. Jones, in

occurred at a constant rate is another question. Archaeological evidence would be our best guide, but very little of it relating to this period has been studied and published. In the broadest of terms it would seem likely that the seventh century, with its known economic and agrarian problems, saw a relative slackening in the rate of new settlement; the sixth, thanks to Solon and Peisistratos, a relative quickening. In equally broad terms there must be a basic correlation between the size of the various demes in 508/7—which, as we shall see, can be gauged with some precision—and the dates of their foundation. The dozen and more demes which have already been mentioned in this chapter had nearly all grown to be substantial townships by the end of the sixth century; and (to invert the argument) the many other demes which were demonstrably large then are likely, sooner or later, to be located and revealed as early settlements by the archaeological record, if this has not happened already. Phlya would be a good example and, as will emerge below, a significant one.

As to the literary evidence, the conclusions which it warrants are for the most part even less exact with regard to date, but it does at least furnish several of the demes with an individual "pre-history." Ikarion, for example, which lies beyond Mt. Pentelikon, "has a special place among Attic demes in its possession of traditions associating it with the advent of Dionysus into Attica and the beginnings of tragedy and comedy."[28] Or there is Plutarch's account (*Theseus* 13.2-3) of the ancient antagonism between the demes Pallene and Hagnous: it is blatantly an explanatory *aition*, but apparently there was something which badly needed explanation—the fact (as it does seem to be) that families from these two communities did not intermarry. Further instances could readily be multiplied, for in fact the vast majority of demes had or laid claim to their own ancestral legends, cults, and customs (cf. Pausanias 1.14.7); and when Kleisthenes came to his task there was an abundance of such material to be exploited.

✳

No more space need be expended upon proving that many of what became the Kleisthenic demes were in existence long before him. Evidence

---

H. F. Mussche et al., eds., *Thorikos and the Laurion in archaic and classical times*, MIGRA 1, Ghent, 1975, pp. 63-136, with discussion 137-144.

[28] Pickard-Cambridge, *Festivals*, p. 48, cf. p. 54 (and fig. 29) on the theater there. For the evidence see A. W. Pickard-Cambridge, *Dithyramb, Tragedy and Comedy*, 2d ed. rev. T.B.L. Webster, Oxford, 1962, pp. 69-89. It has not gone unnoticed that the sole fragment of Susarion, the poet to whom the origination of Old Attic Comedy (in Ikarion) in the second quarter of the sixth century is ascribed, apostrophizes a group of people called δημόται. But it is more likely that this means "citizens" or even (Haussoullier, *Vie*, p. 5) "friends" than "demesmen;" and in any case both the authenticity of the fragment and the historicity of Susarion himself are very dubious.

carries us most of the way in this, common sense the rest. However, the belief that they possessed any official standing then, as units of either central or local government, is neither necessitated nor justified.

We may consider first the use of the *dēmotikon* or deme-name. In the Aristotelian *Ath. Pol.*, noted at the beginning of this chapter, it is stated that one of Kleisthenes' provisions was to make the demotic, rather than the patronymic, the official nomenclature for all Athenians.[29] What this means is that the deme-name was thereafter to be mandatory and universal. What it does not mean is that any pre-Kleisthenic *dēmotika* therefore present us with a difficulty—so long as they are not found in an official context. Such a context, for instance, is not proven and perhaps not even probable for "Myron of Phlya" (Μύρων Φλυεύς), named as such by Plutarch as the man who in the late seventh or early sixth century prosecuted the murderers of the Kylonians.[30] Whether before or after Kleisthenes, a demotic will have been employed *in common usage* if that was the best way of identifying its bearer. And by the same token it did not need a Kleisthenes to urge the use of their deme-name upon those who took a natural pride in it.[31]

Thus, insofar as Hignett was right in insisting that "what is needed to prove [that the deme system was pre-Kleisthenic] is an instance prior to the reforms of Kleisthenes in which the deme is found as the basis of citizen-rights or in which a citizen is officially described by his deme-

---

[29] Note that a distinction seems to be intended in ?Aristot. *Ath. Pol.* 21.4 between προσαγορεύειν and ἀναγορεύειν, the former signifying common parlance and the latter official nomenclature. On how far Kleisthenes' wishes were followed, see Chap. 3A.

[30] Μύρων Φλυεύς: Plut. *Sol.* 12.3. An enormous literature has grown up around Myron, but the discussions of F. Jacoby, *Atthis: the local chronicles of ancient Athens*, Oxford, 1949, p. 368, n. 81, and Hignett, *Constitution*, pp. 120-122, 334-335, should at last have settled the issue. Almost as much weight can be attached to the fact that the tyrant Peisistratos is described in two late sources ([Plato] *Hipparchos* 228B; Plut. *Sol.* 10.2) as a man of the deme Philaidai—which, as we shall see, is almost certainly one of the very small minority of "artificial" demes created at the time of the establishment of the deme network as a whole; thus, the argument runs, that network must indeed go back at least to the seventh century. But here again the evidence has been forced. Some writers found it natural to describe Peisistratos' home as Brauron; others found it equally natural to employ the Kleisthenic deme-name which, in this sense, obliterated Brauron from the map. See Raubitschek, *Dedications*, pp. 469-470; Bicknell, *Studies*, p. 3, n. 9; and below, n. 83.

[31] To this extent, the efforts of Raubitschek in *Dedications* to date all dedications which include demotics to the post-Kleisthenic period (see *Dedications*, pp. 471ff.) are otiose. I do not challenge his dating as such, but simply make the point that *in this respect* it would not matter if he were wrong. The issue is better understood by J. H. Oliver, in his publication (*Hesp.* 5, 1936, p. 230; cf. SEG 10.463) of a sixth-century grave monument which contains the demotic of the deme Aphidna. Oliver comments (ibid., p. 230, n. 1): "the occurrence of the word Ἀφιδναῖος, if my reading is correct, does not oblige us to date the inscription after the reforms of Kleisthenes, because Aphidna was one of the oldest and most important localities of Attica."

name,"[32] one can be equally confident in replying that no such instance is known. In fact, of course, there are other possible proofs which might suffice, but these too can be shown to be inadequate. Bluntly stated, if it was not Kleisthenes who formally created the deme system, there are only two alternative candidates: Solon and Peisistratos. (Given Greek habits of mind, it is not even worth considering the possibility that the individual responsible was unknown or unsung.) In the light of ?Aristot. *Ath. Pol.* 21 the burden of proof falls squarely upon the shoulders of anyone arguing for either of these alternatives; so it will be enough to account in other ways for such data as have been invoked in favor of Solon or Peisistratos in order to vindicate, irrefutably, the case for Kleisthenes.

Solon. There are four items of evidence (other than the ones discussed and dismissed above) which either have been or could be deployed in support of the notion of a Solonic—or for that matter pre-Solonic—deme system. None of them stand up to scrutiny.

1. Writing on the deme Hagnous, the grammarian Stephanus of Byzantium preserves a seemingly genuine extract from the *axones* of Solon, which mentions it: τὸ τοπικὸν Ἀγνουντόθεν, καὶ ἐν τόπῳ Ἀγνοῦντι ἐν τοῖς ἄξοσιν, "ἐπειδὴ Ἀγνοῦντι θυσία ἐστὶ τῷ Λεῷ" (". . . since in (H)agnous there is a sacrifice to Leos").

All that this shows is that the name Agnous/Hagnous—the unaspirated version is the original one, apparently—existed in Solon's time and could be used to specify a topographical location. It is not called a deme, and even if it had been, this would be no proof of its being, already at this time, a deme in the post-Kleisthenic sense.[33]

2. A fragment of the fourth-century philosopher and statesman Demetrius of Phaleron (*FGrH* 228 F31), quoted by a scholiast on Aristophanes *Clouds*, line 37, asserts that "Solon and his associates" created demarchs: καὶ δημάρχους οἱ περὶ Σόλωνα καθίσταντο ἐν πολλῇ σπουδῇ, ἵνα οἱ κατὰ δῆμον διδῶσι καὶ λαμβάνωσι τὰ δίκαια παρ' ἀλλήλων.

There is a flat contradiction, obviously, between this and ?Aristot. *Ath. Pol.* 21.5, where the demarchs are the creation of Kleisthenes. No other evidence suggests that they existed before Kleisthenes, and the phrase

---

[32] Hignett, *Constitution*, p. 120.

[33] Cf. Raubitschek, *Dedications*, p. 469, who again, however, somewhat misconstrues what is at stake: "the question is not whether or not local communities existed in Solon's times, but whether they were called demes." On when and why the demes *were* first called demes, see Appendix 1.

"Solon and his associates" is suspiciously vague.[34] Moreover the judicial functions attributed to the demarchs here may betray confusion, as Jacoby noted, with the Peisistratid *kata dēmous dikastai*. (I differ from him, however, in how I unravel it, as will be seen below.) Considered as information about Solon, the passage must simply be erroneous.

3. In "the texts of two dedications and a series of extracts from a [law of the king-archon], copied originally by three different authors, and preserved only by the omnivorous curiosity of Athenaeus (6.234-235),"[35] there are two allusions to religious *parasitoi* "from the demes" (235A and C) and one to "the Acharnians' *parasitoi*" (234F).

If this law could be securely dated to Solonic or even pre-Solonic times, the conclusion that the demes had some official standing then would be hard to avoid. More probably, though, it reflects ancient, perhaps even unwritten, custom, not formally codified until possibly the late fifth century.[36]

4. Another law which has been regarded as evidence for the official recognition of the demes under the Solonic law code may indeed go back to that code, but its wording is unlikely to be wholly original. The source is the Roman jurist Gaius, as quoted in Justinian's *Digest* (47.22.4): ἐὰν δὲ δῆμος ἢ φράτορες ἢ ἡρώων ὀργεῶνες ἢ γεννῆται ἢ σύσσιτοι ἢ ὁμόταφοι ἢ θιασῶται ἢ ἐπὶ λείαν οἰχόμενοι ἢ εἰς ἐμπορίαν, ὅ τι ἂν τούτων διαθῶνται πρὸς ἀλλήλους, κύριον εἶναι, ἐὰν μὴ ἀπαγορεύσῃ δημόσια γράμματα ("If a deme or members of a phratry or *orgeōnes* of heroes or members of a *genos* or messmates or funerary associates or *thiasōtai* or those away for booty or for trade make arrangements in these matters amongst themselves, they shall be valid unless forbidden by the laws").

Here we have a whole series of "associations," of widely differing types,[37] which are allowed to issue sovereign enactments insofar as they do not contravene public law; and the series opens with "a deme."

---

[34] Glen Bowersock has suggested to me that οἱ περὶ Σόλωνα might be the sort of periphrasis which in fact meant simply Solon himself. This seems, however, to be late usage (see for instance Plut. *Pyrrhos* 20) and thus unlikely to be what Demetrius meant by the phrase—always assuming, of course, that this is indeed the *verbatim* quotation that it purports to be. On the οἱ περί formula, see in general S. Dow, *TAPhA* 91, 1960, pp. 381-409, at 395ff.

[35] R. Schlaifer, *HSPh* 54, 1943, pp. 35-67, at 36, which remains the standard treatment (though see Lewis, "Cleisthenes" pp. 33-34, 39).

[36] R. Schlaifer, *HSPh* 54, 1943, p. 43; cf. Raubitschek, *Dedications*, p. 469. It seems that E. Ruschenbusch did not even contemplate the possibility of this material's being part of the ΣΟΛΩΝΟΣ ΝΟΜΟΙ (*Historia* Einzelschrift 9, Wiesbaden, 1966).

[37] See on this point Finley, *Land and Credit*, pp. 88-89 (whose translation I have given here).

W. S. Ferguson—whose text I have followed here—argued strongly that the list, and the wording of the law as a whole, *was* original, but even he was obliged to make the important concession that the final phrase (χύριον . . .) "is not verbally authentic."[38] Most scholars have rightly concluded that what we have here is a conflation of archaic elements (such as the curious way of describing pirates and traders) with later ones; and Wilamowitz was surely justified in maintaining that "a deme" was one of the latter.[39]

So the evidence which might have supported the idea of officially recognized demes as early as Solon is entirely inconclusive, and this is all that we need to establish in order to reject it. The same goes for the testimony relating to Peisistratos (and his sons).

Peisistratos.   In ?Aristot. *Ath. Pol.* 16.5 we learn of Peisistratos' inauguration of an unspecified number—later thirty—of *kata dēmous dikastai.* If their title is authentic, it is certainly proof of one worthwhile point: that by this time the Attic villages were indeed known as "demes." It does not, however, either indicate or presuppose official recognition of the demes as constitutional entities. On the contrary, it implies if anything a view that the demes were in need of a judicial system but could not provide it for themselves; hence both the *dikastai* and, the writer adds, Peisistratos' own habit of arbitral forays into the *chōra.*

Secondly—and finally—there are the herms of Hipparchos.[40] According to [Plato] *Hipparchos* 228D (cf. 229A), Peisistratos' elder son Hipparchos, "wishing to educate the country people, set up for them Hermai on the roads, midway between the *asty* and each of the demes," with gnomic wisdom inscribed on them. The one surviving example[41] is comfortingly corroborative, for it claims to be "midway between Kephale and the *asty*" and it was found at Koropi/Sphettos which meets that requirement. Beyond that, however, the number and, *pace* [Plato], the purpose of the herms remain a matter for speculation. At any rate the idea that the demes were already formed into a network of political units receives no support from this quarter, for, like Solon's mention of Agnous/

[38] W. S. Ferguson, "The Attic Orgeones," *HThR* 37, 1944, pp. 61-140, at 62-66.

[39] U. von Wilamowitz-Moellendorff, *Antigonos von Karystos*, Berlin, 1881, pp. 278-279; cf. Schoeffer, "Demoi," col. 2; H. T. Wade-Gery, *Essays in Greek History*, Oxford, 1958, p. 153, n. 1; Raubitschek, *Dedications*, p. 469; A. Andrewes, *JHS* 81, 1961, p. 12, n. 40.

[40] Bibliography and discussion in J. F. Crome, "Hipparcheioi Hermai," *AM* 60-61, 1935-1936, pp. 300-313; Raubitschek, *Dedications*, pp. 470-471 (very muddled); *Agora* 11, pp. 112-114 (E. B. Harrison); W. K. Pritchett, *Studies in Ancient Greek Topography, 3: Roads*, University of California Publications in Classical Studies 22, 1980, pp. 160-162.

[41] IG I³1023 (I²837; but see rather J. Kirchner and S. Dow, *AM* 62, 1937, pp. 1ff.).

Hagnous, nothing suggests that at this time the names had more than a topographical denotation and import.

✳

We may be certain, then, that in sixth-century Attica, before Kleisthenes, the many and various nucleated settlements, old and newer, were familiar and in some cases important in topographical terms but had as yet no existence, from the standpoint of the polis, in a political sense.[42] Insofar as the central, synoecized government in Athens needed a local subdivision of the polis for official purposes, the need seems to have been filled by the little-known naukraries—which indeed the Aristotelian *Ath. Pol.*, as we have seen, claims explicitly as the demes' forerunners.[43]

It remains to ask, however, how far the pre-Kleisthenic demes enjoyed an *unofficial* or informal role in local self-government, corresponding to and anticipating the functions which the Kleisthenic constitution was to give them as standard procedure. "It is incredible," W. S. Ferguson once asserted, "that the villages of Attica lacked a local organisation of some sort before they were engrossed as demes of the state in the Kleisthenian system."[44] Unfortunately, given the great dearth of evidence, the issue does indeed become a matter of what one may or may not find "incredible"; and the only safe course is to eschew the sort of all-embracing generalizations which are made by, for example, Frank Kolb in his recent book *Agora und Theater*. Kolb's subject is an important one. Extending the work of W. A. McDonald, Roland Martin, and others, he explores the interconnections between what might be termed sacred and secular gatherings in Greek society, and ranges widely in both time and space for his material. His discussion of the Attic demes is open to criticism on both counts, however, when considered as proof (as it is suggested to be) that "die Mitglieder der Demen sich vor Kleisthenes . . . an einem bestimmten Ort zur Beratung gemeinsamer Angelegenheiten und zu gemeinsamen religiösen Feiern zusammengefunden hätten"—so that Kleisthenes had merely to *extend* the competence of preexisting deme assemblies.[45] On the contrary, even if one could concede the universality of

---

[42] Cf. Lewis, "Cleisthenes," p. 26: "obviously there were centres of population before Cleisthenes. Cleisthenes gave them corporate existence."

[43] On the *naukrariai*, see Hignett, *Constitution*, pp. 68-74; Raubitschek, *Dedications*, p. 469; B. Jordan, *CSCA* 3, 1970, pp. 153-175 (and *Hypomnemata* 55, Göttingen, 1979, pp. 56-62); J.-C. Billigmeier and A. S. Dusing, *TAPhA* 111, 1981, pp. 11-16.

[44] W. S. Ferguson, *HThR* 37, 1944, p. 66. Compare e.g. D. Roussel, *Tribu et Cité*, Paris, 1976, p. 271: "les dèmes n'attendirent pas pour exister, *avec leurs assemblées* et leurs cultes, que Clisthène eût fait d'eux des unités de droit public" (my emphasis); and Kolb, *Agora und Theater*: see next note.

[45] F. Kolb, *Agora und Theater: Volks- und Festversammlung*, Deutsches Archäologisches

Kolb's equation between *Agora* and *Theater*, it must be insisted that few demes, comparatively speaking, are known to have possessed a theater at all, and that even the oldest known deme theater, at Thorikos, the possible function of which as a place of assembly has long been acknowledged, now seems unlikely to have been begun before the last years of the sixth century[46]—that is, just as well after as before Kleisthenes.

So it is idle to pretend that we have *evidence* of the "activités collectives propres"[47] of any, let alone all, pre-Kleisthenic demes, when all one can do is to deal in suppositions. My own supposition would differ from that of Ferguson, Roussel, or Kolb chiefly in that (to reiterate the point) it seems to me imprudent to generalize. Ancient towns such as Eleusis or Marathon, as we have seen, had a continuous history stretching back to Mycenaean times—subsequently given expression as the canon of the Dodekapolis, or "Twelve Cities," of Attica[48]—and very probably they had an almost equally long tradition of local autonomy in both the secular and the sacred spheres. As far as religion is concerned, in addition to activity *within* demes there were also ancient cult organizations which drew some of the demes together in groups;[49] and in general it would be perverse to deny archaic origins for much of the local religious observance which we later encounter in a deme context.[50] Yet in this respect as in others there must have been enormous diversity across the whole gamut of demes, old and new, large and small. How could it have been otherwise, without uniformity and standardization imposed from the center? In the late sixth century, however, with Kleisthenes, the time for some uniformity was at hand.

B. The Kleisthenic Demes

We return, then, after this lengthy preamble, to the key figure of Kleisthenes. The precise nature and objectives of every facet of his program

---

Institut, Archäologische Forschungen 9, Berlin, 1981, pp. 62ff.; the quotation is from p. 63, n. 5.

[46] See H. F. Mussche, in H. F. Mussche et al., eds., *Thorikos and the Laurion in archaic and classical times*, MIGRA 1, Ghent, 1975, pp. 46-47; T. Hackens, *AC* 34, 1965, pp. 39-46 (and *Thorikos* 3, 1965, pp. 75-96); H. F. Mussche, *A Class* 13, 1970, pp. 131-132. The fragmentary official measure found during the excavations there dates from the early fifth century: *Thorikos* 7, 1970-1971, p. 174, no. 38; cf. H. A. Thompson, *Hesp.* Suppl. 19, 1982, p. 135, n. 5. For other demes with theaters, see Chap. 7D.

[47] D. Roussel, *Tribu et Cité*, Paris, 1976, p. 271. For the view that landholding by demes predated Kleisthenes, see Andreyev, "Agrarian conditions," pp. 45-46.

[48] See Strabo 9.1.20; Lewis, "Cleisthenes, p. 33.

[49] See in brief Lewis, "Cleisthenes," pp. 33-34; and below, Chap. 7, n. 46.

[50] I shall take up this point again in the introduction to Chap. 7.

of reforms have been extensively debated since antiquity itself, as has every stage of the historical circumstances which led up to their proposal and which account for their adoption and ultimate success.[51] As this is not a book about Kleisthenes himself but about one, albeit fundamental, feature of his political reorganization, we need not discuss any issue, however intrinsically important, which does not bear directly upon the subject of the deme system, nor aim at doxographic comprehensiveness at every turn. We can and should accept the bulk of the information which the sources preserve about the letter, if not necessarily the spirit, of Kleisthenes' measures as they related to the demes. Our problems arise primarily from the fact that that information is insufficient to allow a complete reconstruction of Kleisthenes' "reform bill"[52] without resort both to the historian's normal procedures of ratiocination and also to extrapolation from what is known of the operation of the Kleisthenic system long after its genesis.

The best and fullest source, as we have seen, is the one quoted and translated at the beginning of this chapter: ?Aristot. *Ath. Pol.* 21, especially sections 4-5. It preserves at least the substance of two central provisions of Kleisthenes' "bill": (*a*) that those living in each deme were to be fellow demesmen and known officially by that deme's name (which modern scholars, though not the ancients themselves, call the *dēmotikon* [*sc. onoma*]); and (*b*) that the demes were to be in the charge of *dēmarchoi*. It further states (*c*) that Kleisthenes determined the names of the demes. This by contrast looks likely, as we shall see, to have been something not embodied in the measures themselves, except in principle, but consequential upon them once approved.

So far as this information goes, it is either verifiable from later evidence (points *a* and *b*) or else unexceptionable *per se* (point *c*); but clearly it raises a host of other questions only to leave them unanswered. We are told, for example, of the *names* of the demes, but what of their *number*? This is one of the writer's most puzzling omissions. He tells of ten tribes (instead of the old four) and of thirty trittyes which in trios made up each tribe,[53] yet did not think to mention the number of the units which formed the basis of this three-tiered edifice—the demes. Scholars once

---

[51] Of the standard modern accounts, I am most in sympathy with Ostwald, *Nomos*, pp. 137-160. (To avoid undue repetition in what follows I shall speak schematically of "Kleisthenes" as responsible for the deme system as a whole, likely though it may be that others were involved both in 508/7 itself and later.)

[52] The phrase is taken from the title of A. Andrewes' article in CQ 27, 1977, pp. 241-248, an admirably sensible reconstruction of "the concrete form in which [Kleisthenes'] proposals were put forward"; I adhere to it on most points, as will be seen, in what follows.

[53] For the little-known *pre*-Kleisthenic trittyes, twelve in number, see Hignett, *Constitution*, pp. 47-48, 71-72.

widely believed that another ancient source, and an even earlier one, supplies the missing figure. According to the received text of Herodotus 5.69.2, Kleisthenes δέκα τε δὴ φυλάρχους ἀντὶ τεσσέρων ἐποίησε, δέκα δὲ καὶ τοὺς δήμους κατένειμε ἐς τὰς φυλάς ("created ten phylarchs instead of four, and assigned ten demes [or: the demes in tens] to the tribes"); and it would seem not unnatural *in vacuo* to construe this as meaning that there were exactly one hundred demes, ten per tribe. Strenuous debate on the question went on throughout the nineteenth century and into the twentieth, with the adherents of the ten-by-ten demes initially in a clear majority but falling away, by degrees, as the countervailing evidence grew ever more arresting. Busolt and Swoboda were the last scholars of that epoch to argue in support of the figure of one hundred Kleisthenic demes, doing so mainly on the grounds of an appeal to Kleisthenes' love of "logical-arithmetical construction";[54] and the only attempt (as far as I am aware) to reestablish the figure in recent years has come in a study of Kleisthenes[55] which, while rich in suggestive insight, likewise allows such considerations of "intellectual coherence"—as another scholar has it[56]—to prevail over the plainest indications of the evidence on this point.

For indeed the figure of one hundred is quite untenable. That Strabo (9.1.16) put the number of the demes at one hundred and seventy or one hundred and seventy-four was of course always realized, and regularly accounted for by the assumption that more demes must have been created over the course of time and added to the original ten tens. However, there was and is no way of evading the fact, once the topographical and epigraphical work of the late nineteenth century had revealed it, that one of the tribes, IX Aiantis, had fewer demes than the "required" ten;[57] and it is inconceivable that a tribe should have lost any of its original quota of demes before the first increase in the number of the tribes (but not of the demes) in 307/6.[58] More broadly, indeed, modern scholars who have paid close attention to the fine details of the deme-trittys-tribe structure

---

[54] For references and discussion, see Schoeffer, "Demoi," cols. 3-5 and Busolt/Swoboda, *Staatskunde*, pp. 873-874; cf. Raubitschek, *Dedications*, pp. 467-468.

[55] P. Lévêque and P. Vidal-Naquet, *Clisthène l'Athénien: essai sur la représentation de l'espace et du temps dans la pensée politique grecque de la fin du VIe siècle à la mort de Platon*, Paris, 1964, pp. 9, 13 with n. 4.

[56] Murray, *Early Greece*, p. 258 (twice!). Murray's excellent discussion, I hasten to add, does not involve a belief in one hundred demes.

[57] See in brief Traill, *Organization*, pp. 96-97. By his criteria for establishing the official canon of Kleisthenic demes (see below), Aiantis had only six (cf. Gomme, *Population*, p. 64)—an even smaller number than some earlier scholars had supposed (see, for instance, Schoeffer, "Demoi," col. 5).

[58] See Traill, *Organization*, p. 26, and the table on p. 102.

and in particular to deme representation in the *boulē* have emerged with the conviction that there is a striking absence of change in these matters, over the period during which we have evidence for them (that is, essentially from the fourth century onwards); and this, they contend, is best explained as conservative adherence to the original political organization of Kleisthenes.[59] Thus, *if* Herodotus really meant to say that the ten Kleisthenic tribes each comprised ten demes, he was mistaken or misinformed. However, as has long been appreciated, we are not obliged to conclude that this is what Herodotus either said or meant. Whether by accepting Lolling's emendation of δέκα to δέκαχα[60] or else by simply understanding δέκα itself in a distributive sense,[61] we may legitimately infer that what Herodotus says and what actually happened are not at variance: the demes were allocated to the tribes *in ten groups*. As to whether Herodotus believed they were ten *equal* groups, that is another question, and necessarily an unanswerable one. But there are no grounds for supposing that this was indeed his belief, and therefore he must obviously no longer be considered as a source of information about the total number of the Kleisthenic demes.

The only figures from antiquity itself for the number of the demes are thus the ones cited by Strabo (9.1.16): one hundred and seventy, or one hundred and seventy-four.[62] Can either of them be accepted? At one time the lists of demes compiled by modern scholars[63] produced aggregates at or even in excess of this level, but more recent estimates have been significantly lower. Peter Bicknell, for instance, concluded from a survey

---

[59] See above all Traill, *Organization*, passim (e.g. pp. 56, 61, 103); cf. Lewis, "Cleisthenes," p. 30, and Bicknell, *Studies*, p. 2, n. 5, and p. 6, with further references. We shall return to this below (n. 73).

[60] H. G. Lolling, *AD* 1889, pp. 24ff. (on the basis of a formula in the Athenian decree enfranchising the Samians in 405: IG I³127, line 34). The emendation has been accepted into the Oxford and Budé texts, amongst others, of Herodotus.

[61] See for example A. Wilhelm *apud* Busolt/Swoboda, *Staatskunde*, p. 873, n. 4; Traill, *Organization*, p. 97.

[62] Strabo 9.1.16: οὗτος (*sc.* Hegesias) μὲν οὖν ἑνὸς ἐμνήσθη τῶν ἐν ἀκροπόλει σημείων· Πολέμων δ᾽ ὁ περιηγητὴς τέτταρα βιβλία συνέγραψε περὶ τῶν ἀναθημάτων τῶν ἐν ἀκροπόλει. τὸ δ᾽ἀνάλογον συμβαίνει καὶ ἐπὶ τῶν ἄλλων τῆς πόλεως μερῶν καὶ τῆς χώρας· Ἐλευσῖνά τε εἰπὼν ἕνα τῶν ἑκατὸν ἑβδομήκοντα δήμων, πρὸς δὲ καὶ τεττάρων, ὥς φασιν, οὐδένα τῶν ἄλλων ὠνόμακεν. See on this text Traill, *Organization*, p. 97 with (especially) n. 86, where he rightly points out that neither of the sources mentioned (Hegesias of Magnesia, mid third century; Polemon "the Periegete" of Ilion, early second century) appears to be the source, strictly speaking, of either of the *figures*; cf. G. C. Richards, *CR* 10, 1898, pp. 383-384.

[63] Chiefly Schoeffer, "Demoi," cols. 35-122 and W. B. Dinsmoor, *The Archons of Athens in the Hellenistic Age*, Cambridge, Mass., 1931, pp. 444-447; see Traill, *Organization*, p. 81.

of "the literary and epigraphic evidence at present available" that there were one hundred and forty demes in the fourth century, which he regarded as the figure fixed by Kleisthenes and not augmented until 224/3 (whereafter, he believed, at least twenty-two demes were newly created from time to time).[64] Now, however, the whole issue has been set upon secure methodological foundations by Traill, whose investigation replaces all previous work.[65] In order for it to be properly counted as a deme in the constitutional sense devised by Kleisthenes, Traill puts up two prerequisite conditions to be fulfilled by any community described as or claimed to be a "deme," either in antiquity or by modern scholars. It must have "a minimal body of citizens," identifiable as such, for each deme, by its *dēmotikon*, together with "representation in the Council," as recorded in or deducible from the bouleutic and prytany lists. And from the combination of these two fundamental criteria—as indeed from either of them alone—it clearly emerges that between about the beginning of the fourth century (when the second criterion, especially, first becomes investigable) and the last quarter of the third century, the number of the constitutional demes was one hundred and thirty-nine. Three more were created and added later, that is, one each in 224/3, 200, and A.D. 126/7.[66] But every other supposed "deme" can be accounted for either by manifest error, ancient or modern, or else (and more usually) by the fact that it was or became a "deme," a village or township, *only in a nontechnical sense.*[67]

Throughout the rest of this book, then, it will be taken for granted that during the classical and early Hellenistic periods there were indeed

[64] Bicknell, *Studies*, pp. 1-17 (with p. 1, n. 4, on the additions after 224/3).

[65] Traill, *Organization*, pp. 73-103. It would be fair to say, however, that Traill's systematic approach was partially anticipated both by Gomme, *Population*, pp. 55-66, and by Bicknell, *Studies*, pp. 1-17. Gomme's total of 139 demes is the same as Traill's but is made up differently: Gomme failed to register Ankyle in II Aigeis as a split deme (see, on this, Bicknell, *Studies*, p. 1, n. 3; Traill, *Organization*, pp. 126-127), while conversely admitting the spurious Kikynna of VII Kekropis (see S. Dow, *Hesp.* 3, 1934, p. 188; Traill, *Organization*, p. 83) as well as the genuine one of V Akamantis. Bicknell's 140 (see above) correctly divided Ankyle but retained the false Kikynna.

[66] (i) Berenikidai: created in 224/3 on the formation of the new tribe Ptolemais, in honor of Berenike, wife of Ptolemy III Euergetes (see W. K. Pritchett, *The Five Attic Tribes after Kleisthenes*, Baltimore, 1943, pp. 13-23; Traill, *Organization* pp. 29-30). (ii) Apollonieis: created in 200 on the formation of the new tribe Attalis, in honor of Apollonis, wife of Attalos I of Pergamon (see Traill, *Organization*, p. 31). (iii) Antinoeis: created either in A.D. 126/7 on the formation of the new tribe Hadrianis or else added to it in A.D. 130 at the death and apotheosis of its eponym, Hadrian's favorite Antinoos (see Pritchett, ibid., p. 37; Traill, *Organization*, p. 31 with n. 18).

[67] See on this Traill, *Organization*, pp. 73, 97-98.

one hundred and thirty-nine constitutional, Kleisthenic demes.[68] That the figure originally arrived at in 508/7 was lower than this remains theoretically possible[69] but highly unlikely, given the fact mentioned above: the extraordinary absence of change and modification in the system from the fourth century onwards, once we have the evidence to appreciate it. Even the six sets of "divided" demes—Upper (καθύπερθεν) and Lower (ὑπένερθεν) Ankyle, Pergase, and the rest[70]—which have been taken by some to be obvious cases of post-Kleisthenic adjustment[71] will on the contrary have been part of the inaugural plan.[72] Furthermore, and for analogous reasons, it seems best to suppose that the quotas for deme representation in the *boulē* which can be determined for the fourth century onwards are the ones fixed *ab initio*.[73]

[68] For a catalog of them, with their tribal affiliation and bouleutic representation, see Appendix 2.

[69] Some scholars injudiciously assert it to be a fact: P. Lévêque and P. Vidal-Naquet, *Clisthène l'Athénien*, Paris, 1964, p. 13, n. 4; Effenterre, "Mobilisation," p. 15 with n. 52.

[70] The full list is as follows. I Erechtheis: Upper and Lower Agryle, Upper and Lower Pergase, Upper and Lower (or Coastal) Lamptrai. II Aigeis: Upper and Lower Ankyle. III Pandionis: Upper and Lower Paiania. IV Leontis: Upper and Lower Potamos, and also Potamos Deiradiotes (though this is perhaps not a tripartite division but a divided pair and a homonym: Traill, *Organization*, pp. 44, 127, n. 1).

[71] See for instance Busolt/Swoboda, *Staatskunde*, pp. 873-874.

[72] See on this Traill, *Organization*, pp. 123-128 (Appendix D) and in *Phoenix* 35, 1981, p. 91: "I do not believe that any deme was divided after the Kleisthenic establishment." Having approached this doctrine with scepticism I am now satisfied that it is correct. The earliest reference to one of the divided demes is the phrase "Λαμπτρεὺς ἔγωγε τῶν κάτω" in Aristoph. fr. 27, from a play, the *Amphiaraus*, which according to the second hypothesis to Aristophanes' *Birds* was staged at the Lenaia of 414; and in IG I³515 (I²398; *Dedications*, no. 167; *Agora 15*, no. 1), where some of the *prytaneis* of I Erechtheis dedicate to Athena in 408/7, all three Erechtheid "divides" are distinguished. These demes remain an enigma nonetheless: note Davies' comment (in *Families*, p. 536) that "we do not yet know enough about split demes to be able to decide whether these two men [one from each Lamptrai] can or cannot have been brothers."

[73] References above, n. 59. For the documentation of bouleutic quotas, see Traill, *Organization*, "Tables of Representation"; and in another form, *Agora 15*, passim, with addenda in *Hesp.* 47, 1978, pp. 269-331. The documentation approaches a satisfactory level only from the mid fourth century onwards: note, however, J. K. Davies, "A reconsideration of IG I²847," *LCM* 4, 1979, pp. 151-156, who carefully and convincingly argues that in this stone (now IG I³1040) we have a fragmentary bouleutic list from the *fifth* century (? ca. 420), in which two demes from different tribes, Gargettos and Phrearrhioi, show the same quotas as later. (The dedication by Erechtheid *prytaneis* of 408/7, referred to in the preceding note, provides evidence for largely different fifth-century quotas only on the assumption that all fifty Erechtheis were listed—but this is unlikely: see *Agora 15*, no. 1, and, on the possible political context, Raubitschek, *Dedications*, p. 191, developed by Bicknell, *Studies*, pp. 13-14.) Hansen, "Political activity," has recently contended that the quotas were revised in or around 403/2. His main argument is the "miraculous" (p. 232) correspondence between the percentages of the total bouleutic representation assigned

We have dwelt here upon the question of the *number* of Kleisthenes'
demes not only because of its inherent importance but because it has
implications of significance for the way in which the Kleisthenic system
was constructed. The number of the demes, one might say, was significant
precisely because it was of no consequence as such![74] Ten tribes, thirty
trittyes—yet one hundred and thirty-nine demes. Here at least, Kleisthenes was no slave to the bewitching aesthetics of decimal arithmetic.
Each tribe was made up of three trittyes, but the number of *demes* in
each tribe varied very considerably: fourteen in I Erechtheis, twenty-one
in II Aigeis, eleven in III Pandionis, twenty in IV Leontis, thirteen in V
Akamantis and VI Oineis, eleven in VII Kekropis, seventeen in VIII Hippothontis, a mere six in IX Aiantis, and thirteen in X Antiochis. Did this
mean that the tribes were correspondingly disparate in size? If the demes
had been of equal or nearly equal size, such an outcome would naturally
have been inescapable; but in fact the size-range within the deme system
was truly enormous. First, there was great variation in the number of
demes which went to make up a trittys as well as a tribe. In some instances
it was as many as eight or nine, in others it was one deme only; the
inland trittys of IX Aiantis, for example, comprised the single deme of
Aphidna. This fact alone reveals at least one purpose of the trittyes: they
were to group together the demes in configurations which avoided "gross
inequalities between tribes;"[75] and in broad terms the success of such an
aim is as plain as its desirability.[76] Secondly, the variation in deme size
is of course directly indicated by the bouleutic quotas, and the quotas

---

to the three regions of Attica—namely (after Traill, *Organization*, p. 71), *asty* 26%, *paralia*
39%, *mesogeios* 35%—and the regional percentages calculable from the known demotics
both of (*a*) fourth-century *rhētores* and *stratēgoi* (cf. Hansen, *GRBS* 24, 1983, pp. 157-
176, plus some demotics without names) and of (*b*) *dikastai* (cf. Kroll, *Allotment Plates*,
pp. 106-258, with seven more which he adds in *GRBM* 10, 1984, pp. 165-171): they are,
for *a*, *asty* 26%, *paralia* 36%, *mesogeios* 38%; for *b*, *asty* 23%, *paralia* 42%, *mesogeios*
35%. Without a post-Kleisthenic adjustment of the quotas, Hansen contends, "the correspondence between bouleutic quotas and actual political participation in the fourth century" (p. 231) could not have been so close, for by then the citizen population "differed
both in size and in geographical distribution from that of the age of Kleisthenes" (p. 231).
But one may concede both points without conceding also their relevance to the question
of quotas. As regards "size" there is no good reason to suppose that, over a lengthy period,
some demes grew or shrank more than others (cf. Bicknell, *Studies*, pp. 18-19); and as
regards "geographical distribution," shifts in deme *residence* did not affect deme *membership*, on which the quotas rested.

[74] Cf. Traill, *Organization*, p. 97, n. 85.

[75] Andrewes, "Reform bill," p. 246.

[76] See further Traill, *Organization*, pp. 70-72, esp. n. 31. Beyond this obvious point we
shall not pursue here the peculiarly complex problems which surround the composition
and significance of the trittyes *per se*; cf. Introduction, n. 19.

themselves are independently corroborated in most instances by general prosopographical statistics (and a small amount of other evidence),[77] a fact which validates what might in any case have been our natural conclusion that the quotas rested upon "a broad general basis of representation according to population."[78] At one extreme of the scale there were a host of tiny hamlets like Acherdous, Hekale, Myrrhinoutta, or Plotheia, which were called upon to provide a single *bouleutēs* only—and in a few cases not even that.[79] At the other extreme stood the "large demes" referred to by the speaker in Demosthenes 57.57, himself from a medium-to-small deme, Halimous. It is hardly to be imagined that he could have quantified the simple large/small dichotomy which his forensic appeal implies, but no doubt he could have enumerated a dozen obviously "large" demes as easily as we ourselves can;[80] and like his fellow Halimousian Thucydides he will have known that Acharnai, with a squad of no fewer than twenty-two councillors, was by far the largest of them all.[81]

As with the question of the *number* of the demes in the Kleisthenic scheme, the fact of their palpable disparity in *size* is of fundamental importance not only in itself but for what it reveals of Kleisthenes' aims and methods. Here, as Andrewes has remarked, "we can only start from the results of the reform as we know them";[82] and those results make it clear beyond doubt that, whatever the artificiality of the two higher tiers (trittyes and tribes) erected upon it, the basis of the system at ground level was an organic and natural one: it was indeed—the switch of met-

---

[77] See Traill, *Organization*, pp. 64-70, improving upon the earlier analysis on the same lines by Gomme, *Population*, pp. 55-66. (I do not accept the "conspiracy theory" of Bicknell, *Studies*, passim, who argues that certain bouleutic quotas were deliberately fixed in such a way as to under-represent the demes of Kleisthenes' opponents while over-representing those of his supporters.)

[78] Traill, *Organization*, p. 56, who notes (n. 1) that "this is the *opinio communis* of scholars" (as indeed it is: see for instance Schoeffer, "Demoi," col. 28; Gomme, *Population*, pp. 37-66 passim; W. K. Pritchett, *Hesp.* 11, 1942, p. 235, n. 25; Hignett, *Constitution*, p. 150; Rhodes, *Boule*, p. 11). However, in the light of the emphasis recently placed upon the *military* significance of Kleisthenes' measures (e.g. Effenterre, "Mobilisation"; for doubts, see A. Andrewes, *CR* 33, 1983, p. 347), it is not impossible that the quotas represented *hoplite* numbers rather than total population.

[79] It looks as though Pambotadai and Sybridai, two small Erechtheid demes, occasionally or even regularly *shared* one bouleutic "seat" between them: Traill, *Organization*, pp. 14-15, 69.

[80] Namely (in order of size, as shown in bouleutic representation), Acharnai, Aphidna, Kydathenaion, Lower Paiania, Eleusis, Alopeke, Euonymon, Anaphlystos, Marathon, Coastal Lamptrai, Peiraieus, Phrearrhioi.

[81] On Acharnai, see Appendix 5.

[82] Andrewes, "Reform bill," p. 241.

aphor is irresistible—the veritable "grass roots." Nobody who sat down
to devise a deme system as an abstract exercise would have produced
one of such unequal units in so irrational a number. As we saw in the
first part of this chapter, the raw materials were ready at hand; and
Kleisthenes gave them their due as such.[83] If Acharnai was in fact larger
than a score of the smallest villages put together, so be it; and likewise
if "Upper" Paiania was dwarfed by, yet nonetheless distinct from, its
"Lower" neighbor and namesake.

The matter of *names*, indeed, will repay further attention. As we have
seen, the Aristotelian *Ath. Pol.* declares that it was Kleisthenes who
named (προσηγόρευσε) the demes, some "after their localities" (ἀπὸ τῶν
τόπων), others "after their founders" (ἀπὸ τῶν κτισάντων); and later
sources are replete with information, of greater or lesser plausibility,
pertaining to instances which fall under both these headings.[84] But how
far—for either category—did Kleisthenes actually invent and impose
wholly new names, and how far did he merely adopt names which were
already current? According to Andrewes, the *Ath. Pol.*'s προσηγόρευσε
"cannot mean that Kleisthenes invented all the names, and need not mean
that he invented any new name."[85] Both parts of this statement seem
fully justified, but some elaboration is required. It is indeed unlikely, and
it is certainly unprovable, that any deme-name *qua* name was newly
coined by or as a corollary of the Kleisthenic reform. There are, to be
sure, well-known instances where, on the usual and surely correct view,
the name of another, older type of organization—most obviously a

---

[83] There was one glaring exception to this "rule"—Brauron (cf. above, n. 30). This ancient
east-Attic town with its major cult of Artemis, included by Philochorus (*FGrH* 328 F94)
in the canon of the twelve poleis of Kekrops (cf. schol. Aristoph. *Peace*, line 874), was
regarded as a deme by Strabo (9.1.22) and explicitly called one by Pausanias (1.23.7, cf.
33.1) and by Stephanus of Byzantium. However, it was not recognized as such in the
Kleisthenic deme system but subsumed, in whole or part, under a deme given the name
Philaidai (Plut. *Sol.* 10.2; [Plato] *Hipparchos* 228B), the nucleus of which probably lay a
little to the west (Traill, *Organization*, p. 41 with n. 13). There can hardly be any other
explanation of this than the close connection of Brauron with the Peisistratid tyrants
(Wilamowitz, *Hermes* 12, 1877, p. 343; Lewis, "Cleisthenes," pp. 26-27). No other "omissions" from the Kleisthenic system seem as blatant as Brauron, though not all the very
small communities of Attica were independently included. In the vicinity of Aphidna, in
particular, several small hamlets such as Thyrgonidai and Titakidai might well have been
given separate status but were not; they did however attain some degree of semi-independent
existence in later times (see Traill, *Organization*, pp. 87ff., 121-122).

[84] See in general *Etym. Magn.* 327.33 (᾽Ελεεῖς), cf. 64.5 (῾Αλιμοῦς); and on particular
demes e.g. Plut. *Sol.* 10.2; Paus. 1.3.1 and 37.2; Harpoc., Θυμαιτάδαι, Κεραμεῖς,
Μελίτη, Οἰῆθεν, Οἶον; Hesych., ᾽Αναγυράσιος, ᾽Ιφίστιος; St. Byz., ᾽Αγνοῦς,
᾽Αγραυλή, Αἰθαλίδαι, ᾽Ανάφλυστος, ῎Αφιδνα, and many more; Suda, Κεραμίς,
Περιθοῖδαι.

[85] Andrewes, "Reform bill," p. 244, n. 3.

genos—was appropriated for that of a deme.[86] Yet should we assume[87] that all or even most of the demes named "after their founders" (many of them, though by no means all, distinguishable by their *-adai* or *-idai* suffix, as if collective patronymics) were lent their names in this way? Is it plausible that before 508/7 such demes were either anonymous[88] or else known by other, presumably topographic names? Since the bulk of the locality names must certainly have been already in use, I believe we may conclude that in naming the demes just as in numbering them, Kleisthenes' resort to artificial invention and contrivance was small.[89] In the majority of cases the names were well established in usage—some of them twice over[90]—and in the new order they were respected accordingly.

The idea that the Kleisthenic deme network was an essentially natural one is not of course new,[91] but its natural aspects seem to have been given increasingly greater emphasis in recent years, and it will be evident from the foregoing discussion that in my judgment this interpretative trend is well directed. Indeed it has perhaps not yet gone far enough: for even those scholars who have argued most cogently for the naturalness of the *rural* demes have lost faith when it came to the *city* demes, seeing them as, by contrast, "artificial."[92] There are no good grounds for this

[86] See Lewis, "Cleisthenes," p. 26, on this phenomenon in general and the clearest example of it—Boutadai: the name of an old and powerful *genos* was "democratized" by being taken over for the name of a small deme just west of the city of Athens along the Sacred Way, where members of one of its two branches held land (cf. Davies, *Families*, pp. 348-349).

[87] As does Traill, *Organization*, pp. 100-103. See rather G. de Sanctis, *Atthis*, 2d ed., Turin, 1912, pp. 62-63.

[88] According to Lewis, "Cleisthenes," p. 26, ?Aristot. *Ath. Pol.* 21.5 "notes that not all places had names." There is a textual problem here, to add to what is anyway an obscure and condensed locution (consult Rhodes, *Commentary*, p. 258; cf. Andrewes, "Reform bill," p. 244, n. 3), but I do not see that any likely version of the text can be made to yield the meaning that some Kleisthenic demes had *never* previously had a name; in any case this seems psychologically implausible for all but the very tiniest and most self-effacing communities.

[89] Cf. Bicknell, "Pendants," p. 147 (who does not, however, properly distinguish between the artificiality of the demes as such and of their names).

[90] On the homonymous (as opposed to the divided) demes, see Traill, *Organization*, pp. 123-125. The fact that the Kleisthenic system tolerated two demes called Eitea, Oinoe, Eroiadai, and so forth, is obviously another strong indication in itself of its conservative policy toward preexisting names. "Modifiers" are known in two instances (Halai Aixonides and Halai Araphenides; Oion Dekeleikon and Oion Kerameikon), but there is no reason to think that they were devised in 508/7.

[91] See for instance Schoeffer, "Demoi," cols. 1-3.

[92] E.g. R. S. Young, *Hesp.* 20, 1951, p. 141; Eliot, *Coastal Demes*, p. 3; Lewis, "Cleisthenes," p. 27; Thompson, "Deme," p. 75; Andrewes, "Reform bill," pp. 243-244; Murray, *Early Greece*, p. 255; Rhodes, *Commentary*, p. 254.

distinction,[93] but the city demes certainly do call for separate consideration.

Let us first define terms. The issue does not concern all the demes of the "city" trittyes—τῶν περὶ τὸ ἄστυ: ?Aristot. *Ath. Pol.* 21.4—for most of them lay well away from the city of Athens itself and were thus no different in character from the "inland" and "coastal" demes. However, within the actual city walls[94] lay five genuinely urban demes (Koile, Kollytos, Kydathenaion, Melite, Skambonidai), and there were others outside (e.g. Diomeia, Keiriadai, and most obviously Kerameis/Kerameikos) which were equally urban or at least suburban in type.[95] Why is it regularly asserted that such demes as these were "artificial"? According to Andrewes, "the area within the city walls was not an agglomeration of distinguishable villages,"[96] but this begs the very question at issue. By Eratosthenes' day, the second half of the third century, it is true that a visitor to the center of Athens apparently found nothing to tell him where Kollytos ended and Melite began; on the other hand, the *asty* of Athens, as of other cities, in the *eighth* century has been characterized by archaeologists as a cluster of distinct villages, so that the question becomes one of estimating how far this was still the case in 508/7.[97] Here unfortunately the archaeological picture lacks sufficient focus to give a simple answer. To deny or underestimate the extent of urbanization which took place in the seventh and particularly the sixth centuries would plainly be foolish. Yet the way in which most cities (ancient or modern) grow seems often to be a process not of simple centrifugal dispersion but, rather, of more or less complex incorporation and absorption of preexisting population centers into an all-embracing whole; and a feature of this phenomenon which anyone familiar with modern cities can con-

---

[93] Cf. Schoeffer, "Demoi," col. 3, and especially Bicknell, "Pendants," p. 147.

[94] On the vexed question of the pre-480 walls of Athens (if any) I am content to follow E. Vanderpool in *PHOROS: tribute to B. D. Meritt*, Locust Valley, New York, 1974, pp. 156-160, who argues for the construction of some sort of *peribolos* by Peisistratos. See also Wycherley, *Stones*, pp. 9-11; F. E. Winter, *Hesp.* Suppl. 19, 1982, pp. 199-204.

[95] Suburbs: in a well-known passage Thucydides calls Kerameis/Kerameikos τὸ κάλλιστον προάστειον τῆς πόλεως (2.34.5); and compare IG II²1191 (decree of the demesmen of Eleusis and Athenians garrisoned there), lines 19-20, οἱ τὸ προάστ|ιον οἰκοῦν[τ]ε[ς]. For an early migration of population from Melite to Diomeia, see Plut. *Moralia* 601B-C (*de exilio*), on which the views of Jane Harrison, *Primitive Athens as described by Thucydides*, Cambridge, 1906, pp. 143ff., seem to me more plausible than those of O. Broneer, *Hesp.* Suppl. 8, 1949, pp. 55-59.

[96] Andrewes, "Reform bill," pp. 243-244.

[97] Eratosthenes *apud* Strabo 1.4.7: see below, with n. 105. Athens as villages: references above, n. 11. (The same could be, and was, said of *Sparta* as late as the *fifth* century—see Thuc. 1.10.2—but that was a special and extreme case: see A. J. Toynbee, *Some Problems of Greek History*, Oxford, 1969, pp. 171-174.)

firm is that, for example, Greenwich Village or Chelsea retain both their names and their identities long after the encroachment of urban Manhattan or south London has engulfed them in its omnivorous maw. Naturally, modern analogies may mislead—yet even if one did pass fairly directly from Kollytos to Melite in late sixth-century Athens, that is no argument against their having been identifiably distinct "villages"[98] both before and after Kleisthenes. In the city no less than in the Attic countryside the Kleisthenic deme system seems to have adopted *names* which were already in use,[99] and altogether there is little to be said for the notion that the *asty* either posed special problems or called for special solutions.

Be that as it may, we can no longer shirk a fundamental conceptual question: what exactly was a Kleisthenic deme? At first sight the answer looks very simple. In the words of ?Aristot. *Ath. Pol.* 21.4, Kleisthenes "divided the country [and, we may add, the city!], by demes, into thirty parts." Even before this text was available to scholars it was regarded as self-evident that Kleisthenes' procedure was indeed one of *territorial division*—in essence a task of cartography, with the fixing of boundaries between demes as the crucial exercise[100]—and this "model" of the deme system has continued to recruit persuasive adherents.[101] Nevertheless it not only entails some uncomfortable corollaries—chiefly the need to postulate a cadastral survey, extending over several years, to define the necessary boundaries[102]—but derives *a priori* from assumptions which do not stand up to scrutiny. Such a scrutiny was conducted in a short but seminal article by Wesley Thompson in 1971;[103] and although in one

---

[98] I use the term *village* deliberately, for there is some reason to suppose that the urban quarters were indeed known, at least in common usage, as *kōmai*. Referring with studied vagueness to the lawgivers of archaic Athens (see above, p. 4), Isocrates 7.46 speaks of them "dividing the city (polis) by *kōmai* and the country by demes" (cf. Haussoullier, *Vie*, p. 183; Raubitschek, *Dedications*, p. 467; O. Broneer, *Hesp.* Suppl. 8, 1949, p. 57, n. 33; Bicknell, "Pendants," p. 147). One would be happier to believe this if it were corroborated elsewhere: *pace* Bicknell, *loc.cit.*, Plato *Laws* 746D (φρατρίας καὶ δήμους καὶ κώμας) is no help, for the relationship in Plato's Magnesia between the *dēmoi* and the *kōmai* is far from clear; cf. G. R. Morrow, *Plato's Cretan City*, Princeton, 1960, p. 126.

[99] See Andrewes, "Reform bill," p. 244 with n. 2; also Bicknell, "Pendants," p. 147, to whose data may be added Herod. 6.103.3 on Koile.

[100] Cf. Haussoullier, *Vie*, p. 2.

[101] E.g. E. Kirsten (for references, see Introduction, nn. 12-13) and Eliot, *Coastal Demes*, pp. 1-2 and passim; cf. Traill, *Organization*, p. 73, n. 6 (quoted below, n. 111).

[102] See Eliot, *Coastal Demes*, pp. 146-147; cf. H. Lauter, *AAA* 15, 1982, pp. 299-315, esp. 305 on "die wohl unter Kleisthenes vorgenommene Grenzregelung der Demenbezirke" (see further below, n. 110).

[103] Thompson, "Deme." Note also the earlier observation (quoted by Thompson) of D. M. Lewis, reviewing Eliot's *Coastal Demes* in *Gnomon* 35, 1963, pp. 723-725, at 724:

respect they need modification, his findings are in full accord with other features of Kleisthenes' approach as we can best envisage it.[104]

First and foremost, if the boundaries between all demes, rural and urban, had really been surveyed and fixed, they would then have been marked out with numerous official boundary-stones (*horoi*). Yet we are explicitly told by Eratosthenes that there were no such stones to be seen between the two inner-city demes of Kollytos and Melite. "When there are no accurate *horoi*, such as slabs (*stēlai*) or enclosures (*periboloi*), as is the case with Kollytos and Melite, one can declare 'Here is Kollytos, there is Melite,' but one cannot point out the *horoi*."[105] Nor is there any good evidence for a public archive in which deme boundaries, once drawn, were kept on record. Haussoullier believed that the *horismoi* which are mentioned by an Aristophanic scholiast referred to such "registres publics,"[106] but Jacoby made out a convincing case for the word's relating, instead, to the title of a scholarly work of (probably) the first century.[107] Thus, "the demes were unquestionably local units, but that does not mean that they had formal boundaries or that these boundaries were of any significance in Kleisthenes' reforms . . . [He] dealt with the demes as a series of isolated villages, not as blocks of territory."[108]

Thompson was in error on one point, however. In declaring that no *horoi* marking the boundary of a deme were known from anywhere in Attica he had overlooked the one from Peiraieus: IG II²2623, an isolated "*horos* of (the) territory of (the) Peiraieis" (ὅρος Π[ει]|ραέων

"for E(liot), [Kleisthenes] was drawing lines on a map; I think he was drawing up deme-registers. E. thinks of a deme as a territory; for me, it is much more the group of people living in that territory."

[104] Andrewes, "Reform bill," pp. 243-245; Bicknell, "Pendants," p. 147.

[105] Eratosthenes *apud* Strabo 1.4.7: μὴ ὄντων γὰρ ἀκριβῶν ὅρων καθάπερ Κολυττοῦ καὶ Μελίτης, οἷον στηλῶν ἢ περιβόλων, τοῦτο μὲν ἔχειν φάναι ἡμᾶς, ὅτι τουτὶ μέν ἐστι Κολυττός, τουτὶ δὲ Μελίτη, τοὺς ὅρους δὲ μὴ ἔχειν εἰπεῖν. Extraordinarily (as Thompson observes, "Deme," pp. 73-74, with references), this passage has often been construed as meaning the exact reverse of what it clearly says; cf. Andrewes, "Reform bill," p. 243.

[106] Schol. Aristoph. *Birds*, line 997: Μελίτη γὰρ ἅπαν ἐκεῖνο, ὡς ἐν τοῖς ὁρισμοῖς γέγραπται τῆς πόλεως; see Haussoullier, *Vie*, p. 2, n. 3 (confining his suggestion, admittedly, to "les dèmes urbains").

[107] Jacoby *apud* FGrH 375 (asserting nonetheless that there must have been a cadastral survey by Kleisthenes and *horoi* marking the deme boundaries!). Note that Haussoullier also drew attention to the existence of magistrates called *horistai* (*Vie*, p. 2, n. 3), but he wisely did not directly suggest that their business was to fix *deme* boundaries. See IG I³84, lines 7-8; Hyper. 4 (*Eux.*)16, apparently an ad hoc board of fifty; IG II²1177, lines 21-24 (deme of Peiraieus); *Lex. Seguer.* V, *Lexeis Rhetorikai*, ὁρισταί [= Bekker, *Anecd. Gr.* 1.287.18].

[108] Thompson, "Deme," p. 72.

[χώ]|[ϱ]ας) datable by its letter-forms to the fourth century or later.[109] What is more, since Thompson wrote, a few more *horoi* have been published and discussed which in some instances may possibly have marked deme boundaries.[110] Yet these too date from the fourth century or later, which is a fact of crucial importance. However necessary or desirable it may have become *later*—perhaps as the result of boundary disputes—to specify for practical purposes the geographical extent of any individual deme,[111] there is still no evidence to contradict Thompson's view of how the Kleisthenic deme system was originally brought into being; for such evidence could only come in the form of *horoi* contemporaneous with Kleisthenes' measures themselves, or at least from the period immediately following them.

It remains true, then, that Thompson's thesis makes possible a simple and satisfactory picture of how the deme network was actually set up. All that Kleisthenes' bill had to do was to ordain "that each man was to register in his home village,"[112] which meant in whichever deme-center he regarded as the focus of his local community.[113] The deme "bound-

---

[109] It is thus distinct in date as well as function from the Peiraieus *horoi* which he did mention ("Deme," p. 73 with n. 10), i.e., those probably connected with Hippodamos' survey in the mid fifth century: see D. K. Hill, *AJA* 36, 1932, pp. 254-259. Note that the three ὅρος Κεραμεικοῦ stones (IG II²2617-2619) have nothing to do—*pace* H. Lauter, *ΑΑΑ* 15, 1982, p. 300—with the deme Kerameis; cf. Wycherley, *Stones*, pp. 254-255.

[110] See esp. J. S. Traill, *Hesp.* Suppl. 19, 1982, pp. 162-171, on a series of six rupestral inscriptions from Lamptrai originally found by Mitsos and Vanderpool (cf. Eliot, *Coastal Demes*, pp. 63-64) and reading OPʃΠΜ; he understands this to mean ὅρ(ος) ʃ π(αραλίας καὶ) μ(εσογαίας), and suggests a date soon after 307/6, when the transference of Upper Lamptrai to the new tribe Antigonis (while Lower Lamptrai remained in Erechtheis) might have made marking part of the boundary necessary or desirable. A more dogmatic approach is taken by H. Lauter, *AAA* 15, 1982, pp. 299-315 (see above, n. 102), independently suggesting the same expansion of ΠΜ, but not making a convincing case for regarding as *deme* boundary markers (which he insists everywhere existed: ibid., p. 300) either the rock-cut OPOC from Vari which he publishes himself or the Roman-period ones discussed by J. Ober, *Hesp.* 50, 1981, pp. 73-77 (see Lauter, p. 315, "Nachtrag"; Ober himself conjectured that they marked the limits of an apiary). The five rupestral OPOC inscriptions cited by H. Lohmann, *Hellenika: Jahrbuch für die Freunde Griechenlands*, 1983, pp. 98-117, at 99-104 (I thank Robin Osborne for a copy of this), do seem to have marked a deme boundary, between Atene and Sounion; but again they date from the (?late) fourth century.

[111] Note Traill, *Organization*, p. 73, n. 6: "... property is often listed in inscriptions with reference to the demes and ... all the territory of Attica, with a few exceptions, must have been associated theoretically, if not actually, with one deme or another." The first of these observations should include the word *later*, while the second concedes the point at issue; until the (?late) fourth century, it seems, the rule was theory, not actuality.

[112] Thompson, "Deme," p. 74; cf. Andrewes, "Reform bill," p. 243.

[113] For most men this will surely have been a simple decision, but two categories of people will have been faced with a choice: those living equidistantly from two, or more,

aries" can thus have taken shape, in this first instance, not *de iure* but *de facto*—not, that is, by being formally drawn up as part of a centralized and laborious cartographic survey but as the accumulated result of tens of thousands of individuals doing what was required of them (presumably within a specified period of time). Quite possibly this natural, multi-centripetal process gave rise to some initial anomalies, especially where two or more deme-centers were quite close to one another, as was the case particularly (though not exclusively) in the inner city.[114] Perhaps there was provision for the more serious ones to be subsequently ex-amined and rationalized. To be sure, this was only the first and doubtless the easiest stage of Kleisthenes' demographic New Deal. Still to come—as the timetable is best envisaged[115]—was the grouping of demes into trittyes, and trittyes into tribes. However, while some degree of super-imposed contrivance and coordination in these later procedures seems as good as certain,[116] this cannot gainsay the likelihood that the whole conception took as its basis a political "map" of Athens and Attica drawn, in a real and important sense, not by one Athenian, Kleisthenes, but by them all.

✳

Before moving on to other problems, this will be a suitable point to take stock of the conclusions which have so far emerged from our long and occasionally tortuous discussion. While the risk of circular argument is ever-present, it is surely significant that the word "natural" has featured so prominently in our reasoning, with regard to (*a*) the *number* of the demes, the arithmetically intransigent one hundred and thirty-nine; (*b*) the *size* of the demes, ranging from tiny Sybridai and the like to giant Acharnai; (*c*) the *names* of the demes, which I have argued were virtually all already in existence (though not, admittedly, all applied to demes); and (*d*) the actual genesis of the demes as units of the Kleisthenic political system. This last, as we have just seen, probably took the form of a concerted act of self-identification by all the members of local commu-nities, in the knowledge (we may surely presume) that those communities

---

deme-centers (see further on this below, with next note) and those with houses or land in two, or more, places (see on this C.W.J. Eliot, *Historia* 16, 1967, p. 285, n. 33; Bicknell, *Studies*, pp. 60-61).

[114] On the matter of deme boundaries in the *asty* it is customary to refer to the theory of R. S. Young, *Hesp.* 20, 1951, pp. 140-143, that some main roads may have served this purpose; but note the comments of Andrewes, "Reform bill," p. 244 with n. 1, who points out that ". . . a road, at least one inhabited on both sides, tends to unify rather than divide."

[115] Andrewes, "Reform bill," pp. 244-246, cf. 248.

[116] On this vexed question, see the sensible remarks of Traill, *Organization*, p. 71, n. 31.

were now to take on a wholly new and challenging role in both central and local government. This knowledge will doubtless have been welcome to some, unwelcome to others—those who had hitherto been secure in their grip on both local and national affairs through the kinship groups. "It is easy to imagine the attraction of the proposal that groups of familiar neighbours should not only manage their own local affairs but play a part in the affairs of the state. To the extent that they were seen as replacing phratries at the lowest level of the organization of the community, the new demes could be seen as another means [besides, that is, the tribes of mixed trittyes] of reducing aristocratic influence, even if in many cases membership of the old phratry and the new deme overlapped."[117] It would be futile to pretend that we can determine with certainty which particular features of Kleisthenes' program played the greatest part in enlisting popular support, or indeed whether the appeal of the measures lay primarily in what they were creating or what they were destroying. But there can be little doubt that the proposals for the demes, as they were discussed and debated, were an important factor in engendering broad-based goodwill and enthusiasm on the part of those who were now to become *dēmotai*.[118]

Although the precise form and timetable of the measures is not given by any source, a likely reconstruction is inherent, as we have seen, in the view of the nature of the demes and of their mode of creation which I have followed and extended here, and at this juncture it may be worthwhile to argue it through explicitly. No obstacle appears to stand in the way of our envisaging that all Kleisthenes' proposals as they related to the demes were embodied in a single "reform bill" (to adhere to Andrewes' phrase), though, if so, some of them will have had to be enacted in principle only and left for practical implementation later. It is therefore

---

[117] Andrewes, "Reform bill," p. 243. For examples of phratry/deme overlap, see IG II²1241 (Dyaleis/Myrrhinous) and probably 1178 (Ikarieis/Ikarion: see lines 4-6, with Lewis, "Cleisthenes," p. 32 and n. 93).

[118] Cf. Ostwald, *Nomos*, pp. 149-160, esp. 151-153. We may take it that the great majority of "those who were now to become *dēmotai*" had previously been—and, whatever Kleisthenes' intentions, continued to be—*phratores*. On the other hand we are told three times that Kleisthenes was responsible for enfranchising new citizens (Aristot. *Pol.* 1275b32-37; ?Aristot. *Ath. Pol.* 21.2 and 4—21.2 being wrongly construed, in my opinion, by Rhodes, *Commentary*, p. 250). The probability that enfranchisements were a merely tangential aim of Kleisthenes' reform is insufficient reason for doubting that they occurred, and indeed one may readily envisage what happened: the men struck off the phratry lists, rightly or wrongly, in the *diapsēphismos* of 510 (?Aristot. *Ath. Pol.* 13.5) were admitted into the deme lists two years later; cf. Ostwald, *Nomos*, p. 152. Yet I am still disposed to believe (see Whitehead, *Metic*, pp. 143-147) that a separate and lesser status, that of *metoikos*, was now created to meet the needs of free inhabitants of Attica who could not lay claim to citizenship on any grounds. On metics in the demes, see Chap. 3D.

equally likely, perhaps, that two or even more "bills" were needed. However, as nothing substantial hinges upon this,[119] we may for simplicity's
sake assume a single package of measures followed by some detailed
work behind the scenes.

Clearly the central clause of the bill itself was the one described in the
words of ?Aristot. *Ath. Pol.* 21.4: "he made (fellow-)demesmen of those
living in each of the demes." This in effect meant that "each man was
to register in his home village" (W. E. Thompson). Thompson is not
entirely clear on the details of how this registration was actually achieved,
but his view should not be taken to imply that the locations (and names)
of the deme-centers were not officially specified.[120] Without such specification, people might naturally have gone, for example, to Brauron rather
than to Philaidai; and in general terms a network of officials surely needed
to be on hand in predetermined places to await the arriving registrants.
On the other hand it is equally improbable that the work of establishing
the canonical list of demes will have been undertaken before the approval
of the idea of demes in principle; so one cannot think that Kleisthenes'
initial measures contained such a list, but simply ordained its speedy
compilation. What the measures must, however, have contained, besides
the basic registration clause, was provision in at least the following two
areas:

1. The registration process itself. It is possible that *ad hoc* commis-
sioners of some sort were appointed to supervise the enrolment, but
perhaps more likely that it was prescribed as the inaugural task of the
dēmarchoi, the principal deme officials, and the only ones actually mentioned in the context of 508/7 (?Aristot. *Ath. Pol.* 21.5). Admittedly,
once the deme system was in operation the demarchs were appointed by,
as well as from, their fellow demesmen, and we are speaking here of the
time before the bodies of demesmen had defined themselves; nonetheless
this first batch of demarchs could conceivably have been chosen in the
city *ekklēsia* or by some other means.[121] But whoever the registrars were,
their *modus operandi* will certainly have been laid down with precision,
for their task was a crucial and sensitive one. Once the bodies of demesmen existed, enrolment in demes just as in phratries could be a matter

---

[119] Cf. Andrewes, "Reform bill," p. 242.

[120] Thompson, "Deme," pp. 74-76; but see rather Andrewes, "Reform bill," pp. 243-
244.

[121] If so, it would not be excessively cynical to suspect that many of them were the old
"political bosses" in another guise; thus, amongst others, Bicknell, *Studies*, p. 35. Indeed,
however and wherever the first demarchs were chosen, they were surely either directly
elected or else (even more directly!) appointed; and the circles from which such men were
naturally drawn cannot have widened overnight.

of collective scrutiny (see below); but again, *before* the definition of these bodies—indeed, for the actual act of defining them—we can say nothing of the procedures involved beyond the fact that they must surely have been centrally prescribed and universally applicable.

2. Deme representation in the council. Even if most scholars are right no longer to disbelieve that Kleisthenes' *boulē* of Five Hundred was a remodelled version of a Solonic *boulē* of Four Hundred rather than a completely new creation,[122] the principle that its members were to be drawn from demes rather than simply from tribes[123] was necessarily and indubitably a novel one in 508/7 and needed approval in principle at this stage. Implementing the principle, however, must have been a lengthy and complicated business. In determining the different deme-centers, Kleisthenes must have had some general inkling of the numbers likely to register at each of them; and, if the view of the registration process which we have taken here is correct, those numbers could quite quickly have become known and exact, thus permitting a *provisional* calculation of the appropriate numbers of bouleutic "seats" in each case. On the other hand, the demes were not represented in the council directly, so to speak, but in their groupings of trittyes (?Aristot. *Ath. Pol.* 44.1) and tribes (ibid., 21.3 and 43.2); so the overall arithmetic cannot have been finalized until the full deme-trittys-tribe structure had been pieced together.

Thus far, I believe, we may progress by means of legitimate inference and reasoning. To go further can only be undisguised speculation. Either in this principal group of Kleisthenes' measures or as a close corollary of it, for example, there must arguably have been some enactment(s) which represented the facts behind the sources' assertion that the demes and their demarchs superseded the *naukrariai* and their *naukraroi* (?Aristot. *Ath. Pol.* 21.5; cf. Pollux 8.108 and Hesych., ναύκλαροι [*sic*]). To be sure, the naukraries apparently continued to exist, suitably adjusted in number (Cleidemus, *FGrH* 323 F8), but that is consonant with Kleisthenes' way of bypassing rather than abolishing the old institutions.[124] How, though, does one determine precisely, or even approximately, what the pre-Kleisthenic naukraries were and what they did?[125] From ?Aristot.

---

[122] There has been a steady move away, on this issue, from the scepticism voiced thirty years ago by Hignett, *Constitution*, pp. 92-96; see for instance Ostwald, *Nomos*, p. 158, n. 3, and p. 162 with n. 5; Rhodes, *Boule*, pp. 208-209 (with references at 208, n. 2); Jeffery, *Archaic Greece*, p. 107, n. 7; Murray, *Early Greece*, p. 306.

[123] This is explicit (for the second half of the fourth century) at ?Aristot. *Ath. Pol.* 62.1, and of course implicit and quantifiable in the bouleutic lists, discussed above.

[124] Cf. ?Aristot. *Ath. Pol.* 21.6 (quoted at the beginning of this chapter) on priesthoods; see on this Chap. 7, n. 3.

[125] For some references, see above, n. 43.

Ath. Pol. 8.3 and other, later sources a very general picture of local divisions with a role in the levying of both taxes and troops is discernible; but there are obscurities at every turn, and nothing useful can be said about either the means or the consequences of the transference of these fiscal and military functions to the demes.[126]

When it comes to estimating what functions of *local* government were entrusted to or required of the demes under Kleisthenes' scheme we are scarcely any better placed, given the all-pervading difficulty of judging the advisability of extrapolating back to 508/7 what is known about the demes' activities in the fifth and especially the fourth centuries. Moreover, this question is further complicated in its turn by the methodological problem of determining the extent to which generalizations about what "the demes" did are proper in any case. How far were uniform procedures laid down for them by Kleisthenes' measures (and others like them, later), and how far were the individual demes left to devise for themselves what suited them best? This latter issue will be probed in Chapter 2B, where it will be argued that *laisser faire* reigned in some respects and stand-ardization was required in others. However, it still remains a moot point how much of this standardization was prescribed in 508/7 itself and how much subsequently. In plain terms, we do not know. As the minimum necessary to provide for local autonomy it will be safe to assume an order to the effect that the demes were to administer their affairs, sacred and secular, through assemblies of all the demesmen,[127] yet one cannot self-evidently proceed from that to assume that anything was said about the timing and/or frequency of such assemblies, or about specific matters with which the meetings should deal.

It seems unlikely, however, that uniformity will not have been required in those facets of the demes' activities where the interests of the whole polis came directly into play—the facets, that is, where local and central government were virtually one and the same. The most obviously im-portant instance of this would be the maintenance of the lists of the *dēmotai*—which amounted, collectively, to the register of *politai*—and the control of those to be entered on or expunged from them. Cynthia Patterson has recently contended that "it is not justifiable to assume that the system [described in ?Aristot. *Ath. Pol.* 42.1-2] of deme scrutiny, registration, review by the Boule and possible appeal to a *dikastērion* emerged full-blown from the head of Cleisthenes. Rather, it would prob-ably have developed during the course of the fifth century, based initially

---

[126] On the theory of Effenterre, "Mobilisation," that the deme registers had primarily a military purpose, see below, n. 130.

[127] Cf. Ostwald, *Nomos*, p. 153.

on phratry procedure but also affected by the growth of the jurisdiction of the popular courts and of the power of the Boule."[128] Fair comment though this is, the point is equally valid in reverse: the uniform procedures well documented in the second half of the fourth century must surely have had their roots in some basic regulations laid down, with the same end in view, by Kleisthenes. Thus, I suggest, we may—indeed we must—envisage from the start the two fundamental elements of scrutiny-examination (*dokimasia*)[129] and registration-enrolment, either in the later-attested ledger called the *lēxiarchikon grammateion* or else some precursor of it.[130]

[128] Patterson, *Citizenship Law*, p. 27; cf. Effenterre, "Mobilisation," p. 8.

[129] Cf. Rhodes, *Boule*, p. 173: ". . . the δοχιμασία of young citizens goes back at any rate as far as Aristophanes' *Wasps* [see line 578], and is unlikely to be a more recent creation than Cleisthenes' deme organization. . . ." Deme registration will be discussed in full in Chap. 4B, sec. 1.

[130] There are three interlocking problems here: when the *lēxiarchika grammateia* (hereinafter "l.g.") were first created; who was included in them; and the meaning of *lēxiarchikon*. With regard to the first, the l.g. are *first securely attested* in an inscription of the third quarter of the fifth century, IG I³138, line 6. This may or may not be held sufficient to indicate that they were created in 508/7; but even if they were not, there must have been something very like them. A more crucial question, in a sense, is the second problem: who exactly was registered in them? It has been argued that IG I³138 shows that the thetes were not included in them in this period (indeed, not until the mid fourth century); for a distinction seems to be drawn between two military categories who are to pay a levy to Apollo—the *hippeis* and [hoplites], from whom payment will be exacted by the demarchs using the l.g., and the archers, citizen and foreign, who will pay through their commanders. As the citizen archers will have been thetes, the argument goes, they are here shown to be excluded from the l.g. See on this e.g. J. Toepffer, *Hermes* 30, 1895, pp. 391-400; Busolt/Swoboda, *Staatskunde*, p. 966, n. 1; and especially C. Habicht, *Hermes* 89, 1961, pp. 1-35, at 5-6, who used this as the basis of his objection to the authenticity of lines 27-31 of the Troizen "Decree of Themistokles" (ML, no. 23), where the l.g. are the source of rowers, i.e. (again) thetes. However, this argument can be challenged by casting doubt upon the orthodox interpretation (as above) of IG I³138: see e.g. H. Berve, *Sitzb. Münch.* 1961, no. 3, pp. 17-18; B. D. Meritt, *Lectures . . . L. T. Semple*, first series, no. 3, 1962 [1967], pp. 123-124; M. H. Jameson, *Historia* 12, 1963, pp. 399-400, and *Archaiognosia* 1, 1980, pp. 216-223; cf. ML, p. 51 and Rhodes, *Boule*, p. 173, n. 3. There has been no entirely satisfactory counter-explanation of what is happening in the Apollo inscription; on the other hand it is hardly the simple proof of the exclusion of thetes from the l.g. that it has been claimed to be, so on balance I see no good reason to doubt that the l.g. existed in 480—one stage nearer Kleisthenes—or that they included such demesmen as were thetes. The problem would doubtless be eased if we knew what the term *lēxiarchikon* means, but we do not (cf. Andrewes, "Reform bill" p. 244, n. 6). In addition to the discussions cited above, see now Effenterre, "Mobilisation," esp. pp. 7-16, with full sources and doxography. I agree with him that the l.g. were probably Kleisthenic and that probably *all* demesmen were listed on them at the age of majority ("Mobilisation," pp. 11, 15); but there my agreement ends. Following a suggestion of Toepffer (*loc.cit.* above) he rejects the common opinion of most lexicographers and most modern scholars alike, which connects *lēxis* with

*

After so much solemn weighing of incorporeal probabilities and possibilities, let us finally turn to the only item of solid (though fragmentary) contemporary evidence. In 1942 Eugene Vanderpool published "an archaic inscribed stele from Marathon,"[131] which preserves on its obverse side the remains of thirteen lines of a unique legal document of the late sixth century:

$$
\begin{array}{l}
[\ldots\overset{8\text{-}9}{\ldots}\ldots]\text{ν βολ}[- - - - - - - - - - - - - - - - -] \\
[\ldots\overset{6\text{-}7}{\ldots}]\tilde{\text{ι}}\alpha \;\vdots\; \textit{ḥ}\text{εκον}[- - - - - - - - - -] \\
[.]\text{σιον, γνοσθεῖ δὲ } [- - - - - - - - - - - -] \\
[.]\text{ν ἀτεχνος} \;\vdots\; \text{μὲ π}[- - - - - - - -ἄλλοθ]\text{-} \\
(5)\quad [\text{ι] δὲ μεδὲ ḥαμō } [- - - - - - - - - - - - - - -] \\
\quad\quad \text{κελεύοσι} \;\vdots\; \text{χινχά[νεν } - - - - - - - - - - -] \\
\quad\quad [\text{ἐ]πιδικάζεν} \;\vdots\; \text{κατ}[- - - - - - - - - - ἐπιδ]\text{-} \\
\quad\quad [\text{ι]καζέτο} \;\vdots\; \text{τὲν λο/}[- - - - - - - - - ḥότα]\text{-} \\
\quad\quad \text{ν ḥαρκτοῦρος ἐπι[τέλλεται} - - - - - - - -] \\
(10)\quad [.]\text{ν τρέπεν} \;\vdots\; \text{ἴστο ḥιΕ}[- - - - - - - - - -] \\
\quad\quad [.]\text{οιας} \;\vdots\; \text{τὰσυρε̄} \;\vdots\; \text{καὶ } [- - - - - - - - - - -] \\
\quad\quad \text{τέταρας ὀβελός} \;\vdots\; \text{ḥυ}[- - - - - - - - - - ḥυ]\text{-} \\
\quad\quad \text{περ πεντέκοντα} \;\vdots\; \text{κ}[- - - - - - - - - - - - -]
\end{array}
$$

The verb χινχά[νεν in the sixth line appears to be an archaic term meaning "prosecute" (so Photius and the Suda, under κιγχάνειν); and in the following lines, 7-8, [ἐ]πιδικάζεν and ἐπιδ]|[ι]καζέτο evidently refer to some official's pronouncing the verdict in a dispute at law. Further down the stone (lines 12-13) the phrases "four obols" and "(?) in excess of fifty" are preserved. To quote from Vanderpool's commentary *ad loc.*: "Aristotle tells us that under Peisistratos a board of circuit judges (οἱ κατὰ δήμους δικασταί) was established whose duty it was to travel round among the demes deciding small cases in which the total amount involved was ten drachmai or less. Kleisthenes appears to have abolished this board (for Aristotle says that it was reestablished in 453/2 B.C.) and must have placed these minor judicial matters in the hands of the indi-

---

the legal capacity to inherit a *klēros*, and instead conjures out of Pollux 8.104 and the (reasonable) connection of *lēxiarchikon* with *lēxiarchos* the remarkable conclusion that the l.g. were military rosters arranged in year-groups. The malady which Effenterre diagnoses is bad, certainly, but his remedy is worse. Without further evidence, the problem seems stale and insoluble.

[131] E. Vanderpool, *Hesp.* 11, 1942, pp. 329-337; the text published as SEG 10.2, with readings by W. Peek and A. E. Raubitschek, was marginally different. (I give here the latest text, IG I³2.)

vidual demes. Our inscription, which dates from the time of Kleisthenes, is probably to be connected with this change and perhaps it defined the duties and powers of the local judges or courts." I would quarrel with these comments only to the extent of pointing out that "Aristotle" (i.e. the author of the *Ath. Pol.*) writes of the ten-drachma limit in the context of the duties of these judges in his own day (53.2); it can be no more than supposition that this had been so from the start. A more important point to make is the fact that no comparable documents have been found in other demes since Vanderpool wrote. His suggestion is worth pursuing nonetheless, for it can perhaps be stated a little more strongly. We considered in section A of this chapter, in connection with Solon, the fragment of Demetrius of Phaleron which runs: καὶ δημάρχους οἱ περὶ Σόλωνα καθίσταντο ἐν πολλῇ σπουδῇ, ἵνα οἱ κατὰ δῆμον (*sic*) διδῶσι καὶ λαμβάνωσι τὰ δίκαια παρ' ἀλλήλων. Jacoby held that Demetrius was in fact talking about the deme dikasts, not about demarchs, which would mean that the (mis?)quotation is quite irrelevant to the scholiast's digest of facts concerning the latter. In any event one may suspect that "Solon and his associates" knew nothing of either. It is just possible, however, that the passage is not as thoroughly garbled as it appears, but preserves a precious crumb of information—that for the half-century between Kleisthenes and 453/2 the demarchs acted as local justices in their demes.

Such then were the Kleisthenic demes and most of what can be said or surmised about their antecedents and about the role which their creator intended for them.[132] Did the latter indeed amount to Hopper's *Basis of the Athenian Democracy*? Modern scholars no longer find it as easy to believe as Herodotus did (6.131.1) that outright democracy was what Kleisthenes had in mind; yet insofar as democracy was the ultimate outcome of the Kleisthenic political organization,[133] the centrality of the demes to them both is clear enough.[134] We would do better, no doubt, when attempting to identify the political principles appropriate to Kleisthenes' own day (and invoked, very probably, by Kleisthenes himself),

[132] The matter of origins will of course recur in subsequent chapters, as particular topics arise.

[133] Cf. Ostwald, *Nomos*, p. 154.

[134] It was inevitable, perhaps, that sooner or later a scholar would suggest that the very word *dēmokratia* did not mean "power to the people (*dēmos*)" but "power to the demes (*dēmoi*)"; see now K. H. Kinzl, *Gymnasium* 85, 1978, pp. 117-127, 312-326, esp. 324-326—"Regierung bzw. Verwaltung nach Demen" (p. 324). To reject this one need only examine the context of every passage which Kinzl himself collects there.

to lay emphasis upon *isonomia*, political equality[135]—improbable though it may be that this alluring slogan was translated into full and practical reality more instantaneously in the microcosmic affairs of the demes than in those of the polis wherein they all lay encompassed. At all events, whatever the prevailing constitutional form and political climate, the deme system had come to Attica to stay; and its one hundred and thirty-nine components provide from now on both the permanent backdrop to the events of Athenian domestic history during the classical and early Hellenistic periods and also, from our own standpoint, an important and distinctive body of evidence about the demes themselves, collectively and individually. To that evidence we must turn in the next chapter.

[135] See Ostwald, *Nomos*, pp. 96-136, cf. 153-160.

CHAPTER 2

SOURCES AND
METHODOLOGY

For more than half a millennium, following its creation in the late sixth century, the Kleisthenic deme system generated directly or indirectly a rich diversity of epigraphic and literary material; and this, insofar as it has been preserved, offers the historian his data for studying the phenomenon itself. We must now classify and evaluate this miscellany of sources, and make an attempt—which is long overdue—at formulating some methodological principles for its use.

A. Sources

What we know of the demes comes from three categories of source material:[1] inscriptions, literary sources, and lexicographers and scholiasts. During the century since Haussoullier wrote *La Vie Municipale* there has been no increase in the last of these, but the second has been augmented in several areas previously deficient, while the first has expanded very considerably indeed. In any event it will be useful to survey here the principal features and contributions of each of the three categories in turn.

1. INSCRIPTIONS

In the public domain the Athenians appear to have begun the practice of committing laws and decrees to stone at or near the very time of the Kleisthenic reforms.[2] It is thus no surprise to find amongst the very earliest Athenian public inscriptions the fragmentary records of decisions which,

---

[1] Cf. the brief review by Haussoullier, *Vie*, pp. ix-xii.

[2] See IG I³1 (concerning the cleruchs on Salamis). Would that Kleisthenes' measures themselves were preserved in this medium!

it would seem, relate to the demes either collectively[3] or individually.[4] But unfortunately this promise of ample epigraphic documentation of the evolving relationship between the polis and its demes[5] remains only very partially fulfilled. To judge, perforce, from what survives, the overall volume of public inscriptions grew ever greater with each decade but the proportion of it which was directly concerned with the demes failed to increase commensurately. The small body of surviving enactments which do pertain to the demes are almost all, one may note, concerned with matters of cult and religion;[6] it is literary sources, curiously enough, which give us the only deme-related decrees on secular subjects, either *verbatim* (Andoc. 1.83-84 and 97) or in paraphrase ([Demosth.] 50.6-8). Otherwise the documents either have not survived or else were never inscribed on stone in the first place. In practice we may "generate" some of them by extrapolation from the results which they produced, but, as will be seen in the second part of the chapter, such a procedure requires the formulation and application of clear methodological principles if it is not to introduce serious distortion into the subject.

In terms of sheer quantity, then, the bulk of the information which epigraphic sources provide about the demes comes from the public inscriptions of the demes themselves, and particularly from the decrees of the individual deme assemblies, which in form as well as in content are closely akin to the enactments of the all-embracing Assembly, the city *ekklēsia*.[7] Such decrees, as noted in the Introduction, have multiplied in number threefold since Haussoullier's day: whereas he had available around thirty of them,[8] the figure is currently in excess of one hundred.[9] Even so it is not nearly enough! As Traill has observed, "evidence for

---

[3] IG I³2 (cf. Chap. 1, p. 36): local jurisdiction, late sixth century.

[4] IG I³3 (on the reverse of I³2): the organization of Herakleian games in Marathon, shortly after 490; see the *editio princeps* by E. Vanderpool, *Hesp.* 11, 1942, pp. 329-337, and Lewis, "Cleisthenes," p. 31. See also IG I³8 on the cults of Sounion.

[5] The complexities of this in the crucial early decades are tantalizingly obscure. See, for example, the seventeen fragments of *leges sacrae* from the period 480-450 which *seem* to include a decree of the deme Melite, (B. D. Meritt, *Hesp.* 36, 1967, pp. 72-84, no. 15; see now IG I³243); cf. Ostwald, *Nomos*, p. 4, n. 4.

[6] IG I³78, 82, 138, 141; IG II²204, 334.

[7] For a "partial list" of deme decrees, see Traill, *Organization*, p. 74, n. 10, with addenda in *Hesp.* 47, 1978, p. 279 (note on line 18). For a full list, see below, Appendix 3.

[8] See Haussoullier, *Vie*, pp. ix-x.

[9] It is difficult to give a precise figure: there are instances where the fragmentary nature of a stone does not allow us to see how many decrees were inscribed thereon (e.g. *AM* 67, 1942, pp. 8-9, no. 6: Halai Aixonides); and it is not always easy—and perhaps not always important—to separate out deme enactments into the distinct categories of decrees, contracts, laws, sacred laws, sacred calendars, etc. (and in Appendix 3, as will be seen, no such attempt is made).

the local functioning of the demes, e.g. deme decrees, though extremely important, is unfortunately very limited."[10]

One obvious limit arises from the provenance of the stones. We do not have about one hundred decrees from about one hundred different demes (which would be approximately two-thirds of all demes) but from no more than about thirty-five of them (which is more like a quarter of them all).[11] Could it be argued that this unequal distribution is advantageous, in that the twenty decrees from Eleusis, the dozen from Rhamnous, or the ten from Aixone provide an especially penetrating insight into those particular demes? Sadly, this is not really the case, for most of the decrees in question are honorific grants of a more or less repetitive kind (see below); so given the option one would eagerly exchange a good many of them for documents from the numerous demes for which the epigraphic record is bare.[12]

A second limit is chronological. Although there is a spread of these decrees across three centuries—from the first half of the fifth century to the first half of the second—the distribution is again unequal, and this time even more grossly so. Two-thirds of them come from the fourth century; what is more, over half of them come from the second half of that century. (The third century is better documented than the fifth, but, even so, poorly.)

Closely linked with this chronological concentration of the deme decrees is the factor of their subject matter, and this gives rise in turn to a third limitation in the information which they can be expected to furnish. Only about one-third of all deme decrees are directly concerned with the deme's internal administrative business, recurrent or extraordinary, secular or (more often) sacred.[13] The other two-thirds grant honors, substantive or symbolic. The honorands are either Athenian political celebrities who have done the deme in question some real or pretended service[14] or, more usually, the deme's own residents and, particularly, officials—most commonly demarchs[15]—and quasi-officials such as deme *chorēgoi*.[16]

---

[10] Traill, *Organization*, p. 74.

[11] Again (cf. n. 9) it is not easy to specify an exact figure: a number of documents are unattributable, and may therefore have been produced equally as well by those demes with securely attributed documents as by those without.

[12] Note the comments of O. Broneer, *Hesp.* 11, 1942, p. 270, on the rarity of decrees from the *city* (-center) demes; cf. Chap. 7, p. 184 with n. 45.

[13] Given the number of fragmentary stones it is again difficult to be more precise than this.

[14] E.g. IG II²1187 (Eleusis) and 1201 (Aixone).

[15] E.g. *Hesp.* 8, 1939, pp. 177-180, and IG II²949, lines 30ff. (both Eleusis); IG II²1178, 1179, and SEG 22.117 (all Ikarion); cf. Demosth. 57.64 (Halimous).

[16] E.g. IG II²1198, 1200, and *AM* 66, 1941, pp. 218-219, no. 1 (all Aixone).

If we had more decrees from before ca. 400, even ca. 350, these proportions would certainly be different. Indeed, as the demes had no equivalent of the city's proxeny decrees (in the broadest sense of that term:
honorific decrees for non-Athenians resident outside Attica), it is safe to
predict that new deme decrees from the century and a half after Kleisthenes will be "business" decrees, and especially valuable on that account. Equally predictable, however, is the likelihood that most new
discoveries will in fact be yet more honorific decrees from the fourth or
third centuries; and one can only hope that they may come from a wider
spread of demes.

These three limitations put together might seem to provoke the gloomy
reflection that we know a great deal about the honorific decrees of Eleusis
in the second half of the fourth century and very little about anything
else. However, it is important to appreciate the areas of bias and distortion
in the corpus of decrees in order that we may then exploit it to the full,
without misunderstanding what it can and cannot reveal. The chronological limitation is surely the most grave, leaving us very seriously un-
derinformed, in a direct way, about the fifth century. It was no doubt
largely on this account that Haussoullier chose to limit himself explicitly
to the fourth century (*"essai sur l'organisation des dèmes au quatrième
siècle"*), and others have done the same.[17] By not doing so, I do not wish
to be understood to be claiming that the chronological spread of the
deme decrees, indeed the evidence *in toto*, is anything other than it has
already been characterized here—a product, primarily, of the second half
of the fourth century; I would claim only that the paucity of direct
testimony about the demes in the first century of their existence cannot
in itself justify our passing over that period in silence. As to the other
two areas of limitation, that of provenance (or geographical spread) will
be considered below, in the second part of the chapter, while the limitation
of subject matter is perhaps the least crippling of the three in any case;
for however banal and uninformative some of the honorific decrees may
be in themselves (if no more so than those of the *ekklēsia* on which they
are modelled), they rarely fail to disclose some incidental details of the
personnel or internal organization of the deme concerned, or else to
employ a vocabulary which is worthy of note.

Most of the foregoing observations apply equally well, *mutatis mutandis*, to other kinds of public inscriptions erected by the demes, though
less obviously so in that the overall numbers of such documents are much
lower. As indicated above, it is not always simple—and perhaps in any
case not essential—to pigeonhole every deme document exactly in terms

---

[17] E.g. Damsgaard-Madsen, "Démarques."

of type. Sometimes, for example, decrees and leasing-contracts may overlap in form,[18] or a sacrificial calendar may incorporate material more appropriate, by evolved standards, to a general *lex sacra*.[19] In broad principle, nonetheless, the following categories of document may be identified:

Accounts All demes, we may properly assume, kept accounts of the annual income which they levied and the expenditure, recurrent or extraordinary, which they were thus enabled to undertake. Where necessary they also made an inventory of any financial resources which continued in existence from year to year in the care of successive officials. If it was standard practice to commit these records to stone, one can only conclude that a wealth of such documents once existing has perished; but more probably it was a rarity (and for reasons which are now quite indeterminable) for matters of this kind to be inscribed. Certainly only a mere handful survives. And here, as with so much else in the public life of the demes, the secular and the sacred are hardly to be differentiated. On the one hand, for example, in the third quarter of the fifth century the inventories of the monies of Nemesis in Rhamnous (IG I³248) and of Dionysos and Ikarios in Ikarion (IG I³253) both refer each year to the deme's *dēmarchos*.[20] In the former case he is admittedly mentioned purely as a mode of dating, but in the latter he is the person actually in charge of these finances. Conversely, at some time—on the most recent assessment—between 425 and 413, Ikarion's neighbor, the tiny deme of Plotheia, decided to preface a decree concerning the administration of debts to the deme with a summary financial statement (IG I³258); and although the whole document is in an obvious sense "secular" in form it is concerned throughout with sums of money whereof the interest is to go to defray religious expenditure.

Leases Around a dozen inscriptions from half as many demes preserve, in whole or part, the record of leases (*misthōseis*)—that is, contracts in which for a specified period and in return for a specified rent the demesmen granted to a named individual or group the use or occupation of land, buildings, or anything else which was theirs to lease.[21] As will

---

[18] See for instance SEG 28.103, decree II (Eleusis); cf. IG II²2492 (Aixone), SEG 24.152 (Teithras).

[19] See for instance IG I³244 (Skambonidai); the all-purpose character of this well-known inscription is little wonder, given its date of ca. 460 or earlier (cf. above, n. 5).

[20] For the name Ikarios, rather than Karios (cf. Herod. 5.66.1), see Lewis, "Cleisthenes," p. 26, n. 45, and (especially) his commentary to IG I³253-254.

[21] Such as the rights to stone quarrying; see SEG 28.103 (Eleusis).

be seen when we study these documents,[22] the form, language, and content of the contracts show reasonably close similarities with one another, as well as with documents of the same kind originating from other bodies; and this gives them a high collective as well as individual value and interest.

Sacrificial calendars   Although all too little of it is attested until the fourth century, the demes always provided a rich and varied religious diet for their members, and this is nowhere more evident than in the surviving portions of deme *fasti* or calendars of recurring festivals and sacrifices. Two specimens have long been known,[23] but in recent years the genre[24] has expanded beyond recognition, and its principal paradigm is now the splendid calendar from Erchia, inscribed in the second quarter of the fourth century—and completely preserved.[25]

"Leges sacrae"   Under this traditional, all-purpose term is subsumed a miscellany of enactments of a religious nature which are not couched in strict decree form. Thus, unlike the *fasti*, there is no recognizable and coherent genre here, but rather a congeries of more or less fragmentary and obscure individual documents.[26] Usually it is clear, or at least likely, that the source of the regulation is the deme assembly and that its implementation is the task of the regular deme officials. But occasionally the issuing authority is a purely priestly one, with the deme as such invoked for purposes of practical enforcement. Thus in IG II²1362 the priest of Apollo Erithaseos promulgates an edict "on behalf of both himself and the demesmen,"[27] to protect the trees within his deity's *hieron*. We learn from the inscription, set up at the end of the fourth century, that the priest is acting in accordance with a decree of the *boulē* and *ekklēsia* (lines 12-13 and 17-18) and that he will be assisted by the demarch in exacting fines from any offenders (lines 14-15).

[22] In Chap. 6A, sec. 2.

[23] IG II²1358, the Marathonian Tetrapolis and its constituent demes, first half of the fourth century; IG II²1363 (now re-edited by Dow/Healey, *Calendar*), Eleusis, ca. 330-270.

[24] I use the word deliberately; see in general Dow, "Six calendars."

[25] SEG 21.541 (Daux, "Démarchie").

[26] For obscurity—though *apparently* the document is complete!—IG I³245, from Sypalettos, must take the prize. Others which are obscure because of their fragmentary state include IG I³242 (Peiraieus, 490-480) and 251 (Eleusis, ca. 445).

[27] The name of the deme is not given, but the find-spot of the stone at Kamatero might suggest Eupyridai (cf. Traill, *Organization*, p. 46)

Horoi   As we saw in the last chapter, the demes normally had no *horoi* to mark off the entirety of their territory from that of their neighbors. Within any deme, on the other hand, *horoi* abounded, of all shapes and sizes and serving a multiplicity of purposes, official and unofficial. When, for instance, the munificence of one Leukios enabled his deme, Sounion, to lay out a spacious new *agora* in the mid fourth century, its prescribed limits were naturally to be shown by *horoi*, within which even the demarch was forbidden to consider building (IG II²1180). There are no surviving examples of such *horoi* as these, set up by demes in their collective official and (to repeat the unsatisfactory but inescapable term) secular capacity; we have only a number of "sacred" *horoi* which proclaim themselves to be the boundary-stones of cult precincts such as that of Aphrodite in Kephale (IG II²2604, cf. Isaeus 2.31). From the fourth century onwards, however, it would seem that one particular type of *horos* took on a specialized legal significance as an indication of the fact that a piece of land, a house, or whatever else it marked, was legally encumbered in some way—most obviously because it had been put up as the security for a loan; and demes which had evidently made such loans duly appear on four of these hypothecation-stones.[28]

Dedications   We find the demes making various kinds of dedication in their collective capacity, either alone or in conjunction with other bodies. If the "Sounians" (Σο]υνιες) who had their demotic engraved on the thigh of a statue in the sanctuary of Athena at Sounion are to be understood as the deme as a whole, rather than a group of individual *dēmotai*, such dedications began to be made in the very earliest days of the demes' constitutional existence.[29] As regards what still survives, however, there is once again little enough until the second half of the fourth century. In that period it is instructive to come upon demes of the old Tetrakomoi still celebrating a festival and recording their victories over each other (IG II²3102, Phaleron; 3103, Xypete); but more apposite to the times are dedications inscribed on the bases of statues of individuals whom a deme has honored or seeks to honor—Demetrios of Phaleron being a prime (if also a special) case.[30]

---

[28] See Appendix 3, nos. 58 (Halai ?Aixonides), 69 (Kerameis), 92 (Phegaia), and 93 (Phlya).

[29] IG I³1024 (I²830b); cf. Raubitschek, *Dedications*, p. 472, who dates it "at the end of the sixth century."

[30] Demetrios: IG II²2971, where "Eleusinioi" join a multiplicity of other bodies who have crowned him; and SEG 25.206 (Sphettioi, alone). Others: e.g. IG II²2837, 2843 (where I would take the second *dēmos*, on the left side, to be the deme), and 3214.

✳

So much, by way of summary, for *public* inscriptions originating from
or relating to the demes as official, collective entities. In the realm of
private epigraphy too there is useful evidence for the character and content of "municipal life."

At the lowest level, one might say, of informativeness it is obvious that
all private inscriptions which contain demotics will indicate that the
individuals concerned were *dēmotai* of one deme or another and, by so
stating, proud of it. Most grave monuments indicate little else; *ante
mortem*, however, a man tended—fortunately for us—to go into more
detail. Unquestionably the most valuable as well as the most widespread
single type of private inscription with relevance to the demes is the local
choregic dedication. Which particular choregies at which particular festivals are being commemorated is not always determinable, though the
rural Dionysia, "a major event in the religious and cultural life of the
rural demesmen,"[31] may generally be postulated in the absence of any
evidence to the contrary.[32] Otherwise the private dedications which bear
upon our study are of such heterogeneity that there is little to be gained
by passing them in review here; it will be more profitable to cite and
discuss them severally as they arise.

2. LITERARY SOURCES

Before August Boeckh and the dawning of the Age of Epigraphy, as we
have seen, scholars were understandably content with what was revealed
of the internal life of the demes by literary sources—taking that to embrace the lexicographers and scholiasts.[33] Nowadays, to draw solely for
our information upon the "classical" authors and their commentators

[31] Mikalson, "Religion," p. 433.

[32] See for instance IG II²3092 (Acharnai), 3096 (?Aigilia), 3090 (Eleusis), 3094, 3095,
3098, 3099 (all Ikarion), 3097 (Paiania). The much-discussed IG II²3091 (now generally
attributed to Halai Aixonides rather than Aixone; see most recently Davies, *Families*, pp.
183-184) probably does not refer to the rural Dionysia, with celebrity appearances by
Sophocles and others, and not even to a single festival at all, but to victories at several city
festivals by the two *chorēgoi* in question; see Pickard-Cambridge, *Festivals*, pp. 54-56, and
Davies, *Families*, pp. 183-184. Note also the amusing choregic dedication in hexameter
verse, from the second half of the fourth century (IG II²3101; its find-spot at Vari indicates
that the deme is Anagyrous), which encapsulates the tale of a son urging his father, evidently
successfully, to emulate his choregic prowess; the son's claim to have brought "honor to
the deme" (δήμωι μὲν κόσμον) must surely mean that the "Dionysia" referred to were city,
not rural; see further, introduction to Chap. 8B.

[33] An example is cited in the Introduction, n. 21.

would be ridiculous; yet the primacy, in most respects, of epigraphic evidence must not blind us to the great variety and richness of the literary testimony, much of it recognized and familiar but some of it still to be exploited to the full. As a complete, discursive chapter will be devoted to examining the image of the demes, collectively and individually, which is projected by comic drama (Chapter 11), it will be sufficient here to summarize and sample the information on offer in the four genres of tragedy, history, oratory, and political thought.

Tragedy We should not of course expect to find the Attic demes in their constitutional aspect figuring prominently in tragic drama, set as it is in a mythologized version of a bygone age. When the three major poets—Aeschylus, Sophocles, Euripides—allude to the towns and villages of Attica or to their cults and traditions,[34] they do not as a rule do so in a manner which sets up any contemporary reverberations, at least on a frequency detectable by our modern ears. But there is a noteworthy exception—Sophocles' *Oedipus Coloneus*. Whereas one has no reason to suppose that *Aeschylus'* (lost) play set in his own deme, Eleusis,[35] was suggestive of anything other than the era of Eumolpos, Sophocles' *OC* is much more tangibly rooted in a context real to both the poet and his audience, and nowhere more so than in the opening scene set in the sacred precinct of this, Sophocles' own deme, and under the gaze of its eponymous hero Kolonos. When the vagrant Oedipus is told in lines 77-80 that the "*dēmotai*" who will decide whether he may stay are those "here, not in the *asty*," is it fanciful to think that a fleeting smile may have passed across the faces of some of the rural demesmen in the audience? In the play as a whole the constitutional position of Kolonos in relation to Athens is left very blurred, not unnaturally; and it must be admitted that the word *dēmotēs* had other, more usual meanings in tragedy.[36] Here, nonetheless, the *dēmotai* who are not the ones "in the *asty*" can only be the demesmen of Kolonos, and thus the allusion can hardly be to anything other than the deme assemblies and their local freedom of action.

History There is no "history of the demes" as such, and the leading historians evince little interest in them for their own sake. In the case of

---

[34] For some references, see Edwards, *Demesman*, pp. 2-3.

[35] Aeschylus, *Eleusinians*; see Plut. *Thes.* 29.

[36] That is, either common men, as distinct from leaders (e.g. Sophocles *Ajax*, line 1071), or simply citizens, or fellow citizens (e.g. Euripides *Alkestis*, line 1057, and *Erechtheus* fr. 362 Nauck, line 25; cf. Pindar, *Nemean* 7, line 65, and, presumably, Susarion fr. 1—see Chap. 1, n. 28).

Thucydides this was clearly the outcome of deliberate policy.[37] His detached, timeless viewpoint (in aim if not always in realization) saw the Athenians as *politai*, not *dēmotai*, a word he never once uses; apart from the exceptional Acharnai (2.19-21) no demes are mentioned *qua* demes, and not a single Athenian is designated by his demotic. Xenophon, moreover, followed Thucydides' lead in this as in other respects. The solitary instance of a demotic in Xenophon occurs not in the *Hellenica* but, amidst single names, at *Memorabilia* 2.7.6; and the demes themselves play the most minor of roles in a narrative to which they had little to contribute.

It is thus Herodotus, approaching Athens and Attica as a foreigner, who presents the demes more prominently than any native Athenian historian, albeit in a slightly uncomprehending manner by virtue of his outsider's perspective. Demes as such, to Herodotus, were nothing uniquely Athenian,[38] and this very fact may well have diluted his awareness of the peculiar significance of the Attic demes in the post-Kleisthenic political system. Collectively (in contradistinction to the *asty*) or individually, with or without the addition of a place-name, before or after Kleisthenes in chronological context, "*dēmos*" in Herodotus is virtually always best and most appropriately translated as "village."[39] Even so, he faithfully reproduces a handful of demotics, with apparent awareness of what they signified;[40] and he shows eyewitness knowledge of at least some of the sites of the demes themselves.[41]

Oratory   In both quantity and quality this is indubitably the richest of the genres for our purposes,[42] but the distribution of the riches is extremely uneven. Six of the canonical Ten Attic Orators—Antiphon, Andocides, Isocrates, Hyperides, Lycurgus, and Dinarchus—make meagre contributions in the form of, perhaps, some preserved doc-

[37] Edwards, *Demesman*, pp. 55-57 is good on this.

[38] See Herod. 3.55.2 (Sparta) and 5.92 (Corinth); cf. 1.170.3 (Ionia).

[39] See F. Jacoby, *Atthis: the local chronicles of ancient Athens*, Oxford, 1949, p. 368, n. 81; Eliot, *Coastal Demes*, p. 79 with n. 12 (cf. Traill, *Organization*, p. 73). See for instance Herod. 1.60.4-5, 1.62.1, 5.81.3. In 5.74.2 Oinoe and Hysiai are called δήμους τοὺς ἐσχάτους τῆς Ἀττικῆς, but only Oinoe (the Hippothontid one, clearly) was a Kleisthenic deme. Even in 5.69.2 (which we discussed in Chap. 1B), on Kleisthenes himself, there is no explicit awareness of the constitutional nature of the demes.

[40] Herod. 6.92.3, 6.109.2, 8.84.1, 8.93.1 (two), 8.125.1, 9.73.1. To illustrate what by contrast looks like a *lack* of awareness of the significance of demotics, one may cite Diod. 14.32.1, Θρασύβουλος Στ(ε)ιριεὺς ὀνομαζόμενος, ὢν Ἀθηναῖος; cf. 17.57.1, Κλεῖτος ὁ μέλας ὀνομαζόμενος!

[41] See especially Herod. 4.99.4. The implication that he had personally sailed along the Attic coast is explicitly confirmed a couple of sentences later.

[42] See in general Edwards, *Demesman*, chap. 6.

uments[43] or the occasional passage which briefly illuminates some facet of deme life.[44] It is frustrating to realize that there was valuable material on the demes in some of their speeches which have not survived.[45] Nevertheless, as matters stand the bulk of our information is drawn from Lysias (especially speeches 13, 16, 20, 23, 27, and 31), from Isaeus (especially speeches 2, 3, 6, 7, 8, 9, and 12),[46] from Aeschines (all three of his surviving speeches), and, above all, from Demosthenes—or rather the whole *corpus Demosthenicum*, genuine and spurious. Here, in addition to more preserved documents[47] and a scatter of other passages of interest,[48] there are three speeches (39, 44, and *imprimis* 57) where events in particular demes are at the very heart of the matter, and we must exploit them to the full in subsequent chapters.

Political thought Under this heading are subsumed, for convenience's sake, three distinctly disparate writers: Plato, Aristotle, and the unknown author of the *Athenaion Politeia* which antiquity knew as Aristotle's.[49] (In principle the category is flexible enough to embrace another *Athenaion Politeia*, that of pseudo-Xenophon, alias the "Old Oligarch," and also the philosophical works of Isocrates and the real Xenophon. In practice, however, this second trinity of authors do not concern themselves with our subject.)[50] Much of the *oeuvre* of Plato could be said to bear comparison in general terms with that of Aristophanes, to the extent that both men—for their

[43] Notably Andoc. 1.83-84 and 97.

[44] E.g. Antiph. 6.12; Isoc. 8.88, 12.179; Hyper. 4 (*Eux.*).3; Lycurg. *Leok.* 76.

[45] E.g. Antiphon, πρὸς Φίλιππον (see Harpoc., δημοτευόμενος); Andocides, (?) πρὸς τοὺς ἑταίρους (see Suda, σκάνδιξ). The heaviest losses, however, are those of Dinarchus: the κατὰ Κηρύκων and the κατὰ Μοσχίωνος ἀπογραψαμένου αὐτὸν Νικοδίκου (see Haussoullier, *Vie*, pp. 47-49, esp. 49, n. 3), and the two *diadikasiai* on behalf of demes (see Haussoullier, *Vie*, pp. 99-102).

[46] With Isaeus, again, relevant speeches have perished: πρὸς Βοιωτὸν ἐκ δημότων ἔφεσις (see Harpoc., Κειριάδης and λῆξις; for Boiotos cf. Demosth. 39) and πρὸς τοὺς δημότας περὶ χωρίου (see Harpoc., Σφηττός, and Dion. Hal. *Isaios* 10, who preserves the (?)opening words).

[47] See [Demosth.] 43.57-58 (law on the disposal of corpses by demarchs) and 71 (law on sacred olive trees); and [Demosth.] 59.104 (decree about the Plataians). Cf. [Demosth.] 50.6-8, documents in paraphrase.

[48] E.g. Demosth. 18.261; [Demosth.] 43.64, 52.28, 59.13 and 122.

[49] Hereby, necessarily, I declare my inability to believe that the *Ath. Pol.* is the work of Aristotle himself, Aristotelian though it may be in spirit and intent; cf. for instance Hignett, *Constitution*, pp. 27-30, and now Rhodes, *Commentary*, pp. 61-63. Naturally I have striven to prevent this belief from affecting the use which I make of *Ath. Pol.* material.

[50] In the case of the Oligarch at least, this silence may fairly be called negative evidence in itself; that is, it is striking that he did not cite the deme system as one means whereby the all-embracing *dēmos* maintained its grip on power.

utterly different purposes—wrote scenes of dialogue which usually take place in a tangible, contemporary Attic setting; and in the earliest works particularly, Plato's setting may naturally run to a mention of some aspect of deme life.[51] Perhaps it was Sokrates more than Plato to whom we should attribute the liking for such allusions? At all events there is little indication that Plato was at heart a "deme man" himself. For one thing, his preferred form of address is the aristocratic one, the patronymic;[52] he gives a score of demotics, all told, but some of them (e.g. *Gorgias* 495D) seem to strike a note of "mock pomposity."[53] Nevertheless, when Plato came to delineate what he saw as the best practically possible community, the Cretan Magnesia of *Laws*, he was either unwilling or unable to break wholly free of his Athenian heritage, and demes of a recognizably Attic stamp were duly included in his scheme of things.[54]

Turning to Aristotle we hope for much but find surprisingly little. One does not expect mention of individual demes (or their demotics) in philosophical writing which, unlike Plato's, eschews an actual physical setting, but it is remarkable that in the list of *archai* in *Politics* 1321b4-1323a10, for example, there is no reference to demarchs.[55] Elsewhere Aristotle mentions demes three times, but always in the most vague and general of terms.[56]

Thus it is the Aristotelian *Ath. Pol.* which is the single most precious item in this category and the weightiest single addition to our stock of literary source material since Haussoullier's day. As regards the first or historical section of the work, we saw in the last chapter how crucial is the *Ath. Pol.*'s account of the work of Kleisthenes, even if it cannot be accepted *tout court*. Other passages in this section shed light on constitutional developments of the fifth century which affected the demes (22.5, 26.2-3) or else aspects of political practice in the period in which they figured (27.3). In the second half of the work, the quasi-systematic description of the Athenian constitution in the writer's own day, the 320s,

---

[51] E.g. Plato *Apology* 33E; *Laches* 180B-D, 187D-E, 197C; *Lysis* 205C-D. Cf. also the spurious works: *Hipparchos* 228D-229A (cf. Chap. 1, p. 14); *Theages* 121D, 127E. For Aristophanes, see below, Chap. 11A.

[52] Cf. Wilamowitz, *Aristoteles*, p. 172.

[53] Edwards, *Demesman*, p. 59, n. 12, with useful examples and discussion.

[54] See Plato *Laws* 746D, 753C; also 738D-E, where the 'μέρη' may well be demes. For discussion, see G. R. Morrow, *Plato's Cretan City*, Princeton, 1960, pp. 124-126, cf. 166ff.; W. E. Thompson, *Eranos* 63, 1965, pp. 134-136; M. Piérart, *Platon et la cité grecque*, Brussels, 1974, pp. 68-71, stressing how little Plato seems to have worked out his deme system in detail.

[55] Cf. W. L. Newman, *The Politics of Aristotle*, vol. 4, Oxford, 1902, p. 552.

[56] Aristot. *Pol.* 1300a24(a)-26, on ways of appointing officials; *EN* 1160a14-25, on the advantages of political *koinōniai; Poetics* 1448a35-38.

we look in vain for any direct information about the internal constitutional machinery of the demes themselves; but there is an extended account of the standard procedures of deme enrolment (42.1-2, cf. 59.4), together with other testimony, not otherwise preserved, which concerns the demes either collectively[57] or individually.[58]

*

One cardinal feature which all the writers mentioned so far have in common is that they are all contemporary writers—contemporary, that is, with the period of the history of the deme system which is the subject of this book, from Kleisthenes to the middle of the third century. A second common feature, less obvious but more significant, is that none of them show any interest whatever in the Attic demes as an object of study in themselves. In every genre of writing considered so far, the demes are always (mutatis mutandis) simply taken for granted as the backdrop to speech or action. By contrast, a number of retrospective writers, whom we must now survey, viewed the demes from a standpoint much more akin to our own—that is, as interesting and important per se, by virtue of their place in the history, the mythology, and the culture of the greatest polis of a bygone age. This classicization of Athens is too large and complex a topic to be pursued very far here, especially as its crucial early stages are virtually undocumented and we can thus only appreciate it once it has already taken shape. Possibly it was the Atthidographers who played the key role, possibly the pupils of Aristotle—Theophrastus, Demetrius of Phaleron, Dicaearchus of Messana, and the rest. Certainly the process appears to have been under way by the mid third century, with the "cursive account of Attica" by Hegesias of Magnesia,[59] and further boosted in the early second century by Polemon "the Periegete" of Ilion.[60]

Neither Hegesias nor Polemon survive to be read today, except in fragments which lack sufficient substance for our purposes here. Both,

---

[57] See ?Aristot. Ath. Pol. 55.3 (questions about demes in the dokimasia of archons), 62.1 (the role of demes in the appointment of city officials), 63.4 (dikastic pinakia with demotics).

[58] Namely, the (literally) extraordinary deme of Peiraieus: see Appendix 4.

[59] Traill, Organization, p. 97, n. 86; see above, Chap. 1, n. 62. The source is Strabo 9.1.16 (FGrH 142 F24); cf. RE 7, 1912, cols. 2607-2608, "Hegesias (13)." See also below, n. 68, on Diodorus "the Periegete."

[60] Again, see Traill, Organization, p. 97, n. 86; cf. above, Chap. 1, n. 62. It was once believed, on the strength of schol. Aristoph. Birds, line 645 (ἀναγράφει δὲ τοὺς ἐπωνύμους τῶν δήμων καὶ τῶν φυλῶν Πολέμων), that Polemon wrote a specific work called the Ἀναγραφὴ τῶν ἐπωνύμων τῶν δήμων καὶ τῶν φυλῶν, but this could simply be an allusion to material included in his four books περὶ τῶν ἀναθημάτων τῶν ἐν ἀκροπόλει, mentioned by Strabo 9.1.16: thus e.g. G. Pasquali, Hermes 48, 1913, p. 178, n. 2; cf. RE 21.2, 1952, cols. 1294-1295.

however, served as sources for a writer to whom we can still turn, the geographer and antiquarian Strabo, who preserves much useful material about individual demes in the eighth and (particularly) ninth books of his *Geography*.[61] So too, and to an even greater extent, does a later writer in the same mould (except inasmuch as he gathered his data more from his own travels and autopsy): Pausanias. The first book of his *Periegesis* is devoted to Attica and involves a firsthand account of the topography and physical remains of many of the demes, garnished with appropriate details of their cults and monuments.

By Pausanias' time (the middle of the second century A.D.) the classicization of Athens and Attica was all but complete. The literature of the fifth and fourth centuries was familiar to cultured Greeks and non-Greeks alike, and the Second Sophistic movement was evoking an intense interest in and nostalgia for the Greek—and above all the Athenian—past.[62] No more striking an exemplar of this could be imagined than Plutarch. His entire *oeuvre*—the *Moralia* as well as the *Parallel Lives*—betrays a man steeped in Athenian literature and lore; he is thus the purveyor of many intriguing data about individual demes which we should not otherwise have.[63] The value of Athenaeus' *Deipnosophistai* (compiled in about A.D. 200) in preserving comic fragments and other such material[64] is enormous; and thanks to the philosophical biographies of Diogenes Laertius, we may still read Plato's will (Diog. Laert. 3.41-42), which is of considerable interest as evidence of the pattern of land tenure in fourth-century Attica.[65] Finally one may mention the writers (of a very different type) who, while admittedly not offering us information of independent worth for the Attic demes in the classical period, derived from their reading a familiarity with that period and its institutions. Such a category would embrace, for instance, the *Letters* of Aelian and Alciphron, but is most prominently represented by the versatile Lucian, whose "knowledge of Athenian antiquities" extended to the demes both individually and collectively.[66]

---

[61] Note also Eratosthenes *apud* Strabo 1.4.7 (quoted in Chap. 1, n. 105) on the absence of *horoi* between demes.

[62] See E. L. Bowie, "Greeks and their past in the Second Sophistic," *P&P* 46, 1970, pp. 1-41, reprinted in M. I. Finley, ed., *Studies in Ancient Society*, London, 1974.

[63] E.g. Plut. *Thes.* 13.2-3, on the ancient hostility between Pallene and Hagnous; *de exilio* 601B-C (see Chap. 1, n. 95), on the *metastasis* from Melite to Diomeia.

[64] Comic fragments: see in general below, Chap. 11. Other material: e.g., Athen. 260A-B (from Hegesander of Delphi) and 614D-E, on the sixty jesters of Diomeia; 297E, cf. 303B (from Antigonus of Karystos), on the tunny festival at (?) Halai—see Chap. 7, n. 188.

[65] See Haussoullier, *Vie*, p. 76, n. 3; cf. below, Chap. 3, n. 37.

[66] See J. Delz, *Lukians Kenntnis der athenischen Antiquitäten*, diss. Basel, 1947 [1950], pp. 5-12 (cf. ibid., pp. 12-17 on tribes, and 18-22 on phratries and *genē*). Mention of

3. Lexicographers

Between the writers mentioned in the last paragraph and those to be surveyed in this third section a distinction in broad principle is clear enough. The former composed works, however derivative, which were independent in their own right; the latter strove to explain and interpret the works of others—the classics—either by continuous or by intermittent commentary upon individual works or else in general handbooks and glossaries. In practice, perhaps, the distinction cannot be rigidly drawn, particularly since such a gulf as there might be in theory is spanned in actuality by, for example, the *Onomasticon* of Julius Pollux. Although composed in the late second century A.D., this has been transmitted to us only *via* incomplete and interpolated copies of a Byzantine epitome; thus, unfortunately, the occasional terminological or substantive items of relevance to the demes (especially in Book 8) are mostly presented in as dry a form as the most mechanical and uncomprehending of the lexica. Similar vicissitudes with similar results befell the work of other learned men who enjoyed access to earlier collections of information about the demes which we do not. To unravel the complex interrelationships of material which emerged in consequence is *par excellence* a task for experts, and (happily) not directly relevant here, where we may confine ourselves simply to a brief evaluation of what the principal lexicographers have to say about the deme system and its components.

Pride of place, for both quantity and quality of information, must go to Harpocration, whose *Lexicon to the Ten Orators* contains many valuable entries on individual demes—besides, it must be said, many which are all but valueless, in the sense that they consist of no more than the tribal affiliation and the form of the demotic. In addition, as befits a work which set out to give an explanation of all significant words and phrases in the orators and elsewhere, it includes glosses on the terms *dēmarchos, diapsēphisis, lēxiarchikon grammateion*, and so forth. Although itself a product of probably the second century A.D., Harpocration's *Lexicon* has come down to us only in the form of a Byzantine epitome and (later, and interpolated) recension; this adds an extra and for practical purposes unwelcome stratum of matters which call for the exercise of erudite *Quellenkritik*.[67] The primary sources, however, are

---

individual demes: *Ikaromenippos* 18. Demotics, of both real and fictitious persons: list (incomplete) in Delz, ibid., pp. 8-11. According to Delz (p. 12) there is "nothing on the internal function of the demes"; see however *Zeus Tragodos* 26, πρόπαλαι μὲν ἐξ ἐφήβων γεγονώς, ἐγγεγραμμένος δὲ ἐς τὸ τῶν δώδεκα ληξιαρχικόν. On *Timon* 43-51, with mock decrees (and two instances of the word *dēmotēs*), see F. W. Householder, Jr., *TAPhA* 71, 1940, pp. 205-212; cf. D. J. Geagan, *Hesp.* Suppl. 12, 1967, p. 40 with n. 37.

[67] Witness for instance the problematical relationship between Harpoc., δήμαρχος, and

usually specified; and it is clear that in addition to the classical literature itself—and more of it than we ourselves can read today—Harpocration's entries, especially on the individual demes, rested upon the authority of the best in Hellenistic and later scholarship.[68]

After Harpocration, information about individual demes, as opposed to the deme system as a whole, comes in largest measure from the sixth-century A.D. grammarian Stephanus of Byzantium. His sixty books of place-names (*Ethnika*) included entries on more than a hundred of the Attic demes,[69] not to mention places such as Brauron and Kynosarges which were not demes in the constitutional sense. Here again, what we actually read and use is sadly not Stephanus' work itself but an epitome, and from the fragments of the original which are preserved by Constantine Porphyrogenitus it is evident that potentially valuable and interesting material was jettisoned in the simple-minded epitomization process. This doubtless included fuller citation of sources—something where, as matters stand, we cannot venture much beyond the presumption that in general Stephanus' immediate authorities were the same as Harpocration's.[70] Furthermore, insofar as it is fair to judge by the epitomized version, many of Stephanus' entries on demes were of a somewhat narrow and formulaic sort, that is, not necessarily comprising anything more than a standard three items (tribal affiliation, demotic, locatives), with any discussion of them confined to their morphology. Occasionally, though, Stephanus did include something substantive on the origin of a deme's name itself,[71] or the collective character of a deme,[72] or a precious fragment of his source material;[73] and the epitomator was kind or careless enough to spare it.

To turn from Harpocration and Stephanus to the rest of the lexicographers is to experience, by and large, the effects of the law of diminishing

---

schol. Aristoph. *Clouds*, line 37; a common source is suggested by J. J. Keaney, *TAPhA* 100, 1969, p. 202, n. 8. The scholia in general present an even more daunting aspect to the nonspecialist than do the lexicographers, and rather than attempting any rash generalizations here we will simply assess their evidence when it becomes necessary to do so.

[68] Most frequently cited is the third-century treatise *On the demes* by Diodorus "the Periegete"; see *RE* 5.1, 1905, col. 662, "Diodorus (37)." Another, later *On the demes*, mentioned twice by Harpocration (under Θυργωνίδαι and Τιτακίδαι), was that of the grammarian Nicander of Thyateira; see *RE* 17.1, 1936, cols. 265-266, "Nikandros (15)."

[69] He also has a *dēmos*-type entry for places other than Athens (see for instance Εὐίππη, Εὐκάρπεια, Ἧτις, Ἱερὰ Κώμη), though to judge from the curious, generic *Dēmos* entry he did regard demes as characteristically Attic. On Stephanus in general, see N. G. Wilson, *Scholars of Byzantium*, London, 1983, pp. 55-56.

[70] See for instance the citations in Stephanus' Τριχόρυνθον (*sic*) entry.

[71] For some references, see above, Chap. 1, n. 84.

[72] See for instance the Αἰξώνεια (*sic*) entry.

[73] See for instance the quotation from Solon's *axones* (quoted and discussed on p. 12).

returns, in terms of the information both about individual demes and about their common institutions. For example, Hesychius (fifth century A.D.) compiled brief entries on around seventy individual demes, as well as on the routine items, as we may call them, of general deme terminology—*dēmarchoi* (sic), *diapsēphisis*, *lēxiarchikon grammateion*, and the rest—but there is little information which cannot be found in a fuller and more reliable form elsewhere. (The same goes for Photius, the Suda, the *Etymologicon Magnum*, and the other lexica.) The most interesting entries in Hesychius, if not always the most useful ones, tend to be those either on individual demes whose names have extrinsic, often proverbial, significance or else for verbs and other words which embody that same significance.[74] Many of these proverbial and quasi-proverbial words and phrases can be traced back to the classical period—particularly to Old Comedy[75]—or even earlier.[76] Their longevity is thus remarkable: they are to be found, naturally enough, in the paroemiographic collections[77] as well as in all the lexicographers,[78] and as far as the latter are concerned, their durability was appreciably higher than that of the more dull and prosaic facts relating to the deme system and its constituent parts.[79]

[74] See for instance ἀθμονάζειν (inexplicable), αἰξωνεύεσθαι, ἀλωπεκίζειν, Ἀναγυράσιος, Δρυαχαρνεῦ, Λακιάδαι, Συπαληττίους (sic), Τιθράσια.

[75] E.g. "Sphettian vinegar:" Aristoph. *Ploutos* line 720; cf. Athen. 67-D; Hesych., ὄξος Σφήττιον; Phot., Σφήττιοι; *Etym. Magn.* 738.44; *Lex Rhet. Cantabr.*, Σφήττιοι (the only individual deme entry!); *Corpus Paroemiographorum Graecorum*, vol. I, p. 440, no. 29, cf. vol. II, p. 213, no. 93.

[76] E.g. ἀλωπεκίζειν (cf. above, n. 74): the drinking song quoted in Aristoph. *Wasps*, lines 1240-1241 (οὐκ ἔστιν ἀλωπεκίζειν, οὐδ᾽ ἀμφοτέροισι γίγνεσθαι φίλον) seems likely to go back to the *stasis* of the second half of the sixth century; Lewis, "Cleisthenes," p. 23. Compare *Lex Seguer.* I, *Phrynichos Arabios*, ἀλωπεκῆσαι· ἐξαπατήσαντα διαδρᾶναι [= Bekker, *Anecd. Gr.* 1.10.15].

[77] See the *Corpus Paroemiographorum Graecorum*, vol. I, p. 46, no. 55 (Ἀνάγυρον κινεῖν; cf. p. 184, no. 25, and vol. II, p. 479, no. 79—see Aristoph. *Lysistr.*, lines 67-68); ibid., p. 131, no. 29 (Οἰνόη τὴν χαράδραν, explicitly of the deme; cf. vol. II, p. 554, no. 50); ibid., p. 219, no. 31 (Ἀναγυράσιος δαίμων; cf. vol. II, p. 286, no. 96); ibid., p. 440, no. 29 (see above, n. 75); ibid., p. 467, no. 43 (ὦ Λακιάδαι); ibid., vol. II, p. 16, no. 90 (Ἀχαρνικοὶ ὄνοι); ibid., p. 257, no. 67 (Αἰξωνιεὺς [sic] ἄλλος); ibid., p. 611, no. 19 (Πειρίθου καὶ Θησέως φιλοξενία); ibid., p. 770, no. 77 (Ῥαμνούσιος εἶ).

[78] See for instance Phot., Μελιτέα κάπρον and Οἰναῖοι τὴν χαράδραν; Suda, Ἀναγυράσιος, Ἀνάγυρος, αἰξωνεύεσθαι, ὦ Λακιάδαι (cf. Πλακιάδαι [sic!]), Περιθοῖδαι, Τίθρασος; *Etym. Magn.* 36.57 and 288.15; *Lex Seguer.* V, *Lexeis Rhetorikai*, Ἀναγυράσιος [= Bekker, *Anecd. Gr.* 1.210.3]; *Lex Seguer.* VI, *Synagoge Lexeon Chresimon*, αἰξωνεύεσθαι [= Bekker, *Anecd. Gr.* 1.353.31].

[79] Useful material has survived here and there; see for instance Suda, δήμαρχοι and διαψήφισις καὶ ἀποψήφισις; *Etym. Magn.* 220.52, 265.20, 327.33; *Lex Seguer.* V, *Lexeis Rhetorikai*, ἀπογράφειν and δημοτελῆ καὶ δημοτικὰ ἱερεῖα [= Bekker, *Anecd. Gr.* 1.199.5 and 240.28].

B. Methodology

Without at this stage further elaborating our summary catalog of the source material currently available, it will be obvious that the data are indeed at hand for a fresh assessment of "municipal life" in Attica. But equally evident, I would contend, is the necessity of establishing some methodological principles for the use of this evidence, old and new, and the limits of what it reveals. We may express the main problem in the form of a question: how far is it legitimate to speak in generalizing terms of "the demes"—or even "the deme"?

The issue of generalizations, of giving due weight alike to diversity and uniformity, is of course familiar to all ancient historians, and some may grow tired of it for that very reason. In this instance at least we must confront it squarely and explicitly. The problem is, in a sense, both apparent and real: on one level it is posed by the present (and foreseeable future) state of the evidence with which we must work, yet it is also a reflection of the actual historical facts of the subject, whether recorded or merely deducible. The most important single and simple feature of the epigraphic, literary, and lexicographic source material which we have just surveyed is that half of it—schematically speaking—is general, and half particular. We learn sometimes of what happens, or ought to happen, in "the demes"; sometimes of what happens, or ought to happen, in the deme Halimous, or Skambonidai, or wherever. Epigraphy provides the clearest illustrations of these two categories of data, in the form of (*a*) laws and decrees of the *boulē* and *ekklēsia* which set up a general prescription (or proscription) for all demes, and (*b*) analogous enactments by deme X or Y in respect, naturally, of its own affairs only. But this basic and crucial distinction is also to be seen, if not always as plainly, in other kinds of epigraphical material and also in the literary and lexicographic testimony; and it is a distinction which throughout this book we must do our utmost to remember and observe. I shall thus refer to "category-*a*" evidence, the general, and "category-*b*" evidence, the particular, to reiterate the point from time to time.

To do this, however, is merely to state the problem, not to solve it. Clearly the category-*a* evidence offers us the opportunity of constructing a body of soundly based generalizations about "the demes" and their doings; yet we still need to determine whether the category-*b* material— the more plentiful of the two—can properly be exploited in the same way. This is the nub of the methodological issue, which has never been satisfactorily aired before.[80] Is the subliminal message of the evidence

---

[80] Haussoullier made no more than a few perfunctory skirmishes at this crucial issue (see

that the demes were (or were made to be) all the same, one hundred and thirty-nine peas in a pod, or that the differences between them outweighed the similarities?

Two extreme positions might theoretically be taken up on this question:

1. On the one hand, such emphasis could be placed upon differences between one deme and another as to render any attempt at a synoptic view worthless and absurd. We saw in the last chapter that there were indeed demonstrable differences, most obviously that of size—a result of Kleisthenes' use of natural centers of population. Again, a rural deme such as Anagyrous or Teithras was necessarily very different in character, and had different problems to face, from an urban one like Melite, its natural population boosted by Attica's largest concentration of immigrants as well as by an admixture of Athenian political celebrities.[81] Thus (the argument would run) "the deme" never existed. There were simply one hundred and thirty-nine demes, for the majority of which we know little or nothing more than the name; and the category-*a* evidence is evidence merely of the minimal amount of procedural uniformity which any central government would have had to impose for its own bureaucratic purposes.

2. The polar opposite view would obviously assign the category-*a* data pride of place and would work on the assumption that both natural and imposed circumstances contrived to produce uniformity in essentials and diversity only in inessentials. Certainly all demes had a *dēmarchos* (see below) and other officials; all demes sent representatives to the *boulē*; all demes enrolled their members by a standard procedure.[82] Thus (the argument would run) the category-*b* evidence is not really a separate category at all but another, invaluable guide as to what happened throughout the whole deme system; and if we should happen to be well informed about the *euthynai* procedure in Myrrhinous (IG II²1183) or the finances of Plotheia (IG I³258) or the *fasti* of Erchia (SEG 21.541), so much the better for our synthetic study of "the deme."

Without pushing these two extreme positions—the Herodotean and the Aristotelian, one might call them—to the point of caricature, it is plain that they are both untenable. The very existence of evidence and arguments for each destroys the other, and we are left, as so often, with the middle ground of compromise. Since the particularist, Herodotean viewpoint would deny any possibility of a worthwhile synoptic treatment,

---

esp. *Vie*, pp. 136-141 on religion); the best attempt at a frontal assault is by Müller, *de demis*, esp. pp. 1-8.

[81] Immigrants (*metoikoi*): see below, Chap. 3D. Political celebrities: witness for instance Themistokles (Plut. *Them.* 22.1-2) and Phokion (Plut. *Phok.* 18.5).

[82] ?Aristot. *Ath. Pol.* 42.1-2, cf. 59.4; see below, Chap. 4B, sec. 1(a).

it is obvious that the tacit assumption which has always underpinned the work of Haussoullier and his iterators is basically the Aristotelian one. It is time to examine how far this is justifiable.

We must begin by returning, briefly, to Kleisthenes, for his "reform bill," or what can be reconstructed of it, is necessarily our prime candidate, both chronologically and substantively speaking, as category-*a* evidence. As the last chapter emphasized, the arithmetical, decimal neatness which was otherwise the hallmark of the Kleisthenic reorganization was sensibly conjured, at ground level, out of (mainly) natural and thus diverse materials. Largely because of that very diversity, however, both evidence and probability would suggest that this formal creation of the deme system as such called for the imposition of a considerable degree of uniformity. According to ?Aristot. *Ath. Pol.* 21.4-5, those living in each deme were to be fellow demesmen, known by their deme's name, and the demes were to be in the charge of demarchs. These are presented as inaugural and universal features of all demes, that is, the writer evidently knew of no exception to them, and there is nothing to suggest that this was ignorance or negligence on his part. The universality of the first provision is indeed quite simply self-evident, for it is inconceivable that any of the demes were constituted in a manner or by a principle other than this. Only their use of the *dēmotikon* requires—and can be given—formal proof.[83] By the same token, the provision (not mentioned in *Ath. Pol.* 21 but deducible from other sources) that demes were to provide, in proportion to their size, the members of the new *boulē* of Five Hundred was necessarily an utterly basic element in the uniformity of the deme network as a whole. The demarchs are another matter, in that, if Kleisthenes had so envisaged it, they might well have represented an area of possible diversity—optional rather than mandatory as the chief official. In fact, however, epigraphic sources ranging from the third quarter of the fifth century to the middle of the second century (together with a few passages in literature) explicitly prove their existence in around thirty individual demes.[84] Thus the presumption that every deme did have

---

[83] See Chap. 3A.

[84] Acharnai (IG II²1206, lines 3-4, 8, 17-18—*if* the stone is of this deme); Agryle ([Plut.] *Vit. X Or.* 834A-B; Walbank, "Confiscation," p. 80, line 1—thus *either* both from Upper or Lower Agryle *or* one from each); Aixone (IG II²1196, lines 4, 6, 18, 22; 1197, lines 10-11, 20; 1198, lines 15-16, 19-20; 1199, lines 15-16; 1202, lines 13-14; 2492, lines 22, 35; *AM* 66, 1941, pp. 218-219, no. 1, line 9); ?Anagyrous (IG II²1210, lines 5-6; also the likeliest deme for IG II²2852); Aphidna (Walbank, "Confiscation," p. 85, line 4); Athmonon (IG II²1203, line 20; cf. IG I³425, line 26); Eleusis (IG II²949, lines 6, 17, 28-29, 31; 1186, lines 19-20, 29, 34; 1187, lines 19-20, 22-23, 29; 1188, lines 31-32; 1189, line [11]; 1191, line 1; 1193, lines 14-15, 22-23, 28-29; 1299, lines 79-80; 2500, lines 5, 13; *Hesp.* 8, 1939, pp. 177-180, lines 7-8, 18-19; *AE* 1971, pp. 126-127, no. 21; SEG 28.103, lines 23, 31, 36, 39, 44, 50); Erchia (Isaeus 12.11; SEG 21.541, E, lines 52-58); ?Eupyridai (IG

a *dēmarchos*—and indeed no more than one at a time[85]—does look a safe one. In the fourth century he was an annually changing official appointed by lot. Originally the method was more probably direct election. It must at any rate be held unlikely that individual demes were allowed in any period to deviate from a mode of appointment laid down for them all.[86]

An obvious question arises: why was it thought necessary to ordain that every deme should have the same chief official, appointed (if one is right to think this) in the same fashion everywhere? Surely for the same basic reason that it was thought necessary—or so we found cause to believe in the preceding chapter—to have from the start a standard procedure for deme registration. It was because the role of the demes was not to be confined to their own internal affairs, where they could be allowed to please themselves,[87] but was to embrace besides a variety of

II²1362, line 15; see above, n. 27); Halai Aixonides (IG II²1174, lines 3, [4], [15]; 1175, line 22; 1598, line 37—though see rather SEG 21.573; *AM* 67, 1942, p. 10, no. 8, line [3]); Halai Araphenides (*AE* 1925-1926, pp. 168-177, lines 11-12, 17-18; *AE* 1932, *Chronika*, pp. 30-32, line 26); Halimous (Demosth. 57, passim; SEG 2.7, lines 5-6, 19-20); Ikarion (IG I³253, lines 1, 5, 8, 11, 15, 21; 254, lines 6, 7, 13; IG II²1178, lines 2, 5-6, 10-11; 1179, line 2; SEG 22.117, line 6); Kerameis (IG I³425, line 30; Walbank, "Confiscation," p. 76, line 24); Kollytos (IG II²1195, line 11); Marathon (IG II²1358, lines [1-2], 23); Melite (IG I³243, line [32]; SEG 22.116, line 24; probably also the deme of IG II²2394, line 2); Myrrhinous (IG II²1182, lines 17-18; 1183, lines 18-19, 21, 25, 26, 33, 39); Oinoe, of tribe IX Aiantis (IG II²1594, line 51); Oion Dekeleikon *or* Kerameikon (*Hesp.* 15, 1946, pp. 181-184, no. 31, lines 32-34 = Walbank, "Confiscation," p. 83, line 13); Otryne ([Demosth.] 44.37); Peiraieus (?Aristot. *Ath. Pol.* 54.8; IG II²1176+, lines 14, 25; 1177, lines 0-2, 14-15, 22-23; 1214, lines 22, 27; 2498, line 1); Phaleron (Walbank, "Confiscation," p. 75, line 7); Plotheia (IG I³258, line 2); Rhamnous ([Plut.] *Vit. X Or.* 834A-B; IG I³248, lines 1, 32, cf. 15, 20, 27; SEG 25.155, line 37); Skambonidai (IG I³244, A, lines 13-14, and C, line 2; cf. Walbank, "Confiscation," p. 85, line 13, with note at pp. 87-88); Sounion (IG II²1180, lines 19, 23-24; cf. 1672, line 273, with Whitehead, "Demarchs," pp. 40-42); Sphettos (Walbank, "Confiscation," p. 76, line 15 of col. I); Teithras (SEG 24.151, lines 1, 4-5, 26, 33-34); unidentifiable deme, which *might* of course be identical with any of the above (IG II²1173, lines 2-3, 12-13).

[85] The only *prima facie* evidence for a plurality of demarchs in any deme is IG II²1174 (Halai Aixonides, 368/7), line 3, οἱ δήμαρχοι κα[ὶ οἱ ταμίαι (cf. lines 4-5, [τὸς δημάρχος κ]αὶ τὸς ταμίας). In line 15, however, Wilhelm's restoration of a single demarch is inescapable; and in any case it is clear on close examination that these *euthynai* regulations are speaking of "the demarchs" as a series extending into the future.

[86] In my opinion the conflicting evidence about the appointment procedure for demarchs is best reconciled on the assumption not of variation between one deme and another in the same period (as tentatively suggested by Schoeffer, "Demarchoi," col. 2707, before thinking better of it in "Demoi," col. 16) but of a change across the board, probably during the second half of the fifth century, from election to sortition. See further, Chap. 4B, sec. 3(b).

[87] For example, while it must have been enacted in general terms that all bodies of demesmen were to meet in assembly to administer their own affairs (cf. Chap. 1, p. 34),

functions in central government, where diversity could obviously have been much more troublesome. We shall consider in later chapters the interaction between local and central government and attempt to trace the boundaries between them, but for the present it must suffice to repeat the point that it was the demarch who seems to have been given the protagonist's part in linking the two spheres together. Thus an element of standardization in his duties and functions will surely have been introduced from the outset. In fact, of course, one can only conjecture how far the known or likely constituents of this go back to Kleisthenes;[88] so it is initially an argument more from probability than from hard evidence which would suggest that one of the readiest and most convenient ways of ensuring procedural uniformity between all the demes was indeed to elaborate and standardize the role of the demarchs. Nonetheless, if we consider as a body the rest of the surviving category-*a* evidence, spread out across the fifth and fourth centuries, standard instructions for the demarchs undeniably constitute the major part of it.

What might be termed the mandate of any demarch—that is, pre-existing standing orders inherited from his predecessors, together with any additions to them during his own term of office, as well as *ad hoc* assignments—came naturally from two sources: his own deme's assembly, and the polis, acting through the *ekklēsia* and the laws. Insofar as we can actually attribute specific data to the one source or the other, we must treat and use them quite differently. As regards instructions from the individual deme assemblies, there seem no grounds in principle why we should expect uniformity across all demes or even most demes. This, in other words, is category-*b* evidence of the plainest kind; and if it enables us to discern parallels between one deme and another, we should not forget that parallels, not archetypes, is what they are. In certain demes, for example, it appears to have been the demarch who was normally ordered to see to the cutting and erection of the stone stelai recording the decrees of the deme assembly (as part of his general role as convenor, president, and executive officer of that body), but elsewhere other officials were given the job.[89] Some demes adopted the idea of dating their documents by reference to the demarch in office—with or without a cross-reference to the city's eponymous archon—while others, if they bothered at all, chose a priest or priestess.[90] On the other hand, with regard to

---

it need not have been laid down how often this should happen, nor whether regularly or irregularly.

[88] For one *very* conjectural element, see Chap. 1, pp. 36-37.

[89] For references see Chap. 4, n. 50.

[90] Demarch alone: IG I³248, Rhamnous (accounts of Nemesis); SEG 24.151, Teithras. (Archon alone: IG II²1202, Aixone.) Demarch and archon: IG II²1191, Eleusis; 2394,

the instructions which demarchs received from central government there are obvious reasons for regarding this as prime category-*a* evidence. Here, therefore, our presumption should always be that all the demes were treated alike and all their demarchs given the same things to do—with only one exception in general, the "super-deme" of Peiraieus,[91] and occasional exceptions in particular, when an individual demarch was singled out for the performance of some special task.[92] There was, in short, a body of laws (*nomoi*) defining what demarchs had to do no less than those which defined the duties of the city officials.[93]

Although the functions of the demarch are to be examined in full in a later chapter, part of that discussion has been anticipated here because it offers us such a good methodological paradigm of the distinction between what we have been calling category-*a* and category-*b* evidence. As far as other deme officials are concerned, however, we are decidedly—I would insist—in the domain of category-*b* testimony, and extreme caution is needed if justifiable use is to be made of it. After paying lip service to such caution, Haussoullier and others proceeded nonetheless to argue or imply that any official attested in any deme existed in them all.[94] Yet, as will be seen in Chapter 5B, a great diversity of titles is to be found, several of them once only. Plainly such officials *may* have existed in other demes too, but as we cannot prove it, we should not presume it.[95] Besides a demarch it is in fact only *bouleutai* (ranging in number between one and twenty-two) whom we can say for certain existed in all demes at all times,[96] and here again a fairly clear category-*a*/category-*b* distinction may be drawn; for over and above their onerous centralized duties—

?Melite; 2498, Peiraieus. Priest: SEG 21.519, Acharnai; IG II²2496, Kytheros. Priestess: SEG 22.116, Melite. The great majority of deme documents, however, are not explicitly dated at all, at least directly in the prescript: see Appendix 3.

[91] See Appendix 4.

[92] E.g., the demarch of Sounion who brought first-fruits from Oropos in 329/8 (IG II²1672, lines 272-273; see Whitehead, "Demarchs," pp. 40-42), or the demarch of Eleusis who in the mid second century reported to the *boulē* and *ekklēsia* on his cult duties (IG II²949).

[93] Note that the demarch of Eleusis who is praised in a deme decree of ca. 300 (*Hesp.* 8, 1939, pp. 177-180) is said in lines 13-14 to have functioned not merely "well" (καλῶς) but also "in accordance with the laws" (κατὰ τοὺς νόμους); this surely does not mean "legally" but "in accordance with the laws (*sc.* which set out a demarch's duties)."

[94] See Haussoullier, *Vie*, pp. 57-62; cf. Schoeffer, "Demoi," cols. 14-17, and Busolt/ Swoboda, *Staatskunde*, pp. 966-967.

[95] Admittedly, certain titles do recur with some frequency (*kēryx, euthynos, hieropoios,* and above all *tamias*), and diversity in titles must in fact have masked a good deal of uniformity, or at least comparability, in functions; see Chap. 5B.

[96] Strictly speaking, one has to say *virtually* all demes at *virtually* all times, for it seems that certain tiny demes might share a councillor between them (Chap. 1, n. 79).

which of course fall into category *a*—councillors *might* also be given work to do by their own demes. An honorific decree from Teithras, dating from either 331/0 or 330/29, praises that deme's four representatives on the *boulē* of the previous year and declares further that they "took fine and zealous care of the sacrifices and the other things which the demesmen ordered."[97] Precisely what this means we cannot divine, but in any event no assumptions from such category-*b* evidence as this would be warranted for other demes. (There is, however, category-*a* evidence also, to suggest that from the point of view of the polis the *bouleutai*, by dint of their very ubiquity, were the obvious people to give local assistance to the hard-pressed demarchs.)[98]

✳

Many other issues might profitably be discussed in terms of this simple diversity/uniformity antithesis, and indeed they will be, in subsequent chapters. My aim here has been to take examples which illustrate principles, and those principles should now be plain. The outcome of our investigation into sources and methodology—and, with it, our response to the question of how far it is valid to generalize about "the demes"— may be expressed as follows:

1. If questions are not to be begged, we cannot allow ourselves to assume that the demes acted uniformly except in areas where the polis obliged them to do so. Strictly speaking, therefore, category-*b* evidence should never be used as the basis for generalizations, especially on matters of detail.

2. Nevertheless, the areas where for its own convenience the polis did require all demes to act in the same or a very similar manner turn out, upon examination, to be extensive enough to permit a worthwhile synoptic study. In any case we may often, with all due caution, find it possible

---

[97] SEG 21.520, lines 7-12: ἐ]πειδὴ κ[αλῶς καὶ φιλ]οτίμως | [ἐπεμελήθησ]αν τῶν θ|[υσιῶν καὶ τῶ]ν ἄλλων | [ὅσα ἐκέλευσ]αν οἱ δη|[μόται.

[98] (*a*) In [Demosth.] 50.6 Aristophon's naval decree requires "the *bouleutai* and the demarchs" to draw up the naval *katalogoi* of their fellow demesmen; see Chap. 5A, sec. 2(c). (*b*) In the same connection ([Demosth.] 50.8, probably indeed the same decree) "the *bouleutai*" are required to submit lists of those possessing sufficient property in their demes as to make them liable for *proeisphora*; although no mention is made this time of the demarch, we must nonetheless suppose that here too the *bouleutai* acted jointly with him, for otherwise in demes with no *bouleutai* (above, n. 97) the task would have been left undone; see Chap. 5A, sec. 2(b). (*c*) When the demarch pursued debtors to the state he was, according to one of the lexicographers, accompanied and assisted by the *bouleutai*: *Lex Seguer.* V, *Lexeis Rhetorikai*, ἀπογράφειν [= Bekker, *Anecd. Gr.* 1.199.5]; see Chap. 5A, sec. 2(a).

to assume common-sense parallels and patterns, in substance if not necessarily in form, simply because of the extent to which all demes had a core of similar business to transact.

This dual principle will therefore serve as our constant rule for the use of evidence in the investigations which now follow.

II

INSIDE THE DEME

CHAPTER 3

THE DEME
AND ITS RESIDENTS

The Kleisthenic deme system, as we saw in Chapter 1B, was in all probability founded upon a concerted act of self-identification by the residents of local communities. Even if links of residence between members of the same *kinship* groups—phratries and the like—were (and remained) more normal than we can now reconstruct,[1] it does not seem appropriate to describe such organizations as either "local" or, in a genuine sense, "communities." The demes, on the other hand, were clearly both. Their whole *raison d'être* was the establishment of community, of bonds between neighbors naturally united by residence within a definable locality and known by its name—the Aixonians, the Erchians, the Sphettians, and so forth. It will remain to be seen, in subsequent chapters, how far this simple terminological egalitarianism represented any real cohesive force in the interplay of social and political relationships both within the deme and in the arena of the polis at large. For the moment we may take the matter on its own valuation and consider not so much the action as the cast of characters—the personnel of a deme, in the various categories to which the deme system itself gave rise.

A. The *Dēmotai*

By registration in the deme where they had or could claim residence in 508/7, all Athenian citizens—so defined by this very act—became members, demesmen (*dēmotai*), of that deme. The registration was once-for-all, hereditary. As is apparent to us from subsequent, indirect evidence (though not, presumably, left unstated at the time), membership of that same deme passed from father to son down the generations; and this was so irrespective of whether either the original registrant or any of his

---

[1] For examples of phratry/deme overlap, see Chap. 1, n. 117.

direct descendants took up domicile elsewhere, in another deme or even outside Attica altogether.[2] The category of residents in any deme who were in fact demesmen of other demes becomes important enough, schematically at least, to call for separate discussion (below, section B); and the problem of the actual extent to which Athenians stayed in or moved away from their ancestral demes over the course of time is a notoriously intransigent one.[3] For our purposes here, however, it is self-evident that the men of primary significance in any deme were its resident members, its *dēmotai* not merely by name but in day-to-day reality.

An item of quasi-technical vocabulary is worth noting first. The word *dēmotēs* itself seems to have carried no inherent implications of actual residence in a deme and (thus) membership of it in a fully active sense. In any case, other and older connotations—not to mention the several facets of the word *dēmos*—persisted to complicate the picture.[4] Accordingly *dēmotēs* (when it meant "demesman"), like *politēs*, denoted in itself a man's fundamental status in theoretical rather than practical terms. Cognate with the noun *politēs*, however, was the verb *politeuesthai*[5] and its participle *politeuomenos*. These by contrast seem to imply, in a sense less banal than the necessary difference between a noun and a verb, some degree of active exercise of and behavior in the role of *politēs*; and the equivalents as regards *dēmotēs* were the verb *dēmoteuesthai* and its participle *dēmoteuomenos*. The lexicographers offer sundry definitions of and glosses on the word. Some of these, admittedly, suggest that it meant simply the condition of being included in a deme register.[6] Most, however, contrive to imply a sense of living and indeed actively participating in one's deme;[7] and this seems fully justified in the light of surviving fourth-

[2] A man could change his deme *membership* (as opposed to *residence*) only by being adopted by a member of another deme; see [Demosth.] 44, etc. See further below, p. 77.

[3] See below, Conspectus.

[4] For *dēmos* and *dēmoi*, see Appendix 1. Fundamentally *dēmotēs* obviously means "man of the *dēmos*," so its meaning in any context is governed by the *dēmos* in question there; for some references, see Chap. 2, n. 36 (and Chap. 1, n. 28). Not until the third quarter of the fifth century do we find instances of *dēmotēs*, as "demesman," in inscriptions referring to demes (Hephaisteia regulations, 421/0: IG I³82, line 12, fragmentary) and in the enactments of the demes themselves (IG I³250, line 14, Paiania; 254, line 3, Ikarion; cf. 258, line 33, Plotheia; and standard thereafter). However, this is surely an accident of source survival, and the usage must go back to 508/7 if not earlier still.

[5] Or *politeuein*; the differences between the active and middle usages need not concern us here.

[6] E.g. *Lex Seguer.* IV, *Dikon Onomata*, δημοτεύεσθαι· τὸ ἐγγράφεσθαι εἰς ἕνα τῶν δήμων καὶ εἶναι ἐν τῷ ληξιαρχικῷ γραμματείῳ δημοτεύεσθαι ἐκαλεῖτο [= Bekker, *Anecd. Gr.* 1.186.2]. Cf. Harpoc., διαψήφισις· ἰδίως λέγεται ἐπὶ τῶν ἐν τοῖς δήμοις ἐξετάσεων, αἳ γίγνονται περὶ ἑκάστου τῶν δημοτευομένων, κτλ.

[7] See esp. Antiph. fr. 67 *apud* Harpoc. and Suda, δημοτευόμενος· δημοτεύεσθαί ἐστι

century usage.[8] The speakers in Lysias 23 and Demosthenes 57 are clear on the point: a body of demesmen could be expected to vouch for one of their number as a *face*, not merely a name on a list—someone whom they knew personally as neighbor, colleague, and fellow *dēmotēs*.[9]

This sense of identity and recognition amongst members of the same deme was no doubt to some extent a simple corollary of the deme system as such and of the size of (most of) its units. Moreover it was a sense which, in many demes at least, will have pre-dated 508/7, and would have persisted thereafter even if Kleisthenes had never lived. In his analysis of the oligarchic counterrevolution of 411, Thucydides describes the fear, helplessness, and ignorance of the Athenian citizen-body at large "because of the great size of the polis and because they did not know one another" (διὰ τὸ μέγεθος τῆς πόλεως καὶ διὰ τὴν ἀλλήλων ἀγνωσίαν: 8.66.3). This would not—could not—have been true of a deme.[10] On the other hand it is equally clear that Kleisthenes sought positively to strengthen and, one might say, to institutionalize this inbuilt sense of unity and community, above all by his prescription of the use of the deme's name by all its members:

And he made (fellow-)demesmen of all those living in each of the demes, in order that they would not, by using patronymics, expose the new citizens, but would call them after the demes; and hence Athenians do call each other after the demes. (?Aristot. *Ath. Pol.* 21.4)

Leaving aside the precise motivation given here, which can have been no more than partially true, we may accept the chief implication of the passage, that it was Kleisthenes' *intention* for the deme-name to supplant the father's name. That it did not in fact do so, in these simple terms, has long been appreciated. Instead the picture is a highly complex one,

---

τὸ τοῦδέ τινος δήμου κοινωνεῖν καὶ χρηματίζειν ἀπ᾽ αὐτοῦ (". . . to *take part in* the deme in question and take one's name from it"). Note also Pollux 3.51 (μετ᾽ ἐμοῦ δημοτευόμενος); Hesych., δημοτεύεσθαι· τὸ μετέχειν δήμου καὶ πολιτείας κατὰ νόμον; St. Byz., δῆμος· . . . δημοτεύομαι ἀντὶ τοῦ οἰκῶ.

[8] Lysias 23.2, ἠρόμην ὁπόθεν δημοτεύοιτο, cf. 23.3, ἐπυνθανόμην εἴ τινα γιγνώσκοιεν Δεκελειόθεν δημοτευόμενον Παγκλέωνα; [Demosth.] 44.39, ἀντεγράψατο Ὀτρυνεὺς εἶναι ἐν Ἐλευσινίοις δημοτευόμενος; Demosth. 57.49, τὸν μὲν ἄλλον ἅπαντα χρόνον δημοτευόμενος μετ᾽ ἐμοῦ καὶ κληρούμενος, cf. 57.55, ἐν οἷς ὁ πάππος ὁ τοῦ πατρός, ὁ ἐμός, ⟨ὁ⟩ πατήρ, ἐνταῦθα καὶ αὐτὸς φαίνομαι δημοτευόμενος. Note also Plato *Laws* 753C. The word does not occur on public inscriptions.

[9] See further, Chap. 8A.

[10] I am speaking of the simple consequences of size, without wishing to pretend that fear, helplessness, and ignorance were unknown in the demes. For the seamier side of deme life, see Chap. 10A.

which repeated discussion has done little to clarify in detail,[11] and such clarification will indeed remain an impossibility unless the evidence improves dramatically both in overall quantity and in the proportion of it which can be dated with any precision. Nothing is to be gained here, therefore, by rehearsing it *in toto* yet again, but a progressive series of observations may be made:

1. Kleisthenes did not invent the *dēmotikon* as such; there is one certain instance and other possible instances of it, preserved in the literary sources, from earlier times.[12] His aim was to make this form of nomenclature mandatory and universal.

2. In the absence, therefore, of what would have been a fundamental *terminus post quem*, we are not positively obliged to regard all late sixth-century *private* inscriptions which include demotics as dating from the years after 508/7, unless there are independent grounds for this.[13]

3. Nevertheless, in the light of Kleisthenes' aim it is possible to discern a sharp increase in the use of demotics *by individuals* in the generation following the Kleisthenic reforms. This is to be seen mainly on dedications,[14] and it presumably reflects in broad terms the employment of demotics in everyday life and speech. As Raubitschek succinctly put it, "in the private inscriptions, especially the dedications, the names occur in the forms people liked."[15]

4. The patronymic, on the other hand, continues to be found even more frequently than the demotic on similar documents in that same period, which makes the conservative preference of another (and larger) group of "the people" equally plain.[16]

---

[11] See Wilamowitz, *Aristoteles*, pp. 169-174; Schoeffer, "Demoi," cols. 6-7; Busolt/Swoboda, *Staatskunde*, p. 876; Kahrstedt, *Staatsgebiet*, pp. 199-214; Raubitschek, *Dedications*, pp. 467-478, esp. 472-476.

[12] See Chap. 1, n. 30.

[13] See Chap. 1, n. 31. For an example of Raubitschek's faulty principle, referred to there, see *Dedications*, p. 15 (on his no. 9): "The occurrence of the demotic (whatever it was) gives as *terminus post quem* the year 508 B.C. The letter forms do not support a date much later than that." Cf. also *Dedications*, p. 43 (on his no. 40): ". . . it may be doubted whether, until Kleisthenes' laws, an inhabitant of an Attic village would describe himself by a surname made from the name of his village."

[14] Raubitschek, *Dedications*, p. 474, lists twenty-six of his documents, "all dated within the generation following the reforms of Kleisthenes," where the dedicator has a demotic (but no patronymic). Even if a few of these, as I have been suggesting, *might* be pre-Kleisthenic, the great majority clearly are not. Note also IG I³995 and 1024 (with Raubitschek, *Dedications*, p. 472). As regards epitaphs, the earliest known to me with a demotic, IG I³1303 (I²1003), has a patronymic also.

[15] Raubitschek, *Dedications*, p. 475.

[16] See Raubitschek, *Dedications*, p. 474 (forty-nine dedications). I mean of course a "larger" group *of those making dedications*.

5. How soon and how enthusiastically the Athenian state, as opposed to individual Athenians, embraced the demotic as the official nomenclature is extraordinarily difficult to assess, given the extreme paucity of documentation for the first half-century after Kleisthenes. One valuable clue to this period is the usage of Herodotus, who gives most Athenians (as most others) their patronymic but also records a number of demotics, some of them from apparently official sources relating to the Persian Wars.[17] Otherwise we can occasionally observe a moment of change quite late, as in the headings of the tribute lists,[18] yet in many contexts the single name remained the norm, most obviously for the eponymous archon.

Overall, then, I am less convinced than was Raubitschek[19] that one can reconstruct a valid and intelligible account of the fluctuations in usage during the first fifty to sixty years after the Kleisthenic reform. But it is evident that Kleisthenes' attempt to change Athenian citizen nomenclature at a stroke was, perhaps inevitably, unsuccessful. The habit of using demotics took root very slowly, even in official documents which one might have expected to give a lead in the matter. Conversely many Athenians, particularly amongst the upper classes, refused to abandon the patronymics which proclaimed their famous names. The long-term result of this, clear to any reader of the literature of the fifth and fourth centuries—especially Thucydides, Aristophanes, Plato, and the orators—was that an individual's choice of demotic or patronymic could become an issue and an expression of class, status, and political values.[20] The polis itself, however, could hardly have tolerated such total and unbridled *laisser faire*—and of course an obvious compromise solution lay at hand. Already in the first half of the fifth century some private dedicators used their *patronymic and demotic together*,[21] and it is possible that some official documents too employed the same conjunction in that period.[22] A prescription that names be recorded by patronymic and demotic

[17] References in Chap. 2, n. 40.

[18] For years 1-3, i.e., 454/3-452/1, the *grammateus* has a single name, without demotic (IG I³259-261), but he is given one in year 4, 451/0 (IG I³262), and regularly thereafter. For other categories of official documents, see Kahrstedt, *Staatsgebiet*, pp. 199-214.

[19] See Raubitschek, *Dedications*, p. 476.

[20] See in general Edwards, *Demesman*, pp. 58-61, "The Significance of the Demotikon." For Thucydides (and Xenophon), see Chap. 2, p. 48; for Aristophanes, Edwards, ibid., pp. 27-28; for Plato, Edwards, ibid., p. 59 with n. 12; for the orators, Edwards, ibid., pp. 31-47.

[21] See Raubitschek, *Dedications*, pp. 475-476. Note also the epitaph IG I³1303 (I²1003).

[22] See Kahrstedt, *Staatsgebiet*, pp. 200-201 (cf. Raubitschek, *Dedications*, p. 473) on the accuser of Themistokles in ca. 472 (Craterus, *FGrH* 342 F11; Plut. *Them.* 23.1; M. H. Hansen, *Eisangelia*, Odense, 1975, p. 70).

(πατρόθεν καὶ τοῦ δήμου) then occurs in a fragmentary decree, or decrees, of ca. 430.[23] Raubitschek has plausibly suggested that "the establishment of the full Athenian name, containing patronymic as well as demotic, was a direct outcome of the Periklean citizenship laws"[24] (of 451/0); and one may fairly extend this by supposing that it was equally the outcome of the reenactment of the Periklean legislation in 403/2, during the general legislative rationalization of that time, that the *"tria nomina"* became the standard citizen nomenclature that we see in the fourth century.[25] Variations and anomalies persisted, even so, both in official documents and especially in quasi-official or unofficial ones.[26] Increasingly, though, a norm and paradigm prevailed: an Athenian was known by his father and by his deme (Demosth. 39.9).

Would Kleisthenes have been disappointed to see this outcome? Possibly so. True, he had quite deliberately left some of the features of the aristocratic state untouched (?Aristot. *Ath. Pol.* 21.6), but others succeeded in surviving into and through the classical period despite his best efforts; and of these none was more cherished or more deep-seated than the patronymic. Even the demes themselves employed it, in their own documents, where it seemed appropriate or convenient to do so. Yet the demotic too was all-pervasive. It became an essential element in the official vocabulary of the democratic political organization of the state as a whole, and it was proudly proclaimed by both individual demesmen and the demes themselves.[27]

[23] IG I³59, lines 6 ([– – – ἀναγράφ]εν πατρόθεν [καὶ τõ δέμο . . ⁚ . .]) and 37 ([– – – πατρ]όθεν καὶ τõ [δέμο – – –]).

[24] Raubitschek, *Dedications*, p. 475, cf. 476.

[25] The earliest fourth-century occurrence of the πατρόθεν καὶ τοῦ δήμου formula is in the last of the decrees (ca. 360) of the Dekeleieis phratry: IG II²1237, lines 119-120. See also IG II²223B, lines 4-5; 478, line 28 (largely restored); *Hesp.* 9, 1940, pp. 104-111, no. 20, lines 24-25; *Hesp.* Suppl. 19, 1982, p. 174, lines 25, 43. Note also ?Aristot. *Ath. Pol.* 55.3 (the *dokimasia* of archons) and 63.4 (the dikastic *pinakia*); Plato *Laws* 753C; schol. Plato *Gorgias* 451B; schol. Aristoph. *Ploutos*, line 277; Hesych., χαλκοῦν πινάκιον.

[26] See for instance IG II²2345, a catalog of contributors from the members of five *thiasoi*; some have single names, some demotics, some patronymics, and there are two *tria nomina* (lines 36-37).

[27] *Patronymics*. The most obvious use of patronymics by the demes is in honorific decrees. Patronymics are virtually universal for the honorands themselves, both when they belong to demes other than the one honoring them (e.g. IG II²1156 [lines 45-51], 1187, 1188, 1192, 1193, 1201, 1204, 1214) and when they are honored in their own demes; rare exceptions are, in one case explicitly (IG II²1178, Ikarion) and in another implicitly (SEG 24.153, cf. 151, Teithras), men honored as demarchs. For other instances of the "honorific patronymic," cf. SEG 24.197 (financial contributors, Athmonon) and, as a rule, those with whom the demes contract leases (IG II²2492, 2496, 2497, SEG 24.152); but here a bureaucratic, identifying function may sometimes be paramount. The proposers of deme decrees (of all kinds) are given their patronymics in about half of all surviving instances.

The great majority of demotics—approximately one hundred and fifteen out of the one hundred and thirty-nine—were adjectival in form. An individual demesman of Eleusis, for example, was an *Eleusinios*, the collectivity of the demesmen the *Eleusinioi*. It is perhaps not too fanciful to think that the adjectival form was a peculiarly apposite one, in conveying the dual idea that "a man of Eleusis" or "the men of Eleusis" were somehow epitomized by membership of that particular deme, and also, conversely, that a deme was very much the sum of its (human) parts. Indeed in over thirty instances the only name of the deme was not a toponym such as "Eleusis" but the demotic in its collective, plural form.[28] Yet anomalies abounded. The singular demotic of the deme of the *Kerameis*, for example, was not *Kerameus* but "*from Kerameis*" (ἐκ Κεραμέων)—one of a small group of seven demotics which took this prepositional ἐκ (or ἐξ) ——— form.[29] Another, larger group (of seventeen) conveyed the same idea of "from ———" by means of a -θεν form of demotic: Ἀμφιτροπῆθεν ("from Amphitrope"), Κεφαλῆθεν ("from Kephale"), Ὀῆθεν ("from Oe"), and the like. The majority of these arose from toponymic deme-names ending in -ή, for which the -θεν form of demotic was for some reason or other found especially apt.[30]

Demotics. As regards their use by the demes themselves, it is naturally found when a deme document mentions a member of another deme (e.g. as honorand: references above), but also and more interestingly with reference to its own demesmen. For example, approximately half of the proposers of deme decrees are given their demotics (in which case they invariably have the patronymic too; IG II²1214, Peiraieus, has the only instance of demotic alone). No overall principles are evident here, merely the requirements of particular circumstances (such as the addition of the deme's decree to another stele: e.g. IG II²1156 [lines 52ff.], 1299 [lines 51ff.]) together with a certain amount of apparently random choice: compare, for instance, SEG 28.103, line 2, with line 8 (Eleusis); or IG II²1202, lines 2-3, with AM 66, 1941, 218-219, no. 1, line 1 (Aixone). Of course, demes commonly and naturally identified their own members by single *nomina*: witness most obviously the demarchs, but cf. also e.g. IG II²1175, lines 1-2; 1180, lines 4-5, 10, 24; 1182, lines 23-24; 2493, lines 2-3.

[28] Twenty-nine of these are the *-adai* and *-idai* demes (all of which, it may be observed, were small or smallish demes, represented by at most three *bouleutai*); the others are Kerameis and Pelekes. On Phrearrhioi, see J. S. Traill, *Hesp.* Suppl. 19, 1982, p. 170 with n. 28.

[29] The other six are ἐκ Κηδῶν, ἐκ Κοίλης, ἐκ Κολωνοῦ, ἐκ Μυρρινού(ν)της, and (twice) ἐξ Οἴου.

[30] I.e., Ἀγγελῆ, Ἀγκυλῆ (twice), Ἀγρυλῆ (twice), Ἀλωπεκῆ, Ἀμφιτροπῆ, Βατῆ, Ἑκαλῆ, Κεφαλῆ, Ὀῆ, and Περγασῆ (twice). In addition, this form was used of the two Kolonai demes (Κολωνῆθεν: thus distinguishable from the ἐκ Κολωνοῦ of Kolonos; cf. D. M. Lewis, *ABSA* 50, 1955, pp. 12-17), of Hestiaia (Ἑστιαιόθεν), and of Oa (Ὤαθεν or Ὄαθεν; on Oa and Oe and their demotics see S. Dow, *AJPh* 84, 1963, pp. 166-181). In some of these cases there is an attested, "normal" plural demotic—e.g. Ἀγγελεῖς, Κολωνεῖς—but in others, as indeed in some of the ἐκ/ἐξ—— group, there is not; on this see below, in text.

There are indications, however, that in everyday usage a -θεν form was prevalent for other demes too.[31]

From these and other such anomalies I believe it is justifiable to conclude that each deme was left to devise its own demotic, in or soon after 508/7, and that no centralized attempt was made to eradicate eccentricities in form, whether they stemmed from preexisting usage or from preferences expressed then for the first time. Where is the sense, for example, in the demotic of the deme Melite being *Meliteus* while that of the deme Xypete—a toponym identical in form—was *Xypetaion*? One can only suppose that each is what the demesmen of that deme wanted and were allowed to have. Thereafter, by degrees, official documents (and most obviously, once they were in existence, the bouleutic lists) will have canonized one particular form of each demotic at the expense of any variant forms.[32] Nonetheless the variants sometimes continued in unofficial currency alongside it, and even the canonical version might be vulnerable to small inconsistencies in orthography.[33]

In a minority of instances a deme does not seem to have wanted, or needed, an adjectival plural demotic at all. If we possessed a deme decree from either of the Oion demes (Dekeleikon or Kerameikon), for example,

[31] See for instance Aristoph. *Clouds*, line 134, Κικυννόθεν instead of Κικυννεύς; Lysias 23.2-3, Δεκελειόθεν instead of Δεκελειεύς. It might be argued that the question "πόθεν τῶν δήμων;" in the archonship *dokimasia* (?Aristot. *Ath. Pol.* 55.3) invited an answer couched in the -θεν form, but in fact the adjectival demotic was evidently no less suitable: note Demosth. 39.30, Ἀκαμαντίδος φυλῆς γέγονας καὶ τῶν δήμων Θορίκιος. For the τῶν δήμων ——— formula in late authors, see e.g. Plut. *Them.* 1.1, *Arist.* 1.1, *Kim.* 4.2, *Per.* 3.1; [Plut.] *Vit. X Or.* 832B-C, 834B, 840A, 841B, 844A, 848D; Diog. Laert. 2.18, 2.48, 3.3, 4.1, 4.16, 4.21, 10.1.

[32] For one *possible* example of uncertainty in the form of a demotic in the early years, see the dedication IG I³779 (*Dedications*, no. 184) by Κολλυτίδες Ἀρχενείδες; it is not, however, certain that Κολλυτίδης is indeed a variant of Κολλυτεύς (thus Raubitschek in *Dedications*, ad loc.) rather than a *genos*-name (thus Wilamowitz, *Aristoteles*, pp. 183-184).

[33] Unofficial variants: examples above, n. 31. Orthographical inconsistencies: Finley, *Land and Credit*, p. 199, n. 20, points to a *horos* from 315/4 (*AJPh* 69, 1948, p. 203, no. 3) where "all three creditors are from Halai [Aixonides] and the demotic is spelled three different ways," namely, Ἁλαεῖ, Ἁλαῖ, Ἁλαιεῖ, and he sees the explanation of such "eccentricities" in the private nature of this type of stone. (For another instance, note two fourth-century dedications at Plotheia, one by a Πλωθεύς, IG II²4607, the other by a Πλωθει[εύς], IG II²4885.) The explanation is doubtless correct, but a more interesting phenomenon is orthographical variation by the demes themselves, in their own documents. Two instances of this were noted by Müller, *de demis*, pp. 47-48: IG II²1214 (τὸν δῆμον τὸν Πειραιέων, line 4; τὸν δῆμον τὸν Πειραιῶ|ν, lines 10-11) and IG I³258 (Πλωθειεῦσι, line 11; Πλωθεῦσι, line 15); cf. the double lambda of Ἁλλιέων in *AE* 1925-1926, pp. 168-177, line 5 (as compared with the same deme's *AE* 1932, *Chronika*, pp. 30-32, lines 8, 16, 20).

it would appear that we should find the demesmen there referring to themselves, if they had occasion to do so, as οἱ ἐξ Οἴου. However, the great majority of demes favored a more direct and personal formulation. The adjectival demotic is the earliest form that we know of,[34] and it naturally recommended itself to most bodies of *dēmotai* as they sought an individual and a collective identity for themselves in the post-Kleisthenic polis.

B. Other Citizens

In and immediately after 508/7, naturally, all *Eleusinioi* lived in Eleusis, all *Skambonidai* in (and as) Skambonidai, and so on. However, the hereditary nature of deme membership, with its result that groups based originally on domicile gradually become groups based on descent, necessarily fashioned, by degrees, a distinction in any deme between residents who were its own *dēmotai* and residents with ancestral deme membership elsewhere. In demes which had nothing in particular to recommend them to outsiders as places to live, this latter group will surely have been small—perhaps even, in some cases, nonexistent. But in certain demes, especially (though not exclusively) those of Athens itself, the category of non-*dēmotai* may well have come to constitute a substantial minority.

Was there a technical name for such people? If there was, we do not know it. To be sure, a fourth-century orator, paraphrasing the words of a city decree, employed a distinction between the "*dēmotai*" and the "*enkektēmenoi*" which we also find reflected elsewhere,[35] and it has often been asserted or assumed that the latter was the name in question.[36] Yet of itself the term *enkektēmenos* merely described a man who *possessed landed property* in a deme other than his own—as well-to-do Athenians regularly did.[37] It gave no indication whatsoever of whether he actually lived on that property or not. Nor, presumably, could it apply to those

---

[34] Myron Φλυεύς: see Chap. 1, n. 30.

[35] [Demosth.] 50.8 Compare Isaeus 3.80, ἐν δὲ τῷ δήμῳ κεκτημένος τὸν τριτάλαντον οἶκον (referring to property in *one's own* deme); and note *Inscr. Délos* 104-8, B, line 14, [Ἀθην]ό[δ]ωρος Ἁγ[ν]όσιος ἐμ Προβ[αλίνθωι ἐγκεκτημένος], as restored by M.-F. Baslez, *REG* 89, 1976, p. 355 with n. 44. On the *enktētikon* tax, see below, n. 38.

[36] See for instance, most recently, Rhodes, *Commentary*, p. 252: ". . . men who live in one deme but are registered in another."

[37] For some examples, see Davies, *Families*, index, under "property holding outside family deme." A splendid illustrative text is Plato's will, as preserved by Diog. Laert. 3.41-42, which mentions adjacent estates in the deme Iphistiadai owned by *dēmotai* of Kollytos (Plato himself), Phrearrhioi, and Cholleidai; and in Eiresidai owned by two Myrrhinousioi and a Xypetaion, as well as Plato himself.

who did live in a deme other than their ancestral deme but owned no property there. Such facts were rarely relevant ones, either to the state or to the deme in question. What usually mattered was landownership, which, irrespective of residence, rendered an *enkektēmenos* fiscally liable—if so it chose—to the deme as well as to the state.[38]

Logically, then, we may say that from the standpoint of any deme the category of *enkektēmenoi* as a whole subsumed the (surely much smaller) group of those *enkektēmenoi* actually domiciled in that deme.[39] For practical purposes, however, to determine whether any individual *enkektēmenos* was indeed so domiciled requires independent information which is often not forthcoming. Where a deme is found decreeing to a nondemesman honorand privileges which could only be exercised within that deme, or which at least only took on real value there, it will generally be safe to infer that the man did live there and participated in as much of the communal life of that deme as was permitted him.[40] Indeed we know of one deme, Ikarion, where, at any rate in the second half of the fifth century, such participation might go to considerable lengths: a deme decree ordains that tragic *chorēgoi* be drawn in pairs not only from the demesmen but also from other residents.[41] In this we have a fascinating, if fleeting, glimpse into the two interlocking and competing "definitions"

---

[38] In IG II²1214, lines 26-28, Kallidamas of Cholleidai (150) is excused payment of τὸ ἐγκτητικόν (*sc.* τέλος) by the Peiraieis—evidently a tax on his landed property in the deme. It has been the standard assumption that all demes levied this tax (see for instance Müller, *de demis*, p. 59; Haussoullier, *Vie*, pp. 67-69, 78; Schoeffer, "Demoi," cols. 17-18; Busolt/Swoboda, *Staatskunde*, p. 970; Lacey, *Family*, pp. 98, 278 [n. 41]; Harrison, *Law* I, p. 238; D. Whitehead, *ZPE* 21, 1976, p. 256; Nemes, "Public property," p. 5; Osborne, *Demos*, pp. 76, 225) though in fact it is mentioned nowhere else but in Peiraieus. Conceivably the "immunity" (ἀτέλεια) granted to individual non-*dēmotai* by Eleusis (IG II²1187) and Coastal Lamptrai (IG II²1204) presupposes it or something like it, but its presumed ubiquity is the purest conjecture. (Haussoullier's attempt in *Vie*, p. 78, to calculate its usual *rate* is thus quite absurd; see rather Müller, *de demis*, p. 20, and Schoeffer, "Demoi," col. 18, both pointing out the likelihood of different rates in different demes.)

[39] It must be reiterated that one is speaking, here as throughout, only of landowners. There will certainly also have been landless men living in demes (especially in the *asty*) other than their own, but of them we can say little or nothing; cf. Schoeffer, "Demoi," col. 13.

[40] For instance, Kallidamas in IG II²1214 (see above, n. 38) evidently did live in Peiraieus, to judge not only from the tax exemption awarded him (lines 25-28) but also and especially from his invitation to share in all but the most private cult observances of the deme (lines 11-19). Compare, on this, Philokedes of Acharnai (62) in IG II²1204 (Coastal Lamptrai); also the *stratēgos* Derkylos of Hagnous (179), who was evidently *enkektēmenos* in Eleusis (IG II²1187, with Davies, *Families*, p. 98) and thus *perhaps* resident there.

[41] IG I³254, lines 3-4: [. . ⸢ . .]ι τὸν δεμοτὸν καὶ τὸν Ἰκα[ριοῖ οἰκόντ]|[ον δύο] τὸν ἀχορεγέτον. It is not known how long this persisted; individual *chorēgoi* in the fourth century are recorded without demotics, which would argue for their all being Ikarieis.

of a deme—as its true members, and as its actual (citizen) population. Quite possibly the second of these conceptions played a larger role in the everyday life and functioning of some demes, at least, than our surviving sources reveal. But there is a grave misunderstanding in the suggestion, by one modern scholar, ". . . that the purchase of the land belonging to an *oikos* in a deme made a man eligible to be enrolled in that deme";[42] for ultimately the more basic and pure conception of a deme as the descent-group of its *dēmotai* was always the stronger.

C. Women

Another, rather different pair of interlocking models—one of which may be termed the theoretical, the other the (more) practical—emerges when one considers the matter of *women* and the deme.

In the strictest sense women were simply ignored by the deme system and, through it, by the polis itself. Every *dēmotēs* was a *politēs* (and *vice versa*); but *politis*, despite its occasional appearances in oratory, was the essentially metaphorical coinage of poets and philosophers,[43] and *dēmotis* was likewise no more than a metaphor.[44] A Kleisthenic deme was technically an all-male entity, and virtually all its public business was the concern of men only. Women belonged to a deme in the same vicarious way that they belonged to an *oikos*—through their relationship with a demesman, their father or husband (or, failing them, some other man), who was their *kyrios*.[45]

The plainest illustration of this is provided by demotics, as they are

[42] The suggestion, admittedly tentative, is that of Lacey, *Family*, pp. 97-98. The sole text to which he can appeal is Demosth. 55.35, where the speaker complains that his opponents are "driving me out of the deme altogther." The allusion is to the deme in which his father Teisias had bought some land which, as is clear from 55.13-14, had once belonged to another family; thus, Lacey infers, "deme-membership was obtainable by purchases of land," and in this instance the speaker's actual deme membership was therefore in jeopardy. However, this argument rests upon an assumption, possibly quite wrong, that Teisias was not already a member of this (unnamed) deme; and in any case—as Lacey himself foresaw—one may counter his view by the simple and surely correct supposition that the speaker was referring to "the deme" in a purely topographical sense (cf. Bicknell, *Studies*, p. 18, n. 53).

[43] See e.g. Sophocles, *Elektra*, line 1227; Euripides, *Elektra*, line 1335; Isoc. 14.51; Plato *Laws* 814C; Aristot. *Pol.* 1275b32 and 1278a28; Isaeus 8.43; [Demosth.] 59.107.

[44] See Aristoph. *Lysistr.*, lines 331-334: ἁρπαλέως | ἀραμένη ταῖσιν ἐμαῖς | δημότισιν καιομέναις | φέρουσ' ὕδωρ βοηθῶ. This seems to be a very loose usage—"comrades" or the like; but note the help motif elsewhere in Aristophanes, with δημότης (*Clouds*, line 1322; *Lysistr.*, lines 684-685; *Ekkles.*, lines 1023-1024).

[45] On the *kyrios*, see in brief MacDowell, *Law*, p. 84.

preserved on grave monuments and elsewhere. During the period covered by this book it is very rare indeed for a woman either to use or be given a demotic of her own. Certainly *adjectival* demotics in a feminine form, exactly analogous to the masculine adjectival form with its epitomizing associations, do not seem to occur before the second century A.D.,[46] by which time the deme system had lost the greater part of its significance; and in the Hellenistic and Roman periods in general, a more subtle version of feminine demotic was regularly employed. This was an ἐκ/ἐξ ———— prepositional construction which, as we have seen, had always been in use for official, masculine demotics in a few demes but which was now evidently regarded as particularly suitable for women, and is attested for around fifty demes in all. Earlier, in the fourth century, a tiny handful of women's demotics are found, all of them in the -θεν form—sometimes for demes where that form was normal anyway,[47] sometimes (more significantly) for demes where the masculine form was regularly and officially adjectival. A nice example of this latter category is to be seen on a mid fourth-century epitaph of (presumably) a husband and wife, from Halai: Hagnotheos Ἁλαι[εύς], but Nikodike Ἁλῆθ[εν]![48] However, this sort of thing—to reemphasize the point—was exceptional, at least in the classical and early Hellenistic periods. The normal practice was for a woman to be given no demotic of her own; instead, what was indicated, explicitly or implicitly, was her relationship with either her father or her husband or both of them, who appeared in the "possessive" genitive case with their own, masculine demotics. Without any explicit indication, the very common epitaphs in the form, for example, Ἀλκιμάχη | Καλλιμάχου | Ἀναγυρασίο apparently refer to the father, not to the husband (if any),[49] but numerous more explicit variations and permutations were also employed.[50] Any changing patterns of usage

---

[46] See for instance IG II²5276, with other references given there.

[47] E.g. IG II²7831 (ca. 400), Φάνυλλα Ὤαθεν. In IG II²7680 (mid fourth century), Εὐκολίνη | Δημητρίου | Φλυῆθεν, the demotic is *presumably* that of the father (see in general below, with n. 49), though one would have expected Φλυέως.

[48] *Hesp.* 37, 1968, pp. 294-295, no. 39 (SEG 25.240). Note also IG II²6285 (first half of the fourth century), Ῥόδυλλα | Ἰκαριόθεν, and 6897 (same period), Λύσιλλα | Μυρρινοντόθ|εν. Attested in later centuries are Ἀνακαιάθεν, Ἀφίδνηθεν, Λαμπτρῆθεν, etc.

[49] The example given is IG II²5450 (first half of the fourth century), lines 6-8. See also e.g. IG I²1063 (line 2), 1077, 1083; IG II²5231, 5263, 5272, 5280, 5327, 5346, 5377, 5495, 5541, 5559, 5571, 5600, 5607, 5639, 5647, 5695, 5696, 5701, 5722, 5755, 5789, 5823, 5926, 6016, 6025, 6042, 6124, 6166, 6181, 6182, 6236, 6276, 6328, 6340, 6361, 6391, 6407, 6588, 6740, 6815, 6939, 7392, 7415, 7807, etc. Although some of these women may have been unmarried, one cannot suppose that they all were. On marriage patterns in classical Athens, see S. Isager, *C&M* 33, 1981-82, pp. 81-96.

[50] Often an explanatory "daughter" (θυγάτηρ) is added: see for instance IG I²1082;

are difficult to trace with any hope of accuracy or likelihood of explanation. The underlying point is quite clear, though: the *members* of a deme, with demotics to prove it, were men, and the association of a woman with a deme or demes was through her menfolk.[51] Even when a deme sought to praise and honor an outstanding woman and recorded its gratitude on stone, the point could not be stretched. Thus Satyra, the zealous and munificent priestess of the Thesmophoroi in Melite in the first half of the second century, was ceremoniously designated in the only proper way: "Satyra, wife of Krateas of Melite" (Σατύρα Κρατέου Μελιτέως γυν[ή]).[52]

Yet this very document furnishes a perfect illustration of the ambivalent role and status of women in the demes—formally, terminologically, excluded and ignored, but in reality (as a small but significant corpus of both literary and epigraphic evidence makes manifest) fulfilling functions of great importance in communal life. While the deme in its narrowly political aspect necessarily remained an all-male preserve, the sphere of religion and cult operated under a different, older set of imperatives, and "in the sacred and ritual activities of the community the active presence of women in the public world [was] not merely tolerated but required."[53] As the topic of religion in the demes is to be dealt with in a later chapter, it will suffice to note here in brief that within a penumbra of miscellaneous allusions to priestesses and other women in deme documents,[54] it is the

---

IG II²5233, 5242, 5257, 5338, 5360, 5404 (lines 4-7), 5424, 6666, 6727, 6834, 7246, 7802, 7836, 7837, 7841. Sometimes, though, the father goes unmentioned and the woman is "wife" (γυνή): IG II²5295, 5324, 5438, 7452, etc. More common is the dual designation as daughter *and* wife (IG II²5332, 5367, 5393, 5407, 5451, 6580, 7071, 7376, 7798, 7844, etc.), which was itself open to variation: "daughter" understood, "wife" explicit (IG II²6715, 7231, 7259); "wife" first, "daughter" second, both explicit (IG II²5664, 5685); "wife" first understood, "daughter" second explicit (IG II²6344, 6478). For a more elaborate classification, see A. S. Henry, *CQ* 19, 1969, pp. 298-305 (Hellenistic period only).

[51] See on this J.P.A. Gould, "Law, Custom and Myth: aspects of the social position of women in classical Athens," *JHS* 100, 1980, pp. 38-59, at 45.

[52] *Hesp.* 11, 1942, pp. 265-274, no. 51, line 2; Satyra is 293.

[53] J.P.A. Gould, *JHS* 100, 1980, p. 50.

[54] (*a*) In SEG 22.116 (decree of Melite, ca. 330), the document is itself dated by reference to a priestess, ἐπὶ Χαιρύλλης ἱερείας (line 5); she was evidently the priestess of Artemis Aristoboule, a cult founded by Themistokles (see Plut. *Them.* 22.1-2, cf. *de Herod. mal.* 869C-D; J. Threpsiades and E. Vanderpool, *AD* 19, 1964, pp. 26-36; W. R. Connor, *Historia* 21, 1972, pp. 569-574; Wycherley, *Stones*, pp. 189-192); given this dating formula it would seem that the priestess changed regularly, perhaps even annually. (*b*) In IG II²1175 (decree of Halai Aixonides, ca. 360), lines 21-24, priestesses join priests and secular officials in swearing an oath. (*c*) In IG II²1356 (*lex sacra* of (?)Halai Aixonides, early fourth century), the perquisites of six or seven priestesses are detailed. (*d*) In *Hesp.* 39, 1970, pp. 47-53 (*lex sacra* of Phrearrhioi, mid third century), line 11, there is a reference to "the priestesses" doing something. (*e*) In IG II²1213 (decree or *lex sacra* of (?)Erchia, fourth century), line

exclusively female cult of Demeter Thesmophoros, with its early-autumn festival of the Thesmophoria, of which our sources tell us most. The evidence—none of it earlier than the fourth century—either originates from or else pertains to at least six demes, more probably seven,[55] and there seems to be sufficient internal agreement in it to warrant a general reconstruction. The speaker in Isaeus 8.19-20 describes how "the wives of the demesmen" chose two women, including his own mother, to hold office for the Thesmophoria and perform the customary rituals (8.19, αἵ τε γυναῖκες αἱ τῶν δημοτῶν μετὰ ταῦτα προὔκριναν αὐτὴν μετὰ τῆς Διοκλέους γυναικὸς τοῦ Πιθέως ἄρχειν εἰς τὰ Θεσμοφόρια καὶ ποιεῖν τὰ νομιζόμενα μετ᾽ ἐκείνης; cf. 8.20, μήτε τὰς τῶν ἄλλων δημοτῶν γυναῖκας αἱρεῖσθαι ἂν αὐτὴν συνιεροποιεῖν τῇ Διοκλέους γυναικὶ καὶ κυρίαν ποιεῖν ἱερῶν). These two women will be the "officials" (archousai) of the Cholargos decree IG II²1184, lines 3-18, who are to work with the priestess of the cult[56] and provide her, jointly, with the cereals, wine, and other necessities (including money) which the rituals required.

This evidence relates, some scholars believe, to local celebrations of the Thesmophoria by and in demes.[57] Others, however, have argued that it refers at most to local arrangements for celebrating the *city*'s Thesmophoria.[58] With some of the data it seems frankly impossible to decide. However, as we have explicit mention of a Thesmophorion in one deme (Peiraieus: IG II²1177) and, more important, of an independent Thesmophoria festival in another, Halimous,[59] it is manifestly the case that observance of the Thesmophoria was not confined to the city of Athens. In any event it was evidently a time when *all* the "wives of the demesmen" were involved. Having chosen their pair of representatives to help the priestess, they could all look forward to the festival itself (Isaeus 6.49-

---

3, there is a broken reference to "the women in office" (ταῖς ἀρχούσαις; cf. IG II²1184 and Isaeus 8.19, below in text). (*f*) In *Hesp.* 3, 1934, pp. 44-46, no. 33 (decree of Peiraieus, early third century), line 11, the reading is αὐτῶν καὶ γυναικῶ[ν – – –]. See also next note.

[55] Cholargos (IG II²1184), Eleusis (Dow/Healey, *Calendar*), Halimous (see below, n. 59), Melite (the Satyra decree: see above, n. 52), Peiraieus (IG II²1177), Pithos (Isaeus 8.19-20), and the unidentifiable deme of Isaeus 3.80, which of course *might* be one of these six.

[56] Note that in IG II²1184, line 4, the reading τῆς ἱερείας is obviously a mistake for τῆι ἱερείαι: O. Broneer, *Hesp.* 11, 1942, p. 272, n. 81. In IG II²1177 the Thesmophorion of Peiraieus is in the joint charge of the priestess and the demarch.

[57] E.g. Haussoullier, *Vie*, p. 139; Dow/Healey, *Calendar*, p. 36; cf. Davies, *Families*, p. xxiv.

[58] E.g. Deubner, *Feste*, p. 57; O. Broneer, *Hesp.* 11, 1942, pp. 270-274; Mikalson, "Religion," pp. 426, 429.

[59] Schol. Aristoph. *Thesm.*, line 80, δεκάτη [Πυανεψιῶνος] ἐν Ἁλιμοῦντι Θεσμοφόρια ἄγεται (cf. Paus. 1.31.1); Mikalson, *Calendar*, p. 71; cf. Parke, *Festivals*, p. 88.

50), and perhaps also—at least in demes like the one described in Isaeus 3.80—to a feast provided by the wealthiest of their husbands. Such liberation from the severe restrictions of their daily round of duties must have been welcome indeed, and will also have been enjoyed on other occasions when, under the deme's auspices, "the women [came] together in the traditional way."[60]

D. Metics

One further, important group of deme residents remains to be mentioned—the metics (*metoikoi*). I have argued elsewhere[61] the case for believing that the status of metic, or officially registered immigrant, was created either as a part of Kleisthenes' measures themselves or else as a fairly direct consequence and corollary of them in the first quarter of the fifth century. What this means, if true, is that from a very early stage in their existence, and perhaps from the very outset, the individual demes, in addition to evolving their own corporate life and activities as bodies of *dēmotai*, were also required to take formal note of any immigrants who chose to settle within their particular bailiwicks—just as the polis itself had now resolved to monitor the immigrant community as a whole—and to *begin* to devise a broad balance between rights for them and obligations upon them. No doubt each deme was left to do this at its own pace and to its own preferred extent. Some procedure and mechanism for registration and the maintenance of lists and records will surely, however, have been instituted across the board, for, with metics no less than with the citizen demesmen themselves, the creation of concessions and responsibilities alike presupposes some means, however rudimentary, of distinguishing specific individuals for whom they were intended. Thus, in a *lex sacra* of ca. 460, the deme Skambonidai permitted "the metics" to participate in one of its sacrifices (apparently to the tribal hero Leos): καὶ] τὸς μετοίχ[ος λαχ]|ἐν.[62] As well as the obvious intrinsic importance of this early example of a deme's having decided upon such a concession, the provision demonstrates not merely that the deme recognizes the presence of metics but also that it commands a means of determining which of them were living in Skambonidai and not elsewhere.

This document from Skambonidai is by far our earliest piece of evidence for any individual deme's devising rights or duties for its immigrant residents. Unfortunately, besides being early it is also virtually unique;

---

[60] IG II²1177 (Peiraieus), lines 11-12, συνέρχονται αἱ γυναῖκες κα|τὰ τὰ πάτρια.

[61] Whitehead, *Metic*, pp. 140-147.

[62] IG I³244, C, lines 4-10, esp. 7-9.

and one must candidly admit not only that we are entirely ignorant about how the vast majority of the individual demes treated their metics but also, and accordingly, that to proffer generalizations about the deme system as a whole, in this respect as in others, would be most unwise. Taxation can serve as a paradigm of this. In the middle of the fourth century the deme Eleusis thanked and rewarded a number of Thebans who either were at the time, or else had been, resident in the deme.[63] Amongst the honors granted them is "immunity from those taxes over which the Eleusinians have authority" (ἀτέλεια ὧν εἰσιν κύριοι Ἐλευσίνιοι). The natural interpretation of this formula is, no doubt, that this deme exacted a tax or taxes from its immigrant residents, which would certainly have been an obvious option for a deme like Eleusis with a larger than average concentration of such people (see below). In other decrees, however, the Eleusinians grant "immunity" to Athenian citizens,[64] and it is not clear what, if any, fiscal distinctions were drawn between metics and (citizen) *enkektēmenoi*.[65] As to small demes with few metics, some of them *may* have ignored the group for tax purposes altogether. At all events the documents of the demes themselves yield no further enlightenment on the matter.

We can, though, turn to another source and form of information in respect of the *distribution of metics amongst the demes*—something which, in the absence of any indication to the contrary, may be seen as a consequence of where the immigrants themselves chose to make their homes.[66] For something over a hundred years, from the last quarter of the fifth century to the last quarter of the fourth, individual metics (both men and women) who appeared in catalogs, accounts, and similar documents of the Athenian state itself were identified by a standard designation which recorded their deme of residence: "living (οἰκῶν, or for a

---

[63] IG II²1185-1186 (three decrees in all); see Whitehead, *Metic*, p. 32.

[64] IG II²1187 (see above, n. 40), lines 16-17, and IG II²1188 (mid fourth century), lines 28-30; cf. IG II²1204 (Coastal Lamptrai, late fourth century), lines 11-12. In IG II²1214 (Peiraieus: see above, nn. 38, 40) the formula is τελεῖν δὲ αὐτὸν τὰ αὐτὰ τέλη ἐν | τῶι δήμωι ἅπερ ἂγ καὶ Πειραιεῖς καὶ μὴ ἐγλέγειμ παρ᾽ αὐτοῦ τὸν δήμαρχον τὸ ἐγκτ|ητικόν (lines 25-28); but the logical relationship between the two clauses is not clear.

[65] Any such distinctions between (citizen) *enkektēmenoi* and the mass of ordinary metics will doubtless have been reduced, and perhaps entirely eliminated, in the case of any of the latter who secured (from the Athenian state) the rare privilege of *enktēsis* (see Whitehead, *Metic*, p. 30, for instances), and were thus eligible to acquire a house or land in the deme of their choice.

[66] That is, there are no grounds for believing either that individual demes denied metics admission (or would have been permitted to do so) or that the polis itself maintained any overall controls; cf. Whitehead, *Metic*, p. 100, n. 31.

woman οἰχοῦσα) in Melite," or "in Eleusis," or wherever it might be.[67] Unlike the citizen/demesman's *dēmotikon*, which remained immutable whatever his real deme of residence and however often he changed it, the οἰχῶν/οἰχοῦσα nomenclature would have been useless and nonsensical if it had not indicated the metic's actual, current deme of residence.[68] Accordingly, whereas a citizen's demotic *may* be a thoroughly treacherous guide to his real domicile,[69] the deme designations of metics are necessarily a direct and genuine index to their actual distribution throughout Attica. Drawing upon the epigraphic sources which contain the formula,[70] a succession of scholars have compiled lists of individual metics and plotted their distribution amongst the demes; and the concentration of metics in the urban and suburban demes has been repeatedly noted.[71] What has not been so often remarked upon, yet is surely of no little interest, is the overall number of demes in which metics are attested. I have collected the figures afresh (from epigraphic sources; the negligible contribution of literary sources is best ignored), and they are as follows:

1. The deme residence of some 366 metics is currently known.[72]

2. The highest figures, in order, are Melite 75, Peiraieus 69, Kollytos 42, Alopeke 31, Kydathenaion 31, Skambonidai 28, Keiriadai 16, Eleusis 10. (No other deme has a total in double figures.)

3. Thus 302 metics lived in just these eight demes, that is, 82.5 percent of those we know. The two main components of this subtotal are 223—almost 61 percent—from urban and suburban Athens,[73] and 69—almost

---

[67] Whitehead, *Metic*, pp. 31-32, 72-75.

[68] Whitehead, *Metic*, p. 74.

[69] Cf. Gomme, *Population*, p. 40.

[70] The principal ones are: IG I³475-476; IG II²1553-1578, 1654, 1672-1673, 1951; *Hesp.* 28, 1959, pp. 203-238; *Hesp.* 37, 1968, pp. 368-380. For more scattered ones, see Diller, *Race Mixture*, pp. 176-177 (cf. next note).

[71] U. von Wilamowitz, *Hermes* 22, 1887, pp. 107ff.; M. Clerc, *Les métèques athéniens*, Paris, 1893, pp. 384-386, 450-457; K. Scherling, *Quibus rebus singulorum Atticae pagorum incolae operam dederint, Leipziger Studien zur klassischen Philologie* 18, 1898, pp. 89-95; H. Hommel, *RE* 15, 1932, col. 1433; P. Gerhardt, *Die attische Metoikie im vierten Jahrhundert*, diss. Königsberg, 1933 [1935], pp. 15-16; Diller, *Race Mixture*, pp. 120-122, 161-179, esp. 177; cf. Davies, *Wealth*, p. 51.

[72] That is: the 330 known to Diller, *Race Mixture*, pp. 161-179; a net gain of 29 from the new fragments and new readings of the *phialai exeleutherikai* dedications by D. M. Lewis in *Hesp.* 1959 and 1968 (references above, n. 70); one in the fragment of the Erechtheion accounts published by B. D. Meritt, *AJA* 38, 1934, pp. 69-70, no. 7 (SEG 10.283); two in D. M. Lewis' re-edition of those accounts as IG I³475-476 (see 475, lines 152—with SEG 10.274—and 234-235); and now four in the fourth-century leases of sacred property published by M. B. Walbank, *Hesp.* 52, 1983, pp. 100-135 (see pp. 125, 128, 132-133).

[73] Actually a little more than that, if one includes the small totals from Agryle, Diomeia, Kerameis, Koile, etc.

19 percent—from Peiraieus. The significantly large group from the other atypical deme,[74] Eleusis, is also noteworthy.

4. However, the remaining 64 metics (17.5 percent) are scattered across more than thirty demes, in all parts of Attica:[75] Acharnai, Agryle, Aigilia, Anaphlystos, Ankyle, Cholargos, Diomeia, Epikephisia, Hagnous, Iphistiadai, Kephisia, Kerameis, Koile, Kolonos, Korydallos, Lakiadai, (?)Lamptrai,[76] Leukonoion, Myrrhinoutta, Oa, Oe, (?)Paiania,[77] Pergase, Perithoidai, Phearrhioi, Rhamnous, Semachidai,[78] Sounion, Sphettos, Thorikos, Thymaitadai, and Xypete.

There may, admittedly, be some elements of distortion in these figures,[79] but the major source of them (the fourth-century *phialai exeleutherikai* dedications) does seem to be a genuinely random sample as regards deme distribution. And if it is, *both* the dense concentration of metics in Athens itself and Peiraieus *and* the existence of small pockets of them throughout Attica as a whole will be valid representations of the general picture. Obviously one cannot assert as a fact that every deme contained metics, but very many demonstrably did, and we may venture to think that an entirely metic-less deme was a rarity.

Within each deme, as emphasized earlier, the position of the metics may well have varied tremendously in the extent to which they were admitted into or kept excluded from the life of the local community. (There is no evidence that the state had any prescription to make on the matter, beyond the initial and all-important act of registration.)[80] But even in demes where metics were numerous and where they were made welcome—which were not necessarily the same demes—the lines of demarcation were plainly drawn. It should be needless to say that in no sense was a metic a *member* of his deme of residence, or any other deme,[81] and any who attempted to infiltrate a body of demesmen did so at their

---

[74] Cf. Haussoullier, *Vie*, pp. 187-193.

[75] Note also various non-demes: ?Kynosarges (see Lewis, *Hesp.* 28, 1959, p. 231, note on line 98); Oropos (see Lewis, *Hesp.* 37, 1968, p. 371, cf. 373-374); Pentele (IG II²1673, line 37; possibly also IG II²1555, lines 9-10, though not printed in Lewis, *Hesp.* 28, 1959, p. 212; on Pentele, see Traill, *Organization*, p. 92); Salamis (IG II²1570, line 42; 1574, lines 4 and 10; etc.).

[76] See Lewis, *Hesp.* 28, 1959, p. 209.

[77] Probably not (*pace* Clerc and Scherling: references above, n. 71) the two men in IG II²1566; but see instead Lewis, *Hesp.* 28, 1959, pp. 222 (line 60) and 224 (line 214).

[78] IG I³475, line 152.

[79] In that the building accounts possibly yield an over-representation of metic workmen who lived in Athens (or, in the case of IG II²1672-1673, Eleusis).

[80] See Whitehead, *Metic*, p. 75. Note that Sophocles *OC*, lines 77-80 (discussed in Chap. 2, p. 47), would suggest, if taken *au pied de la lettre*, that individual demes could decide whether or not to accept an alien—a good reason for not so taking it.

[81] Whitehead, *Metic*, pp. 72-74.

peril.[82] One is constantly brought back to the crucial point that, in the microcosm of deme society, men knew one another. As the Dekeleians could recollect nobody in their number called Pankleon, he was evidently a metic (Lysias 23.2-4); conversely, if Euxitheos had been a metic, how could he have held deme office in Halimous (Demosth. 57.48)?

So the metics were inevitably a group apart—and in the course of this study, indeed, we shall not often find reason to discuss them again. From now on, our concern will be with the demesmen themselves.

[82] Witness for instance the case of Agasikles in Halimous (M. H. Hansen, *Eisangelia*, Odense, 1975, p. 105; Whitehead, *Metic*, pp. 50 and 53). It will be discussed, with other examples of corruption and/or maladministration in the demes, in Chap. 10A.

CHAPTER 4

THE DEME ASSEMBLY

"Toute association a ses réunions, tout dème a son assemblée. Ceux-là seulement sont membres du dème qui ont le droit de venir à l'assemblée, d'y parler, d'y prendre part aux délibérations et aux votes. L'assemblée, c'est le dème même."[1] Although no source tells us so directly, it may legitimately be assumed that a provision for every deme, great and small, to meet in assembly and administer its own affairs had been part of Kleisthenes' inaugural measures, and was never revoked thereafter (at least during the period covered in this study). "A deme" stands first, as we have seen, in the list of bodies within the Athenian polis which a "Solonic" law declared competent to make their own sovereign decisions and enactments—short of contravening those of the state itself;[2] and the bulk of this chapter will be given over to an attempt to establish what this amounted to in practice, that is, what the business of a deme assembly was. First, however, it is appropriate to consider not the content but the form of deme assemblies: the questions of place, time, and procedure.

A. Place, Time, and Procedure

1. THE PLACE OF ASSEMBLY

It has been customary to believe that the normal venue for a deme's assembly to meet was within the deme itself,[3] and there does seem to be good evidence from individual deme decrees to support this. In a decree of 324/3, for example, the demarch and treasurers of Peiraieus are instructed to set up an inscription "in the agora of the demesmen"; and similar provisions, using the single word *agora*, also occur in decrees of

[1] Haussoullier, *Vie*, p. 5.
[2] See Chap. 1, p. 13. On the local autonomy of demes, see Sophocles *OC*, lines 77-80 (discussed in Chap. 2, p. 47).
[3] Müller, *de demis*, pp. 39, 44-45; Haussoullier, *Vie*, p. 5; Schoeffer, "Demoi," col. 13; Busolt/Swoboda, *Staatskunde*, p. 969; cf. Hopper, *Basis*, pp. 14-15 (implicit).

Halai Aixonides and Sounion.[4] Thus, as Haussoullier put it, "ordinairement, l'assemblée se tenait au milieu du dème, sur l'agora ou dans le théâtre."[5]

Difficulties arise, however. First, the word *agora*—as has always been appreciated—possessed a range of interlocking meanings, even in contexts which relate specifically to demes. Sometimes its sense is almost purely locative, with overtones not so much political as religious or commercial.[6] More important, like other words of its type it can refer to a meeting itself quite as naturally as to the place of that meeting.[7] Strictly as a matter of terminology, therefore, a deme's *agora* (as "meeting") *need* not have been convened within the deme at all, but rather in the city.[8] What is more, in the case of the only meeting of a deme assembly which our sources depict in any detail—that of Halimous, in Demosthenes 57—the venue was indeed in the city (though precisely where is not revealed). In 57.10 the speaker recounts how, towards the end of the long day's proceedings, the older *dēmotai* had already "gone back to their farms; for with our deme, jurymen, being thirty-five stades away from the *asty*, and the majority living there, most had gone back."

This text has not of course passed unnoticed, but scholars have either been content to mark it down as an exception, without further comment,[9]

---

[4] Peiraieus: IG II²1176+, line 27. Halai: IG II²1174, lines 13-15. Sounion: IG II²1180, lines 21-25 (where the decree itself is concerned with a new *agora* for the deme: see further below, n. 6).

[5] Haussoullier, *Vie*, p. 5. For the erection and display of deme decrees in a theater, see references below, n. 51.

[6] In IG II²1180 (Sounion: see above, n. 4) the new deme *agora* is to provide εὐρυχωρία Σουνι|εῦσιν ἀγοράζεν καὶ ἄλ|λωι τῶι βουλομένωι (lines 13-15). IG II²2500 (Eleusis, late fourth century) concerns an *agora* to which the men of Thria as well as of Eleusis have access. Deme *agorai* are also attested for Erchia (SEG 21.541,E, lines 50-51: annual sacrifice to Hermes ἐν ἀγορ|ᾶι Ἐρχιᾶσι), Skambonidai (IG I³244, A, lines 9 and 20-21, and C, lines 9-10: sacrifices in the *agora*), and Besa (the *agora*, and roads to it, used to locate mines in mining leases: *Hesp.* 26, 1957, p. 4, no. S2, lines 31 and 40; ibid., p. 15, no. S6, lines 6-8; ibid., p. 17, no. S14, lines 33-34; *Hesp.* 19, 1950, p. 237, no. 14, line 34; cf. Eliot, *Coastal Demes*, p. 120).

[7] *Lex Seguer.* VI, *Synagoge Lexeon Chresimon*, ἀγορά· συνέδριον φυλετῶν ἢ δημοτῶν, οἱονεὶ σύλλογος [= Bekker, *Anecd. Gr.* 1. 327.23]. IG II²1202 (Aixone, 313/2) is headed ἐπὶ Θεοφράστου ἄρχοντος ἐν τεῖ ἀγοραῖ τεῖ κυρίαι; see below, in text, on this. [Demosth.] 44.36 describes an episode in Otryne ἐν τῇ τῶν ἀρχόντων ἀγορᾷ. In SEG 28.103, decree II, lines 23-24 the demarch of Eleusis is to lease out stone-quarrying rights ἐν τῆι ἀγοραῖ τῶν δημοτῶν; cf. IG II²1176+ (Peiraeus), quoted above, in text! For comparable, though rarer, ambiguity with the word *ekklēsia*—which, as Haussoullier noted (*Vie*, p. 5), is never used of *deme* assemblies—see Philochorus *apud* schol. Aristoph. *Birds*, line 997; and cf., in general, O. Broneer, *Hesp.* 11, 1942, pp. 253-254.

[8] Needless to say, this issue concerns those demes—the great majority—which were not located in the city anyway.

[9] Thus e.g. Schoeffer, "Demoi," col. 13; Busolt/Swoboda, *Staatskunde*, p. 969.

or else they have offered explanations for it—that is, reasons why it might be regarded as abnormal; and indeed such reasons, as we shall see, are not far to seek. Latterly, however, Geoffrey de Ste. Croix has cited it in an attempt to reverse the orthodox picture of deme assemblies taking place in demes. Starting from the observation that ". . . nothing is said to suggest that [meeting in the city] was unusual, although it would have suited the speaker's case if he could have discredited the meeting," de Ste. Croix concludes as follows: "Doubtless the deme Assemblies originally met in the agorai of the demes; but perhaps the venue was changed to Athens, in certain cases at least, at some time in the late fifth or fourth century, when a fair proportion of the members of some country demes possibly no longer lived in them."[10]

At first sight this challenging argument is difficult to counter, for in terms of formal proof there is in fact not a single deme assembly meeting which can be simply shown *not* to have been held in the city! Yet is it really credible that each year in the fourth century the city of Athens played host to hundreds, possibly thousands, of deme assembly meetings, none of them (save the one in Demosthenes 57) finding the faintest echo in the evidence? To be sure, de Ste. Croix cautiously postulates his change "in certain cases at least," but how would they have been determined? His own suggestion that the criterion—and the reason for the reform—was the migration of rural *dēmotai* to the city is not implausible in itself, but it is demonstrably inapplicable in the instance to hand, where we are expressly told that most Halimousioi still lived in Halimous. Surely, then, we should not erect a generalization upon Demosthenes 57 but rather look for a reason why the Halimousioi were meeting in Athens *in this instance*. "Nothing is said to suggest that this was unusual"; de Ste. Croix is justified in so observing. However, his point that Euxitheos would have "discredited" the meeting if possible is valid only if the city venue had been somehow *improper*, not merely "unusual." It may indeed have been unusual—if deme assemblies were normally held locally—but still perfectly proper in special circumstances. Here, at least two "unusual" conditions obtained:

1. Though the wording of Demosth. 57.8 is oddly vague, it certainly appears to indicate that in the year of this case, 346/5, Euboulides was not only demarch of Halimous but also one of its representatives on the (city) council;[11] and it *may*, for all we know, have been open to anyone

---

[10] G.E.M. de Ste. Croix, *The Origins of the Peloponnesian War*, London, 1972, pp. 400-401 (Appendix 47).

[11] Demosth. 57.8: καὶ βουλεύων . . . καὶ κύριος ὢν τοῦ θ' ὅρκου καὶ τῶν γραμμάτων ἐξ ὧν ἀνεκάλει τοὺς δημότας (the latter being a recognizable periphrasis for demarch: see below, in text); cf. Rhodes, *Boule*, p. 174, n. 3. (There are no good grounds for supposing

fulfilling this onerous dual role to convene his deme in Athens, where he himself was obliged to spend so much of his time.[12]

2. The case itself had arisen out of the decree of Demophilos, ordering a general, *extraordinary* scrutiny of the membership rolls of all demes by the bodies of demesmen concerned;[13] and it is not unlikely that such a tricky exercise, in the atmosphere of suspicion (and, specifically, distrust of the demes' normal procedures) which had given rise to it, was required to take place in the city—possibly (though not necessarily) at a time when the demesmen might be there for other purposes.[14]

Here then are two possible reasons—neither of which would have afforded Euxitheos legitimate grounds for complaint—why the deme assembly depicted in Demosthenes 57 may indeed have been, as regards its venue, unusual. Otherwise the Halimousioi surely did not have to travel four or five miles for their *agorai*.

There is one other item of evidence which lends ostensible support to the idea that the assemblies of demes outside Athens regularly took place in the city. In the second of the two recently published deme decrees of Eleusis (from 332/1) it is enacted that rent for the lease of stone-quarrying rights shall, for the future, be paid "in the month Metageitnion, when the demesmen meet in assembly in the Theseion to choose magistrates" (εἰς τὸν Μεταγειτνιῶνα μῆνα ταῖς ἀρχαι|ρεσίαις, ὅταν οἱ δημόται ἀγοράζωσιν ἐν τῶι Θησείωι).[15] As there is no known Theseion *in Eleusis*, this must be taken to refer to the one in Athens.[16] But even so, there are several interrelated problems of interpretation here, which will be considered in detail in Chapter 9. I believe—to anticipate that dis-

---

that the demes had their own *boulai*: see Müller, *de demis*, p. 33; Haussoullier, *Vie*, pp. vii, 115, 131, n. 1; Busolt/Swoboda, *Staatskunde*, p. 970. In the Eleusinian decree IG II²1189 the *boulē* of line 3 is clearly that of the city.) It may be remarked that, as well as any personal ambition on Euboulides' part, his duplication of roles was perhaps forced upon him to some extent. To fulfil its bouleutic quota it has been calculated that a deme needed a minimum population of 32.5 men over thirty years of age for each "seat" (Osborne, *Demos*, pp. 43-44). Thus Halimous, with three "seats," needed at least ca. 100 *dēmotai* to fill them each year. In fact, in 346/5, there were only something over 80 (Demosth. 57.10 with 15).

[12] Cf. Müller, *de demis*, p. 39; Haussoullier, *Vie*, p. 42, n. 3. (On meetings of the *boulē*, see Rhodes, *Boule*, p. 30; Mikalson, *Calendar*, pp. 193ff.; M. H. Hansen, *GRBS* 22, 1981, p. 367 with n. 74.)

[13] See below, sec. B.1(b).

[14] Cf. Haussoullier, *Vie*, p. 5 ("puis l'opération si importante de la revision du registre civique avait sans doute eu lieu à l'époque de quelque fête publique, et ce jour-là les habitants d'Halimonte étaient plus nombreux à Athènes qu'au village"); Hopper, *Basis*, p. 23, n. 115.

[15] SEG 28.103, decree II, lines 27-28.

[16] I am indebted to Professor Homer Thompson for discussion of this point.

cussion—that the *archairesiai* in question were concerned with the choice of officials not, as some scholars have supposed, for the deme itself[17] but for the city. More controversially, perhaps, I shall further argue that the assembly referred to is that of the *tribe* (VIII Hippothontis) to which the Eleusinians belonged, not that of their deme. At all events we have here anything but a clear and simple indication that deme assemblies in Athens were common or customary.

To sum up: in the second half of the fourth century there seem to have been circumstances—possibly routine, more probably occasional and extraordinary—where rural as well as urban demes held their assemblies in the *asty*; otherwise, for normal purposes and at other times, it is overwhelmingly likely that "the *agora* of the demesmen" was a gathering in, as well as for, the deme itself.

2. THE TIMES AND REGULARITY OF ASSEMBLY

The lexicographers tell us that demarchs called their fellow demesmen together in assembly "whenever necessary."[18] While this should not, as will emerge below, be taken to signify that the demarchs enjoyed sole and undirected control over the times and frequency of meetings, it does point to a strong likelihood of variation and disparity, in this respect, between one deme and another. Furthermore, in view of the extreme paucity of evidence even for individual demes, generalization is not only difficult but also, beyond a general formulation of "theory" (see below), unwise.

Much has been made here of the tantalizing heading of a deme decree of Aixone, dating from 313/2: ἐν τῆι ἀγορᾶι τῆι κυρ|ίαι (IG II²1202, lines 1-2). On the strength of this it has been asserted that deme assembly meetings were either, like this one, "ordinary" (*kyria*)—meaning regular—or extraordinary; and, on the pattern of what ?Aristot. *Ath. Pol.* 43.3-4 says about the city *ekklēsia*, the elements of a fixed agenda for the "ordinary" meetings have been confidently reconstructed, and a fixed, recurrent time for them presupposed.[19] However, the tacit assumption here—that a framework of these ordinary/regular meetings was centrally ordained for all demes—is a questionable one. We now possess more than one hundred deme decrees, yet nowhere else is an *agora kyria*

---

[17] Thus, the editors of SEG 28.103, S. N. Coumanoudis and D. C. Gofas, *REG* 91, 1978, p. 298 (demarch and treasurer); Osborne, *Demos*, p. 77 (demarch only).

[18] Harpoc., δήμαρχος· . . . συνῆγον τοὺς δήμους ὁπότε δεήσειεν; cf. Suda, δήμαρχος, and schol. Aristoph. *Clouds*, line 37.

[19] See esp. Schoeffer, "Demoi," col. 13; cf. Müller, *de demis*, p. 44, and Haussoullier, *Vie*, p. 6.

attested.[20] In the second half, and particularly the last quarter, of the fourth century the Aixoneis seem, if one may judge by their surviving decrees, to have been a peculiarly active body of demesmen, and there is nothing to have prevented them from adopting the idea of *agorai kyriai* for themselves. What is more, we do not know (and cannot deduce from IG II²1202) whether its prime purpose was to ensure a fixed *time* for certain meetings—that is, presumably, irrespective of the demarch's initiative—or else a fixed *agenda*, or both.

From other demes the data are scantier still. The most substantial item comes in a decree of Myrrhinous, dated by Köhler to the period after 340 (IG II²1183). In lines 36ff. there is specified what amounts to an agenda in advance, for a future meeting when certain matters (and not, apparently, others) are to be debated: τῆι δὲ ἐνάτει ἐπὶ δέκα τοῦ Ποσιδεῶν[ος] μην[ὸς] χρηματίζ]|[ε]ιν πε[ρὶ Διο]νυσίων, τὰ δὲ ἄλλα πάντα τ[– – – – – – – – – –]|[. . . .¹⁰ . . . . χρη]ματίζειν πλὴν τοῦ δ[– – – – – – – – – –]. Again, generalizations have been built upon this text.[21] Deme decrees of this "business" type are relatively few; the absence of parallels for what the Myrrhinousioi are prescribing here is thus, arguably, not significant. But even so, the usefulness of these lines as a general model of procedure would be limited, for we have no means of telling whether a meeting would have been held on 19 Posideion anyway or whether it is the date as well as the agenda which is being fixed here;[22] and the decrees of other demes offer no guide.[23]

It must be reiterated, then, that we have no satisfactory *evidence* to warrant a supposition either (*a*) that the state laid down any universal principles to govern the time or frequency of deme assembly meetings, or the business to be transacted at them; or even (*b*) that any individual deme, save apparently Aixone in the late fourth century, did so for itself. Quite possibly some demes met more often than others, with the date of the next assembly being determined *ad hoc* on each occasion, or even left open for the demarch to fix (as the lexica put it) "whenever necessary."

[20] The restoration τ|αῖς ἀγοραῖ[ς κυρίαις in IG II²2493 (lease-document of the Rhamnousioi: see Jameson, "Leasing"), lines 14-15, offers no secure basis for argument.

[21] See the references above, n. 19.

[22] A meeting at *around* this time in Posideion will surely have been customary, to discuss matters arising from the recent rural Dionysia. (On χρηματίζειν as an indication that the festival will already have taken place by then, see A. Wilhelm, *Urkunden dramatischer Aufführungen in Athen*, Vienna, 1906, pp. 238ff.; cf. Deubner, *Feste*, pp. 134-135.)

[23] In SEG 28.103, decree II, lines 26-28, *one* "standing item" is laid down for a particular meeting—but possibly that of the tribe rather than the deme (see above, in text). In IG II²1174, lines 10-12, it is enacted that the *euthynai* of deme officials in Halai Aixonides are to be heard within a particular month (for "in the following year, before the month Metageitnion" means in plain terms "in Hekatombaion").

And broadly speaking, as Haussoullier observed, a disinclination to meet more frequently than was indeed "necessary" may surely be taken for granted. "Ce qui est certain, c'est que l'assemblée ne se réunissait que le moins souvent possible; d'abord les affaires n'étaient pas nombreuses, puis les démotes, les gens des petits dèmes surtout, ne quittaient pas volontiers leurs champs."[24] The demarch's task was therefore to weigh this disinclination (if it applied in his deme) against the fact that for certain purposes—some those of the deme, some those of the polis as a whole—the deme assembly *had* to meet. These purposes of course represent and reflect the various functions of the deme assembly itself, and as such will be treated in the second part of this chapter. As their irreducible minimum, new members had to be admitted to the body of demesmen itself, and officials for both local and central government had to be chosen and appointed. Since we know of two instances where the same meeting seemingly served both of these functions,[25] it may theoretically have been possible for a deme to get by with only a single assembly a year. In practice, however, one may think this unlikely; for even if extra meetings required by the state (such as the *diapsēphiseis* of 346/5) were by definition extraordinary,[26] the routine internal administration of even the small demes was doubtless such as to necessitate a number of assemblies at key stages in both the sacred and the civil calendar year.

3. FORM AND PROCEDURE

Here, by contrast, the general, composite picture which successive scholars have presented[27] need not be challenged in its essentials, for it is justified on two counts:

1. The central role of the demarch is clear, both from the generalizing lexicographers and from what we know of individual demes; and much if not all of this is likely to have been acted out in accordance with state legislation.[28]

2. It is in any case evident from the surviving deme decrees, together

[24] Haussoullier, *Vie*, pp. 6-7.

[25] Isaeus 7.27-28 (deme indeterminable); [Demosth.] 44.39 (Otryne).

[26] That the *diapsēphiseis* of 346/5 did indeed take place at extra(ordinary) meetings is admittedly no more than an assumption, but one warranted primarily by the fact that they took place in Athens (see above, in text). Note, however, that routine business was transacted at them even so; Demosth. 57.9.

[27] Haussoullier, *Vie*, pp. 8-10; Schoeffer, "Demoi," cols. 13-14; Busolt/Swoboda, *Staatskunde*, pp. 967-970.

[28] See Chap. 2B (esp. n. 93), and, more fully, Chap. 5A.

with other testimony, that in broad terms the procedure of deme assemblies was modelled on that of the city *ekklēsia*.

The position of the demarch as not merely convenor but also president of his deme assembly is shown most graphically in Demosthenes 57. There, sadly for us, the meeting was not only improperly conducted—if the speaker is to be believed—but also atypical in itself, its main object being the wholesale scrutiny of the deme's membership required under the decree of Demophilos. Nonetheless it involved elements of procedure which are attested elsewhere. The demarch is described, for example, as "master of the oath" (κύριος τοῦ ὅρκου: 57.8), that is, the oath by which all the demesmen swore to vote honestly upon the validity of each man's claim to belong amongst them. One clause from it is quoted, apparently *verbatim*, later in the speech.²⁹ Such an oath, sworn over sacrificial victims, seems to have been the prelude to all votes of this kind, at the regular annual *dokimasia* as well as at any extraordinary *diapsēphiseis*.³⁰ But in addition we also find the demarch administering an oath in two deme decrees concerned with the *euthynai* of officials.³¹ It would thus seem fair to presume that the demarch was indeed "master of the oath" on any occasion when either the demesmen as a whole or else deme officials were required to swear one. And it is perhaps possible to infer, further, that such occasions were any which called for a formal ballot rather than a simple show of hands (see below).

The actual mechanics of the vote followed the general pattern with which we are familiar from other spheres of the Athenian democratic *politeia*. The demarch handed out the ballots;³² the voters placed them

---

²⁹ Demosth. 57.63: τὸ ψηφιεῖσθαι "γνώμῃ τῇ δικαιοτάτῃ καὶ οὔτε χάριτος ἕνεκ᾽ οὔτ᾽ ἔχθρας." (Euxitheos claims that Euboulides and his accomplices had removed this clause.) From the context, however, it is possible that this oath was taken at the *euthynai* of the demarch; cf. Chap. 10, n. 29.

³⁰ For the *dokimasia*, see ?Aristot. *Ath. Pol.* 42.1 (διαψηφίζονται περὶ αὐτῶν ὀμόσαντες οἱ δημόται); cf. Isaeus 7.28 (ὀμόσαντες καθ᾽ ἱερῶν ἐνέγραψάν με) and Demosth. 57.61 (ἡνίκ᾽ ἐνεγράφην ἐγὼ καὶ ὀμόσαντες οἱ δημόται δικαίως πάντες περὶ ἐμοῦ τὴν ψῆφον ἔφερον). Note also Demosth. 57.26 and 61 for the same at the διαψηφίσεις ἐξ ἀνάγκης occasioned by the loss of the deme register.

³¹ IG II²1174 (Halai Aixonides, 368/7), lines 15-18: ἐξορκούτω [δὲ ὁ δήμαρχος τὸν ε]|[ὔ]θυνον καὶ τὸς πα[ρέδρος εὐθύνεν κα]|[τ]ὰ τὸ ψήφισμα τὸ ἐ[ν τῆι ἀγορᾶι ἀναγε]|[γ]ραμμένον. IG II²1183 (Myrrhinous, after 340), lines 18-22: τὴν δὲ ψῆφον διδότω [ὁ ν]|[έ]ος δήμαρχος καὶ ἐξορκού[τ]ω αὐτοὺς ἐναντίον τῶν δημο[τῶ]|[ν]· εἶναι δὲ καὶ ἔφεσιν αὐτῶι [ε]ἰς ἅπαγτας τοὺς δημότας· ἐ[ὰν] | [δ]έ τις ἐφῆι, ἐξορκούτω ὁ δήμα[ρ]χος τοὺ[ς] δημότας καὶ διδό[τω] | [τ]ὴν ψῆφον κτλ. These two *euthynai* procedures are discussed at the end of this chapter.

³² Harpoc., δήμαρχος; Suda, δήμαρχος; schol. Aristoph. *Clouds*, line 37; Demosth. 57.13; the deme decrees cited in the preceding note.

in an urn (*kadiskos*).³³ According to Pollux, the votes themselves were not the customary pebbles (*psēphoi*), but leaves (*phylla*).³⁴ As Euxitheos speaks explicitly and repeatedly of *psēphoi* (Demosth. 57.13-14 and 16, cf. 61) it has been usual to disbelieve Pollux,³⁵ who may have been confused, as von Schoeffer suggested, with the *ekphyllophoria* procedure by which the *boulē* expelled any delinquent members from its ranks.³⁶ What Pollux says has been supported by E. S. Staveley;³⁷ but there is no justification in Staveley's claim that only thus is the malpractice described in Demosth. 57.13 intelligible. So, while voting with leaves may have been adopted, when appropriate, by the *boulē* (and other organizations),³⁸ it does not seem to have played any part in the procedure of the assemblies of the demes.

That a formal vote with pebbles was always or even often necessary need not, of course, be imagined. True, the routine business of a deme assembly, just like that of the city *ekklēsia*, was the enactment of decrees, *psēphismata*,³⁹ either honorific or administrative. As regards the *ekklēsia*, however, we know that the noun *psēphisma* and the verb *psēphizesthai* were employed, at least in the fourth century, metaphorically rather than literally, that is, with reference not to a method of voting but to a type of decision; also, the normal "vote" was actually a simple show of hands (*cheirotonia*).⁴⁰ The same must surely have been true in the demes. What is more, the strong likelihood that in a *cheirotonia* in the *ekklēsia* the show of hands was not precisely counted but simply estimated⁴¹ will

---

³³ Demosth. 57.13. It is not clear whether ballots of two kinds were deposited in a single urn or whether Euxitheos ought properly to have referred to two urns (as in Lysias 13.37).

³⁴ Pollux 8.18: φύλλοις δὲ ἐψηφίζοντο οἱ κατὰ δήμους δικάζοντες, οἷς ἐπέγραφον, εἴ τις ὡς παρέγγραπτος ἐκρίνετο.

³⁵ See e.g. Haussoullier, *Vie*, p. 44, n. 1; Schoeffer, "Demoi," col. 14; Busolt/Swoboda, *Staatskunde*, p. 967, n. 5.

³⁶ Schoeffer, "Demoi," col. 14. On the *ekphyllophoria*, see Aeschin. 1.110-112 (with Rhodes, *Boule*, pp. 144-146); and note that it needed to be confirmed, in order to be valid, by an orthodox ballot.

³⁷ Staveley, *Elections*, pp. 114-115.

³⁸ In a parenthetical note *apud* Busolt/Swoboda, *Staatskunde*, p. 967, n. 5, "A(dolf) W(ilhelm)" drew attention to IG II²1328 (decree of *orgeōnes*, 182), lines 15-16: κύριοι δ' ἔστωσαν καὶ τὸ φύλλον τά[ξ]α[ι] | ὑπὲρ τῆς ἀπειθούσης.

³⁹ ψηφίσματα: Demosth. 57.9; and regularly in the decrees on stone. But note also ἐψηφισμένα (SEG 28.103, decree II, Eleusis; SEG 25.155, Rhamnous) and even γράμματα (IG II²1184, Cholargos).

⁴⁰ See Rhodes, *Boule*, p. 39 (and *Commentary*, pp. 498-499); M. H. Hansen, "How did the Athenian *Ecclesia* vote?" *GRBS* 18, 1977, pp. 123-137, at 124 (= idem, *The Athenian Ecclesia*, Copenhagen, 1983, pp. 103-117, at 104).

⁴¹ See M. H. Hansen, *art. cit.* in preceding note (with addenda in *The Athenian Ecclesia*, pp. 118-121).

again, we may take it, have been reflected in the practice of the demes. An exact count may have been necessary or desirable in particular circumstances—and will have been a more practicable undertaking at a gathering numbering hundreds, or less, rather than thousands. Still, the only instances we know of where exactitude in numbers was known or necessary all seem to have involved a formal ballot. In Demosth. 57.9 Euxitheos is able to assert that he was one of seventy-three Halimousioi who took the pre-vote oath on the day of the *diapsēphiseis* (though he was apparently able only to estimate the number of those who actually cast ballots: 57.13). In IG II²1183 the demarch of Myrrhinous is instructed, in the deme's *euthynai* procedure, not to administer oaths and distribute voting-pebbles if fewer than thirty demesmen are present.[42] A similar quorum requirement appears, a century earlier, in a decree of Lower Paiania.[43] Haussoullier's suggestion that every deme may have fixed such a quorum for itself, appropriate to its own membership, is thus not an outrageous one as such conjectures go.[44] But the figure may have been determined in and for specific circumstances—as seems to be the case in the Myrrhinous and Paiania documents—rather than permanently laid down for all purposes; and it is perhaps unlikely that a quorum was ever necessary for routine decrees but rather for the sort of business which, while administratively important, was unattractive to the ordinary demesman.[45]

The basic substance of a deme assembly meeting, then, is doubtless accurately enough encapsulated in Euxitheos' bitter description of the proceedings of the Halimousioi in 346/5: a day of speeches and decrees.[46] All demesmen were presumably eligible to speak if they felt moved to

---

[42] IG II²1183, lines 21-22: ἐξορκούτω ὁ δήμα[ρ]χος τοὺ(ς) δημότας καὶ διδό[τω] | [τ]ὴν ψῆφον ἐὰν παρῶσιν μὴ ἐλάττους ἢ ΔΔΔ.

[43] IG I³250 (from the period 450-430), lines 11-14: τὰ χσυνγεγραμμ|ένα μὲ ἔναι ἀναφσεφίσα[ι] | ἐὰμ μὲ ℎεκατὸν παρõσιν | τõν δεμοτõν. (For the term ἀναψηφίζειν cf. Thuc. 6.14.) It is possible that in this period, the mid fifth century, the procedure referred to was a formal ballot, but one cannot be sure; if it was not, this would be the sole known instance of a quorum required for a simple *cheirotonia*.

[44] Haussoullier, *Vie*, p. 7; cf. (more cautious) Schoeffer, "Demoi," col. 13.

[45] The indications are (cf. Haussoullier, *Vie*, p. 7) that attendance at deme assembly meetings was low. A multiplier of *at least* 32.5 men aged thirty or over to fill each seat on the *boulē* (see above, n. 11) sets our two known quorum figures in some sort of perspective and suggests that in Lower Paiania, with eleven *bouleutai*, the quorum of a hundred was possibly one-quarter of all the demesmen, while the figure of thirty in Myrrhinous, with six *bouleutai*, may have been more like one-seventh. Comparison with attendance at the city *ekklēsia* mitigates the gloomy implications of these figures somewhat; see most recently M. H. Hansen, *GRBS* 17, 1976, pp. 115-134 (= *idem, The Athenian Ecclesia*, Copenhagen, 1983, pp. 1-20, with addenda at pp. 21-23); and below, Conspectus, n. 29.

[46] Demosth. 57.9: κατέτριψε τὴν ἡμέραν δημηγορῶν καὶ ψηφίσματα γράφων.

do so, though we do not know whether substantive motions could be made from the floor or whether it was more usual (as in IG II²1183, lines 36ff., discussed above) for the demarch to adhere to a predetermined agenda. Occasionally the wording of a decree gives the *impression* that it has arisen from a motion *ad hoc* (or *ad hominem*),[47] but obviously one cannot be certain, and in the great majority of cases the phraseology is too bland and standardized to permit any conclusions in this regard. At all events, once a decree was passed the final decision to be made was whether it merited the distinction (and the expense) of being inscribed on stone. No doubt many, probably most, did not. In that case they may either not have been recorded at all—but simply implemented—or else preserved only in memoranda kept by the demarch.[48] Sometimes, though, whether to honor further the beneficiary of an honorific decree (and to guarantee his rewards) or to keep important administrative decisions in the public eye, inscription on stone was the course adopted. If so, we usually find that the last clause of the decree itself consisted of instructions to the deme's officials to pay out the necessary monies[49] and have a stele cut and set up[50] in an appropriate public place.[51]

[47] See for instance IG II²1175 (Halai Aixonides, ca. 360), lines 1-3: Ἀστύφιλος εἶπεν· περὶ ὧν Νικο|[μ]ένης λέγει, [δ]εδόχθαι τοῖς δη|μόταις – – –.

[48] Note SEG 2.7 (Halimous, 330-325), lines 18-21: ἀναγράψαι δὲ τ|ὸ ψήφισμα τὸν δήμαρχο|ν Κύβερνιν εἰς τὰ κοιν|ὰ γραμματεῖα κτλ. On the *koinon grammateion*, see below, n. 60.

[49] IG II²1206 (?Acharnai), lines 16-19 (demarch); IG II²1186 (Eleusis), lines 33-34 (demarch); SEG 28.103 (Eleusis), decree II, lines 49-51 (demarch); AM 67, 1942, pp. 7-8, no. 5 (Gargettos), lines 5-9 (*tamias*); AD 11, 1927-1928, pp. 40-41, no. 4 (Halai Aixonides), line 13 (*tamias*); AE 1932, Chronika, pp. 30-32 (Halai Araphenides), lines 28-31 (*tamias* τῶν θ|[ε]ίων); Agora 16, no. 54 (Kydathenaion), A, lines 4-5, and B, lines 5-6 (*tamias*); IG II²1182 (Myrrhinous), lines 21-25 (?honorand and *antigrapheus*); SEG 25.155 (Rhamnous), line 43 (*tamias*); cf. SEG 14.81 (deme unknown), lines 5-6, restored by B. D. Meritt from IG II²1206 (above). In other cases it is not stated who will disburse the money.

[50] This was sometimes the task of the demarch: IG II²1197, 1198, 1199 (all Aixone); IG II²1203 (Athmonon); IG II²1188, 1193 (both Eleusis); AE 1925-1926, pp. 168-177 and AE 1932, Chronika, pp. 30-32 (both Halai Araphenides); SEG 2.7 (Halimous); SEG 22.116 (Melite); IG II²1182 (Myrrhinous); also restored in AM 67, 1942, p. 10, no. 8 (Halai Aixonides). But sometimes others assist him: IG II²1202 (Aixone), with *tamiai*; IG II²1187 (Eleusis), with fathers of "ephebes"; IG II²1299, lines 51-80 (Eleusis), with *hieromnēmones*; SEG 28.103 (Eleusis), with priest; IG II²1176+ (Peiraieus), with *tamiai*; IG II²1177 (Peiraieus), with *horistai*; SEG 25.155 (Rhamnous), with *epimelētai* (= garrison officers); IG II²1180 (Sounion), with donor of the new *agora*. And sometimes another official does it: *grammateus* in IG II²1206 (?Acharnai); *hieropoioi* in SEG 22.120 (Rhamnous); *ad hoc* choice in IG II²1186 (Eleusis); *tamiai*, singular or plural, in AM 66, 1941, pp. 218-219, no. 1 (Aixone), SEG 28.102 (Eitea), IG II²1185 (Eleusis), Hesp. 11, 1942, pp. 265-274, no. 51 (Melite, restored), IG II²1212 (deme unknown), and probably the unnamed officials of IG II²1184 (Cholargos).

[51] The *agora*: IG II²1188 (Eleusis, restored); IG II²1174 (Halai Aixonides); IG II²1176+

B. The Business of the Assembly

We may now turn to the actual business which a body of demesmen had to transact when their demarch had called them together in assembly. As Haussoullier emphasized, the deme assembly was above all else "une assemblée d'affaires";[52] and—fortunately for our synoptic study—some of the most important ones can be seen to have been conducted in the same way, or at least on the same lines, throughout the deme system as a whole.

1. EXAMINATION AND REGISTRATION OF MEMBERS

(a) Regular Registration

Indisputably the most crucial of the functions of a deme assembly[53] was its control over its own membership. It was crucial because, in the absence of centralized lists of all citizens,[54] becoming a *dēmotēs* and becoming a *politēs* were effectively one and the same act; and conversely, a man could prove his citizen-status, if need be, only by proving his membership of a deme.[55] It was thus vital to the state as a whole as well as to the

(Peiraieus); IG II²1180 (Sounion). The theater: IG II²1197, 1198, 1202, and *AM* 66, 1941, pp. 218-219, no. 1 (all Aixone); IG II²1185 (Eleusis). But most commonly in temples and sacred precincts: IG II²1206 (?Acharnai); IG II²1199 (Aixone); IG II²1203 (Athmonon); IG II²1184 (Cholargos); *SEG* 28.102 (Eitea); IG II²1186, 1187, and *SEG* 28.103 (all Eleusis); *AM* 67, 1942, pp. 7-8, no. 5 (Gargettos); *AD* 11, 1927-1928, pp. 40-41, no. 4, and *AM* 67, 1942, p. 10, no. 8 (both Halai Aixonides); *AE* 1925-1926, pp. 168-177, and *AE* 1932, *Chronika*, pp. 30-32 (both Halai Araphenides); *SEG* 2.7 (Halimous); *SEG* 22.117 (Ikarion); *Agora* 16, no. 54 (Kydathenaion); *SEG* 22.116 (Melite); *Hesp.* 11, 1942, pp. 265-274, no. 51 (Melite, restored); IG II²1182 (Myrrhinous); IG II²1177 and 1214 (both Peiraieus); *SEG* 22.120 (Rhamnous); *SEG* 24.153 (Teithras); cf. IG II²2496, *locatio* of Kytheros. (Note also IG II²1156, lines 45-63, decrees of Eleusis and Athmonon on the same stele as an ephebic monument and tribal decree.) Clearly it was normal for the place of display to be specified in the decree; note, however, IG II²1193 (Eleusis), lines 30-31, where the demarch is empowered to set up the stone ὅπου ἂν δο[κ]εῖ ἐν καλλί|[στ]ωι εἶναι.

[52] Haussoullier, *Vie*, pp. 9 and esp. 56-57.

[53] Cf. Haussoullier, *Vie*, p. 12, cf. 53-56.

[54] On the illusion of the central hoplite *katalogos*, see M. H. Hansen, *SO* 56, 1981, pp. 24-29.

[55] The significance, after Kleisthenes, of *phratry* membership has been frequently debated, and some scholars have argued or asserted that it remained "a condition of citizenship" (thus Hignett, *Constitution*, p. 143). It is certainly noteworthy that individuals naturalized by decree of the *ekklēsia* were regularly invited to choose a phratry as well as a deme and tribe (for the full corpus of such decrees, see now M. J. Osborne, *Naturalization in Athens*, vols. 1 and 2, Brussels, 1981-1982); on the other hand the Plataians enfranchised in 427 apparently joined demes and tribes only (see [Demosth.] 59.104). Harrison, *Law* I, pp. 64-

individual demes that precise records be kept, and that admission to (or exclusion from) a body of demesmen be a process not merely enacted under controlled and standardized conditions but overseen and, if necessary, overturned by a higher authority.

All this is demonstrably true, at any rate, of the fourth century, whence as always the great bulk of our evidence comes. How great is the risk of anachronism in assuming that in the early *fifth* century the concern to protect and preserve the citizen "descent group"[56] was as obsessive, or the means to that end as elaborate, as in the later classical period? I have already argued[57] that general considerations make it close to inconceivable that the demes were not obliged, from the very outset of the deme system, to record and control their membership in a manner acceptable not merely to themselves but to the polis at large. In her recent and robust study of the Periklean citizenship law of 451/0, Cynthia Patterson has advanced the avowedly revisionist theory that before Perikles' law there existed no city legislation to regulate and standardize admission to a deme; instead, she contends, the demes simply employed traditional (and variable) norms and criteria modelled on those of the phratries, so that "through the early fifth century citizenship was determined by one's neighbors and kin on a traditional and familial basis."[58] However, as the argument is one of silence either way, I prefer to suggest that the Kleisthenic deme legislation either itself embodied or else swiftly called into being general regulations under which deme assemblies would meet every year to scrutinize the credentials of the sons of demesmen who had reached the age of eighteen[59] and, if all was well, to vote that the demarch enrol them in the *lēxiarchikon grammateion*.[60]

Obviously it would be idle to pretend that the details of procedure on

---

65 reasonably concludes that membership of a phratry remained normal but not indispensable.

[56] See in general Davies, "Descent group."

[57] Chap. 1, pp. 34-35.

[58] Patterson, *Citizenship Law*, p. 3, and chap. II (esp. pp. 13-14 and 25-28; quotation from p. 28).

[59] The age of eighteen: see below, n. 78.

[60] See Chap. 1, n. 130, for the problem of whether the *grammateion* existed from the time of Kleisthenes and included *all* citizens. (I incline to believe that, on both counts, it did.) For the demarch as its custodian, see [Demosth.] 44.37; Demosth. 57.8 and 26; Harpoc., δήμαρχος; Suda, δήμαρχος; schol. Aristoph. *Clouds*, line 37. Note that the term κοινὸν γραμματεῖον (or κοινὰ γραμματεῖα) could sometimes be used (Demosth. 57.60 with 26; cf. *Lex Seguer.* V, *Lexeis Rhetorikai*, κοινὸν γραμματεῖον [= Bekker, *Anecd. Gr.* 1.272.27]) but was much wider in connotation, embracing all the demarch's records (cf. above, n. 48), and sometimes indeed those of bodies other than demes (phratries, IG II²1237, lines 97-98; phratries and *genē*, Isaeus 7.1 and 16-17, cf. Harpoc. and Suda, κοινὸν γραμματεῖον καὶ ληξιαρχικόν).

these occasions (before the fourth century; see below) can be recon-structed, but their essential purpose will have been for the demesmen to satisfy themselves that each candidate for registration met the require-ments of age[61] and, perhaps especially, status. Before Perikles' law, the latter criterion was simply met, by the citizen status—in practice, the deme membership—of the youth's father and by the legitimacy of his parents' marriage;[62] the status of the mother was *per se* immaterial.[63] Then the Periklean law stipulated that "anyone not born of *both* citizen parents would not have a share in the polis";[64] and this was the definition of citizenship,[65] restated in 403/2 after the irregularities and ideological controversies of the preceding decade,[66] which remained in force for eighty years thereafter as the fundamental element in the corpus of Athe-nian citizenship law.[67]

For the period *before* 403/2 (but after Perikles' law) the most impen-etrable problem concerns the Egyptian grain episode of 445/4, when it is alleged that no fewer than 4,760 men were disfranchised as "improperly enrolled aliens" (ξένοι παρεγγεγραμμένοι).[68] Apart from the figure itself, which deserves no credence,[69] the chief difficulty here is that of deciding exactly how this "alien expulsion" (*xenēlasia*), as Philochorus colorfully dubbed it, actually occurred. There would seem to be two, equally hypothetical possibilities. One is that a general *diapsēphismos* or *diapsēphisis* was carried out in the demes under general decree of the

---

[61] Cf. ?Aristot. *Ath. Pol.* 42.1, διαψηφίζονται . . . εἰ δοκοῦσι γεγονέναι τὴν ἡλι-κίαν τὴν ἐκ τοῦ νόμου, with Rhodes, *Commentary*, p. 499; see further below, in text.

[62] I follow those scholars who have argued that bastards (*nothoi*) were not entitled to Athenian citizenship; references and discussion in Rhodes, *Commentary*, pp. 496-497. See also D. Lotze, "Zwischen Politen und Metöken: Passivburger im klassischen Athen?" *Klio* 63, 1981, pp. 159-178.

[63] The suggestion of R. Sealey, *A History of the Greek City States, 700-338 B.C.*, Berkeley, 1976, p. 299 (quoted with approval by Patterson, *Citizenship Law*, p. 29, n. 1), that before 451/0 some demes were insisting on doubly endogamic qualifications seems to me fantastic.

[64] ?Aristot. *Ath. Pol.* 26.4; cf. Plut. *Per.* 37.2-5; Aelian, *VH* 6.10; Suda, δημοποίητος; see Patterson, *Citizenship Law*, pp. 1-2. (While it is now generally accepted that the law was not retroactive in the sense of disfranchising anyone *registered* before 451/0, it very probably did disfranchise and disinherit those born at any time after 469/8, whom the demes would reject when they came up for enrolment: see S. C. Humphreys, *JHS* 94, 1974, pp. 88-95, esp. 92-94.)

[65] I cannot see the force of Patterson's insistence (*Citizenship Law*, pp. 8, 146) that this, the usual way of referring to what the law created, is misleading and that it merely laid down a "minimum necessary condition."

[66] See on this Patterson, *Citizenship Law*, pp. 140-147.

[67] For this corpus, see in brief Diller, *Race Mixture*, pp. 95-97.

[68] Philochorus, *FGrH* 328 F119 (*apud* schol. Aristoph. *Wasps*, line 718); cf. Plut. *Per.* 37.4.

[69] Discussion in Whitehead, *Metic*, p. 169, n. 51.

state; in effect, a precursor of what happened in 346/5. The other is that a host of individual prosecutions, *graphai xenias*, were brought which added up to much the same result. With Diller, I incline on balance to the latter alternative[70] (though it admittedly does little more than shift the problems to another area);[71] and if this is correct, the episode has no direct bearing on the practice of the demes as such, least of all upon their *regular* procedures of scrutiny and registration in the fifth century. For that, we have but two items of evidence. In Lysias 21.1—probably delivered in 403/2 or soon afterwards—the speaker introduces his record of liturgical and other outlay with the fact that he passed through his (citizen's) *dokimasia* in the archonship of Theopompos, 411/0. This is of course thoroughly uninformative as regards any possible procedural differences in the *dokimasia* before and after 403/2;[72] and the fuller context yields up only one additional fact, that this man's *dokimasia*, in his indeterminable deme, took place within the early months of the administrative year.[73] More interesting and important is line 578 of Aristophanes' *Wasps*, where Philokleon claims that one of the pleasures of being a juror is gazing at the genitals of youths undergoing their *dokimasia* (παίδων τοίνυν δοκιμαζομένων αἰδοῖα πάρεστι θεᾶσθαι).[74] According to the procedures described in the Aristotelian *Ath. Pol.*, to which we shall next turn, "there was a possibility of reference from the deme-assembly to the courts on the criterion of freedom, and compulsory

[70] See Diller, *Race Mixture*, p. 93 with n. 42; for an intermediate view, Patterson, *Citizenship Law*, pp. 95-96, and esp. 122-123, n. 63.

[71] Namely, the actual conduct of such cases in this period, which raises problems beyond the scope of this book. On the *nautodikai* (and *xenodikai*) see Harrison, *Law* II, pp. 23-24; MacDowell, *Law*, pp. 222-231; Patterson, *Citizenship Law*, pp. 108-112; Rhodes, *Commentary*, p. 662 (on *Ath. Pol.* 59.3: by this time *graphai xenias* went before the *thesmothetai*).

[72] For similarly bald phrases from the fourth century, see e.g. Lysias 10.31 (cf. 11.2), 26.21, 32.9; Demosth. 27.5; Isoc. 12.28.

[73] I do not share the conviction of e.g. R. Sealey (*CR* 7, 1957, p. 195), MacDowell (*Law*, p. 69), and Rhodes (*Boule*, p. 172 with n. 2; *Commentary*, p. 497) that there is any proof *here*—for other passages see below, n. 86—that the *dokimasia* was held at or near the beginning of the year. The speaker simply mentions his registration in general terms before recalling his first liturgies at the Dionysia (implicit) and the Thargelia, so his registration *could*, theoretically, have occurred at any time between Hekatombaion and Anthesterion in the year of Theopompos. In practice, admittedly, this period must be shortened to allow for the young man actually to perform the preliminary part of his *chorēgia*, but the real (and unanswerable) question is when he was *appointed* to it; and ἔπειτα in ?Aristot. *Ath. Pol.* 56.3 (cf. Rhodes, *Commentary*, p. 623) does not seem to me sufficient proof that this had been at the beginning of the archon-year.

[74] For the significance of the passage, see Lacey, *Family*, p. 95 with n. 56. I do not accept the inference drawn from [Xen.] *Ath. Pol.* 3.4 by Harrison, *Law* II, p. 206, n. 3, that only orphans were involved.

reference to the boule on the criterion of age."[75] Since Philokleon seems to be referring to the *dikasts'* assessment of *age*, as measured in sexual maturity, it is obviously possible that there were procedural changes here as between the fifth and fourth centuries. Yet that is not an absolutely necessary inference, as Rhodes has observed: "the *Athenaion Politeia's* account may be incomplete, and it may be that both courts and boule were entitled to take notice of all criteria for citizenship" (see further below); alternatively Aristophanes has perhaps allowed himself comic licence on the basis of the simple connection between the *dokimasia* and the *dikastēria*.[76]

At all events, the *Ath. Pol.*'s account runs as follows:[77]

It is men born of citizens on both sides who share in citizen-rights, and they are enrolled amongst the demesmen when they have attained the age of eighteen.[78] Whenever they are being enrolled, the demesmen decide by vote under oath, first, whether they appear to have reached the age which the law prescribes—and if they do not so appear, they return to being "boys" once again—and, secondly, whether (each one) is free[79] and was born in accordance with the laws. Then, should they vote against him as being *not* free, he appeals to the jury-court,[80] and the demesmen choose five of their number as accusers;[81] if it is decided (by the court) that he has no right to

---

[75] Rhodes, *Boule*, p. 173.

[76] Rhodes, *Boule*, p. 173 (and *Commentary*, p. 500). In either case these παῖδες δοκιμαζόμενοι will have been only those initially *rejected* for deme enrolment; see below.

[77] ?Aristot. *Ath. Pol.* 42.1-2: μετέχουσιν μὲν τῆς πολιτείας οἱ ἐξ ἀμφοτέρων γεγονότες ἀστῶν, ἐγγράφονται δ᾽ εἰς τοὺς δημότας ὀκτωκαίδεκα ἔτη γεγονότες. ὅταν δ᾽ ἐγγράφωνται διαψηφίζονται περὶ αὐτῶν ὀμόσαντες οἱ δημόται, πρῶτον μὲν εἰ δοκοῦσι γεγονέναι τὴν ἡλικίαν τὴν ἐκ τοῦ νόμου, κἂν μὴ δόξωσι, ἀπέρχονται πάλιν εἰς παῖδας, δεύτερον δ᾽ εἰ ἐλεύθερός ἐστι καὶ γέγονε κατὰ τοὺς νόμους. ἔπειτ᾽ ἂν μὲν ἀποψηφίσωνται μὴ εἶναι ἐλεύθερον, ὁ μὲν ἐφίησιν εἰς τὸ δικαστήριον, οἱ δὲ δημόται κατηγόρους αἱροῦνται πέντε ἄνδρας ἐξ αὑτῶν, κἂν μὲν μὴ δόξῃ δικαίως ἐγγράφεσθαι, πωλεῖ τοῦτον ἡ πόλις· ἐὰν δὲ νικήσῃ, τοῖς δημόταις ἐπάναγκες ἐγγράφειν. (2) μετὰ δὲ ταῦτα δοκιμάζει τοὺς ἐγγραφέντας ἡ βουλή, κἂν τις δόξῃ νεώτερος ὀκτωκαίδεκ᾽ ἐτῶν εἶναι, ζημιοῖ τοὺς δημότας τοὺς ἐγγράψαντας. As well as the excellent guidance in Rhodes, *Commentary* (see the following notes), consult Rhodes, *Boule*, pp. 171-174; and C. Pélékidis, *Histoire de l'éphébie attique des origines à 31 avant J.-C.*, Paris, 1962, pp. 83-101.

[78] This should probably be understood to mean "having attained their eighteenth birthday" (rather than "in their eighteenth year"); for bibliography and discussion on the point, see Rhodes, *Commentary*, pp. 497-498.

[79] That is, not a slave: see on this, Gomme, "Problems," pp. 130-140; cf. Rhodes, *Commentary*, pp. 499-502.

[80] Under the presidency of the *thesmothetai*, as we learn from a later passage (59.4: εἰσάγουσιν δὲ καὶ . . . τοὺς ἀπεψηφισμένους ὑπὸ τῶν δημοτῶν).

[81] It is possible (cf. Rhodes, *Commentary*, p. 501) that οἱ αἱρεθ|έντες ὑπὸ τῶν δημοτῶν

be enrolled, the polis sells him (into slavery), but if he wins the demesmen are obliged to enrol him. After this the *boulē* scrutinizes those who have been enrolled, and if it is decided that someone is younger than eighteen, the demesmen who enrolled him are fined.

While this is by far the fullest and most informative account of procedure that we have, it is not necessarily either a complete or a completely accurate one. There is no difficulty in the notion that the *boulē* scrutinized all candidates, including any who had been rejected by their deme but reinstated by the court, whereas the courts dealt only, as stated, with *apepsēphismenoi* (?Aristot. *Ath. Pol.* 59.4)—and indeed only with such of them as chose to exercise their right of appeal. However, it has been reasonably surmised that the ostensible precision of the *Ath. Pol.* as to the separate criteria tested by the *boulē* (age) and the courts (status) is misleading, and that both bodies would examine all relevant criteria,[82] just as the deme assembly itself had done. What is noteworthy, at all events, is that in all cases the initial decision of the deme assembly was subject to and if necessary reversed by a higher authority, in respect of both areas of possible abuse. The courts sought to ensure that nobody was improperly *ex*cluded; the council was watchful lest anyone be improperly *in*cluded.

We may take it, then, that this careful procedure in three (possible) stages—*diapsēphisis* in the deme assembly, *ephesis* (if need be) to a jury-court, and *dokimasia* by the *boulē*[83]—was the standard one in the fourth century, if not earlier,[84] for the regular enrolment or registration[85] of Athenian citizens in their deme. It was this solemn act of communal

κατή|γοροι Νεοκλέους who are praised in a deme decree of Epikephisia (IG II²1205, from the late fourth century) had been acting—evidently successfully—under this provision; however, there were other reasons why a deme might take an individual to court (see Haussoullier, *Vie*, pp. 97-102, and below, Chap. 5A, sec. 1(c)).

[82] Rhodes, *Commentary*, pp. 500, 502; cf. J. M. Moore, *Aristotle and Xenophon on Democracy and Oligarchy*, London, 1975, p. 275.

[83] The term *dokimasia* could also be applied to the part played by the deme (e.g. [Demosth.] 44.41, τοῦ δήμου τὴν δοκιμασίαν; cf. Demosth. 57.62) and by the court (Aristoph. *Wasps*, line 578), and was doubtless used in common parlance, not unreasonably, of deme registration as a whole.

[84] That the procedure described in the *Ath. Pol.*, and especially the right of *ephesis*, was not introduced until Demophilos' decree of 346/5 was argued by A. Diller, *TAPhA* 63, 1932, pp. 193-205 (cf. *CPh* 30, 1935, pp. 302-311, and *Race Mixture*, pp. 98-99) but this is unlikely: see Gomme, "Problems," pp. 123-130.

[85] ἐγγράφειν/ἐγγραφῆναι (εἰς τοὺς δημότας/ἄνδρας/τὸ ληξιαρχικὸν γραμματεῖον) is the technical term: ?Aristot. *Ath. Pol.* 42.1; Isaeus 7.27-28; Demosth. 18.261, 39.5, 57.61; [Demosth.] 44.35-39; Lycurg. *Leok.* 76; etc. Failure to attend was termed *ekleipsis*: Suda, ἔκλειψις καὶ ἐξέλιπεν; *Lex Seguer.* V, *Lexeis Rhetorikai*, ἔκλειψις [= Bekker, *Anecd. Gr.* 1.259.21].

admission and recognition by his fellow demesmen that a man would invoke if ever, subsequently, his status was called into question (Demosth. 57.60-62; etc.). The significance of the act, moreover, to the polis as a whole as well as to the individual demes may be further gauged by the likelihood that the regular *diapsēphiseis* of all the demes were synchronized at or near the beginning of the administrative year.[86]

In certain circumstances, though, the procedure was simpler. In addition to the year's crop of eighteen-year-olds, the deme assembly might also have to consider two other, special categories of applicant for enrolment: adoptive rather than natural sons of demesmen,[87] and newly enfranchised aliens.[88] Insofar as the candidates in both these categories were normally adults, there was presumably no question of the confirmatory *dokimasia* by the *boulē*.[89] And in the case of an alien *dēmopoiētos*, indeed, the procedure must have been simpler still; his basic right to citizenship had already—in a reversal of the normal timetable of events— been affirmed by the *ekklēsia*, and thus could scarcely be challenged at local level. In such cases the deme's acceptance of any persons who chose it[90] or else were allocated to it[91] was no more than the acknowledgment of a *fait accompli*.[92]

The *lēxiarchikon grammateion*, as we have seen, furnished a record

---

[86] The actual evidence for this, however, is slighter than has sometimes been claimed. Lysias 21.1 (referring to 411/0) is inconclusive (see above, n. 73); at most it is no obstacle. As regards the fourth century there is no explicit indication of time in either Demosth. 39 or [Demosth.] 44 (though note ἐν τῇ τῶν ἀρχόντων ἀγορᾷ in 44.36); and the view that, in Isaeus 7.27-28, Thrasyllos' enrolment (in an indeterminable deme) could be dated to either Hekatombaion or Metageitnion because at the time he was away at the Pythian Games (see Haussoullier, *Vie*, p. 16) was rendered untenable by the demonstration that ἐκ τῆς Πυθαΐδος refers to the *Pythaïs*, the (occasional) sacred pilgrimage from Athens to Delphi: see A. Boëthius, *Die Pythais*, Upsala, 1918, pp. 19ff.; H. W. Parke, *JHS* 59, 1939, pp. 80-83. The generalization thus rests upon Demosth. 30.15, which shows that he himself was enrolled in Paiania in either the last month of the old year (Skirophorion) or, perhaps more probably, the first of the new (Hekatombaion). Cf. Rhodes, *Commentary*, p. 497.

[87] See Haussoullier, *Vie*, pp. 23-28, cf. 17, n. 1, on Isaeus 7 and [Demosth.] 44.

[88] See Haussoullier, *Vie*, pp. 28-31.

[89] Those adopted as adults would indeed already have undergone it. For youths adopted before the age of eighteen and for the sons of *dēmopoiētoi*, the full procedures were of course appropriate.

[90] For individual honorands free choice was normal. Instances of the registration of a *dēmopoiētos* in the deme of whoever had sponsored his enfranchisement are noted by Davies, *Families*, p. 430-431, 558, 566, 571.

[91] The block enfranchisements of both the Plataians ([Demosth.] 59.104) and the Samians (IG I³127, lines 33-34) instruct that the honorands be allotted amongst the demes and/or tribes; for the exact phraseology, see D. Whitehead, *ZPE* 52, 1983, pp. 113-114.

[92] To that extent the disgust of, e.g., Isoc. 8.88 (cf. Andoc. 2.23) at both the quantity and the quality of *dēmopoiētoi* was not the fault of the demes themselves.

of everyone duly enrolled in a deme. In [Demosth.] 44.35, however, another document is mentioned, evidently distinct from it—the *pinax ekklēsiastikos*, in which (in this instance) Leostratos succeeded in having himself included prior to his enrolment in the *grammateion*. This was presumably an improper reversal of the normal order of events.[93] It has been generally assumed that all demes kept such a *pinax*, as a list or notice of those eligible to attend (which meant, in the fourth century, to be paid for attending) the city *ekklēsia*.[94] The necessity for such a list, over and above the *lēxiarchikon grammateion*, is not altogether clear, except inasmuch as the theoretical eligibility to attend the *ekklēsia* which came with deme enrolment at eighteen may have been at odds with a convention that actual attendance there was inappropriate, or even practically impossible, before the age of twenty.[95] Certainly a second, effectively routine registration at twenty, for those who had discharged their two years as ephebes, would help to explain why some lexicographers mistakenly placed enrolment in the *lēxiarchikon grammateion* after, not before, the ephebic service.[96] This is not, to be sure, a wholly satisfactory nexus of arguments;[97] and it is curious, to say the least, that, if the *pinakes* really were a feature of every deme's record keeping in this period, they passed unmentioned elsewhere in our (surviving) contemporary sources and unnoticed by the lexicographers and scholiasts; but perhaps their existence was a brief one.

(b) Extraordinary Registration

Once a man had been duly enrolled in his deme's register by decision of the assembly of his fellow demesmen, confirmed by the *boulē* where

[93] Alternatively, Leostratos' audacity consisted in enrolling *himself* on the *pinax*; but see Haussoullier, *Vie*, pp. 112-113.

[94] See for instance Haussoullier, *Vie*, pp. 111-113; Schoeffer, "Demarchoi," col. 2709; Busolt/Swoboda, *Staatskunde*, pp. 944, n. 5, and 966; Rhodes, *Boule*, p. 173 (and *Commentary*, pp. 494-495).

[95] On the efforts of Glaukon to seek political prominence οὐδέπω εἴκοσιν ἔτη γεγονώς, see Xen. *Mem.* 3.6.1. To attend (and address) the *ekklēsia* at his age was evidently unusual, though equally evidently (as Rhodes rightly notes, *Commentary*, pp. 494-495) it was not impossible. But it may have become, in practical terms, impossible once the *ephēbeia* had been converted, in ca. 335/4, into "a period of full-time national service for all young citizens" (Rhodes, *Commentary*, p. 495, with bibliography and discussion).

[96] Pollux 8.105; Harpoc. and Suda, ἐπιδιετὲς ἡβῆσαι; cf. Lucian, *Zeus Tragodos* 26 with scholiast.

[97] The main problem, obviously, is that Glaukon (see above, n. 95) *did* attend the Assembly—presumably exercising a right to do so—before the age of twenty, which would seem to cast doubt upon the notion of a gap of two years between enrolment in the *grammateion* and in the *pinax* (cf. Müller, *de demis*, pp. 15-16). But perhaps one sought inclusion in the *pinax* (cf. above, n. 93) as soon as, and not before, attendance was actually possible.

appropriate and by the courts if necessary, he might reasonably expect that his status as a *bona fide* member of both deme and polis would be beyond challenge thereafter, as a matter of record and of common knowledge. And so, in the vast majority of cases, it will have been. Yet what if the record itself were lost or destroyed? In Demosthenes 57, Euxitheos recalls a bizarre episode in Halimous when his opponent's father, Antiphilos, as demarch, had announced one day that the *lēxiarchikon grammateion* had been lost! "Forced ballotting" (διαψηφίσεις ἐξ ἀνάγκης) had been held, under solemn oath, and ten men expelled—nine of them subsequently reinstated by the jury-court.[98] Euxitheos claims, not unnaturally, that Antiphilos and his henchmen had deliberately destroyed or suppressed the register, with the twofold aim of having their enemies expelled from the deme and of making money from those who were prepared to pay to stay in.

Whatever the truth of this claim, the prime point here is what it led to. In form (*diapsēphiseis* under oath, with appeal to the courts for *apepsēphismenoi*) the procedure appears to be at least closely modelled on and possibly identical with the regular scrutiny and enrolment of youths and any others applying for deme membership for the first time. At any rate no differences can be detected. However, what Euxitheos (or Demosthenes) unfortunately failed to make clear is whether the procedure was mandatory in these circumstances. Haussoullier suggested that a more informal solution *could* have been adopted—that of simply convening the deme assembly and "retrieving" the names by a communal effort of memory, and then perhaps checking the resulting list against the *pinax ekklēsiastikos* (see previous section)—but instead Antiphilos wanted, and secured, formal and individual *diapsēphiseis*. This seems unlikely. We are told, admittedly, that Antiphilos "persuaded" (ἔπεισε) the Halimousioi to hold *diapsēphiseis* (Demosth. 57.60), but if a simpler and less contentious course had been available, it is astonishing that Euxitheos does not say so; as an ex-demarch himself (57.63) he would certainly have known of it. The term διαψηφίσεις ἐξ ἀνάγκης sounds very like a technical or quasi-technical one,[99] and we must surely postulate a law under which Antiphilos was at least allowed and very likely obliged to act as he did.[100] It is inconceivable that any deme assembly, let alone any demarch, could have taken a decision not merely to reconstruct but

---

[98] Demosth. 57.26 and 60-62. See Haussoullier, *Vie*, pp. 52-53; Schoeffer, "Demoi," col. 12.

[99] Cf. Haussoullier's own use of it as a section heading (*Vie*, p. 52). Even if ἐξ ἀνάγκης is an adverbial phrase to be construed with ἐγένοντο, it would still indicate that Antiphilos was acting under standing orders; see further below, in text.

[100] Which indeed, *if* he was the man whom Euxitheos portrays, he will have wanted to do anyway.

actually to revise its register unless a law of the state had permitted and required it. Such a law undoubtedly underpinned the normal, regular procedure,[101] and these extraordinary *diapsēphiseis* in Halimous must have been warranted by either the same law or another on similar lines.

We do not hear of any comparable episodes in other demes, but that fact represents no proof that none occurred. That this one instance was drawn to "national" attention (and hence to our own) is utterly fortuitous, and others like it could well have happened without occasioning anything beyond local and unrecorded scandal. True, it can hardly have been commonplace for demarchs to lose, or claim to have lost, their registers. Provided they did not do so, the registers *as such* were above challenge, on the crucial assumption that they were wholly composed of individuals who had been admitted in the proper manner; and any individual who came, rightly or wrongly, under suspicion might find himself the object of a *graphē xenias*.[102] Yet what if it was, rather, the fundamental assumption itself which was brought into question—the question of whether, across the board, the demes had indeed been admitting only the right people in the right way?

This question is not of course rhetorical. It arose in concrete form in 346/5, when (as Euxitheos puts it: Demosth. 57.49) "the whole polis was provoked to anger at those who had outrageously forced their way into the demes"; and the upshot of this anger was the formulation, acceptance, and implementation of Demophilos' proposal for a scrutiny of *every* deme register and a formal vote on *everyone* therein.

Our information about this episode is considerable,[103] and in view of the furore which it understandably created[104] the likelihood that other, similar extraordinary general scrutinies were held on other occasions yet passed unmentioned in the record must be decidedly remote.[105] The procedure is described most fully by Libanius in his *hypothesis* to Demosthenes 57, and is partially to be seen in action in that speech itself. It is

[101] Cf. Gomme, "Problems," p. 124.

[102] See Diller, *Race Mixture*, pp. 95-97.

[103] Demosth. 57, with Libanius' *hypothesis*; Aeschin. 1.77-78 (with scholiast on 77), 86, 114, and 2.182; Isaeus 12, with Dion. Hal. *Isaios* 17; Dion. Hal. *Deinarchos* 11; Harpoc., διαψήφισις. (It is probable that much lexicographic material on *diapsēphiseis* in general derives from this episode.) For some salient items in an extensive bibliography, see: Haussoullier, *Vie*, pp. 38-52 (including a detailed study of Demosth. 57); W. Wyse, *The Speeches of Isaeus*, Cambridge, 1904, pp. 714ff.; Gomme, "Problems"; the articles of Diller cited above, n. 84; and Rhodes, *Commentary*, pp. 500-502.

[104] See Demosth. 57.1-7 and passim; Aeschin. 1.77. In court in 343, Aeschines expected goodwill on the grounds of not having been responsible for anyone's exclusion (2.182)!

[105] I agree, nonetheless, with Gomme ("Problems," p. 124) that there must have been an "enabling law" which made such things always *possible*.

closely akin to that of the regular one as set out in the Aristotelian *Ath. Pol.* (discussed above): *diapsephiseis* on every man by his deme's assembly, and right of appeal (*ephesis*) to the jury-courts for *apepsephismenoi*,[106] who were vindicated as citizens if their appeal was upheld but sold as slaves if it was rejected.[107] No mention is made of the council, but this is understandable for a procedure concerned with adults. Additional detail has been sought in the accounts of the litigation to which some of the *apepsephismenoi* resorted, though much of it raises more questions than it solves.[108]

Even the initial proceedings at deme level—which for most individuals will have been the only ones necessary—leave a number of points unclear to us, despite our good fortune in possessing the vivid picture depicted in Demosthenes 57. The great problem with Euxitheos' account of what happened in Halimous is not so much that of extracting a model of what ought, properly, to have taken place from this description of what did, improperly, take place—for the speaker offers us every assistance, direct and indirect, in making due allowance for his opponents' malpractice. It is rather the problem of determining how far, if at all, the proceedings at this extraordinary meeting differed from those of a regular deme assembly; and in this the dilemmas obviously arise from the fact that Demosthenes 57 is our only detailed picture of *any* sort of deme assembly meeting at any time. We have seen, for example, that the Halimousioi were convened on this occasion *in Athens* (Demosth. 57.10). I have argued above, on general grounds, that all the demes may, on this occasion, have been required to do likewise but that normally they did not;

---

[106] But metic status for those who chose to abide by the deme's judgment. (This was probably the case in the regular *diapsephiseis* also; cf. Rhodes, *Commentary*, p. 502.)

[107] Gomme, "Problems," pp. 130-140 argued strongly that slavery was only the penalty for those who were slaves anyway; see however Rhodes, *Commentary*, pp. 501-502.

[108] Besides Demosth. 57, the principal cases known are those of Euphiletos *vs.* Erchia (Isaeus 12), Philotades *vs.* Kydathenaion (Aeschin. 1.114-115), and the cases for which Isaeus wrote Πρὸς Βοιωτὸν ἐκ δημοτῶν ἔφεσις (see Davies, *Families*, p. 365) and Dinarchus two speeches which are now lost: Κατὰ Κηρύκων (subtitled λόγος περί τινος ἀποψηφισθέντος) and Κατὰ Μοσχίωνος ἀπογραψαμένου αὐτὸν Νικοδίκου. I have little beyond conjecture to contribute to any of the well-known problems of procedural disparity which these cases seem to present (see, most searchingly, Gomme, "Problems," pp. 125-130). How, for example, could the prosecutor on behalf of Kydathenaion against Philotades properly have been Timarchos of Sphettos? Why did Euphiletos—if Isaeus 12 is not spurious!—go first to arbitration (when Euxitheos, it would seem, did not), and then, at first, claim not *ephesis* but a *dike*? These and other puzzles are most intractable, though an important observation of Gomme's is worth reiterating: "of course other actions [than an *ephesis*] might arise out of appeals from deme scrutinies, even against non-members, as for slander, bribery, or false witness" (Gomme, "Problems," p. 130 with n. 16). See also MacDowell, *Law*, p. 207.

however, neither part of this argument, especially the first, is as secure as one would wish. Certainly *if* all the deme assemblies did take place in the city, it would be difficult to follow Haussoullier in believing that they were all held at the same time,[109] though possibly within a fixed *period* of time. Again, Euxitheos asserts—and there is no good reason to doubt him—that the vote on his own case could have been left for the following day, when in any event the meeting would have had to be reconvened to consider the remaining quarter of the cases (see Demosth. 57.16, cf. 10). Presumably therefore the whole proceedings did take up two days. Was this extraordinary in itself? It is arguably likely that normal deme assembly meetings transacted their business in one day, but in truth we do not know.[110] What seems certain, though, is that the *diapsēphiseis* of 346/5 entailed meetings of very varying duration, depending upon the size of the deme. Demophilos' decree will simply have ordained that the demesmen meet and vote on everyone (cf. Demosth. 57.15). A medium-to-small deme like Halimous doubtless took longer over this than did the tiniest demes with only a few dozen members, but much less long than did a deme whose membership ran into several hundreds—and whose demarch allowed the opportunity for the testimony of witnesses and counterwitnesses which Euxitheos claims he was denied by Euboulides (Demosth. 57.12).

The sponsors of this whole singular, Augean episode must have believed, and persuaded their fellow citizens to believe, that nothing short of wiping the slate clean and beginning again would have sufficed to eradicate deep-rooted and widespread laxity and corruption throughout the entire deme network. Unquestionably the problems did exist; there is a body of evidence for them which is too substantial to be dismissed as the product of malice and exaggeration.[111] Yet the solution adopted stood at some risk of being self-defeating, by offering corrupt demes and deme officials unprecedented scope for expelling qualified *dēmotai* with no more justification than they had admitted unqualified ones.[112] Here, clearly, the role of the courts as a corrective was an absolutely vital one—as Euxitheos did not fail to observe (Demosth. 57.6 and 56). We do not know whether he himself was reinstated, but surely many were (cf. Demosth. 57.60). Many, however, were not; for when, in the crisis after the defeat at Chaironeia eight years later, Hyperides proposed a series of

---

[109] Haussoullier, *Vie*, p. 41.

[110] Were the earlier *diapsēphiseis* in Halimous, after the "loss" of the register (Demosth. 57.26 and 60-62), completed in a single day? We are not told; but in any case the circumstances there might have called for a special, and especially long, meeting.

[111] We shall look at some of this evidence in Chap. 10A.

[112] For alleged discrimination within the same family, see Demosth. 57.58; cf. Isaeus 12.

rewards and incentives to secure the support of underprivileged groups such as slaves and metics, the *apepsēphismenoi* (for whom the prize was presumably reinstatement) were worthy of special mention.[113] One need not interpret this as an admission that their disfranchisement had been unjust or improper; the proposals as a whole were not based on such thinking—and were probably not implemented in any case.[114] Yet perhaps at least some Athenians felt uneasy with the continuing human legacy of the 346/5 *diapsēphiseis*; and the community as a whole was evidently satisfied, thereafter, that any individuals illegally enrolled in the demes could be efficaciously caught by a line and hook rather than by a seine.[115]

2. OTHER ASPECTS OF STATE ADMINISTRATION PERFORMED BY DEMES

If a deme's examination and registration of its own membership was a matter of concern to both deme and state in broadly equal measure, the other attested functions of the deme assemblies fall more readily (if not totally) into the one category or the other; that is, they are more easily divisible into functions of what today we would term local government, where the demes administered their own internal affairs, and central government, where the demes fulfilled duties delegated to them by the state. This section deals with some of the latter.[116]

An obvious distinction is to be drawn here between functions which were regular or recurrent and tasks which were created or imposed *ad hoc*. Given the haphazard nature of the evidence, it is at first sight paradoxical but in fact quite understandable that by and large we are told more about the latter than about the former. Andocides furnishes two examples from the last decade of the fifth century. In 410 a decree of the *ekklēsia* ordered all Athenians to take an oath "by tribes and by demes" (κατὰ φυλὰς καὶ κατὰ δήμους) to kill anyone attempting to subvert the newly reestablished democracy (Andoc. 1.97). A procedure "by tribes and by demes" presumably means not that the oath was sworn twice over but that the demesmen took it, by demes, at the tribal assemblies; and we shall see further cause in Chapter 9A for surmising that it was not uncommon for tribal assemblies to work as groups of demes. The second instance comes from 403, when the decree of Teisamenos refers to five hundred *nomothetai*—apparently required for "a procedure

---

[113] See Haussoullier, *Vie*, pp. 50-51; Diller, *Race Mixture*, pp. 111-112; C. Mossé, *Athens in Decline: 404-86 B.C.*, London, 1973, pp. 72-74; Whitehead, *Metic*, pp. 162-163.

[114] See Diller, *Race Mixture*, p. 112; Whitehead, *Metic*, p. 162 with n. 118.

[115] The metaphor is Diller's (*Race Mixture*, p. 97), of the *graphē xenias*.

[116] See further, Chap. 9.

for one particular occasion"[117]—whom "the demesmen" had chosen (Andoc. 1.84, ... οἱ νομοθέται οἱ πεντακόσιοι, οὓς οἱ δημόται εἵλοντο). While this was admittedly an extraordinary event in extraordinary circumstances,[118] the mode of appointment may in itself have been not especially uncommon, at least in the fourth century. In 330 we find Aeschines alluding in general terms to "(officials) whom the tribes and the trittyes and the demes choose from amongst themselves to administer public monies" (Aeschin. 3.30, ... οὓς αἱ φυλαὶ καὶ αἱ τριττύες καὶ οἱ δῆμοι ἐξ ἑαυτῶν αἱροῦνται τὰ δημόσια χρήματα διαχειρίζειν). The example of this which he is discussing, the tribally appointed *teichopoioi* (3.27-30), are attested elsewhere;[119] and he implies that the tribes were not unused to undertaking such tasks (3.30). Unfortunately it is impossible to provide an instance, either actual or even hypothetical, of what he meant by comparable officials chosen by and from the demes (or for that matter the trittyes), but it is hard to see why he should have made a point of mentioning them unless they were indeed called into existence as and when the occasion demanded.[120]

Besides such occasional tasks, the demes also discharged regular or recurrent business on behalf of the polis as a whole, and we catch glimpses of this from time to time. [Demosthenes] 44.37, for example, refers to the distribution of *theōrika* during the Great Panathenaia, when "the other demesmen" (of Otryne) duly received theirs but the alleged Eleusinian interloper, Leostratos, was thwarted in an attempt to do likewise (and to have himself enrolled in the *lēxiarchikon grammateion*). The clear implication here is that *theōrika* were distributed not merely "by demes"[121] but actually at meetings of the deme assemblies,[122] to demesmen who presented themselves there in person.[123] However, this is best regarded not so much as a function of the assemblies themselves, strictly speaking, but as an instance of deme officials—here presumably the demarch[124]—performing a task of central government in a local context.[125]

---

[117] D. M. MacDowell, *JHS* 95, 1975, p. 62; cf. A.R.W. Harrison, *JHS* 75, 1955, p. 33.

[118] Cf. Haussoullier, *Vie*, p. 56.

[119] See Hansen, "*Archai*," p. 154, n. 8.

[120] In his discussion of this passage Haussoullier first envisages this only "en temps de guerre" (*Vie*, pp. 56-57), but later expresses this, reasonably enough, as "souvent" (*Vie*, p. 121)!

[121] Müller, *de demis*, p. 23.

[122] Haussoullier, *Vie*, p. 129.

[123] See Hyper. 5 (*Demosth.*), col. 27, where a Paianian is prosecuted for taking it on behalf of his absent son. (The same case is apparently referred to by Dinarch. 1. [*Demosth.*] 56.)

[124] Cf. Haussoullier, *Vie*, p. 129.

[125] For this see further Chap. 5A, sec. 2.

The most direct way in which deme *assemblies* as such could be required to make a contribution to the normal administration of the polis was to have them do routinely what Aeschines, as we saw, spoke of their doing occasionally, namely, to choose officials, not for their own internal purposes but to hold office in and for the city itself. The role of the demes in the appointment of the *boulē* and of the numerous boards of major and minor city magistrates may be mentioned here, but left for discussion—for there are many problems and obscurities—until Chapter 9C.

3. THE DEMES' OWN BUSINESS

We have so far discussed or previewed those aspects of the business of deme assemblies which in effect constituted the performance at local level of some of the administrative workload of the polis as a whole, and which were therefore (or so it would seem) transacted in the same or else a very similar way throughout the deme system. The universal, standardized nature of such operations as the maintenance of the *lēxiarchika grammateia* or the appointment of *bouleutai* is of course reflected in their documentation not only by evidence from or concerning individual demes but also and more particularly by literary and lexicographical testimony which deals in generalizations—and rightly so. To turn, however, to the deme assembly as arbiter of the deme's own internal life and activities is to confront source material—principally the epigraphically recorded enactments of the demes themselves[126]—where the rules of evidence are quite different.[127] We know that a deme assembly could legally bind its members to do anything short of illegality itself,[128] and there is ample proof that this freedom gave rise, as it naturally would, to all kinds of variation in the ways in which individual demes organized themselves internally. Thus we must often rest content with observing parallels (or their absence) rather than extrapolating archetypes, and the rationale of our general model must be the determination of the sort of things which deme assemblies did rather than the precise way in which they did them.

Here again there is an obvious distinction to be drawn, in theory at any rate, between occasional and recurrent business.

(a) Occasional Business

Given the grossly unequal distribution of surviving inscriptions from the various individual demes,[129] it stands to reason that no more than a tiny

---

[126] Cf. Haussoullier, *Vie*, p. 57.

[127] See above, Chap. 2B, for the distinction to be drawn between "category-*a*" evidence, the general, and "category-*b*" evidence, the particular.

[128] For this "Solonic" law see Chap. 1, p. 13 (and above, p. 86).

[129] See Chap. 2A, sec. 1. Major demes from which we have no public inscriptions at all

fraction of the occasional, *ad hoc* business which a deme assembly might transact can now be appreciated. What is more, even when a relevant document does survive, its fragmentary state and/or our ignorance of its background and context may leave all the important questions unanswered. Two examples will serve as illustration. A decree of Halai Aixonidcs, prosopographically datable to ca. 360, seems to have been occasioned by some internal scandal, possibly of a religious nature; for the demarch, the treasurers, the priests, and the priestesses are all to swear an oath "that nothing of the kind shall happen in the deme in future."[130] Later—at the beginning of the third century—an unidentifiable deme evidently suffered some calamitous damage to the fabric of its cult center: an extraordinary levy (*eparchē*) was imposed on the deme's officials, and those unable to pay it at once will have been duly grateful to their rich fellow demesman who met the expense in advance.[131] Such tantalizing instances as these do little more than reemphasize the lamentably lacunose evidence on which we are obliged to rely.

Taking that evidence on its own terms, however, it is plain that in some demes at least, and in the fourth century especially, the enactment of honorific decrees was one of the most common and characteristic of a deme assembly's "occasional" activities[132]—so common indeed, in certain demes, as to be reckoned recurrent *de facto*.[133] Honorific decrees of all kinds, as we noted in Chapter 2, make up fully two-thirds of all surviving deme decrees. To be sure, one may reasonably suspect that they did not constitute anything like so high a proportion of all deme decrees *enacted*, for it was surely more usual to commit to stone an honorific decree than many an example of ephemeral decision making (cf. Demosth. 57.9) which did not warrant preservation in so durable and public a

---

include Alopeke, Anaphlystos, Aphidna, Euonymon, Hagnous, Kephale, Kerameis, Oe, Prospalta, and Thria.

[130] IG II²1175, lines 19ff.; dating by Wilhelm, by reference to IG II²1174 and 2820 (see under Appendix 3, no. 52). Unfortunately Foucart's copy apparently made no sense of lines 3-18, from which we would surely have learned more of what the affair was about. But it may be significant that all three men whom, besides the demarch, the decree mentions by name appear, together with the son of one of them, on curse-tablets: see **184, 190, 195, 196**. For an interpretation and reconstruction see A. Wilhelm, *JÖAI* 7, 1904, pp. 114-118; cf. Davies, *Families*, p. 197.

[131] IG II²1215; the find-spot at Kypseli *may* suggest that the deme was the little-known Erikeia (Traill, *Organization*, p. 39, cf. p. 74, n. 10). For discussion of the stone and its background, see Müller, *de demis*, p. 59; Haussoullier, *Vie*, pp. 52 and esp. 77; Schoeffer, "Demoi," col. 18.

[132] Cf. Schoeffer, "Demoi," cols. 24-25.

[133] It is a fair assumption, for example, that in the last quarter of the fourth century at least, the deme Aixone honored local *chorēgoi* as a matter of routine.

form.[134] Nor do we know for a fact that every deme had the inclination and, where expense was involved, the funds to pass honorific decrees at all. We can only say that they were all *entitled* to do so,[135] and that probably most of them did. Following the lead set by the polis itself, even a tiny deme like Epikephisia sought to proclaim itself a body which promoted *philotimia* and rewarded it accordingly.[136]

One other occasional function of a deme assembly is worth noting here, namely, arbitration, where the assembly effectively took on the role of a court of law. As Haussoullier rightly emphasized, only a single instance of this is known, on an inscription from Aixone, and the absence of any parallels either from other inscriptions or from literary sources such as the orators indicates that it can hardly have been an everyday occurrence.[137] That a deme assembly *could* act in this way is nonetheless of some significance. The stone in question is IG II²1196, from the year 326/5,[138] and it is concerned with the details of a leasing agreement of *ennomion*, which seems to mean rights of pasturage.[139] Owing to its extremely fragmentary state as well as its elliptical phraseology, it presents multiple problems of interpretation.[140] However, in the best-preserved portion of the stele (lines 6-13) a situation is envisaged where, if the lessees have seen reason not to pay their dues (and have thus become, from the deme's standpoint, debtors), they may, before resort to a jury-court,[141] submit their case to arbitration by the deme assembly (ἐπι-τρέπειν τοῖς δημό|[ταις, lines 8-9). In that event the deme's side of the story will be stated by the demarch, assisted by *syndikoi*,[142] and the

---

[134] Cf. discussion above, p. 96.

[135] Within certain limits imposed by the state: see Chap. 9A.

[136] IG II²1205. On *philotimia* and the demes, see Chap. 8B.

[137] See Haussoullier, *Vie*, pp. 84-92, esp. 87ff. On the deme assembly of Myrrhinous as a court of appeal in its (presumably regular) *euthynai* procedure (IG II²1183), see next section.

[138] For the date, see Whitehead, "Demarchs," pp. 38-39.

[139] IG II²1196, A, line 7, ἐννόμιον; B, lines 10-11, ἐννόμια. Compare IG II²2498 (*locatio* of Peiraieus), line 13; and for deme leases in general, see Chap. 6A, sec. 2.

[140] As well as Haussoullier, *Vie*, pp. 87ff., see the *editio princeps* of Lolling (AM 4, 1879, pp. 199ff.) and Dittenberger's notes to *Syll.* 914, many of which were reproduced by Kirchner in IG II².

[141] *Pace* Haussoullier, *Vie*, pp. 89-90, there is no loose use of the term *dikastērion* here (lines 2, 9, 21-22) with reference to the role of the deme assembly; see rather Dittenberger's note *ad loc.* in *Syll.* 914. (On *dikazein*, of the deme assembly, see below, n. 143.)

[142] δικάζεσθαι δὲ τὸν δήμαρ[χον − −], line 6; [− −]ον καὶ οἱ σύνδικοι, line 17; δήμαρχος μετὰ τῶν συν|[δίκων, lines 18-19; τῶ]ι δημάρχω[ι], line 22. (For the *syndikoi* of Aixone, see also IG II²1197, lines 13-14.) The mention of *hieropoioi* in line 5 might suggest that the land in question was "sacred."

assembly will give "judgment"[143] by a vote (ψηφίσωνται, line 12). The decision of the arbitrating body, having been voluntarily sought, is to be final (lines 11-12); this is in line with the rules of private arbitration by *individuals*,[144] and it probably entitles us to infer that the lessees were themselves Aixoneis.

(b) Recurrent Business

The recurrent or regular business of a deme assembly in relation to its own internal affairs fell under three principal headings:[145] the regulation of income and expenditure (including the management of communal land and other property); the administration of cults and festivals; and the appointment of deme officials, secular and sacred, and the assessment of their performance by *euthynai*. As the first and second of these areas will be dealt with elsewhere[146] we may confine ourselves here to the third.

The multiplicity and variety of deme officials has already been noted (in Chapter 2B), and their duties and functions will be investigated, as far as this is possible, in Chapter 5. But how were they selected, appointed, and, after their term of office was over, held to account? There is neither evidence nor probability that the fine details of such matters were centrally regulated and thus standardized, save in the crucial instance of every deme's chief executive official, the demarch. On the contrary, local variation is certain. Nevertheless, the degree of uniformity, or at least comparability, in the *principles* governing the choice and the evaluation of deme officials may still have been considerable, by dint of imposed standardization *in general terms*, or the natural imitation by demes of the procedures of central government, or a combination of the two.

Method of appointment   To pose the question of whether "the demes" appointed their officials by election (*hairesis, cheirotonia*) or by sortition (*klērōsis*, possibly though not necessarily from *prokritoi*) would be fruitless. Both methods are attested[147]—in the same deme at the same time,

---

[143] ἕως ἂν δικάζωσιν οἱ δημόται, line 11. This use of *dikazein* is, strictly speaking, untechnical: Harrison, *Law* II, p. 36, n. 3.

[144] Harrison, *Law* II, p. 65; MacDowell, *Law*, p. 209.

[145] Cf. Schoeffer, "Demoi," col. 14.

[146] Income and expenditure, Chap. 6; cult and religion, Chap. 7.

[147] Sortition: see for instance IG II²1199 (Aixone), lines 1-2 (οἱ | λαχόντες ἱεροποιοί of Hebe); *Hesp.* 8, 1939, pp. 177-180 (Eleusis), line 7 ([λ]αχὼν δήμαρχος); Demosth. 57.25, cf. 49 (Halimous), ἀρχὰς ἔλαχεν; ?Aristot. *Ath. Pol.* 54.8 (Peiraieus), κληροῦσι . . . εἰς Πειραιέα δήμαρχον; IG I³258 (Plotheia), lines 2ff. (financial officials, perhaps including demarch). (Sortition from *prokritoi*: Demosth. 57.46-48, cf. 62, Halimous, priesthood of Herakles; Isaeus 8.19, Pithos, *archousai* for the Thesmophoria.) Election: see for instance IG II²1205 (Epikephisia), lines 3-5 (elected *katēgoroi*; see above, n. 81); SEG 2.7

in two instances.[148] Applying general considerations, however, we may perhaps perceive two processes at work—one a development over time, the other an administrative principle which emerged once that development had taken place. The likelihood must be that originally all deme officials were elected, by election procedures which were naturally, on that account, called *archairesiai* (Isaeus 7.28; [Demosth.] 44.39). One may suppose, however, that a change to sortition occurred in the second half of the fifth century, imposed by the state in respect of demarchs,[149] and adopted, perhaps more gradually and unsystematically, by the demes themselves for their other officials. At all events, by the fourth century the *archairesiai*—still so called—will in fact have been occasions for the appointment by lot, with or without *prokrisis*, of most if not all a deme's regular officials; for it is a significant feature of nearly all the attested *elective* appointments (or provisions for election) that there is something special, unusual, temporary, or *ad hoc* about them.[150] This, it thus appears, is an important distinction which is not only reflected, albeit rather dimly, in the evidence but also intelligible and justifiable in itself: sortition for routine (i.e., in the main annual) magistracies; election, less formal but more immediate, to extra duties and positions as and when they arose.

With regard to every deme's principal magistrate, the demarch, I have already made clear my belief that the polis had good reason from the outset to standardize the method of his appointment throughout the deme network as a whole.[151] What that method was—election or sortition— is a question which scholars made surprisingly heavy weather of at one time. For the fourth century at least, the careful study of Aksel Damsgaard-Madsen leaves scant room for doubt that the procedure used was sortition;[152] and it may be noted that prosopographical evidence offers hitherto unnoticed corroboration of this.[153] That sortition was the way

---

(Halimous), lines 2ff. (someone elected to act ὑπὲρ τοῦ δημάρχου: see Chap. 5, n. 160); IG II²1183 (Myrrhinous), lines 16-18 (the ten αἱρεθέντες in the *euthynai* procedure; see below, p. 119; IG II²1176 + (Peiraieus), lines 23-24 (provision for electing three *epitimētai*).

[148] (a) IG II²1215 (?Erikeia: see above, n. 131): αἱρούμενοι of some sort in lines 2-3, sortitive *archai* in lines 14-15. (b) AC 52, 1983, pp. 150-174 (*fasti* of Thorikos): lines 58-65 distinguish between sortitive *archai*—though only that of the *euthynos* himself, according to the latest restoration of line 58 (ἔλαχ[ον, not ἔλαχ[εν), by Daux, "Calendrier"—and, in lines 64-65, elective ones.

[149] See Chap. 2, n. 86, and further below.

[150] For examples, see above, n. 147; a full list will be dressed in Chap. 5B.

[151] See Chap. 2B, esp. n. 86.

[152] Damsgaard-Madsen, "Démarques."

[153] Had demarchs been *elected*, it would be reasonable to expect a fairly high proportion of them to have been men of some prominence; a sortition process, by contrast, would

of appointing demarchs from 508/7 is not itself utterly inconceivable, though we should regard it as more likely that sortition replaced election in the 450s or 440s. But under either system the appointment will presumably have taken place in the deme assembly.[154] (For the special case of the demarch of Peiraieus, see Appendix 4.)

Dokimasiai Although we only have explicit evidence of it from one deme, Halimous (see below), it seems not unreasonable to suppose that, once appointed, deme officials just like city officials would be expected to undergo some kind of formal scrutiny (*dokimasia*) before actually taking up their duties.[155] It would be "le plus souvent une formalité sans importance," in Haussoullier's estimation[156]—a final verification of the candidate's basic right to be standing for office, with an opportunity for anyone who challenged that right to make his objections known. In demes which employed a *dokimasia* procedure, however, the important fact would be that such a challenge was always a possibility. When Euxitheos refers to local offices (*archai*) which he and his father have held in Halimous, he makes a point of mentioning the *dokimasiai* involved (Demosth. 57.25,46,67), as these were other occasions—besides the *diapsēphiseis*—when the family's citizen status might have been called into question.

Euthynai In IG II²1199, an honorific decree of Aixone from the year 320/19, *hieropoioi* are praised and rewarded for having fulfilled their sacrificial duties justly and zealously and for having rendered due account of themselves in this respect: "they gave a *logos* and *euthynai*" (καὶ λόγον καὶ εὐθύνας δεδώκα|σιν, lines 6-7). In view of the all-pervading importance of the principle and practice of *euthynai* under the radical Athenian democracy,[157] it must be highly probable that all demes were en-

---

have produced a high proportion of men otherwise unknown to us; and it can be seen from the Prosopography (nos. 1-50) that very few demarchs are otherwise attested. (Osborne, *Demos*, pp. 83-87, has simultaneously made much the same observations.) Haussoullier's brief foray into prosopographical evidence (*Vie*, pp. 59-62, cf. 130-133), which by implication suggests the opposite conclusion, is vitiated by his failure to separate out demarchs from other men who appear in deme documents.

[154] Osborne, *Demos*, p. 77, suggests that all demarchs were centrally appointed in Athens, for he believes that this is what is meant by the *archairesiai* in the Theseion which are mentioned in the recently published deme decree of Eleusis (SEG 28.103, lines 27-28). But in my opinion it is *city* officials who are appointed at such meetings: see above, sec. A.1, and further in Chap. 9C.

[155] Cf. Müller, *de demis*, p. 52.

[156] Haussoullier, *Vie*, p. 79.

[157] See most recently M. Piérart, *AC* 40, 1971, pp. 526-573.

couraged and perhaps even compelled to devise and operate *euthynai* procedures *of some sort* for their own officials.[158] As early as the second quarter of the fifth century we find officials of the deme Skambonidai being required to swear that they will "render the necessary (τὸ καθῆκον) to the *euthynos*";[159] and a *euthynos* is also attested in Eleusis,[160] Halai Aixonides,[161] Myrrhinous,[162] Thorikos,[163] and a deme which cannot be identified.[164]

What we cannot assume, though, is that the procedure was exactly the same in all demes. Indeed there is positive evidence that it was not. The two-stage process undergone by the *hieropoioi* of Aixone (above)— financial accounting (*logos*) and general examination (*euthynai*)—conforms to what is known of the state procedure,[165] which certainly offered an obvious paradigm for the demes to copy. But there is no reason why

---

[158] Osborne, *Demos*, pp. 77-78, argues that the *euthynoi* who appear in various deme documents are *city* officials, and this, as he rightly says, would be an important aspect of control of, even interference in, the affairs of the demes by central government. His case is groundless, however. Its only apparently solid support comes from the Thorikos *fasti* (*AC* 52, 1983, pp. 150-174) and their use of the word *horkōmosion*: ὀρκωμόσιον πα[ρέ]χεν ἐς εὐθύνας, line 12, cf. line 52. This Osborne, following Dunst, "Opferkalender," p. 252, takes to refer to *the* Horkomosion in Athens, mentioned by Plut. *Thes.* 27.5. More probably, though, the word is simply ὀρκωμόσιον, meaning "assertion on oath" (see e.g. Plato *Phaidros* 241A, *Kritias* 120B) and, by extension from that, as here, the provision of a victim to solemnize such an oath. Nor can one readily believe that a deme could require a city official to swear an oath (cf. Haussoullier, *Vie*, p. 81, n. 4), as the *euthynos* does not only in this Thorikos document (lines 57ff.) but also in IG II²1183 (Myrrhinous: see below). See further, Chap. 9, n. 19.

[159] IG I³244, B, lines 9-10 and 20-21. Who the officials are is not clear; see Haussoullier, *Vie*, p. 79, n. 2.

[160] SEG 28.103, decree II, lines 41-43: the *euthynos* and the *synēgoros* are to charge fines on anyone attempting to reverse certain decisions, or else be liable themselves.

[161] IG II²1174, lines 15-18: the demarch is to make the *euthynos* and (?his) *paredroi* swear to conduct the *euthynai* in accordance with the decree just enacted; on this document, see below, in text.

[162] IG II²1183, line 16 (cf. also lines 8-13, the end of an oath which is probably that of the *euthynos*); on this document see below, in text.

[163] *AC* 52, 1983, pp. 150-174, lines 57ff.: oath of the *euthynos* and his *paredroi*; cf. above, n. 158.

[164] IG II²1216, fr. *a*, lines 7 and 10. (As one must constantly note, this deme *might* be one of those already mentioned.)

[165] See, for instance, Aeschin. 3.26 (πρὶν ἂν λόγον καὶ εὐθύνας δῷ); Lysias 24.26; ML no. 58A, lines 25-27; and the deme decree of Halai Aixonides (IG II²1174), requiring *euthynai* on the basis of *logoi*—see below, in text. Either term could refer inclusively to both stages of the state procedure (see e.g. Lysias 30.4-5 for *euthynai*, Demosth. 19.211 for *logos*), and the same was perhaps true in the demes (see e.g. *AC* 52, 1983, pp. 150-174, line 12, for *euthynai* in Thorikos; *AD* 11, 1927-1928, pp. 40-41, no. 4, line 6, for *logoi* in Halai Aixonides—see next note; also *logos* in SEG 22.117, line 4, Ikarion).

a *euthynos*, or indeed any special official, was essential; *euthynai* could simply have been conducted by the demarch, in the deme assembly, as was apparently the case with the priest of Apollo Zoster in Halai Aixonides who "gave *logoi* of his superintendence to the demesmen."[166] Small demes in particular might have preferred such a simple and direct form of accountability for their officials, without seeing a need to create extra ones—a *euthynos*, perhaps a *logistēs*,[167] with *paredroi*[168] or *synēgoroi*[169] in attendance—who would themselves have to be kept under surveillance.[170]

At all events there are two instances (both from the fourth century) where we can see how an individual deme assembly devised a means of calling its officials to account.

For Halai Aixonides, IG II²1174 sets out a procedure for the *euthynai* of demarchs and treasurers[171] which, it seems, has been voluntarily tried out (line 9) by the officials of the current archon-year, 368/7, and is to be standard practice for the future. Once a month during their year in office the officials are to deposit in a box a *logos* of receipts and outgoings, and are to undergo their *euthynai* (in the first month of the succeeding year)[172] on the basis of those *logoi* and no others. The demarch[173] is to administer oaths to the *euthynos* and the *paredroi*; and at the point where the stone breaks off it seems that penalties are being specified in case of improper performance of their task by these special officials.[174] Whether the deme assembly was involved, either regularly or as a possible "court of appeal" (cf. below, Myrrhinous), is not stated.

---

[166] *AD* 11, 1927-1928, pp. 40-41, no. 4, line 6: λόγους τῆς ἐπιμελείας ἔδωκεν τοῖς δημόταις.

[167] Attested in Myrrhinous: IG II²1183, lines 13-14.

[168] Attested in Halai Aixonides (IG II²1174, line 16) and Thorikos (*AC* 52, 1983, pp. 150-174, lines 57-58 and 61-62).

[169] Attested in the singular in Eleusis (SEG 28.103, decree II, lines 41-42) and in the plural in Myrrhinous (IG II²1183, lines 14-16).

[170] By the admission of oaths; see below, in text.

[171] Cf. Chap. 2, n. 85.

[172] IG II²1174, lines 11-12: τῶι [ὑ]στέρωι ἔτει πρὸ [τὸ Μεταγειτνι]|ῶνος μηνός. Compare SEG 22.117 (Ikarion), line 4, *logos* of the demarch "in the month Hekatombaion." In the Thorikos procedure (*AC* 52, 1983, pp. 150-174), as Daux, "Calendrier," p. 164, has now pointed out, the *euthynos* and his *paredroi*, appointed at the end of the old administrative year (lines 57ff.), are expected to come forward with their findings during the second month, Metageitnion, of the new one (line 12).

[173] Obviously the one who has just taken up office. (The Myrrhinous procedure, discussed below in text, explicitly distinguishes between "the new demarch," lines 18-19, and his predecessor, line 26.)

[174] For this (and in general) see the re-edition of the stone by A. Wilhelm, *BCH* 25, 1901, pp. 93-104.

For Myrrhinous, IG II²1183—or what is left of it—reveals a procedure not only more explicitly outlined but more elaborate in itself.[175] What is envisaged is a meeting of the deme assembly, early in the administrative year, with the new demarch (lines 18-19) presiding over the *euthynai* of his predecessor (line 26).[176] Various specialist officials are to be sworn in by the demarch, to perform the examination itself: a *euthynos*, a *logistēs*, and an unspecified number of *synēgoroi*.[177] The duties of the *synēgoroi* apparently include some sort of preliminary vote (ψ[ηφ]ιεῖσθαι, line 15); however, the vote which really matters is that of the ten "elected men" (αἱρεθέντες), who are sworn in by the demarch in front of their fellow demesmen and who vote in a secret ballot.[178] If a majority of the ten are satisfied, the *euthynos* destroys the accounts and the proceedings are at an end. If not, they impose a fine—but in that event the ex-official has the right of appeal (*ephesis*) to the assembly as a whole; after checking that at least thirty demesmen are present,[179] the presiding demarch administers an oath to them and distributes votes, and this final "court of appeal" may either reverse the decision of the ten or else confirm their vote of condemnation[180] and increase the fine originally imposed by 50 percent in consequence.

*

Two other important elements of the deme assembly's recurrent business—the financial and the religious—remain to be discussed in later chapters; nevertheless, the evidence and issues reviewed here should have sufficed to create a general picture both of the scope and significance of that business and also of the role and character of the assembly itself. The picture is, necessarily, a general one, for both negative and positive reasons. The negative reasons arise because our surviving evidence furnishes little more than fleeting glimpses of the variation and individuality

[175] See Müller, *de demis*, pp. 4-6, 45-53; Haussoullier, *Vie*, pp. 80-83; Schoeffer, "Demoi," col. 15.

[176] No other officials liable to *euthynai* are mentioned in what survives of the document, though obviously they may have been enumerated in the lost, first part. (Perhaps the *antigrapheus* of IG II²1182, lines 23-24?)

[177] *Pace* Haussoullier, *Vie*, p. 81, no *paredroi* are mentioned here. Evidently he was generalizing from the example of Halai Aixonides. In point of fact *paredroi* and *synēgoroi* are not found together: see above, nn. 168-169.

[178] Since the opening provisions of the document are not preserved, one cannot entirely rule out the possibility that the *synēgoroi* and the ten "elected men" are one and the same (and if they are, only one vote was taken); but this does not *seem* to be so, unless the terminology is more than usually confused and confusing.

[179] On this quorum cf. above, p. 95.

[180] Only the latter course is actually mentioned explicitly.

which must surely have characterized the ways in which one hundred
and thirty-nine demes, of all shapes and sizes, devised and implemented
their own brand of local self-government. But another, more positive
creator of generality is the fact that much of the actual business of any
deme assembly was basically modelled, sometimes *de iure*, sometimes *de
facto*, on standard paradigms derived from the principles and practice
of democratic government in the polis as a whole. On matters of procedure (discussed in the first part of this chapter) unanswered questions
proliferate, as they did for Haussoullier. Indeed it is hard to foresee a
time when, in this area, there will ever be enough solid facts as ballast
for the airy construction of arguments from probability. By the same
token, though, it is some comfort that Haussoullier's strong overall evocation of what, essentially, a deme assembly was (and was not) is one
which can still be endorsed. Within its own microcosm—and subject to
the ultimate control of the state—it was "souveraine," "toute-puis-
sante."[181] Its meetings may have been infrequent and, at times, poorly
attended. What is more, its proceedings were largely and inevitably dominated in practice by the rich, the experienced, and the articulate.[182]
However, that fact served only to temper, not to nullify, its role as an
instrument and expression of local autonomy and, if not *dēmokratia*, at
least *isonomia*.[183] As far as the demes are concerned, the Kleisthenic
political system found unworthy heirs in the likes of Euboulides of Halimous, yet the achievement represented by the system itself is not to be
diminished on that account; and, of its cardinal principles, those of communal decision making and responsibility at local as well as national
level—not only "enacted by the *dēmos*" (ἔδοξε τῷ δήμῳ) but also "enacted by the demesmen" (ἔδοξε τοῖς δημόταις)—stand inseparable in
significance.

[181] See Haussoullier, *Vie*, pp. 9-10, 92-93.
[182] See further, Chaps. 8B and 10A.
[183] Cf. Chap. 1, pp. 37-38.

CHAPTER 5

---- ✳ ----

THE DEMARCH AND
OTHER OFFICIALS

The deme assemblies, as we have seen in Chapter 4, transacted business and passed resolutions like the city *ekklēsia*. Yet no deme assembly, however small, was small enough to act as its own executive—and no deme, as far as we know, possessed an equivalent of the city's *boulē*.[1] To implement what the demesmen had resolved, and also to apply such regulations of central government as affected local administration—in short, to administer the deme's affairs from day to day—it was therefore necessary for individual *dēmotai* to take on the labor and the responsibility of being deme officials. We have already discussed how these officials were appointed, vetted, and (their duties done) called to account. The subject of this present chapter is the functions and character of the officials themselves.[2]

A. The Demarch

Three reasons make it appropriate to deal with the demarch separately. First, his is the only post which we know to have been created at the very inauguration of the Kleisthenic deme system itself (?Aristot. *Ath. Pol.* 21.5). Secondly, it is the only post which may legitimately be assumed to have existed in all one hundred and thirty-nine demes.[3] And thirdly,

[1] See Chap. 4, n. 11.

[2] I shall use the word "officials" throughout, but two points should be borne in mind. First, from the deme's point of view they are divisible (at least in theory) into *archontes* (such as the demarch, and the *tamiai* if any), *epimelētai* (such as *hieropoioi* and those fulfilling tasks *ad hoc*: see sec. B), and *hypēretai* (such as a herald); cf. Müller, *de demis*, p. 49. Secondly, from *the city's* point of view even the demes' "*archontes*" (see [Demosth.] 44.36, etc.) were not, technically speaking, holders of an *archē*: Hansen, "*Archai*," p. 173, and *GRBS* 22, 1981, pp. 347-351; for the special exception of the demarch of Peiraieus, see Appendix 4.

[3] See Chap. 2B, esp. the documentation in n. 84.

a considerable body of evidence makes it clear, in consequence, that the demarch was the most important of deme officials, for besides the duties (recurrent or *ad hoc*) laid upon him by his own fellow demesmen, he was also the crucial pivot between the spheres of local government and central government, deme and polis.

The methodological principles which need to be applied to this body of evidence have already been discussed (in Chapter 2B), and they require a distinction to be drawn between these twin sources of authority which provided the component elements of any demarch's mandate. His most important functions were laid down by the state and enshrined in a body of *nomoi*.[4] Some of these tasks were performed in the deme, some outside it; and they can be reconstructed not only from epigraphic, literary, and lexicographic testimony of a generalizing character but also, with due caution, from certain of the enactments of the demes themselves. This is what we have termed "category-*a*" evidence, and it may be taken to hold good, by and large,[5] for the deme system as a whole. On the other hand, within the general *nomoi* there was scope for an individual deme assembly to use its own demarch in a variety of ways and for a miscellany of purposes, ordinary or extraordinary. This we see from the "category-*b*" evidence, which is thus, of necessity, illustrative rather than normative, and which we shall consider first.

1. THE DEMARCH AS AGENT OF HIS DEME ASSEMBLY

As we saw in the last chapter, there was a basic and inescapable relationship between every demarch and his deme assembly, in that it was the demarch who convened the assembly (by virtue of the *lēxiarchikon grammateion* which was in his charge),[6] who supervised its proceedings, including any oaths and votes, and who executed its decisions. That his activities within the deme should be built around these three fundamental duties was undoubtedly laid down by central, polis legislation, and to that extent they formed a common "theoretical" core of responsibilities to be discharged by all demarchs alike. Equally clearly, however, a possibility of variation between demes in the *actual* duties undertaken by or imposed on the demarch—as indeed on any other deme official—necessarily follows from the fact of each deme assembly's freedom to resolve whatever it saw fit; and variation is what the evidence duly reveals.

One minor illustration of this has already been cited: the fact that the

---

[4] Cf. Chap. 2, n. 93.

[5] Again (cf. above, n. 2) one must always allow for exceptional practices in Peiraieus, a deme which was literally a law unto itself; see Appendix 4.

[6] Demosth. 57.8: κύριος ὤν . . . τῶν γραμμάτων ἐξ ὦν ἀνεκάλει τοὺς δημότας.

task of arranging the cutting and erection of inscriptions recording some
of the deme assembly's decrees was sometimes given to demarchs, sometimes to others;[7] and a number of other *possible* duties for a demarch
likewise arise from what one might call the mechanics of implementing
a decree, especially an honorific decree. In two fourth-century honorific
decrees of Eleusis, for instance, the crowns awarded to the honorands
are to be proclaimed at the next celebration of the (deme's) Dionysia, by
whoever is then demarch.[8] Also, both in these same two decrees and in
two others from the same deme, a standing order is laid upon all demarchs
in future—the formula is ὁ δήμαρχος ὁ ἀεὶ δημαρχῶν—to ensure that
the honorand actually receives the privilege(s) voted to him,[9] or else to
take care of his needs in future.[10] (Other demes too, for a variety of
reasons, created such standing orders for their demarchs, using either
this same formula or one very like it.)[11] Generally in these cases the major
privilege which the honorand has been voted is that of *proedria* in the
deme's theater,[12] and sometimes the task of the demarch each year is to
summon him officially to take his seat.[13] Needless to say, such a privilege,

---

[7] See Chap. 4, n. 50.

[8] IG II²1186, lines 19-24 (ὁ μετὰ Γνᾶθιν δήμα|ρχος, lines 19-20); IG II²1193, lines
13-21 (τὸν δήμαρχον τὸν μετὰ Ἴσ|αρχον δημαρ[χ]οῦντα, lines 14-15). These formulas
obviously suggest that both decrees were passed in the second half of an administrative
year, i.e., after the Dionysia of that year. (Compare, for this, IG II²1199 (Aixone), lines
13-16: the stele to be inscribed and erected by "the demarch after the archon Neaichmos";
the decree was evidently enacted near the end of the administrative year 320/19.) Note
that elsewhere a *herald* may do the announcing: references below, nn. 118 (Halai Araphenides), 119 (Ikarion), 120 (Peiraieus), 122 (Rhamnous). The announcing official is
unspecified in IG II²1202 (Aixone), lines 14-18.

[9] IG II²1187, lines 16-23; IG II²1193, lines 21-24; *Hesp.* 8, 1939, pp. 177-180, lines 18-
21 (including a fine if he fails in this). Note also IG II²1189 (also Eleusis), lines 11-12,
where the formula to be restored is different but probably meant the same thing.

[10] IG II²1186, lines 28-30.

[11] See IG II²1206 (?Acharnai), lines 2-12, an annual task for the demarch and treasurer
[οἳ ἂν ἀεὶ ἄρ]χωσιν; IG II²1197 (Aixone), lines 9-11, τὸν δήμα]ρχον τὸν ἀεὶ
δημ[αρχοῦντα to guarantee *proedria* (on which see next note); IG II²1177 (Peiraieus),
lines 0-2, τὸν δήμαρχον] . . . τὸν [ἀεὶ δημαρχ][οῦ]ντα, with a priestess, to care for the
Thesmophorion; SEG 24.151 (Teithras), lines 32-34, taxes to be paid each year in the
month Elaphebolion τῶι δημάρχωι [τῶι] | [ἀεὶ δημαρχόντι.

[12] Grants of *proedria* are attested in Aixone (IG II²1197, lines 9-11*), ?Anagyrous (IG
II²1210, lines 4-6, partially restored*), Eleusis (IG II²1185, line 4; 1186, line 24; 1187,
lines 17-20*; 1189, lines 11-12*; 1192, line 10; 1193, lines 21-24*; *Hesp.* 8, 1939, pp.
177-180, lines 17-19*), Halai Araphenides (*AE* 1932, *Chronika*, pp. 30-32, lines 20-24),
Myrrhinous (IG II²1182, lines 2-4), Peiraieus (IG II²1214, lines 19-25*; cf. 1176+, lines
11-16), and Rhamnous (SEG 22.120, lines 5-6). For the asterisks, see next note.

[13] This is so in the seven cases marked with an asterisk in the preceding note. Again (cf.
above, n. 8), however, note that a *herald* sometimes does this: Halai Araphenides (cited in
preceding note).

and thus such a duty for the demarch, existed only in demes which possessed a theater of their own.[14]

A deme assembly might also see fit to lay down a standing order to *prohibit* its demarch from doing something. Thus for example an Eleusinian decree obliges him not to divert a specific source of income (from the lease of stone-quarrying rights) from being used for a festival of Herakles;[15] a decree of Peiraieus instructs him not to demand the *enktētikon* tax from a particular individual who has been granted immunity from it;[16] and a decree of Sounion forbids his building within the *horoi* of a new deme *agora*.[17]

The evidence as a whole indicates a possibility of duties for the demarch in three main areas—finance, religion, and law—which we may survey in turn.

(a) Finance

Despite the existence in many, perhaps most, demes of one, two, or more treasurers (*tamiai*),[18] the demarchs are nonetheless found discharging financial functions of various kinds. For example,[19] one of the earliest surviving deme decrees, from fifth-century Ikarion, requires the demarch to supervise any *antidoseis* arising from the appointment of *chorēgoi* in the deme;[20] and the accounts which are inscribed on the other side of the stone comprise a record of the funds of Dionysos and the deme's eponymous hero Ikarios[21] handed over, for six (presumably consecutive) years, by "X the demarch."[22] No *tamiai* are attested for Ikarion, and if indeed none existed we may well surmise that the duties of the Ikarians' demarch in the financial sphere were more than usually onerous.[23] Yet it does not seem to have been the case that in demes where *tamiai* or their equivalent were appointed, the demarch was necessarily freed

[14] The evidence for deme theaters will be marshalled in Chap. 7D.

[15] SEG 28.103, decree II, lines 36-38 (applying also to the *hieromnēmones*).

[16] IG II²1214, lines 26-28.

[17] IG II²1180, lines 17-21.

[18] See below, sec. B.

[19] And examples, as one must constantly remember, are all we have. (On *enechyrasia*, however, where tentative generalizations seem warranted, see below.)

[20] IG I³254, lines 3-7.

[21] For Ikarios see Chap. 2, n. 20.

[22] Compare the accounts of Nemesis of Rhamnous (IG I³248), where, however, it is *hieropoioi* (line 33) who control the money, and the demarch is mentioned only for dating purposes (lines 1-2, 15-16, 20-21, 27-28, 32-33).

[23] It may be significant in this respect that, in the fourth century at least, the demarch of Ikarion was frequently honored by his fellow demesmen: see IG II²1178, 1179, and SEG 22.117 (the last of which explicitly mentions financial expertise: lines 4-6).

thereby from financial responsibilities. Rather, demarch and treasurer(s) might work in concert, and one generally cannot separate out their individual functions.[24]

To reconstruct in simple terms a dossier of financial duties performed by every demarch in every deme is thus impossible; and if the evidence were more plentiful than it is, or more explicit, it would doubtless serve only to multiply the variations, not to iron them out into a picture of bland uniformity. On one important matter, however, assistance towards a general view is forthcoming from literary and, especially, lexicographic testimony. In setting out the general responsibilities of demarchs, the lexicographers declare that they "ἠνεχυρίαζον,"[25] that is, seized the property of debtors.[26] We know that demarchs were involved in the proceedings taken against debtors *to the state*, and this—which must be presumed to be a consequence of central legislation to that effect—will be considered later in the chapter. However, there were two other sets of circumstances in which *enechyrasia* by the demarch was possible: in debts to the deme itself, and to private individuals who sought the demarch's assistance.

The first of these circumstances is envisaged in a lease document of Aixone, from the year 346/5 (IG II²2492, lines 7-9): "if the tenants do not pay their rent, the Aixoneis shall have right of seizure (*enechyrasia*) both from the fruits of the estate and from all the other properties of the defaulter" (ἐὰν δὲ μὴ ἀποδιδῶσιν, εἶναι ἐνεχυρασίαν Αἰ|ξω-νεῦσιν καὶ ἐκ τῶν ὡραίων τῶν ἐκ τοῦ χωρίου καὶ | ἐκ τῶν ἄλλων ἁπάντων τοῦ μὴ ἀποδιδόντος). No doubt it would be the demarch who, if need be, carried this out.[27] In Demosth. 57.63-64, Euxitheos recalls his year as demarch of Halimous, during which he made enemies for himself by the forcible extraction of rents and other monies due to the

---

[24] Thus for instance two honorific decrees of Aixone direct "the demarch [who is named] and the *tamiai*" to give the honorands money to offer a sacrifice: IG II²1198, lines 13-16; AM 66, 1941, pp. 218-219, no. 1, lines 8-10. Note also IG II²1202 (also Aixone), where the same conjunction of officials is to provide the money for the honorands' crowns (lines 12-14) and also to see to the erection of the stele (lines 18-21). In IG II²1206 (?Acharnai) a standing order is imposed upon the demarch and the *tamias* together (cf. above, n. 11), yet only the demarch is to pay out for the inscription of the stele (lines 16-18). See also IG II²1176 + (Peiraieus), lines 25-27.

[25] Harpoc., δήμαρχος; Suda, δήμαρχος; schol. Aristoph. *Clouds*, line 37; cf. Hesych., δήμαρχοι and esp. δήμαρχον (which simply glosses it as τὸν ἐνεχυραστήν); Lex Seguer. V, *Lexeis Rhetorikai*, δήμαρχοι [= Bekker, *Anecd. Gr.* 1.242.16].

[26] See Finley, *Land and Credit*, p. 222, n. 6; Harrison, *Law* II, pp. 244-247.

[27] Possibly, though, with some assistance: note IG II²1183 (Myrrhinous), lines 34-35, a distribution of sacrificial meat τοῖς π[αροῦσιν κ]|αὶ συναγοράζουσιν καὶ συνενε-χυράζουσιν (with Haussoullier, *Vie*, p. 106, n. 5).

deme, and although the words *enechyrasia* and *enechyrazein* are not used, the procedure may well have been.

More common, perhaps, were bad debts between individuals,[28] and here too the demarchs were active. According to Harpocration (under δήμαρχος), "Aristophanes in *Skenas Katalambanousai* shows that demarchs used to seize the property of debtors" (ὅτι δὲ ἠνεχυρίαζον οἱ δήμαρχοι δηλοῖ Ἀριστοφάνης ἐν Σκηνὰς Καταλαμβανούσαις). But as the *Skenas Katalambanousai* is lost, we have no idea of the episode or remark which gave rise to this statement, and we must look instead to a play which does survive—the *Clouds*. Strepsiades' debts, incurred by and on behalf of his spendthrift son, are central to the plot of *Clouds*. When the play opens he has already lost lawsuits brought by some of his creditors, and others are threatening him with *enechyrasia* (lines 34-35). He later tells Sokrates that he is actually suffering it (τὰ χρήματ' ἐνεχυράζομαι, line 241). But how? When the two creditors appear, in lines 1214-1302, there is no *enechyrasia*. The first of them, accompanied by a witness, simply delivers a summons upon Strepsiades to attend court (lines 1218-1222), and the second threatens to do so (lines 1277-1278). In the opening scene, however, Strepsiades complains that his disturbed night is the result of being bitten by something in the bedclothes—some *demarch* (line 37)—"and it is a fair inference from this passage that [a demarch] had the authority to enforce the surrender of securities by a debtor to a private creditor."[29] Thus, as Haussoullier observed, as soon as Strepsiades thinks of the menace of his creditors he pictures the demarch too—even though the latter's presence might in fact be some guarantee (of orderly proceedings) for him, besides a reinforcement of the rights of his creditors.[30]

Yet the question arises: from where did the demarch's authority in this matter derive? Haussoullier assumed (without argument) that the demarch's role in *enechyrasia* was one of several "fonctions de police," both civil and religious, with which he was charged by the laws of the state.[31] While this is perfectly possible—and there can presumably be no doubt

---

[28] And the aggravation arising from them. In Aristoph. *Ekkles.* lines 565-567 Praxagora speaks thus of the advantages of the womens' utopia: μὴ λωποδυτῆσαι, μὴ φθονεῖν τοῖς πλησίον,| μὴ γυμνὸν εἶναι μὴ πένητα μηδένα,| μὴ λοιδορεῖσθαι, μὴ 'νεχυραζόμενον φέρειν; and by this last she *presumably* means safety for private debtors from seizure by their creditors.

[29] K. J. Dover, *Aristophanes: Clouds*, Oxford, 1968, p. 98 (with an inconclusive discussion of whether the correct reading is δάκνει μὲ δήμαρχός τις ἐκ τῶν στρωμάτων or τις δήμαρχος). According to the excellent scholion on the line, ἔδει οὖν τὸν δήμαρχον ἀγαγεῖν εἰς τοὺς οἴκους τοὺς ἐνεχυριαζομένους.

[30] Haussoullier, *Vie*, p. 106.

[31] See Haussoullier, *Vie*, pp. 95, 103-104, 106; cf. Harrison, *Law* II, p. 189.

that in all forms of *enechyrasia* the demarch was not exceeding the limits of his legal competence—it does not automatically follow that demarchs were, strictly speaking, the agents of the state if they accompanied and assisted private creditors in this way. At least the first of Strepsiades' two creditors in *Clouds* is a demesman of the same deme (lines 1218-1219), Kikynna (lines 134 and 210). *Conceivably*, then, a demarch's role here was restricted to debts incurred within his deme, and arose from a natural extension of the authority vested in him by his deme assembly to act against debtors to the deme as a whole.[32]

(b) Religion

The possible existence of *tamiai* or their equivalents in a deme did not, as we have seen, necessarily free the demarch of that deme from financial and fiscal responsibilities. Likewise in the sphere of religion a deme may have appointed *hieropoioi, hieromnēmones,* or *epimelētai*[33]—and the cults which it administered or helped to administer will generally have had their own priests and/or priestesses[34]—yet the demarch may still be found with religious duties to undertake, corresponding at local level to those incumbent upon many of the civil magistrates of the city itself.[35] Thus, in the testimony from or concerning individual demes we find the demarchs discharging a range of tasks such as the care of cult monies,[36] the collection of rent from sacred land out on lease,[37] the organization of the rural Dionysia,[38] and the maintenance of both the decorum and the physical fabric of temples and their precincts.[39]

[32] I hope I have made it plain that this is a tentative hypothesis only. Note, however, that both the potential debtors in IG II²2492 and the actual ones in Demosth. 57.63-64 are also *dēmotai* of the deme in question.

[33] See below, sec. B.

[34] See Chap. 7A, sec. 2.

[35] For this distinction between priests (et al.) and civil officials with religious duties, see Aristot. *Pol.* 1322b18-29 (discussed in Chap. 7A, sec. 2).

[36] IG I³253 (Ikarion).

[37] Demosth. 57.63 (Halimous).

[38] IG II²1178 (Ikarion), lines 6-8. Note also IG II²1173 (deme unknown, but *possibly* Acharnai), where the honorand, who is *probably* a demarch, has "taken care of" what has been restored as a festival!

[39] In IG II²1177 (Peiraieus) the "demarch in office" (cf. above, with n. 11), with the priestess (*sc.* of the Thesmophoroi), is to take care of the deme's Thesmophorion and to forbid improper or unseasonal use of it. The decree also mentions wood gathering (*hylasia*), which is to be dealt with under "the ancient laws on the subject" (lines 17-21). On the demarch's power, attested here, to impose fines, see Appendix 4. Note also IG II²1362 (*Lois*, no. 37), the late fourth-century edict of the priest of Apollo Erithaseos in (?)Eupyridai (see Chap. 2, n. 27), "on behalf of himself and of the demesmen and of the Athenian people" (lines 3-5). It too is concerned with *hylasia* and lays down punishments for those,

What is sufficiently widespread in these documents, however, as to be accounted common practice is a role for the demarch in offering sacrifices. We find this in Eleusis,[40] Halimous,[41] Ikarion,[42] Kollytos (probably),[43] Marathon,[44] Myrrhinous,[45] Plotheia,[46] and perhaps elsewhere.[47] In two demes—Eleusis and Myrrhinous—the demarch's task extends to distribution of the sacrificial meat;[48] and in two others—Erchia and Skambonidai—he is himself allotted special perquisites (*gera*).[49] None of this, we need suppose, was prescribed by state legislation. As the deme's chief official it was simply natural for the demarch to be involved.

(c) Law

If for any reason a deme was obliged or inclined to go to law, whether as plaintiff or defendant, it obviously needed to be represented in court by a particular individual or individuals. Provided that this person or group was acting officially in the name of the whole collectivity of the

free or slave, who are caught at it; and the fifty-drachma fine imposed upon free men (while slaves receive fifty lashes!) is to be exacted "with the demarch" (line 15). It is noteworthy that this priest twice emphasizes that he is acting "in accordance with the decree of the *boulē* and the Athenian people" (lines 12-13, 17-18); and it *may* be that we possess the decree in question in IG II²204 (from the year 352), which, *inter alia*, makes demarchs responsible, with other officials, for the holy places in their demes (lines 16-23, esp. 21). This is of course "category-*a*" evidence; see further below, sec. 2(d).

[40] *Hesp.* 8, 1939, pp. 177-180, lines 8-10: [τ]ὴν θυσίαν τῶι Δ|ιονύσωι ὑπὲρ ὑγιε[ί]ας καὶ σωτηρία|ς τῶν δημοτῶν παρ' αὑτοῦ ἔθυσεν.

[41] SEG. 2.7, lines 4-6: ἐπεμελή|(θ)η τῶν θυσιῶν ὑπὲρ τοῦ | δημάρχου Ἰσχυρίου. (N.B. θυσιῶν is the correction, suggested by several scholars when the stone was first published, for οὐσιῶν.)

[42] SEG 22.117, lines 1-2: τά τε ἱερὰ ἔθυσεν ἅπασιν τοῖς θεοῖς | [οἷς πάτριον ἦν.

[43] IG II²1195, τὸν δήμαρχον in line 11, [πό]πανα καὶ πελανο[ύς in line 12; see Haussoullier, *Vie*, p. 145, n. 3. (For Sokolowski's restorations of lines 6-13, for *Lois* no. 38, see SEG 25.145.)

[44] IG II²1358, col. II, line 23 (from which lines 1-2 are restored): τάδε ὁ δήμαρχος ὁ Μαραθωνίων θύει.

[45] IG II²1183, lines 33-34: θυέτω τὴν πληροσίαν ὁ δήμαρχος τῶ[ι] Διὶ ἀπὸ[Ͱ δραχμῶν κ]|αὶ νεμέτω τὰ κρέα.

[46] IG I³258, line 2: [δη]μάρχωι Χ; that is, a thousand drachmas (or more probably the *revenue* from it: see Chap. 6B, sec. 2) for the year's sacrifices to be offered by him (cf. line 3, [τα]μίαιν ἐς τὰ δι' ἔτος ἱερὰ Ͱ, with Haussoullier, *Vie*, p. 145).

[47] E.g. Erchia, *if* the heading Δημαρχία ἡ μέζων in the *fasti* (SEG 21.541) refers to the demarch; but see Chap. 6B, sec. 2, on this vexed question.

[48] Eleusis: IG II²1187, lines 20-23, νέμειν δὲ αὐτ|ῶι καὶ μερίδα ἐκ τῶν ἱερῶν καθά|περ Ἐλευσινίοις τὸν δήμαρχον | τὸν ἀεὶ δημαρχοῦντα (where the sacrifices are not necessarily all *performed* by the demarch himself). Myrrhinous: see above, n. 45.

[49] Erchia: SEG 21.541, E, lines 52-58 (with Dow, "Six calendars," p. 186). Skambonidai: IG I³244, A, lines 13-14 (skins).

demesmen, it is unlikely from the state's point of view that it much mattered who they were. As we saw in the preceding chapter, for example, the official response to any appeals by men voted off a deme register could apparently be presented by any five of the demesmen elected as prosecutors (*katēgoroi*) to appear before the jury-court and justify there the vote of rejection which their deme assembly had taken (?Aristot. *Ath. Pol.* 42.1). Often, no doubt, the demarch was one of the five, but we are not told that he had to be.[50]

From the standpoint of the demes themselves, nevertheless, their demarch—with or without any *syndikoi* or *synēgoroi* appointed to assist him—will generally have been the obvious choice to speak for the deme in court, just as he represented it in other ways in the context of the polis at large.[51] In a mid fourth-century decree of Peiraieus, for instance, the demarch is instructed to "take to the jury-court" (εἰσάγει[ν] εἰσστὸ δι|καστήριον) anyone who violates the sanctity of the deme's Thesmophorion.[52] A fragmentary honorific decree of Ikarion, from the same period, apparently congratulates a demarch for services performed in court cases.[53] The Aixone decree concerning arbitration by the deme assembly in disputes over pasturage rights seems also to envisage possible action in a *dikastērion*, where the deme will be represented by the demarch and *syndikoi*.[54] And from Isaeus 12 we learn that Euphiletos' first attempt to secure reinstatement in Erchia took the form of a *dikē* against "the community of the demesmen and the demarch then in office" (τῷ κοινῷ τῶν δημοτῶν καὶ τῷ τότε δημαρχοῦντι, 12.11).

Circumstantial though some of this evidence is, it probably entitles us to follow Haussoullier in assuming that it was the demarch who was the principal spokesman for his deme even in cases where we are not told this explicitly.[55] Three such cases are numbered amongst the lost speeches

---

[50] Cf. Haussoullier, *Vie*, p. 101, on the αἱρεθέντες ὑπὸ τῶν δημοτῶν κατήγοροι Νεοκλέους of IG II²1205, Epikephisia (who perhaps acted in such a case: see Chap. 4, n. 81).

[51] Haussoullier, *Vie*, p. 101.

[52] IG II²1177, lines 13-17. The phrase εἰσάγειν εἰς τὸ δικαστήριον seems to be used "only in a loose sense" here (Harrison, *Law* II, p. 36 with n. 3; cf. Busolt/Swoboda, *Staatskunde*, p. 966), that is, meaning *not* introducing the case as presiding magistrate but simply bringing the prosecution (cf. Demosth. 24.10); but for the contrary view, see Hansen, "Archai," p. 173, n. 56.

[53] IG II²1179, lines 3-4: ἐπιμελεῖται|[ι τῶν Ἰκαριέων? ἐν τ]αῖς δίκαις (with demarch in lines 2-3).

[54] IG II²1196 (see Chap. 4, pp. 113-114), line 2, δικαστηρίωι; line 4, τὸν δήμαρχον Δωρ[–; line 9, πρὶν εἰσάγεσθαι εἰς τὸ δικαστήριον; line 17, –]ον καὶ οἱ σύνδικοι καί; lines 18-19, δήμαρχος μετὰ τῶν συν|[δίκων; lines 21-22 εἰσαγ]όντων [εἰ]ς δι[κ]|[αστήριον; line 22, τῶ]ι δημάρχω[ι].

[55] Haussoullier, *Vie*, p. 101.

of the fourth-century orators. One is Isaeus' *Against the demesmen concerning an estate* (Πρὸς τοὺς δημότας περὶ χωρίου), mentioned both by Dionysius of Halicarnassus (*Isaios* 10) and also by Harpocration in his entry for the deme Sphettos (from which we may infer that the Sphettians were the "demesmen" involved). Its exordium is preserved by Dionysius and reveals that Isaeus' client, a youngish man (νεώτερος ὤν), was prosecuting the members of his own deme; and Dionysius himself explains that the "estate" at issue had been offered to the deme as a pledge—he does not say whether for a lease or for a loan—and now seized.[56] In the two other cases the deme, and the demarch on its behalf, is described by Haussoullier as plaintiff instead of defendant,[57] though in point of fact both were *diadikasiai*, "where there is no defendant or plaintiff and the function of the court is simply to decide which of the parties before it has the better right to a thing or to escape from a duty."[58] The titles of the two lost speeches—both by Dinarchus—are Διαδικασία Ἀθμονεῦσι περὶ τῆς μυρρίνης καὶ τῆς μίλακος and Διαδικασία Φαληρέων πρὸς Φοίνικας ὑπὲρ τῆς ἱερωσύνης τοῦ Ποσειδῶνος. We thus know the identity of the demes concerned, Athmonon and Phaleron, and we can deduce that both cases arose out of religious disputes; the rest is conjecture.[59]

2. THE DEMARCH AS AGENT OF THE STATE

We have so far attempted to define and illustrate the chief areas of activity in which an individual demarch might operate, mostly within his deme but sometimes outside it, as agent or representative of his own deme assembly. It has not always proved easy to employ in practice the distinction of principle between "category-*a*" and "category-*b*" evidence, for two reasons: whether a particular duty was discharged, ultimately, in the name of the deme or of the state is not clear in every instance;[60] and, more important, it *is* clear that some of every demarch's most essential functions had a dual significance and authority, that is, they were laid down in broad outline by city legislation but implemented (and varied) in detail by the individual deme assemblies. The plainest example of this, as we have seen, was the demarch's actual dealings with the deme assembly itself, including his maintenance of its records of membership; and no more need be said of that here. Instead we may turn to the evidence

---

[56] See further Haussoullier, *Vie*, pp. 98-99.
[57] Haussoullier, *Vie*, p. 99.
[58] Harrison, *Law* II, pp. 79-80; cf. MacDowell, *Law*, pp. 145-146.
[59] For which see Haussoullier, *Vie*, pp. 100-101.
[60] Witness for instance the discussion above, in sec. 1(a), of *enechyrasia* for private debts.

of how the demarchs also acted, in effect, as one hundred and thirty-nine local agents of the central government.

(a) Apographai

According to the lexicographers, demarchs "used to make the *apographai* of the estates in each deme" (τὰς ἀπογραφὰς ἐποιοῦντο τῶν ἐν ἑκάστῳ δήμῳ χωρίων).[61] Earlier scholars, including Haussoullier, took this to mean the maintenance of a permanent land-register, which they regarded as an obvious desideratum in any case; but, as M. I. Finley showed, the necessity for such a cadaster is illusory, and the *apographai* were in fact publicly declared inventories, as and when they were required, of property forfeit to the state.[62]

A well-known instance of this occurred in the year 411, when Archeptolemos and Antiphon were convicted of treachery, and the demarchs of their demes—Agryle and Rhamnous, respectively—were instructed to "declare" their property.[63] Epigraphic sources provide further examples. A few years earlier than the case of Archeptolemos and Antiphon came the double scandal of the profanation of the Mysteries and the mutilation of the Hermai; and in the so-called Attic Stelai of 415-413, listing the confiscated property of the culprits, there are five instances of demarchs making *apographai*.[64] Twelve years later, in 402/1, as Michael Walbank has recently established, there was a grand confiscation and sale by the *pōlētai* of the real property of the Thirty Tyrants and their adherents, with *apographai* by eight demarchs in what survives of the series of stelai.[65] Another example occurs in the records of sales by the *pōlētai* in

---

[61] Harpoc., δήμαρχος; Suda, δήμαρχος; schol. Aristoph. *Clouds*, line 37. See also *Etym. Magn.* 265.20 (ἀπεγράφετο τὰς οὐσίας ἑκάστῳ πρὸς τὰ δημόσια ὀφλήματα); cf. *Lex Seguer.* V, *Lexeis Rhetorikai*, δήμαρχος [= Bekker, *Anecd. Gr.* 1.237.8]. According to *Lex Seguer.* V, *Lexeis Rhetorikai*, ἀπογράφειν [= Bekker, *Anecd. Gr.* 1.199.5], the action was taken by ὁ δήμαρχος σὺν τοῖς βουλευταῖς; see Chap. 2, n. 98.

[62] Finley, *Land and Credit*, pp. 13-14, esp. nn. 19-20. See also Harrison, *Law* II, pp. 186, 211-212.

[63] [Plut.] *Vit. X Or.* (Antiphon) 834A-B: τὼ δὲ δημάρχω ἀποφῆναι τὴν οὐσίαν αὐτοῖν. The document as a whole is generally taken to be genuine: Müller, *de demis*, pp. 1-2; cf. D. M. Lewis in *Ancient Society and Institutions: studies presented to Victor Ehrenberg*, Oxford, 1966, p. 183 with n. 40.

[64] IG I³425, col. II, lines 23, 26-27, 30-31, 41, 44.

[65] See in detail Walbank, "Confiscation." He observes on pp. 95-96 that "whether the rubric of Stele III can be taken as typical of the whole series is a moot point, but in every case where both the deme of the denouncer and the location of the property are known, they are the same, so that the implication is that in every case the demarch was responsible for the denunciation." The rubric of Stele III is ο]ἰκίαι ἃς οἱ δήμ[αρχοι ἀπέγραψαν], which might in fact justify an assumption that other denouncers were somewhere involved; nonetheless I tentatively follow Walbank in presuming that "all denunciations were handled by the demarchs."

ca. 350.[66] Obviously the demarchs were called on for this procedure because they were "the local officials who could be expected to know who owned what in their deme";[67] and we shall see further instances below of this same local knowledge being put to use.[68]

(b) Eisphorai

In his recent book *Wealth and the Power of Wealth in Classical Athens*, John Davies has offered the thesis that, until the reforms of 378/7 and their creation of the symmory system (Philochorus, *FGrH* 328 F41), *eisphorai* were collected locally in the demes by the demarchs.[69] His argument is circumstantial, but compelling. The author of the Aristotelian *Ath. Pol.*, at any rate, believed that Kleisthenes had given the demarchs this duty;[70] there is no evidence, before 378/7, for any other machinery; yet there *is* evidence that other financial tasks on behalf of central government were performed locally by demarchs "in a way exactly analogous to that which we would have to posit for them if they were the local administrative officers for the eisphora."[71] Collection by demarchs from their fellow demesmen will have been both a natural and an efficient system until the later fifth and fourth centuries, when (as Davies observes) the emergence of a more complex economic pattern—changes of residence, fragmentation of estates, and increased "invisible property" (ἀφανὴς οὐσία)—necessitated the adoption of a nonterritorial approach.

If all this is as sound as it appears to be, then Davies must be accounted equally justified in his interpretation of one of the provisions of Aristophon's naval decree of 362. The clause is paraphrased thus by Apollodoros in [Demosth.] 50.8: "you resolved that ⟨the demarchs and⟩ the *bouleutai*, on behalf of the demesmen, should declare the names of those,

---

[66] *Hesp.* 15, 1946, pp. 185-187, no. 32, line 25: [οἱ δήμαρ]χοι ἀπέγ[ραφον – –].

[67] D. M. Lewis, *loc. cit.* (above, n. 63).

[68] It may be noted here *faute de mieux* that at least three demarchs (16, 35, 47) also appear, selling pieces of land in their demes, in the intractable *rationes centesimarum* (ἑκατοστή) documents from the last quarter of the fourth century; see in general D. M. Lewis in M. I. Finley, ed., *Problèmes de la terre en Grèce ancienne*, Paris and The Hague, 1973, pp. 187-212; also Osborne, *Demos*, pp. 56-59.

[69] Davies, *Wealth*, pp. 143-150.

[70] See ?Aristot. *Ath. Pol.* 21.5 (Kleisthenes' demarchs given the same *epimeleia* as "the previous *naukraroi*") with 8.3 (ἦν δ᾽ ἐπὶ τῶν ναυκραριῶν ἀρχὴ καθεστηκυῖα ναύκραροι, τεταγμένη πρός τε τὰς εἰσφορὰς καὶ τὰς δαπάνας τὰς γιγνομένας). It is of course possible that *eisphorai* in 8.3 simply means revenue in general; cf. Rhodes, *Commentary*, p. 153.

[71] Davies, *Wealth*, p. 147, citing the decrees concerning the first-fruits for Eleusis (IG I³78) and the levy for Apollo Lykeios (IG I³138); for both, see below, sec. 2(d).

both demesmen and *enkektēmenoi*,[72] who were to pay the *proeisphora*."[73] Expanding a suggestion of J. H. Lipsius, Davies takes Apollodoros' description of what was involved here as a "*proeisphora*" to be misleading, and probably deliberately so. Aristophon's aim seems to have been to circumvent the exemption rules against two simultaneous liturgies—in this case *proeisphora* and trierarchy—which would otherwise have hamstrung either the naval or the financial preparations for the despatch of the fleet (50.4-7). Be that as it may, what was authorized was in effect a return, presumably temporarily, to the old deme-based system of *eisphora* collection, and a protagonist's role for the demarchs therein.

(c) Naval Conscription

Aristophon's decree of 362 (above) also made provision for the levying of naval manpower for the expedition. Apollodoros' paraphrase runs thus: "you voted that the trierarchs launch the ships and convey them to the jetty, and that the *bouleutai* and the demarchs make lists of the demesmen and submit (lists of) sailors."[74]

As Davies rightly comments, "the provision that the levy of man-power should be carried out through the demarchs and the Councillors is a notable departure from the usual procedure."[75] The fact that it had to be spelled out in the decree at all is arguably proof enough of this, but in any case we know that from at least the later fifth century onwards, the "usual procedure" was for the trierarchs themselves to make up their crews by recruitment of volunteers,[76] by no means all of whom would be Athenian citizens;[77] and there is no call to visualize any role for the demes or their officials in this process.

What is much less clear-cut, however, is whether—as many scholars have inferred—the procedure created by Aristophon's decree remained

[72] For the *enkektēmenoi*, see Chap. 3B.

[73] [Demosth.] 50.8: δόξαν γὰϱ ὑμῖν ὑπὲϱ τῶν δημοτῶν ⟨τοὺς δημάϱχους καί, Meier⟩ τοὺς βουλευτὰς ἀπενεγκεῖν τοῖς πϱοεισοίσουσας τῶν τε δημοτῶν καὶ τῶν ἐγκεκιη-μένων. (Note that in Davies' translation of 50.8-9, in *Wealth*, p. 143, one or more lines, including this key phrase, have fallen out.) Meier's supplement, accepted by Gernet in the Budé edition though not by Rennie in the Oxford text, is surely correct, since in 50.6 both demarchs and councillors are to draw up the lists of sailors (see below, sec. 2(c)); and in general it has been fairly assumed that 50.6-8 refer to the same decree, attributed to Aristophon in 50.6.

[74] [Demosth.] 50.6: ἐψηφίσασθε τάς τε ναῦς καθέλκειν τοὺς τϱιηϱάϱχους καὶ παϱακομίζειν ἐπὶ τὸ χῶμα, καὶ τοὺς βουλευτὰς καὶ τοὺς δημάϱχους καταλόγους ποιεῖσθαι τῶν δημοτῶν καὶ ἀποφέϱειν ναύτας. (For παϱακομίζειν ἐπὶ τὸ χῶμα, cf. Tod no. 200, lines 184-186.)

[75] Davies, *Wealth*, p. 144.

[76] Lysias 21.10; Demosth. 21.154.

[77] On the composition of the crews, see in brief Whitehead, *Metic*, pp. 84-86.

the standard one thereafter.[78] Certainly it was a far from satisfactory one if Apollodoros is to be believed. He claims that in his own case, when "the sailors listed by the demesmen" (οἱ ναῦται οἱ καταλεγέντες ὑπὸ τῶν δημοτῶν) did not materialize, save for a group inadequate in number and unacceptable in quality, he was obliged to hire his own crew in the traditional way ([Demosth.] 50.7)—only to see most of them later desert (50.16). So did the Athenians persist with this system? In plain terms we do not know, but may doubt it. Conscription as such, rather than volunteer recruitment, was evidently more common in and from the 350s than ever before, and perhaps even the norm (cf. Isoc. 8.48, Demosth. 4.36). Furthermore it is deducible from Demosth. 21.155 that Periandros' law of 357 which established the trierarchic symmories also laid down, or else entailed as a corollary, that the state provided the crews (πληρώμαθ' ἡ πόλις παρέχει). But how? Not necessarily by the deme-based procedure of Aristophon's decree, and indeed not necessarily by the same procedure every time. The crews did not always consist of Athenian citizens (see Demosth. 4.36); and even when they did, wholly or partially, the levy may still have been made centrally by the generals, either exercising a right of direct access to the *lēxiarchika grammateia*[79] or else relying on the local knowledge of the demarchs.

(d) Religion

Besides the religious duties imposed upon an individual demarch by his deme assembly, it is clear from a small but significant body of evidence, largely epigraphic, that all demarchs were required to discharge religious responsibilities, regularly or from time to time, on behalf of the state as a whole. They may be divided into (1) those which the demarch performed, initially at least, within his own deme and (2) those where the bulk of his work lay outside it.[80]

[78] Thus e.g. Haussoullier, *Vie*, pp. 119-120; Schoeffer, "Demarchoi," col. 2709; Busolt/ Swoboda, *Staatskunde*, p. 969 with n. 4; M. Amit, *Athens and the Sea: a study in Athenian sea-power*, Collection Latomus 74, Brussels, 1965, p. 48, cf. 35-38. Müller, *de demis*, pp. 28-29 was, typically, more circumspect; his belief, however, that a distinction is drawn in [Demosth.] 50.6 between hoplite *katalogoi* and lists of sailors is ruled out by the phrase οἱ ναῦται οἱ καταλεγέντες ὑπὸ τῶν δημοτῶν in 50.7; cf. M. H. Hansen, SO 56, 1981, p. 32, n. 24.

[79] One is naturally reluctant to cite the Troizen "Decree of Themistokles" (ML no. 23) in support of an argument which is in any case speculative, but note lines 27-30: ἀνα-γράψα[ι δὲ κα[ὶ τοὺς ἄλλους κατὰ] ναῦν τοὺς στρατηγοὺς εἰς λ]ευκώ[ματα, τοὺς μὲν Ἀ]θηναίους ἐκ τῶν ληξιαρχικῶν γρ]αμματεί[ων, κτλ. See on this M. H. Jameson, *Historia* 12, 1963, pp. 398-399, rightly stressing the uniqueness of this *total*, emergency conscription. For the levy of *hoplites* ἐκ καταλόγου by the generals, cf. Lysias 9.4 and 14.6.

[80] It is not certain in which of these categories one should place IG I³141, a city decree

1. The most important document here is a city decree of 352 which charges not only a series of city officials (including the *boulē*) and "those whom the law prescribes in each case" but also "the demarchs" with the permanent care, thereafter, of all holy places (*hiera*).[81] As I suggested earlier,[82] we *may* possess an instance of local reinforcement of this in the edict of the priest of Apollo Erithaseos in (?)Eupyridai, who declares, "in accordance with the decree of the *boulē* and the Athenian people," that he will fine, "with the demarch," any free man who gathers wood in the *hieron* and report his name to the king-archon (IG II²1362). On the other hand it is obviously quite possible that the priest is referring to some other decree, perhaps more specific and more recent. Certainly we may well suppose that there were a number of laws or decrees, enacted at various times, under which demarchs were either empowered or obliged to enforce law and order in a religious context.[83]

We have already noted the distribution of *theōrika* in the deme assemblies ([Demosth.] 44.37), which must in practice have meant distribution by the demarchs.[84] That the demarchs were also asked to *collect* either money or other contributions from their fellow demesmen is attested in two inscriptions from the second half of the fifth century. IG I³138, a city decree of (?)ca. 440,[85] imposed a modest tax upon the Athenian land forces—cavalry, hoplites, and archers—to be collected, in the case of those enrolled in the *lēxiarchika grammateia*, by the demarchs;[86] they were to deliver it to two treasurers of Apollo Lykeios (chosen by and

on a religious subject dating from some time between 440 and 425; the fragmentary line 31 reads [. . . . . .²⁵. . . . . β]ολὲς· τὸς δὲ δεμά[ρχος – – – –].

[81] IG II²204 (*Lois* no. 32), lines 16-23: ἐπι]μελεῖσθαι [δ]ὲ τῆς ἱερᾶς ὀργάδος καὶ τῶν ἄλλω|[ν ἱερῶν ἁπάντ]ων τῶν Ἀθήνησιν ἀπὸ τῆσδε τῆς ἡμέρας εἰς τὸν | [ἀεὶ χρόνον οὕ]ς τε ὁ νόμος κελεύει περὶ ἑκάστου αὐτῶν καὶ τ|[ὴν βουλὴν τὴν] ἐ[ξ] Ἀρείου πάγου καὶ τὸν στρατηγὸν τὸν ἐπὶ τὴ|[ν φυλακὴ]ν τῆς χ]ώρας κεχειροτο-νημένον καὶ τοὺς περιπολά|[ρχ]ους καὶ τοὺς [δη]μάρχους καὶ τὴν βουλὴν τὴν ἀεὶ βουλεύου|[σαν] καὶ τῶν ἄλλ[ων Ἀθηναίων τὸμ βουλόμενον τρόπωι ὅτωι ἂν | [ἐπ]ίστω[ν]ται.

[82] See above, n. 39.

[83] On IG II²1177 (Peiraieus) see above, n. 39. I am tempted to think that the mysterious line ὑπέλυσε δήμαρχός τις ἐλθὼν εἰς χορόν, from an unknown play of the fifth-century comic poet Pherecrates (fr. 171) might refer to the demarch's role in "policing" cults and festivals; for a full discussion, see Chap. 11A.

[84] See Chap. 4, p. 110.

[85] The new corpus text has been prepared by M. H. Jameson; for his excellent discussion (on which I rely here) of all aspects of the inscription and the cult with which it is connected, see *Archaiognosia* 1, 1980, pp. 213-236; note, however, that the text printed there is faulty (see SEG 30.5).

[86] IG I³138, lines 5-7: ἐκπραττόντον δὲ ℎοι δέμαρ[χοι παρὰ ἁπάντον τὸν] | ἐς τὸ λεχσιαρχικὸν γρ(α)μματ[εῖον γραφέντον, οἱ δ]|[ὲ] τόχσαρχοι παρὰ τὸν τοχσοτ[ὸν. Collection by the *toxarchoi* was necessary because some of the archers were foreign mercenaries; see Jameson, *Archaiognosia*, 1, 1980, pp. 217-218, 222-223.

from the *bouleutai*) for the upkeep of that god's *temenos*. The levy was
to be an annual one (line 4), but we do not know for how many years
it lasted. And the demarchs also figure in IG I³78, the city decree concerning first-fruits for Eleusis, of (?)ca. 422.[87] "In accordance with tradition and the oracle from Delphi," all Athenian farmers were required
to set aside *aparchai* of both wheat and barley for the Eleusinian Goddesses; the demarchs were to collect them in their own demes and hand
them over to *hieropoioi*, who had to make a record of what they received
from each individual demarch on behalf of his deme. Again, how long
this system remained in operation is not known. The accounts of the
aparchai received a century later, in 329/8, list totals for the ten tribes,
but that in itself is no indication that the system of actual collection by
the demarchs had by then been discontinued.[88]

2. The collection of both the tax for Apollo Lykeios and the *aparchai*
for the Goddesses involved the demarchs in acting first in their own demes
and then, to deliver what they had collected to other officials, going
outside them. Furthermore, both of these duties—and any others like
them—were little different in character from the demarchs' exaction of
eisphorai, in that they will have tended to emphasize a psychological gulf
between the demarch, appearing as the agent of the state, and the rest
of the demesmen, passively submitting to the authority thereby vested in
him. To counterbalance this, however, there were other, regular occasions
when the feelings universally engendered between demarchs and their
fellow *dēmotai* must have been those of solidarity and communal celebration. In the organization of most of the great city festivals there are
no grounds for supposing that any account was taken of the demes as
such or of their demarchs *ex officio*, but to this there was one probable
exception, the Hephaisteia,[89] and another certain (and very important)
one—the Panathenaia.

It was the demarchs, according to the Suda lexicon (under δήμαρχοι),
who "marshalled the festival of the Panathenaia" (διεκόσμουν τὴν
ἑορτὴν τῶν Παναθηναίων). Although this information appears in more
accurate and intelligible form in the scholion to Aristophanes' *Clouds*,

---

[87] IG I³78 (ML no. 73; *Lois* no. 5), lines 8-30, esp. 8-10: ἐγλέγεν δὲ [τὸς δ]εμ|άρχος
κατὰ τὸς δέμος καὶ παραδιδόναι τοῖς ἱεροποιοῖς τοῖς | Ἐλευσινόθεν Ἐλευ-
σῖνάδε.

[88] See IG II²1672, lines 263-271. IG II²140 (*Lois, Suppl.* no. 13) is a resolution of the
nomothetai, from 353/2, which amends "the law of Chairemonides" on the *aparchai*, but
no mention is made of demes or demarchs.

[89] The Hephaisteia regulations of 421/0 (IG I³82; *Lois*, no. 13) include the contextless
line 12: [. . . . . . .¹⁶. . . . . . . .τ]οῖς δεμότεσι ἐγ [. . . . . .³¹. . . . .].
On the document (and festival) as a whole, see Parke, *Festivals*, pp. 171-172.

line 37—the demarchs "marshalled the *procession* (τὴν πομπήν rather than τὴν ἑορτήν) of the Panathenaia"[90]—it is hard to tell, even so, exactly what the demarchs' duties amounted to. The components of the procession were many and various,[91] and it would seem improbable that it was the demarchs who "marshalled" all of them. Nor is it clear whether we are being told about the Great (quadrennial) or the Lesser (annual) Panathenaia.[92] However, on the assumption that the two celebrations differed more in scale than in substance,[93] it is perhaps reasonable to invoke for further guidance the city decree of ca. 355/4 which made regulations for the annual festival. There the *hieropoioi* are ordered to distribute the sacrificial meat "to the Athenian people in the Kerameikos, just as in the other distributions of meat," and to "assign the portions to each deme in accordance with the numbers of those in the procession which each deme provides."[94] Thus the individual demes apparently determined for themselves the size of their contingents to take part in the procession and to share in the ensuing sacrifice. Perhaps the demes' officials were always expected to do so *ex officio*, together with any other demesmen who cared to make the journey;[95] and the demarchs' *diakosmēsis* was doubtless necessary not only for the ordering of the procession but also to assist the *hieropoioi* in identifying by deme those who were to be allotted their meat.[96]

(e) Burial of the Dead

With the exception of those ceremonially interred by the state, burying the dead was the duty, both moral and legal, of their relatives—or in the case of slaves, their masters. If they failed in this, however, the law required the demarchs to take action. The procedure is laid down in one of a number of *nomoi* (and other documents) preserved in [Demosthenes] 43:[97]

---

[90] For the phrase cf. Thuc. 1.20.2, the murder of Hipparchos τὴν Παναθηναϊκὴν πομπὴν διακοσμοῦντι.

[91] See Parke, *Festivals*, pp. 37-45.

[92] J. A. Davison, *JHS* 78, 1958, pp. 23, 31-33, contended that in official documents (i.e., inscriptions) there is no instance "in which Παναθήναια alone necessarily, or even probably, refers to anything other than the great Panathenaea." Be that as it may, one cannot feel the same certainty about the usage of lexicographers and scholiasts.

[93] Cf. Parke, *Festivals*, p. 47.

[94] IG II²334 (*Lois*, no. 33), lines 24-27 (of what is now fragment B: see D. M. Lewis, *Hesp.* 28, 1959, pp. 239-247).

[95] Cf. Haussoullier, *Vie*, p. 129: "le démarque paraît donc à la tête de ses démotes, entouré de tous les magistrats et prêtres du dème."

[96] Cf. Haussoullier, *Vie*, p. 129, n. 3.

[97] [Demosth.] 43.57-58: τοὺς δ' ἀπογιγνομένους ἐν τοῖς δήμοις, οὓς ἂν μηδεὶς

If nobody takes up (for burial) those who die in the demes, let the demarch give notice to the relatives to take them up and bury them and to purify the deme, on the day of decease in each case. As regards slaves he shall give notice to the master, and as regards free men to those in possession of the property; and if the deceased had no property, he shall give notice to the deceased's relatives. If, after the demarch has given notice, the relatives do not take up (the body and bury it), let the demarch contract for the taking-up and burial and for the purification of the deme on the same day, at the lowest possible price;[98] and if he does not (so) contract, he shall owe a thousand drachmas to the public treasury. Whatever he spends (on this) he shall exact double from those liable; and if he does not exact it, he shall himself owe it to the demesmen.

The two equally important objectives of this law are made clear, as Haussoullier noted, by repetition. The dead must receive their last rites (and rights), and the deme must be purified from the taint of a corpse— both without delay.[99] Moreover, the responsibilities imposed upon the demarch are considerable. If he fails to ensure that the relatives do their private duty (as the law seems to expect), the problem thereby becomes a public one. To resolve it, the state compels him to act—and will fine him heavily if he does not—by spending his deme's money. That is a step which he would normally take only on the authorization of his deme assembly, and as if to recompense them for this usurpation of their authority, the demesmen may look to their demarch to exact twice what he has spent. If he fails in this too, however, the law allows the deme to regard him as personally liable for the reimbursement. The whole procedure is a fascinating paradigm of the demarch's Janus-like position in such matters, intermediate between deme and polis.

ἀναιρῆται, ἐπαγγελλέτω ὁ δήμαρχος τοῖς προσήκουσιν ἀναιρεῖν καὶ θάπτειν καὶ καθαίρειν τὸν δῆμον, τῇ ἡμέρᾳ ᾗ ἂν ἀπογένηται ἕκαστος αὐτῶν. ἐπαγγέλλειν δὲ περὶ μὲν τῶν δούλων τῷ δεσπότῃ, περὶ δὲ τῶν ἐλευθέρων τοῖς τὰ χρήματ' ἔχουσιν· ἐὰν δὲ μὴ ᾖ χρήματα τῷ ἀποθανόντι, τοῖς προσήκουσι τοῦ ἀποθανόντος ἐπαγγέλλειν. ἐὰν δὲ τοῦ δημάρχου ἐπαγγείλαντος μὴ ἀναιρῶνται οἱ προσήκοντες, ὁ μὲν δήμαρχος ἀπομισθωσάτω ἀνελεῖν καὶ καταθάψαι καὶ καθῆραι τὸν δῆμον αὐθημερόν, ὅπως ἂν δύνηται ὀλιγίστου· ἐὰν δὲ μὴ ἀπομισθώσῃ, ὀφειλέτω χιλίας δραχμὰς τῷ δημοσίῳ. ὅ τι δ' ἂν ἀναλώσῃ, διπλάσιον πραξάσθω παρὰ τῶν ὀφειλόντων· ἐὰν δὲ μὴ πράξῃ, αὐτὸς ὀφειλέτω τοῖς δημόταις. There seems no good reason to doubt the authenticity of this law; cf. Müller, de demis, pp. 54-56.

[98] See IG II²1672, line 119, for the removal of a corpse from "the Raria" (cf. line 257, lease of it) by a metic paid to do so.

[99] See Haussoulier, Vie, pp. 108-109. S. C. Humphreys, JHS 100, 1980, p. 98, hazards the attractive guess that the law was passed "as a result of the experiences of the plague in 430."

*

With such duties as these, recurrent or occasional, the demarch was ensured of a busy year in office.[100] Circumscribed though his powers of initiative were by the control both of his own deme assembly and of the organs of state, it is, one may say, entirely understandable that under the developed democratic constitution such an official should have been appointed by lot and not by election.[101] Perhaps, also, a man could serve as demarch only once in his life, on the model of the great majority of the city offices (?Aristot. *Ath. Pol.* 62.3). At any rate no instances of iteration are known. On the other hand, certain basic aptitudes—not least, literacy—were essential for the performance of the job at all;[102] for, whatever assistance they received at times from other officials, the demarchs discharged the core of their responsibilities single-handed. It would thus seem improbable that the appointment was made by simple sortition amongst the whole body of demesmen in any deme. Rather, either by some formal process of preselection (*prokrisis*)[103] or else by informal, mutually agreed exclusion of those likely to prove incompetent, we may surmise that the pool of genuine candidates was distilled down to those willing and able (οἱ βουλόμενοι καὶ δυνάμενοι) and the lots were cast between them.

B. Other Officials

To turn from the demarch to other deme officials[104] is to encounter a quite different methodological dilemma. With the demarchs there is a high degree of standardization in their activities in all demes, as a reflection of the extent to which they all received a common mandate from the state. It is on such a basis that one attempts to distinguish the evidence for this—the "category *a*" evidence—from the data concerning any individual demarch's duties in and for his own deme only. As regards all

---

[100] That Euboulides was simultaneously demarch of Halimous and one of its *bouleutai* (Chap. 4, n. 11) is remarkable—unless he was the villain he is made out to be!

[101] See Damsgaard-Madsen, "Démarques" (and above, Chap. 4, n. 153).

[102] Cf. Haussoullier, *Vie*, p. 130: "il faut qu'il écrive couramment, qu'il ait l'intelligence et l'habitude des affaires." Haussoullier's whole peroration on the demarchy (*Vie*, pp. 130-133) is well worth reading, though an unsound prosopographical basis (see above, Chap. 4, n. 153) led him to fix the socioeconomic status level of demarchs too high, and to regard them accordingly as men filling local office as a stepping-stone to higher things; see on this Chap. 10B, sec. 3.

[103] Cf. Schoeffer, "Demoi," cols. 16-17.

[104] For the term "officials" see above, n. 2.

other deme officials, however, the data belong entirely in "category *b*," originating from and relating to one particular deme or another, and this forces our approach to be, if not nihilistic, at least severely empirical. We simply cannot assume that an office existed in any deme besides those in which it is expressly attested. And it may not even be the case that an official with the same name in different demes performed the same functions in each, beyond any *general* indications conveyed by this title. From the state's point of view the principle was evidently *laisser faire*: the demes could appoint whatever officials they liked, to assume whatever responsibilities they saw fit.

As the extreme illustration of this, several posts—none of them outlandish ones, to all appearances—are known from only a single deme:

1. *?Acharnai.* In IG II²1206, lines 12-16, a secretary (*grammateus*)[105] is charged with the task of having the decree inscribed on stone and set up in the *hieron* of Athena Hippia.[106] (Elsewhere other officials, sometimes the demarch, do this;[107] here the demarch is mentioned, but his job is to disburse the necessary twenty drachmas.)

2. *Aixone.* In IG II²1196, lines 17-18, the arbitration procedure for disputes concerning pasturage rights[108] mentions advocates (*syndikoi*), of unspecified number, working in conjunction with the demarch; and *syndikoi* are also, it would seem, the honorands in the acephalous IG II²1197.[109]

3. *Athmonon.* In IG II²1203, six named individuals designated as "the *merarchai* of the year of the archon Antikles" (οἱ μεράρχαι οἱ ἐπ' Ἀντικλείους [325/4] ἄρχοντος) are praised and crowned by the deme for their zeal and efficiency in supervising sacrifices and discharging other public duties.

4. *Kytheros.* In IG II²2496, deme property is leased out by eight named individuals designed as "the *meritai* of (the) Kytherioi" (Κυθηρίων οἱ μερῖται).

5. *Myrrhinous.* In IG II²1182, lines 21-25, the sum of thirty drachmas

---

[105] Osborne, *Demos*, p. 235, n. 34 wrongly sees a deme *grammateus* in IG II²1195, lines 1-2; the first five lines of the stele, before the deme decree of Kollytos begins, belong to the end of a city decree.

[106] There is a problem with the IG restoration of lines 13-14, τὸν γραμ[μ]|[ατέα μετὰ τ]ῶν δημοτῶν: how can the demesmen *in general* do this "with the secretary"? Neither τὸν γραμ[μ]|[ατεύοντα τ]ῶν δημοτῶν nor τὸν γραμ[μ]|[ατιστὴν τ]ῶν δημοτῶν seem very convincing alternatives; perhaps, rather, one may simply substitute ὑπέρ for μετά.

[107] See Chap. 4, n. 50.

[108] See Chap. 4, pp. 113-114.

[109] Note lines 12-14: εἶναι αὐτοῖς τὰς αὐτὰς [δωρεὰ]|ς ὅσαιπερ καὶ τοῖς συνδί-κοι[ς] | τοῖς περὶ Λάχητα. This formula *might* indicate that the *syndikoi* had some sort of chief or chairman, but is perhaps more likely to be simply an informal, nontechnical way of referring to a particular group of *syndikoi* in terms of its best-known member.

for the inscription of the stele is to be apportioned by (or between?) "Pheidippos and the *antigrapheus* Meixias" (lines 23-24). Haussoullier took Pheidippos to be the demarch,[110] but as he is not so called, this is unconvincing. More probably he is the honorand of the decree, who has held some unnamed financial office, possibly *tamias*.[111] Meixias' position, that of *antigrapheus*, is also evidently financial, but its relationship with the post held by Pheidippos is not made clear.[112]

We may note also the Myrrhinousian "reckoner" (*logistēs*) in IG II²1183, lines 13-14. Although some sort of *euthynai* procedure must have been devised and operated by most demes,[113] this is again the sole appearance of this particular official, charged with calculating expenditure therein.

6. *Peiraieus.* In IG II²1177, lines 21-24, the task of inscribing and erecting the inscription goes to "the *horistai* with the demarch" (lines 22-23). The name of these officials (of unknown number) obviously suggests duties concerned with the fixing or defining of boundaries (*horoi*),[114] but why they were needed here is not at all certain.[115]

On the other hand several *titles*, at least, do recur:

1. *Kēryx* (herald). This post—perhaps a long-term one—is attested in seven demes: Aixone,[116] Erchia,[117] Halai Araphenides,[118] Ikarion,[119] Peiraieus,[120] Phrearrhioi,[121] and Rhamnous.[122] In four instances the herald's duty is that of proclaiming the award of an honorific decree,[123] and, in one case, summoning the recipient of a grant of *proedria* to take his

---

[110] Haussoullier, *Vie*, p. 80.

[111] See lines 4-11: εἶν[αι] | [δ'α]ὐτῶι καὶ τῶν λοιπῶν χϱ[η]|[μ]άτων ἐπιμεληθέν[τ]ι τῆς [ἀ]|[π]οδόσεως ὑπὲϱ τῶν δημοτώ|[ν] εὑϱέσθα[ι] τι ἀγαθὸν παϱὰ |[τ]ῶν δημοτῶν καθότι τιμηθ[ή]σεται ἀξίως τῶν εὐεϱγετ[ημ]άτων.

[112] For conjecture as to the functions of this *antigrapheus*, see Haussoullier, *Vie*, p. 80. (For the city's *antigrapheus*, see Rhodes, *Commentary*, p. 601.)

[113] See Chap. 4, pp. 116-119.

[114] Cf. Chap. 1, n. 107.

[115] In other deme decrees of Peiraieus this task is given to the demarch and *tamiai* (IG II²1176+, lines 25-27) or else, implicitly, the demarch alone (IG II²1214, lines 36-38).

[116] IG II²1199, lines 20-22: Charikles the herald praised and crowned, with others, φιλοτιμίας ἕνεκα τῆς πεϱὶ τὴν παννυχίδα.

[117] SEG 21.541, E, lines 47-58: herald to sacrifice a ram to Hermes on 4 Thargelion, and to receive τὰ γέϱα.

[118] AE 1932, *Chronika*, pp. 30-32, lines 14-24: herald to announce an honorific award at the Tauropolia festival and to summon the honorand to take up his *proedria*.

[119] IG II²1178, lines 3-8: herald to announce honors for a demarch.

[120] IG II²1176+, lines 13-16, *proedria* for the herald; IG II²1214, lines 28ff., herald to announce an honorific award in the theater during the Dionysia tragic contest.

[121] *Hesp.* 39, 1970, pp. 47-53, line 6: herald to share in a sacrificial feast.

[122] SEG 22.120, lines 6-7: herald to announce an honorific decree during the Dionysia.

[123] See above, nn. 118 (Halai Araphenides), 119 (Ikarion), 120 (Peiraieus), and 122 (Rhamnous).

seat.[124] Elsewhere both of these tasks could be performed by the demarch,[125] but it does not automatically follow from this that the herald,
where he existed, was formally attached to the demarchy, in the manner
of the archon's *kēryx* in the city (?Aristot. *Ath. Pol.* 62.2); the post *seems*
to be an independent one, and, in certain demes at least, one of higher
status than we might have expected. It is particularly striking that in
fourth-century Erchia the herald acted as a priest, on at any rate one day
of the year, and was entitled to perquisites (*gera*) accordingly.[126]

2. *Euthynos* (examiner). This post, as we saw in the last chapter, is
found in either five or, more probably, six demes: Eleusis, Halai Aixonides, Myrrhinous, Skambonidai, Thorikos, and the unidentifiable deme
which enacted IG II²1216.[127]

3. *Hieropoioi*. Boards of these officials with religious duties are also
attested in six demes: Aixone,[128] Halai Araphenides,[129] Paiania,[130] Phrearrhioi,[131] Rhamnous,[132] and Skambonidai.[133] They appear always in the
plural,[134] but only in one instance (the four men of IG II²1199, Aixone)
can their actual number be determined. Nor is any very clear pattern to
be seen in what they do, save in the most general of terms,[135] and it
would probably be ill-advised to attempt to impose one. The religious
life of the demes was diverse in the extreme, and one important reason
for this was the fact that "the demes" *per se* represented the conceptual
and organizational framework for only a part of it. At what might be
termed the secular end of the range of possibilities, a deme could appoint

[124] See above, n. 118 (Halai Araphenides).

[125] Proclamation: IG II²1186, lines 19-24; IG II²1193, lines 13-21 (both Eleusis). Summons: IG II²1187, lines 18-20; IG II²1193, lines 22-24; *Hesp.* 8, 1939, pp. 177-180, lines
18-21 (all three Eleusis); cf. also IG II²1214 (Peiraieus), lines 22-25, with a different formula.

[126] See above, n. 117 (with Daux, "Démarchie," p. 631; cf. Dow, "Demarkhia," pp. 206-
207). For the status of the herald, see also above, nn. 116 (Aixone), 120 (Peiraieus), and
121 (Phrearrhioi).

[127] References in Chap. 4, nn. 159-164.

[128] IG II²1196, line 5 (context lost, but see Chap. 4, n. 142); IG II²1199, lines 1-13,
honorific decree for four named individuals, οἱ | λαχόντες ἱεροποιοὶ εἰς τὸ τῆς Ἥβη|ς
ἱερόν, for their sacrifices to Hebe and to other deities.

[129] *AE* 1925-1926, pp. 168-177, lines 8-10: *hieropoioi* (*sc.* of Artemis Tauropolos) to
allot a share of sacrificial meat to each of a group of honorands.

[130] IG I³250, lines 9-11: ῥαβδοχὲν τὸς | ℎιεροποιὸς καὶ ℎὸς ἂν κελ|εύοσιν.

[131] *Hesp.* 39, 1970, pp. 47-53, lines 1 and 10 (context lost).

[132] IG I³248 (ML no. 53), accounts of Nemesis in the charge of *hieropoioi* (line 32); SEG
22.120, lines 7-9, *hieropoioi* to inscribe a stele and set it up in the *hieron* of Nemesis.

[133] IG I³244, C, lines 3-4: τὸς ℎι[εροποι]|ός.

[134] Note, however, the single individual in SEG 2.7 (Halimous) who has performed τὰς
ἱεροποία|ς ὅσας οἱ δημόται προσ|έταξαν (lines 8-10). Whether he is himself a *hie-
ropoios*, strictly speaking, is not clear; see below, n. 160.

[135] Compare the case of the various boards of city *hieropoioi*; see Rhodes, *Boule*, pp.
127-130 (and *Commentary*, pp. 605-610).

either *hieropoioi* or other officials of a similar type,[136] as well as entrusting religious responsibilities to its demarch.[137] However, the cult personnel in most demes would also embrace a miscellany of priests and/or priestesses, not necessarily appointed by the deme as such, and thus not directly relevant here.[138]

4. *Tamiai* (treasurers). Either one, or two, or more *tamiai* are known from at least thirteen demes: ?Acharnai,[139] Aixone,[140] Antiochid Eitea,[141] Eleusis,[142] Gargettos,[143] Halai Aixonides,[144] Halai Araphenides,[145] Kydathenaion (restored),[146] Melite (restored),[147] Peiraieus,[148] Plotheia,[149]

---

[136] E.g. the (?two) *sophronistai* of the *hieron* of Hebe in Aixone (IG II²1199, lines 17-20). Note also various *hieromnemones*: IG II²1596(A), line 5 (Alopeke); IG II²1184, lines 1-2 (Cholargos); IG II²1299, line 80, and SEG 28.103, line 38 (both Eleusis).

[137] See above, sec. A.1(b).

[138] But they may still act on the orders of the deme assembly: witness IG II²1175 (Halai Aixonides), where the priests and priestesses as well as the demarch and *tamiai* are to swear an oath (lines 21-24). Note also the dating of "secular" documents by reference to a priest or priestess: see Chap. 2, n. 90. For priests and priestesses in general, see Chap. 7A, sec. 2.

[139] IG II²1206, lines 3 and 8: a single *tamias* sharing annual financial tasks with the demarch.

[140] IG II²1198, lines 13-18 (demarch and *tamiai* to give honorands ten drachmas "from the revenue of the demesmen," for sacrifice); IG II²1202, lines 12-14 and 18-21 (demarch and *tamiai* to provide money for the honorands' gold crowns and to inscribe and set up the stele); IG II²2492, lines 20-24 ("the *tamiai* of the year of the demarch Demosthenes" to inscribe and erect two stelai recording a leasing agreement, and *horoi* on the land itself) and lines 34-36 (demarch and *tamiai*, with others, to let out a contract); AM 66, 1941, pp. 218-219, no. 1, lines 9-11 (demarch and *tamiai* to give honorands ten drachmas for sacrifice, and *tamiai* to inscribe and erect the stele).

[141] SEG 28.102, lines 15-22: "the *tamias* of the year of the archon Niketes" to have the stele inscribed and set up and to account to the demesmen for what this costs.

[142] IG II²1185, lines 5-8: *tamias* to inscribe and set up the stele.

[143] AM 67, 1942, pp. 7-8, no. 5, lines 5-9: *tamias* to pay out "from the communal revenues" whatever is expended on the inscription of the stele.

[144] IG II²1174, lines 3 (restored) and 5, "the *tamiai*" (and "the demarchs") and their *euthynai*; IG II²1175, lines 21-24, *tamiai* amongst others to swear an oath; AD 11, 1927-1928, pp. 40-41, no. 4, line 13, *tamias* to disburse and account for the money needed to inscribe a stele. (This last was conceivably a separate ταμίας τῶν θείων, as in Halai Araphenides; see next note.)

[145] AE 1932, Chronika, pp. 30-32, lines 12-13 ("the *tamiai*" to give the honorand money for sacrifice) and lines 28-32 (the ταμίας τῶν θείων to pay out twenty drachmas for the inscription of the stele and to account for it to the demesmen).

[146] Agora 16, no. 54, A, lines 4-5, and B, lines 5-6 (identical formulas): "[the *tamias*] of the demesmen" to pay for the inscription of the stele. This restoration is modelled on an earlier one, by O. Broneer, in a decree of Melite: see next note.

[147] O. Broneer, Hesp. 11, 1942, pp. 265-274, no. 51, lines 13-15: "[the *tamias*] of the demesmen" to pay out for, inscribe, and set up the stele.

[148] IG II²1176 +, lines 25-27: demarch and *tamiai* to have the terms of a lease inscribed and set up in the *agora*.

[149] IG I³258, line 3: (the income from) five thousand drachmas allotted to two *tamiai*

Rhamnous,[150] and probably Skambonidai.[151] One may say "at least" these thirteen demes not only because it would be rather fortuitous if the unknown deme responsible for IG II²1212 (with ταμία[ς in line 12) were one of those already listed but also, and more especially, because we are perhaps entitled to regard as *tamiai* certain undesignated financial officials elsewhere.[152] Thus, apart from the altogether different case of the demarchs themselves, *tamiai* are the most widely attested of deme officials. In at least two, possibly five, cases they served annually.[153] As to their functions, the one most commonly mentioned is precisely what their name would suggest: they paid out money (for which they generally had to account later), and thus presumably also received and kept it. That all demes were encouraged, or even obliged, to appoint an official or officials other than the demarch to administer their financial affairs is not, to be sure, utterly inconceivable, but the impression which the evidence gives is, rather, that each deme took its own course and divided out the responsibilities as it liked.[154] Possibly in some demes, the very smallest ones, the demarch alone was thought sufficient. Sometimes we see the demarch and treasurers working together; sometimes the duties of the latter seem to have been distinct. There are parallels between groups of demes, but no overall uniformity.

Diversity, then, is all-pervasive, both in the titles of officials and in the functions they performed. Some demes, in order to administer cults and

---

for τὰ δι' ἔτος ἱερά. (For the ἄρχοντες τοῦ ἀργυρίου of lines 11ff., see below, n. 154.)

[150] SEG 25.155, line 42: *tamias* to pay out for the inscription and account for it to the demesmen.

[151] IG I³244, C, line 1: τα]μία (i.e. two of them, as in Plotheia: above, n. 149) read by Hicks, though the IG I³ editor, D. M. Lewis, reckons this "*dubium.*"

[152] In IG II²1184 (Cholargos), lines 21-25, οἱ ἐπὶ Κτησικλέους ἄρχοντος are to inscribe and set up the stele and to account for it to the demesmen; this looks very like a board of *tamiai*, and indeed one might suspect that the mason omitted the word in error. In IG II²1182 (Myrrhinous), lines 4-9, the post held by Pheidippos is perhaps that of *tamias*; see above, p. 141.

[153] Explicitly in Aixone (IG II²2492: see above, n. 140), in Eitea (see above, n. 141), and in Cholargos *if* the officials concerned are indeed *tamiai* (see preceding note); implicitly in ?Acharnai (see above, n. 139) and Halai Aixonides (IG II²1174: see above, n. 144).

[154] For the (?)ταμίας *and* ἀντιγραφεύς of Myrrhinous, see IG II²1182, discussed above. A decree of Plotheia contains provisions for financial officials to be selected by lot (IG I³258, lines 12-14): τὸς μὲν ἄρχοντας τὸ ἀργυρίο ἀ[ξ]|[ιό]χρεως κυαμεύεν ὅσο ἑκάστη ἡ ἀρ[χ]|[ὴ ἄ]ρχει. I agree with Damsgaard-Madsen ("Démarques," p. 107, n. 20, and in general pp. 105-107; cf. Müller, *de demis*, p. 50, and Schoeffer, "Demoi," col. 15) that οἱ ἄρχοντες τοῦ ἀργυρίου here does not refer to a specific board of officials

festivals unique to them or else to deal with other matters peculiar to their own circumstances and needs, will have created officials for whom there was no *exact* equivalent elsewhere. All demes, though, were faced with a common basic minimum of routine administration, and if they felt that this represented too heavy a workload for the demarch they could appoint other officials with whom some of it was shared or to whom some of it was transferred. A division of financial responsibilities appears to have been particularly common, and was doubtless effected so as not only to lighten the load of the officials concerned but also to create checks and balances to safeguard the community's interests. And there were others besides the demes' own, internal officials who might be put to work. A fourth-century decree of Teithras reveals that that deme's four representatives on the *boulē* of the previous year had discharged not only their civic duties in the city but also various tasks, including sacrifices, entrusted to their care by their own fellow demesmen in assembly.[155]

Furthermore, there was another option besides the appointment of permanent or regular officials. The documents of the individual demes offer numerous instances of the election[156] of individuals or groups *ad hoc*, to perform a specific task either in concert with the regular officials or by themselves:

1. *Acharnai.* In SEG 21.519, lines 11-12, reference is made to "the elected men" (οἱ αἱρεθέντες) who have reported what it will cost to build altars for Ares and Athena Areia.

2. *Aixone.* In IG II²2492, lines 31ff., it is resolved to elect men who, with the demarch and the *tamiai* and the lessee of land from the deme, will sell to the highest bidder the rights to the olive trees on it (lines 34-36); and the names of the three men chosen are appended (lines 46-47).

3. *Eleusis.* In IG II²1186, lines 30-33, it is resolved that someone be elected forthwith to take care of the inscription and erection of the stele (for which the demarch will furnish him with ten drachmas: lines 33-34).[157]

4. *Epikephisia.* In IG II²1205 rewards are decreed for "those elected

---

but is a general term for *all* the deme's officers who discharge financial duties: the demarch (line 2), the two *tamiai* (line 3), and possibly others besides (note lines 31-33: τὸς ἄρχο[ντας] | [ο]ῖ̈ ἂν ἄρχωσι τὸ ἀργυρίο τὸ ἐς τὴ[ν ἀτ]|[έ]λειαν).

[155] SEG 21.520, esp. lines 7-12 (quoted in Chap. 2, n. 97).

[156] Literally: see Chap. 4, n. 147, and further below.

[157] Note also IG II²1187 (also Eleusis), lines 27-29, where this task falls, "with the demarch," to the fathers of the youths whom the honorand, the *stratēgos* Derkylos, has provided with informal ephebic training; see in general F. W. Mitchel, *Hesp.* 33, 1964, pp. 337-351.

by the demesmen to prosecute Neokles" (οἱ αἱρεθέντες ὑπὸ τῶν
δημοτῶν κατήγοροι Νεοκλέους), who have evidently won the deme's
case against him in the jury-court.[158]

5. *Halai Aixonides*. (*a*) IG II²2820 records a dedication to Aphrodite
by twenty-four named individuals, "elected by the Halaieis to make the
agalma for Aphrodite (and) crowned by the demesmen" ([οἱ αἱ]-
ρεθέ[ν]τ[ες ὑπ]ὸ ῾Αλα[ιῶν] | [τὸ ἄγ]αλμα ποήσασθαι τἔι ᾿Αφ-
[ροδίτει] | [στεφα]νωθέντες ὑπὸ τῶν δη[μοτῶν], lines 1-3). (*b*) In *AD*
11, 1927-1928, pp. 40-41, no. 4, mention is made of "those elected from
the demesmen" (οἱ αἱρεθέντες ἐκ τῶν δημοτῶν, lines 4-5) who have
assisted the honorand of the decree, the priest of Apollo Zoster, in the
preparation or adornment of *agalmata*; the four individuals—one of them
also in IG II²2820—are named and, like the priest himself, awarded
crowns of laurel.

6. *Halimous*. In SEG 2.7 Charisandros Charisiadou is praised and
crowned in gold for having zealously performed "the sacrifices[159] on
behalf of the demarch Ischyrias" (lines 5-6)—a charge to which he was
elected by the demesmen (lines 6-8)—and "the rites (*hieropoiiai*) which
the demesmen enjoined" (lines 8-10).[160]

7. *Myrrhinous*. In IG II³1183, lines 17-24, the elaborate procedure for
euthynai involves ten "elected men" (αἱρεθέντες) besides a number
of regular officials.[161]

8. *Peiraieus*. In IG II²1176 +, lines 23-24, a provision is enacted for
the election of three of the demesmen as "valuers" (*epitimētai*) whenever
the lease of the theater changes hands.

9. *Sounion*. In IG II²1180, lines 6ff., it is resolved that three men be

---

[158] It is *possible* (see Chap. 4, n. 81) that this is an example in action of the procedure
outlined in ?Aristot. *Ath. Pol.* 42.1, where a deme elects five of its members as *katēgoroi*
to represent it in any appeals by *apepsēphismenoi*. Be that as it may, the procedure was
presumably used whenever necessary and is thus relevant here.

[159] See above, n. 41.

[160] The background to this has been variously interpreted. In his *editio princeps* (*ABSA*
24, 1919-1921, pp. 151-160) J.J.E. Hondius argued that Ischyrias had been suspended
from his duties and that Charisandros had been chosen as substitute demarch; however,
at that stage Hondius had not accepted the correction of οὐσιῶν in line 4 (see above, n.
41), and in any case his thesis requires ὑπὲρ τοῦ δημάρχου to be construed as "*in place
of* the demarch," which, as Damsgaard-Madsen observes ("Démarques," pp. 108-111), is
not its only, and not even its most natural, sense. Rather than a substitute demarch, then,
we seem to have here a man undertaking religious tasks, some of which (the sacrifices)
were on behalf of, or in the name of, the demarch. Damsgaard-Madsen's own view, however,
that Charisandros was simply a routinely appointed *hieropoios* seems to ignore the clear
indications in the decree's phraseology that its circumstances were indeed, somehow or
other, extraordinary.

[161] See Chap. 4, p. 119.

elected forthwith to mark out, together with the man who has provided it, the new *agora*.

10. *Teithras*. In SEG 24.151, lines 24-28, it is resolved that "three men in addition to the demarch" (line 26) shall make any necessary changes in the inscribed terms of a particular lease.

Within these eleven instances, as already indicated, certain differences are noteworthy. In two cases (3, 6) the task goes to an individual, otherwise to a group (of between three and twenty-four, where the numbers are known). Sometimes the task is performed in conjunction with regular deme officials or priests (2, *5b*, 7, 10), sometimes—or so it would seem—independently. More important perhaps, it may be legitimate to infer that the actual circumstances and method of appointing the individuals or groups concerned ranged from a genuine, formal election at one extreme (e.g. 6, 7) to a much more summary, off-the-cuff nomination and choice at the other (e.g. 3, 9)—the latter perhaps arising unforeseen during discussion in the deme assembly and implemented there and then (see 2). But what they all demonstrate is that demes were in the habit of dealing with administrative tasks as and when they arose, and of sharing them out amongst a wider circle of demesmen than those who happened to be the officeholders of the moment.

A rather different but perhaps more significant illustration of this principle of division than the eleven already given has recently been noted by Michael Jameson, in his study of the two virtually identical versions of a Rhamnousian lease from the second half of the fourth century.[162] In both versions the lessors are designated as "the demesmen from the *meros* of Archippos and Stesias" (οἱ δημόται οἱ ἐκ[163] τοῦ ᾽Αρχίππου μέρους καὶ Στησίου). The word *meros* is "protean" (Jameson), but has connotations which suggest that it must mean here a division of those participating in something, or making up a part of it, or taking turns to do it. At all events it begs comparison with two cognate terms which we have already encountered in the documents of other demes: the eight *meritai* of Kytheros (IG II²2496), who lease three buildings in Peiraieus to Eukrates of Aphidna—and who undertake to pay him and his descendants a thousand drachmas in the event of failure to maintain the lease; and the six *merarchai* of Athmonon, praised by their deme in IG II²1203. "We have to do, I believe, with liturgists who took upon themselves tasks which, in the majority of demes, the demarch would have had difficulty in managing alone. Individual benefactors of organizations are familiar. But for more routine business demesmen able to serve would

---

[162] Jameson, "Leasing," esp. pp. 72-73.

[163] See Jameson, "Leasing," p. 68, correcting the [μετ]ά of IG II²2493, line 3.

have been divided into groups and shared the costs and, in the case of leases, perhaps also the risks."[164]

It may, in point of fact, be unwarranted to imagine that such groups invariably "took upon themselves" their particular tasks, for, as Jameson himself suggests, two rather different types of activity seem to be exemplified here. On the one hand, the Rhamnousian "*meros* of Archippos and Stesias" and the Kytherian *meritai* give the impression of being entrepreneurs, groups of associates who have perhaps voluntarily, and primarily for business reasons, made a contract with their deme and are now in effect subcontracting it.[165] By contrast, "the *merarchai* of the year of the archon Antikles" in Athmonon (IG II²1203, lines 2-4) might almost be called quasi-magistrates, or at least, as Jameson has it, liturgists;[166] and gratitude is expressed in particular for their zealous performance of sacrifices (lines 4-5). It is not necessarily to be presumed that in this they acted together; and if in fact they acted separately there may be a close and instructive parallel to the situation here, as Jameson points out, in the fourth-century *fasti* from Erchia, "where an extensive list of small sacrifices is divided into five groups, corresponding one supposes to the responsibilities of five liturgists or groups of liturgists."[167]

To be sure, with further documentation this distinction may turn out to need modifying or even abandoning altogether, given the interplay in all these cases of social and religious imperatives with strictly financial considerations.[168] But at all events what this sort of evidence has revealed is that, by the fourth century at any rate, the demes often found it necessary to share out in various ways not merely their administrative workload but also the actual expense of sustaining their communal life and activities. In short, income and expenditure were constant preoccupations; so the income and expenditure of the demes must be the subject of the next chapter.

[164] Jameson, "Leasing," p. 73.

[165] See (on the *meritai*) Haussoullier, *Vie*, pp. 72-74. He adduced for comparison (as does Jameson, "Leasing," p. 72) IG II²1176 +, the leasing of the Peiraieus theater; only two of the four ὠνηταί there are demesmen (lines 38-40), but otherwise the parallel seems a valid and instructive one.

[166] For their designation, cf. two decrees of Aixone: IG II²1198, lines 2-4 (οἱ χορηγ|οὶ (οἱ) ἐπὶ Χρέμητος ἄρχοντος), and IG II²1200, lines 3-4 (οἱ χορηγοὶ οἱ ἐπὶ Δημ|ογένους ἀρχο[ν]τος).

[167] Jameson, "Leasing," p. 73. We shall return to this matter in Chap. 6C.

[168] Cf. Jameson, "Leasing," pp. 73-74.

CHAPTER 6

INCOME AND
EXPENDITURE

The communal life of the demes, as of the state itself, was ultimately fuelled by money. Through its assembly and its officials every deme derived an income, from a variety of sources, and spent it (or part of it) in a variety of ways; and a concern with finance—especially the maintenance and, if possible, increase of revenue(s) (*prosodos, prosodoi*)—naturally figures prominently in many of the demes' enactments.[1] Broadly speaking, it may be assumed that each deme had to formulate its own budget (*dioikēsis*),[2] that is, a balance between income and expenditure,[3] at a level determined by its own resources and its own needs. However, the evidence does not allow us to reconstruct the full budget of any individual deme, large or small. Rather, we must assemble a composite picture of "deme income and expenditure," supported by detailed documentation where it can be found.[4]

---

[1] In *Hesp.* 8, 1939, pp. 177-180, a demarch of Eleusis is praised and rewarded because (*inter alia*) "he has made the *prosodos* more" (line 12). Compare SEG 28.103 (also Eleusis), lines 14-16, ἐπαινέσαι δ|ὲ Μοιροκλέα Εὐθυδήμου, ὅτι τοῖς δημόταις ἐ|πιμελεῖται, ὅπως ἂν ἦι πρόσοδος ὡς πλείστη; SEG 22.117 (Ikarion), where the demarch-honorand ἀποφαίνει χρήματα περιόντα (i.e., surplus) λογισάμενος τὰς προσόδους καὶ τὰ | ἀγ-[αλώματα (lines 5-6); and IG II²1176 + (Peiraieus), lines 34-35, with Chap. 8, n. 121. Other references to *prosodos/prosodoi*: IG II²1198 (Aixone), lines 17-18; SEG 28.103 (Eleusis), lines 19-20 and 51; *AM* 67, 1942, pp. 7-8, no. 5 (Gargettos), lines 7-8; IG II²1182 (Myrrhinous), lines 22-25.

[2] For the term *dioikēsis*, see IG II²1202 (Aixone), lines 11-12, ἐκ τῆς διοικήσεως ἐκ τῶν περιόντων χρημάτων | τῶν ἐπὶ Θεοφράστου ἄρχοντος. The phrase κοινὴ διοίκησις is partially restored in IG II²1206 (?Acharnai), lines 10-11, and wholly restored (by O. Broneer) in *Hesp.* 11, 1942, pp. 265-274, no. 51 (Melite), line 15; note also IG II²1173 (deme unknown), lines 3-4, [τῆς διοικήσεω]ς τῶγ κοινῶν.

[3] Cf. Haussoullier, *Vie*, pp. 76-77. On the balance, however, see below, sec. C.

[4] See in general Müller, *de demis*, pp. 58-62; Haussoullier, *Vie*, pp. 62-79; Schoeffer, "Demoi," cols. 17-20; Finley, *Land and Credit*, pp. 95-97.

A. Income

A deme's income varied from year to year—not least because certain of its elements were potential rather than, in practice, actual, and thus in any given year might not in fact be forthcoming. For example, fines, in cases of misconduct by deme officials or misdemeanours by others,[5] obviously might not actually be incurred; so no deme can have relied on them as a regular source of revenue.[6] In the normal course of events three forms of income must have been fixed and predictable, at any rate in general terms: taxes and liturgies, rents, and the interest on loans.

1. Taxes and Liturgies

In IG II²1214, lines 25-28, one of the privileges granted to Kallidamas of Cholleidai by the demesmen of Peiraieus was the right to pay "the selfsame taxes in the deme as the Peiraieis (pay)" and to be exempt from the *enktētikon* tax.[7] In IG II²1185, lines 4-5, and IG II²1186, lines 25-26, the Eleusinians conceded to resident Theban benefactors of the community "immunity from the (taxes) over which the Eleusinioi have authority" (ἀτέλεια ὧν εἰσιν κύριοι Ἐλευσίνιοι). In IG II²1187, lines 16-17, and IG II²1188, lines 29-30, the same deme granted "immunity" to Athenian honorands who were members of other demes; and the demesmen of Coastal Lamptrai did the same in IG II²1204, lines 11-12.

Largely negative though it is, this evidence invites the assumption that deme taxation *of some kind* was widespread; but detailed generalizations can only be tentative. The *enktētikon* tax, for instance, may not have been anything like as universal as is commonly supposed.[8] Nor, more generally, can Eleusis or (particularly) Peiraieus necessarily be regarded as fiscally typical demes. The Eleusinian documents, especially, give the impression that deme assemblies were more inclined to tax *enkektēmenoi* and metics than their own members. This would be most instructive, if true, but may actually tend to mislead. Certainly IG II²1214 shows that the Peiraieis did pay "taxes" (τέλη) themselves, at least in the first half of the third century; and so, in the second half of the *fifth* century, did the demesmen of a much smaller and otherwise more representative deme,

---

[5] E.g. [Demosth.] 43.58 (general); *Hesp.* 8, 1939, pp. 177-180 (Eleusis), lines 18-21; SEG 28.103 (Eleusis), lines 39-41; IG II²1362 (?Eupyridai), lines 14-16; IG II²2496 (Kytheros), lines 17-20; IG II²1183 (Myrrhinous), lines 22-24, 26, 30-32, 40; IG II²1177 (Peiraieus), line 14; SEG 21.644 (Prasiai), lines 4-11; IG I³245 (Sypalettos), lines 5-12.

[6] *Pace* Schoeffer, "Demoi," col. 18, and Finley, *Land and Credit*, p. 96.

[7] Quoted in Chap. 3, n. 64.

[8] See Chap. 3, n. 38.

which is more significant. In IG I³258, lines 28-29, reference is made to *hiera* in Plotheia "for which all the Plotheians must pay money" (ὅποι ἂν δέ[ηι Π]|λωθέας ἅπαντας τελεν ἀργύριο[ν). Here the τέλη would seem to be not so much taxes for general administrative purposes as subsidies for particular cult activities in which the contributors themselves participate.[9] The same may well be true of the τέλη in Peiraieus in IG II²1214, to judge from the whole context (lines 11ff.); it is similarly implied in the Eleusinian grants by the conjunction of *ateleia* with *proedria* (IG II²1185, 1186, 1187), and in Lamptrai by its association with participation with the demesmen in sacrificial feasts (IG II²1204).

We have some slight indication, then, that any routine and undesignated "secular" taxation in the demes was imposed upon those who were not demesmen, while the latter preferred if possible to make contributions in a way which in itself reinforced their collective identity as *dēmotai*. This was perhaps especially significant for the Peiraieis, surrounded as they were by so many cults which took no account of the status of their adherents.[10] On the other hand, *if* the Eleusinian "immunity" did indeed relate to τέλη of a comparable sort, it looks as though at least some of the Eleusinians' *hiera* were not similarly restricted to the demesmen, or even to Athenian citizens. What is more, Damasias, the Theban honorand in the Eleusinian decree IG II²1186 (lines 1-35), is praised, together with his "pupils," for benevolence "towards *all* those living in the deme" (lines 4-5). This had taken the form, *inter alia*, of the provision of both men's and boys' choruses at his own expense for the deme's Dionysia (lines 6-13). But these should perhaps be regarded as merely unofficial *chorēgiai* on his part (and, even as such, unparalleled elsewhere for a metic), in a deme which seems to have been more than usually liberal in including non-demesmen in its cult activities. It is true that the two tragic *chorēgoi* in fifth-century Ikarion were drawn not only from demesmen but also

---

[9] Cf. Schoeffer, "Demoi," col. 18. Lines 28-33 actually make the following provision: καὶ ἐς τἆλλα ἱερά, ὅποι ἂν δέ[ηι Π]|λωθέας ἅπαντας τελεν ἀργύριο[ν ἐς] | [ἱ]ερά, ἢ ἐς Πλωθέας ἢ ἐς Ἐπακρέα[ς ἢ ἐς] | [Ἀ]θηναῖος, ἐκ το κοινο τὸς ἀρχο[ντας,]|[ο]ἳ ἂν ἄρχωσι το ἀργυρίο τὸ ἐς τὴ[ν ἀτ]||[έ]λειαν, τελεν ὑπὲρ τῶν δημοτῶν. The method of financing is thus being changed, it would seem, from individual contributions by the demesmen to payment on their collective behalf by financial officials in charge of a component of the deme's monies designated τὸ ἐς τὴν ἀτέλειαν. See the comments of Kirchner *apud* IG II²1172 (quoted by D. M. Lewis *apud* IG I³258), which derive in part from V. Thumser, *de civium Atheniensium muneribus eorumque immunitate*, Vienna, 1880, pp. 144ff.; also Müller, *de demis*, pp. 60-62.

[10] See in brief on this M. Amit, *Athens and the Sea: a study in Athenian sea-power*, Collection Latomus 74, Brussels, 1965, pp. 84-88. It is noteworthy that even the favored Kallidamas in IG II²1214 is to join in the feasting ἐν ἅπασι τοῖς ἱεροῖς πλὴν | εἴ που αὐτοῖς Πειραιεῦσιν νόμιμόν ἐστ|ιν εἰσιέναι (lines 15-17).

from other residents of the deme,[11] but liturgists in other demes seem always to be *dēmotai*.

The elusive subject of deme "taxation" thus shades naturally into that of deme liturgies. These are somewhat better documented, though one cannot draw up a complete list even for any individual deme. An honorific decree of Halai Araphenides, for example, praises a man whose principal "choregy" (lines 3-4) had been the provision of Pyrrhic dancers; it then tantalizingly refers to his discharge, besides, of "all the other liturgies in the deme."[12] However, *chorēgia* (at the rural Dionysia) is explicitly attested in seven demes[13] and must have been widespread.[14] In addition we hear of *gymnasiarchia*,[15] *hestiasis*,[16] and women's liturgies connected with the Thesmophoria.[17] It may be assumed that only the wealthier demesmen were called on to be liturgists, though the expense entailed must have been considerably less than that of most liturgies for the state.[18]

2. RENTS

A variety of literary and epigraphic sources reveal that the demes—*qua* collectivities of demesmen[19]—regularly owned landed property and de-

---

[11] See Chap. 3, n. 41. I take this to mean other *Athenian* residents.

[12] *AE* 1932, *Chronika*, pp. 30-32, lines 3-7: τοῖς τε πυρριχισταῖς ἐ|χορήγησεν καὶ τὰς ἄλλας λ|ειτουργίας ἀπάσας τὰς ἐν | τῶι δήμωι καλῶς καὶ φιλοτ|ίμως λελειτούργηκεν. This phraseology indicates that the Pyrrhic dance in question was not the one which formed part of the Panathenaia in Athens (for which see Parke, *Festivals*, p. 36) but a liturgy within the deme. For comparable vagueness in the overall formulation, cf. Isaeus 3.80, θεσμοφόρια ἑστιᾶν τὰς γυναῖκας καὶ τἄλλα ὅσα προσῆκε λητουργεῖν ἐν τῷ δήμῳ (the deme is indeterminable).

[13] Acharnai: IG II²3092 and 3106. Aigilia: IG II²3096. Aixone: IG II²1198 and 1200, and *AM* 66, 1941, pp. 218-219, no. 1. Eleusis: IG II²1186 and 3090. Ikarion: IG I³254; IG II²1178, 3094, 3095, 3098, 3099. Paiania: IG II²3097. Rhamnous: IG II²3108 and 3109. See in general Haussoullier, *Vie*, pp. 168-170; Schoeffer, "Demoi," cols. 23-24. (It is unlikely that either IG II²3091, from Halai Aixonides, or IG II²3101, from Anagyrous, commemorate deme *chorēgiai*; see Chap. 2, n. 32.)

[14] For example, *chorēgoi* must have been required for the comic and tragic performances at the Dionysia in Kollytos: Aeschin. 1.157 and Demosth. 18.180; see Haussoullier, *Vie*, p. 169. On the general point, see below, Chap. 7D.

[15] Isaeus 2.42 (with W. Wyse, *The Speeches of Isaeus*, Cambridge, 1904, p. 267; Davies, *Families*, p. xxiii), deme indeterminable (but *perhaps* Kephale or Acharnai: see Chap. 8, n. 6); IG II²3109, Rhamnous.

[16] Theophr. *Char.* 10 (μικρολογίας).11, general; Isaeus 3.80 (see above, n. 12), deme indeterminable. Cf. Menander *Sikyonios*, lines 183-191, Eleusis.

[17] See Chap. 3C, esp. the references in n. 55.

[18] Note the comments of Davies, *Families*, pp. xxiii-xxiv, on Isaeus 2 and 3.

[19] See Finley, *Land and Credit*, pp. 88-90; cf. Harrison, *Law* I, pp. 235, 241-242.

rived part of their income from leasing it out for rent (*misthōsis*).[20] In Demosth. 57.63-64, for example, Euxitheos recalls how as demarch of Halimous he made enemies of many of his fellow demesmen from whom he had to exact μισθώσεις τεμενῶν, that is, rents from (the lease of) sacred precincts.[21] In an even smaller deme, Plotheia, the (?total) *misthōsis* income for one year somewhere in the last quarter of the fifth century was recorded as 134 drachmas and 2½ obols[22]—a sum which, together with the interest from monies out on loan, was earmarked for cult purposes.[23] Around the middle of the fourth century the demesmen of Teithras passed a summary decree instructing their demarch to set up an epigraphic record of deme properties rented out on a permanent basis (κατάπαξ), "so that the common property may be safe for the demesmen, and the Teithrasioi may know their resources and their income";[24] and in 321/0 the Peiraieis saw fit to lay down general rules for the leasing of their *temenē* and *ennomia*.[25] In addition, several inscriptions from other individual demes record actual *misthōsis* contracts in which specific items of deme property are leased out to a named person or group, and the terms of the lease as they affected both parties are set out. Six of these contracts are leases of land (or, in one instance, buildings),[26] in form

[20] See in general Haussoullier, *Vie*, pp. 69-74; Schoeffer, "Demoi," col. 17; O. Schulthess, *RE* 15, 1932, cols. 2095-2129 (with Finley, *Land and Credit*, p. 216, n. 68); Andreyev, "Agrarian conditions," esp. pp. 38-44; Nemes, "Public property"; and other references below, in n. 30.

[21] For the leasing of *temenē* by a deme, see IG II²2498 (Peiraieus), lines 2-3 and 10-11; IG II²2493 (Rhamnous: see Jameson, "Leasing"), lines 4-5 and passim. Note, however, Andreyev's suggestion ("Agrarian conditions," p. 26) that "from an economic point of view" the word *temenos* could have described any type of (public) landholding. There was undeniably a degree of interchangeability, to say the least, in deme leases between the terms *temenos* and *chōrion* (see, for instance, IG II²2493, with Jameson, "Leasing," p. 68, n. 6; IG II²2498; SEG 24.151, lines 11-12); and probably a deme's communal land was indeed mainly, sometimes even wholly, of this "sacred" type.

[22] IG I³258, line 10: [μ]ισθώσεων ΗΔΔΔΗΗΗΙΙC. The view of M. Guarducci, *Historia: studi storici per l'antichità classica* (Milan/Rome) 9, 1935, pp. 205-222, that this figure refers to *expenditure* on μισθώσεις was refuted by V. Arangio-Ruiz, *Studia et documenta historiae et iuris* 2, 1936, pp. 450-451; cf. Finley, *Land and Credit*, p. 96 with n. 39. The document as a whole is quoted below, sec. B.2.

[23] IG I³258, lines 22-28. On loans, see below, sec. 3.

[24] SEG 24.151, lines 2-5: ὅπως ἂν σᾶ ἦι τ|οῖς δημόταις τὰ κοινὰ καὶ εἰδῶσι Τειθράσιοι τὰ ὑπάρχ|ο[ντα] καὶ τὰ προσιόντα ἀναγρά[ψαι τὸ]ν δήμαρχο|[ν] ὁπ-[όσ]οι κατάπαξ μεμίσθωνται τῶν κοινῶν. (SEG 24.152 looks like part of such a record.)

[25] IG II²2498. For *ennomia* (line 13) cf. IG II²1196 (Aixone), discussed at Chap. 4, pp. 113-114.

[26] Land: IG II²2492 (Aixone); IG II²2493 (Rhamnous: see Jameson, "Leasing"); IG II²2497 (Prasiai); SEG 21.644 (Prasiai); SEG 24.151 (Teithras). Buildings (in Peiraieus): IG II²2496, which I believe should be accepted as a document of the deme Kytheros; see

broadly similar both with one another and also with the leasing documents of other bodies such as phratries and *orgeōnes*.[27] Others—of a rather different type—deal with the leasing of a theater[28] or the right to quarry stone.[29]

Most of these inscriptions, general or particular, throw up problems and obscurities which can hardly be fully considered except in a detailed commentary on each document;[30] for our purposes here a more summary treatment will suffice.

1. *Length of lease.* For reasons which cannot be divined, some leases were agreed in perpetuity (εἰς τὸν ἅπαντα χρόνον, κατάπαξ),[31] others for finite periods—five years in the case of the Eleusinian stone quarries,[32] ten years in Peiraieus and Rhamnous,[33] forty years in Aixone.[34]

2. *Amount of rent.* Only three figures are clearly preserved: 54 drach-

---

Appendix 3, no. 72. If it is, the idea that one deme could not hold property in another—thus D. M. Lewis in M. I. Finley, ed., *Problèmes de la terre en Grèce ancienne*, Paris and The Hague, 1973, p. 192—seems clearly untenable, though as always the unique position *qua* deme of Peiraieus complicates the issue.

[27] See for instance IG II²1241 (*Pachturkunden*, no. 36) for a phratry, IG II²2499 (*Pachturkunden*, no. 39) for *orgeōnes*.

[28] Much the best-preserved instance, though incomplete even so, is that of the theater of Peiraieus (IG II²1176 +), "sublet" in 324/3 to four πριάμενοι/ὠνηταί who between them put up, unequally, 3,300 drachmas—a sum quite outside the normal range of deme *misthōseis* (cf. Finley, *Land and Credit*, p. 285, n. 40). Revenue from the theater at (?)Acharnai is referred to in IG II²1206, lines 4-6.

[29] SEG 28.103 (Eleusis, 332/1). The second and longer of the two decrees on the stele enacts that revenue for the cult of Herakles-in-Akris shall be generated by leasing out, to the highest bidder (lines 23-24), the rights to the stone quarries in the deme (τὰς λιθοτομίας τὰς Ἐλευσῖνι, line 21). The other decree, inscribed first, commends and rewards both the proposer of the scheme and the demesman who has purchased the concession for five years at 150 drachmas *per annum* (lines 6-8; note the error here in the *editio princeps*, REG 91, 1978, pp. 289-306 at 300-301, i.e., 50 drachmas instead of 150, as correctly translated on p. 291).

[30] For some bibliography and references, see Appendix 3 (*via* nn. 26, 28, and 29, above). I have included there the numbers from Behrend, *Pachturkunden*, chap. 3, but it should be noted that he provides *no texts*—a fact which, together with the excessively schematic nature of his chap. 2 ("Eine Theorie der μίσθωσις"), has attracted adverse comment from reviewers: see esp. M. I. Finley, *Tijdschrift voor Rechtsgeschiedenis* 40, 1972, pp. 559-561, and R. S. Stroud, *AJPh* 95, 1974, pp. 84-86. A more unassuming yet no less useful work is Kussmaul, *Synthekai*, esp. pp. 37-61.

[31] Kytheros: IG II²2496, lines 11-12. Prasiai: IG II²2497, lines 6-9 (and presumably also SEG 21.644, judging by the mention of the descendants in lines 8-9). Teithras: SEG 24.151, lines 5 and passim (and SEG 24.152, lines 5-6).

[32] SEG 28.103, line 7.

[33] Peiraieus: IG II²2498, lines 17-21. Rhamnous: IG II²2493, lines 10-13.

[34] IG II²2492, lines 2-3.

mas *per annum* for the Kytherians' buildings in Peiraieus,[35] 150 for the Eleusinian quarries,[36] and 152 for the Phelleis land in Aixone;[37] in addition, the figure in the full lease from Teithras is perhaps at least 200 drachmas.[38] Most of these sums, it may be noted, are higher than what is presumably the totality of rents payable to the Plotheians (134 drachmas and 2½ obols; see above), the constituents of which doubtless included some very small rents indeed—not least, the one calculated to the nicety of 2½ obols! Even the much larger and wealthier deme of Peiraieus collected rents of less than 10 drachmas.[39] Given this range of figures, an estimate of the "average" rent received by a deme cannot be expressed in anything but the most vague of terms.[40]

3. *Method of payment.* As with the length of lease, considerations which we cannot fathom led some demes to stipulate a single, annual payment,[41] while others preferred two instalments, equal or unequal.[42] It is surely accidental that only examples of the first type specify that payment shall be made to the demarch.[43]

4. *Eisphorai and taxes.* "Unlike the state itself, all subdivisions of the state were subject to private law. Land owned by the demes was taxable like privately owned land; the incidence of the *eisphora* was a matter of agreement whenever a deme leased out some of its holdings."[44] In the

---

[35] IG II²2496, lines 12-15.

[36] See above, n. 29.

[37] IG II²2492, lines 3-4.

[38] The reading (SEG 24.151, line 16) is I.Ḥ..H, and Wilhelm suspected a later alteration here (*APF* 11, 1933-1935, p. 193). Andreyev, "Agrarian conditions," pp. 39-40 reads 200.

[39] IG II²2498, lines 3-6; see further below, under "*Safeguards for the deme.*" The figure is surprisingly low (cf. Finley, *Land and Credit*, p. 96), but must be taken as proof that rents of ten drachmas or less *existed* in this deme.

[40] See Andreyev, "Agrarian conditions," pp. 38-43, concluding that the average was "in the vicinity of several hundred drachmas"; cf. Finley, *Land and Credit*, p. 96, "probably never more than several hundred drachmas."

[41] Aixone: IG II²2492, lines 5-7 (month of Hekatombaion). Eleusis: SEG 28.103, lines 26-28 (month of Metageitnion, at the *archairesiai* in the Theseion). Rhamnous: IG II²2493, lines 13-15 (month of ?Gamelion, at the *agora ?kyria*). Teithras: SEG 24.151, lines 32-34 (month of Elaphebolion; here I follow Behrend's restoration in *Pachturkunden*, p. 79, τ[ὰ]|[ς δὲ μισθώσεις ἀπο]διδόναι, in preference to Kirchner's τ[ὰ] | [δὲ τέλη αὐτοὺς ἀπο]διδόναι).

[42] Kytheros: IG II²2496, lines 12-15 (30 drachmas in Hekatombaion, 24 in Posideion). Peiraieus: IG II²2498, lines 11-15 (half in Hekatombaion, half in Posideion). Prasiai: IG II²2497, lines 9-14 (half in Metageitnion, half in ?Mounichion).

[43] Eleusis: SEG 28.103, lines 31-33. Rhamnous: IG II²2493, line 14 (partially restored). Teithras: SEG 24.151, lines 33-34.

[44] Finley, *Land and Credit*, p. 93. See also Kussmaul, *Synthekai*, pp. 53-55; Behrend, *Pachturkunden*, pp. 119-120.

five documents where such a provision survives, the tenant pays in two instances,[45] the deme in three.[46] The deme's decision as to whether the property should be "immune" (ἀτελές) from its *own* point of view seems to have been a separate issue.[47]

5. *Safeguards for the tenant.* These were of two main kinds. Sometimes damage to the property from invasion or other enemy action is envisaged. In that case the deme and the tenants are to bear the misfortune in equal measure.[48] Sometimes, on the other hand, the potential hazards to the tenant are internal rather than external, and the deme sees fit to protect him against any alteration (from its own side) in the terms of the lease,[49] or else, in one instance, to furnish a warranty of his rightful title.[50]

6. *Safeguards for the deme.* As well as those inherent in the provisions already mentioned, as also in any positive or negative stipulations as to the *use* of the property,[51] safeguards for the deme as lessor generally meant its requiring initial guarantees of the tenant's capacity to pay his rent.[52] These guarantees took the form of the nomination either of persons to act as sureties (ἐγγυηταί) or of property to be valued as security (ἀποτίμημα).[53] (A third and simpler option was to emphasize a right of *ad hoc* seizure, *enechyrasia*;[54] the Aixoneis do this at lines 7-9 of IG

[45] Kytheros: IG II²2496, lines 25-28. Teithras: SEG 24.151, lines 31-32.

[46] Aixone: IG II²2492, lines 24-27. Peiraieus: IG II²2498, lines 7-9. Prasiai: IG II²2497, lines 4-6. Compare, for bodies other than demes, IG II²1241 and 2499.

[47] Note IG II²2496 (Kytheros), line 13, ἀτελὲς ἁπάντων—yet the tenant is to pay *eisphorai*; see above, at n. 45. In IG II²2497 (Prasiai), lines 4-6, the phrase is ἀτ|[ελὲς κ]αὶ ἀνεπιτίμητον εἰσφορ|[ᾶς καὶ] τῶν ἄλλων ἁπάντων; cf. IG II²2498 (Peiraieus), lines 6-7, ἐπὶ τοῖσδε μ|[ι]σθοῦσιν ἀνεπιτίμητα καὶ ἀτελῆ, with the *eisphora* clause immediately following.

[48] Aixone: IG II²2492, lines 12-14. Prasiai: SEG 21.644, lines 11-16. Teithras: SEG 24.151, lines 17-21. See Behrend, *Pachturkunden*, pp. 120-121.

[49] In IG II²2492 (Aixone), lines 29-31, the tenant is granted a suit for damages (δίκη βλάβης) against any demesman making a proposal contrary to the terms of the lease, for as long as it lasts; see on this Behrend, *Pachturkunden*, pp. 127-130, and D. M. Lewis in *PHOROS: tribute to B. D. Meritt*, Locust Valley, New York, 1974, p. 82, n. 7. In SEG 24.151 (Teithras), lines 21-28, provision is made for setting aside any contrary conditions enacted in earlier documents. In IG II²2497 (Prasiai), lines 14ff., regular payment apparently guarantees security of tenure; see Behrend, *Pachturkunden*, p. 84 with n. 158.

[50] Kytheros: IG II²2496, lines 22-24, βεβαιοῦν δὲ τὴν μίσθωσιν Κυθηρίων τοὺς μερί|τας Εὐκράτει καὶ τοῖς ἐγγ[όνοις] αὐτοῦ, εἰ δὲ μή, ὀφείλειν | δραχμὰς Χ.

[51] See, for instance, IG II²2492 (Aixone), lines 4-5, 14-18, 31ff.; IG II²2498 (Peiraieus), lines 9-11, 15ff.; SEG 21.644 (Prasiai), lines 16ff.; IG II²2493 (Rhamnous), lines 7-10, 15ff.

[52] See Kussmaul, *Synthekai*, pp. 47-50; Behrend, *Pachturkunden*, pp. 124-127.

[53] On the concept and practice of *apotimēma*, see Finley, *Land and Credit*, pp. 38-52 (esp. 45-47) and 95-97.

[54] On *enechyrasia* see Chap. 5A, sec. 1(a).

II²2492, which, though a complete document, makes no mention of either sureties or security.)

Why, in any given circumstances, one of these forms of guarantee might be more acceptable to the deme than the other is not clear. In their general leasing rules of 321/0 the demesmen of Peiraieus stipulate that tenants whose annual rent exceeds ten drachmas must put up appropriate *security*, while those paying less than this shall nominate a *surety* who, if need be, is to make good the tenant's default out of his own pocket.[55] This line of demarcation, set "ridiculously low,"[56] will obviously have ensured that tenants of all but the very smallest deme properties provided security rather than personal sureties; and such must have been, in part at least, its object. On the other hand, annual rents of 54 drachmas in Kytheros and 150 drachmas in Eleusis are backed by sureties,[57] and, as Finley observed, when the financial officials in Plotheia are instructed to make loans *either* on the basis of security *or* by demanding sureties, "the language implies that the choice rested with the official and was not determined by the size of the loan."[58]

Whatever the considerations, then, which made the Peiraieis favor the *apotimēma* system, they were evidently not universal. On the face of it, the Peiraieus procedure debarred those without land or houses (to serve as the security) from leasing the choicest of the deme's *temenē*, and it is possible that the covert aim of this was to keep out the metics, of whom Peiraieus housed so many.[59] Most other demes will not have faced such a problem. Nevertheless, as scholars have rightly emphasized,[60] a significant feature of the whole body of public *misthōsis* documents is the fact that the great majority of tenants are themselves members of the leasing organization or group. Certainly in all known deme *misthōseis*[61] demesmen (of the deme concerned) outnumber non-demesmen by at least three

---

[55] IG II²2498, lines 3-6: τοὺς μισθω|[σ]αμένους ὑπὲρ : Δ : δραχμὰς καθιστάναι ἀποτίμημα τῆς μ|[ι]σθώσεως ἀξιόχρεων, τοὺς δὲ ἐντὸς Δ δραχμ(ῶ)ν ἐγγυ(η)τὴ|[ν] ἀποδιδόμενον τὰ ἑαυτοῦ τῆς μισθώσεως. On the meaning of the second clause here, see Finley, *Land and Credit*, pp. 283-284, n. 38.

[56] Finley, *Land and Credit*, p. 96; cf. above, n. 39.

[57] Kytheros: IG II²2496, lines 20-22 (one named surety, the tenant's father). Eleusis: SEG 28.103, lines 29-31 (two sureties to be provided).

[58] IG I³258, lines 20-22, ὃς ἂν [πεί]|[θ]ηι τὸς δανείζοντας ἄρχοντα[ς τιμ]|ήματι ἢ ἐγγυητῆι; see Finley, *Land and Credit*, p. 97 (and pp. 242-243, n. 51, on the use of *timēma* for *apotimēma*).

[59] S. Isager, *Forpagtning af jord og bygninger i Athen*, Copenhagen, 1983, pp. 32-33.

[60] Notably Andreyev, "Agrarian conditions," pp. 43-44; cf. Jameson, "Leasing," pp. 73-74.

[61] Including the Halimousian ones presupposed by Demosth. 57.63.

to one.[62] This in itself offers strong support for Andreyev's contention that deme *misthōseis* were not primarily a financial or commercial exercise but rather a manifestation of "patriarchal traditions, the privileges of citizens and mutual collective aid";[63] and the language of some of the documents themselves confirms the point. In SEG 24.151, lines 6ff., the Teithrasioi resolve to lease to Xanthippos on the grounds, it would seem, of services he has rendered to the community: ἐπε[ι]δὴ Ξ‖[άνϑι]ππό[ς] ἐστι ἀνὴρ ἀγαϑὸς περ[ὶ] τ[ὰ κ]οινὰ τὰ [Τ]ε‖[ι]ϑ[ρασ]ί[ων]. Thus the decree is tantamount to being honorific, with permission to lease a prime deme property as its reward. And what is implicit here becomes explicit both in IG II²1176 +, where the four "purchasers" of the theater in Peiraieus are crowned (lines 37-40), and also in SEG 28.103, where the same mark of gratitude is decreed by the Eleusinians for Moirokles, whose successful bid for the stone-quarrying rights was made with a view to maximizing the revenue to his fellow demesmen (lines 14-17, cf. 6-9). No contradiction need be seen in the idea that to lease from the deme was both a privilege and a meritorious service; they were the two sides of the same coin.[64] "The lessors' concern was to secure a dependable income for the regular performance of cult with the attendant entertainment of the organizations' members, to avoid the absence of a tenant and the consequent neglect of the property for more than a short period, and, insofar as it was consistent with these aims, to assist members of the organization. The honoring of lessees points to their contributions to the benefit of the organization while the granting of leases over many years or in perpetuity . . . suggests benefits available to the lessees. On both sides the religious and social aspects may have been at least as important as the strictly financial."[65]

3. LOANS

The third source of regular deme revenue was interest on loans.[66] Our most informative text here is again the financial decree of the Plotheians (IG I³258), a provision of which deals with this very subject. Financial officials are charged with furnishing their fellow demesmen with the income from loans of two kinds: those where the terms (including the

[62] Non-demesmen: Eukrates of Aphidna in IG II²2496 (Kytheros); Melesias of Lamptrai and Arethousios of Pelekes—two out of four—in IG II²1176 + (Peiraieus); Euthynos of Oa, jointly with a demesman, in SEG 24.152 (Teithras).

[63] Andreyev, "Agrarian conditions," p. 43.

[64] Cf. Nemes, "Public property," pp. 7-8.

[65] Jameson, "Leasing," pp. 73-74.

[66] See in general Haussoullier, *Vie*, pp. 74-76; Schoeffer, "Demoi," col. 18; Finley, *Land and Credit*, pp. 95-97.

rate of interest) have been laid down by decree and those made annually on the initiative of the officials themselves, free to choose the highest rates of interest and the most suitable guarantees.[67]

Both of these forms of loan are attested in other demes. In IG II²2492, lines 31ff., the Aixoneis resolve that the olive trees ceded by the tenants of the Phelleis estate shall be sold to the highest bidder and the proceeds loaned out ἐπὶ δραχμεῖ, that is, at the commonly found rate of one drachma *per* mina *per* month, or 12 percent *per annum*. On the other hand, the priests whom in IG II²1183 the Myrrhinousioi instruct, if necessary, to make loans may evidently fix whatever rates of interest they can secure; the decree stipulates only that they must take guarantees in the form of security (land, house, or tenement) and that they must place a *horos* on the property in question to indicate to which god the loaned money belongs—or else owe it themselves.[68]

This last provision is of especial interest for its insistence upon the use of *horoi*. M. I. Finley has drawn attention to "the unmistakable infrequency with which demes entered into transactions involving *horoi*," concluding that "loans by the deme[s] were not numerous, were made in relatively small amounts, and were generally not backed by hypothecation publicized through the medium of the *horoi*."[69] While this may be valid as an overall picture, it is important to stress that there was clearly great variation within it, both in procedural terms and also in terms of the scale of the loans in question. As regards procedure, the Myrrhinousioi did insist upon the use of *horoi*, and so presumably did several other demes, the ones which figure on the *horoi* stones themselves—Halai,[70] Kerameis,[71] Phegaia,[72] and Phlya.[73] And as to the sums

---

[67] IG I³258, lines 12-22: τὸς μὲν ἄρχοντας τὸ ἀργυρίο ἀ[ξ]||[ιό]χρεως κυαμεύεν ὅσο ἑκάστη ἡ ἀρ[χ]|[ὴ ἄ]ρχει, τούτος δὲ τὸ ἀργύριον σῶν [π]||[αρ]έχεν Πλωθεῦσι, περὶ μὲν ὅτο ἐστ[ὶ] | [ψ]ήφισμα δανεισμὸ ἢ τόκος τεταγμέ]νος κατὰ τὸ ψήφισμα δανείζοντα[ς κ]|[α]ὶ ἐσπράττοντας, ὅσον δὲ κατ' ἐν[ιαυ]||[τ]ὸν δανείζεται δανείζοντας ὅ[στι]|ς ἂν πλεῖστον τόκον διδῶι, ὃς ἂν [πεί]||[θ]ηι τὸς δανείζυντας ἄρχοντα[ς τιμ]|ήματι ἢ ἐγγυητῆι. On the syntax of lines 12-14, see Damsgaard-Madsen, "Démarques," p. 106, n. 16.

[68] IG II²1183, lines 27-32: ἐὰν δέ τ[ινι δέ]|ει ἀργύριον, δανείζειν τοὺς ἱερέα[ς] ἀξιοχρείωι ἐπ[ὶ χωρίω]|ι ἢ οἰκίαι ἢ συνοικίαι καὶ ὅρον ἐφ[ισ]τάναι, οὗ ἂν ἐι [θεοῦ πα]|ραγράφοντα ὅ[[υ]]του ἂν ἐι τὸ ἀργύριο[ν· ἐὰν δὲ μὴ ὁρί[σηι αὐτά?], ὀφείλειν τὸν ἱερέα οὗ ἂν ἐι θεοῦ ἱερεὺς καὶ τὰ χρ[ήματα αὐ]|τοῦ ὑποκείσθω τῶι θεῶι οὗ ἂν ἐι ἱερε[ι]ωμένος.

[69] Finley, *Land and Credit*, pp. 95, 97.

[70] IG II²2761B: *horos* of a town house pledged to the Halaieis for 200 drachmas.

[71] *Hesp.* Suppl. 9, 1951, pp. 12-13, no. 23: *horos* of a town house sold subject to redemption to the Kerameis for 3,000 drachmas.

[72] *Hesp.* 41, 1972, pp. 279-280, no. 5: *horos* of a town house sold subject to redemption to the Phegaieis for either 300 or 700 drachmas.

[73] IG II²2670: *horos* of an estate (in Phlya) put up as *apotimēma* for the dowry of

involved, the largest specified on a *horos* is the three thousand drachmas lent by the Kerameis, which surely falls outside Finley's "relatively small amounts." Other evidence is more suggestive still. The key document here is IG I³248, the accounts of the financial resources, in reserve or on loan, of the cult of Nemesis of Rhamnous, for five (presumably consecutive) years between ca. 450 and ca. 440. Unsystematic as they are, these accounts reveal not only that the total resources during the period in question ranged between eight and ten talents[74] but also that initially 75 percent and ultimately 90 percent of this money was out on loan; 37,000 drachmas were in the hands, throughout, of "the 200-drachma borrowers," and in the fourth and fifth years loans of 300 drachmas are mentioned, totalling at first 13,500 and finally 14,400 drachmas.[75] Finley's protestation that this requires us to envisage 185 borrowers of 200 drachmas and 48 (initially 45) of 300—"fantastic numbers," in his view— would appear to be satisfactorily met by Pouilloux's suggestion that 200 and 300 drachmas were standard sums on offer *in multiples*, according to the capacity of each borrower, together with the observation of Meiggs and Lewis that the Nemesis cult was in any case one of supra-parochial stature and may thus have attracted borrowers from outside the deme.[76]

The obvious question arises: can the situation here be regarded as in any way indicative of the general scale of loaning by demes? Obviously we cannot say for certain. Nonetheless it cannot readily be demonstrated either that the total resources available, through the Nemesis cult, to the Rhamnousioi were grossly incommensurate with a deme of this size or that the proportion of them out on loan was exceptional.[77]

Hippokleia, daughter of Demochares of Leukonoion, to the value of one talent, and hypothecated by whatever its worth exceeded that valuation to the (tribe) Kekropidai, the (*genos*) Lykomidai, and the Phlyeis. On multiple creditors, see Finley, *Land and Credit*, pp. 107ff.; on the connection between Phlya and the Lykomidai, Plut. *Them.* 1.3 and 15.2.

[74] The totals (assuming the years to be consecutive) are as follows: year 1, 49,729 drachmas and 3 obols; year 2, 51,397 drachmas and 5 obols; year 3, 48,723 drachmas and 2 obols; year 4, 55,712 drachmas and 1 obol; year 5, 56,606 drachmas and 4 obols.

[75] See the *editio princeps* of P. D. Stavropoullos, *AE* 1934-1935, pp. 128-132; Pouilloux, *Forteresse*, no. 35.

[76] Finley, *Land and Credit*, p. 285, n. 43; Pouilloux, *Forteresse*, no. 35 (at p. 149); ML, no. 53. It is usually assumed (e.g. by ML) that the cult of Nemesis at Rhamnous was under state, not deme, control; for the opposite view, see J. S. Boersma, *Athenian Building Policy from 561/0 to 405/4*, Groningen, 1970, p. 78, and T. Linders, *The Treasurers of the Other Gods in Athens and their functions*, Beiträge zur klassischen Philologie 62, Meisenheim am Glan, 1975, p. 13 with n. 38.

[77] Comparison may be made with Ikarion (IG I³253) and Plotheia (IG I³258) in the same period. (*a*) Total resources: 8-10 talents for a deme the size of Rhamnous (bouleutic representation 8) *is* broadly comparable with 4-4½ talents in Ikarion (b.r. 5 or 4) and 3⅔ talents in Plotheia (b.r. 1); it is however quite possible that the Rhamnousioi commanded

B. Expenditure

The ordinary, recurrent expenditure of a deme divides obviously into two principal parts:[78] *administrative* expenses and *cult* expenses—both construed in the broadest sense.

1. ADMINISTRATION

One may assume that the majority of demes kept their day-to-day administrative expenditure as low as possible. For example we have no evidence, from any deme, of salaries for the demarch[79] or for other officials.[80] Nor is it at all likely even in the fourth century that payment was made for attendance at meetings of the deme assemblies. The evidence suggests, instead, that significant expenditure was entailed only by the actual activity of the assemblies, that is, as a direct or indirect consequence of their individual decisions and enactments.[81]

Whether to have the decree (or whatever the document might be) inscribed on stone was the first choice to be made. If this was thought necessary or desirable, instructions would be given—usually recorded as part of the document itself—to one or more of the deme's officials to pay out the money needed and have the stele cut and set up in an appropriate public place.[82] In the majority of cases no specific sum of money is mentioned; those made responsible for the task were presumably free, within reasonable limits, to spend whatever was called for, provided they duly accounted for it afterwards.[83] Occasionally a figure was, however,

---

other funds besides those of Nemesis. (*b*) Extent of loaning: a more difficult comparison, in both cases; the Ikarion accounts record only funds in reserve, and it is a matter of supposition (see for instance Schoeffer, "Demoi," col. 20) how much *if any* was out on loan; in Plotheia, conversely, the sums mentioned were all out on loan (according to the most satisfactory interpretation of the document; see below, section B.2), and it would perhaps be surprising if a deme of this size had much in reserve besides.

[78] Cf. Haussoullier, *Vie*, p. 63; Schoeffer, "Demoi," cols. 18-19.

[79] The sum allotted "to the demarch" in the Plotheia accounts (IG I³258, line 2) must, from the context, refer to sacrifices for which the demarch was responsible: Haussoullier, *Vie*, p. 145.

[80] A wage for such posts as "Schreiber" and "Herold" is nonetheless envisaged, gratuitously, by Schoeffer, "Demoi," col. 19.

[81] The only obvious expense entailed by the assembly meetings *per se* was the cost of any sacrifices which the proceedings required (see Isaeus 7.28, etc.).

[82] See Chap. 4A, sec. 3, especially the documentation in nn. 49-51.

[83] I.e., λογίσασθαι τοῖς δημόταις (or some similar phrase): see IG II²1184 (Cholargos), lines 24-25; SEG 28.102 (Eitea), lines 20-22; *AD* 11, 1927-1928, pp. 40-41, no. 4 (Halai Aixonides), line 13; *AM* 67, 1942, p. 10, no. 8 (Halai Aixonides), lines 5-6; SEG 25.155 (Rhamnous), lines 41-43; cf. *AM* 67, 1942, pp. 7-8, no. 5 (Gargettos), lines 5-9.

fixed in advance. It is thirty drachmas in one surviving instance,[84] but otherwise either ten[85] or—apparently more usually—twenty.[86] A norm, if such it was, of twenty drachmas in the fourth century would seem to be lower than the sum devoted to inscribing a typical city decree in the same period,[87] and might help to account for the poor quality of the engraving of some, at least, of the demes' inscriptions.[88]

Secondly, the implementation of the decree's provisions frequently entailed expense, particularly if (as was so often the case) its purpose was to bestow honors. Sometimes, for example, the honorand was granted a sum of money—anything between ten and a hundred drachmas—with which to offer sacrifice.[89] However, a more standard and significant item of expense might result from the award of a wreath or crown (στέ-φανος); for, at deme as at city level and elsewhere, this became the habitual honorific mode of the fourth and subsequent centuries. In the demes as in general, these crowns were either of foliage—usually olive (θαλλός), occasionally ivy (κιττός), laurel (δάφνη), or myrtle (μυρ-ρίνη)[90]—or else of gold. It was not the case that poor demes awarded

---

Note that such a stipulation was sometimes combined with a stated sum; references below, n. 86.

[84] IG II²1182 (Myrrhinous), lines 21-25.

[85] IG II²1186, lines 33-34, and SEG 28.103, lines 49-51 (both Eleusis).

[86] IG II²1206 (?Acharnai), lines 16-19; AE 1932, Chronika, pp. 30-32 (Halai Araphenides), lines 28-32; both add a λογίσασθαι clause (see above, n. 83). In addition the figure is possibly twenty drachmas in three other decrees: SEG 14.81 (deme unknown), lines 5-6, where Meritt explicitly modelled his restoration on IG II²1206 (above); and Agora 16, no. 54 (Kydathenaion), A, line 5, and B, line 6 (though the texts are not stoichēdon and would permit other restorations).

[87] I have not verified this systematically, but a perusal of Tod's selections reveals three stones costing twenty drachmas (Tod nos. 131, 135, 142) as against eight costing thirty (Tod nos. 117, 136, 139, 147, 167, 173, 178, 181).

[88] Note above all Köhler's complaints about the Myrrhinous decree IG II²1183 (cited by Kirchner ad loc.; and cf. Müller, de demis, p. 47). Haussoullier, Vie, p. 65, made a generalization of this: "les inscriptions des dèmes sont gravées moins soigneusement que les inscriptions d'Athènes." This is indeed true in many cases, but one should not overlook such examples of fine craftsmanship (and drafting) as IG II²1202 (Aixone); cf. Müller, de demis, pp. 46-47.

[89] Ten: IG II²1198 (Aixone), lines 13-18; AM 66, 1941, pp. 218-219, no. 1 (Aixone), lines 8-10. (?)Fifty: AE 1932, Chronika, pp. 30-32 (Halai Araphenides), lines 12-13. A hundred: IG II²1186 (Eleusis), lines 34-35; cf. SEG 24.153 (Teithras), lines 5-6, which may have been a simple gift. Note also IG II²1206 (?Acharnai), lines 2-12, where twenty drachmas "for the sacrifice" is to be paid annually; it is however not certain that this is an honorific decree at all, at least of the usual type.

[90] Olive: IG II²1199 (Aixone), lines 7-8, 18-19, and (presumably) 26; IG II²1210 (?Ana-gyrous), lines 3-4; IG II²1185 (Eleusis), lines 2-3 (restored); IG II²1156 (Eleusis), lines 48-49 (restored), cf. IG II²1189, line 7; SEG 28.103 (Eleusis), line 17; Hesp. 8, 1939, pp. 177-180 (Eleusis), lines 24-25; AE 1925-1926, pp. 168-177 (Halai Araphenides), lines 1-2; IG II²1176+ (Peiraieus), lines 35ff.; SEG 24.153 (Teithras), lines 4-5; IG II²1173 (deme un-

the former and wealthy demes the latter:[91] foliage crowns are found granted by demes whose resources were as great as any,[92] while small demes could crown in gold when they saw fit.[93] Evidently the choice was made on grounds of *ad hoc* appropriateness which to us usually remain opaque.[94] At all events, crowning in gold was the more common practice. Where the cost of the crowns is mentioned,[95] it ranges between a hundred drachmas[96] and a thousand,[97] but is most frequently five hundred.[98] Thus any self-respecting deme which wanted to praise and reward its magistrates, *chorēgoi*, or other benefactors, will have found it extremely difficult (in the second half of the fourth century, at any rate) to avoid substantial expense in doing so.[99]

2. CULT

The costs of cult—upkeep of temples and shrines, offering of regular sacrifices, celebration of recurrent festivals[100]—surely represented, for any

---

known), lines 9-10. *Ivy*: IG II²1178 (Ikarion), lines 3 and 9-10. *Laurel*: AD 11, 1927-1928, pp. 40-41, no. 4 (Halai Aixonides), lines 8 and 10. *Myrtle*: Hesp. 11, 1942, pp. 265-274, no. 51 (Melite), lines 9-10.

[91] *Pace* Haussoullier, *Vie*, p. 66.

[92] E.g. Aixone, Eleusis, Peiraieus; references above, n. 90.

[93] E.g. Eitea, Halimous; references below, n. 98.

[94] Certainly no idea of foliage crowns for "sacred" services and gold for "secular" is tenable in the great majority of instances; nor does the magnitude or value of the service itself seem to have been a determinant.

[95] It was not so mentioned, apparently, in the following cases: IG II²1189 (Eleusis), lines 9-10; IG II²1193 (Eleusis), lines 12-13; SEG 22.116 (Melite), lines 20-21; SEG 22.120 (Rhamnous), lines 2-3; SEG 21.520 (Teithras), lines 2-6. Note also crowning in gold κατὰ τὸν νόμον in the second half of the third century: IG II²1299 (Eleusis), line 75; SEG 25.155 (Rhamnous), lines 35-36; SEG 31.112 (Rhamnous), lines 6-8.

[96] AM 66, 1941, pp. 218-219, no. 1 (Aixone), lines 4-5 (two crowns, each of a hundred drachmas); SEG 28.103 (Eleusis), lines 10-14 (where the suggestion in the *editio princeps*—REG 91, 1978, pp. 289-306, at 303—that this is the same sum contributed by Moirokles, lines 8-9, is misconceived: the latter was explicitly destined εἰς τὰ Ἡ[ρ]||[ά]κ[λ]εια).

[97] IG II²1186 (Eleusis), lines 17-18; SEG 22.117 (Ikarion), line 7; IG II²1212 (deme unknown), lines 7-10.

[98] Aixone: IG II²1200, lines 8-10 (two crowns, each of five hundred drachmas); IG II²1202, lines 8-14 (the same); cf. also IG II²1198, lines 9-11, where the figure for the two crowns should doubtless be read as five hundred drachmas. Athmonon: IG II²1156, lines 57-58 and 59-60 (two crowns, each of five hundred drachmas); IG II²1203, lines 6-15 (*six* crowns, each of five hundred drachmas). Eitea: SEG 28.102, lines 12-13. Eleusis: IG II²1187, lines 8-9; IG II²1188, lines 18-20; IG II²1192, lines 5-7. Halai Araphenides: AE 1932, *Chronika*, pp. 30-32, lines 10-11. Halimous: SEG 2.7, lines 13-16. Unknown demes: IG II²1173, lines 5-7; IG II²1209, lines 15-16 (indeterminable plurality of crowns, each of five hundred drachmas).

[99] See further below, sec. C.

[100] Cf. Schoeffer, "Demoi," col. 18.

deme, the major object of regular expenditure,[101] and indeed the fundamental *raison d'être* of the budget as a whole. "The Attic demes functioned, of course, as religious units as well as political units";[102] and the access, during the last quarter-century, of so much fresh documentation relating to the religious life of the demes[103] has underscored not only how rich and varied it was but also the extent to which its financing was a constant concern.[104] The point is well illustrated by the pair of Eleusinian decrees found in 1970 and published in 1978. Their aim was to maximize the revenues and (thus) optimize the sacrifices for the cult of Herakles-in-Akris by leasing out stone-quarrying rights in the deme to the highest bidder. There are strict stipulations against using the money for any other purpose, and both the proposer of the scheme and his fellow demesman who successfully bid for the contract over a five-year term are praised and crowned accordingly.[105]

But what is lacking here, unfortunately, is any indication of the significance of this particular, hitherto unknown cult, and of the annual sum which was evidently sufficient for its maintenance, within the context of the Eleusinians' religious budget as a whole and the total income which that budget required from all sources.[106] From other demes there are other figures, more useful because more general, yet with attendant problems of their own. For example, the total cost of the fifty-nine annual sacrifices detailed in the fourth-century *fasti* from Erchia is approximately 547 drachmas, with no individual item exceeding 12 drachmas.[107] But does the document cover *all* of this (larger than average) deme's publicly financed sacrifices in the period? Sterling Dow has claimed that it does,[108] as a corollary of his controversial thesis that the heading of the stele, "the greater *dēmarchia*" (δημαρχία ἡ με(ί)ζων), does not refer to the demarch[109] but signifies "the increased scope of deme authority," that is, in taking over the financing of these sacrifices. For Dow there is thus no need to postulate the existence of another, concurrent document which set out the elements of the "lesser" demarch's calendar.[110] It has been

---

[101] Cf. Haussoullier, *Vie*, p. 63.

[102] Mikalson, "Religion," p. 424.

[103] Notably their *fasti* (calendars of festivals): see Chap. 7B.

[104] See esp. Dow, "Six calendars," p. 185, and Jameson, "Calendar," pp. 155-156.

[105] SEG 28.103; see above, n. 29.

[106] The Eleusinian *fasti* from somewhere between 330 and 270 (SEG 23.80; Dow/Healey, *Calendar*) offer scant assistance, since so little of the document has survived; cf. Dow, "Six calendars," pp. 171, 175.

[107] Dow, "Demarkhia," p. 187. The stone is SEG 21.541 (= Daux, "Démarchie").

[108] Dow, "Demarkhia," p. 210.

[109] As naturally supposed by Daux in the *editio princeps* (Daux, "Démarchie," p. 633).

[110] Dow, "Demarkhia," pp. 195-197 (and "Six calendars," pp. 182-183).

objected, however, that this interpretation entails construing both δημαρχία and με(ί)ζων in an unnatural sense;[111] and in any case these *fasti* make no mention of any biennial or quadrennial festivals.[112] Thus the likelihood must be that 547 drachmas represented only a proportion (if arguably a high one) of the recurrent cult expenses of Erchia in this period, and that in consequence the *totality* of such expenses in a deme can still, after a century and a half of new and varied data, be assessed only in the single and frequently debated case of Plotheia.

The inscription in question here (IG I³258, formerly IG II²1172),[113] parts of which have been quoted or cited already in this chapter, must now be set out and considered in its entirety:

```
          [κεφ]άλαια
          [δη]μάρχωι Χ
          [τα]μίαιν ἐς τὰ δι'ἔτος ἱερὰ ⌐ˣ
          [ἐ]ς τὸ Ἡρακλεῖον ⌐ˣ ΧΧ
(5)       [ἐ]ς Ἀφροδίσια ΧΗΗ
          [ἐ]ς Ἀνάκια ΧΗΗ
          [ἐ]ς τὴν ἀτέλειαν ⌐ˣ
          [ἐ]ς Ἀπολλώνια ΧΗ
          [ἐ]ς Πάνδια ⌐ Η
(10)      [μ]ισθώσεων ΗΔΔΔΗΗΗΙC
          [ἔδ]οξεν Πλωθειεῦσι· Ἀριστότιμος [ε]-
          [ἶπ]ε· τὸς μὲν ἄρχοντας τὸ ἀργυρίο ἀ[ξ]-
          [ιό]χρεως κυαμεύεν ὅσο ἑκάστη ἡ ἀρ[χ]-
          [ὴ ἄ]ρχει, τούτος δὲ τὸ ἀργύριον σῶν [π]-
(15)      [αρ]έχεν Πλωθεῦσι, περὶ μὲν ὅτο ἐστ[ὶ]
          [ψ]ήφισμα δανεισμὸ ἢ τόκος τεταγ[μέ]-
          νος κατὰ τὸ ψήφισμα δανείζοντα[ς κ]-
          [α]ὶ ἐσπράττοντας, ὅσον δὲ κατ' ἐν[ιαυ]-
          [τ]ὸν δανείζειυι δανείζυντας ὅ[στι]-
(20)      ς ἂν πλεῖστον τόκον διδῶι, ὃς ἂν [πεί]-
          [θ]ηι τὸς δανείζοντας ἄρχοντα[ς τιμ]-
          ήματι ἢ ἐγγυητῆι. ἀπὸ δὲ τὸ τόκο [τε κ]-
          αὶ τῶμ μισθώσεων ἀντὶ ὅτο ἂν τ[ῶν κε]-
          φαλαίων ὠνήματα ἦι μί[σ]θωσιν φ[έρο]-
(25)      γτα, θύεν τὰ ἱερὰ τά τε ἐς Πλωθεί[ας κ]-
          οινὰ καὶ τὰ ἐς Ἀθηναίος ὑπὲρ Πλ[ωθέ]-
```

---

[111] See Jameson, "Calendar," pp. 154-155, esp. 155, nn. 1-2.

[112] Mikalson, "Religion," pp. 427-428.

[113] Kirchner (for IG II²) had dated the stone ca. 400, but D. M. Lewis (IG I³) advocates Köhler's original fifth-century date, between 425 and 413.

[ω]ν τὸ κοινὸ καὶ τὰ ἐς τὰς πεντετ[ηρί]-
[δ]ας· καὶ ἐς τἆλλα ἱερά, ὅποι ἂν δέ[ηι Π]-
λωθέας ἅπαντας τελὲν ἀργύριο[ν ἐς]
(30) [ἱ]ερά, ἢ ἐς Πλωθέας ἢ ἐς Ἐπακρέα[ς ἢ ἐς]
['Α]θηναίος, ἐκ τὸ κοινὸ τὸς ἄρχο[ντας],
[ο]ἳ ἂν ἄρχωσι τὸ ἀργυρίο τὸ ἐς τὴ[ν ἀτ]-
[έ]λειαν, τελὲν ὑπὲρ τῶν δημοτῶν· [καὶ]
[ἐ]ς τὰ ἱερὰ τὰ κοινὰ ἐν ὅσοισιν ἐσ[τι]-
(35) [ῶ]νται Πλωθῆς οἶνον παρέχεν ἡδὺ[ν ἐ]-
[κ τὸ] κοινὸ, ἐς μὲν τὰ ἄλλα ἱερὰ μέχρ[ι]
[ἡμίχο ἑ]κάστωι τοῖς παρδσι Πλωθέ[ω]-
[ν, ...⁷... δὲ τῶ]ι διδασκάλωι κάδο[ν]
[......¹³...... ἀ]ποκαίοντι κ[....]
(40) [.......¹⁶.......] δημιοργ [....]
- -

Interpretation of this unique document must begin from the assumption
that the decree (lines 11ff.) and the figures listed before it are interde-
pendent. The main provisions of the decree, as they survive (lines 11-
33), may be paraphrased as follows. (*a*) An unspecified number of financial officials, capable of discharging the duties of each office, are to
be chosen by lot,[114] to safeguard the Plotheians' money.[115] (*b*) Insofar as
this money is the product of interest on loans, the officials are to manage
it either in accordance with preexisting decrees on the subject, where
they are applicable, or else, for loans made afresh each year, by con-
tracting with the individuals who offer the highest rates of interest (and
suitable guarantees).[116] (*c*) The income from both loan interest and leases
is to finance the sacrifices at festivals for the Plotheians, for the Athenians
on the Plotheians' behalf, and for the quadrennial festivals.[117] (*d*) Other
festivals—again of three kinds—which have hitherto been financed from
sums paid by all Plotheians individually, are to be financed on their
collective behalf from common funds by the officials in charge of the
"immunity money."[118]

Above the decree, and under the heading [κεφ]άλαια, appear eight
sums in drachmas earmarked for particular purposes: 1,000 to the demarch; 5,000 "to the two *tamiai* for the *hiera* through the year"; 7,000

[114] An alternative is to take τὸς ἄρχοντας as *subject* of κυαμεύεν—thus Haussoullier,
Vie, p. 75, but see Müller, *de demis*, p. 16, followed by Damsgaard-Madsen, "Démarques,"
p. 106, n. 16.
[115] For the phrase ἀργύριον σῶν παρέχειν, cf. Aristoph. *Lysistr.*, line 488.
[116] See above, sec. A.3.
[117] See on this Mikalson, "Religion," p. 426.
[118] See above, n. 9.

for the Herakleion; 1,200 each for the Aphrodisia and the Anakia; 5,000 "for the immunity"; 1,100 for the Apollonia; and 600 for the Pandia—the whole amounting to 22,100 drachmas. (Appended, in line 10, is the figure of 134 drachmas and 2½ obols, described as "of leases.")

What then are the [κεφ]άλαια? Two interpretations have been advocated over the years. One is that they are *consummationes, Ausgaben*, sums actually *spent* (or to be spent) in the ways specified.[119] The other is that they represent *Kapitalien*, funds out on loan, the *income* from which—a far smaller amount of money, necessarily—is being allocated.[120] The latter view has much more to recommend it, on two major counts:

1. *The figures themselves.* Those scholars, notably von Schoeffer and Guarducci, who have argued for the figures being actual expenditure have done so largely because "the income alone would have been too small to meet their idea of the deme's needs."[121] But in reality this argument operates in reverse; for it is inconceivable that the tiny deme of Plotheia could have spent three and two-thirds talents on its cult activities in one year. Finley noted the comparison with the accounts of Nemesis of Rhamnous, a deme several times the size of Plotheia, where the total cash holdings during a period of five years in the 440s ranged between eight and ten talents.[122] And one may now cite also the Erchia *fasti*, discussed above, where—in a deme far closer in size to Rhamnous than to Plotheia—one major category of regular cult *expenditure* (the annual festivals) required an outlay of ca. 547 drachmas in the second quarter of the fourth century. Arguments from one deme to another must obviously be used with circumspection, for size and wealth may not always have been in perfect correlation with each other; all the same it is evident that even the *income* on more than 22,000 drachmas will have given the Plotheians a surprisingly large amount to spend (see further, below).

2. *The internal logic of the document.* This, as already stated, presupposes that the [κεφ]άλαια and the decree are interconnected. Since the burden of the decree is concerned with the management of loans, the

[119] Thus e.g. Köhler *apud* IG II 570; Schoeffer, "Demoi," cols. 19-20 (responding to Szanto and Haussoullier; see next note); Kirchner *apud* IG II² 1172; Busolt/Swoboda, *Staatskunde*, p. 968, n. 5; M. Guarducci, *Historia: studi storici per l'antichità classica* (Milan/Rome) 9, 1935, pp. 205-222.

[120] Thus e.g. E. Szanto, *Untersuchungen über das attische Bürgerrecht*, Vienna, 1881, pp. 39-42; Haussoullier, *Vie*, pp. 63-64, 75-76; Finley, *Land and Credit*, pp. 284-285, n. 39; D. M. Lewis *apud* IG I³258. For κεφάλαιον as loan capital cf. e.g. Demosth. 27.64, Plato *Laws* 742C, and especially the accounts of Nemesis of Rhamnous (IG I³248, passim).

[121] Finley, *Land and Credit*, pp. 284-285, n. 39.

[122] Finley, *Land and Credit*, pp. 284-285, n. 39; for the exact figures see above, n. 74. (We cannot necessarily assume, however, that *all* the funds of the Rhamnousioi were kept with Nemesis; cf. above, n. 77.)

figures which precede it may thus be naturally held to relate to such loans. Were *they themselves* taken as totals of *interest*, they would represent, at a rate of, say, 12 percent a year,[123] a capital holding of more than thirty talents—an absurdity. To regard them as *Kapitalien* is therefore inescapable. (Admittedly line 10, on this view, records a figure of a different kind, the actual income from leases,[124] but in this summary context it could hardly have done otherwise.)

Assuming, then, an overall interest rate of 12 percent *per annum*,[125] the figures for *expenditure* emerge as follows: 120 drachmas to the demarch, 600 to the treasurers, 840 for the Herakleion, 144 each for the Aphrodisia and the Anakia, 600 for the "immunity" fund, 132 for the Apollonia, and 72 for the Pandia—a total of 2,652 drachmas. But we may follow Haussoullier in discounting, as an item of *recurrent* outlay, the ca. 840 drachmas of interest on the 7,000 drachmas earmarked for the Herakleion—this presumably refers to the refurbishing of a temple or the like—and the figure thus falls to 1,812 drachmas.[126] With the addition to this of the stated income from leases,[127] the grand total for the recurrent cult expenses of the Plotheians in this unknown year during the last quarter of the fifth century turns out to be of the order of 1,946 drachmas and 2½ obols, or something under one-third of one talent.

In view of the size of Plotheia it is obviously likely that most demes spent more than this, some many times more. On the other hand, other demes of the same or similar size may well have spent less. The level of expenditure in Plotheia, in short, should arguably be located near, though not necessarily at, the bottom of what was surely an extensive *range* of routine deme expenditure on cult; and it is in this—not in any support derivable for the unhelpful notion of a deme's "average" expenditure in this area[128]—that the value and importance of the figure lies.

As to the detailed allocation of the sums, the document as a whole answers some of our questions while leaving others in suspension. The decree distinguishes, from the viewpoint of financing, between two main groups of *hiera*, each of them in three parts. The first (lines 22-28) is to be funded out of the income from loans and leases; the second (lines 28ff.), hitherto financed from payments by individuals, from a common

---

[123] For 12% cf. e.g. IG II²2492 (Aixone), lines 36-38; but see below, n. 125.

[124] Which is what it must be: see above, n. 22.

[125] Cf. Haussoullier, *Vie*, p. 64, cf. 79. In fact the interest rates will doubtless have varied, if the officials did their job as instructed (lines 18-22).

[126] Haussoullier, *Vie*, p. 64.

[127] *Pace* Haussoullier, *Vie*, p. 64, lines 22ff. of the decree seem clearly to earmark for cult purposes the income from leases as well as from loans.

[128] For otiose calculations based on such an "average," see Schoeffer, "Demoi," col. 20.

"immunity" fund. How precisely these two groups differed from each other *per se* is obscure,[129] but the components of the [κεφ]άλαια must surely correspond to this basic fiscal distinction, even though the modest rent-income is not explicitly allocated to either.[130] If, *faute de mieux*, we adhere to Haussoullier's figures calculated on the basis of an annual interest rate of 12 percent, 600 drachmas are destined for the "immunity" fund and therefore, evidently, to the second category of *hiera*. This leaves 1,212 drachmas for the first category. But within (it would seem) this first category some administrative distinctions are drawn: another 600 drachmas are allotted to the two *tamiai*, "for the *hiera* through the year," yet 120 drachmas go directly to the demarch, presumably for cult duties discharged by him personally; and four festivals—conceivably biennial or even quadrennial rather than annual ones?—are given a separate budget, to the tune of a further 492 drachmas in all. The fact that the rural Dionysia receives no special mention is somewhat surprising, but in this as in other respects the rationale of the distribution of funds lies beyond our divination.

C. Balancing the Budget

From the evidence so far discussed, patchy and problematical though it is, the following general picture of deme finances seems to emerge. To meet its regular expenditure, on administration and (especially) on cult, a deme would command any or all of five sources of income: taxes (τέλη), exacted particularly, perhaps, from non-citizens and from non-demesmen resident or owning property in the deme; levies (sometimes also called τέλη) on the demesmen for specific cult purposes; liturgies of various kinds; rents from the deme's land and other assets; and the interest from whatever proportion of the deme's capital resources was out on loan. Sundry fines might represent a sixth source, but only as and when they were actually incurred.

How exactly these monies were handled, administratively speaking, was up to each individual deme acting through its assembly, but one recurring phenomenon is worthy of note. In the Eleusinian decree of

---

[129] The two overt differences between the two groups are obviously that the first includes the quadrennial festivals and that the second embraces ἱερὰ . . . ἐς Ἐπακρέα[ς (on which see R. J. Hopper, *ABSA* 56, 1961, pp. 217-219; and cf. now *AE* 1980, pp. 94-95, line 1— see Appendix 3, no. 97). But we have no clue to the distinction, other than the financial one, between e.g. ἱερὰ . . . ἐς Πλωθει[ᾶς κ]οινά and ἱερὰ . . . ἐς Πλωθέας.

[130] As the stele is not acephalous, the belief (Schoeffer, "Demoi," col. 20) that it was so allocated, in a lost opening section of the document, is erroneous.

332/1 which earmarked the revenue from the leasing of stone-quarrying rights in the deme for the cult of Herakles-in-Akris, the demarch is ordered to provide ten drachmas "from the *prosodos* of the god" for the inscription of the stele.[131] Whether this refers only to the lease-income which is the subject of the decree or whether this cult had other (evidently inadequate) sources of *prosodos*, what is revealed here is that at least part of the financial resources managed by the Eleusinians' deme assembly was regarded as belonging to the god rather than to the deme. The same— and to a more significant extent—was true in Rhamnous, where in the 440s sums of between eight and ten talents were held in the name of the goddess Nemesis and administered by the *hieropoioi* of her cult.[132] "The so-called temple funds," as Moses Finley has observed, "were deme funds, of course, and the administrative technique, common in Athens and elsewhere, of handling such moneys through the temple had no special significance, legally or otherwise."[133] Certainly such funds were *in fact* under the "secular" control of the deme itself. Just as a deme rented out its deities' *temenē*,[134] so it could also—if it saw fit—order the loaning of cult funds. This, implicit in the Nemesis accounts with their dating by demarchs, is made explicit in the decree of the Myrrhinousioi, from the second half of the fourth century, which laid down the procedure to be followed, "if money is needed," by the priests in lending the *chrēmata* of their various (unspecified) deities.[135]

Whether all demes used temple funds as a means of managing their finances is necessarily indeterminable, and even those which demonstrably did so are unlikely to have found it a convenient or appropriate system for all purposes. To borrow the terminology of modern banking, a good deal of a deme's routine income and expenditure will surely have passed uncomplicatedly through its current account; that is, it will have been paid in to the demarch or other officials, kept by them,[136] and paid out again sooner rather than later. On this same analogy the temple funds, if any, may be regarded as the deme's deposit account(s), accumulated capital reserves which might ideally, once they had met the expenses of their own cults, be left undisturbed[137] but which were perhaps

[131] SEG 28.103, lines 49-51.

[132] IG I³248; *hieropoioi* in line 33.

[133] Finley, *Land and Credit*, p. 95.

[134] See above, n. 21.

[135] IG II²1183, lines 27-32 (quoted above, n. 68).

[136] And if necessary passed between them—most commonly, no doubt, from *tamias* (or *tamiai*) to demarch; see for instance AE 1932, *Chronika*, pp. 30-32 (Halai Araphenides), lines 25ff.

[137] As they apparently were in Ikarion in the third quarter of the fifth century (IG I³253;

more likely to be employed, in part, in the generation of income from loans—a course of action envisaged as a possibility by the Myrrhinousioi and illustrated at work in Plotheia and Rhamnous.

＊

By these means, then, the demes sought to balance their budgets, to the extent of ensuring income sufficient to meet foreseeable expenditure. But did they succeed?

One very obvious yet unavoidable practical problem lay in the fact that not all expenses *were* foreseeable, or at any rate not routine and recurrent in the normal budgetary sense, but arose *ad hoc* out of particular circumstances and needs. The Acharnians, for example, were confronted by such circumstances when, shortly after the middle of the fourth century (and in accordance with an oracle from Delphi), they resolved to construct altars for Ares and Athena Areia, having received the report of a commission of the demesmen elected to examine the costs of this.[138] Another, earlier instance of building expenditure seems to occur, as we saw, in the summary budget of the Plotheians, where the income—possibly ca. 840 drachmas—on a loan or loans of 7,000 drachmas is designated "for the Herakleion."[139] Here the demesmen were fortunate, in apparently being able to absorb this item of expenditure within their normal cult budget, by lending out a larger proportion of their reserves than they might otherwise have done.

But not all demes had such surplus funds available, or at least not at the right moment. For example, no such deposits were seemingly at the disposal of the deme which, to judge from its fragmentary decree on the subject, suffered catastrophic damage to the fabric of its cult center at the beginning of the third century; instead the decree refers to a levy (*eparchē*) on officeholders, for the building of *hiera* and *anathēmata*.[140] At much the same time the demesmen of Peiraieus were also faced with the task of financing the construction or repair of buildings, but their (equally fragmentary) decree on the subject suggests that their preferred solution was a different one: it either consisted in or at least included a

---

see above, n. 77), where between 4 and 4½ talents was simply passed, for six years, from the custody of one demarch to his successor.

[138] SEG 21.519.

[139] IG I³258, line 4.

[140] IG II²1215; cf. Chap. 4, n. 131. A similar background and purpose might be suggested for SEG 24.197, a list (from the beginning of the fourth century) of names and patronymics from Amarousi (= Athmonon); see Appendix 3, no. 15. There, however, the contributions may have been required from a larger section of the demesmen, for the number of names—thirty-six survive—seems too large for officeholders.

call for gifts (*epidoseis*), both in cash and in kind.[141] This perhaps warrants the conjecture that the Peiraieis could if necessary have funded the project(s) adequately out of normal resources and revenues; the role played by *epidoseis* (whether solicited or spontaneous) in other demes sometimes looks more like that of gilding the lily—enriching an already rich communal life—than that of bringing the deme through a budgetary crisis.[142] Be that as it may, for demes which found themselves in genuine financial embarrassment the immediate problem may have been not so much choosing an appropriate "theoretical" means of raising the money as actually laying hands on it quickly enough—in short, a problem of liquidity. Here a *deus ex machina* was required: a demesman or other benefactor wealthy enough, like the honorand in (?)Erikeia, to meet at least part of the cost in advance out of his own pocket.[143]

So we see here four possible methods of financing extraordinary, large-scale deme expenditure: putting reserve funds, if any, out to interest; ordering a special levy; inviting *epidoseis*, in cash and/or kind; and—to expedite the actual outlay—individual prepayment. All but the first of these represented a direct appeal to the public spirit, and the purses, of a particular section of the demesmen. They were not necessarily the very rich, except in liquidity crises, and not necessarily the magistrates and officials, who may not always have been men of property, but rather the wider spectrum of demesmen definable—for us—by this very criterion, their participation as individuals in the community's affairs and, especially, their expenditure of both money and time on the community's behalf. Examples of the multifarious activities of such men have already been marshalled and discussed,[144] and in many cases it can be seen that the tasks which they fulfilled were specific, short-term, and nonrecurrent: witness for instance the twenty-four men elected in Halai Aixonides in ca. 360 to "make" (ποήσασθαι)—which surely entailed paying for—an *agalma* for Aphrodite.[145] For this service they were crowned by their

---

[141] *Hesp.* 3, 1934, pp. 44-46, no. 33; gifts of stones are mentioned in line 7, and monetary donations (probably) in lines 18-19, cf. 8-10.

[142] It is noteworthy that individual *epidoseis* (some so-called, others so to be regarded) are attested most frequently in wealthy Eleusis. See, for instance, IG II²949, lines 33-34; IG II²1191, lines 21-23; SEG 22.127, line 18; *Hesp.* 8, 1939, pp. 177-180, lines 8-10; SEG 28.103, lines 8-9; also the epidosis-liturgies, as we may term them, of the metic Damasias (IG II²1186, lines 11-14). We have of course more inscriptions from Eleusis than from any other deme, but that in itself is some index of the deme's prosperity.

[143] IG II²1215, lines 9ff., esp. 12-13, προαναλίσκων τοῖς δημόται|ς παρ᾽ ἑαυτοῦ ἐπὶ τε̄ι ἐπαρχε̄ι κτλ. Other examples: SEG 21.519 (the Acharnian altars, see above), lines 17-18; IG II²1191 (Xenokles' bridge in Eleusis), lines 21-23.

[144] Chap. 5, pp. 145-148.

[145] IG II²2820.

grateful fellow demesmen; and so too were the six *merarchai* of Ath-monon who in the year 325/4 were declared to have supervised sacrifices and discharged other public duties with zeal and efficiency.[146]

Yet with this latter instance the ground of our investigation has begun to shift, and significantly, for here the deme is apparently reliant upon these six men not merely to assist in extraordinary expenditure but actually to assume responsibility for some of the ordinary cult outlay of the Athmoneis in the year in question. It is not impossible that these *merarchai* were magistrates or quasi-magistrates whose function was to disburse common funds; but more probably, as Michael Jameson has suggested, they were "liturgists," spending their own resources on the deme's behalf[147]—and doing so as part of the regular, institutional structure of its budgeting. Did the six act together or separately? We cannot say, but an attraction of assuming that each of the six took on his own *meros* is the parallel which would then suggest itself with what we find in Erchia several decades earlier. In his *editio princeps* of the Erchia calendar Georges Daux drew attention to the curious fact that its five columns (headed with the letters A through E) represented a "découpage," a vertical division, of the sacrifices listed; and this indicated to him a division of administrative responsibility between "cinq commissions ou commissaires . . . sous l'autorité du démarque."[148] Sterling Dow, however, raised a somewhat different possibility. From the fact, chiefly, that the costs of the sacrifices in the five columns each amounted to almost exactly the same total sum (apparently between 108 and 111 drachmas) Dow plausibly inferred that the *raison d'être* of the document was primarily a financial one, namely, the allocation of these cult expenses between five liturgists.[149] Moreover, in his subsequent, comparative examination of six Athenian sacrificial calendars Dow found good reason to suggest that the *fasti* of the Marathonian Tetrapolis (IG II²1358), also from the first half of the fourth century, likewise show signs of "semi-voluntary tax-donations."[150]

---

[146] IG II²1203.

[147] Jameson, "Leasing," pp. 72-73; see above, Chap. 5, pp. 147-148, the argument of which I now reiterate and expand.

[148] Daux, "Démarchie," pp. 615-617.

[149] Dow, "Demarkhia," pp. 187, 193-195, and 213 (where the suggestion that this was a novice liturgy for young men spoils a sound chain of inferences with a gratuitous conjecture). See also Dow, "Six calendars," pp. 172, 175, 180, 182-183.

[150] Dow, "Six calendars," pp. 181-182, cf. 175. His observations are founded upon the readings of seven lines of face B by W. Peek, *AM* 67, 1942, pp. 12-13, no. 10. It seems to be a list of names and figures; the names have the (abbreviated) demotics of Marathon and Oinoe, and the best-preserved figure is apparently 131 drachmas and 1 obol. "The appearance, of course, is that of a list of taxpayers with their payments, and the natural

The impression which this evidence creates, then, is that liturgical financing—in a broader and more basic sense than the one assumed earlier in this chapter[151]—was an important element in the *regular* cult budgeting of at least some of the demes (and by no means only the smallest ones) in the fourth century. It cannot of course be conclusively demonstrated that this was not equally true of the fifth century, given the exiguous documentation from that period. We have no idea, for example, when the *merarchai* of Athmonon were first appointed. Yet the fact is, as Dow has emphasized, that the Athenian sacrificial calendars display a preoccupation with financing; and at least three individual demes (Eleusis, Erchia, Teithras) and one grouping of demes (the Tetrapolis) betrayed this preoccupation in their fourth-century *fasti*. Thus they were apparently shorter of money than before and devising new ways to raise it.[152]

But even if this is the right line of interpretation to take, its full significance is difficult to appreciate without a context. For Dow, what these documents illustrate is "the devolution from private to public" as regards the type and source of the funding.[153] "Formerly," he maintains, "the rich Gennetai could and did pay for most of the sacrifices in the Deme. . . . Now, however, the rich were poorer. The situation was desperate enough so that an elaborate system of allotment had to be devised in order to get the sacrifices paid for . . . [namely] the taking over of the financing of the sacrifices, and of the control, by public authority, that is, by the Deme." This may be so. Yet it is possible to argue, from another point of view, that what we glimpse here is quite the contrary: a devolution, in real terms, *from public to private*. Dow's scenario depends very heavily, as he acknowledges, upon the Erchia calendar, and especially upon an understanding of its heading δημαρχία ἡ με(ί)ζων in a sense which, as we have seen, there is good reason to dispute.[154] In Plotheia, as we have also seen, the "scope of deme authority"—that is, the *dēmarchia* as Dow construes it—was apparently being exercised over the cult budget already in the last quarter of the fifth century, in that it was paid for then out of common revenues and resources; and we know far too little about the financing of cult activities in the demes in that period to dismiss this

---

suggestion is that the demesmen named were paying for the sacrifices" (Dow, "Six calendars," p. 182).

[151] See sec. A.1.

[152] Dow, "Six calendars," passim. The *Thorikos* calendar (as will be seen in Chap. 7B, sec. 4) is something of an exception to Dow's generalization, but it remains valid enough.

[153] Dow, "Six calendars," p. 183 (and the following quotations from pp. 180 and 182-183); cf. his "Demarkhia," p. 197.

[154] See above, pp. 164-165.

as an anomaly, in favor of Dow's model of wholly private financing by the *genē*.

Thus, to reiterate the point, if it is justifiable to discern any overall change at all in the method of cult financing in the demes as between the fifth century and the fourth, that change was probably not the assumption by the demes, for the first time, of responsibility for cults and festivals hitherto funded and managed privately. It was, rather, an increased resort, by demes faced with a chronic fiscal shortfall, to the resources of individuals to pay for what had once come out of general community monies. Naturally the activities funded in this way were "public" just as before, but they were also "private" in the sense of now relying, more than before, on the public spirit and generosity of individual demesmen. Having been formerly responsible only for the jam, one might say, such men were now the providers of much of the bread-and-butter besides,[155] and due gratitude was expressed to them.[156] This in itself, we should remember, could be an expensive business: the six *merarchai*, for example, were each crowned in gold by their fellow Athmoneis to the tune of five hundred drachmas.[157] The pursuit of income thus led on to further expenditure for the deme, in a never-ending cycle.

[155] By the jam I mean liturgies in the narrow, technical sense, as in fifth-century Ikarion (IG I³254).

[156] Note the phrase καλῶς καὶ φιλοτίμως in the decree honoring and crowning the *merarchai* of Athmonon (IG II²1203, line 4), and the same concept in numerous other deme decrees of the second half of the fourth century; see on this Chap. 8B.

[157] IG II²1203, lines 14-15.

CHAPTER 7

RELIGION

A. Preliminaries

In *La Vie Municipale* Haussoullier divided his subject into two parts, dealing first with the "constitution civile" of the deme and then with its "constitution religieuse." The neatness of this bipartition was more apparent than real, however, for under the first heading he had, inevitably, to investigate such matters as the control of cult expenditure by the deme assemblies and the role of the demarchs in the religious sphere. Likewise, in the different format adopted in this present book, several important aspects of deme religion have already arisen for discussion, whether summarily or in detail. In particular we have seen (in Chapter 5) how religious duties were undertaken both by the demarchs—acting sometimes as agents of their demes, sometimes on behalf of the state—and by other deme officials, ordinary or extraordinary; and (in Chapter 6) how expenditure on, and thus income for, cult activities was central to any deme's budget. Indeed it is perfectly proper to claim as a *datum*, not a *demonstrandum*, of the subject the observation that the demes "functioned . . . as religious units as well as political units,"[1] so few are the recorded facets of deme life in which the sacred and the secular are not found closely interwoven.

Yet this very fact creates its own problems, which make it idle to pretend that deme religion is anything but an amorphous and intractable topic to treat in its own right. Whatever obstacles block a clear view of the functioning of the demes as "political units," they are multiplied several times over when one adjusts one's terms of reference and attempts to look at them as "religious units." To some extent, as we shall see, this is a difficulty of marshalling and organizing the evidence. But in truth the problems arise at a more fundamental level than that of practical methodology; they stem from the very nature and history of the Kleisthenic demes as such. In Chapter 1A I was at some pains to contest the

---

[1] Mikalson, "Religion," p. 424. (I am much indebted, throughout this chapter, to Mikalson's succinct but well-directed study.) For the provision of religious activities by the demes, the *locus classicus* is Aristot. *EN* 1160a14-25; cf. Plato *Laches* 187D-E; etc.

idea—which some scholars have felt to be self-evident—that the collective, communal activities of most of the demes pre-dated to any significant degree the reforms of Kleisthenes, which gave the demes an official standing for the first time.[2] For the demes as "political units" (to adhere to Mikalson's terms) the importance of 508/7 as *terminus ante quem non* is plain. It is far from plain, however, in the religious sphere, where arguably the likelihood is quite the reverse: whatever deme cults and festivals were inaugurated in or after 508/7, many more had surely come down from archaic times, to be incorporated *to a greater or lesser extent* into the new local institutional frameworks.[3] When Thucydides in 2.14-16 described the evacuation of Attica in 431, at the beginning of the Peloponnesian War, he noted how distressing it was for the country people—who made up the majority of "the Athenians" (2.14.2)—to leave behind ancestral holy places which were a permanent heritage of their origins as a community (ἱερὰ ἃ διὰ παντὸς ἦν αὐτοῖς ἐκ τῆς κατὰ τὸ ἀρχαῖον πολιτείας πάτρια, 2.16.2). It was apparently not impossible for Athenians of Thucydides' generation to describe the Kleisthenic reforms themselves, or what had resulted from them, as "ancestral";[4] nonetheless in this instance—that of people of whom it could be said in all seriousness that they had only recently reestablished themselves after the evacuation of 480 (2.16.1)—it is surely clear that many if not all of the cults in question were genuinely ancient ones. Indeed we have very few instances where it is certain that a deme cult is post-Kleisthenic, as one can say of Artemis Aristoboule in Melite, the work of Themistokles.[5] Rather, when Strabo (9.1.17-22) and, especially, Pausanias (1.1-39) list what seemed to them the most noteworthy cults and cult monuments of the demes, the probability must be that many, even most, pre-dated the epoch which saw an official political identity conferred upon the communities in which they were located.[6]

[2] See Chap. 1, pp. 15-16.

[3] According to ?Aristot. *Ath. Pol.* 21.6 Kleisthenes "left everyone free to belong to clans and brotherhoods and to hold priesthoods as tradition dictated" (τὰ δὲ γένη καὶ τὰς φρατρίας καὶ τὰς ἱερωσύνας εἴασεν ἔχειν ἑκάστους κατὰ τὰ πάτρια). There is no warrant for Feaver's translation of τὰς ἱερωσύνας as "the priesthoods *belonging to the various demes*" (Feaver, "Priesthoods," p. 133, with my emphasis); indeed, in context it would be more natural to understand "the old priesthoods attached to particular γένη and phratries" (thus Rhodes, *Commentary*, p. 258); but Kleisthenes' non-interference with priesthoods may well have *included* those in the demes.

[4] See, most obviously, ?Aristot. *Ath. Pol.* 29.3 (Kleitophon and the "ancestral laws" of Kleisthenes), with M. I. Finley, *The Use and Abuse of History*, London, 1975, pp. 36-40.

[5] For references, see Chap. 3, n. 54.

[6] One should strictly say "*most* of the communities in which they were located," for not every center of *cult* significance was recognized as a Kleisthenic deme: witness, most glaringly, Brauron (Chap. 1, n. 83), on which see now Osborne, *Demos*, chap. 8.

For this reason alone, then, the whole idea of a "deme cult" is a problematic one, but the term need not be abandoned if it is used with care.[7] Obviously the impact of 508/7 is impossible to assess in any detail, but in broad terms what the creation of the Kleisthenic deme system did, in the religious domain, was to superimpose upon a varied pattern of preexisting cult activity a new framework of local institutions which itself embodied the capacity, *sooner or later*, both to generate new cults and festivals of its own and to assume partial or total control of the old ones. Indeed "control"—in the twin senses of the financing of the cult or festival, and the personnel found in charge of it—is clearly the criterion which can best bring the notion of a "deme cult" into sharper focus.

1. CULT FINANCING

The question of who paid for due religious observance in classical Athens, with its emphasis on the public execution of sacrifices and other ritual acts, was an ever-present one. In the lexicographers we find a fundamental distinction drawn on this basis between cults financed by a deme (δημοτικά) and by the *dēmos* as a whole, the state (δημοτελῆ).[8] The distinction is both clear and clearly important; it carries implications, as we shall see, for the organization and timing of festivals as well as for their finance; but no doubt, like so much other lexicographical lore, it is derived from the fourth century,[9] and thus reflects the end of a process which in practice will have been both lengthy and in some respects incomplete. In IG I³258, lines 25ff., the demesmen of Plotheia in the last quarter of the fifth century identified one of the three categories of sacrifices for which deme money was being provided as "for the Athenians on behalf of the community of the Plotheians" (τὰ ἐς Ἀθηναίος ὑπὲρ Πλ[ωθέω]ν τὸ κοινὸ). As Mikalson points out, the surviving deme calendars and *leges sacrae* provide examples, of two kinds, of what must be meant by this: first, local observances of state festivals, and second, the contribution by demes of either sacrificial victims or money to state festivals held outside the deme (that is, usually, in the city).[10] Under the first heading come, for instance,

---

[7] For a useful discussion of "the cult of the deme," exploring some of the subtleties of the relationship between local cults and the demes as political units, see Osborne, *Demos*, pp. 178-182.

[8] *Lex Seguer.* V, *Lexeis Rhetorikai*, δημοτελῆ καὶ δημοτικὰ ἱερεῖα διαφέρει· τὰ μὲν δημοτελῆ θύματα ἡ πόλις δίδωσιν, εἰς δὲ τὰ δημοτικὰ οἱ δημόται κτλ. [= Bekker, *Anecd. Gr.* 1.240.28]. Cf. Harpoc., δημοτελῆ καὶ δημοτικὰ ἱερά; Hesych., δημοτελῆ ἱερά; Suda, δημοτελῆ. For δημοτελῆ cf. Thuc. 2.15.2, Plato *Laws* 935B, etc.

[9] In the law preserved in [Demosth.] 43.71 the terminology is slightly different: ἱερὸν Ἀθηναίων δημόσιον ἢ δημοτικόν.

[10] Mikalson, "Religion," pp. 426-431.

two groups of sacrifices enshrined in the *fasti* from Erchia. On 27 Gamelion, the day of the Theogamia in Athens, there were four sacrifices in Erchia (all in the sanctuary of Hera, whose festival it was), to Zeus Teleios, Poseidon, Kourotrophos, and Hera herself;[11] and on 3 Skirophorion, almost certainly the day of the Arre(to)phoria in Athens, there were six sacrifices in Erchia (all "on the akropolis," ἐμ Πόλε)—to Kourotrophos again, with Athena Polias, Aglauros, Zeus Polieus, Poseidon, and [Pandrosos].[12] What is common to these and other instances, as Mikalson observes, is that the festivals celebrated are those which concerned the family and were observed primarily or even exclusively by women.[13] As regards the rather different matter of the participation of demes, *qua* demes, in festivals or sacrifices outside the deme itself, three or four demes offer illustrations of this: Skambonidai and the Synoikia, on 16 Hekatombaion;[14] Eleusis and (possibly) Thorikos and the Pyanopsia, on 7 Pyanopsion;[15] and Erchia and (possibly) Thorikos and the Diasia, on 23 Anthesterion.[16]

Instances such as these necessarily blur the δημοτικός/δημοτελής distinction from all points of view including the financial. But they do so

[11] SEG 21.541, B, lines 32-39 (Kourotrophos and Hera); Γ, lines 38-41 (Zeus Teleios); Δ, lines 28-32 (Poseidon). See F. Salviat, *BCH* 88, 1964, pp. 647-654; Mikalson, *Calendar*, pp. 106-107, 189 (and "Religion," p. 429).

[12] SEG 21.541, A, lines 57-65 (Kourotrophos and Athena Polias); B, lines 55-59 (Aglauros); Γ, lines 59-64 (Zeus Polieus); Δ, lines 56-60 (Poseidon). Pandrosos is restored in E, lines 65-70, by Jameson, "Calendar," pp. 156-158. See also W. Burkert, *Hermes* 94, 1966, p. 5, n. 2; Mikalson, *Calendar*, pp. 166-167, and "Religion," p. 431. On the Arre(to)phoria in general, see Deubner, *Feste*, pp. 9-17.

[13] Mikalson, "Religion," p. 429, cf. 431. Another example which he gives is that of the Skira, whose celebration in the deme of Peiraieus is attested in IG II²1177, line 10 (mid fourth century); cf. IG I³250, A, line 6 (Paiania).

[14] IG I³244, C, lines 16-19, with Mikalson, "Religion," p. 430 (and *Calendar*, pp. 29-31); cf. Parke, *Festivals*, pp. 30-32. Note that Thuc. 2.15.2 explicitly calls this a ἑορτὴ δημοτελής; was it one in the 460s?

[15] Eleusis: SEG 23.80, fr. A, col. I, lines 8-19, with Mikalson, "Religion," p. 426 (and *Calendar*, pp. 69-70). Thorikos: *AC* 52, 1983, pp. 150-174, line 27 (where the reading Πυανοψίοις is plain enough but doubt attaches to whether this was an offering made in Athens or a local observance; cf. below, p. 197).

[16] Erchia: SEG 21.541, A, lines 37-43, with Jameson, "Calendar," pp. 159-172; see also Mikalson, *Calendar*, pp. 117, 120-121, and "Religion," pp. 429-430. No connection with known state festivals can be established for the Erchians' four sacrifices in Athens on 12 Metageitnion (A, lines 1-5, Apollo Lykeios—see M. H. Jameson, *Archaiognosia* 1, 1980, pp. 213-236, esp. 227-228; B, lines 1-5, Demeter ἐν Ἐλευσι(νίωι)—on the locative see Daux, "Démarchie," p. 624; Γ, lines 13-18, Zeus Polieus; Δ, lines 13-17, Athena Polias), nor for their offering to Zeus Epakrios ἐν Ὑμηττῶι on 16 Thargelion (E, lines 59-64). Thorikos: *AC* 52, 1983, pp. 150-174, lines 34-35 (= 22-23 Vanderpool), with Mikalson, "Religion," p. 430; again (cf. preceding note) the *place* of this offering is the doubtful point; cf. below, p. 197.

only, so to speak, in one direction: the demes contribute—at times—
towards the state cults, but the state does not reciprocate. Thus a "deme
cult" is *par excellence* a cult such as that of Herakles-in-Akris, the subject
of the Eleusinians' two decrees of 332/1 in which the revenue from deme
property is devoted to its maintenance;[17] and by the same obvious token
the Erchia calendar alone offers fifty-nine examples of "deme sacrifices."
But for how long had this been so? Before Kleisthenes, local cults had
presumably been paid for by the *genē* and other kinship groups, and—
as argued above—it is unlikely that 508/7 brought an immediate change
in this. Rather, the process whereby the demes took over financial responsibility will have been a gradual and piecemeal one, beginning in
the fifth century and largely completed during the fourth.[18]

2. CULT PERSONNEL

Here much the same general pattern—the gradual, unsystematic, and
complex integration of the new secular officialdom of the Kleisthenic
demes into preexisting cult duties—may be suggested. In *Politics*
1322b18-29 Aristotle distinguishes between two kinds of religious superintendence (ἐπιμέλεια ἡ πρὸς τοὺς θεούς). One comprises priests
(ἱερεῖς),[19] superintendents of the fabric of temples and other cult duties
(ἐπιμεληταὶ τῶν περὶ τὰ ἱερὰ τοῦ σῴζεσθαί τε τὰ ὑπάρχοντα
καὶ ἀνορθοῦσθαι τὰ πίπτοντα τῶν οἰκοδομημάτων καὶ τῶν ἄλλων
ὅσα τέτακται πρὸς τοὺς θεούς), *hieropoioi*,[20] temple guardians (να-
οφύλακες), and treasurers of sacred monies (ταμίαι τῶν ἱερῶν
χρημάτων). The other consists of officials who perform "all the communal sacrifices which the law [or custom?] does not assign to the priests"
(τὰς θυσίας . . . τὰς κοινὰς πάσας, ὅσας μὴ τοῖς ἱερεῦσιν ἀπο-
δίδωσιν ὁ νόμος) but "to those who derive their office from the common
hearth" (ἀπὸ τῆς κοινῆς ἑστίας ἔχουσι τὴν τιμήν); that is, secular
officials whose functions involve, *inter alia*, the offering of sacrifices on
behalf of the community which they represent. As Haussoullier commented when citing this passage, the plainest illustration of this second
category as far as the demes are concerned is obviously that of the demarch,[21] whose role in the religious domain, especially though not exclusively in the offering of sacrifices, has been outlined in Chapter 5A. The

---

[17] SEG 28.103; cf. Chap. 6, n. 29.

[18] See Chap. 6, pp. 174-175.

[19] This may be taken to embrace priestesses (ἱέρειαι).

[20] The word defies translation. For *hieropoioi* in the demes, see Chap. 5B (esp. the
documentation in nn. 128-133) and further below.

[21] Haussoullier, *Vie*, pp. 136-137.

deme's chief magistrate, his arrival on the scene in 508/7 heralded the beginning of a process of penetration by the deme in its secular guise into areas of responsibility previously monopolized by priests and the like; and, as we have seen, in addition to the extent to which individual demes cared to assign cult duties, old or new, to their demarchs,[22] the state itself gave all demarchs religious functions both recurrent and occasional, some to be discharged within their demes and some outside.[23]

Aristotle's first category of religious *epimeleia* raises some problems of taxonomy, however. We hear of priests, priestesses, *hieropoioi, epimelētai,* and so forth, in the demes; and one feature which is apparently common to them all, and which does therefore properly differentiate them from such an official as the demarch, is the fact that their responsibilities, unlike his, were wholly religious ones. Yet Aristotle's own distinction seemingly pivots around the criterion of the source of the authority of the "official" in question, and here the difficulty arises; for, in a deme context at any rate, is it in fact so obvious that not only *hieropoioi* and the like but also in some instances priests could not equally well be described as "deriving their office from the common hearth"?

Their mode of appointment must constitute one cardinal test, and the extent to which they were subject to deme authority another. We may take priests (and priestesses) as the extreme case, in that they might be thought to represent the area of cult personnel upon which the Kleisthenic deme framework impinged to a negligible degree if at all.[24] In Demosth. 57.46-48 and 62 we learn of the method of appointing a priest of Herakles in fourth-century Halimous. The demesmen nominated a short list of "best-born" (εὐγενέστατοι) candidates,[25] who then drew lots; and the priest's duties involved offering sacrifice on behalf of the demesmen (57.47). May one generalize from this? There is no warrant for Haussoullier's repeated assertion that all such priests were appointed for a one-year term.[26] We know that some were, from the fact, significant in itself, that demes sometimes dated their decrees or other public documents by reference to a priest or priestess in office.[27] But in other instances there

[22] See Chap. 5A, sec. 1(b).

[23] See Chap. 5A, sec. 2(d).

[24] Note Aeschin. 3.18 on the "surprising" (ἐπὶ τῶν παραδόξων) fact that the city's priests and priestesses were subject to *euthynai*; and see in general Feaver, "Priesthoods."

[25] "Best-born" did not, evidently, mean "aristocratic"; the requirement was simply valid citizen ancestry on both sides (cf. Haussoullier, *Vie*, pp. 137-138).

[26] Haussoullier, *Vie*, pp. 140, 149.

[27] SEG 21.519 (cf. Tod no. 204, the ephebic oath), the priest of Ares and Athena Areia in Acharnai; IG II²2496, the priest of an unspecified cult in Kytheros; SEG 22.116, the priestess of Artemis Aristoboule in Melite; cf. IG II²3109, priestesses of Themis and Nemesis to date liturgies in Rhamnous.

is no means of telling whether the term of office was annual (or otherwise finite) or for life.[28] Nevertheless, Haussoullier's view that "le prêtre est un simple magistrat"[29] is not an unreasonable one. Whether or not *appointed* by the deme assembly like the priest of Herakles in Halimous,[30] priests and priestesses could unquestionably be *controlled* by that body. Four clear examples of this have been cited in previous chapters. In SEG 28.103, lines 47-49, the Eleusinians order the priest of Herakles-in-Akris to take joint charge (συνεπιμεληθῆναι), with the demarch,[31] of the erection of the inscription in the god's sanctuary. In IG II²1183, lines 27-32, the Myrrhinousians instruct "the priests" to make any necessary loans, on guarantee of land or house or tenement, and to place *horoi* on the property in question to indicate to which deity the loaned money belongs; and failure to set up such *horoi*, it is decreed, will transfer the debt to the priests themselves.[32] In IG II²1175, lines 20-24, the Halaieis Aixonides order an oath (necessitated, it would seem, by an internal deme scandal of some kind) to be taken not only by the demarch and treasurers but also by "the priests and the priestesses";[33] and in another decree of the same period (*AD* 11, 1927-1928, pp. 40-41, no. 4) the same deme thanks and rewards the priest of Apollo Zoster, who "has given accounts

---

[28] As well as Demosth. 57.46-48 itself this is true of, e.g., the priestess of Athena Hippia in Acharnai (IG II²1207, lines 2-3), the priest of the Herakleidai and the priestess of Hebe and Alkmene in Aixone (IG II²1199, lines 22-25), the priest of Herakles-in-Akris in Eleusis (SEG 28.103, lines 47-49), the priest of Apollo Erithaseos in ?Eupyridai (IG II²1362, line 2), the priest of Apollo Zoster in Halai Aixonides (*AD* 11, 1927-1928, pp. 40-41, no. 4, lines 1-9), and the priestess of the Thesmophoroi in Peiraieus (IG II²1177, lines 1-2 and 7).

[29] Haussoullier, *Vie*, p. 149.

[30] Despite his own warning about the hazards of generalization in this respect (*Vie*, p. 136), Haussoullier proceeded nonetheless (*Vie*, pp. 137-150, esp. 137-140) to conclude that sortition—usually if not invariably preceded by *prokrisis*—in the deme assembly was the normal method of making priestly appointments. It should be noted, however, that only one of his three chosen examples of this concerns a *priest* (the one in Demosth. 57); the other two relate to *hieropoioi*, in Aixone (IG II²1199, lines 1-2) and Pithos (Isaeus 8.19-20). Of texts unknown to Haussoullier, only the second-century decree of Melite (*Hesp.* 11, 1942, pp. 265-274, no. 51) is of any relevance here: in lines 1-2 Broneer restored ἡ ἱέρεια τῶν Θεσμοφό|[ρων προκεκριμένη ὑπὸ τῶν] δημοτῶν; irrespective of the restoration the word δημοτῶν guarantees that the deme assembly had been somehow involved in her appointment. By contrast, nothing can be safely deduced, as regards the priest of Apollo Zoster in Halai Aixonides, from the tantalizing phrase ἱερεὺς γενόμενος in *AD* 11, 1927-1928, pp. 40-41, no. 4, line 2, unless one presses dangerously hard the later reference (lines 9-10) to the four men αἱρεθέντας μετ᾽ αὐτοῦ εἰς τὴν ἐπιμέλειαν τοῦ ἱεροῦ.

[31] For another demarch and priest working together, cf. IG II²1362 (?Eupyridai).

[32] Quoted in Chap. 6, n. 68.

[33] Cf. Chap. 4, n. 130.

of his superintendence to the demesmen" (λόγους τῆς ἐπιμελείας ἔδωκεν τοῖς δημόταις, line 6), together with the four demesmen elected to assist him.[34]

By the same twin yardsticks—the role of the deme assembly in appointing and/or directing the personnel concerned—what is true of priests and priestesses will generally hold good a fortiori for hieropoioi and the like. We know for instance that the four hieropoioi attached to the cult of Hebe in fourth-century Aixone were appointed (annually?) by lot, and that they rendered account of their duties and expenses to the deme.[35] Also in the fourth century, the Halaieis Araphenides are found instructing hieropoioi (of the cult of Artemis Tauropolos, it would seem) to take action for the benefit of an honorand.[36] From ca. 460 the multipurpose lex sacra of Skambonidai includes a partially preserved oath to be taken, possibly, by hieropoioi.[37] In the middle of the third century we have the Rhamnousians ordering hieropoioi to set up an honorific decree in the sanctuary of Nemesis[38]—a task which, in another decree only slightly later, they give jointly to the demarch and to (military) epimelētai.[39] In their measures to ensure income for the Herakles-in-Akris cult, the Eleusinians take care to stipulate that no proposal to use the money for other purposes will be entertained; anyone making such a proposal or even putting it to the vote will incur a fine, payable to the god, of twice the sum in question; and the officials specified who may not "put it to the vote" (ἐπιψηφίσαι) are the hieromnēmones and the demarch.[40] (A cen-

---

[34] I am not persuaded by the argument of T. Linders, The Treasurers of the Other Gods in Athens and their functions, Beiträge zur klassischen Philologie 62, Meisenheim am Glan, 1975, pp. 81, n. 38, and 83-84, n. 45 that the state, not the deme, controlled the Apollo Zoster cult; see rather J. S. Boersma, Athenian Building Policy from 561/0 to 405/4, Groningen, 1970, p. 36, cf. 40-41. But the indications are undeniably confusing; compare the Nemesis cult in Rhamnous (Chap. 6, n. 76).

[35] IG II²1199, lines 1ff., esp. 2 (λάχοντες) and 6-7 (λόγον καὶ εὐθύνας δεδώκα|σιν). The decree also praises either three or more probably two (see 88, 92, 98) sōphronistai (lines 17-20), a herald (lines 20-21), the priest of the Herakleidai (lines 22-24), the priestess of Hebe and Alkmene (lines 24-25), and the cult's "archon" (lines 25-26).

[36] AE 1925-1926, pp. 168-177, lines 8-12, νέμειν δὲ | [καὶ μερίδ]α αὐτῶν ἑκατ|[έρωι τοὺς] ἱεροποιοὺς | [....⁸....] π[οι]οῦντας Ἀ|[ρχ]ίαν τὸν] δήμ[α]ρχον. On Artemis Tauropolos, see: Euripides Iphigeneia in Tauris, lines 1450-1461; Menander Epitrepontes, line 451 (with Gomme/Sandbach, Menander, p. 330); Strabo 9.1.22; Deubner, Feste, pp. 208-209; J. Papademetriou, PAAH 1956, pp. 87-89.

[37] IG I³244, B (21 lines surviving); see Haussoullier, Vie, p. 140. Note also, a generation later, IG I³250 (Paiania), where at lines 9-11 the deme assembly issues instructions to hieropoioi.

[38] SEG 22.120, lines 7-9.

[39] SEG 25.155, lines 36ff. On the interaction of deme and garrison in Rhamnous, see Appendix 6.

[40] SEG 28.103, lines 36-41. For hieromnēmones in other demes, see: IG II²1596(A), line

tury later, a decree of the same deme instructed the same conjunction of officials to superintend the proclamation of an honorific crown and the manufacture and positioning of an inscription to commemorate it,[41] but one would never have guessed from this alone that the *hieromnēmones* as well as the demarch could put proposals to the vote in the Eleusinian deme assembly.)[42] Finally—in terms of Aristotle's examples—the sole instance of a "treasurer of sacred monies" (ταμίας τῶν ἱερῶν χρημάτων, or rather, here, ταμίας τῶν θ[ε]ίων) occurs in fourth-century Halai Araphenides, where an honorific decree orders him to pay out twenty drachmas for the inscription of the stele and to account for it to the demesmen.[43] He is thus clearly a deme official, but his relationship to the plurality of treasurers mentioned earlier in the same decree[44] is uncertain.

✳

By the fourth century if not earlier, then, the demes had imposed themselves upon the complex pattern of local cult activity in one or, more usually, both of two ways: they financed many of the cults, festivals, and sacrifices in question, and they either supplied or at any rate controlled the principal cult personnel involved in them. Naturally, much still remained outside the scope of the deme framework. This was so not only in the city itself, where state cults and festivals may have supplied many of the religious needs of the inhabitants of the city demes,[45] but also in the countryside of Attica, where there were major cult-centers—some of them demes (e.g. Eleusis, Rhamnous), others not (e.g. Brauron)—whose "constituencies" took little or no account of the political work of Kleisthenes. Nor should one overlook the stubborn survival, into the fourth century and beyond, of such archaic cult-organizations as the Tetrapolis,

---

5 (Alopeke); IG II²1184, lines 1-2 (Cholargos); and see next note. Like *hieropoioi* (above, n. 20) the word is untranslatable.

[41] IG II²1299, lines 78-80. Compare IG I³243, side B, lines 31-32: τός τε νῦν hι]-ερομνέμοy|ας κ[αὶ τὸν δέμαρχον τὸν Μελι]τέον; but it is not certain, from the fragmentary context, that they are *deme* officials, and in any case Meritt's restoration derived from the view that "it was normal for *hieromnemones* and a demarch to co-operate in setting up a stele" (*Hesp.* 36, 1967, pp. 72-73), a generalization supported only by IG II²1299.

[42] If indeed they still could do so by that time; clearly we cannot tell.

[43] *AE* 1932, *Chronika*, pp. 30-32, lines 28-32.

[44] *AE* 1932, *Chronika*, pp. 30-32, lines 12-13; they give the honorand money "for sacrifice."

[45] Cf. O. Broneer, *Hesp.* 11, 1942, p. 270, who regarded this as the explanation for the relative scarcity of decrees from the city demes; but as so many deme decrees are honorific this can be no more than partially true.

the Trikomoi, the Tetrakomoi, and the League of Athena Pallenis, their component parts canonized as demes by Kleisthenes yet at least some of their cult activity transcending those parts.[46] But it is not the task of this chapter, or indeed of this book, to set the religion of the demes in the context of this whole bewildering array of religiosity manifested in classical Attica, nor to pose the (impossible) question of the relative importance, to individual Athenians, of the religious program provided by their demes by comparison with what was on offer elsewhere. The literary and epigraphic evidence for what Jon Mikalson has called the "distinctive features of the religious life in the demes" is what concerns us here, and we may follow his example in taking the sacred calendars of the demes as the most suitable framework in which to marshal it.[47]

B. The Sacred Calendars

It would be no exaggeration to say that the discovery, within only the last twenty-five years, of sacred calendars (fasti) from the demes has brought a new dimension to the study of deme cults and religion. Two such documents, admittedly, have long been known—though neither of them to Haussoullier, as they were both published in 1895. What remains of the mid fourth-century calendar of the Marathonian Tetrapolis and its constituent demes was published by its American excavators in that year[48] (and ultimately edited by Kirchner as IG II²1358). So also were two fragments of the calendar of Eleusis, from the period ca. 330-270;[49] Kirchner presented them as IG II²1363, and in 1965 they were re-edited by Sterling Dow and R. F. Healey.[50] But our own generation has now

[46] The *Tetrapolis* (Marathon, Oinoe, Probalinthos, Trikorynthos—see Strabo 8.7.1): IG II²1358, with W. Peek, *AM* 67, 1942, pp. 12-13, no. 10; Lewis, "Cleisthenes," pp. 30-33, esp. 31. The *Trikomoi* (Eupyridai, Kropidai, Pelekes—see St. Byz., Εὐπυρίδαι): no documents survive. (Lewis, "Cleisthenes," p. 34 n. 111, conjecturally cited the fragmentary IG II²1213, with παρὰ τῶν τριχώμων in line 4 and τὸν τριχώμαρχ[ον in line 6; however, as P. J. Bicknell points out in *REG* 89, 1976, pp. 599-603, the discovery of the Erchia *fasti* at Spata—also the provenance of IG II²1213—rules out any connection with the Eupyridai Trikomoi, and Bicknell himself postulates the existence of another one, consisting of Erchia, Konthyle, and Kytheros.) The *Tetrakomoi* (Peiraieus, Phaleron, Thymaitadai, Xypete—see Pollux 4.105): IG II²3102 and 3103; Lewis, "Cleisthenes," p. 33. The *League of Athena Pallenis* (probably Acharnai, Gargettos, Paiania, Pallene—see Lewis, "Cleisthenes," pp. 33-34 and addendum on p. 39): Athen. 234F-235C; W. Peek, *AM* 67, 1942, pp. 24-29, no. 26; R. Schlaifer, *HSPh* 54, 1943, pp. 35-67.

[47] Mikalson, "Religion," p. 424.

[48] Richardson, "Epakria."

[49] A. N. Skias, *AE* 1895, pp. 97-100, no. 12.

[50] Dow/Healey, *Calendar* (SEG 23.80).

seen the appearance of three more such documents, two of them of major importance, which all date from the first half of the fourth century. In 1961 J. J. Pollitt published a fragment (representing about one month) of the sacrificial *fasti* of Teithras;[51] two years later, in 1963, came the publication by Georges Daux of the virtually complete calendar from Erchia;[52] and Daux has now also, in 1983, provided the first autoptic edition of the *fasti* of Thorikos—previously known only through the imperfect copies edited by Vanderpool, Dunst, and Labarbe—which are well preserved for ten of the twelve months.[53]

All but the last of these *fasti* came under scrutiny in Sterling Dow's synoptic study of "Six Athenian Sacrificial Calendars."[54] There Dow brought out clearly the generic format of these documents, and both he and Michael Jameson have emphasized their overriding concern with the costs of the sacrifices which they detail. As Jameson has written, "this is a forceful reminder that the majority of our epigraphic so-called *leges sacrae* and *fasti sacri* are not in the first instance ritual texts, though such may be included or alluded to, but severely practical documents of public and private organizations assigning official and financial responsibilities. . . . The ritual information is precious, but it is incidental, even casual."[55]

1. TEITHRAS

The Teithras calendar (SEG 21.542) may be considered first, since all that survives of it is two short passages. Of these the latter (Side B, lines 1-10) is too fragmentary to be informative. Side A, lines 1-12, however, preserves (in line 2) the rubric Βοηδ[ρομιῶνος] and the gist of three sacrifices—presumably local, annual ones[56]—to take place during that

[51] J. J. Pollitt, *Hesp.* 30, 1961, pp. 293-297, no. 1 (SEG 21.542).

[52] Daux, "Démarchie," with corrected readings *BCH* 88, 1964, pp. 676-677 (SEG 21.541).

[53] *AC* 52, 1983, pp. 150-174 (Daux, "Calendrier"); for other references see Appendix 3, no. 127. After its mysterious whereabouts in the 1960s and 1970s the stele is now in the J. Paul Getty Museum, Malibu, where I myself saw and examined it on 13 April 1982, and where Daux had prepared his edition the previous autumn. When we come to discuss this document, below, no attention will normally be paid to readings and restorations which autopsy now shows to be impossible.

[54] Dow, "Six calendars." The other two of his "Six" are the one preserved fragment of the late fifth-century *fasti* of the Athenian state itself (J. H. Oliver, *Hesp.* 4, 1935, pp. 5-32; S. Dow, *Hesp.* 10, 1941, pp. 31-37) and the complete calendar of the Salaminioi *genos* from 363/2 (W. S. Ferguson, *Hesp.* 7, 1938, pp. 1-74, no. 1).

[55] Jameson, "Calendar," pp. 155-156. The *Thorikos* calendar, as we shall see, is something of an exception here.

[56] Mikalson, "Religion," p. 426.

month, the third of the Athenian year. On either 4 or 14 Boedromion[57] a ram worth seventeen drachmas was to be offered to Zeus; and on 27 Boedromion a sheep worth four drachmas to Athena and, to Zeus, a sucking-pig and *prothy[mata]* (line 9). These last—unique to this calendar—were probably offerings of grain or meal, indicating worship of the god in his chthonic aspect;[58] it is perhaps significant that what seems to have been the Teithrasians' principal *hieron* was something not attested in any other deme, a Koreion.[59] Either or both of the sacrifices to Zeus took place, we may surmise, either there or at the *"temenos* of Zeus" ([Δ]ιὸ[ς] τέμενος) mentioned in SEG 24.151, line 12. The cult personnel is not specified.[60]

Since no other deme is known to have had a sacrifice on 28, 29, or 30 Boedromion we may take it that these three events accounted for all the local, annual cult observance in Teithras during this month. In the same month there were eight sacrifices (of an equivalent kind) in the larger deme of Erchia, though nothing between the fifth day and the twenty-seventh.[61] The middle days of Boedromion were dominated by the celebration of the Eleusinian Mysteries,[62] during which much local cult activity was in abeyance.[63]

---

[57] That is, either τετρ[άδι ἱσταμένου] or τετρ[άδι ἐπὶ δέκα]; Dow, "Six calendars," p. 176, declares for the former, presumably (though he does not say so) because the 14th fell within the period of the Eleusinian Mysteries (cf. below, at n. 62). No state festival is attested for either day, but in Erchia there was a wineless holocaust sacrifice of a white ewe-lamb to Basile on 4 Boedromion (SEG 21.541, B, lines 14-20).

[58] Thus Pollitt in the *editio princeps* (above, n. 51), citing schol. Aristoph. *Ploutos*, line 661, and Eustathius, *Commentarii ad Homeri Iliadem* I 449, par. 132, 23. As he notes, there may have been different terminology elsewhere for the same thing, e.g. the ἀλφίτων ἑκτεύς of the Marathonians (IG II²1358, col. II, lines 45 and 50); cf. perhaps the [πό]πανα καὶ πελανο[ύς of Kollytos (IG II²1195, line 12). Note that 27 Boedromion was a day of five offerings in Erchia—to the Nymphs, Acheloos, Alochos, Hermes, and Ge (SEG 21.541, Α, lines 12-16; Β, lines 21-25; Γ, lines 26-30; Δ, lines 24-27; E, lines 16-21); but no state festival is known.

[59] SEG 24.151, lines 21-22, στήλην [δ]ὲ στῆσαι ἐν τῶι Κορ[ε]‖[ίωι]; SEG 24.153, lines 6-8, ἀναγρά|ψαι δὲ τόδε τὸ ψήφισμα ἐν στή[λ]ηι λιθίνηι καὶ στῆσα|ι ἐν τῶι Κο-ρείωι. It is tempting to suggest this restoration also for SEG 21.520, lines 20-21: στῆσα|ι ἐν τῶ|[ι Κορείωι].

[60] The fact that in SEG 21.520, lines 9-12, the duties of the four Teithrasian *bouleutai* are said to have included sacrificing may or may not be relevant here.

[61] To Basile on the 4th (see above, n. 57); to Epops on the 5th (SEG 21.541, Δ, lines 18-23, and E, lines 9-15); to the Nymphs et al. on the 27th (see above, n. 58).

[62] 15-23 Boedromion: see Mikalson, *Calendar*, pp. 54-60, 65.

[63] Note the annual sacrifice "in Boedromion before the Mysteries" (Βοηδρομιῶνος πρὸ μ[υ]στ[η]ρ[ίων) in the Marathonian calendar (IG II²1358, col. II, line 5). Mikalson, "Religion," p. 428, claims an absence of local cult activity during such "major state festivals," besides the Mysteries, as the Panathenaia (probably 23-30 Hekatombaion: see Mikalson,

2. ELEUSIS

If the whole of the Teithras calendar, as is likely, was in the form manifested by its one surviving fragment, we may presume that that form was the purest and simplest one possible for such documents, that is (under monthly and daily rubrics), price, deity, victim, perquisites.[64] Almost equally little is preserved of the Eleusis calendar (SEG 23.80), but the painstaking study of Dow and Healey has shown it to have had a rather different form and (thus) purpose. It gives, they conclude, "the appearance of a supplement to some extensive Calendar, which provided the full complement of sacrifices, etc."; the chief concern of its three surviving portions (totalling some forty-one lines) seems to be to pay not so much for the sacrifices themselves as for expenses incurred by the cult personnel in the performance of their duties, and for various "petty extras."[65] For example, one and a half drachmas are provided for the lunch (ἄριστον) of the *hierophantēs* and *(hiero)kēryx*[66] on the day of

---

Calendar, pp. 34, 199), the Pyanopsia (7 Pyanopsion: *Calendar*, pp. 69-70), the Stenia (9 Pyanopsion: *Calendar*, p. 71), the Haloa (26 Posideion: *Calendar*, pp. 94-95), the Lenaia (within 12-21 Gamelion: *Calendar*, pp. 109-110), the Anthesteria (11-13 Anthesterion: *Calendar*, pp. 113-114), and the Thargelia (7 Thargelion: *Calendar*, pp. 153-154). As regards the city Dionysia Mikalson writes ("Religion," p. 428) that "we find only a goat sacrifice at Marathon on Elaphebolion 10 (col. II, 17-18) and in Erkhia a sacrifice to Dionysos and Semele on Elaphebolion 16 [SEG 21.541, A, lines 44-51; B, lines 33-40], the very end of the festival." This reflects his earlier conclusion, in *Calendar*, pp. 124-130, 137, that the Dionysia occupied 10-16 Elaphebolion; but it has been objected that 10 Elaphebolion is "the only necessary day of the ἑορτή, the rest is the ἀγών, of variable length" (D. M. Lewis, reviewing *Calendar* in *CR* 27, 1977, p. 216). This point, if taken, would strengthen Mikalson's own, important argument that "the demesmen went to Athens or Eleusis to celebrate these major festivals, and ... the demes did not provide local observances of them" ("Religion," p. 428). But in fact the argument is vulnerable on three counts. (*a*) With *days* of the month not normally specified, the Marathon calendar *might* include more exceptions to Mikalson's suggested rule than the one he cites; and the same goes for the calendar from Thorikos. (*b*) His definition of a "major state festival" is questionable and ought arguably to include (e.g.) the Bendideia of 19 Thargelion, when the Erchieis sacrificed to the possibly associated Menedeios (see Jameson, "Calendar," pp. 158-159). (*c*) With superior texts of the Thorikos calendar than the one available to Mikalson, we now know that that deme celebrated, *perhaps* locally, the Pyanopsia, the (?)Anthesteria, and the Plynteria (*AC* 52, 1983, pp. 150-174, lines 27, 33-34, 52-53). A clear pattern thus remains elusive.

[64] See Dow, "Six calendars," pp. 170-171. Perquisites: side A of the Teithras calendar specifies (*a*) cash ἱερειώσυνα of 1 drachma and 2 obols for the ram sacrifice to Zeus (line 7) and (*b*), for the sucking-pig sacrifice, [ἱ]ερεώσυ[να] (*sic*), cost not preserved, [εἰς] ἐσθῆτ[α λευκήν] (lines 11-12; reading and restoration by Dow, "Six calendars," p. 184). For other demes, see below.

[65] Dow/Healey, *Calendar*, p. 45.

[66] On this "herald" see Dow/Healey, *Calendar*, pp. 18-19. For the provision of ἄριστον

their trip to Athens, on 5 Pyanopsion, for the proclamation of the Proerosia (lines 3-7); and in the last preserved line (line 27) of column I
there is a reference to "wood for the altar" (ξύλα ἐπὶ τὸν βωμόν) at
the Thesmophoria.

Four festivals are in question. The only one mentioned by name is the
Proerosia (line 7), but the goat-sacrifice to Apollo Pythios on 7 [Pya-
nopsion] must refer to the Pyanopsia itself;[67] further down column I, on
fragment B, mention of "the two Thesmophorian deities" (τοῖν
Θεσμο|[φόροιν, lines 25-26) indicates that we are still in the month of
Pyanopsion, with the Thesmophoria;[68] and the fragmentary beginnings
of lines 33-41, including an offering to Poseidon (Ποσ[ειδῶνι, line 37),
suggested to Dow and Healey the Skira, celebrated on 12 Skirophorion.[69]
This last identification is especially significant for the layout of the document, in that if it is correct it proves two things: that there were only
two columns; and that, consequently, while column I covered only four
months (Hekatombaion to Pyanopsion), column II, which is in any case
shorter, covered twice that period, the eight months from Maimakterion
to Skirophorion.[70]

Such an imbalance would be puzzling if this Eleusinian calendar were
a list, and a complete one, of the annual religious observances *in Eleusis*.
But patently (as Dow and Healey show) it is not; indeed quite possibly
it has no strict bearing upon *local* cult activity at all. The crux here is
the Thesmophoria of fragment B. According to Dow and Healey, "the
presence of the Priestess of Plouton at the festival [line 24] seems to be
an indication that it was a local celebration of the Thesmophoria and
not the city one."[71] Roux and Mikalson have both doubted this, however;[72] and if, as Mikalson notes, this is in fact the city's Thesmophoria
and not a local one, the Eleusinian calendar as a whole will then, evidently, "detail expenditures to be made by the Eleusinians for festivals
being announced or celebrated in Athens itself. ... It would thus be
internally consistent and would be similar to the second group of ἱερά
of the Plotheians [in IG I³258], i.e., those offerings and ceremonies provided to the state on behalf of the deme." If this analogy is as valid as

---

compare lines 3-4 and 15-16 of the Thorikos calendar (*AC* 52, 1983, pp. 150-174), discussed below, sec. 4.

[67] Dow/Healey, *Calendar*, pp. 21-31; cf. Mikalson, *Calendar*, pp. 69-70.

[68] Dow/Healey, *Calendar*, pp. 32-38; cf. Mikalson, *Calendar*, pp. 71-73.

[69] Dow/Healey, *Calendar*, pp. 39-41; cf. Mikalson, *Calendar*, p. 170.

[70] Dow/Healey, *Calendar*, pp. 42-45.

[71] Dow/Healey, *Calendar*, p. 36.

[72] G. Roux, reviewing Dow/Healey, *Calendar* in *AC* 35, 1966, pp. 562-573, at 562 and
esp. 573; Mikalson, "Religion," pp. 426-427.

it is attractive, the internal proportions of SEG 23.80 will have been determined simply by the significance, to this deme at this time, of the various festivals of the *state* calendar; and Dow and Healey themselves observe that, for Eleusis, the Synoikia (in Hekatombaion) and particularly the Eleusinia (Metageitnion) and Mysteries (Boedromion) will have loomed larger in the sacred year than anything in its remaining nine months.[73]

3. MARATHON

The Marathonian calendar (IG II²1358) too, as Mikalson has shown,[74] may usefully be compared with the Plotheians' classification (IG I³258, lines 25-28), to the extent that column II, which relates to the deme of Marathon itself,[75] falls clearly into two sections. Both sections refer exclusively, it would seem, to sacrifices to be offered locally, within the deme, but lines 1-33 detail the annual ones (corresponding to the Plotheians' *hiera* τὰ ἐς Πλωθε[ᾶς κ]οινά) while lines 34-53 list the biennial ones (a category analogous to the Plotheians' quadrennial *hiera*, τὰ ἐς τὰς πεντετ[ηρίδ]ας). These latter fall in turn into two divisions, headed τάδε τὸ ἕτερον ἔτος προτέρα δραμοσύνη (line 34) and τάδε τὸ ἕτερον ἔτος θύεται μετὰ Εὔβουλον ἄρχ[ο]|ντα Τετραπολεῦσι ὑστέρα δραμοσύνη (lines 39-40), that is, two alternating series.[76]

In other respects, however, both form and content here create a distinctly archaic impression. As to form, one negative and one positive feature are worthy of comment. The negative feature is the fact that, with only two exceptions (and only one of them in column II), the month alone is given, not the day.[77] Presumably it was felt that the day would

[73] Dow/Healey, *Calendar*, pp. 43, 45. For the dates see Mikalson, *Calendar*, pp. 29-31 (Synoikia), 46 (Eleusinia), 54-60 with 65 (Mysteries).

[74] Mikalson, "Religion," pp. 426-427.

[75] The "demarch of the Marathonians" is mentioned, as sacrificer, in line 23, from which lines 1-2 are restorable to give the same. Three lines of the *fasti* for Trikorynthos (lines 54-56), "presumably much shorter" (Dow, "Six calendars," p. 174), end what survives of the column. The entries in col. I probably concern—and I shall assume this in what follows—offerings made by the Tetrapolis as a whole rather than by its constituent demes; thus J. von Prott, *Leges graecorum sacrae, I: fasti sacri*, Leipzig, 1896, no. 26; Kirchner *ad loc.*

[76] See on this rubric (and esp. the word δραμοσύνη, which Kirchner restored also in line 39 of col. I) S. Dow, *Historia* 9, 1960, pp. 282-283, developing Richardson's comments in the *editio princeps* ("Epakria," p. 213).

[77] The exceptions are a Tetrapolis offering to [Apollo] Apotropaios on (?)7 Hekatombaion (col. I, lines 24-26; [ἑβδόμηι ἱστα]μένου is Kirchner's restoration, following Wilamowitz; Richardson, "Epakria," p. 210, had given [τρίτηι ἱστα]μένου) and a deme goat-sacrifice to (?)Ge on 10 Elaphebolion (col. II, lines 17-18; cf. above, n. 63, and Mikalson, *Calendar*,

be known to the cult personnel involved; yet, of the other calendars, only the one from Thorikos, as we shall see, is based on a similar assumption. The positive feature of interest is the use of what might be termed super-rubrics which group the offerings into units of three months: πρώτης τριμήνο (i.e., Hekatombaion to Boedromion), δευτέρας τριμήνο (Pyanopsion to Posideion), τρίτης τριμήνο (Gamelion to Elaphebolion), and τετάρτης τριμήνο (Mounichion to Skirophorion). These are most obvious in column I (lines 4, 20-21, 23-24, 27, 29, 32-33, ?37, 40, 42, 44) but occur also as divisions of the *annual* sacrifices in column II, for both Marathon (lines 7, 11, 19) and Trikorynthos (line 54). As Dow has comprehensively observed, "the reason for this seasonal arrangement is not revealed in the Calendar. Evidently totals were not given for any of the successive periods—no totals of any kind appear in the many lines we possess; for Marathon itself it can be stated positively that no totals were given. The trimenial division might conceivably be very ancient and primitive, dating back to a time when the seasons determined everything. The approximation to the seasons is however approximate only, and in the cults themselves the trimenial divisions have no meaning obvious to us."[78]

Many of the cults themselves, too, look "very ancient and primitive."[79] Straightforward Olympians are few: three manifestations of Zeus (Anthaleus,[80] Horios,[81] Hypatos),[82] one of Athena (Hellotis),[83] one of Apollo

---

pp. 126-127). Three times a *relative* indication is given: Βοηδρομιῶνος πρὸ μ[υ]στ[η]ρ[ίων (col. II, line 5) and Σκιροφοριῶνος πρὸ Σκίρων (col. II, lines 30 and 51).

[78] Dow, "Six calendars," p. 181.

[79] Cf. Lewis, "Cleisthenes," p. 31.

[80] Or Anthales (Lewis, "Cleisthenes," p. 31); "apparently in the role of a farmer" (Richardson, "Epakria," p. 216). The reference is col. II, line 47, a biennial sacrifice in Metageitnion.

[81] Col. I, line 11, a Tetrapolis sacrifice in (?)Skirophorion. There was a sacrifice to this god of boundaries in Erchia on 16 Posideion (SEG 21.541, E, lines 22-30; Mikalson, *Calendar*, pp. 91-92); cf. in general Plato *Laws* 842E.

[82] Col. II, line 13, an annual sacrifice in Gamelion. Richardson, "Epakria," p. 210, restored a ewe-sacrifice here *exempli gratia*, but it is noteworthy that, according to Paus. 1.26.5, no living creature was offered on the altar of Zeus Hypatos at the entrance to the Erechtheion.

[83] Col. I, line 55, Tetrapolis sacrifice; col. II, lines 34-36 and 41, biennially alternating offerings of a *suovetaurilia* (an ox, three sheep, and a pig) and a ewe. The preferred form of the goddess' name was actually Athenaia, itself archaic (cf. Aeschylus *Eumenides*, line 288; ML no. 18; and the Thorikos calendar, AC 52, 1983, pp. 150-174, lines 23, 53, 54). For the epithet Hellotis, cf. Pindar *Olympian 13*, line 40 (56), with scholiast; Athen. 678A-B; Hesych. and *Etym. Magn.*, Ἑλλωτίς; St. Byz., Γόρτυν. Note also the Marathonians' sacrifice ἥρῳ παρὰ τὸ Ἑλλώτιον (col. II, line 25).

(Apotropaios),[84] and—in Trikorynthos, not Marathon—one of Hera;[85] to these may perhaps be added Demeter in the guise of Chloe, Eleusinia, and Achaia.[86] For the rest, the evident importance of Kourotrophos[87]— no other deity is mentioned so frequently—is paralleled in the Erchia calendar,[88] where we also meet the Tritopatreis.[89] But otherwise many of the names make strange reading: the Akamantes, Galios, Telete, Nea-

[84] Col. I, lines 24-26; see above, n. 77. (The restoration Διὶ ἀποτροπ]αίῳ by Richardson, "Epakria," p. 211, in col. I, line 34, is speculative at best, and Kirchner prudently ignored it.) In Erchia there were two goat-sacrifices to Apollo Apotropaios on 8 Gamelion (SEG 21.541, A, lines 31-36; Γ, lines 31-37). The Marathonians' Δαφνήφοροι (col. II, line 38) suggest a cult of Apollo in another form: Richardson, "Epakria," p. 216.

[85] Col. II, line 55, annual sacrifice (*suovetaurilia?*) in Metageitnion. On the significance of Hera-worship in Trikorynthos (but not, apparently, Marathon) see Richardson, "Epakria," p. 219, n. 23. In Erchia there were sacrifices to Hera Thelchinia on 20 Metageitnion (SEG 21.541, A, lines 6-11) and to Hera et al. on 27 Gamelion, the day of the Theogamia in Athens (see above, p. 179); with the latter cf. line 32 of the Thorikos calendar (*AC* 52, 1983, pp. 150-174), Γαμηλιῶνος, Ἥραι, Ἱερῶι Γάμωι.

[86] *Chloe*: col. II, line 49, biennial offering in Anthesterion Χλόῃ παρὰ τὰ Μειδύλου, of a ὗς κύου[σα; for Chloe alone cf. Aristoph. *Lysistr.*, line 835; as epithet of Demeter cf. Paus. 1.22.3, IG II²1356 (line 16), IG II²5006 (line 4). *Eleusinia*: col. II, line 48, biennial offering in Anthesterion of a ὗς κύουσα; as epithet of Demeter cf. Sophocles *Antigone*, lines 1120-1121, etc. The epithet was restored by Dunst, "Opferkalender," p. 244, in line 38 of the Thorikos calendar, under Elaphebolion, but Daux, "Calendrier," reads Δήμητρι, τὴν χλο[ῖαν, and takes the phrase to indicate a *day* ("la journée dite Chloïa"), tantamount to the first day of spring; see further below, n. 100. *Achaia*: col. II, line 27, annual ram-sacrifice in Thargelion; as epithet of Demeter cf. Herod. 5.61.2.

[87] See col. II, lines 6 (annual sacrifice in Boedromion), 14 (annual sacrifice in Gamelion), 31 (annual sacrifice in Skirophorion), 37 and 42 (biennially alternating sacrifices of a ewe and a piglet in Hekatombaion), 46 (biennial sacrifice in Metageitnion), and—in Trikoryn-thos—56 (annual sacrifice in Metageitnion). On the status of Kourotrophos, see: Daux, "Démarchie," p. 631; T. H. Price, *Kourotrophos*, Leiden, 1978 (pp. 101-131 on Attica); and further, next note.

[88] Apart from Zeus and Apollo under their various epithets (references below, nn. 156-158), no deity is mentioned so frequently in Erchia: see SEG 21.541, A, lines 23-30 and 57-65; B, lines 6-13 and 32-39; Γ, lines 1-12; Δ, lines 1-12. As Daux, "Démarchie," p. 631, pointed out, in all six instances the offering, of a piglet, was in some sense preliminary to a (presumably) more important sacrifice in the same place on the same day (respectively, to Apollo Delphinios, Athena Polias, Artemis Hekate, Hera, and, twice more, Artemis). A similar role has been seen for Ko(u)rotrophos in the Thorikos calendar (*AC* 52, 1983, pp. 150-174), i.e., "preliminary" to Demeter in lines 20-22, to Athena in lines 22-23, and to Leto, Artemis, and Apollo in lines 41-43; see Dunst, "Opferkalender," p. 254, and Labarbe, *Thorikos*, p. 61, n. 13. But is is hard—and perhaps improper—to detect such a thing in the Marathonians' practice.

[89] In Marathon: col. II, lines 32 (annual ewe-sacrifice in Skirophorion) and 52-53 (biennial "table," τράπεζα, also in Skirophorion; see in general S. Dow and D. M. Gill, "The Greek Cult Table," *AJA* 69, 1965, pp. 104-114, and other instances in the calendars of Eleusis and Thorikos). In Erchia: SEG 21.541, Δ, lines 41-46 (wineless ram-sacrifice on 21 Mounichion).

nias,[90] Νύμφη Εὐίς,[91] Hyttenios,[92] and a string of anonymous heroes and heroines. The most surprising absentee is unquestionably Herakles, with whom the Tetrapolis in general and Marathon in particular were so strongly associated.[93] In the calendar we find only a fragmentary reference to a Tetrapolis sacrifice in Elaphebolion παρὰ] τὸ Ἡράκλειον—which is presumably the same Herakleion mentioned by Herodotus in his account of the events of 490 (6.108.1 and 116)—and an annual deme sacrifice in Gamelion to Herakles' nephew and associate Iolaos.[94]

Upon this nexus of archaic cult observance the deme of Marathon had nonetheless succeeded—by this time, the first half of the fourth century— in superimposing some of its own practices and concerns. As regards personnel, for example, the only figure explicitly mentioned is the demarch, who performs two groups of the annual sacrifices, one in Hekatombaion or Metageitnion (col. II, lines 1-4) and one in Mounichion (col. II, lines 23-26).[95] Furthermore the document as a whole displays the preoccupation with costs which is characteristic and symptomatic of its period. Everything from ox-sacrifices of ninety drachmas down to *hierōsyna* of one drachma is priced. Hence a comparison may be made, on the basis of the annual sacrifices only, with the calendar from Erchia. In the latter, fifty-nine offerings cost the deme (or rather the five liturgists) some 547 drachmas.[96] In what survives of the annual calendar of Marathon—a larger deme than Erchia—only about forty offerings are made, but their total, including *hierōsyna*, is more than 820 drachmas. By

[90] Col. II, lines 19-20 (annual *suovetaurilia* in Mounichion). In the Thorikos calendar (*AC* 52, 1983, pp. 150-174, lines 26-27) there is an offering to Neanias on 16 Pyanopsion. (I read νεανίας, not Νεανίας, in Paus. 1.33.8.)

[91] Thus Richardson, "Epakria," p. 211 (Kirchner read Νυμφαγέτης); col. I, line 45, Tetrapolis sacrifice in Mounichion. A plurality of Nymphs received cult in Erchia (*SEG* 21.541, A, lines 12-16; E, lines 44-46; annual offerings on 27 Boedromion and 8 Gamelion, respectively), in Lamptrai (*IG* I³256), and in Phlya (Paus. 1.31.4); see in general Solders, *Kulte*, pp. 59-61.

[92] Col. II, lines 30-31, Σκιροφοριῶνος πρὸ Σκίρων. Hyttenia was the ancient name of the Tetrapolis itself: St. Byz., Τετράπολις τῆς Ἀττικῆς.

[93] Paus. 1.15.3 and 32.4; schol. Sophocles *OC*, line 701 (= Istrus, *FGrH* 334 F30). The fragmentary *IG* I³3 concerns the state organization of Herakleian Games at Marathon shortly after 490: see E. Vanderpool, *Hesp.* 11, 1942, pp. 329-337 (the *editio princeps*); Lewis, "Cleisthenes," p. 31; Davies, *Wealth*, p. 111.

[94] The Herakleion: see E. Vanderpool, *AJA* 70, 1966, pp. 319-323, and S. Marinatos, *PAAH* 1972, p. 6. Iolaos (cf. Euripides *Herakleidai*, line 32 and passim): col. II, line 14.

[95] It would appear, though, that no *hierōsyna* were allotted to him; on the twenty occasions where the word is used it must presumably refer to priests and priestesses whose management of the cult in question was too obvious to require specification.

[96] Dow, "Demarkhia," p. 187.

comparison with Erchia the Marathonians' choice was thus to sacrifice more expensive victims to fewer deities on fewer occasions.[97]

4. THORIKOS

The most recently discovered of the deme *fasti*, those of Thorikos (*AC* 52, 1983, pp. 150-174), call to mind in one respect the fifth-century *lex sacra* of Skambonidai (IG I³244). Both documents include an oath; in the case of Thorikos it is that of the deme's *euthynos* and his *paredroi*.[98] The stipulation that this oath be inscribed, followed by some provisions for the *euthynai* of deme officials,[99] gives the document something of the character of a secular deme decree of its period. So also does the fact that it was cut in the *stoichēdon* style (with thirty letters to the line), unlike the calendars of Teithras, Eleusis, and Marathon; even the Erchia calendar is only quasi-*stoichēdon*. But otherwise it is a sacred calendar in the normal form, with monthly rubrics—all but the second, for Metageitnion, surviving—though perhaps only two explicit indications of the *day* of the month, which is somewhat surprising.[100] And very surprising indeed is the relative absence of overt concern with prices or other mundane practicalities.[101] It is thus the nearest thing we possess to a calendar of purely religious significance.[102]

[97] Cf. Mikalson, "Religion," p. 425.

[98] *AC* 52, 1983, pp. 150-174, lines 57-62; cf. Chap. 4, n. 158.

[99] Lines 62-65: ἀναγρά{ι}ψαι δὲ τὸν ὅρκ]|[ο]ν ἐστήλη καὶ καταθε̄ναι π[αρὰ τὸ Δελ⟨φί⟩)]|[ν]ιον, ὅσαι δ᾽ἂν ἀρχαὶ αἱρεθῶ[σι . . . .⁶. . .]|σιν ὑπευθύνος ε̄ναι ἁπάσα[ς]. (Daux's αἱρεθῶ|σιν is unwarrantable.)

[100] Daux, "Calendrier," pp. 161-162, makes out a good case for restoring the Μετα-γειτνιῶνος rubric in line 10. Explicit indications of the day: lines 26 (ἕκτη ἐ[πὶ δέκα], of Pyanopsion) and 33 (δω[δεκάτη], of Anthesterion). But in addition Daux, "Calendrier," pp. 162-163 sees day-specifications in the phrases τὴν πρηρο[σ]|[ίαν (lines 5-6) and τὴν χλο[ΐαν (line 38), which, he supposes, were days fixed each year by the deme assembly to mark the advent of, respectively, autumn and spring. Note also his *exempli gratia* restoration ("Calendrier," p. 163) of line 8, ἐντὸς τὸ̄ μ]ηνός.

[101] The only mentions of price are the stipulations that the ox-sacrifices for the heroes Thorikos (lines 28-30, Maimakterion) and [Kepha]los (lines 54-56, Skirophorion) should cost between 40 and 50 drachmas, and—if Daux's brilliant interpretation of the puzzling οἶ⟨Δ⟩ν in line 57 is correct—that an offering to Poseidon in Skirophorion should cost no more than 20 drachmas; see on this "Calendrier," p. 169. Note also the provision of lunch (ἄριστομ), by a priest for his ἀκολουθῶν in lines 15-16 and (as restored by Daux, "Calendrier," p. 162) τῶι φύλα]κι καὶ τοῖ|[ς ἀκολούθοις αὐτὸ πᾶσι in lines 2-3; the connection, if any, between the latter clause and δρα]χμὴν ἑκατερ|[ο or ω (lines 4-5) is not clear.

[102] Apart from the oath of the *euthynos* and *paredroi* (lines 57-62), no deme officials are mentioned, only the cult personnel spoken of in connection with the provision of lunches (see preceding note), and the (?)"singing women" (ἐπαϋτομένας; see Daux, *CRAI* 1980,

The calendar inscription from Thorikos.
Courtesy of the J. Paul Getty Museum.

Considered as such, its interest and importance remain indubitable nonetheless. The sacrifices—annual ones, we must suppose—are set out on the main face of the stone, with small omissions supplied on the left and right sides both by the original mason and in other, later hands.[103] With only one certain exception, though other possible ones, all the sacrifices may be presumed to have taken place within the deme itself. The certain exception to this is the offering of a lamb "to Poseidon at Sounion" (ἐπὶ Σούνιον Ποσειδῶνι) in Boedromion.[104] Two of the possible exceptions occur in lines 3-4 and 15-16, where lunch is provided for the cult personnel. In the Eleusinian calendar, as we saw earlier, a similar provision was laid down for 5 Pyanopsion, in respect of the two officials who would go then to Athens for the proclamation of the Proerosia; so it must be accounted at least a possibility that in one or both of these instances from Thorikos a comparable journey beyond the deme was entailed. The context of lines 3-4 is lost, but lines 13-16 read: Βοη-δρομιῶνος. Πρηρόσια. Διὶ Πολιεῖ· κρ|ιτὸν οἶν: χοῖρον κριτόν, ἐπαϊτομένας, | χοῖρον ὠνητὸν ὁλόκαυστον, τῶι ἀκολου|θõντι ἀρι-στομ παρέχεν τὸν ἱερέα. The Erchians, we know, offered sacrifices to Zeus Polieus and Athena Polias on the city akropolis on 12 Metageitnion, as well as on their own akropolis on 3 Skirophorion,[105] but it is hard to know how far, if at all, that is relevant. A further difficulty is whether these Thorikian offerings to Zeus Polieus were connected with or distinct from the "Prerosia" (or in other words the practical difficulty of punctuation in line 13). The editors, including now Daux, have assumed them to be distinct, so that the "Prerosia" would be a self-contained entry comparable to the "Dionysia" in line 31. So it may be; but if, on the contrary, the offerings to Zeus Polieus were actually *part of* the "Prerosia,"[106] the calendar from Eleusis offers some grounds, as we have seen, for supposing that they may have been made in Athens.

The Pr(o)erosia (or Plerosia) itself remains problematical, however. Its principal locale was Eleusis, where those who responded to the proclamation of 5 Pyanopsion foregathered on the following day;[107] but schol-

---

pp. 468-469, and "Calendrier," pp. 171-174) of lines 14 and 47. It must therefore be likely that priests (and priestesses?) were the sacrificers throughout.

[103] See Dunst, "Opferkalender," p. 264, citing W. Burkert; Labarbe, *Thorikos*, p. 64, n. 41; and above all Daux, "Calendrier," pp. 156-160.

[104] Lines 19-20. (The words ἐπὶ Σούνιον are not an epithet; cf. Labarbe, *Thorikos*, p. 61, n. 12.) Perhaps on the eighth day (see Mikalson, *Calendar*, pp. 19-20)? For the Poseidon cult in Sounion, see IG I³8, line 6.

[105] SEG 21.541, Γ, lines 13-18 and 59-64.

[106] Cf. Mikalson, "Religion," p. 434.

[107] Dow/Healey, *Calendar*, pp. 14-20; Mikalson, *Calendar*, p. 68.

ars disagree as to whether it was a festival of the state[108] or of the deme.[109] In any case "the references to the festival from other areas indicate that the ritual ploughing was also celebrated locally and at slightly different times of the year":[110] in Boedromion (and earlier?) in Thorikos, as we have seen;[111] on [5] Posideion in Myrrhinous;[112] and at an indeterminable time in Peiraieus and Paiania.[113] On balance, then, the way in which the Thorikioi celebrated their "Prerosia" is perhaps *un*likely to have necessitated a visit to Athens (or Eleusis), but it remains a possibility that the sacrifices to Zeus Polieus did.

An analogous problem is presented by one of the entries under Anthesterion, which reads: Δ]|ιασίοις· Διὶ Μιλιχίωι· οἶν πρα[τόν (lines 34-35). The likelihood must be that this refers to the chief, state celebration of the Diasia, in Agrai, on 23 Anthesterion,[114] but as Mikalson notes, "the possibility remains that this offering was made at one of the numerous altars and sanctuaries of Zeus Meilichios in the Attic countryside."[115] And similarly it is not certain whether the sacrifices in connection with the Pyanopsia (line 27, with addendum on the left side) and the Plynteria (lines 52ff.) were local observances of state festivals or offerings made in the city.[116]

At all events, the cults attested in the Thorikos calendar are many and various. Olympians are decidedly more to the fore than in Marathon,

---

[108] E.g. Dow/Healey, *Calendar*, pp. 15-17.

[109] E.g. Mikalson, *Calendar*, pp. 68-69.

[110] Mikalson, "Religion," p. 434.

[111] The contextless AI τὴν πρηρο[σ]|[ίαν (lines 5-6) remains enigmatic, despite Daux, "Calendrier," pp. 162-163 (see above, n. 100).

[112] IG II²1183, lines 32-33, τῆι [δὲ πέμπτ]ει θυέτω τὴν πληροσίαν ὁ δήμαρχος τῶ[ι] Διί. The only month mentioned is Posideion (line 36); and the suggestion of L. Ziehen, *RE* 21.1, 1951, col. 234, that Πυανοψιῶνος stood almost thirty lines earlier, in line 5, is utterly gratuitous.

[113] Peiraieus: IG II²1177, line 9; *if* the festivals mentioned are in chronological order, the Prerosia in Peiraieus came after the Thesmophoria, i.e., in Pyanopsion or later. Paiania: IG I³250, A, lines 8 and 15ff. (and B, line 4).

[114] See above, with n. 16.

[115] Mikalson, "Religion," p. 430, citing Pfister, *RE* 15, 1931, cols. 340-342. Thucydides' statement that at the Diasia the Athenians sacrificed πανδημεί (1.126.6) has generally been taken to indicate a single, collective celebration by the demes rather than separate local ones (C. Wachsmuth, *RhM* 23, 1868, p. 178, n. 31; Jameson, "Calendar," p. 165), but there may have been exceptions.

[116] The Pyanopsia took place on 7 Pyanopsion (Mikalson, *Calendar*, pp. 69-70). The date of the Plynteria is stated by literary sources to be either 25 or 29 Thargelion (Deubner, *Feste*, pp. 17-18; Mikalson, *Calendar*, pp. 160-161, 163-164, arguing for the former); however, the Thorikos calendar lists the Plynteria under Skirophorion, and the festival in Thargelion was doubtless the closely associated Kallynteria; see Dunst, "Opferkalender," p. 260, and Labarbe, *Thorikos*, p. 63, n. 34.

accounting here for approximately half of the sixty or so sacrifices preserved. Zeus heads the list, appearing not only as M(e)ilichios and Polieus, discussed already, but also as Kataibates and Herkeios (and epithetless);[117] it is disappointing, though, to find no mention of the cult named on the fourth-century ὅρος ἱεροῦ Διὸς Ἀυαντῆρος (IG II²2606). Poseidon receives four sacrifices at various times of the year.[118] There are either three or four for Apollo,[119] three for Athena,[120] three for Demeter,[121] and three—counting in the rural Dionysia itself—for Dionysos.[122] Artemis receives two,[123] and there is one each for Hekate[124] and Hera.[125] Of the remaining, miscellaneous half, the most interesting comprise a group of offerings made to minor deities closely linked with this particular deme. In the *editio princeps* Vanderpool picked out the names of Kephalos and his wife Prokris, daughter of Erechtheus, who receive offerings—of a sheep and a sacrificial table, respectively—every Boedromion (lines 16-17); and Daux has now very plausibly restored [Kepha]los as the recipient of a major sacrifice, that of an ox, in Skirophorion (lines 54-55). Their connection with the deme Thorikos is well attested in lexicographic sources;[126] and local links may also account for the presence of at least some of the other minor deities in the calendar, such as Nisos and Philonis.[127] What is more, the deme's eponymous hero

---

[117] Kataibates: lines 10-12 (with Zeus restored in line 10), under ?Metageitnion, and 25-26, under Pyanopsion. Herkeios: line 22, under Boedromion; and note also -]ι Ἑρκείωι οἶν on the left side (with Daux, "Calendrier," pp. 157-158) and [Διὶ Ἑρ]κείωι οἶν on the right side (with Daux, "Calendrier," p. 160). Epithetless: lines 39 (Elaphebolion) and 47-48 (Thargelion).

[118] Lines 19-20 (cf. above, p. 196) and 23-24, under Boedromion; line 27 (with left-side addendum), under Pyanopsion; lines 56-57 (cf. above, n. 101), under Skirophorion.

[119] Lines 20 and 24, under Boedromion, and line 43, under Mounichion. In line 41 the curious formulation ἐς Πυθίο Ἀπόλλωνος τρίτ[τοαν could be either a fourth offering to Apollo or simply a designation of locale.

[120] Lines 23 (Boedromion) and 52-54 (twice in Skirophorion, the first Π]|λυντηρίοις; cf. above, n. 116).

[121] Lines 21-22 (Boedromion), 38-39 (Elaphebolion; cf. above, n. 86), and 43-44 (Mounichion).

[122] Lines 31 (the Dionysia), 33-34 (goat-sacrifice on the day of the Anthesteria, 12 Anthesterion; cf. above, n. 100), and 45-46 (Mounichion).

[123] Lines 40-41 (as Mounichia) and 42-43 (securely restored in the company of Leto and Apollo); both Mounichion.

[124] Line 7 (?Hekatombaion).

[125] Line 32 (the Theogamia in Gamelion; see above, with n. 11).

[126] See Labarbe, *Thorikos*, nos. 19-21.

[127] Nisos: line 49 (Thargelion); see Labarbe, *Thorikos*, p. 63, n. 30, for a possible link between Nisos and Kephalos. Philonis: lines 44-45 (Mounichion); for the local connection, see Labarbe, *Thorikos*, no. 14. Thargelion was evidently the key month for offerings to heroes: see lines 48-51, for (as well as Nisos) Hyperpedios, Thras[. . ⁵ . .], Sosineos, Rhogios, and Py[lochos], and see also next note.

himself, Thorikos, who is otherwise explicitly mentioned only by Hesychius (under *Thorikos*), occupies a position of significance. He receives
not only a ram every Boedromion (line 18) but also, in Maimakterion,
an ox worth between forty and fifty drachmas (lines 28-30)—clearly a
major sacrifice, and one otherwise offered, it appears, only to [Kepha]los
(above). Also, and in association, "the heroines of Thorikos" are offered
a sacrificial table twice a year, in Boedromion (lines 18-19) and Maimakterion (line 30).[128] This is the best illustration yet, as we shall see,
for the cult of the eponymous hero which has always been assumed—
on very little evidence indeed—to have played a protagonist's role in the
religious life of the demes.

5. Erchia

The Erchia calendar (SEG 21.541), cited already many times in this
chapter and earlier, is on many counts the most approachable and, one
might even say, rational of its genre. Its precise form is unique, admittedly.
No other *fasti*—whether those of a deme or of any other body—parade
their financial preoccupations so openly as to divide out the year's sacrifices into five parallel vertical columns, representing concurrent series
of offerings to be paid for, in calculatedly equal measure, by five individual
liturgists.[129] However, with the inscription so excellently preserved (only
about 14 lines out of a total of ca. 339 are missing)[130] it is a simple
mechanical task to reconstitute the single, original "master-list"[131] and,
with the help of the magisterial studies by Daux and Dow, to appreciate
the unrivalled insight into the cult activity of a fourth-century deme which
the document makes possible.

Precision is its keynote throughout. Under monthly and daily rubrics,
with the day specified in all but one instance,[132] appear the deity in

---

[128] Labarbe's note (*Thorikos*, p. 61, n. 11) that "les Héroines en question ne sont pas
caractérisées comme appartenant à la localité ou au dème, mais comme des parèdres du
héros" is borne out, as he observes, by parallels elsewhere in the calendar; see lines 48-49
(Hyperpedios and his heroines: Dunst, "Opferkalender," p. 253; Labarbe, *Thorikos*, p. 62,
n. 29) and 50-51 (Pylochos and his heroines: Dunst, "Opferkalender," p. 253; Labarbe,
Thorikos, p. 63, n. 32); in both instances the heroines are offered a sacrificial table (for
which see above, n. 89). But the offering ['Hρ]ωΐνησιν Κορωνέων (addendum to the left
side; see Daux, "Calendrier," pp. 158-159, superseding both Dunst, "Opferkalender," pp.
259-260, and Labarbe, *Thorikos*, p. 64, n. 42) *seems* to belong in a different category.

[129] See Dow, "Demarkhia," pp. 187, 193-195.

[130] Dow, "Demarkhia," p. 184.

[131] See Daux, "Démarchie," pp. 617-618; more fully and graphically, Dow, "Demarkhia,"
pp. 189-191. For formal proof of the existence of such a "master-list" see Daux, "Démarchie," pp. 616-617, and Dow, "Demarkhia," p. 193.

[132] Namely, A, lines 37-38, Ἀνθεστηριῶνο|ς, Διασίοις. Presumably it was thought
supererogatory to specify the twenty-third day (schol. Aristoph. *Clouds*, line 408; Mikalson,

question, the location of the sacrifice, the victim to be offered, and its price, ranging between three drachmas for a piglet and twelve for a ram.[133] Of these four constant elements the second is the most striking; indeed the *invariable* specification of locale is unique to this calendar.[134] Six sacrifices are offered outside the deme itself: to Apollo Lykeios, Demeter, Zeus Polieus, and Athena Polias in Athens on 12 Metageitnion;[135] to Zeus Meilichios (for the Diasia in Agrai) on [23] Anthesterion;[136] and to Zeus Epakrios "on Hymettos" on 16 Thargelion.[137] More surprising, arguably, is the explicit indication in all other cases that the sacrifice will be, where one would anyway have assumed it to be, in the deme. Here the formula is either simply "in Erchia" (Ἐρχι/Ἐρχιᾶ/Ἐρχιᾶσι/ Ἐρχιᾶσιν: twenty-one times)[138] or else the same with an additional, precise locative phrase such as "on the Paianian side" (πρὸς Παια-νιέων),[139] "in (the *temenos*) of the Sotidai" (ἐς Σωτιδῶν),[140] or "in (the *hieron*) of Hera" (ἐν Ἥρας).[141] The most frequent of such phrases are "on the akropolis" (ἐμ Πόλε(ι): seven times)[142] and, especially, "in the Pagos" (ἐμ Πάγωι: nine times)[143]—the latter being evidently "the major cult center."[144]

Calendar, p. 117); but note the ewe-lamb offered to Athena Γαμηλιῶνος | ἐνάτηι ἱστα|μένο, Ἡροσου|ρίοις, the only other festival (see on it Daux, "Démarchie," p. 620) mentioned by name.

[133] It is noteworthy that no ox-sacrifices or *trittoia* are mentioned (cf. Daux, "Démarchie," p. 632), so that "the most striking feature about the sacrifices themselves is their small quantity" (Dow, "Demarkhia," p. 192). On the offering to Athena Polias, on 3 Skirophorion, of a ewe ἀν|[τ]ίβους (A, lines 64-65) see Daux, "Démarchie," p. 630, and Jameson, "Calendar," pp. 157-158.

[134] Cf. Dow, "Demarkhia," p. 212.

[135] A, lines 1-5, ἐν ἄστει (precise location unspecified); B, lines 1-5, ἐν Ἐλευσι(νίωι) ἐν ἄστει; Γ, lines 13-18, ἐμ Πόλε(ι) ἐν ἄστει; Δ, lines 13-17, ἐμ Πόλε(ι) ἐν ἄστε(ι). Cf. above, n. 16.

[136] A, lines 37-43. Cf. above, nn. 16, 132.

[137] E, lines 59-64. Cf. above, n. 16.

[138] Explicitly nineteen times: A, line 29; B, lines 12-13, 17, 37-38, 44, 48-49; Γ, lines 35, 45, 51; Δ, lines 20-21, 36, 44, 50, 54; E, lines 11-12, 25-26 (taking ἐμ Πετρῆι with Διί rather than with Ἐρχιᾶσιν: see Jameson, "Calendar," p. 158), 28-29, 35-36, 42-43. In addition two offerings are made "on the same altar" (ἐπὶ τοῦ αὐτοῦ βωμοῦ) as others which are explicitly in the deme: A, lines 44-51 (Semele), cf. Δ, lines 33-40 (Dionysos); E, lines 44-46 (Nymphs), cf. 39-43 (Apollo Nymphegetes). See further below, n. 166.

[139] A, lines 34-35. See Daux, "Démarchie," p. 625.

[140] Γ, lines 4-5 and 8-9. See Daux, "Démarchie," p. 624.

[141] B, lines 34-35; Γ, lines 40-41; Δ, line 31.

[142] A, lines 60 and 63; B, lines 29-30 and 58; Γ, line 62; Δ, lines 59-60; E, lines 68-69 (as restored by Jameson, "Calendar," p. 157). Surprisingly, ἐπὶ τὸ Ἄκρο (Δ, lines 4-5 and 8-9) apparently signified somewhere different (though see Dow, "Demarkhia," p. 211).

[143] A, lines 8-9 and 15; B, lines 22-23 and 53-54; Γ, lines 21-22, 29, 56-57; Δ, line 26; E, line 18.

[144] Mikalson, "Religion," p. 424. The cults located there were those of Hera Thelchinia,

Various stipulations relating to "rituel" (Daux) are appended to approximately half of the fifty-nine entries.[145] The commonest of them is the phrase οὐ φορά, sometimes abbreviated to οὐ φορ or οὐ φο, which appears twenty-two times (including three added after—perhaps long after—the main part of the inscription had been completed).[146] This seems to mean that none of the sacrificial meat was to be carried away from the scene of the sacrifice itself.[147] If Dow is right, the prohibition reflected purely secular considerations rather than any (obscure) requirements of ritual propriety. Immediate consumption of the meat helped to ensure that it was equitably shared amongst all present, not unfairly preempted by priests or other officials. By contrast, in other instances the cult personnel, and other groups with a special interest of some kind, did enjoy some perquisites. In the case of three local sacrifices to Apollo in Gamelion and Thargelion the beast was "to be handed over to the Pythaistai" (παραδόσιμος Πυθαϊσταῖς);[148] and for the offerings, on the same altar, to Dionysos and Semele on 16 Elaphebolion it was "to be handed over to the women" (γυναιξὶ παραδόσιμος)—οὐ φορά, in both cases.[149] The priestesses of Dionysos and Semele—if they were not one and the same[150]—had to content themselves, on 16 Elaphebolion, with bearing off the beast's skin; and such a grant, ἱερείαι (or ἱερέας) τὸ δέρμα, was made also to the priestesses of Hera and (twice) of the Heroines.[151]

That only priestesses, not priests, are mentioned in this Erchia calendar is not the least of its noteworthy features; and the explanation must be

the Nymphs, Acheloos, Apollo Paion, Zeus Epopetes, Alochos, Zeus (other, evidently, than Epopetes), Hermes, and Ge; references in preceding note. For the probable location of the Pagos within the deme, see E. Vanderpool, *BCH* 89, 1965, pp. 21-26, at 23.

[145] For the total of fifty-nine, see Dow, "Demarkhia," pp. 186-187; for the three unknown to Daux ("Démarchie," p. 619), see Dow, "Demarkhia," p. 191.

[146] Original entries: A, lines 5, 10-11, 21, 51; Γ, lines 6-7, 10, 17-18, 53, 64; Δ, lines 6-7, 10-11, 38, 46, 55; E, lines 6-7, 20-21, 26-27, 30, 63-64. Added later: B, lines 44 and 59; E, lines 36-37; see Daux, "Démarchie," pp. 612, 628, and on the date of the additions—apparently third or even second century—Dow, "Demarkhia," p. 185.

[147] Daux, "Démarchie," p. 628, followed and developed by Dow, "Demarkhia," pp. 208-210.

[148] B, lines 45-51, Apollo Pythios on 4 Thargelion; Γ, lines 31-37, one of two offerings to Apollo Apotropaios on 8 Gamelion; E, lines 31-38, Apollo Lykeios on 7 Gamelion. To the last of these οὐ φορά has been added (cf. above, n. 146).

[149] A, lines 44-51; Δ, lines 33-40. See Dow, "Demarkhia," p. 209.

[150] Cf. Dow, "Demarkhia," p. 209.

[151] A, lines 17-22, Heroines, 14 Pyanopsion; B, lines 37-39, Hera, 27 Gamelion; E, lines 1-8, Heroines, 19 Metageitnion. The priestess of Artemis, on the other hand, was twice given skins deliberately spoiled by being torn: see Daux, "Démarchie," p. 630, on the phrase τὸ δέρμα κατα(ι)γίζειν in Γ, lines 8-12, and Δ, lines 8-12 (both on 21 Hekatombaion). Note also the four holocausts, where the victim was entirely burned up: B, lines 14-20 (Basile, 4 Boedromion); Γ, lines 19-25 (Zeus Epopetes, 25 Metageitnion); Δ, lines 18-23, and E, lines 9-15 (Epops, 5 Boedromion; see Mikalson, "Religion," p. 430).

that the prerogatives of the latter were known and secure.[152] But what the document unfortunately fails to make clear is the precise extent to which the priests and priestesses were the people who performed the actual sacrifices. In this respect the long entry under 4 Thargelion (E, lines 47-58) is tantalizing: Θαργηλιῶνο|ς τετράδι ἱ|σταμένο, Ἑρ|μῆι, ἐν ἀγορ|ᾶι Ἐρχιᾶσι, | κριός, τούτ|ωι ἱερεῶσθ|αι τὸν κήρυ|κα καὶ τὰ γέ|ρα λαμβάνε|ν καθάπερ ὁ | δήμαρχος, Δ. This ram-sacrifice to Hermes is the only offering of the year which is made in the deme's *agora*, and it involves the only mention of the herald. No doubt he was present *qua* herald at many other sacrifices besides this one, but here he steps out into the limelight to act as priest (ἱερεῶσθαι) in an offering to the god of heralds, and he receives prime portions (*gera*) "just as does the demarch."[153] The implication here, as Dow observes, is not only that demarch and herald shared the *gera* on this particular day but also that such *gera* for the demarch may be postulated for all the offerings which the calendar lists. All the same, it may be wrong to infer that the demarch personally *offered* all the sacrifices. Some he surely did, as in Marathon (and elsewhere); but otherwise the priests and priestesses of the various cults are likely to have played out their traditional roles.[154]

As to the cults themselves, a brief and selective summary must suffice. Thirty-two of the fifty-nine sacrifices go to Olympians, that is, approximately the same proportion as in Thorikos; and it is the Olympians, moreover, who usually receive the larger victims.[155] The dominant figures are Zeus, to whom six offerings are made within the deme[156] and three outside it,[157] and Apollo, who receives eight sacrifices (all but one in the

---

[152] Cf. Dow, "Demarkhia," p. 207: "Where are the Priests? It seems unavoidable to conclude that the Priestesses are mentioned to make it certain that they got what was theirs. Where no Priestess is specified as the recipient, the hide goes to some other official, most often, perhaps always, to the Priest." Yet *if* more of the deme's cults had priestesses (rather than priests) than this argument implies, the principles at work here would remain unfathomable.

[153] See Dow, "Demarkhia," p. 206.

[154] See Dow, "Demarkhia," pp. 206-207, cf. 192 and 196.

[155] Dow, "Demarkhia," p. 204, commenting that "though she was always a minor deity, there would be sense in grouping Kourotrophos with the Olympians, since sacrifices to her [in this calendar] are always *prothymata* to Olympian sacrifices;" cf. above, p. 192 and esp. n. 88. Note that Dow's table on p. 203 of "Demarkhia" omits one of the Zeus sacrifices (Γ, lines 55-58; see next note).

[156] Γ, lines 19-25 (Zeus Epopetes, 25 Metageitnion; on the epithet see Daux, "Démarchie," p. 622); Γ, lines 38-41 (Zeus Teleios, 27 Gamelion; see above, with n. 11); Γ, lines 55-58 (Zeus without epithet, 4 Thargelion; see above, n. 144); Γ, lines 59-64 (Zeus Polieus, 3 Skirophorion; see above, with n. 12, and next note); E, lines 22-27 (Zeus ἐμ Πετρῆι, 16 Posideion; see above, n. 138); E, lines 28-30 (Zeus Horios, also 16 Posideion; cf. above, with n. 81).

[157] A, lines 37-43 (Zeus Meilichios at the Diasia, 23 Anthesterion; see above, with n.

deme itself) under six epithets.[158] Athena receives three, two of them as Polias;[159] there are two each for Artemis,[160] Dionysos,[161] Hera,[162] Hermes,[163] and Poseidon;[164] and one each for Demeter[165] and the syncretized Artemis Hekate.[166] Amongst the non-Olympians it is puzzling to find no reference to Herakles, who we know had a *temenos* in the deme (IG II²2609, its *horos*). And it is disappointing to find no mention of the eponymous hero Erchios, who was linked with Demeter (St. Byz., under *Erchia*). Indeed there are no deities or heroes who were particularly associated—so far as is known—with Erchia. To say this, however, may simply betray the extent of our ignorance of cult observance not only in this deme (which, as Mikalson notes, "is mentioned by neither Pausanias nor Strabo as being remarkable for its cults or sanctuaries")[167] but in general. Why, for example, should the Erchieis have made offerings to the Sican hero Leukaspis,[168] or to Epops the hoopoe?[169] The questions must remain rhetorical ones; we do not know, and can scarcely guess. Other names, however, offer more of a foothold. The ram offered to the

---

16); Γ, lines 13-18 (Zeus Polieus on the city akropolis, 12 Metageitnion; cf. preceding note); E, lines 59-64 (Zeus Epakrios "on Hymettos," 16 Thargelion).

[158] Apotropaios (cf. above, with n. 84): A, lines 31-36, and Γ, lines 31-37 (both 8 Gamelion). Delphinios: A, lines 28-30 (7 Gamelion). Lykeios: A, lines 1-5 (12 Metageitnion, ἐν ἄστει) and E, lines 31-38 (7 Gamelion). Nymphegetes: E, lines 39-43 (8 Gamelion). Paion: B, lines 52-54 (4 Thargelion). Pythios: B, lines 45-51 (4 Thargelion).

[159] Athena Polias in A, lines 62-65 (3 Skirophorion; on the victim see above, n. 133), and Δ, lines 13-17 (12 Metageitnion, on the city akropolis); without epithet in B, lines 26-31 (9 Gamelion, Ἡροσουρίοις; cf. above, n. 132).

[160] Γ, lines 8-12, and Δ, lines 8-12 (both 21 Hekatombaion). On Artemis Hekate see below, at n. 166.

[161] Γ, lines 42-47 (2 Anthesterion); Δ, lines 33-40 (16 Elaphebolion, with Semele "on the same altar"; cf. above, n. 138).

[162] A, lines 6-11 (Hera Thelchinia, 20 Metageitnion; on the epithet see Daux, "Démarchie," p. 622); B, lines 37-39 (without epithet, 27 Gamelion; see above, with n. 11).

[163] Δ, lines 24-27 (27 Boedromion); E, lines 47-58 (4 Thargelion; quoted above, in text).

[164] Δ, lines 28-32 (27 Gamelion; see above, with n. 11); Δ, lines 56-60 (3 Skirophorion; see above, with n. 12).

[165] B, lines 1-5 (12 Metageitnion, ἐν Ἐλευσι(νίωι) ἐν ἄστει).

[166] B, lines 11-13 (16 Metageitnion). (Dow, "Demarkhia," p. 203, lists Hekate as an epithet of Artemis, while Daux, "Démarchie," p. 622, regards Hekate as the predominant element.) Although it is only the piglet for Kourotrophos which is expressly said (B, line 8) to be offered ἐν ['E]κάτης (*sc.* ἱερόν), and the nanny goat for Artemis Hekate simply "in Erchia," both surely *were* sacrificed in the same place; this is explicit in three of the other Kourotrophos-linked dual offerings (A, lines 57-65; Γ, lines 1-12; Δ, lines 1-12) and implicit in the other two (A, lines 23-30; B, lines 32-39).

[167] Mikalson, "Religion," p. 424.

[168] Γ, lines 48-53 (20 Mounichion). See Daux, "Démarchie," pp. 622, 632, and esp. G. Dunst, "Leukaspis," BCH 88, 1964, pp. 482-485.

[169] Δ, lines 18-23, and E, lines 9-15 (both 5 Boedromion, the day of the city Genesia—but no connection with it is evident: Mikalson, "Religion," p. 430).

otherwise unattested Menedeios on 19 Thargelion, for instance, has been tentatively (but plausibly) linked by Michael Jameson with the state festival which took place on that day, the Bendideia.[170] The Herakleidai (B, lines 40-44; 4 Mounichion) *are* attested elsewhere, and to an extent which allows one to say that their cult in the demes seems to have been widespread; a priest of the Herakleidai is known from Aixone (IG II²1199, lines 23-24), a *hieron* of the Herakleidai in Kydathenaion (*Agora 16*, no. 54, A, lines 4-5, and B, lines 4-5), and a Ἡρακλειδῶν ἐσχάρα, sacrificial hearth, in Prasiai (IG II²4977). And as for the cult of Basile, well attested in the city,[171] it was unknown in a deme before the discovery of the Erchia calendar with its wineless holocaust sacrifice to her on 4 Boedromion (B, lines 14-20), but now we also have an honorific decree from Antiochid Eitea which was set up in her *hieron* there (SEG 28.102, lines 18-19).

✳

Even this brief resumé of the contents and scope of the five surviving *fasti* should have served to bear out my claim that these documents have opened up an extra dimension in the study of religion in the demes. As well as sifting through scattered and disparate data from a miscellany of literary and epigraphic sources—data which may be individually suggestive and significant but difficult to put into any sort of context[172]—we can also, now, observe something of how the demes themselves, in the fourth century, shaped and organized a complex nexus of (often) archaic cult activity into a more or less coherent program of sacrifices and festivals. Nevertheless, invaluable as they are, the *fasti* by no means provide answers to all the questions that one wants to ask, so that evidence from other quarters retains its importance both (1) *per se* and also (2) as a control upon inferences which the calendars alone might prompt us to draw:

---

[170] Δ, lines 52-55, with Jameson, "Calendar," pp. 158-159; cf. above, n. 63.

[171] Plato *Charmides* 153A; IG I³84 (city decree of 417 on the *hieron* of Kodros, Neleus, and Basile); *Hesp.* 7, 1938, p. 123, no. 25 (priestess and ?temple of Basile in 239/8); R. E. Wycherley, "Neleion," *ABSA* 55, 1960, pp. 60-66. In IG II²4546, A (= line 4), from Phaleron ca. 400, Lolling's emendation of Ἰασίλη to Βασίλη has perhaps, however, been too readily accepted: see B. D. Meritt, *Hesp.* 11, 1942, p. 284; Wycherley, *art. cit.* p. 60; Daux, "Démarchie," p. 621.

[172] Examples are legion, and many will appear in the following pages, if indeed they have not been cited already. It will suffice to mention here the case of Halimous, where we know from a variety of sources that there were cults of Demeter Thesmophoros and Kore (Paus. 1.31.1, and Chap. 3, n. 59), Dionysos (SEG 2.7, line 23), Herakles (Demosth. 57.46-48 and 62) and Hestia (SEG 21.813, *lex sacra* of the fourth or third century); but what was their relationship to each other in the context of the deme's sacred calendar as a whole?

1. No surviving calendar mentions, for example, whether the festivals and sacrifices with which it is concerned were restricted to demesmen[173] or open more widely. Here our information has to come from documents of other kinds, chiefly honorific decrees. The fullest and clearest instance is IG II²1214, where in the first half of the third century the deme of Peiraieus honored a man, Kallidamas of Cholleidai, who was palpably not a member of the deme but who may reasonably be supposed to have been resident in it.[174] The relevant clauses read: "whenever the Peiraieis sacrifice in the communal *hiera*, Kallidamas shall have a portion too, just like the others, (the) Peiraieis; and Kallidamas is to dine together with the Peiraieis in all the *hiera* except any where entry is customarily restricted to the Peiraieis themselves and not others; and he is to be assigned to whichever *triakas* he likes" (ὅταν θύωσι Πειραιεῖς ἐν τοῖς κοιν|οῖς ἱεροῖς νέμειν καὶ Καλλιδάμαντι με|ρίδα καθάπερ καὶ τοῖς ἄλλοις Πειραιεῦ|σιν, καὶ συνεστιᾶσθαι Καλλιδάμαντα με|τὰ Πειραιέων ἐν ἅπασι τοῖς ἱεροῖς πλὴν | εἴ που αὐτοῖς Πει-ραιεῦσιν νόμιμόν ἐστ|ιν εἰσιέναι, ἄλλωι δὲ μή· κατανεῖμαι δὲ α|ὐτὸν καὶ τριακάδα ἣν ἂν αὐτὸς βούλη|ται).[175] The interesting point here is that, despite the great favors granted to this honorand (and to three others like him in other demes),[176] there remained a nucleus of *hiera* from which, according to the dictates of *nomos*, even he had to stay excluded. For Peiraieus, in other words, one can distinguish between two categories of *hiera*, those which could and those which could not be shared with privileged outsiders. Yet what not one of these four cases reveals is whether a third category too should be envisaged, namely, those in which others besides the demesmen were *normally included*. Apart from the evidence that the rural Dionysia did embrace outsiders (see below, section D) our only clues here are very fragmentary ones. They come in *leges sacrae* from Skambonidai (ca. 460), where the deme's metics are allowed to participate in one of its festivals, and from Phrearrhioi (mid third-century), concerned principally with the rites of Demeter and Kore, where one line begins with the tantalizing phrase "for demesmen with the others" ([δημ]όταις μετὰ τῶν ἄλλων).[177]

---

[173] And/or, on appropriate occasions, their womenfolk.

[174] Cf. Chap. 3, n. 40.

[175] IG II²1214, lines 11-19. On the *triakades*, see Pollux 8.111; Schoeffer, "Demoi," col. 24.

[176] Eleusis: IG II²1187, lines 20-23, νέμειν δὲ αὐτ|ῶι καὶ μερίδα ἐκ τῶν ἱερῶν καθά|περ Ἐλευσινίοις τὸν δήμαρχον | τὸν ἀεὶ δημαρχοῦντα. Halai Araphenides: AE 1925-1926, pp. 168-177, lines 8-12 (quoted above, n. 36). Lamptrai: IG II²1204, lines 12-17, νέμειν|ν αὐτῶι κρέα ἐν τοῖς | ἱεροῖς οἷς ἂν θύωσ[ι]ν οἱ δημόται Λαμπτρ|[ᾶσι καθ]άπερ Λαμπτρ|[εῦσι.

[177] Skambonidai: IG I³244, C, lines 7-9; see Chap. 3, p. 81. Phrearrhioi: *Hesp.* 39, 1970, pp. 47-53, line 7; the restoration, an irresistible one, is Vanderpool's *ad loc*. Note

It is probably legitimate to assume that most demes did divide their cults and festivals threefold on these lines, but the criteria by which they did so remain as obscure to us as they were, doubtless, clear to them.

2. Of the many kinds of information which the deme *fasti* have yielded, one of the most valuable—to which reference has been made from time to time in the foregoing pages—is their indication of the relative importance, in the demes, of the cults of the various Olympian and non-Olympian deities. According to Mikalson, "what should be particularly noted is the importance of Zeus and Apollo in the cults listed on the deme calendars, whereas their importance in state cult appears somewhat limited."[178] A fuller text of the Thorikos calendar than was available to Mikalson, who based his comments on the *fasti* from Erchia and Marathon, confirms, as we have seen, the general prominence of Zeus and Apollo. But it also, arguably, elevates that of Athena to a level not far below them—as indeed Pausanias' generalization in 1.26.6 already hinted: "even those who in their demes have an established worship of other gods hold Athena in honor nonetheless" (ὅσοις θεοὺς καθ-έστηκεν ἄλλους ἐν τοῖς δήμοις σέβειν, οὐδέν τι ἧσσον τὴν Ἀθηνᾶν ἄγουσιν ἐν τιμῇ). At all events, other sources bear out the ubiquity of cults of these three major Olympians.[179] On the other hand,

---

also the recruitment of tragic *chorēgoi* in fifth-century Ikarion from residents as well as members of the deme (IG I³254, lines 3-4); see Chap. 3, n. 41, and further below, sec. D.

[178] Mikalson, "Religion," pp. 432-433.

[179] ZEUS. *In the calendars*: see above, under Teithras, Marathon, Thorikos, and Erchia. *Elsewhere (e.g.)*: ?Bate (IG I³1084; see Traill, *Organization*, p. 39, on its find-spot, Ambelokipi); Hekale (Plut. *Thes.* 14; Hesych., Ἑκάλειος Ζεύς; St. Byz., Ἑκαλή); Myrrhinous (IG II²1183, lines 32-36); Peiraieus (Paus. 1.1.3; etc.); Phaleron (Paus. 1.1.4); Phlya (Paus. 1.31.4); Teithras (SEG 24.151, line 12); Thorikos (IG II²2606). See in general Solders, *Kulte*, pp. 1-6.

APOLLO. *In the calendars*: see above, under Eleusis, Marathon, Thorikos, and Erchia. *Elsewhere (e.g.)*: Acharnai (Paus. 1.31.5; ec.); Cholargos (IG II²1184, line 23); Eleusis (Paus. 1.37.6-7); ?Eupyridai (IG II²1362); Halai Aixonides (*AD* 11, 1927-1928, pp. 40-41, no. 4; etc.); Ikarion (*Hesp.* 17, 1948, p. 142, no. 2; IG II²4976, with W. R. Biers and T. D. Boyd, *Hesp.* 51, 1982, pp. 15-18); Kikynna (schol. Aristoph. *Clouds*, line 134); Lamptrai (IG II²2967); Phlya (Paus. 1.31.4; Plut. *Them.* 15.2, cf. Athen. 424F); Plotheia (IG I³258, line 8; and cf. now *AE* 1980, pp. 94-95, line 2—see Appendix 3, no. 97); Prasiai (Paus. 1.31.2); Skambonidai (IG I³244, C, line 20). See in general Solders, *Kulte*, pp. 16-21.

ATHENA. *In the calendars*: see above, under Teithras, Marathon, Thorikos, and Erchia. *Elsewhere (e.g.)*: Acharnai (IG II³1206, 1207; SEG 21.519; Paus. 1.31.5); ?Bate (IG I³1084; see Traill, *Organization*, p. 39, on its find-spot, Ambelokipi); Halai Aixonides (Paus. 1.31.1; etc.); Kolonos (Paus. 1.30.4); Lakiadai (Paus. 1.37.2); Lamptrai (IG II²1035, line 51); Marathon (*PAAH* 1933, p. 42); Peiraieus (Paus. 1.1.3); Phaleron (Paus. 1.1.4, cf. 36.4); Phlya (Paus. 1.31.4); Prasiai (*Lex Seguer.* V, *Lexeis Rhetorikai*, Προναία Ἀθηνᾶ [= Bekker, *Anecd. Gr.* 1.299.6]); Sounion (IG I³1024; Paus. 1.1.1). See in general Solders, *Kulte*, pp. 9-16.

as Mikalson also points out, "the relative importance of deities obviously varied significantly from area to area,"[180] and it is vital that the general patterns which the calendars suggest should not lead us to forget or discount this. Cults of three other Olympians—Aphrodite (who does not figure in any of the *fasti*), Artemis, and particularly Dionysos—are well attested,[181] while that of the non-Olympian Herakles, all but absent from the *fasti*,[182] could nonetheless hardly be described as anything but widespread.[183] In addition, "individual demes might devote special worship to a deity closely linked with their own locality."[184] This seems to be true, for example, of Ares in Acharnai,[185] Hebe in Aixone,[186] and the Dioskouroi (Anakes) in Kephale.[187] A coastal deme might for obvious

[180] Mikalson, "Religion," p. 432.

[181] APHRODITE. Cults at (e.g.) Athmonon (Paus. 1.14.7), Eleusis (Paus. 1.37.7), Halai Aixonides (IG II²2820), Kephale (IG II²2604; Isaeus 2.31), Peiraieus (Paus. 1.1.3; etc.), ?Phaleron (Paus. 1.1.4; Strabo 9.1.21 wrongly assigns the cult of Aphrodite Kolias to Anaphlystos; Cape Kolias itself, modern Cape Agios Kosmas, is in Halimous, however; cf. J. Day, *AJA* 36, 1932, pp. 1-11, esp. 1-2), Plotheia (IG I³258, line 5; cf. IG II²4607). See in general Solders, *Kulte*, pp. 32-37.

ARTEMIS. *In the calendars*: see above, under Thorikos and Erchia. *Elsewhere (e.g.)*: Athmonon (IG I²865, *horoi*; IG II²1203, line 17; Paus. 1.31.4-5; see Mikalson, "Religion," p. 432), Besa (*Hesp.* 19, 1950, p. 214, no. 5, lines 76-77, and p. 256, no. 18, lines 35-36), Eleusis (Paus. 1.38.6), Halai Aixonides/Zoster (Paus. 1.31.1; etc.), Melite (see Chap. 3, n. 54), Myrrhinous (IG II²1182, lines 19-21; Paus. 1.31.4-5), Phlya (Paus. 1.31.4). See in general Solders, *Kulte*, pp. 21-30.

DIONYSOS. See below, sec. D.

[182] Only at Thorikos (*AC* 52, 1983, pp. 150-174, line 36, under Elaphebolion), in conjunction with his mother Alkmene (line 37); note, however, that R.C.T. Parker, *ZPE* 57, 1984, p. 59, persuasively reads Ἡρακλείδα[ις τέλεον instead of Daux's Ἡρακλεῖ δά[μαλιν, οἶν. For the Marathonian Tetrapolis, see above, p. 193.

[183] Cf. Mikalson, "Religion," p. 433. Herakles cults are attested at (e.g.) Acharnai (Paus. 1.31.5; IG I³971), Besa (*Hesp.* 19, 1950, p. 255, no. 18, lines 12 and 21-22), Eleusis (SEG 28.103), Erchia (IG II²2609, *horos*—but not in the *fasti*), Halimous (Demosth. 57.46-48 and 62), Iphistiadai (IG II²2611, *horos*, and Diog. Laert. 3.41, Plato's will; see G. Klaffenbach, *AM* 51, 1926, pp. 21-25), Kephisia (IG II²2610, *horos*), Marathon (Paus. 1.15.3 and 32.4), Phegaia (IG II²1932, line 14), Plotheia (IG I³258, line 4), Teithras (SEG 24.151, line 11), the unidentifiable deme responsible for IG II²1211 (B, line 4), and possibly Peiraieus (IG I³242, *lex sacra* of 490-480, where the editor, D. M. Lewis, regards the trace in line 1 as "potius ϸεϱ[[ακλ- quam ϸ]ιεϱ"). See in general Solders, *Kulte*, pp. 77-81, and esp. S. Woodford, "Cults of Heracles in Attica," in D. G. Mitten et al., eds., *Studies presented to George M.A. Hanfmann*, Mainz, 1971, pp. 211-225. (The Herakleia of Kynosarges, in Diomeia, was a *state* festival: see Deubner, *Feste*, p. 226; S. C. Humphreys, *JHS* 94, 1974, pp. 88-95; Parke, *Festivals*, p. 51.)

[184] Mikalson, "Religion," p. 432.

[185] Cult of Ares and Athena Areia: SEG 21.519, cf. Tod no. 204; note also IG II²2953, dedication to Ares and Augustus by τὸ κοινὸν τῶν Ἀχαρνέων. I know of no other Ares cult in a deme.

[186] IG II²1199, passim; IG II²2492, lines 22-23; cf. IG II²1035, line 58.

[187] Paus. 1.31.1. Other demes: Erchia (SEG 21.541, Δ, lines 47-51, annual sacrifice on

reasons pay particular attention to Poseidon.[188] And as regards the cults of heroes—whose tombs, together with the sanctuaries of gods and the graves of men, were seen everywhere by Pausanias as he travelled the roads of Attica (1.29.2)—local traditions and links must obviously have been the determining consideration. This, however, raises again the question, which merits separate discussion, of the eponymous heroes of the demes.

C. The Eponymous Hero

"Un seul culte était à la fois pratiqué dans tous les dèmes: celui du héros éponyme. Le dème d'Araphène honorait le héros Araphène qui lui avait donné son nom et qui était son patron; celui de Dioméia, Diomos; celui d'Hékalé, l'héroïne Hékalé. Tous ces cultes existaient-ils avant que Clisthène eût divisé l'Attique en cent dèmes? Cela est peu probable. Clisthène en établit un certain nombre, s'autorisant sans doute des traditions anciennes et des légendes, auxquelles il n'eut qu'à donner un corps."[189]

Haussoullier's confident statement, echoed by von Schoeffer,[190] has been briefly criticized,[191] but never to my knowledge examined in de-

---

4 Thargelion), Phegaia (IG II²1932, line 15), Plotheia (IG I³258, line 6, Anakia festival), Thorikos (*AC* 52, 1983, pp. 150-174, line 37, sacrifice in Elaphebolion in conjunction with their sister Helen).

[188] Besides the obvious examples of Sounion (see above, p. 196) and Thorikos (see above, p. 198), note Athen. 297E: Ἀντίγονος ὁ Καρύστιος ἐν τῷ περὶ λέξεως τοὺς Ἁλαιέας λέγει θυσίαν ἐπιτελοῦντας τῷ Ποσειδῶνι ὑπὸ τὴν τῶν θύννων ὥραν, ὅταν εὐαγρήσωσι, θύειν τῷ θεῷ τὸν πρῶτον ἁλόντα θύννον, καὶ τὴν θυσίαν ταύτην καλεῖσθαι θυνναῖον (Θυνναῖα, Meineke); for the MS ἁλιέας, Kaibel (Teubner) adopted Wilamowitz' Αἰολέας, but I prefer Toepffer's Ἁλαιέας. Poseidon cults were not of course *confined* to coastal demes: witness (e.g.) Erchia (see above, p. 203), Kolonos (Sophocles *OC*, lines 54-55 and 888-889; Paus. 1.30.4), and Lakiadai (Paus. 1.37.2). See in general Solders, *Kulte*, pp. 7-9.

[189] Haussoullier, *Vie*, p. 151.

[190] Schoeffer, "Demoi," col. 21.

[191] By O. Broneer, *Hesp.* 11, 1942, p. 270, n. 74, objecting that Haussoullier cited insufficient examples to back up his categorical statement that *all* demes had eponymous hero cults. Broneer's point has much validity, as will be seen below, though it must be stated in Haussoullier's defence that both he (*Vie*, p. 151, n. 1) and von Schoeffer ("Demoi," col. 21) made reference to the collection of (forty) deme eponyms compiled by H. Sauppe, *de demis urbanis Athenarum*, Leipzig, 1846, pp. 6-8, and indeed to the fact that similar material, apparently, was collected in antiquity itself by Polemon "the Periegete" of Ilion (schol. Aristoph. *Birds*, line 645; see Chap. 2, n. 60). Broneer also observed that "if such cults existed in all the Attic demes, they had, of course, only local significance and thus would not be frequently mentioned either in inscriptions or in literature." Yet the inscriptions *of the demes themselves* were precisely concerned with what was of "local significance," and so may, indeed must, be scrutinized for signs of these hero cults; see below.

tail.[192] The main problem which it raises is not of course that of the "cent dèmes," a figure long untenable.[193] It is not even the supposition, which is likely enough, that in some instances such cults were formally established in 508/7 itself. The problem is this categorical assertion that *all* demes paid cult to a "héros éponyme." The fact that no ancient author, as far as we know, made such a claim is not in itself sufficient to disprove it, but examination of the evidence may at least indicate a more complex, less uniform pattern of observance.

Two general observations will help to put this evidence, such as it is, into perspective. First (and pedantically), some demes cannot possibly have had a cult of their *eponymous* hero, for they were not eponymously named. In ?Aristot. *Ath. Pol.* 21.5, it will be recalled, Kleisthenes is said to have "named some of the demes after their localities, others after their founders, as (founders) no longer existed for all the places" (προσηγόρευσε δὲ τῶν δήμων τοὺς μὲν ἀπὸ τῶν τόπων, τοὺς δὲ ἀπὸ τῶν κτισάντων· οὐ γὰρ ἅπαντες ὑπῆρχον ἔτι τοῖς τόποις). Whether Kleisthenes' role was that of creator or merely (as I have argued) canonizer of most of the deme-names,[194] the distinction between the two types of name is plain enough;[195] and Elaious, Halai Aixonides, Halimous, Potamos, Rhamnous, and all the other demes in the first category necessarily lacked a "héros éponyme" and, *a fortiori*, a cult thereof. What such demes *may* have had instead is a cult of a "founder-hero" (ἥρως ἀρχηγέτης) or *Schutzpatron*, either named or anonymous, such as is attested for Rhamnous.[196]

[192] The deme heroes are not discussed by Mikalson, "Religion."

[193] See Chap. 1, pp. 17-23.

[194] See Chap. 1, pp. 24-25. As well as the general statement in ?Aristot. *Ath. Pol.* 21.5, we have one other piece of evidence linked with Kleisthenes' allocation of deme-names. The rediscovery of the *Ath. Pol.*, in conjunction with the realization that there were many more than one hundred demes, put an end to the old nineteenth-century argument over whether the "hundred heroes" of the lexica (e.g. Hesych., Πολύξενος) were those of the demes or—as is now universally accepted—the one hundred preselected *archēgetai* from whom the Pythia picked out the eponyms for the ten Kleisthenic tribes (?Aristot. *Ath. Pol.* 21.6, unnecessarily doubted by U. Kron, *Die zehn attischen Phylenheroen*, AM Beiheft 5, 1976, pp. 29-31): see Schoeffer, "Demoi," cols. 3-4; Busolt/Swoboda, *Staatskunde*, p. 874. But what happened to the ninety not chosen? In a note in *RPh* 16, 1892, p. 167, Haussoullier drew attention to the entry Ἀραφήν· εἷς τῶν ἑκατὸν ἡρώων in Herodian, περὶ μονήρους λέξεως 17.8 (= II p. 293 Lentz); and one may compare schol. Euripides *Hippolytos*, line 455, Κέφαλος εἷς ἐστι τῶν (ἑκατόν, Wilamowitz). It would seem possible, then, that *some* of the unused tribal eponyms (certainly not all of them: witness Hesych., Πολύξενος, and Phot., Πάνοψ) were adopted for or by demes—but only, no doubt, if a genuine local link existed.

[195] At least in theory. On occasion the antiquarians seem to have hedged their bets; note for instance Harpoc., Κεραμεῖς, and St. Byz., Πίθος.

[196] See W. Peek, *Mnemosyne* 4, 1936, p. 16 (= Pouilloux, *Forteresse*, no. 26), ἀρχεγέτει ἥροι ἄ[γ]αλμα (late sixth or early fifth century), and especially IG II²2849 (= Pouilloux,

Secondly, a deme with either an eponymous hero (or heroine) or simply a founder-hero (or -heroine) need not automatically be assumed to have paid cult to him (or her). On the presumption that the subject of the verb in the *Ath. Pol.*'s οὐ γὰρ ἅπαντες ὑπῆρχον ἔτι τοῖς τόποις is indeed *founders* rather than *demes*,[197] the passage appears to mean that in some demes the original eponym or founder had lapsed into obscurity, so that (again *a fortiori*) any ancient cults of them no longer existed.[198] There is no justification for supposing that Kleisthenes was concerned to revive any such cults, even if he could have done so; each deme, surely, took its own decision. Thus for example no offerings to Erchios are mentioned, as we have seen, in the exceptionally well-preserved Erchia *fasti*, so it must be a reasonable inference that none were made, at any rate annually; and by the same token one has no right to postulate a *cult* in each of the many instances where the lexicographers and scholiasts speak only— and sometimes, to all appearances, conjecturally—of a *hero*.[199]

The evidence for *cults* is as follows:

1. *Anagyrous*. There was a *"temenos* of Anagyros in the deme of the Anagyrasioi" (τέμενος Ἀναγύρου ἐν τῷ δήμῳ τῶν Ἀναγυρασίων), according to the Suda lexicon (under *Anagyrasios*); and Zenobius refers in *Proverbs* 2.55 to the eponym's *heroön*.

2. *Diomeia*. A priest of Diomos (cf. St. Byz. under *Diomeia*) is mentioned in a mid third-century decree of the Mesogeioi: IG II²1247, line 24. This suggests, though it does not quite prove, a cult of Diomos *in Diomeia*; compare 3, below.

3. *Hekale*. According to Plut. *Thes.* 14.2, citing Philochorus (*FGrH* 328 F109), "the demes round about used to assemble and sacrifice in Hekale to Zeus Hekaleios, and they honored Hekale, calling her by the

---

Forteresse, no. 25), offering to Dionysos by the ἱερεὺς ἥρῳ ἀρχηγέτου (fourth century); see P. Lévèque and P. Vidal-Naquet, *Clisthène l'Athénien*, Paris, 1964, p. 70 with n. 4. A deme ἀρχηγέτης of Aixone is mentioned by Plato *Lysis* 205D, but not a *cult*; see below, in text, for this distinction.

[197] As I have indeed assumed in my translation of the passage; for the problem consult Rhodes, *Commentary*, p. 258.

[198] Cf. P. Lévèque and P. Vidal-Naquet, *Clisthène l'Athénien*, Paris, 1964, p. 70, n. 3.

[199] Thus (besides Aixone, Araphen, and Kephale: see above, nn. 194, 196): Agryle (St. Byz., Ἀγραυλή), Aigilia (Athen. 652E), Aithalidai (St. Byz., s.v.), Anaphlystos (Paus. 2.30.9; St. Byz., s.v.), Aphidna (Plut. *Thes.* 31-34; St. Byz., s.v.), Boutadai (St. Byz., s.v.), Deiradiotai (St. Byz., Δειράδες), Dekeleia (Herod. 9.73.2; St. Byz., s.v.), Eleusis (Paus. 1.38.7), Erchia (St. Byz., s.v.), Euonymon (St. Byz., Εὐωνύμεια), Gargettos (Paus. 6.22.7; St.Byz., Ἀλήσιον), Iphistiadai (Hesych., Ἰφίστιος), Kollytos (St. Byz., Διόμεια), Krioa (schol. Aristoph. *Birds*, line 645), Lousia (St. Byz., s.v.), Melite (Harpoc., s.v.), Oe (Harpoc., Οἴηθεν), Oinoe (Paus. 1.33.8), Perithoidai (Phot. and Suda, s.v.), Philaidai (Plut. *Sol.*10.2; St. Byz., s.v.), Phlya (Paus. 4.1.5), Phrearrhioi (St. Byz., Φρέαρροι), Pithos (St. Byz., s.v.), Semachidai (St. Byz., s.v.), Sphettos (Paus. 2.30.9; St. Byz., s.v.), Teithras (schol. Aristoph. *Frogs*, line 477), Thymaitadai (Harpoc., s.v.).

diminutive name Hekaline" (ἔθυον γὰρ Ἑκαλῆσιν οἱ πέριξ δῆμοι συνιόντες Ἑκαλείῳ Διί [cf. Hesych., Ἑκάλειος Ζεύς; St. Byz., Ἑκαλή], καὶ τὴν Ἑκάλην ἐτίμων, Ἑκαλίνην ὑποκοριζόμενοι κτλ). The cult was expressly located in Hekale itself, though the scope of οἱ πέριξ δῆμοι is hardly determinable.

4. *Ikarion.* The monies of Ikarios recorded on IG I³253, from the third quarter of the fifth century, testify to a cult of the eponym.

5. *Kerameis.* Both Harpocration (under *Kerameis*), citing Philochorus (*FGrH* 328 F25), and the Suda (under Κεραμίς) assert—what Paus. 1.3.1 does not—that sacrifice was offered to the hero Keramos.

6. *Kolonos.* The opening scene of Sophocles' *Oedipus Coloneus* is set in a precinct sacred to Poseidon Hippios (lines 16, 37-38, and esp. 54-55; cf. Paus. 1.30.4), within which there is an equestrian (?)statue of the eponymous *archēgos* Kolonos (lines 58-65). The detail here has been subject to a certain amount of poetic licence,[200] but a cult of this hero seems clearly indicated.[201]

7. *Lakiadai.* Paus. 1.37.2 reports "a *temenos* of the hero Lakios" (Λακίου τέμενος ἥρωος).

8. *Marathon.* Having in 1.15.3 mentioned the eponymous hero Marathon—or, according to Plut. *Thes.* 32.4, Marathos—Pausanias adds in 1.32.4 that the demesmen paid cult to him. (It is a matter of conjecture whether he should be identified with any of the five unnamed heroes to whom the Marathonians, as we know, offered annual sacrifice: IG II²1358, col. II, lines 3, 4, 15, 23-24, 25.)

9. *Phaleron.* Pausanias saw (1.1.4) an altar of either Phaleros himself or his children (βωμοὶ . . . παίδων τῶν Θησέως καὶ Φαλήρου).

10. *Rhamnous* and 11. *Thorikos.* The cults of the founder-hero in Rhamnous and of Thorikos in Thorikos have been noted above.[202]

Other demes besides these eleven may or may not have had a cult of their eponymous hero or founder-hero, as well as other heroes or heroines with local connections;[203] quite simply, we cannot tell.

[200] In the fact, for example, that the cult-site of Prometheus (lines 55-56) was actually in the nearby Academy (Paus. 1.30.2).

[201] Despite its beguiling title there is nothing of relevance here in G. Méautis, *L'Oedipe à Colone et le culte des héros*, Neuchâtel, 1940.

[202] Rhamnous: see above, p. 209 with n. 196. Thorikos: see above, pp. 198-199.

[203] Sometimes these connections are known or deducible (e.g. Kephalos and Prokris in Thorikos: see above, p. 198), but more often they elude us. In Teithras, for example, where there is no sign of a cult of the eponym T(e)ithras, son of Pandion (schol. Aristoph. *Frogs*, line 477)—though admittedly only a fragment of the *fasti* wherein such a cult might have figured—we find a χῶρι{ι}ο|[ν] ἥρ[ωος Δα]τύλ[ο (SEG 24.151, lines 11-12), whose link with the deme is quite unknown; cf. the ἀργύρι[ον] | Δατύλλ[ο] in the 429/8 accounts of the Treasurers of the Other Gods (IG I³383, lines 75-76).

D. The Rural Dionysia

Unlike the cults of the heroes, the rural Dionysia (τὰ κατ' ἀγροὺς Διονύσια) and the evidence relating thereto has by no means wanted for
discussion;[204] and most of the problems—if not always the solutions to
them—are now well defined.

The festival was celebrated in the winter month of Posideion. This is
stated as a generalization by Theophrastus (Ποσιδεῶνος δὲ ⟨τὰ⟩ κατ'
ἀγροὺς Διονύσια: *Char*. 3 (ἀδολεσχίας).5) and by lexicographers
and scholiasts;[205] in addition it is confirmed by epigraphic evidence either
from or pertaining to three individual demes, Myrrhinous,[206] Peiraieus,[207]
and now Thorikos.[208] The solitary counter-indication—Athenaeus' assertion that both comedy and tragedy were invented, in Ikarion, "at the
very time of the vintage" (κατ' αὐτὸν τὸν τῆς τρύγης καιρόν), that
is, in late summer—may therefore be disregarded.[209] But the festivities
were not held everywhere on the same *day* (or days) of that month. In
Plato *Republic* 475D, Glaukon is made to speak of people rushing from
one festival to another out of passion for theater and music; and a similar
"cycle" is implied in Demosthenes' jeering allusions to Aeschines' days
as a jobbing actor.[210] If there was no attempt at precise synchronization
in the mid fourth century, there surely never had been any; within Posideion, individual demes could do as they liked.[211]

Most scholars who have written about the rural Dionysia have wisely
taken care not to claim—though they may nonetheless have implied—
that each and every deme celebrated it. It is certainly true, and significant,
that some degree of evidence can be found relating to the festival in as

[204] The standard accounts are those of Deubner, *Feste*, pp. 134-138, and esp. Pickard-
Cambridge, *Festivals*, pp. 42-56. See also Parke, *Festivals*, pp. 100-103; Mikalson, "Religion," pp. 433-434.

[205] *Lex Seguer*. V, *Lexeis Rhetorikai*, Διονύσια [= Bekker, *Anecd. Gr.* 1.235.6-8];
schol. Plato *Republic* 475D; schol. Aeschin. 1.43.

[206] IG II²1183, lines 36-37; cf. Chap. 4, n. 22.

[207] IG II²1496, etc.; see Pickard-Cambridge, *Festivals*, p. 45, n. 8. The degree of state
involvement in the Peiraieus Dionysia (see ?Aristot. *Ath. Pol.* 54.8 and other evidence cited
by Pickard-Cambridge, *Festivals*, pp. 44, 46-47) make it tantamount to, and perhaps even
actually, a state festival: Deubner, *Feste*, p. 137; Mikalson, *Calendar*, p. 97.

[208] *AC* 52, 1983, pp. 150-174 (the *fasti*), line 31: Ποσιδειῶνος, Διονύσια.

[209] Athen. 40A-B; cf. Pickard-Cambridge, *Festivals*, p. 42 with n. 8 (more circumspect).

[210] Demosth. 18.180 and 262; cf. Aeschin. 1.157. See Pickard-Cambridge, *Festivals*, pp.
43, 52; Parke, *Festivals*, pp. 102-103.

[211] Mikalson, *Calendar*, p. 97, suggests that the different dates for the rural Dionysia
might "partially explain" the fact that not many meetings of the *ekklēsia* in Posideion are
attested.

many as fourteen different demes (as well as in Brauron and Salamis),²¹² which goes to make the rural Dionysia "more widely attested than any other festival of the Attic countryside."²¹³ Yet none of these demes are small ones. The smallest—in terms of bouleutic representation—is Kollytos, which as a deme inside the city walls has to be acknowledged a special case,²¹⁴ and most of the rest were much larger. Whether every single one of the one hundred and thirty-nine demes observed the festival is thus open to some doubt, though it is obviously conceivable that many did so in modest ways which have gone unrecorded.

The *Hauptakt* (as Deubner put it) of the festival was evidently the procession (πομπή), which "doubtless . . . varied greatly in elaboration from deme to deme."²¹⁵ In Eleusis and, especially, Peiraieus it was a grand and formal *cortège*, supervised by the demarch and other officials,²¹⁶ but elsewhere one can envisage something more along the lines of Plutarch's nostalgic evocation of "the ancestral festival of the Dionysia" (ἡ πάτριος τῶν Διονυσίων ἑορτή)—a cheap and cheerful affair of wine jar, vine twig, billy goat, dried figs, and "above all" phallus²¹⁷— or else the well-known scene in Aristophanes' *Acharnians* (lines 237-279). There Dikaiopolis organizes his own rural Dionysia and procession. "It is headed by his daughter as κανηφόρος, carrying as an offering a cake or flat loaf on which she pours porridge with a ladle; behind her is the slave Xanthias as φαλληφόρος (with another slave), carrying the

---

²¹² Demes: Acharnai, Aigilia, Aixone, ?Anagyrous (IG II²1210), Eleusis, Halai Araphenides (the unpublished decree reported in *Ergon* 1957, pp. 24-25 = *PAAH* 1957, pp. 45-47), Ikarion, Kollytos, Myrrhinous, Paiania, Peiraieus, Phlya (Isaeus 8.15-16), Rhamnous, Thorikos; cf. Pickard-Cambridge, *Festivals*, p. 45, on the difficulty, at times, of deciding whether "Dionysia" means city or rural. Brauron: schol. Aristoph. *Peace*, line 874. Salamis: IG II²1227 (lines 30ff.) and 3093; Pickard-Cambridge, *Festivals*, p. 51.

²¹³ Mikalson, "Religion," p. 433.

²¹⁴ Its *actual* population in the fourth century will doubtless have been far larger than a "representation" of three *bouleutai* presupposed. That the Dionysia in such a thoroughly urban deme could still be called κατ᾽ ἀγρούς (Aeschin. 1.157) is worthy of incidental note.

²¹⁵ Deubner, *Feste*, p. 135; quotation from Pickard-Cambridge, *Festivals*, p. 44.

²¹⁶ Eleusis: IG II²949, lines 31-32, praise for a second-century demarch who τοῖς Δι][ονυσί]οις ἔθυσεν τῶι Διονύσωι καὶ τὴν πομπὴν ἔπεμψεν. Peiraieus: IG II²380 (streets to be prepared by the *agoranomoi*) and other evidence cited in Pickard-Cambridge, *Festivals*, p. 44 with nn. 1-2.

²¹⁷ Plut. *Moralia* 527D (*de cupiditate divitiarum*): ἡ πάτριος τῶν Διονυσίων ἑορτὴ τὸ παλαιὸν ἐπέμπετο δημοτικῶς καὶ ἱλαρῶς, ἀμφορεὺς οἴνου καὶ κληματίς, εἶτα τράγον τις εἷλκεν, ἄλλος ἰσχάδων ἄρριχον ἠκολούθει κομίζων, ἐπὶ πᾶσι δ᾽ ὁ φαλλός. (I agree with Pickard-Cambridge, *Festivals*, p. 44, n. 4, that "δημοτικῶς probably conveys no reference to celebration by demes.") The usefulness of Plutarch's picture will not be much reduced even if he was thinking of Boiotia rather than Attica: Deubner, *Feste*, p. 136, n. 2; Pickard-Cambridge, *Festivals*, p. 44; Parke, *Festivals*, p. 101.

phallos upright on a pole, and lastly Dikaiopolis himself, perhaps representing a body of revellers, singing a chant to Phales, the personified symbol of fertility, and greeted as a companion of Bacchus."[218] In view of another remark of Plutarch's, elsewhere in the *Moralia*, the participation of Dikaiopolis' slaves here would seem to be an authentic feature of the festival as a whole, if not necessarily of the procession itself.[219]

It was once commonly supposed that another integral event or activity of the rural Dionysia was the so-called *askōliasmos*, a grotesque sport in which the players attempted to jump on to and then maintain their balance on an inflated wineskin (*askos*) covered in oil or grease. The term is explained thus both by a scholiast to Aristoph. *Ploutos*, line 1129, citing Didymus, and also in a long aetiological entry in the Suda (under ἀσκὸς Κτησιφῶντος; cf. Pollux 9.121). Deubner reasonably rejected the scholiast's assertion that there was a specific festival called the Askolia, at which this activity took place "to honor Dionysos" (εἰς τιμὴν τοῦ Διονύσου).[220] He also disputed the purported connection with the Choes, the second and central day of the Anthesteria,[221] insisting that a link with the rural Dionysia, and that festival alone, is made clear both by a passage in Vergil's *Second Georgic*[222] and by the statement of Cornutus in *de natura deorum* 30 (p. 60, 23 Lang) that "in the villages of Attica the young farmers leap on to the wineskin" (εἰς τὸν ἀσκὸν ἐνάλλονται κατὰ τὰς Ἀττικὰς κώμας οἱ γεωργοὶ νεανίσκοι). However, this link is not cogent. "Doubtless the game took place at many festivals, and it is doubtful whether it should be associated with the Rural Dionysia in particular."[223] What is more, Kurt Latte has shown that there is deep-seated confusion in the evidence as a whole, and that the derivation of *askōliasmos* from *askos* is etymologically unsound:[224] in fifth- and fourth-century texts (and the most reliable later ones) the meaning of the verb *askōliazein* is simply "to hop on one leg."[225] Thus the term

---

[218] Pickard-Cambridge, *Festivals*, p. 43.

[219] Plut. *Moralia* 1098B (*non posse suaviter vivi secundum Epicurum*): καὶ γὰρ οἱ θεράποντες ὅταν Κρόνια δειπνῶσιν ἢ Διονύσια κατ᾿ ἀγρὸν ἄγωσι περιιόντες, οὐκ ἂν αὐτῶν τὸν ὀλολυγμὸν ὑπομείναις καὶ τὸν θόρυβον, ὑπὸ χαρμονῆς καὶ ἀπειροκαλίας τοιαῦτα ποιούντων καὶ φθεγγομένων.

[220] Deubner, *Feste*, p. 135 with n. 3; cf. Latte, "*Askoliasmos*," p. 390; Pickard-Cambridge, *Festivals*, p. 45, n. 6.

[221] Deubner, *Feste*, pp. 117-118, 135.

[222] Vergil, *Georgic* 2, lines 380-384: non aliam ob culpam Baccho caper omnibus aris | caeditur et veteres ineunt proscaenia ludi, | praemiaque ingeniis pagos et compita circum | Thesidae posuere, atque inter pocula laeti | mollibus in pratis unctos salvere per utres.

[223] Pickard-Cambridge, *Festivals*, p. 45; cf. Latte, "*Askoliasmos*," pp. 389-390.

[224] Latte, "*Askoliasmos*"; cf. Pickard-Cambridge, *Festivals*, p. 45.

[225] Aristoph. *Ploutos*, line 1129 (*pace* the scholiast *ad loc.*: see Latte, "*Askoliasmos*," p. 386); Plato *Symp.* 190D; Aristot. *de incessu animalium* 705b33 (easier to do it on left leg);

askōliasmos has been wrongly applied to the game with the wineskin. Such a game is, admittedly, attested in the fourth century, in a fragment of the comic poet Eubulus,[226] but its name, if any, is unknown. The game *may* have been played at the rural Dionysia and other rustic festivals, as may also the several forms of genuine *askōliasmos*—contests to hop the most times or the longest distance, and a game in which one hopper tried to "tag" the other players with his free leg.[227]

In the midst of such simple entertainments, however, some demes at least organized also a more sophisticated spectacle: the performance of comic and/or tragic drama. We do not know when this began,[228] but it is appropriate that the *terminus ante quem* should be provided by the deme associated with the very genesis of both genres—Ikarion. A cult of Dionysos in Ikarion at least as early as the 520s is attested by both epigraphical and archaeological remains from that time: a dedication to Dionysos (and Apollo ?Pythios),[229] and a colossal statue of the god (perhaps set up in the "Dionysion" mentioned in a fourth-century deme decree).[230] And from the second half of the *fifth* century we have an Ikarian decree, IG I³254, which though fragmentarily preserved plainly reveals the existence of regularly organized dramatic festivals in honor of Dionysos (named in line 24) in the deme. Its main surviving provision, in lines 3-4, concerns the choice of [two] *chorēgoi* from amongst those who have not performed the liturgy before ([. . ? . .]ι τὸν δεμοτὸν καὶ τὸν Ἰκα[ριοι οἰκόντ]|[υν δύο] ιὸν ἀχορεγέιον). These men are later referred to as *prōtochoroi*,[231] and a procedure of *antidosis*—the earliest mention of it anywhere in Attica, including the city[232]—is made available to them if they approach the demarch within twenty days (lines 5-7).

Three points are noteworthy, in the context both of other, later documents from Ikarion and of the evidence from other demes. First, as lines 3-4 (quoted above) show, the *chorēgoi* here were to be drawn not only from the demesmen but also from other men merely resident in the deme.

cf. Plut. *Moralia* 621E-F, Pollux 2.194 and 9.121, and other testimony in Latte, "Askoliasmos," p. 386. On the aberrant version, traceable *via* Didymus to Eratosthenes, see Latte, "Askoliasmos," pp. 386-388; cf. LSJ, ἀσχωλιάζω.

[226] Eubulus fr. 8: καὶ πρός γε τούτοις ἀσκὸν εἰς μέσον | καταθέντες εἰσάλλεσθε καὶ καχάζετε ἐπὶ τοῖς καταρρέουσιν ἀπὸ κελεύσματος. For commentary see R. L. Hunter, *Eubulus*, Cambridge, 1983, pp. 93-94.

[227] Pollux 9.121 (cf. schol. Aristoph. *Ploutos*, line 1129, and Suda, ἀσχωλίαζε); see Parke, *Festivals*, p. 102.

[228] Pickard-Cambridge, *Festivals*, p. 43.

[229] *Hesp.* 17, 1948, p. 142, no. 2.

[230] I. B. Romano, *Hesp.* 51, 1982, pp. 398-409; references to this *agalma* in IG I³254, lines 10-12, and IG II²2851 (fourth-century repairs to it).

[231] IG I³254, lines 15 and 17. On the meaning of the word, see C. D. Buck in the *editio princeps*, *AJA* 5, 1889, pp. 304ff.; cf. Schoeffer, "Demoi," col. 24.

[232] Davies, *Families*, p. xxii, n. 8.

As already noted,[233] we do not know how long this practice lasted, but individual *chorēgoi* in Ikarion in the fourth century appear without demotics both in a deme decree (IG II²1178, lines 8-9) and in their own dedications (IG II²3094, 3095, 3098, 3099), which would strongly suggest that they were Ikarieis. As regards the evidence from other demes—all of it from the fourth century or later still—the only case of a non-demesman *chorēgos* is actually that of a non-*citizen*, the Theban Damasias who paid for both boys' and men's dithyramb in Eleusis in the middle of the fourth century (IG II²1186, lines 11-13); but the language in which this and his other services to the deme is couched points to their having been voluntarily undertaken, and thus no real exception to what seems to have been the general rule, in Eleusis as elsewhere, that *chorēgoi* were demesmen.

The second point which arises from the Ikarian decree about *chorēgoi* is the fact that it is not stated, and thus not certain, whether comedy as well as tragedy was performed there. Only tragedy is mentioned, both in this document (lines 9, 21, 34) and in the deme decree of ca. 330 (SEG 22.117, line 9); and of the four Ikarian choregic dedications cited in the last paragraph the only two which are explicit on the matter refer to tragic *chorēgiai* (IG II²3095 and 3099). In IG II²3094 one cannot determine whether the *didaskalos* Nikostratos is the comic poet of that name, purportedly son of Aristophanes, or the dithyrambic poet Nikostratos attested in IG I³961 (after 450)[234]—if indeed he is either of them. From the evidence as a whole it looks as though we may conclude that the individual demes could stage any or all of tragedy, comedy, and dithyramb, as they pleased and as they felt able.[235]

The third issue raised by IG I³254 is that of the *number* of the liturgists appointed. In Ikarion alone this seems to vary rather surprisingly. If the norm there, both in the fifth century and the fourth, was two (IG II²1178, lines 8-9, which supports the restoration in IG I³254, line 4, quoted above), then unless the dedications deceive us there were deviations from it in both directions. Three men commemorate a choregy on IG II²3095 (a father and two sons) and 3098 (the same, *possibly*), while in IG II²3094 and 3099 the dedicant is a single individual. And comparable variation—though never, perhaps significantly, within the same deme—is to be found

[233] Chap. 3, n. 41.

[234] Pickard-Cambridge, *Festivals*, pp. 48-49.

[235] Cf. Pickard-Cambridge, *Festivals*, pp. 51-52. In terms of explicit evidence, the following events are attested: Acharnai, dithyramb and comedy (IG II²3106); Aixone, comedy (IG II²1202; *AM* 66, 1941, pp. 218-219, no. 1); Eleusis, dithyramb, tragedy (IG II²1186), and comedy (IG II²3090 and 3100); Ikarion, tragedy and *either* dithyramb *or* comedy (see discussion above, in text); Kollytos, comedy (Aeschin. 1.157) and tragedy (Demosth. 18.180 and 262); Paiania, tragedy (IG II²3097); Peiraieus, comedy and tragedy (Demosth. 21.10); Rhamnous, comedy (IG II²3108 and 3109).

elsewhere: one *chorēgos* in Paiania (IG II²3097, for tragedy) and Rha-
mnous (IG II²3109, for comedy); two in Acharnai (IG II²3092), Aixone
(IG II²1198 and 1200; AM 66, 1941, pp. 218-219, no. 1), and Eleusis
(IG II²3090);[236] and three, again a father and his sons, in Aigilia (IG
II²3096). Collaboration by *three* liturgists has been seen as a sign of
(their) "poverty,"[237] rather than any wish to share in the kudos of the
enterprise—yet men like **68** and, especially, **221** were scarcely paupers.
At all events the overall evidence for variation in the number of the
chorēgoi, with pairs most usual, is clear enough.

But did the members of such pairs work in collaboration or in competition with each other? Haussoullier was adamant that any notion of
competition would have been inappropriate in an intra-deme context.
"Les chorèges qui se disputaient le prix au théâtre de Dionysos étaient
les représentants de leur tribu: c'est pour elle qu'ils luttaient, c'est sur
elle que rejaillissait l'honneur de la victoire, c'est son nom qui figure à
la première ligne des inscriptions gravées sur les monuments choragiques.
Au contraire, les chorèges qui paraissent sur les théâtres de Thorikos ou
d'Aixoné sont des habitants d'un même bourg: il n'y aura donc pas de
lutte, pas de concours (ἀγών). Les chorèges, peu nombreux d'ailleurs,
feront cause commune et s'uniront pour donner plus d'éclat au spectacle
(θέα)."[238] This view was accepted and developed by von Schoeffer, who
observed that the crowning of pairs of *chorēgoi* in Aixone and Ikarion
could not naturally be interpreted as reflecting a victory by one of the
individuals over the other.[239] His point is a good and reasonable one.
The word *synchorēgos* is never used, yet that is what these pairs (and,
in the dedications cited above, trios) of *chorēgoi* patently were—a team.
Equally patent, however, is the fact that they are a *victorious* team. In
answer to Haussoullier's thesis, C. D. Buck rightly drew attention to the
explicit claims of victory in the choregic dedications from Ikarion;[240] and
one may add that the same is true elsewhere.[241] It must first be proved,
objected von Schoeffer, that these victories were not won at *city* festivals;
and indeed we have already noted that certain dedications once associated
with the rural Dionysia may more plausibly be related to the city Dio-

---

[236] On IG II²3090, see Pickard-Cambridge, *Festivals*, pp. 47-48.

[237] Pickard-Cambridge, *Festivals*, p. 48.

[238] Haussoullier, *Vie*, pp. 169-170, citing, for θέα, IG II²1182 (Myrrhinous), lines 2-4
(quoted below, n. 264).

[239] Aixone: IG II²1198 and 1200; AM 66, 1941, pp. 218-219, no. 1. Ikarion: IG II²1178.
See Schoeffer, "Demoi," col. 24; cf. A. Koerte, *Gnomon* 11, 1935, p. 634, on Aixone.

[240] IG II²3094 ([ν]ικήσας), 3095 (νικῶντες), 3098 (νικήσαντες), 3099 (ἐνίκα); see
C. D. Buck, *AJA* 5, 1889, pp. 29-30.

[241] Acharnai (IG II²3106, νικήσας); Aigilia (IG II²3096, νικήσαντες); Eleusis (IG
II²3090, ἐνίκων αι ι ἑτέρα νίκη; 3107, νι[κήσας]); Paiania (IG II²3097, ἐνίκα); Rhamnous (IG II²310′ , νικήσας).

nysia.[242] But can this be true of all of them—particularly if, as seems likely, *synchorēgia* in Athens lasted only one year, 406/5?[243] The word *contest* (ἀγών), brushed aside by Haussoullier and von Schoeffer, is used by the demesmen of ?Anagyrous,[244] Eleusis,[245] Halai Araphenides,[246] Ikarion,[247] and Peiraieus.[248] Thus, as far as the rural Dionysia is concerned the evidence is plain in attesting *synchorēgia* (as well as *chorēgia*) and competition together;[249] and when pairs of *chorēgoi* are honored by their deme, they are honored as victors.

Did the victories of Epikrates and Praxias in Ikarion (IG II²1178) and of the three pairs of *chorēgoi* thanked and rewarded in Aixone entail any disparagement of the efforts of their defeated rivals? We need not suppose so; and in point of fact it might be suggested that we possess one instance where the deme thought it fitting to give the latter, too, some recognition. In *AM* 66, 1941, pp. 218-219, no. 1, the Aixoneis, on the motion of Glaukides Sosippou, honored a pair of their *chorēgoi*, Auteas and Philoxenides, for their fine and zealous *chorēgia* (lines 1-3). As they were to be crowned in the deme's theater "at the comedies of the year after the archonship of Theophrastos" (τοῖς κω|μωιδοῖς τοῖς μετὰ Θεόφραστον ἄρχοντα, lines 5-6), we know that their liturgy was discharged during Theophrastos' year itself, 313/2.[250] (The decree is the last in a series of three in which such pairs of *chorēgoi* are commended, IG II²1198 relating to the year 326/5 and IG II²1200 to 317/6.) Yet in IG II²1202, headed "in the archonship of Theophrastos," we find the same man,

---

[242] See Chap. 2, n. 32, on IG II²3091 and 3101.

[243] E. Capps, *Hesp.* 12, 1943, pp. 1-11, at 5-8; Pickard-Cambridge, *Festivals*, pp. 48, 87, 102.

[244] IG II²1210, lines 4-6 (quoted below, n. 261).

[245] IG II²949, line 33: as well as offering the sacrifice to Dionysos and despatching the procession (see above, n. 216), the demarch Pamphilos ἔθηκεν δὲ καὶ τὸν ἀγῶνα ἐν τῶι θεάτρωι; cf. IG II²1189, lines 10-11, the announcement of honors τῶι ἀγ[ῶνι - -] |[. . . . . . .]¹⁵. . . . . .τ]ῶν [Δ]ιονυσίων.

[246] References below, n. 263.

[247] IG II²1178, lines 6-8: the demarch Nikon καλῶς καὶ δικαίως τῶι Διο|νύσωι τὴν ἑορτὴν ἐποίησεν καὶ τὸν ἀγῶ|να.

[248] IG II²1214, line 29, announcement of a crown τραγωιδῶν τῶι ἀγῶνι; cf. Aelian, *VH* 2.13, Πειραιοῖ δὲ ἀγωνιζομένου τοῦ Εὐριπίδου.

[249] Further evidence of competition has been seen in one of the symbolic representations on the Hagios Eleutherios calendar-frieze (variously dated between the late Hellenistic period and the Imperial): in the place corresponding to Posideion, and hence the rural Dionysia, three judges sit behind a table on which are set five crowns, and before which appear a palm-branch and two fighting-cocks. See Deubner, *Feste*, pp. 138, 248-254 (esp. 251), with plates 34-40 (esp. 37 section 13); cf. Pickard-Cambridge, *Festivals*, p. 51; and see further below, n. 252.

[250] Rather than the archon-year of an earlier Theophrastos, 340/39: see Pickard-Cambridge, *Festivals*, p. 49 with n. 3.

Glaukides Sosippou, proposing an honorific decree in favor of two individuals who have been "good and zealous men towards the deme of
the Aixoneis" (lines 4-5).[251] Beyond this all-purpose phrase the services
of this second pair, Kallikrates and Aristokrates, are not specified; all the
same, the fact that their crowns too were to be proclaimed in the theater
"at the comedies of the Dionysia" (lines 14-15) surely prompts the conjecture that they too were *chorēgoi*, defeated in competition by Auteas
and Philoxenides but nonetheless thanked and rewarded by their grateful
fellow demesmen as the men who *proxime accesserunt*.[252]

Such performances and contests (whether of comedy, tragedy, or dithyramb) at the rural Dionysia would seem naturally to presuppose the
existence of either a stone or at least a wooden theater in the demes in
question, if such a structure is not attested in any case. Conversely,
archaeological, epigraphical, or literary evidence for a theater—or for
the privilege of *proedria* exercisable there—may presumably be taken as
grounds for postulating Dionysiac contests in a deme, whether or not
there is other, explicit testimony to them. We have direct evidence of a
theater in seven demes: Acharnai,[253] Aixone,[254] Euonymon,[255] Ikarion,[256]
Peiraieus,[257] Rhamnous,[258] and Thorikos.[259] To these seven[260] inference

[251] Again (cf. preceding note) this must be the Theophrastos of 313/2, not 340/39, for
not only the archon and the proposer but also the demarch Hegesileos are the same as in
AM 66, 1941, pp. 218-219, no. 1; cf. Pickard-Cambridge, *Festivals*, p. 19, n. 3.

[252] To pile Pelion on Ossa, I suggest further that the contest may have been between five
pairs of *chorēgoi*: witness the five comic masks inscribed above the decree for Auteas and
Philoxenides (see Pickard-Cambridge, *Festivals*, fig. 25, following p. 48), and compare the
five crowns in the Hagios Eleutherios frieze (see above, n. 249). During the fifth and fourth
centuries the contest at the *city* Dionysia (and the Lenaia) was also, normally, a five-way
one: see Pickard-Cambridge, *Festivals*, p. 83 with n. 1.

[253] IG II²1206, lines 2ff. (use of the revenue from it).

[254] IG II²1197, line 21; IG II²1198, line 22; IG II²1202, lines 15-16 and 20-21; *AM* 66,
1941, pp. 218-219, no. 1, lines 5 and 11; cf. the grant of *proedria* in IG II²1197, lines 9-
11.

[255] See O. Tzachou-Alexandri, *Ergon* 1980 [1981], pp. 24-25, *PAAH* 1980 [1982], pp.
64-67, and *Ergon* 1981 [1982], pp. 44-45 (mid fourth-century theater at Trachones =
Euonymon); cf. H. W. Catling, *AR* 1981-1982, p. 12, and 1982-1983, p. 11.

[256] See W. R. Biers and T. D. Boyd, *Hesp.* 51, 1982, pp. 1-18, at 12-14, on the "theatral
area"; references to older work in Pickard-Cambridge, *Festivals*, p. 54, n. 2.

[257] Thuc. 8.93.1; Lysias 13.32; Xen. *Hell* 2.4.32; IG II²1176 + (leasing of the theater in
324/3; cf. *proedria* in lines 11 and 13-16); IG II²1214, lines 19-25 (inc. *proedria*) and 28.
For the meagre archaeological remains, see *AD* 22B.1, 1967, p. 143; Wycherley, *Stones*,
pp. 263-264.

[258] IG II²1311, line 7; cf. *proedria* in SEG 22.120, lines 5-6. See in general Pouilloux,
Forteresse, pp. 73-78; Pickard-Cambridge, *Festivals*, pp. 53-54.

[259] For references see Chap. 1, n. 46.

[260] I do not know the archaeological evidence claimed by Osborne, *Demos*, pp. 233-234

adds seven more: we have grants of *proedria* from ?Anagyrous,²⁶¹
Eleusis,²⁶² Halai Araphenides,²⁶³ and Myrrhinous;²⁶⁴ there are choregic
dedications from Aigilia and Paiania;²⁶⁵ and reference has already been
made to the performances of both tragedy and comedy at the "rural"
Dionysia in the inner-city deme of Kollytos.²⁶⁶ It will hardly be imagined
that only in these fourteen instances did deme theaters exist, and archaeological or documentary evidence for more of them will surely come
to light in future years. Until it does, we are quite unable to say whether
even all the larger demes normally possessed a theater or not.

What can, however, be said is that in those demes which did have
one—built either in the early days or in the fourth century, "the great
era of settled, moderate prosperity in Attica"²⁶⁷—the observance of the
rural Dionysia served two connected but distinguishable ends. The original and prime one was of course the worship of Dionysos, a deity with
a character and attributes which would have made him a widespread
object of cult in the demes even without the special focus of the rural

---

(n. 24) for the theater—unless he means the *telestērion?*—at Eleusis (there is indirect
epigraphical evidence only; see below, n. 262), nor his epigraphic evidence for the theater
at Kollytos (there is indirect literary evidence only; see above, n. 235). His claim of epigraphic evidence for a theater in Plotheia is presumably based on IG II²1172, line 38 (ἐς
Διονύσια δὲ] διδασκάλωι κάδο[v]); for the IG I³258 text, however, D. M. Lewis reads
an extra letter, which rules out the restoration of the Dionysia (. . . ?. . . δὲ τῶ]ι διδασκάλωι); and without it Osborne's concatenation of assumptions is too fragile, for there
is no clue here to who the *didaskalos* is and what he does.

²⁶¹ IG II²1210 (from Vari = Anagyrous; cf. Pickard-Cambridge, *Festivals*, p. 50, n. 3),
lines 4-6: εἶναι δὲ αὐτῶ[ι καὶ προεδρίαν τραγωιδῶν τῶι ἀγ]|ῶνι ὅταν ποιῶ[σι τὰ
Διονύσια καὶ καλείτω αὐτὸν ὁ δή]|μαρχος εἰς τὴ[v προεδρίαν; these restorations
seem inescapable. Note also the late fifth-century choregic dedication from Varkiza, SEG
23.102 (cf. SEG 26.225), with Euripides as *didaskalos*; but there is no reason to relate this
to the rural Dionysia.

²⁶² IG II²1185, line 4; IG II²1186, line 24; IG II²1187, lines 17-20; IG II²1189, lines 11-
12; IG II²1192, line 10; IG II²1193, lines 21-24; *Hesp.* 8, 1939, pp. 177-180, lines 17-19.

²⁶³ *AE* 1932, *Chronika*, pp. 30-32, lines 20-24, εἶναι δὲ καὶ προε|δρίαν αὐτῶι ἐν
τοῖς ἀγῶσι|v ἅπασιν, οἷς ἂν ποιῶσιν Ἁλ|αιῆς, καὶ τὸν κήρυκα καλεῖ|v εἰς τὴν
προεδρίαν αὐτόν; cf. the unpublished decree reported in *Ergon* 1957, pp. 24-25 (=
PAAH 1957, pp. 45-47), in which ἀναφέρονται ἀγῶνες τελούμενοι κατὰ τὰ Διονύσια
ἐν Ἁλαῖς.

²⁶⁴ IG II²1182, lines 2-4, πρ]οεδρί[αν ἐν] | [ταῖς θέ]αις πάσαις αἷς πο[ι]|[ο]ῦσι
Μυρρινούσιοι; for the Dionysia in general, IG II²1183, lines 36-37.

²⁶⁵ Aigilia: IG II²3096. Paiania: IG II²3097.

²⁶⁶ References above, n. 235. From the lack of archaeological findings Schoeffer, "Demoi,"
col. 23, presumed that the theater in Kollytos was a wooden structure.

²⁶⁷ Pickard-Cambridge, *Festivals*, p. 52, pointing out how much of *all* the evidence for
the rural Dionysia comes from the fourth century. The theater at Euonymon was, it appears,
built in the fourth century (cf. above, n. 255), and the one at Thorikos elaborated then
(references in Chap. 1, n. 46).

The theater at Thorikos. Courtesy of the Comite voor Belgische opgravingen in Griekenland.

Dionysia[268] and which, once associated with rites and rituals far more primitive,[269] may well have meant that the "religious content" of the rural Dionysia lasted longer than that of the great state festivals.[270] But

[268] The rural Dionysia aside, there is ample evidence of Dionysos cults in the demes. For Dionysos in the *fasti* see above, pp. 198 (Thorikos) and 203 (Erchia). A "Dionysion" is known in four demes: Eleusis (IG II²1186, lines 32-33, cf. schol. Aristoph. *Frogs*, line 343; note also *Hesp.* 8, 1939, pp. 177-180, lines 8-10 and 20-21, for a demarch's sacrifice to D. and funds for him), Halimous (SEG 2.7, line 23), Ikarion (SEG 22.117, line 8; note also monies of D. in IG I³253), and Thorikos (*Hesp.* 19, 1950, p. 264, no. 20, line 15). In addition there was a "*temenos* of Dionysos" in Gargettos (*AM* 67, 1942, pp. 7-8, no. 5, lines 4-5), Kerameis (Paus. 1.2.5), and Peiraieus (IG II²1176+, line 4); and a "*hieron* of Dionysos" in Marathon (IG II²1243, lines 21-22) and Rhamnous (SEG 3.122, line 15). Epithets include Lenaios in Rhamnous (IG II²2854, with Pickard-Cambridge, *Festivals*, p. 42), Kissos in Acharnai (Paus. 1.31.5), Melpomenos in Acharnai (Paus. 1.31.5) and Kerameis (Paus. 1.2.5), and Anthios in Halai Aixonides (IG II²1356, lines 9-10) and Phlya (Paus. 1.31.4). (Dionysos Anthios has no connection with the Antheia festival in Paiania, attested in IG I³250: see M. P. Nilsson, *Eranos* 42, 1944, pp. 70-76, at 74.) See in general Solders, *Kulte*, pp. 37-45.

[269] Cf. Pickard-Cambridge, *Festivals*, pp. 42-43.

[270] Pickard-Cambridge, *Festivals*, p. 51 (including the phrase quoted).

in addition, the festival took on a more secular importance of its own, as the deme drew upon all its communal resources for the creation of an annual display of pomp and circumstance. A (doubtless) excited throng of demesmen and other onlookers[271] saw the demarch or herald solemnly escort benefactors and other dignitaries to their front seats;[272] crowns and other honors for the most recent of these benefactors were proclaimed;[273] and the audience as a whole settled down to enjoy competitive performances of comedy, tragedy, and dithyramb—sometimes by leading poets[274]—and to applaud or deride the judges' verdicts. All this was imitation of the polis itself, naturally. Yet at the same time, and indeed for that very reason, the demes were concerned "to assert their identities as states within the state."[275] In the preliminaries to this chapter we referred to Thucydides' account of the forced evacuation of Attica at the beginning of the Peloponnesian War. There Thucydides tells us that, for each individual countryman, what he was abandoning seemed to be nothing less than his own polis (Thuc. 2.16.2). It was surely at the rural Dionysia that such a combination of instinctive attachment and conscious pride was most deeply felt and most potently expressed.

[271] Other onlookers: see Plato *Republic* 475D. Both they and the demesmen had presumably to *pay* for entry (we know of no local equivalent of the *theōrika*), especially if the theater had been leased to entrepreneurs, as in Acharnai (IG II²1206) and Peiraieus (IG II²1176 +); cf. Haussoullier, *Vie*, p. 171.

[272] References in Chap. 5, nn. 12-13. IG II²1214, lines 22-25, suggest that in Peiraieus in the first half of the third century priests enjoyed προεδρία *ex officio*.

[273] It seems natural to suppose that such "proclamation" (the decrees use the word ἀνειπεῖν) incorporated the crowning ceremony itself. In one instance what is specified is indeed the actual crowning (Aixone: *AM* 66, 1941, p. 218-219, no. 1, lines 3-8), while in others the crowning appears to be implied by the proclamation of it: Aixone (IG II²1202, lines 14-18), Eleusis (IG II²1186, lines 19-24; IG II²1187, lines 9-16; IG II²1189, lines 10-11; IG II²1193, lines 13-21), Ikarion (IG II²1178, lines 3-8 and 10-11; SEG 22.117, lines 8-9), Peiraieus (IG II²1214, lines 28ff.), and Rhamnous (SEG 22.120, lines 6-7). Similar "proclamation" at other festivals: IG II²1203, line 17 (the Amarousia in Athmonon); *AE* 1932, *Chronika*, pp. 30-32, lines 13-20 (the Tauropolia in Halai Araphenides). According to Aeschin. 3.41-45, demes (and tribes) were prohibited from announcing their award of crowns at the city theater.

[274] We know that in the fifth century Euripides produced in Peiraieus (Aelian, *VH* 2.13) and both Sophocles and Aristophanes in Eleusis (IG II²3090, with Pickard-Cambridge, *Festivals*, pp. 47-48); however, *pace* Haussoullier, *Vie*, p. 170, there is no certainty, perhaps even no likelihood, that they were premières. For the fourth century the only evidence, for Kollytos, is of a fifth-century "classic" revival in tragedy (Sophocles' *Oinomaos*: Demosth. 18.180) and a contemporary comedy (Aeschin. 1.157; again, not necessarily a first performance).

[275] Pickard-Cambridge, *Festivals*, p. 51.

CHAPTER 8

———————— ✳ ————————

DEME SOCIETY

It is as true today as it was when Haussoullier wrote *La Vie Municipale* that the inner life of the demes is largely impenetrable. We cannot—and we surely never shall—know Melite or Myrrhinous as we know Montaillou or Myddle.[1] The concentrated dossier of evidence which has made possible the detailed study of such villages in mediaeval and early modern times is lacking for any ancient Attic deme, even in the fourth century. Accordingly the only practicable means of approaching the topic of deme society is, once again,[2] to assemble a composite picture within which the data from one deme or another serve to illustrate the testimony of a general nature. In such a picture, so constructed, two interwoven aspects of deme life will come to the fore: the degree to which there were genuine ties of solidarity and community between men of the same deme, and the way active individuals and families, in the demes no less than in the polis as a whole, sought and maintained positions of prominence and influence.

A. The Deme as Ideal Community

The Kleisthenic deme system institutionalized the bonds which naturally existed between those resident in a given locality and known by its name—the Acherdousians, the Paianians, or whatever.[3] The deme name,

---

[1] Montaillou: see E. Le Roy Ladurie, *Montaillou: village occitan de 1294 à 1324*, Paris, 1975; there is a translation by B. Bray, *Montaillou: Cathars and Catholics in a French village, 1294-1324*, London, 1978. Myddle: see D. Hey, ed., *Richard Gough, The History of Myddle*, Harmondsworth [Penguin Books], 1981. I have eschewed explicit comparisons between this sort of material (and/or the fruits of the study of villages in present-day Greece and the Balkans, such as E. Friedl, *Vasilika: a village in modern Greece*, New York, 1963) and the infinitely more fragmentary data from or relating to the Attic demes.

[2] Cf. the introduction to Chap. 6.

[3] See the introduction to Chap. 3, and cf. O. Aurenche, *Les groups d'Alcibiade, de Léogoras et de Teucros: remarques sur la vie politique athénienne en 415 avant J.-C.*, Paris, 1974, p. 85: "le sentiment d'appartenir à un groupe homogène et localisé remplace, pour

the *dēmotikon*, might or might not be favored by individual demesmen (in circumstances where they had a choice in the matter), but as a collective designation in the plural it became not only an indispensable element in the official vocabulary of the political organization of the state as a whole but also an assertion of identity and unanimity by the individual bodies of demesmen. Mundane instances of this are too numerous to be cited *in extenso*, but one might pick out three of the more striking declarations: by the Peiraieis in 321/0, of the terms under which they would lease out their common property; by the Aixoneis in or after 326/5, of the honors which they would bestow upon future deme *chorēgoi*; and by the Phalereis and the Xypetaiones, of their respective victories in the inter-deme festival of the Tetrakomoi.[4] (This last instance is especially noteworthy for the fact that the two bodies of demesmen were proclaiming their superiority over three other *particular* demes, the other member-demes of the Tetrakomoi. Such superiority was of course both temporary and, one assumes, amicably won; but the relations between one deme and another were not always so friendly.)[5]

The self-esteem of individual demes and the solidarity of their bodies of demesmen brought no very tangible benefit, perhaps, to the operation of the constitutional machinery of the polis as a whole. On the other hand the polis itself continued to make important contributions to such feelings of intra-deme cohesion, not least in the military sphere. In Isaeus 2.42 the speaker insists that he had earned respect as the adoptive son of Menekles not only by performing the *gymnasiarchia* liturgy in his deme[6] but also by "serving in his tribe *and in the deme* on all the campaigns which took place during that period" (καὶ τὰς στρατείας, ὅσαι ἐγένοντο ἐν τῷ χρόνῳ τούτῳ, ἐστράτευμαι ἐν τῇ φυλῇ τῇ ἐκείνου

---

ceux que les liens familiaux n'attachaient pas à un clan, et renforce, pour les autres, le besoin de se regrouper au sein d'un ensemble où l'on retrouve des problèmes et des intérêts communs"; on "les relations de bon voisinage" see his pp. 83-85 as a whole, which cite some of the evidence presented below.

[4] Peiraieus: IG II²2498, esp. line 2. Aixone: IG II²1198, lines 22-28. Phaleron and Xypete: IG II²3102 and 3103, respectively.

[5] The *locus classicus* for hostility between two particular demes is Plut. *Thes.* 13.2-3, on the (long-standing) avoidance of intermarriage between Hagnous and Pallene. As a general argument for use in court, note, for example, [Demosth.] 43.64, where Sositheos asserts that the mother of the defendant Makartatos was kept in ignorance of the death of Hagnias of Oion as a consequence of the fact that she belonged to another deme, Prospalta (cf. 43.48); and in 43.65 Makartatos' claim to the estate of Hagnias is implicitly prejudiced by the description of him as ἐκ τῆς Ἀπολήξιδος τοῦ Προσπαλτίου θυγατρός.

[6] The mention of Kephale in 2.31 is the best clue as to what that deme might be; the other possibility is Acharnai, since Menekles is said to have been φίλος καὶ ἐπιτήδειος of the speaker's father, Eponymos of Acharnai (2.3). Deme *gymnasiarchia* is otherwise attested only in Rhamnous (IG II²3109).

καὶ ἐν τῷ δήμῳ). It has been customary—but in my view incorrect—to follow Dobree in obelizing the words "and in the deme" (καὶ ἐν τῷ δήμῳ) as dittography after "I performed the *gymnasiarchia* in the deme" (ἐγυμνασιάρχουν ἐν τῷ δήμῳ). Wyse in his commentary on the passage offered two independent, substantive reasons for doing so.[7] He first argued that, while there are adequate parallels for referring to a tribal regiment simply as a *phylē* (e.g. Thuc. 6.98.4 and 101.5, Lysias 13.79), "no such defence can be put forward for the singular expression στρατεύεσθαι ἐν τῷ δήμῳ τῷ ἐκείνου." Secondly, he contended, "while Greek habits make it probable that members of the same deme were kept together as far as was practicable, it is not likely that each of the ten tribal regiments of infantry was permanently distributed into unequal groups each composed of men of one deme. The subdivisions (Xen. *Hell.* 1.2.3, τῶν ὁπλιτῶν δύο λόχοι) must have followed a different principle and have sometimes involved the breaking up of the contingent furnished by a deme." This second argument is perfectly valid. Xen. *Hell.* 1.2.3 is, in point of fact, the only explicit allusion to *lochoi* in the *Athenian* army,[8] but neither this nor any other mode of internal subdivision of the tribal regiments which may have been employed from time to time can have been *based on* the necessarily unequal deme contingents. Yet is this what Isaeus' client is really asking us to believe? Surely all one can deduce from the passage is (in Wyse's own words) that "members of the same deme were kept together as far as was practicable." The speaker is not saying that he had fought in any official subdivision of the Athenian army called (even *un*officially) a "deme." He is saying that the men who would verify, from a military standpoint, his wholehearted assumption of the role of adoptive son of Menekles would be those in whose company he had spent the campaign—his fellow tribesmen and his fellow demesmen.

This interpretation and defence of the manuscript reading in Isaeus 2.42[9] is lent support by other evidence. Lysias 16.14 speaks of demesmen assembling together before setting out on campaign (συλλεγέντων τοίνυν τῶν δημοτῶν πρὸ τῆς ἐξόδου κτλ.). This, as Wyse rightly observed, "merely shows that men of the same place, when called out, sometimes started from home in a body."[10] But [Lysias] 20.23 is less easily dismissed. There the son of Polystratos avers that the people who

---

[7] W. Wyse, *The Speeches of Isaeus*, Cambridge, 1904, p. 268.

[8] Cf. Rhodes, *Commentary*, p. 685, suspecting that Xenophon may have used the term untechnically. For *lochagoi*, however, see ?Aristot. *Ath. Pol.* 61.3 (and Xen. *Mem.* 3.1.5 and 3.4.1).

[9] Cf. Müller, *de demis*, pp. 32-33. The problem is ignored by Haussoullier, *Vie*, p. 121.

[10] W. Wyse, *The Speeches of Isaeus*, Cambridge, 1904, p. 268. There is more to be said, however, on this passage: see below.

knew best and could best testify to the number of campaigns on which his father had served without shirking his duty would be his fellow demesmen. And an even clearer vignette occurs in Theophrastus *Characters* 25(δειλίας).3: "on campaign, when ⟨the⟩ infantry are marching out to the rescue, (the Coward) is apt to call his ⟨fellow demesmen⟩ and insist that they stand near him and have a look round first—remarking how hard it is to tell which side are the enemy" (καὶ στρατευόμενος δὲ ⟨τοῦ⟩ πεζοῦ ἐκβοηθοῦντος τοὺς ⟨δημότας, Ilberg⟩ προσκαλεῖν, κελεύων πρὸς αὐτὸν στάντας πρῶτον περιιδεῖν, καὶ λέγειν, ὡς ἔργον διαγνῶναί ἐστι, πότεροί εἰσιν οἱ πολέμιοι). Ilberg's supplement has been generally accepted, as the demesmen appear later, in section 6: "he is apt to bring in his fellow demesmen and tribesmen to see the casualty, and to describe to each of them how he himself with his own hands brought the man back to camp."[11] In general one cannot deny the likelihood that the requirements of battle formation may have cut across some of the deme contingents, especially the larger ones; and as to a man's off-duty company, that was apparently his own concern.[12] Nonetheless the evidence as a whole leaves us in little doubt that warfare (on land, at any rate) in all its aspects would normally draw an individual closer to his fellow demesmen and, within the limits of normal human likes and dislikes, would strengthen the bond between them.

There were thus many ways, both positive and negative, in which an Athenian could perceive himself as being part of (say) "the Anaphlystians," and many ways, outside as well as inside the deme, in which that group could engage in partially or wholly concerted action and so reinforce the sense of identity of its members. As a simple corollary of size, most of the members of even the largest demes must have known each other by sight or by name or both;[13] and the consequences of this fact are everywhere evident in our sources, particularly oratory, comedy, and the early dialogues of Plato. To discredit the claim of Pankleon to be a Dekeleian, for example, all that was necessary was to establish that the Dekeleians had never heard of him (Lysias 23.2-4). From an early age a *dēmotēs*,[14] as Nikias says of Sokrates in Plato's *Laches*, would have

---

[11] Theophr. *Char.* 25.6: καὶ εἰσάγειν πρὸς τὸν κατακείμενον σκεψομένους τοὺς δημότας ⟨καί, Gesner⟩ τοὺς φυλέτας καὶ τούτων ἅμ' ἑκάστῳ διηγεῖσθαι, ὡς αὐτὸς αὐτὸν ταῖς ἑαυτοῦ χερσὶν ἐπὶ σκηνὴν ἐκόμισεν. Gesner's καί is clearly preferable to either toleration of the asyndeton (e.g. J. M. Edmonds in the Loeb edition) or obelization of τοὺς δημότας (Diels in the Oxford text).

[12] See Plato *Symp.* 219E on Alkibiades and Sokrates as messmates at Poteidaia—two men not merely from different demes (Skambonidai and Alopeke, respectively) but from different tribes, IV Leontis and X Antiochis.

[13] Contrast Thuc. 8.66.3 on the polis as a whole.

[14] Not, admittedly, a *dēmopoiētos*, as Pankleon pretended to be. We cannot enter here

accompanied his father to *hiera* and other gatherings of the demesmen[15]—
occasions on which the demesmen might naturally be expected to notice
the company kept by any one of their number and to testify, if need be,
to his presence or absence. Such at least is the contention of the speaker
in Isaeus 9.21, anxious to cast doubt on the attitude of Astyphilos to
Kleon.[16]

Indeed *the demesman as witness* (potential or actual) was a ubiquitous
figure in the Athenian courts. Aeschines in 343 threatened to invoke the
collective memory of "the senior Paianians" to prove Demosthenes guilty
of ingratitude to the man who had facilitated his deme registration;[17]
and the actual appearance of demesmen *qua* demesmen in court was
commonplace, as they testified not only to this crucial matter of enrolment
into their ranks (or else to aspects of family background, adoption, wills,
and other things material to it)[18] but also to a whole range of other
circumstances of which their knowledge, as demesmen, was of relevance
and significance. To cite just three examples: in Lysias 31.15-16 the
members of an *ad hoc* committee of the Acharnians are called to prove
that Philon had not, like others, provided funds for the war effort against
the Thirty in 404/3;[19] in Isaeus 3.80 the speaker's concluding argument

into the complexities of Plataian status in Athens at this time; see most recently M. J.
Osborne, *Naturalization in Athens*, vol. 2, Brussels, 1982, pp. 11-16.

[15] Plato *Laches* 187D-E: ὦ Λυσίμαχε, δοκεῖς μοι ὡς ἀληθῶς Σωκράτη πατρόθεν
γιγνώσκειν μόνον, αὐτῷ δ' οὐ συγγεγονέναι ἀλλ' ἢ παιδὶ ὄντι, εἴ που ἐν τοῖς
δημόταις μετὰ τοῦ πατρὸς ἀκολουθῶν ἐπλησίασέν σοι ἢ ἐν ἱερῷ ἢ ἐν ἄλλῳ τῳ συλ-
λόγῳ τῶν δημοτῶν. The deme is Alopeke.

[16] Isaeus 9.21: εἰς τὰς θυσίας τοίνυν, ἐν αἷσπερ οἱ ἄλλοι Ἀθηναῖοι ἑστι-
ῶνται, πρῶτον μὲν δημότην ὄντα, ἔπειτα ἀνεψιόν, ἔτι δὲ τὸν υἱὸν τὸν τούτου μέλ-
λοντα ποιεῖσθαι, εἰκὸς δήπου ἦν, ὁπότε περ ἐπιδημοίη, μηδὲ μεθ' ἑνὸς ἄλλου
ἰέναι τὸν Ἀστύφιλον ἢ μετὰ Κλέωνος. ὡς τοίνυν οὐδέποτ' ἦλθε μετ' αὐτοῦ, ὑμῖν
τῶν δημοτῶν μαρτυρίαν ἀναγνώσεται. The deme is Araphen (9.18).

[17] Aeschin. 2.150: οὕτως ἀναιδὴς καὶ πόρρωθεν ἀχάριστος εἶ, ὃς Φιλόδημον τὸν
Φίλωνος πατέρα καὶ Ἐπικράτους οὐκ ἀγαπᾷς οὐδὲ προσκυνεῖς, δι' ὃν εἰς τοὺς
δημότας ἐνεγράφης, ὡς ἴσασιν οἱ πρεσβύτεροι Παιανιέων. (For the phrase οἱ πρεσβύτεροι Παιανιέων, cf. Demosth. 57.10 and 61, and esp. Isaeus fr. 10a Thalheim: οὐ
τοίνυν μόνον, ὦ ἄνδρες δικασταί, ταύτην τὴν μαρτυρίαν παρέξομαι, ἀλλὰ καὶ ἐκμαρτυ-
ρίαν ἑτέραν Μυρωνίδου, ὃς ἦν τῶν δημοτῶν πρεσβύτατος.) When Demosthenes, in
later years, referred to Aeschines' deme enrolment he chose a cruder kind of innuendo:
ἐπειδὴ δ' εἰς τοὺς δημότας ἐνεγράφης ὁπωσδήποτε, (ἐῶ γὰρ τοῦτο,) ἐπειδή γ' ἐνεγράφης κτλ. (Demosth. 18.261).

[18] See, for instance, Isaeus 2.14-17 and 44, 6.10 and 64 (cf. 9.8); [Demosth.] 43.35-36,
44.44; Demosth. 57.19, 23-27, 40, 46, 67-69; perhaps IG II²1205; and cf. in general
?Aristot. *Ath. Pol.* 42.1-2 and 59.4 with Chap. 4B, sec. 1(a). In some of these cases the
plaintiff or defendant is an individual demesman, in others the deme as a whole.

[19] Lysias 31.15-16: ὑπολείπεται τοίνυν αὐτῷ λέγειν ὡς τῷ μὲν σώματι δι' ἀσθέ-
νειάν τινα γενομένην ἀδύνατος κατέστη βοηθῆσαι εἰς τὸν Πειραιᾶ, ἀπὸ δὲ τῶν
ὑπαρχόντων ἐπαγγειλάμενος αὐτὸς ἢ χρήματ' εἰσενεγκεῖν εἰς τὸ πλῆθος τὸ ὑμέτερον ἢ ὁπλίσαι τινὰς τῶν ἑαυτοῦ δημοτῶν, ὥσπερ καὶ ἄλλοι πολλοὶ τῶν πο-

that the sister of the defendant Nikodemos had not, as claimed, made a legitimate marriage with the wealthy Pyrrhos is the testimony of Pyrrhos' fellow demesmen that he had not, on such a wife's behalf, either provided the obligatory feast for the demesmen's wives at the Thesmophoria or fulfilled any of the other deme duties incumbent upon the possessor of a three-talent fortune;[20] and in Isaeus 9.18 we are told that the quarrel between Thoudippos, father of Kleon, and Astyphilos' father Eukrates— a quarrel so violent that it resulted in the latter's death—*could* have been described by the many Araphenian onlookers, if only any of them had been prepared to come forward.[21]

This last example, of course, leaves a question hanging in the air: *why* were none of the demesmen of Araphen willing to talk of this affair? The suspicion arises that it must have been unwise, in fourth-century Araphen, to speak out against either Thoudippos himself, who had been an associate of the fearsome fifth-century leader Kleon, or any other member of his "slightly raffish family";[22] and if so, such a fact, together with other evidence of a similar kind, points to an element of unpleasant intimidation possibly to be found in deme society which we must consider in Chapter 10A. Self-evidently, rather than making enemies of powerful individual *dēmotai* it was advisable to cultivate the esteem and approval of one's fellow demesmen as a whole. Such approval is claimed, for instance, by the speaker in Isaeus 2, for his (and his wife's) solicitous care of his adoptive father Menekles both before (2.18) and after (2.36) the latter's death.[23]

λιτῶν αὐτοὶ οὐ δυνάμενοι λητουργεῖν τοῖς σώμασιν ... (16) καί μοι κάλει Διό-τιμον τὸν Ἀχαρνέα καὶ τοὺς αἱρεθέντας μετ' αὐτοῦ τοὺς δημότας ὁπλίσαι ἀπὸ τῶν εἰσενεχθέντων χρημάτων.

[20] Isaeus 3.80: καὶ ἐν δὲ τῷ δήμῳ, κεκτημένος τὸν τριτάλαντον οἶκον, εἰ ἦν γε-γαμηκώς, ἠναγκάζετο ἂν ὑπὲρ τῆς γαμετῆς γυναικὸς καὶ θεσμοφόρια ἑστιᾶν τὰς γυναῖκας καὶ τἆλλα ὅσα προσῆκε λητουργεῖν ἐν τῷ δήμῳ ὑπὲρ τῆς γυναικὸς ἀπό γε οὐσίας τηλικαύτης. οὐ τοίνυν φανεῖται οὐδὲν τούτων γεγενημένον οὐδεπώποτε. οἱ μὲν οὖν φράτορες μεμαρτυρήκασιν ὑμῖν (*sc.* that there had been no marriage-feast in the phratry)· λαβὲ δὲ καὶ τὴν τῶν δημοτῶν τῶν ἐκείνου μαρτυρίαν. The particular deme is indeterminable.

[21] Isaeus 9.18: ὡς δὲ ταῦτ' ἐστὶν ἀληθῆ, ἴσως μὲν καὶ Ἀραφηνίων [καὶ] πολλοὶ τῶν τότε συγγεωργούντων μαρτυρήσειαν ἄν μοι, διαρρήδην δὲ περὶ τηλικούτου πράγματος οὐκ ἂν ἔχοιμι ὅπως ὑμῖν παρασχοίμην.

[22] The phrase is Davies' (*Families*, p. 228). For the Kleon connection, see B. D. Meritt and H. T. Wade-Gery, *AJPh* 57, 1936, p. 392, n. 36.

[23] Isaeus 2.18, ... καὶ ἐγὼ τὸν αὐτὸν τρόπον ὥσπερ γόνῳ ὄντα πατέρα ἐμαυτοῦ ἐθεράπευόν τε καὶ ᾐσχυνόμην, καὶ ἐγὼ καὶ ἡ γυνὴ ἡ ἐμή, ὥστε ἐκεῖνον πρὸς τοὺς δημότας ἐπαινεῖν ἅπαντας; 2.36, ... καὶ τελευτήσαντα ἔθαψα ἀξίως ἐκείνου τε καὶ ἐμαυτοῦ, καὶ ἐπίθημα καλὸν ἐπέθηκα, καὶ τὰ ἔνατα καὶ τἆλλα πάντα ἐποίησα τὰ περὶ τὴν ταφὴν ὡς οἷόν τε κάλλιστα, ὥστε τοὺς δημότας ἐπαινεῖν ἅπαντας.

A more complex—because more tendentious—exploitation of both this sort of appeal and others associated with it occurs in [Lysias] 20.[24] According to his son (or whoever else the speaker of chaps. 1-10 may be), it was his record as a good "deme man" as well as a good democrat which had led his tribe to choose Polystratos Deiradiotes as *katalogeus* under the Four Hundred in 411 (20.2).[25] However, the price of having mentioned the demesmen was to remind the jurors of the prosecution's attempt (20.11) to link Polystratos with the murdered extremist Phrynichos. Polystratos' son flatly denies the allegation that his father was either a relative (συγγενής, ἀναγκαῖος) or a "friend" (φίλος; see below on this term) of Phrynichos (20.11-12),[26] but he is still left with the embarrassing fact that the two men were, irrefutably, fellow demesmen— embarrassing because the (to us) dubious implication that demesmen of the same deme were tarred with the same brush might sometimes, apparently, carry weight with an Athenian jury.[27] To this the speaker has two replies, one direct and one diversionary. The direct reply is simply to challenge the logic of the idea. Where is the justice, he asks, in a jury comprised of Phrynichos' fellow *citizens* absolving themselves of the blame which they are being invited to attribute to his fellow *demesman*?[28] Obviously he is seeking here to suggest, and not unreasonably, that there were good and bad demesmen no less than good and bad citizens. The categorization of Phrynichos, on either count, is left unspoken, but Polystratos' claim to have deserved well of the Deiradiotai as well as of the Athenians as a whole is made explicit: as *katalogeus*, we are told, his aim had been "not to make an enemy of any of his fellow demesmen"

[24] On the speech and its political background the best discussion is that of Andrewes in A. W. Gomme, A. Andrewes, and K. J. Dover, *A Historical Commentary on Thucydides*, vol. 5, Oxford, 1981, pp. 201-206.

[25] [Lysias] 20.2: οὗτος γὰρ ᾑρέθη μὲν ὑπὸ τῶν φυλετῶν ὡς χρηστὸς ὢν ἀνὴρ καὶ περὶ τοὺς δημότας καὶ περὶ τὸ πλῆθος τὸ ὑμέτερον.

[26] Indeed it is claimed that they scarcely even met. As youths the πένης Phrynichos was tending sheep ἐν ἀγρῷ while Polystratos ἐν τῷ ἄστει ἐπαιδεύετο; as men it was Polystratos who ἐγεώργει while Phrynichos ἐλθὼν εἰς τὸ ἄστυ ἐσυκοφάντει! The morality of these various phases of life is left to speak for itself.

[27] It is (subtly) used, for example, in Lysias 13.55: Hagnodoros of Amphitrope, who has secured a decree of immunity for the informer Menestratos, is introduced as the latter's fellow demesman (as well as Κριτίου κηδεστὴς τοῦ τῶν τριάκοντα). Why the speaker in Antiph. 6.12 bothered to mention that his son-in-law Phanostratos (on whom see Davies, *Families*, pp. 530-531) was of the same deme as his accusers is not clear. Note also Aristoph. *Ach.*, line 855, Lysistratos Χολαργέων ὄνειδος (with S. Halliwell, *LCM* 7.10, December 1982, p. 153); there, however, exoneration of the general body of the demesmen may be the implication.

[28] [Lysias] 20.12: εἰ δ᾽ ἦν δημότης, οὐ δίκαιος διὰ τοῦτο βλάπτεσθαί ἐστιν ὁ πατήρ, εἰ μὴ καὶ ὑμεῖς ἀδικεῖτε, ὅτι ὑμῶν ἐστι πολίτης.

but to oblige any and all of them who sought either inclusion in or exclusion from the Five Thousand.[29]

The clear element of factual improbability in these claims[30] in no way diminishes, for us, the interest of the particular line of argument employed, especially the notion that a quarrel with a fellow demesman was always something best avoided or, if unavoidable, a matter for regret. In the speeches of Isaeus, for example, so often concerned with issues of inheritance and succession, the view that it is distressing to be in a fight with one's *relatives* (who are thus morally in the wrong for not feeling the same) is naturally something of a cliché.[31] But we know also that at least one of his clients, the young (?)Sphettian for whom he wrote the speech *Against the demesmen, concerning an estate* (Πρὸς τοὺς δημότας περὶ χωρίου), indulged in the same lament in deme terms. "Men of the jury," he begins, "I should have much preferred not to be wronged by any one of my fellow citizens, or failing that, to find opponents with whom a quarrel would cause me no concern. But as it is I am faced by the worst of all worlds: I am being wronged by my fellow demesmen. I cannot easily overlook the fact that they are robbing me, yet it is unpleasant to incur the hatred of men with whom one is obliged to share sacrifices and attend communal gatherings."[32] The force of such a plea for sympathy may admittedly have been augmented in this case not only by the speaker's tender years (νεώτερος ὤν, as he goes on to say) but also by the fact that his adversary was the deme itself, not merely a

---

[29] [Lysias] 20.13: πῶς δ' ἂν ⟨τις⟩ γένοιτο δημοτικώτερος, ἢ ὅστις ὑμῶν ψηφισαμένων πεντακισχιλίοις παραδοῦναι τὰ πράγματα καταλογεὺς ὢν ἐνακισχιλίους κατέλεξεν, ἵνα μηδεὶς αὐτῷ διάφορος εἴη τῶν δημοτῶν, ἀλλ' ἵνα τὸν μὲν βουλόμενον γράφοι, εἰ δέ τῳ μὴ οἷόν τ' εἴη, χαρίζοιτο.

[30] See Andrewes (reference above, n. 24), p. 205.

[31] See for instance Isaeus 1.6-7, 21, 27-29, 45-47; 3.73; 5.30, 35, 39; 9.25. (On the importance of forensic cliché, note Davies' remarks in *Families*, p. xviii.) I shall not argue or imply that the link between fellow demesmen was *more* significant than ties between, say, members of the same family, phratry, or *genos*; many times more data than we have now would be needed before the separability of these various loyalties became more striking than the interaction between them. On this interaction see now Osborne, *Demos*, chap. 7; his equation there between neighbors and fellow demesmen is unexamined but justifiable (see below).

[32] Isaeus fr. 4 Thalheim = 15 Sauppe (Dion. Hal. *Isaios* 10; cf. Harpoc., Σφηττός— which is therefore presumably the deme in question): μάλιστα μὲν ἐβουλόμην, ὦ ἄνδρες δικασταί, μηδ' ὑφ' ἑνὸς ἀδικεῖσθαι τῶν πολιτῶν, εἰ δὲ μή, τοιούτων ἀντιδίκων τυχεῖν πρὸς οὓς οὐδὲν ἂν ἐφρόντιζον διαφερόμενος· νῦν δέ μοι πάντων πραγμάτων λυπηρότατον συμβέβηκεν· ἀδικοῦμαι γὰρ ὑπὸ τῶν δημοτῶν, οὓς περιορᾶν μὲν ἀποστεροῦντας οὐ ῥάδιον, ἀπέχθεσθαι δὲ ἀηδές, μεθ' ὧν ἀνάγκη καὶ ⟨θύειν καί, Sauppe⟩ συνουσίας κοινὰς ποιεῖσθαι. The speech was delivered, according to Dion. Hal. *loc. cit.*, in support of a claim for the restoration of an estate retained by the demesmen, who had received it as a pledge; see Haussoullier, *Vie*, p. 98.

member or members of it.[33] However, the gravity of even individual
demesmen being at loggerheads with each other is equally evident elsewhere. In Aristophanes' *Clouds*, for instance, the first of the two creditors
who unsuccessfully attempt to recover their money from Strepsiades expresses his discomfiture that, on top of everything else, he will become
an enemy of his fellow demesman.[34] And Apollodoros' line of argument
in [Demosth.] 52.28 is that Archebiades' willingness to testify against
Kallippos can mean only one thing: since it would be unthinkable to give
(perjured) evidence against a fellow demesman, what he says must be
the truth.[35]

The basic character of the relationship between fellow demesmen which
all this testimony invites us to formulate is in fact openly revealed on
many occasions. Just as most demesmen were likely, for good or ill, to
be *neighbors* (γείτονες) of one another,[36] so that "neighbors" and
"demesmen" are often mentioned in the same breath,[37] it is even more
common to find an association and a semantic overlap between *dēmotai*
and *philoi*. To be sure, *philos* was a term with so broad a connotation
as to embrace relatives as well as (the standard rendering) "friends"; yet
this very broadness meant that, under the latter heading if not the former,
dēmotēs and *philos* were frequently tantamount to being one and the
same.[38] The plays of Aristophanes provide five good examples of this.

[33] He is aware, naturally, of the danger that either of these considerations could work
just as well against him as for him.

[34] Aristoph. *Clouds*, lines 1218-1219: γενήσομαι | ἐχθρὸς ἔτι πρὸς τούτοισιν ἀν-
δρὶ δημότῃ.

[35] [Demosth.] 52.28: καὶ ὁ Ἀρχεβιάδης εἰς τοῦτο φαυλότητος ἥκει, ὥστε τοῦ
Καλλίππου δημότου ὄντος αὐτῷ καὶ πολιτευομένου καὶ οὐκ ἰδιώτου ὄντος καταμαρ-
τυρεῖ, καὶ φησὶν ἡμᾶς μὲν ἀληθῆ λέγειν, τοῦτον δὲ ψεύδεσθαι, καὶ ταῦτα εἰδὼς
ὅτι, ἂν οὗτος βούληται ἐπισκήψασθαι αὐτῷ τῶν ψευδομαρτυριῶν καὶ ἄλλο μηδὲν
ποιῆσαι ἢ ἐξορκῶσαι, ἀνάγκη αὐτῷ ἔσται πίστιν ἐπιθεῖναι ἣν ἂν κελεύῃ οὗτος.

[36] See in general Ehrenberg, *People*, chap. 8 ("Family and Neighbours"), esp. pp. 155-
158.

[37] See e.g. Aristoph. *Clouds*, line 1322, where Strepsiades, attacked by his son, shouts
for help to his γείτονες καὶ ξυγγενεῖς καὶ δημόται. As K. J. Dover notes *ad loc.*
(*Aristophanes: Clouds*, Oxford, 1968, p. 249), while the assumption that one's *neighbors*
are within earshot is to be seen also in Trygaios' ἴτε δεῦρο δεῦρ' ὦ γείτονες (*Peace*,
line 79) and natural and unremarkable enough in itself, the (to us) less natural assumption
that such a cry would be heard also by one's fellow demesmen is no less "true to life"
(Dover), or at least true to the picture of Kikynna presented in this play, especially at lines
210-211. Compare *Ekkles.*, lines 1114-1115, where Praxagora's maid glosses ὑμεῖς θ'
ὅσαι παρέστατ' ἐπὶ ταῖσιν θύραις with οἱ γείτονές τε πάντες οἵ τε δημόται.

[38] See Connor, *Politicians*, pp. 30-31, on the meaning of *philos* (and pp. 3-32, in general,
on the constituents of *philia* groupings; demesmen are mentioned, all too briefly, at p. 22,
n. 35), and pp. 35-84, on the behavior of *philoi* towards each other. His belief (pp. 75-
79) that "the poor" were included in *philia* relationships only, so to speak, vicariously may

In *Acharnians,* lines 325ff., the coal scuttle taken hostage by Dikaiopolis is both *philos* (line 326) and *dēmotēs* (line 333, cf. 349) of the Acharnians.[39] In *Knights,* lines 319-320, Demosthenes declares that his deception by Kleon made him the laughingstock of his *dēmotai* and *philoi.* In *Clouds,* lines 1206-1210, Strepsiades injudiciously forecasts that a song in envy of himself and his son will be sung by his *philoi* and his *dēmotai.* In *Ekklesiazousai,* lines 1023-1024, a young man expresses the hope— a forlorn one in the circumstances—that one of his *dēmotai* or *philoi* will come and save him from his sexual obligations to his elderly admirer.[40] And in *Ploutos,* lines 253-254, the slave Karion summons the chorus of honest farmers, men who "eat the same thyme" as his master Chremylos, with the appellation "*philoi* and *dēmotai.*"[41] (We may note the variation here in respect of which of the two terms gives rise to the other; and it should be supererogatory to point out that in phrases like these Greek usage regularly drew no distinction—quite the reverse, in fact—between the two elements linked by καί.) In court too the same conjunction is found. The speaker in [Lysias] 6.53 asks, rhetorically, what sort of *philos* or relative or *dēmotēs* of Andokides should incur the open enmity of the gods by doing him a favor in secret (that is, by voting for him);[42] and Lysias 27.12 anticipates and denounces what was evidently a familiar forensic gambit, the hackneyed spectacle of a guilty defendant's *dēmotai* and *philoi* tearfully begging for mercy on his behalf.[43]

What Lysias had in mind when he wrote 27.12 was not, to be sure, the orchestrated histrionics of the Kothokidai (or whoever it might be) *en masse,* but merely of a sufficient number of them to lend practical force to the idea of "the deme as ideal community"; and in these foregoing pages we have seen enough evidence of enough kinds to show that under

---

be true of high politics and political organization (in the fifth century); that it is less true of other aspects of life is evident from the passages which we shall now examine.

[39] Aristoph. *Ach.*, line 326, ἀνταποκτενῶ γὰρ ὑμῶν τῶν φίλων τοὺς φιλτάτους; line 333, ὁ λάρκος δημότης ὅδ᾽ ἔστ᾽ ἐμός; lines 348-349, ὀλίγου τ᾽ ἀπέθανον ἄνθρακες Παρνήθιοι, | καὶ ταῦτα διὰ τὴν ἀτοπίαν τῶν δημοτῶν.

[40] Aristoph. *Ekkles.*, lines 1023-1024: τί δ᾽ ἦν ἀφαιρῆταί μ᾽ ἀνὴρ τῶν δημοτῶν | ἢ τῶν φίλων ἐλθών τις;

[41] Aristoph. *Ploutos,* lines 253-254: ὦ πολλὰ δὴ τῷ δεσπότῃ ταὐτὸν θύμον φαγόντες, | ἄνδρες φίλοι καὶ δημόται καὶ τοῦ πονεῖν ἐρασταί. Cf. Chremylos himself at lines 322-323: χαίρειν μὲν ὑμᾶς ἐστιν ὦνδρες δημόται | ἀρχαῖον ἤδη προσαγορεύειν καὶ σαπρόν.

[42] [Lysias] 6.53: ποῖον φίλον, ποῖον συγγενῆ, ποῖον δημότην (Blass: δικαστὴν MSS) χρὴ τούτῳ χαρισάμενον κρύβδην φανερῶς τοῖς θεοῖς ἀπέχθεσθαι; (Whether or not this "speech" was ever delivered in court is immaterial here.)

[43] Lysias 27.12: καὶ νῦν ἴσως ποιήσουσιν ἄπερ καὶ πρότερον ἦσαν εἰθισμένοι καὶ δημόται καὶ φίλοι, κλαίοντες ἐξαιτεῖσθαι αὐτοὺς παρ᾽ ὑμῶν.

normal circumstances the relationships between fellow demesmen were
indeed such as to make that ideal, and the efforts of those who strove
to attain it, one of the identifiable vectors which went to shape deme
society. Contact, familiarity, and help—Aurenche's "relations de bon
voisinage"—were normal and natural. When Sokrates, in Plato's *Apology*, observes that the fathers and other relatives of the young men whom
he has allegedly been corrupting have come to court to aid not in his
conviction but in his acquittal, his eye falls first on Kriton, his "contemporary and fellow demesman."[44] Sokrates' active presence as a *dēmotēs*
of Alopeke is further attested in the *Laches*, not only, as we have seen,
in 187D-E but also in 180B-D. There, after Laches has expressed surprise
that Lysimachos is not asking for advice about the education of his sons
from his fellow demesman Sokrates, Lysimachos duly does so.[45] Not
every deme enjoyed the advantage of a Sokrates to counsel its young
men, but perhaps the more conventional wisdom of a fellow demesman
might be solicited as arbitrator of a private dispute, before it came to a
court-case. This, according to Aeschin. 1.63, is what Hegesandros had
done—whereat his fellow Sounian Diopeithes had obligingly procrasti-
nated.[46] And no doubt this sort of thing had its equivalent at less exalted
levels of deme society also,[47] the levels at which the assistance to be
expected from fellow demesmen would normally be more simple and
immediate.[48]

   Thus the rewards of cultivating close and amicable relations with one's
fellow demesmen were many and various. And such rewards did not

[44] Plato *Apology* 33E: πρῶτον μὲν Κρίτων οὑτοσί, ἐμὸς ἡλικιώτης καὶ δημότης, Κρι-
τοβούλου τοῦδε πατήρ. For ἡλικιώτης καὶ δημότης, cf. [Plato] *Theages* 121D.

[45] Plato *Laches* 180B-D: (Laches speaks) ὅτι δ᾽ ἡμᾶς μὲν συμβούλους παρακαλεῖς
ἐπὶ τὴν τῶν νεανίσκων παιδείαν, Σωκράτη δὲ τόνδε οὐ παρακαλεῖς, θαυμάζω,
πρῶτον μὲν ὄντα δημότην, ἔπειτα ἐνταῦθα ἀεὶ τὰς διατριβὰς ποιούμενον ὅπου
τί ἐστι τῶν τοιούτων ὧν σὺ ζητεῖς περὶ τοὺς νέους ἢ μάθημα ἢ ἐπιτήδευμα καλόν
... (Lysimachos speaks) ἀλλ᾽ εἴ τι καὶ σύ, ὦ παῖ Σωφρονίσκου, ἔχεις τῷδε τῷ σαυτου
δημότῃ ἀγαθὸν συμβουλεῦσαι, χρὴ συμβουλεύειν. 187D-E is quoted above, n. 15.

[46] Aeschin. 1.63: προϊόντος δὲ τοῦ χρόνου ἐπέτρεψαν διαγνῶναι τὸ πρᾶγμα (*sc.*
the status of the slave Pittalakos) Διοπείθει τῷ Σουνιεῖ, δημότῃ τε ὄντι τοῦ
Ἡγησάνδρου, καὶ ἤδη ποτὲ καὶ χρησαμένῳ, ὅτ᾽ ἦν ἐν ἡλικίᾳ· παραλαβὼν δὲ τὸ
πρᾶγμα ὁ Διοπείθης ἀνεβάλλετο χαριζόμενος τούτοις χρόνους ἐκ χρόνων.

[47] On the families of Diopeithes and Hegesandros, see Davies, *Families*, pp. 167-169 and
209-210 respectively. Note that both were members of the Sounian branch of the *genos*
of the Salaminioi.

[48] As well as Aristoph. *Clouds*, line 1322 (see above, n. 37), and *Ekkles*. lines 1023-
1024 (see above, n. 40), note two instances of the assistance motif in *Lysistrata*: lines 331-
334, ἁρπαλέως | ἀραμένη ταῖσιν ἐμαῖς | δημότισιν καιομέναις | φέρουσ᾽ ὕδωρ βοη-
θῶ; and lines 684-685, καὶ ποιήσω τήμερον τοὺς δημότας βωστρεῖν σ᾽ ἐγὼ πεκτού-
μενον.

necessarily lapse with an individual's death, for we know of one instance (and we may surely visualize others) where the service rendered by one *dēmotēs* to another was, quite literally, the last thing he could have wished for—a decent burial.[49]

B. Wealth, Honor, and Service

At some time in the second half of the fourth century an epigram (IG II²3101) was set up near Vari—thus in the deme Anagyrous—by a man whose choregic victory at the "Dionysia" had prompted his father to try for, and attain, a similar success:

ἡδυγέλωτι χορῶι Διονύσια σ[ύ]μ ποτ' ἐν[ίκων],
μνημόσυνον δὲ θεῶι νίκης τόδε δῶρον [ἔθηκα],
δήμωι μὲν κόσμον, ζῆλον πατρὶ κισσοφο[ροῦντι]·
τοῦδε δ' ἔτι πρότερος στεφανηφόρον [εἶλον ἀγῶνα].

Early editors, down to Kirchner, took the "Dionysia" in question (line 1) to be the *rural* Dionysia, but they were surely mistaken. Such "honor for the deme" (δήμωι . . . κόσμον, line 3) can only have been won outside it, namely, at the Dionysia in the city.[50] The commemoration of these two comic victories[51] thus belongs in the small but significant tradition of choregic dedications by demesmen who preferred to advertise their urban successes not in the city but in their own demes;[52] and δήμωι . . .

[49] See SEG 12.100 (records of the *pōlētai* of 367/6), lines 25-30: Theophilos of Xypete (and his wife) buried by Isarchos of Xypete. There is no indication that the two were related, nor other grounds for thinking so (see 353 and 358 for Isarchos and his family); conversely, the fact that Isarchos claimed, and was awarded, thirty drachmas for his pains is scarcely proof of cynical opportunism. Beyond that, the context is irrecoverable.

[50] Thus, rightly, A. Koerte, *Gnomon* 11, 1935, p. 634; cf. Pickard-Cambridge, *Festivals*, p. 50, and esp. Davies, *Families*, p. 576 (under A21). Koerte's other reason for arguing this was misconceived, however: since Vari is not Aixone but Anagyrous (see Eliot, *Coastal Demes*, p. 43), the proof supposedly furnished by IG II²1198 etc. that the rural Dionysia in this deme involved no contest between the *chorēgoi* obviously lapses—and in any case we have seen reason in Chap. 7D to conclude that the rural Dionysia in general regularly did entail such competition.

[51] Comedy is indicated by the phrase ἡδυγέλωτι χορῶι: Wilamowitz, *Hermes* 65, 1930, p. 243.

[52] Cf. Davies, *Families*, p. 576 (under A21), citing the other two known—or rather, strictly speaking, highly probable—instances: IG II²3091, from (?)Halai Aixonides (see Chap. 2, n. 32), ca. 380 but relating to victories of the mid fifth century; and SEG 23.102 (cf. SEG 26.225), from the late fifth century, and probably also from Anagyrous (see Chap. 7, n. 261, both for this and for IG II²1210, the "evidence for dramatic performances at Anagyrous" overlooked by Davies, *Families, loc.cit.*).

κόσμον makes explicit one, at least, of the prime reasons for doing so. Unless the phrase is a thoroughly empty one, there was evidently some reflected glory for the deme as a whole in such achievements: perhaps a congratulatory announcement in the deme assembly; at the least, ample scope for any Anagyrasian (to keep to this, concrete example) to give vent to emotions of pleasure and pride.

To this extent these unknown *chorēgoi*, father and son, would surely have argued that they had made a striking contribution to the notion of "the deme as ideal community" which we examined in the first part of this chapter. Yet there is an obvious distinction to be drawn between the surge of *campanilismo* which a body of demesmen (or members thereof) might derive on the one hand from something for which the credit was genuinely theirs as a community[53] and on the other from a success which in real terms was nothing to do with the deme at all. Whatever the *kosmos* for the Anagyrasioi as a whole in the achievements recorded on IG II²3101, it was of necessity less than that for the individuals and the family whose ambitions and financial resources had brought them about. Already in this book we have seen far too much evidence of the role of energetic and wealthy individuals in deme life for the observation that some demesmen were more active and/or prosperous than others to come as anything more than a truism at this stage of our study. Even so, some of the most notable items and categories of evidence remain to be examined; and in the process of doing this, something of the ideological context within which such behavior was accommodated to the needs of deme society may be elucidated.

✳

We may begin by quoting in full a deme decree of Aixone, from the year 313/2, to which frequent reference has been made in earlier chapters. It reads as follows:

> Gods.
> On the proposal of Glaukides Sosippou. Since the *chorēgoi* Auteas Autokleous and Philoxenides Philippou performed the choregy with a fine love of honor, the demesmen resolved to crown each of them with a golden crown worth one hundred drachmas in the theater at the time of the comedies in the year after Theophrastos' archonship, in order that such a love of honor may also be shown by other *chorēgoi* who perform the choregy in future. It was further resolved that the demarch Hegesileos and the treasurers should give them ten

---

[53] Such as victories in an *inter-deme* festival (e.g. IG II²3102 and 3103; see above, p. 224).

drachmas for a sacrifice, and that the treasurers should have this decree inscribed on a stone stele and set up in the theater in order that the Aixoneis may always make their Dionysia as fine as possible.[54]

It would not be unreasonable to describe this as a "typical" honorific deme decree (of the type, at any rate, committed to stone) of its period, as regards both the individuals involved and the language employed; and in both respects the document can serve to introduce important observations about the evidence as a whole.

PERSONNEL

The demarch. Hegesileos (5) is mentioned in another, similar deme decree from this, his year in office (IG II²1202), but he is not otherwise attested either in the deme or outside it, and his family background is indeterminable. In this he is representative of demarchs in general.[55] Of the fifty known (forty of them by name), it would be an abuse of prosopographical licence to suggest either other personal appearances in the source record or else identifiable family ties for even half of them. In fact, given the ever-present risk of error in making such connections, between one-third and one-quarter would be a safer estimate.[56] For all the lacunae and uncertainties in our knowledge of individual Athenians, even in the comparatively lavishly-documented fourth century, the conclusion that most demarchs were men neither of great personal ambition nor of high socioeconomic status seems quite inescapable.[57] There is good

---

[54] *AM* 66, 1941, pp. 218-219, no. 1: Θεοί. | [Γ]λαυκίδης Σωσίππου εἶπεν· ἐπειδὴ οἱ χορηγοὶ Αὐτ[έα]|ς Αὐτοκλέους καὶ Φιλοξενίδης Φιλίππου καλῶς [κα]|[ὶ] φιλοτίμως ἐχορήγησαν· δεδόχθαι τοῖς δημότ[α]|[ι]ς στεφανῶσαι αὐτοὺς χρυσῶι στεφάνωι ἑκά-τε||[ρ]ον ἀπὸ ἑκατὸν δραχμῶν ἐν τῶι θεάτρωι τοῖς κω|μωιδοῖς τοῖς μετὰ Θεόφρασ-τον ἄρχοντα, ὅπως ἂν | [φ]ιλοτιμῶνται καὶ οἱ ἄλλοι χορηγοὶ οἱ μέλλον-τες | [χ]ορηγεῖν, δοῦναι δὲ αὐτοῖς καὶ εἰς θυσίαν δέκα δ|ραχμὰς τὸν δήμαρχον Ἡγησίλεων καὶ τοὺς ταμί|ας, ἀναγράψαι δὲ καὶ τὸ ψήφισμα τόδε τοὺς ταμία|ς ἐν στήληι λιθίνηι καὶ στῆσαι ἐν τῶι θεάτρωι, ὅπως | ἂν Αἰξωνεῖς ἀεὶ ὡς κάλλιστα ⟨τὰ⟩ Διονύσια ποιῶσιν. For the date see Chap. 7, nn. 250-251.

[55] Cf. Chap. 4, n. 153, and Chap. 5, n. 102.

[56] See 6, 7, 10, 11, 13, 15, 16, 17, 18-19, 20, 21, 22, 29, 31, 34, 40, 41, 42, 46, 47, 49.

[57] The conclusion of Sundwall, *Beiträge* pp. 53-58 (esp. 55-57), on the basis of the thirteen fourth-century demarchs known to him (our nos. 3-6, 10-13, 18-20, 29, and 37) was that "die Begüterten ein entschiedenes Übergewicht in den Demen hatten" (*Beiträge* p. 57). However, with the data now available this is simply not borne out *by demarchs*, from whom Sundwall (like Haussoullier before him: see Chap. 4, n. 153) failed to distinguish other categories of deme personnel—categories to which his dictum, as we shall see, does more properly apply. (On Sundwall's use of the terms *reich* and *wohlhabend* in his study as a whole, see Davies, *Families*, p. xix; "die Begüterten" evidently embraces both.)

(and independent) reason to believe that, in the fourth century at least, demarchs were appointed by sortition rather than election,[58] and it is of course entirely consonant with this to discover that the typical demarch was, prosopographically speaking, a nonentity[59]—plucked, as it were, by lot from a life of decent obscurity into which he would gratefully relapse once he had discharged his year in office to the best of his ability.[60]

There are, nonetheless, *some* demarchs who, if not demonstrably prosperous and/or (otherwise) active themselves, belonged to demonstrably prosperous and/or active families—"active" not, with only one major exception, at city level[61] but in the deme (and sometimes by extension the tribe) itself.[62] In fourth-century Eleusis (10, 11) and third-century Rhamnous (42) especially we catch glimpses of such families—as we surely would in every deme, given only comparable depths of documentation. And the glimpses give way, progressively, to clearer and fuller impressions if we leave the demarchs and consider other categories of deme personnel.

The proposer.   Glaukides Sosippou (80), who proposed the Aixonian decree we are dissecting, was also the proposer of another in the same year (IG II²1202), and he has been justifiably described as one of the "vermögende Leute" in the decree-proposer category.[63] The discovery of his father's grave monument at Glyphada indicates a family still resident in the deme itself, and Glaukides' (presumably younger) brother Smikythos is attested as a *hippeus*. In all, fifty-nine proposers of deme decrees are known—all but twelve of them by their full name[64]—and two features of the group as a whole are noteworthy: it overlaps with the demarch group only in one (probable) instance (13); and here a significantly higher proportion of "vermögende Leute," perhaps as much as half, is discernible.[65] Furthermore one can again detect the relative predominance of

[58] See Damsgaard-Madsen, "Démarques."

[59] I use the term entirely neutrally, meaning by it simply that, if he did do anything (in the deme or elsewhere) other than be demarch for a year, it has gone unrecorded.

[60] Would it be too fanciful to suggest that Theophilos of ?Anagyrous (7) might be such a man, moved to commemorate his demarchy and the unwonted celebrity which it brought him in a dedication?

[61] Euthydemos of Eleusis (10), whose father Moirokles *may* be the prominent city politician of that name (see 163). See also 19, 22, 47.

[62] See 6, 10, 11, 13, (?)15, 16, 18-19, 20, (?)21, (?)34, 40, 42, 47, 49.

[63] Sundwall, *Beiträge*, p. 56, citing also our nos. 95, 96, 163, 169, and 304.

[64] The twelve are 64, 159, 172, 173, 229, 294, 307, 335, 336, 337, 351, and 368. A patronymic—and thus a prosopographical foothold—is known for 159, 172, 307, and 335; cf. below, n. 71.

[65] See 73, 78, 80, 95, 96, 146, 152, (?)158, 159, 163, 165, 169, 171, 172, 176, 184,

certain families, members of which were apparently prompted to move deme decrees either by particular, short-term circumstances[66] or else in accordance with a longer-standing tradition of local activity.[67]

Unlike the demarchs, the proposers of decrees were presumably a self-selected group; and although in the deme assembly just as in the city *ekklēsia* it was surely open to anyone to frame a motion, the fact that those who actually did so tended to be "les hommes d'affaires du dème"[68] is natural enough. Only a single demarch, as noted earlier, is known also as the (probable) proposer of a decree, but we have six instances where the proposer of one decree is the honorand in another.[69] And it is with honorands, quite clearly, that one arrives at the highest echelons of deme society.

The honorand. In the Aixonian decree which we have been taking as our starting point and paradigm, the pair of honorands, who have discharged the (?comic) choregy at the deme's Dionysia of 313/2, are Auteas Autokleous (**74**) and Philoxenides Philippou (**97**). Each was no ordinary *dēmotēs*. Auteas, in association with his father, had since 345/4 been the lessee of a deme estate (IG II²2492), while a likely relative of theirs had served the city as Treasurer of the Goddess a few years before that (see under **75**). Philoxenides was almost certainly from a family which was not only prosperous but connected, by the marriage of Philoxenides' sister, with the distinguished house of the statesman Lykourgos. They are nonetheless quite as representative of the overall category of honorands in deme decrees as the demarch and the proposer of this decree were found to be of their respective (smaller) groups. Between 113 and 116 individuals honored by either their own or another deme[70]

190, 192, 278, 289, 298, 304, 307, 322, 324, 325, 329, and 344. I exclude cases where the only relevant fact is a *bouleutēs* in the family, but *in*clude those where a grave monument is known, either for the proposer himself or for a relative; on this latter criterion, however, note the comments of Davies, *Families*, p. xix.

[66] The most striking instance of this is that of the two Aixonian brothers Philaios (**95**) and Philoktemon (**96**): the latter moved IG II²1198 in the year, 326/5, when their father Chremes was eponymous archon; Philaios followed suit in 320/19, with IG II²1199; and IG II²1200, from 317/6, was again the work of Philoktemon.

[67] See for instance **169** and **325**.

[68] Haussoullier, *Vie*, p. 62 (speaking of deme magistracies).

[69] See **73**, **163**, **165**, **184**, **190**, and **344**. Nine *demarchs* are also honorands: see **11**, **14**, **20**, **29**, **31**, **32**, **42**, **49**, and **50**; however, in all but one instance (**49**) they are honorands *qua demarchs*, and thus a special category.

[70] That is, 113 certain cases plus **92**, **177**, and **296**. (For men honored in demes other than their own, see **56**, **62**, **69**, **105**, **150**, **153**, (?)**177**, **179**, **230**, **279**, **280**, **290**, **300**, **308**, **309**, **314**, **340**, and **352**.) Naturally I include not only men actually named as honorands in honorific decrees themselves but also those whom other epigraphic sources (e.g. IG II²2820 and 2845) or even literary sources (e.g. Demosth. 57.64; see **20**) reveal as such.

are known—all but thirteen of them by their full name.[71] If we set aside the nine demarchs, the figure falls somewhere between 104 and 107, and of these almost three-quarters can be assigned some sort of personal or family background of prosperity and/or activity either in the deme or outside it or both.[72]

The predominance of individuals of wealth and standing amongst the honorands in demes which habitually honored their *chorēgoi* and other liturgists, or which sought, habitually or more occasionally, the favor of men influential in the city (whether fellow demesmen or not), was obviously an inevitable consequence of either or both of those practices. But equally obviously it is none the less significant for being so. On the contrary, one's attention is thus profitably drawn not so much to that predominance itself as to the circumstances which produced it. From the deme's point of view—as will be seen most clearly when we turn, below, to the language of the honorific decree—the active support of its most able and prosperous members, their energies competed for by numerous other bodies including the state itself, was vital. To be sure, some honorands were humbler folk—a demarch, say, who had discharged his office conscientiously, or someone whose service to the community either regular (e.g. 76) or extraordinary (e.g. 214, 305) had been equally praiseworthy. Yet if the Aixoneis truly wanted to "make their Dionysia as fine as possible" (*AM* 66, 1941, pp. 218-219, no. 1, lines 11-12), they were well aware of the necessity to look for this to the sector of deme society represented by the likes of Auteas and Philoxenides.

In the deme of Halai Aixonides, just before the middle of the fourth century, we can gain an unusually clear view of this class of demesman, not only from a clutch of three deme decrees[73] but also, and especially, from IG II²2820. This records a dedication to Aphrodite by twenty-four elected demesmen who have been concerned with and crowned for the erection of a statue to the goddess. Two interconnected features of the group are striking: just as with our honorand category as a whole, 75

---

[71] The thirteen are 32, 50, 65, 82, 100, 101, 102, 210, 232, 301, 314, 349, and 350. A patronymic—and thus a prosopographical foothold—is known for 100, 101, 102, and 210; cf. above, n. 64.

[72] See 56, 62, 71, 72, 73, 74, 77, 81, 84, 85, 86, 87, 89, 90, 97, 98, 99, 100, 101, 102, 105, 112, 131, 133, 150, 151, 155, 163, 165, 170, 174, 178, 179, 180, 182, 183, 184, 185, 186, 187, 188, 189, 190, 192, 193, 195, 196, 198, 199, 203, 207, 210, 214, 219, 226, 232, 279, 280, 292, 293, (?)296, 300, 302, 305, 308, 309, 340, 344, 352, and 364. Although I have taken account of the evidence of grave monuments (on which see above, n. 65), this list is in general a conservative one; such additions as the other three *merarchai* of Athmonon (110, 116, 144) and the otherwise unattested Halaieis Aixonides from IG II²2820 (discussed below, in text)—181, 194, 201, 202, 204, 208—could arguably be made.

[73] IG II²1174 and 1175; *AD* 11, 1927-1928, pp. 40-41, no. 4. Only the last of these, as it happens, is honorific.

percent of these individuals—eighteen of the twenty-four—are otherwise known as active in the deme or outside it,[74] and as many as sixteen of the twenty-four may reasonably be identified as relatives of one another by either birth or marriage.[75] Here we see the men and families which, for all the real extent of democracy and egalitarianism in its formal organization, in fact dominated deme society. They were men and families which, besides taking their turn as demarch (for Halai Aixonides, see 180 with 16) and supplying the bulk of the proposers of decrees (see 184, 190, 192), were the natural choice of their fellow demesmen when the need arose for particular individuals to spend their time—and, as often as not, their money—on the community's behalf.[76] And their reward

[74] The eighteen are 180, 182, 183, 184, 185, 186, 187, 188, 189, 190, 193, 195, 196, 198, 199, 203, 207, and 210; the probability that the other six are men of the same type must therefore be high (cf. above, n. 72). It is instructive to compare these twenty-four Halaieis Aixonides with formally equivalent "samples" from two other demes, Athmonon and Upper Lamptrai.

SEG 24.197 gives the names of either thirty-five or more probably (see 147-148) thirty-six Athmoneis who made some kind of financial contribution to their deme in the early fourth century. Only a third of them at most can be given any sort of prosopographical background whatever (see 107, 108, 111, 123, 125, 127, 132, 137, 140, 141, 145, 147, and 148; the others are 106, 109, 113, 114, 115, 117, 118, 119, 121, 122, 124, 126, 128, 129, 130, 134, 135, 136, 138, 139, 142, 143, and 149); this would seem to suggest that, whatever this payment was, it had reached further down the socioeconomic scale than the honorand-liturgist class represented by IG II²2820.

IG II²2967 gives the names of at least thirty-six (Upper) [Lamp]treis who made a dedication to Apollo in the mid fourth century. Of the twenty-five whose names are preserved or restorable in full, only three are demonstrably men of substance (256, 260, 264) and at most only six others—thus again a total of about one-third—have *any* sort of prosopographical background (see 245, 249, 252 with 253, 255, 262, and 269; the remaining fifteen are 244, 246, 247, 251, 254, 257, 259, 263, 265, 267, 268, 270, 271, 272, and 274). A genuine cross section of deme society? See further, next note.

[75] The sixteen fall into six groupings: 182 and 183 (brothers); 184, 195, and 198 (father, son, and nephew); 208 and 201 (father and son: an element of ranking in the list would suggest this relationship rather than the reverse); 188 and 203 (brothers); 196 and 193 (?uncle and ?nephew: note again the ranking positions); 190, 189, 187, and 207 (father and three sons, of whom the first is son-in-law to 185). Again one may cite for comparison the "samples" from Athmonon and Upper Lamptrai (see preceding note). In the Athmonon group there are only three likely family groupings, embracing seven men in all: 121 and 122 (brothers); 140 and 141 (relationship indeterminable); 147, 148, and 107 (perhaps grandfather and two grandsons). In the Lamptrai group *no* interrelationships are apparent, but for all we can tell there may be some; the document's lack of patronymics (save to distinguish between the homonyms 252 and 253), without which many possible links are of course obscured, is perhaps a fact of some (political) significance in itself.

[76] As well as IG II²2820 itself (where the phrase [τὸ ἄγ]αλμα ποήσασθαι surely indicates that they *paid* for the work), see *AD* 11, 1927-1928, pp. 40-41, no. 4, which thanks and rewards not only the priest of Apollo Zoster but also the four αἱρεθέντες μετ' αὐτοῦ εἰς τὴν ἐπιμέλειαν τοῦ ἱεροῦ (see 180, 191, 197, 205).

came of course not only in explicit form but in a renewal of individual and family prestige.

As far as Halai Aixonides is concerned the prime examples of such families are those of Astyphilos (184) and Euthemon (190). But similar *domi nobiles*—Sallust's phrase is irresistible[77]—may also be detected, in varying measure, in other demes besides: in Eleusis and Rhamnous, as noted above;[78] in Aixone, for which Haussoullier drew attention to the comparative wealth of documentation within a short time-span;[79] and— in fleeting glimpses—in Acharnai,[80] Ikarion,[81] Kytheros,[82] Melite (possibly),[83] Paiania,[84] and Xypete.[85] Can it be doubted that they were ubiquitous?[86] The demes as communities could hardly have eliminated or neutralized such people and their influence even if they had wanted to, and to have wanted to would have been self-defeating. Far better to promote their goodwill and encourage their continuing contribution— and to say so, for all to see, in appropriate language.

LANGUAGE

The language of Glaukides' decree in honor of Auteas and Philoxenides (*AM* 66, 1941, pp. 218-219, no. 1) embodies two phrases, conveying the same idea, which repay attention. The Aixoneis recognize that the pair have performed their choregy "with a fine love of honor" (καλῶς [κα]‖[ὶ] φιλοτίμως),[87] and they resolve to crown them "in order that such a love of honor may also be shown by other *choregoi* who perform

[77] Sallust *Bellum Catilinae* 17.4 (echoing the singular form common in Cicero). For the use of the phrase in a deme context, cf. Davies, *Families*, p. 99.

[78] For Rhamnous, see also 323, 324, and 326.

[79] Haussoullier, *Vie*, pp. 60-62, pointing to our nos. 71, 73, 81, 85, 86, 87, 95, 96, 100, 101, and 102—to which one could add 72, 74, 75, 77, 78, 80, 84, 89, and 93. Note that the only known connection with a demarch (contrary to the thrust of Haussoullier's argument; cf. Chap. 4, n. 153) is through 100, surely the son of 6.

[80] See 55 and 63; 60 and 61.

[81] See 221, 227, and 228.

[82] See 236 and 242; 238, 239, 240, and 241.

[83] See 34, 286, and 287.

[84] See 299.

[85] See 353 and 358; 356 and 359.

[86] Other examples, whether from these same demes or others, will come to light with new documents and persons, and may also be revealed (by such new data) within our current prosopographical stock, from which I have picked out here only the more obvious cases. Arguably, for instance, Antiphilos (18) and his son Euboulides (19) represent a leading family of fourth-century Halimous, though the fact that both were demarchs would not prove this, and Euboulides' political methods both inside and outside the deme smack of the opportunist *novus homo*.

[87] See Dover, *Morality*, pp. 72-73 on καλός and καλῶς as "a reinforcement to other words."

the choregy in future" (ὅπως ἂν | [φ]ιλοτιμῶνται καὶ οἱ ἄλλοι χορη-
γοὶ οἱ μέλλοντες | [χ]ορηγεῖν).⁸⁸

I have attempted elsewhere to trace the history and significance of the
concept of *philotimia*—literally "love of honor *(timē)"*—in classical and
early Hellenistic Athens.⁸⁹ In particular I have sought to demonstrate
that the clearest proof of that significance is the prominent role which
the word (and its cognates) came to play in honorific decrees of the fourth
and third centuries. This is most obvious in the decrees of the city itself
but it is exemplified also in those of other, lesser bodies, the demes
amongst them.

All such bodies faced the same basic problem. Viewed as an abstraction,
the individual pursuit of honor might be declared to be a natural thing,
even a laudable one;⁹⁰ and yet—as Thucydides, for instance, noted on
several occasions⁹¹—it could, when taken to excess, be harmful and dis-
ruptive to the wider communities of which the individuals were members.
Hence the hazards which unbridled personal ambition might pose were
frequently aired at the levels of philosophy and political thought.⁹² In
the realm of practical politics, however, a practical solution came to be
formulated during the fourth century which in most respects very satisfactorily harmonized the needs of the community and of the individual
alike. This was the notion of *dēmosia philotimia* (Demosth. 18.257, cf.
Aeschin. 1.129)—zealous ambition with, as its principal and proper beneficiary, the community as a whole. Built upon a recognition that *philotimia* was a basic and even necessary feature not only of the individual
human character but also of the successful operation of a democratic
society, the idea found underlying our evidence is that the only practicable
course was to accept it (as both) and to exploit it; to harness it, and its
objectives and results, for the profit of the wider social group; and thus

---

⁸⁸ Conceivably these "other *chorēgoi*" referred to are merely the ones about to be involved
(μέλλοντες χορηγεῖν) in the 312/1 Dionysia itself, directly after the crowning; but we
shall see below that the normal purpose of such clauses (including ones framed by the
Aixoneis themselves: IG II²1198, lines 22-28; cf. IG II²1197, lines 15-18) was to promote
φιλοτιμία *for the foreseeable future*. I therefore strongly suspect that οἱ μέλλοντες
χορηγεῖν in Glaukides' decree means the same as οἱ ἀεὶ μέλλοντες χορηγεῖν in IG
II²1198, lines 23-24.

⁸⁹ See Whitehead, *"Philotimia."* It would be inappropriate here to do more than summarize the argument of this article, though naturally I extract and expand what concerns
the demes.

⁹⁰ Thus most obviously Xenophon: see *Hieron* 7.3-4 and other passages cited in Whitehead, *"Philotimia,"* p. 70, n. 6.

⁹¹ Thuc. 2.65.7, 3.82.8, 8.89.3; cf. Pindar fr. 210 Schroeder and Euripides *Phoinissai,*
lines 531-567.

⁹² See e.g. Plato *Republic* 548C-550B and 586C; Aristot. *EN* 1107b21-34 and 1125b1-
25; Isoc. 3.18 and 12.81. Note also Protagoras' treatise Περὶ φιλοτιμίας (Diog. Laert.
9.55).

to give it a central position within a known and accepted ideology of effort and reward. The effort came, of course, from the *philotimoi* themselves, who used it to lay claim to *charis* and thereby to build up "a political investment in goodwill."[93] The reward came from the community—sometimes the polis itself, sometimes a subgroup thereof—which geared itself not merely to accommodate but actively to welcome and promote *philotimia*. The only proviso was that the community itself (rather than any restricted, élite peer group within it) was acknowledged to be the only legitimate source of the honor and thus the only legitimate object of the energy and/or expense that the *philotimoi* sought to lay out.

From the individual standpoint this simple but effective set of ideas is attested most copiously in forensic arguments deployed throughout the whole corpus of fourth-century Attic oratory.[94] But the public, official approval and endorsement of *philotimia* which formed the context and the justification of such arguments emerge nowhere more plainly, as stated earlier, than in honorific decrees. Apparently in the late fifth century,[95] honorific decrees of the city began to include in their stereotyped citations of the services or achievements of the honorand(s) a number of general attributes—notably *andragathia*[96] but also *aretē, dikaiosynē, eusebeia*, and others—which in the fourth century (and beyond) came to represent, in effect, a canon of cardinal civic virtues, publicly recognized and rewarded *sub specie aeternitatis* as behavior which called for praise and recompense. Around the middle of the fourth century, it would seem, *philotimia* joined this canon,[97] and remained integral to it thereafter, not only throughout the rest of the classical period but for as long afterwards as such decrees were enacted. We possess too few deme decrees from before the middle of the fourth century to reveal how far if at all the demes were already by then copying this general development in epigraphic phraseology.[98] As far as *philotimia* is concerned, however, the

[93] Davies, *Families*, p. xvii; see pp. xvii-xviii as a whole, and more fully now in *Wealth*, pp. 92ff.

[94] See e.g. Isoc. 18.61; Lysias 16.18-20, 19.56, 21.22, 26.3; Isaeus 7.35-40; Demosth. 18.257, 19.223, 20.5 and passim, 21.159-166, 28.22, 42.24-25, 45.66, 50.64, 51.22; Aeschin. 1.129 and 196, 2.105, 3.19-20; Hyper. 1 (*Lyk.*).16; Lycurg. *Leok.* 15 and 140. For some counterarguments, see e.g. Lysias 14.21, 26.4; Demosth. 8.71, 21.169; Aeschin. 2.177, 3.45.

[95] See Whitehead, "*Philotimia*," pp. 61-62, esp. n. 22.

[96] On the connotation of *andragathia*, a much wider one than the common rendering "courage," see Whitehead, "*Philotimia*," pp. 61 and (esp.) 69-70.

[97] See Whitehead, "*Philotimia*," p. 62. I concentrate here on *philotimia* itself, but the canon as a whole is of some significance.

[98] To be included in this "general development" are not only single abstract nouns or pairs of nouns in the standard phrase with ἕνεκα (e.g. ἀνδραγαθίας ἕνεκα, or ἀρετῆς ἕνεκα καὶ δικαιοσύνης) but also the adverbial phrase καλῶς καὶ (e.g.) φιλοτίμως (cf.

earliest examples from the demes are closely contemporaneous with those from the city itself;[99] and the concept of *dēmosia philotimia* quite clearly had as important a role to play in the demes as anywhere else. Without resort either to decrees in which the key word or phrase is restored (however plausibly)[100] or to documents which are not demonstrably those of demes,[101] one may still amass thirty-two instances where demes describe those whom they are honoring as men who have displayed *philotimia*. All but two of these emanate from the century ca. 350 to ca. 250,[102] and the remaining thirty[103] display all the features, both linguistic and substantive, which can be shown to have been characteristic of the totality of such decrees (that is, from all bodies) within that period.[104]

As regards language, this was obviously the means by which the community's attitude to *philotimia*, present and future, was made plain; and this could be done in a number of possible ways.

1. Most simply and commonly the adverbial phrase "with a fine love of honor" (καλῶς καὶ φιλοτίμως) was appended—as we saw in the case of Auteas and Philoxenides in Aixone—to the verb(s) which related what the honorand had done.[105] Clearly this was little more than a cliché, but

---

above, p. 241) and indeed any adjectival, adverbial, or verbal cognate of the virtue in question. On this basis there are two relevant deme decrees, both dated "ante med.s.IV" in the Corpus: IG II²1178 (Ikarion), line 6, management of the Dionysia καλῶς καὶ δικαίως by a demarch; IG II²1173 (deme indeterminable), lines 10-11, [καλῶς καὶ φιλοτί]μως.

[99] Namely, decrees of Eleusis (IG II²1186), Halai Araphenides (*AE* 1925-1926, pp. 168-177; *AE* 1932, *Chronika*, pp. 30-32), and Myrrhinous (IG II²1182), all dating from the mid fourth century. IG II²1173 is apparently earlier still (see preceding note) and is thus at present our earliest example of a *philotimia* phrase in a decree of *any* body; but it is scarcely imaginable (cf. Whitehead, "*Philotimia*," p. 72, n. 25) that this terminology originated in the demes.

[100] E.g. SEG 22.127 (IG II²1219 + 1288), lines 19-23, at 23 (Eleusis, mid third century).

[101] E.g. IG II²1208; see Appendix 3, no. 140.

[102] One of the two is earlier than that period (IG II²1173; see above, n. 98), the other much later: IG II²949, lines 30ff. (Eleusis, 165/4) uses the phrase σπου]δῆς καὶ φιλοτιμίας οὐθὲν ἐλλείπων of the demarch **14**.

[103] IG II²1156 (lines 45ff.: Eleusis and Athmonon), 1176+, 1182, 1186, 1187, 1191, 1192, 1197, 1198, 1199, 1200, 1202, 1203, 1204, 1210, 1212, 1214; SEG 2.7, 21.520, 22.116 and 117, 24.154; *Hesp.* 3, 1934, pp. 44-46, no. 33; *Hesp.* 8, 1939, pp. 177-180; *AD* 11, 1927-1928, pp. 40-41, no. 4; *AD* 24, 1969, pp. 6-7; *AE* 1925-1926, pp. 168-177; *AE* 1932, *Chronika*, pp. 30-32; *AM* 66, 1941, pp. 218-219, no. 1 (see above, n. 54). Six of these come from Aixone, six from Eleusis, and the remaining eighteen from fourteen other demes; that is, a predictable concentration but a reasonable spread.

[104] See Whitehead, "*Philotimia*," pp. 62-68.

[105] As well as *AM* 66, 1941, pp. 218-219, no. 1, lines 2-3, see: IG II²1156, lines 45-46 (Eleusis) and 60 (Athmonon); IG II²1198 (Aixone), lines 6-7; IG II²1200 (Aixone), line 6; IG II²1203 (Athmonon), line 4; IG II²1210 (?Anagyrous), lines 1-2; IG II²1212 (deme indeterminable), lines 4-5; SEG 2.7 (Halimous), lines 3-4; SEG 21.520 (Teithras), lines 7-8; SEG 22.117 (Ikarion), line 2; SEG 24.154 (Rhamnous), lines 6-7; *AD* 24, 1969, pp. 6-

its very ubiquity testifies to the constant need to stipulate the "fine" *philotimia* that was called for. Alternatively or additionally, the verb of resolution to crown the honorand was accompanied by the phrase "on account of *philotimia*" (φιλοτιμίας ἕνεκα), mentioned either alone or in tandem with other attributes.[106] Between them these two types of simple formula—both echoing the usage of city decrees—supplied most demes with the means of expressing what they wanted to say, though some degree of local idiosyncracy and independence (especially in Eleusis) is also to be seen.[107]

2. More directly, a qualifying phrase or clause was frequently added to the mention of the honorand's *philotimia*, to make it quite clear that it was the demesmen as a whole who had reaped its benefits.[108] Here again the city's own usage offered the general model.

---

7 (Kephisia), lines 1-2; *AE* 1932, *Chronika*, pp. 30-32 (Halai Araphenides), lines 2-3 and 6-7. See also IG II²1199 (Aixone), line 3, δικαίως καὶ φιλοτίμως. For φιλοτίμως alone, see below, n. 107.

106 IG II²1187 (Eleusis), lines 14-15, ἀρετῆς ἕνεκα καὶ φιλο|τιμίας; IG II²1192 (Eleusis), lines 7-8, ἀρετῆς | [ἕνεκα καὶ φι]λοτιμίας; IG II²1198 (Aixone), lines 11-12, φιλοτιμίας | ἕνεκα καὶ ἐπιμελείας; IG II²1199 (Aixone), lines 11-12, δικαιοσύνης ἕνεκα κ|αὶ φιλοτιμίας, 21-22, φιλοτιμίας ἕν|εκα, and 27-28, εὐσεβείας καὶ φιλοτιμί|ας ἕνεκα; IG II²1200 (Aixone), lines 10-11, φιλ[οτ]||[ιμίας ἕνεκα - -]; IG II²1204 (Lower Lamptrai), lines 10-11, φιλοτιμίας ἕνε|κα; *AE* 1925-1926, pp. 168-177 (Halai Araphenides), lines 3-4, [δικαιοσ]ύνης ἕνεκα | [καὶ φιλοτι]μίας; *AE* 1932, *Chronika*, pp. 30-32 (Halai Araphenides), lines 17-19, δικαι|οσύνης ἕνεκα καὶ φι[λ]οτιμ|ίας.

107 See IG II²1156 (Athmonon), line 56, πάντα ποιοῦντας φιλοτίμως, of ephebes; IG II²1176+ (Peiraieus), line 33, φιλοτιμεῖται; IG II²1186 (Eleusis), lines 7-8, ἐσπούδασε [ν κ]||αὶ ἐφιλοτιμήθη; IG II²1187 (Eleusis), line 2, φιλοτιμεῖται; IG II²1191 (Eleusis), lines 14-15, φιλοτίμ[ω]ς τὰ ἐν τ[αῖς ἀρχα]ῖς ἔπραξεν; IG II²1202 (Aixone), line 4, ἄνδρες ἀγαθοὶ καὶ φιλότιμοι; IG II²1204 (Lower Lamptrai), lines 4-5, φιλότιμός ἐστι|ν εἰ[ς] τὰς θυσίας κτλ.; *Hesp.* 3, 1934, pp. 44-46, no. 33 (Peiraieus), line 12, κοινῆι τε φιλοτιμ[- - ; *Hesp.* 8, 1939, pp. 177-180 (Eleusis), line 11, πεφιλοτίμηται; *AD* 11, 1927-1928, pp. 40-41, no. 4 (Halai Aixonides), line 3, [λί]αν φιλοτίμ[ω]ς; *AD* 24, 1969, pp. 6-7 (Kephisia), line 8, καὶ τἆλλα φι[λ]ότιμός ἐστι (restoration by J. and L. Robert, *Bull. Epig.* 1971, no. 286).

108 IG II²1176+ (Peiraieus), lines 33-34, φιλοτιμεῖται πρὸς τοὺς δημότας καὶ νῦν καὶ ἐν τῶι | ἔμπροσθε χρόνωι; IG II²1187 (Eleusis), lines 2-3, φιλοτιμεῖται π|ερὶ τὸν δῆμον τὸν Ἐλευσινίων, and 14-16, ἀρετῆς ἕνεκα καὶ φιλο|τιμίας τῆς εἰς τὸν δῆμον τὸν Ἐλ|ευσινίων; IG II²1192 (Eleusis), lines 7-9, ἀρετῆς | [ἕνεκα καὶ φι]λοτιμίας τῆς εἰς τ|[ὸν δῆμον τὸν Ἐλ]ευσινίων; IG II²1198 (Aixone), lines 11-13, φιλοτιμίας | ἕνεκα καὶ ἐπιμελείας τ|ῆς εἰς τοὺς δημότας; IG II²1199 (Aixone), lines 11-13, δικαιοσύνης ἕνεκα κ|αὶ φιλοτιμίας τῆς εἰς τοὺς δημότα|ς; IG II²1202 (Aixone), lines 4-5, ἄνδρες ἀγαθοὶ καὶ φιλότιμοι περὶ τὸν δῆμο|ν τὸν Αἰξωνέων; *Hesp.* 8, 1939, pp. 177-180 (Eleusis), line 11, εἰς τοὺς δημότας πεφιλοτίμηται; *AD* 24, 1969, pp. 6-7 (Kephisia), lines 8-9, φι[λ]ότιμός ἐστι πρὸς] | τὸν δῆμον τὸν Κ[ηφισι]έων (first restoration by J. and L. Robert, *Bull. Epig.* 1971, no. 286); *AE* 1925-1926, pp. 168-177 (Halai Araphenides), lines 3-5, [δικαιοσ]ύνης ἕνεκα | [καὶ φιλοτι]μίας τῆς ⟨ε⟩ἰς | [τὸν δῆμον τ]ῶν Ἁλλιέων; *AE* 1932, *Chronika*, pp. 30-32 (Halai Araphenides), lines 17-20, δικαι|οσύνης

3. Most directly of all, deme decrees provide six instances of what I have termed a manifesto-clause; that is, a clause at or near the end of the resolution which expressed the fact that the honors voted were to represent not merely the community's approval of the particular manifestation of *philotimia* in question in the decree itself but its desire for more of it, from others, in future. We have already seen the example of such a clause—yet again, a feature borrowed from the city's own decrees—in the Aixonian decree for Auteas and Philoxenides, and another very like it occurs, partially restored, in a decree of Melite: "in order that others too may display *philotimia* towards the demesmen."[109] And a further degree, still, of explicitness is embodied in the other four cases (two from Aixone again, and one each from Myrrhinous and Peiraieus), with the unambiguous and reassuring policy declaration that *philotimia* from the individual will bring appropriate rewards from the deme.[110]

By the use of this kind of language, then, a deme let it be plainly known that the pursuit of honor in a community context would be certain to be a successful pursuit, and that examples of this in action should serve as a spur to others. The demes (like the city itself) were deliberately fostering not only a positive spirit of emulation amongst the *philotimoi* but also the idea that *philotimia* was tantamount to a duty incumbent upon those who possessed the means to fulfil it. Quite apart from these decrees, such an idea infuses, for example, the courtroom argument of the somewhat ingenuous young man Mantitheos in Lysias 16.14. Upon discovering, he says, that some of his honest fellow demesmen who were about to set off with him as hoplites (to the relief of Haliartos in 395) had no provisions, he not only declared that "the haves" (τοὺς ἔχοντας) had a duty to provide for those who found themselves in need, but then proceeded to practice what he preached by personally giving thirty drach-

---

ἕνεκα καὶ φι[λ]οτιμ|ίας τῆς περὶ τὸν δῆμον τὸν | ʽΑλαιέων. Much the same idea is conveyed by other means in SEG 21.520 (Teithras), lines 7-12, and SEG 24.154 (Rhamnous), lines 6-7. Note also IG II²1186 (Eleusis), lines 7-10, ἐσπούδασε[ν κ]|αὶ ἐφιλοτιμήθη πρὸς τοὺς θεοὺς κ[αὶ τ]|ὸν δῆμον τὸν ᾽Αθηναίων καὶ ᾽Ελευσιν[ίω]|[ν; for φιλοτιμία περὶ τοὺς θεούς cf. IG II²1199, Aixone, lines 27-28.

[109] Aixone: see above, n. 54. Melite: SEG 22.116, lines 26-27, [ὅπως ἂν καὶ οἱ ἄλλοι] φιλοτιμῶνται πρ|[ὸς τοὺς δημότας].

[110] IG II²1182 (Myrrhinous), lines 11-16, ὅπως ἂν καὶ ο[ἱ] ἄλλο|[ι π]άντες φιλοτι-[μ]ῶ[ν]ται εἰ|[ς] τοὺς δημότας εἰδό[τες] ὅτ[ι] χάριτας [ἀ]πολ[ή]ψον[ται πα]|[ρ]ὰ τῶν δημοτῶν ἀξίας [τῶν ε]|[ὐ]εργετημ[ά]των; IG II²1197 (Aixone), lines 15-18, ἵνα καὶ οἱ | ἄλλοι φιλοτιμῶνται εἰδότες | ὅτι χάριτας ἀπολήψονται παρὰ τῶν δημοτῶν; IG II²1198 (Aixone), lines 22-28, ὅπω|ς ἂν εἰδῶσιν οἱ ἀεὶ μέλλ|οντες χορηγεῖν Αἰξωνε|ῦσι ὅτι τιμήσει αὐτοὺς | ὁ δῆμος ὁ Αἰξωνέων τοὺς | εἰς ἑαυτοὺς φιλοτι-μου|[μ]ένους; IG II²1214 (Peiraieus), lines 33-36, ὅπως ἂν εἰδῶσι πά|ντες ὅτι ἐπίστανται Πειραιεῖς χάριτα|ς ἀξίας ἀποδιδόναι τοῖς φιλοτιμουμέν|οις εἰς αὐτούς.

mas each to two men who would bear witness to that fact; and he did this, he insists, not to represent himself as a rich man patronizing the poor but in order to set an example to the others of his type.[111]

The honorific decrees too furnish no lack of instances where *philotimia* had taken the natural form of financial generosity, direct or indirect. Liturgists, not surprisingly, form the largest single group,[112] but a wide range of other benefactions is also attested. To cite just four prime examples:

1. The general Derkylos of Hagnous (**179**) earned the gratitude of the Eleusinians in 319/8 by his generous provision of military training for the youth of the deme (in which he certainly owned property and may well have been actually resident) during the suspension of the *ephēbeia* under the pro-Macedonian oligarchy.[113]

2. At around the same time the Eleusinians (and other Athenians garrisoned amongst them) also thanked another non-demesman, Xenokles of Sphettos (**340**), whose construction, at his own expense, of a stone bridge across the Kephisos during his tenure of the office of superintendent of the Mysteries was a valuable amenity for locals as well as visitors.[114]

3. An equally celebrated figure, Neoptolemos Antikleous (**292**), was honored by his own deme, Melite, in ca. 330 for benefactions—surely financial—to the deme's cult of Artemis Aristoboule.[115]

---

[111] Lysias 16.14: συλλεγέντων τοίνυν τῶν δημοτῶν πρὸ τῆς ἐξόδου, εἰδὼς αὐτῶν ἐνίους πολίτας μὲν χρηστοὺς ὄντας καὶ προθύμους, ἐφοδίων δὲ ἀποροῦντας, εἶπον ὅτι χρὴ τοὺς ἔχοντας παρέχειν τὰ ἐπιτήδεια τοῖς ἀπόρως διακειμένοις. καὶ οὐ μόνον τοῦτο συνεβούλευον τοῖς ἄλλοις, ἀλλὰ καὶ αὐτὸς ἔδωκα δυοῖν ἀνδροῖν τριάκοντα δραχμὰς ἑκατέρῳ, οὐχ ὡς πολλὰ κεκτημένος, ἀλλ᾽ ἵνα παράδειγμα τοῦτο τοῖς ἄλλοις γένηται. καί μοι ἀνάβητε. (On ἐφόδια see W. K. Pritchett, *The Greek State at War*, part I, Berkeley, 1974, pp. 33-34, esp. 33, n. 16.) Mantitheos does not explicitly call this an act of *philotimia*, but he does go on to describe himself as a *philotimos* in 16.18-20.

[112] See IG II²1186 (Eleusis), lines 7-14 (voluntary dithyrambic liturgies by a non-citizen); IG II²1198 (Aixone), lines 2-13 (*chorēgia*); IG II²1200 (Aixone), lines 3-7 (*chorēgia*); AE 1932, *Chronika*, pp. 30-32 (Halai Araphenides), lines 2-7 ("all the liturgies in the deme"); AM 66, 1941, pp. 218-219, no. 1 (Aixone), lines 1ff. (*chorēgia*). The pair of honorands in IG II²1202 (Aixone) *may* also be *chorēgoi*—see Chap. 7, pp. 218-219; and the six *merarchai* of Athmonon (IG II²1203) might be described as liturgists in the broad sense, see Chap. 5, pp. 147-148.

[113] IG II²1187; cf. Chap. 3, n. 40. For the date, the interpretation of ὅπως ἂν οἱ παῖδες παιδεύωνται, and all other matters, see F. W. Mitchel, *Hesp.* 33, 1964, pp. 337-351, esp. 341-348.

[114] IG II²1191, lines 15-23. The bridge was commemorated in an epigram (*Anth. Palat.* 9.147).

[115] SEG 22.116, esp. lines 8-13—which break off before telling us *exactly* what he did. For Artemis Aristoboule, see Chap. 3, n. 54.

4. In the only surviving decree from this deme, "Phro——[232] seems to have deserved well of the demesmen of Kephisia by looking out for their sacred chores, making his private estate available, repairing their palaistra and its dressing room, fencing off the fountain house to control entrance to it, and in various other ways."[116]

All these four men are commended for their *philotimia*; and since three of them (all but Phro——) are known to have been figures of some celebrity, one may perhaps legitimately detect the implication, brought out in the manifesto-clause in the decree for Neoptolemos, that if such individuals as these could exert themselves on behalf of their deme (actual or "adoptive") they were setting an obvious example, *a fortiori*, for lesser men. Neoptolemos, we know, had a city-wide reputation as the recipient of honors for his personal generosity in the superintendence of numerous public works.[117] A man like him was in any case invaluable to his fellow demesmen as a source of liason with the whole network of other "very rich"[118] and/or politically prominent citizens—indeed, one might well say, with the Athenian governing class.[119] If in addition to that he saw fit to act as benefactor to his deme as a whole, there was little justification for those with fewer extra-deme commitments not to do likewise. And we have no reason to suppose that any such justification was sought by, for instance, the four men of Halai Aixonides (**180, 191, 197, 205**) whose *philotimia* in charge of the *hieron* of Apollo Zoster was only exceeded by that of their fellow demesman the priest whom they had been elected to assist;[120] nor by Theaios (**306**), whose record of *philotimia* towards

---

[116] *AD* 24, 1969, pp. 6-7 (second half of the fourth century); quotation from E. Vanderpool, ibid., p. 6. "This is the first instance of a palaistra in an Attic deme outside the immediate environs of the city" (Vanderpool, ibid., p. 7). We cannot, as Vanderpool rightly implies, assume that Phro—— had actually *provided*, in the first place, either the palaistra or its *apodytērion*, in the way that the wealthy Leukios of Sounion (**338**) presented an *agora* to his fellow demesmen in the same period (IG II²1180).

[117] See Demosth. 18.114, πολλῶν ἔργων ἐπιστάτης ὤν, ἐφ᾽ οἷς ἐπέδωκε τετίμηται. For an instance of this, see [Plut.] *Vit. X Or.* 843F; in general, Davies, *Families*, pp. 399-400.

[118] Demosth. 21.215 describes Neoptolemos and others as σφόδρα πλούσιοι.

[119] Osborne, *Demos*, pp. 88-92 has some perceptive observations on this. I doubt, however, his (admittedly tentative) suggestion that the *trittyes* played any significant part in this informal "mediation of power" (p. 90). He supposes "that Athenians felt a closer bond with other members of the same trittys than they did with fellow tribesmen as a whole"; yet whereas there is ample evidence for bonds between men of the same tribe (e.g. Aristoph. *Birds*, line 368; Andoc. 1.150; [Lysias] 20.2; Lysias 21.6; Demosth. 21.81 and 126, 23.206, 29.33), there is no equivalent for the *trittyes*.

[120] *AD* 11, 1927-1928, pp. 40-41, no. 4, lines 1-9, on the priest (**200**) who [λί]αν φιλοτίμ-[ω]ς [ἐπ]ε|σκεύακεν τὸ ἱερὸν κτλ.; lines 9ff. on the four αἱρεθέντες μετ᾽ αὐτοῦ εἰς τὴν ἐπιμέ|λειαν τοῦ ἱεροῦ (**180, 191, 197, 205**).

his fellow Peiraieis in the past was cited in the decree honoring him for his efforts in connection with the leasing of the deme's theater.[121] Furthermore, the demes welcomed *philotimia* not only and exclusively from their own members but from anyone resident in the deme or connected with it (by, most obviously, the ownership of landed property there). Derkylos of Hagnous and Xenokles of Sphettos were both benefactors of Eleusis, as we have seen,[122] and although the great majority of the honorands in the *philotimia* decrees were being thanked and rewarded by their own demes, a noteworthy minority were non-demesmen,[123] even non-citizens.[124]

Yet the ideology of *philotimia* would hardly have played the central role that it did in deme society—indeed in polis society—if its sole objective had been to harness the competitive instincts of those in whom they were felt to be natural, or to tap the financial resources of those who could easily command them. Such an objective indubitably represented one, vital aspect of the idea of *dēmosia philotimia*, the aspect which was concerned with shaping and exploiting to collective advantage the energy and outlay of individuals who sought honor for much the same reasons (if not always in the same spheres) as their ancestors had done. In the view of Xenophon, individuals with a passion for honor and praise were real *men* (ἄνδρες), not merely human beings (ἄν-

---

[121] IG II²1176+, lines 32ff. In "*Philotimia*," p. 64, I chose Theaios as an example of *philotimia* taking the direct form of the expenditure of money (as it often did). In fact, however, he πεπόηκεν τριακοσίαις δρα|χμαῖς πλέον εὑρεῖν τὸ θέατρον (lines 34-35), i.e., he produced four lessees for the theater—two of them fellow demesmen (302, 305), with two others (279, 308)—who between them put up 3,300 drachmas (lines 29-31); evidently the deme had only been expecting 3,000.

[122] I take Phro—— (see above, p. 248) to be a Kephisieus, but only because there is no positive indication that he was not.

[123] As well as Derkylos (IG II²1187) and Xenokles (IG II²1191), see IG II²1192 (a Φ]υλάσιος in Eleusis), IG II²1204 (an Acharnian in Coastal Lamptrai), IG II²1212 (a Π[αιονίδης—see 301—in a deme which, though indeterminable, cannot from the provenance of the stone be Paionidai), and IG II²1214 (a Cholleides in Peiraieus). It is perhaps natural that a deme like Eleusis—if indeed there were any quite like it—should have especially attracted non-demesmen benefactors (cf. further, next note), and for other reasons the same could be said of a "garrison deme" like Rhamnous which from the late fourth century onwards would regularly find itself with a non-demesman (as the general 362 in SEG 24.154 probably was) in charge of its guard-post. On the garrison demes, see Appendix 6.

[124] See IG II²1186 (Eleusis), decree I (i.e., lines 1-35), honoring the Theban Damasias Dionysiou, οἰ[κήσ]ας Ἐλευσῖνι, for (voluntary) contributions to the deme's Dionysia and *epidoseis* to Demeter and Kore. It is likely enough that other Theban honorands in Eleusis at around the same time (IG II²1185; IG II²1186, decree II) were also praised for their *philotimia*.

θρωποι);[125] and it was that sort of attitude which the community, be it a deme or whatever, wished to hold up as an example to others. But to whom, exactly? In some measure, no doubt, to anyone who needed to be convinced or reminded that under the democracy his innate inclination to seek prominence and acclaim ought properly to express itself in ways beneficial to and sanctioned by the community at large. Democratic Athens, however, could not rely on Xenophon's ἄνδρες alone, either at city level or in the demes; ἄνθρωποι too were needed, to serve the community in capacities less striking, for the most part, but no less valuable overall.

And with this, patently much larger group in view, the doctrine of *dēmosia philotimia* thus changed its effect from that of a rein to that of a spur, in attacking apathy and keeping the cumbersome wheels of the democratic administration in motion. In short, *philotimia* was held to be the appropriate civic virtue not only of private individuals but also of those holding office—small as well as great, and sortitive as well as elective. This is true of the city and its decrees,[126] and it is equally true of the demes, where we find *philotimia* ascribed to honorands who are demarchs,[127] *bouleutai*,[128] financial officials,[129] a herald,[130] *syndikoi*,[131] *hieropoioi*,[132] and other cult officials.[133] No matter that the honor won by, say, the members of a board of *syndikoi* was likely to be more modest than that owed to a lavish financial benefactor.[134] In its way it was no less deserved, as the reward for the satisfactory discharging of office in the community's service; and those unable to serve their community simply by the ancient equivalent of nonchalantly writing out a check will

---

[125] Xen. *Hieron* 7.3: οἷς δ᾽ ἂν ἐμφύῃ τιμῆς τε καὶ ἐπαίνου ἔρως, οὗτοί εἰσιν ἤδη οἱ πλεῖστον μὲν τῶν βοσκημάτων διαφέροντες, ἄνδρες δὲ καὶ οὐκέτι ἄνθρωποι μόνον νομιζόμενοι.

[126] For examples, see Whitehead, "*Philotimia*," p. 73, n. 32.

[127] SEG 22.117 (Ikarion); *Hesp.* 8,. 1939, pp. 177-180 (Eleusis), where the honorand (10) is a member of a well-known family; see also above, n. 102, for IG II²949. In SEG 2.7 (Halimous) the honorand Charisandros (215) has acted ὑπὲρ τοῦ δημάρχου Ἰσχυρίου; see, on this, Chap. 5, n. 160.

[128] SEG 21.520 (Teithras), with reference to duties imposed upon them *in the deme*; see lines 7-12, quoted in Chap. 2, n. 97.

[129] Pheidippos (296) in IG II²1182 (Myrrhinous)—if indeed he is the honorand there; and the quasi-liturgist *merarchai* of Athmonon (IG II²1203).

[130] IG II²1199 (Aixone), lines 17-22.

[131] IG II²1197 (Aixone).

[132] IG II²1199 (Aixone), lines 1-16.

[133] IG II²1199 (Aixone), lines 17-22 (*sōphronistai*) and 22-30 (priest, priestess, and cult archon). Their *philotimia* is glossed as περὶ τοὺς θεούς; compare, for this, IG II²1186 (Eleusis), line 8.

[134] Both in the general sense of the esteem of their fellows and also in the actual "gifts" (δωρεαί: IG II²1197, lines 12-13) voted in the decrees.

have taken particular note of any manifesto-clause—such as the one, indeed, in the decree for the *syndikoi* of Aixone (IG II²1197)—which made it clear that those who could justly boast of their *philotimia* were not only the rich and influential but anyone at all who was willing to devote time and effort to his deme and his fellow demesmen.

✳

The extent to which I have emphasized *philotimia* as a central concept in deme society, just as in Athenian society at large, may possibly appear excessive; yet it is from the demes themselves that the emphasis really comes, for reasons which the foregoing pages have attempted to explain. And it is surely needless to add that what is important is, precisely, the concept, which was even more pervasive than the words which describe it.[135] In an ideal world, all members of the community[136] would have served it eagerly and unstintingly, albeit in ways and to degrees determined by their individual circumstances. In the actual world—that, at least, of the fourth century and beyond—there was a danger that the reality would be all too sadly different: the Few either abusing property-power and hereditary influence for their own ends or else disdaining local involvement in favor of more potent satisfactions to be found elsewhere; the Many thus left chronically disenchanted and apathetic. So how could the ideal be approached, even imperfectly? In part, naturally, by the institutional framework. Assigning liturgies and other expenses to those fit to bear them reminded the wealthy of their local obligations;[137] appointing demarchs (and others) by lot extended the burdens—and the pleasures—of administration to those who might not otherwise have experienced them. Institutions alone could go only a certain way, however, unless they were animated by a known and accepted value-system rooted in both individual and social psychology.

The concept of *dēmosia philotimia* became the fundament of that system, its effectiveness lying in its threefold impact. As far as their demes were concerned, men like Neoptolemos of Melite were *philotimoi* if amidst all their other honorific enterprises elsewhere they did not forget

---

[135] That is, the words could have been (but were not) used to describe the behavior of, for example, the honorands in SEG 22.120 (Rhamnous) and SEG 24.153 (Teithras).

[136] I mean the community of the deme; but much of what follows is applicable, *mutatis mutandis*, to the community at large, the polis.

[137] Witness for instance Isaeus 3.80 (quoted above, n. 20): in a deme which unfortunately cannot be determined, the liturgical duties of a rich man included that of providing a feast for his fellow demesmen's wives during the Thesmophoria; see on this Davies, *Families*, pp. xxiii-xxiv. On deme *hestiasis* in general, note Theophr. *Char.* 10 (μικρολογίας).11: the Skinflint (*mikrologos*) would cut up the meat too small!

that charity (and indeed *charis*) began at home. Men like Philoxenos of Halai Araphenides (**214**), active and generous within the deme but not, as far as is known, outside it, were *philotimoi* if more of the same activity and generosity were forthcoming from them and others of their ilk. And men like Nearchos of Aixone (**94**) were *philotimoi* if, when picked out by the lot—possibly with others better known than themselves—for official duties,[138] they discharged them competently and enthusiastically. To the extent that, and for as long as, demesmen of all three types knew what was expected of them and acted accordingly, the viability of the deme unit and the cohesion of deme society was assured.

[138] Nearchos' colleagues are **71**, **72**, and **99**.

III

※

DEME AND POLIS

※

CHAPTER 9

LOCAL GOVERNMENT AND CENTRAL GOVERNMENT

A. An Interlocking System

In a sovereign (nonfederal) nation-state, a model of the relationship between local government and central government can often be a fairly simple one. Irrespective of whether, historically speaking, administrative powers have been concentrated centripetally or devolved centrifugally, some of the functions of government (notionally the major ones) are exercised by all-embracing organs and agencies of the state as a whole, while others (notionally the minor ones) fall to subdivisions of the state— usually though not necessarily territorial subdivisions—with their own deliberative bodies and executive officials. Every citizen of the state is also a member of a local subdivision and is subject to the decrees and decisions of both.[1] The powers of local government itself extend as far as, but no further than, central government sees fit; for while the need for local autonomy is recognized and respected, central government, both as general policy and in particular circumstances, not only legislates for the community *tout court* but also reserves the right to instruct the local authorities to do certain things and to prohibit them from doing others.

The *partial* applicability of such a model to post-Kleisthenic Athens is plain enough. That the enactments of a deme assembly were binding upon the members of that deme is, and was, so obvious that it hardly ever needed stating.[2] No Athenian (or metic) can have failed to come

---

[1] I assume simple bipartition for simplicity's sake, but obviously in practice there may be more than one tier of "local government (e.g. in classical Athens the trittyes and tribes as well as the demes); the principle remains the same, however.

[2] A rare exception occurs in SEG 28.103 (Eleusis): lines 43-47 ordain that the demarch shall preserve the decree on stone ὅπως ἂν τὰ ἐψ|ηφισμένα ὑπὸ τῶν δημοτῶν κύρια ἔι εἰς τὸν ἀεὶ χρόνον | κ[αὶ μ]ὴ καταλύηται; and even here the emphasis is perhaps less upon the binding nature of the decisions than upon their intended permanence.

under the jurisdiction of at least one deme assembly;[3] and few of them, surely, would have agreed with the *obiter dictum* of the nonagenarian Isocrates that the power (*dynamis*) of the demes was negligible.[4] However, if not negligible, the power of the demes was indubitably circumscribed and restricted. Over the heads of the demes and their doings—and this is conceivably what Isocrates had in mind—stood the laws and decrees of Mr. Demos of the Pnyx (Δῆμος Πυκνίτης: Aristoph. *Knights*, line 42), the sovereign democracy itself, which not only determined how the Athenians should act as individuals but also delimited the areas within which the demes could make their own, lesser rules and regulations. As I have emphasized in Chapter 2B and reiterated throughout this book, our evidence for the functioning of the Kleisthenic demes must be divided, if we are to understand and use it legitimately, into two fundamentally different categories. One represents the enactments of the demes themselves, concerned with matters and procedures in respect of which the central government saw no need to insist upon unnatural uniformity across the diversity of the deme network as a whole. The other reveals, albeit imperfectly, those areas of deme activity where the polis did have a direct interest in (and justification for) securing such uniformity, by either prescriptive or proscriptive means, and legislated accordingly. And the basic relationship between these two sources of authority was enshrined, as we have seen, in "Solonic" law. Like the members of other properly constituted organizations within the state, the bodies of demes-

[3] For the metics in demes, see Chap. 3D. As regards citizens, they have to be described as subject to "at least one" deme assembly on account of the indeterminable proportion of them who moved away from their ancestral demes to others. In theory the deme assembly of, say, Kephale was sovereign over not only those Kephaleis actually resident in Kephale but also those who lived elsewhere (and who were doubtless less likely to attend and vote in the assemblies of their fellow Kephaleis); and for some purposes the ancestral link evidently remained a real and important one—above all, of course, for deme registration itself. But in practice deme assemblies sometimes concerned themselves not so much with the totality of their membership in this legalistic sense but with the realities of life and population in the deme as an actual community in a physical location (witness again IG I³ 254, the appointment of *chorēgoi* in fifth-century Ikarion from others besides the *dēmotai*); and from the individual's standpoint the power of (e.g.) the deme assembly of Peiraieus to demand an *enktētikon* tax (IG II² 1214, lines 26-28) from a member of another deme who owned property in Peiraieus was a fact of no less significance than were the decisions and policies of his own deme.

[4] Isoc. 12.179 (on the early Spartans' creation of their perioikic communities): διελόντας τὸ πλῆθος αὐτῶν ὡς οἷόν τ' ἦν εἰς ἐλαχίστους εἰς τόπους κατοικίσαι μικροὺς καὶ πολλούς, ὀνόμασι μὲν προσαγορευομένους ὡς πόλεις οἰκοῦντας, τὴν δὲ δύναμιν ἔχοντας ἐλάττω τῶν δήμων τῶν παρ' ἡμῖν (". . . groups who in name were spoken of as living in poleis, but who in reality had less power than the demes with us"); see Haussoullier, *Vie*, pp. 202-204. One wonders whether the events of 346/5 stand behind this comparison, peripheral though it is to Isocrates' main point here.

men could legally bind themselves to anything short of illegality (that is, contravention of the *dēmosia grammata*) itself.[5]

A good example of this, involving two *proscriptive* measures of central government in relation to local, is the control of crowning and other honorific activities on the part of the demes (and, by association, the tribes). In the third quarter of the fourth century, as is well known, the award of honors became a particularly contentious issue in the political life of the city, and evidently the reverberations of this were felt at lower levels also. Both the honors themselves and the means of bestowing them were regulated. A deme decree of Aixone dating from ca. 330 granted a board of *syndikoi* "as many honors as the laws allow."[6] A decree of the Eleusinians and other Athenians garrisoned in Eleusis, a decade later, speaks of what seems to have been a legal requirement to cite in the honorific decrees of demes—and surely of other bodies too—any benefactions of the honorand to the city.[7] And Aeschines alludes to a prohibition upon both tribes and demes announcing their award of crowns at the theater "in town."[8]

Are we entitled, then, to conclude that the domains of local and of central government were defined and separated with absolute clarity in classical Attica? Nobody who has read Part II of this book could be happy with any such conclusion. Of course it may to some extent be that what lacks clarity for *us* was plain and unambiguous enough at the time. With regard, for instance, to cult and religion, one is still left, after distinguishing in general terms the main areas of deme and city responsibility,[9] with a stubborn residue of activity which on current data cannot be decisively assigned to the one or the other. Perhaps more information will make this possible; that at least seems preferable to suggesting, as even a provisional solution, some species of *joint* responsibility which is

[5] The law is quoted and discussed in Chap. 1, pp. 13-14.

[6] IG II² 1197, lines 14-15: ὅσαι (*sc.* δωρεαί) κατὰ το|ὺς νόμους δέδονται.

[7] IG II² 1191, lines 7-10: ὁ [νό]μ[ος κ]ελεύε[ι] πϱ[οσγ]||[ϱ]άφειν ἐν [τῶι ψ]ηφίσ[ματι τὸν λ]||[α]μ[β]άνοντα δ[ω]ϱεὰν ὅ[τι] ε[ὐεϱγέ]||[τ]ηκεν τὴν πό[λι]ν. The phraseology here is a little odd, but the intention cannot have been to prevent demes from honoring those whose benefactions were purely local.

[8] Aeschin. 3.41-45. (Announcement could of course still be made in the demes' own theaters: references in Chap. 7, n. 273.) For a link between crownings by demes and by tribes, see *Hesp.* 9, 1940, pp. 104-111, no. 20, with the comments of O. Broneer, *Hesp.* 11, 1942, p. 272, n. 85: the tribal taxiarchs of 302/1, here honored, have already been crowned by *ad hoc* committees elected from their fellow demesmen (lines 15-17, καὶ ἐστ|εφάνωσαν αὐτοὺς οἱ ἐπὶ ταῦτα αἱ[ϱ]|εθέντες ἐκ τῶν δήμων), perhaps in accordance with a tribal decree to that effect. (Does ἐκ rather than ὑπό imply an event in the *tribal* assemblies?)

[9] See Chap. 7A.

very difficult to envisage in practical operation.[10] In other respects, however, present evidence is already quite sufficient to show that under the Athenian democratic system the workings of central and local government were intricately and deliberately interlocked with each other.

There could be no more graphic or more significant illustration of this than the principles and procedures devised for the control of membership of the citizen-body itself.[11] The status of a citizen of Great Britain or the United States in our own time depends upon criteria which are not merely nationally determined but also nationally administered; it does not stem, *a fortiori*, from being (say) a Mancunian or a New Yorker (though registration as such may, to be sure, be a prerequisite for the actual exercise of certain civic rights). Post-Kleisthenic Athens adopted the opposite policy. An Athenian citizen was an Athenian citizen because, both logically and chronologically prior to that, he was a demesman of Alopeke or Themakos or wherever it might be. In other words, central government entrusted to local government the protagonist's role in an administrative process so crucial to the fabric and well-being of the state that—to our modern eyes—for the state itself to have laid claim to it would have been entirely understandable.

The rationale (had it ever been consciously formulated) for devolving both this and other aspects of routine administration onto the demes is not to be sought primarily, one may suspect, within the realm of constitutional "theory";[12] rather, it was essentially a matter of practical convenience and collective common sense. The key factor was local knowledge. To us, the Athenian polis as a whole seems a small and administratively manageable body. Yet, in the absence of our modern methods of data collection, storage, and retrieval, the problem (described in Thuc. 8.66.3) of one individual's keeping track of his fellows would, without local involvement, have had its counterpart at the bureaucratic level also. Thus for certain tasks, recurrent or occasional, the demes were objectively the obvious and sensible bodies to call on, as the information needed was either in their hands already or else could most conveniently be assembled by them. Who better than a demarch to know those entitled to *theōrika*, to make *apographai* of the property of convicted debtors, to collect *eisphorai* (and assign *proeisphorai*), to facilitate the levying of naval manpower, to organize the collective contribution of his fellow demesmen to the religious life of the polis, and to insist, if need be, that

---

[10] See Chap. 6, n. 76 (Nemesis and Rhamnous), and Chap. 7, n. 34 (Apollo Zoster and Halai Aixonides).

[11] See Chap. 4B, sec. 1, for detailed justification of what follows.

[12] For such "theory" see below, sec. C. (I should also stress that I am not speaking of devolution as an actual historical process in this case.)

the dead were properly buried?[13] And what better organ than the deme assembly to determine its own membership, and thus in aggregate the membership of the polis as a whole? Under the developed constitution at any rate (and in some sense, as I have argued, from its Kleisthenic origins themselves), the cardinal necessity for each individual Athenian was to convince his fellow demesmen that he had the right to be enrolled amongst them. To produce satisfactory witness of such enrolment remained thereafter the most telling and reliable guarantee of his citizen status. Failure to do so put that status in serious jeopardy. Local knowledge—and local goodwill—was paramount.

It would have been astonishing, all the same, if central government had abnegated a role in so vital a matter as citizen registration to the extent of allowing the demes unadulterated power over it; and of course we know that this was not the case. Fundamental and indispensable though it was, the initial *diapsēphisis* of the deme assembly, as we have seen, was controlled (and if necessary overturned) by state authority in respect of both areas of potential error or abuse: the candidate's right of appeal to a jury-court was designed to ensure that nobody was unjustly excluded from his deme; the *dokimasia* by the city council made it less likely that anyone was improperly included. The *dokimasia* procedure is especially noteworthy, both for being a necessary, regular component of the whole registration process rather than something which arose only *ad hominem*, and also because rejection by the *boulē* of what the demesmen had decided led not only to the reversal of their decision but, in addition, to the imposition of a fine upon them.[14] We do not hear of any such (or similar) action being taken against demes in the event of any of their members' unsuccessfully defending a *graphē xenias*, but obviously the demes involved were obliged to acquiesce in the overruling of those particular individuals' accreditation as citizens.[15] And in relation to one, albeit specialized, category of enrolments—those of *dēmopoiētoi*,

[13] For all these duties, see Chap. 5A, sec. 2.

[14] ?Aristot. *Ath. Pol.* 42.2. I can find no basis for the assertion of MacDowell, *Law*, p. 69, that "the deme-members could appeal to a court against the fine." See rather Harrison, *Law* II, p. 206: "there is no evidence that there was ... any appeal from the decision of the boule to a dikastery, either for the excluded candidate or for the fined demesmen" (though he adds that "we should rather have expected that there would have been"; cf. ?Aristot. *Ath. Pol.* 45.2-3 and 55.2 for possible grounds, by analogy, for such an expectation).

[15] As well (quite possibly) as bearing the brunt of public ridicule if this happened too often. A nice example is Anaxandrides *Anchises* fr. 4, lines 3-4: πολλοὶ δὲ νῦν μέν εἰσιν οὐκ ἐλεύθεροι, εἰς αὔριον δὲ Σουνιεῖς ("today a slave, tomorrow a Sounian!"). Haussoullier, *Vie*, p. 197 with n. 3, oddly misunderstands this as an allusion to the "richesse" of the Sounieis. On deme corruptibility, see in general Chap. 10A.

whether individuals or groups—the powers of the demesmen were reduced to a mere formality, as they simply accepted men who had chosen
or been allotted to their deme as a corollary of a sovereign decree of the
ekklēsia.[16]

By these various means, then, the state reserved to itself ultimate power
over membership of the citizen-body; what the demes shared in was the
work of maintaining it. The demes were reckoned to know their own
people best, and be best able to put them forward as *prima facie* citizens,
but the risk of error, honest or dishonest, was too great nonetheless to
allow any deme's decision to bind the polis as a whole. Hence the need,
as regular procedure, for a multiplicity of safeguards—principally a scrutiny by the one executive organ of central government, the *boulē*, which
could be regarded as actually rather than merely notionally representative
of all one hundred and thirty-nine demes;[17] and hence also the justification for an extraordinary episode like the *diapsēphiseis* of 346/5.[18]

✳

As regards our ability to separate out the elements contributed to the
classical Athenian *politeia* by central and by local government, the example of the citizenship procedures can hardly be better described than
by the word used, several pages ago, to introduce it: the two were interlocking. But if, in the light of what was said in the opening paragraph
of this chapter about centrifugal and centripetal processes, we now turn
to consider the constitutional machinery of central government itself as
it related to the demes, and especially the appointment and responsibilities
of various city magistrates, the subject would seem to call for discussion
under two complementary headings: how the city impinged upon the
demes; and—more fundamental, as will be seen—what the demes contributed to the city.

B. From the Center to the Periphery

For the administration of their own internal affairs the demes enjoyed,
as we have seen, considerable local autonomy. Insofar as central government saw a need to control and standardize the demes' activities at
all, the preferred method was clearly that of regulating the demes' own
officials—above all the demarchs, with their dual role as agents both of

---

[16] See Chap. 4, p. 103.
[17] See below, sec. C.1, where the question of "representation" will be taken up.
[18] See Chap. 4B, sec. 1(b).

their own deme assemblies and of the state—rather than that of imposing centrally appointed magistrates.[19]

In terms of personnel, then, the impact of the center upon the periphery would appear to be represented by only one board of magistrates, the *dikastai kata dēmous*; and it was an impact which, while it lasted, was beneficial rather than adverse in its effects.

The *dikastai kata dēmous*, according to ?Aristot. *Ath. Pol.* 16.5, had originally been created (in unknown numbers) by Peisistratos, in order to obviate the necessity for time-wasting journeys by the country people into the *asty*.[20] While this explanation is not altogether implausible, "it is unlikely that the minor disputes which these magistrates will have been competent to settle will previously have been brought to Athens, and more probable that Pisistratus was substituting representatives of the central authority for whatever arbitration the disputants had been able to obtain locally—usually, no doubt, from the local nobility."[21] At all events, the revival of the institution in the mid fifth century (see below) obviously indicates that the appointment of these itinerant magistrates had lapsed at some time before then; and the fall of the tyranny itself in

[19] Osborne, *Demos*, pp. 77-83, claims three instances of "men appointed by a central mechanism [who] are responsible for local action" (ibid., p. 83), namely, the *dikastai kata dēmous*, the *euthynoi*, and the *diaitētai* (arbitrators); but in fact only the first of these (discussed below, in text) properly fulfils that definition—and, even so, only in the fifth century. Osborne's theory that deme officials were answerable to centrally appointed *euthynoi* is in my opinion misconceived (see Chap. 4, n. 158); I am certain that when we meet *euthynoi* in a deme context they are deme officials. As to the *diaitētai*, his contention is that "the demes must have been involved at some stage in the identification of the men of the requisite age" (ibid., p. 81) and that "it is possible that men with relevant local knowledge could be chosen if they were available." However, the age of the arbitrators, as ?Aristot. *Ath. Pol.* 53.4 clearly states, was δῆλον ἐκ τῶν ἀρχόντων καὶ τῶν ἐπωνύμων (that is, an automatic consequence of progression through the forty-two-year cycle of liability for military service; cf. Hansen, "*Archai*," p. 172). And the "local knowledge" idea, undeniably valid in other areas, appears to be baseless in this instance. The law in Demosth. 21.94 which allows a *choice* of arbitrator refers not to public but to private arbitration; in any event it is quite possibly spurious, as (certainly) is the deposition in 21.93 to the effect that Demosthenes *chose* Straton of Phaleron to arbitrate in his dispute with Meidias. Demosthenes' own words in 21.83 show that the hapless Straton was *allotted* to the case, and the fact that Straton belonged to a different tribe (Aiantis) from either Demosthenes (Pandionis) or Meidias (Erechtheis) adds evidence to probability that the arbitrators, like the Forty with whom they were linked, were quite deliberately assigned to tribes other than their own (cf. Rhodes, *Commentary* p. 594).

[20] ?Aristot. *Ath. Pol.* 16.5: τοὺς κατὰ δήμους κατεσκεύασε δικαστὰς . . . ὅπως μὴ καταβαίνοντες εἰς τὸ ἄστυ παραμελῶσι τῶν ἔργων. On their number see below, n. 24.

[21] Rhodes, *Commentary*, p. 216; cf. e.g. Hignett, *Constitution*, pp. 115, 218. That these Peisistratid dikasts were empowered to settle only "minor disputes" is an inference (but not an unreasonable one) from the competence of their fourth-century descendants (?Aristot. *Ath. Pol.* 53.2: see below, p. 263).

510 is generally seen as the likeliest occasion for this.[22] If so, there were no *dikastai kata dēmous* in existence when Kleisthenes came, only a few years later, to create the deme system. That system may, as I have very tentatively suggested in an earlier chapter, have called upon the *demarchs* to act in some way as local justices in their demes.[23] The hypothesis is too fragile to press hard; but *if* this is what was happening during the first half of the fifth century, it would obviously represent a considerable triumph for local over central government; for never before, and never again, were the demes' own officials given such scope in a judicial capacity, and the small change of Athenian justice not merely decentralized but actually devolved.

Be that as it may, in 453/2 the *dikastai kata dēmous* were revived.[24] This time the author of the *Ath. Pol.* offers neither any explanation for the measure[25] nor any details of either the appointment or the responsibilities of the thirty men. Their number suggests some connection with the Kleisthenic trittyes;[26] and it is commonly supposed that they were empowered to decide suits for sums up to ten drachmas, as was the case in the fourth century (see below).[27] Further possible inferences from what we know of fourth-century practice would be that they were appointed by lot (Demosth. 24.112, cf. ?Aristot. *Ath. Pol.* 53.1) and that they functioned not as a single group of thirty but in (?tribal) subdivisions.[28] The second of these inferences should indeed be classified as probable rather than merely possible, in view of the only thing that one can say for certain about the fifth-century *dikastai kata dēmous*: they lived up to their name by actually going out to the demes, in the manner of their Peisistratid predecessors, to do their work (?Aristot. *Ath. Pol.* 53.1: κατὰ

[22] E.g. Hignett, *Constitution*, p. 218; Rhodes, *Commentary*, pp. 215, 257, 331; S. Hornblower, *The Greek World 479-323 B.C.*, London and New York, 1983, p. 113.

[23] See Chap. 1, pp. 36-37.

[24] ?Aristot. *Ath. Pol.* 26.3: ἐπὶ Λυσικράτους ἄρχοντος οἱ τριάκοντα δικασταὶ κατέστησαν πάλιν οἱ καλούμενοι κατὰ δήμους. The definite article—"*the* thirty dikasts"—suggests, without fully justifying, the inference that Peisistratos' dikasts had also numbered thirty; cf. Rhodes, *Commentary*, pp. 215, 331.

[25] "It may have been an attempt to decentralize jurisdiction in order to relieve in some measure the pressure of business on the dikasteria and the magistrates, or it may have been a concession to the rural population, so that they could get their disputes settled on the spot and need no longer make the journey to Athens" (Hignett, *Constitution*, p. 219; similarly Rhodes, *Commentary*, p. 331). My theory about the demarchs would, if correct, obviously undermine the second of these suggestions at least.

[26] That is, one *assigned to* each trittys (cf. Rhodes, *Commentary*, p. 331), or one *appointed from* each trittys, or both.

[27] E.g. Hignett, *Constitution*, p. 219; Rhodes, *Commentary*, pp. 331, 589, 591. (MacDowell, *Law*, p. 206, eschews this and other speculation.)

[28] ?Aristot. *Ath. Pol.* 48.5 and 53.1-2; cf. Lysias 23.3. See further below.

δήμους περιόντες ἐδίκαζον). There, liaison with the demarchs may safely be assumed;[29] and ten panels of dikasts could perhaps have covered Attica to the extent of visiting each deme once a month.

But in (or soon after) 403/2 the system underwent a very radical reform. Describing the constitution of his own day, the author of the *Ath. Pol.* wrote as follows. "The Forty are also appointed by lot, four from each tribe, and (plaintiffs) bring other suits to them. Previously there were thirty of them, who used to try cases on a circuit through the demes, but after the oligarchy of the Thirty (Tyrants) they became forty. Up to the sum of ten drachmas they have the authority to settle cases themselves, but beyond that valuation they hand them over to the arbitrators."[30] The arbitrators, we learn, would attempt first to reconcile the disputants and would pronounce their own verdict only after failing to do so. If both parties accepted the verdict the issue was at an end. If, however, either party chose to appeal to the courts, the Forty were again involved, in that it was the four dikasts assigned to the defendant's tribe—a subgroup to which, in fact, it is likely that the plaintiff had originally applied— who brought the case before an appropriately sized jury.[31]

Quite clearly, then, the whole character of these fourth-century *dikastai kata dēmous* was different from that of their predecessors and namesakes in the sixth and fifth centuries.[32] The increase in their number is of interest

[29] Haussoullier, *Vie*, p. 126. (Note that Haussoullier's whole discussion of the *dikastai* was written without the benefit of the Aristotelian *Ath. Pol.*)

[30] ?Aristot. *Ath. Pol.* 53.1-2: κληροῦσι δὲ καὶ (τοὺς) τετταράκοντα, τέτταρας ἐκ τῆς φυλῆς ἑκάστης, πρὸς οὓς τὰς ἄλλας δίκας λαγχάνουσιν· οἳ πρότερον μὲν ἦσαν τριάκοντα καὶ κατὰ δήμους περιόντες ἐδίκαζον, μετὰ δὲ τὴν ἐπὶ τῶν τριάκοντα ὀλιγαρχίαν τετταράκοντα γεγόνασιν. (2) καὶ τὰ μὲν μέχρι δέκα δραχμῶν αὐτοτελεῖς εἰσι δ[ικ]άζειν, τὰ δ᾽ ὑπὲρ τοῦτο τὸ τίμημα τοῖς διαιτηταῖς παραδιδόασιν. These "other suits" are private suits other than those mentioned in 52.2-3, but the writer is somewhat simplifying the true picture, as Rhodes, *Commentary*, p. 587, explains; see also Harrison, *Law* II, pp. 19-21, and MacDowell, *Law*, pp. 206-207. For the ten-drachma limit, cf. *Ath. Pol.* 52.3 (the *apodektai*) and the currency law of 375/4 (*Hesp* 43, 1974, pp. 157-188, lines 23-26: various boards of magistrates). As Rhodes observes (*Commentary*, p. 587), neither the *Ath. Pol.* nor any other text suggests "a right of appeal against decisions given by a magistrate on a case within his competence, and we must assume that such decisions were final."

[31] See ?Aristot. *Ath. Pol.* 53.2-5, with Rhodes' comments (*Commentary*, p. 590) on παραδιδόασι τοῖς δ᾽ τοῖς τὴν φυλὴν τοῦ φεύγοντος δικάζουσιν. Note also 48.5 (with Rhodes, *Commentary*, p. 563) for the dikasts' role—again in their tribal subdivisions—in connection with *euthynai*.

[32] On their name see below, n. 34. As regards the date of the reform, *Ath. Pol.* 53.1 (quoted above, n. 30) would suggest that it was either in or at least soon after 403/2; and D. M. MacDowell, *RIDA* 18, 1971, pp. 267-273, esp. 270-271, has pointed out that there is no sign in the second chapter of Lysias 23 (a speech to be dated, as he demonstrates, not before 400/399) that the speaker had to *go to* Dekeleia in order to call Pankleon πρὸς

in itself, in appearing to reflect (as ?Aristot. *Ath. Pol.* 53.1 implies) a revulsion, irrational but understandable, after the regime of the Thirty Tyrants against any more boards of that size.[33] But the really crucial change lay in the fact that, despite the perpetuation of their old name alongside their new numerical one, the Forty,[34] their connection with the demes had in fact been completely severed. The author of the *Ath. Pol.* does not state in so many words in 53.1 that they now remained in the city instead of travelling through the demes, but that is without doubt what he meant, and what forever afterwards was the case.[35] As Peter Rhodes has observed, "we are not told when or why they ceased to travel on circuit, but may guess that administrative convenience came to outweigh the convenience of litigants . . . Probably the judges discontinued their travels in the last period of the Peloponnesian War, when Decelea was occupied by the Spartans and the citizens were confined to Athens and the Piraeus, and after the war it was decided that they should continue to work in the city."[36] At all events, the "deme dikasts" were transformed, in effect, into *tribe* dikasts;[37] this (benign) imposition of the center upon the periphery came to an end; and the decentralization of justice remained, for the rural demesmen as they journeyed to Athens, no more than a memory.

C. From the Periphery to the Center

If the role of city magistrates in the demes was both limited and short-lived, the same could by no means be said of the contribution which the demes were required to make toward the appointment of the personnel of central government: the five hundred *bouleutai* and the numerous

τοὺς τῇ Ἱπποθωντίδι δικάζοντας. MacDowell further argues (against L. Gernet, *REG* 52, 1939, pp. 389-414, esp. 392-395 = *Droit et société en Grèce ancienne*, Paris, 1955, pp. 103-119, esp. 105-107) that there was a very short period between the institution of the Forty and that of the public arbitrators, who first took office in (as he shows) 399/8; and in view of the absence of any mention of public arbitration in Lysias 23.3, the speech must belong to that period.

[33] Cf. Rhodes, *Commentary*, p. 331.

[34] The old name, *dikastai kata dēmous*, is used by Demosth. 24.112 and in ?Aristot. *Ath. Pol.* 48.5 (cf. above, n. 31; Rhodes, *Commentary*, p. 563 believes that this was the term used "in the law on which A. P.'s account is based"). They are called the Forty in (e.g.) ?Aristot. *Ath. Pol.* 53.1, Isoc. 15.237, and Demosth. 37.33.

[35] Cf. e.g. Schoeffer, "Demoi," col. 29; Hignett, *Constitution*, pp. 218-219; Harrison, *Law* II, p. 18; MacDowell, *Law*, p. 206; Rhodes, *Commentary*, pp. 331, 588.

[36] Rhodes, *Commentary*, p. 588.

[37] Cf. MacDowell, *Law*, p. 206.

boards of city magistrates (*archontes*), major and minor.[38] Simple administrative pragmatism, I suggested earlier, is enough to account for much of the extent to which the business of operating the Athenian democratic constitution was transacted at its "grass roots" in the demes as well as at the central seats of government. But can we entirely exclude, on a different plane of explanation, considerations of constitutional theory—or, if "theory" strikes the wrong note, constitutional principle—and in particular the idea of representative (central) government? One would be reluctant to think so; but if we are to talk in such terms they must be properly understood.

The constitution of classical Athens was characterized not by representative government, strictly speaking, but by representation *in* government, and thus government (in the executive sphere at any rate) by representative individuals. The democratic *politeia* neither consisted of nor even anywhere contained a body or bodies of mandated delegates; it was, nonetheless, a *politeia* designed to reflect—and so "represent" in that sense—the entirety of the citizen-body. J.A.O. Larsen opened his investigation of *Representative Government in Greek and Roman History* with the following formulation. "Representative government, for the purposes of the present study, can be defined simply as government in which the ultimate decisions on important questions are made by representatives acting for their constituents and having authority to make such decisions according to their own best judgment . . . They are true representatives and not messengers merely recording the will of their constituents."[39] In classical Athens the "ultimate decisions" were of course taken by the *ekklēsia*, the sovereign assembly of all the citizens, to which each man went as the representative, in constitutional terms, of nobody but himself. Larsen's definition, though, is hardly the less applicable to Athens on that account: for as regards the executants of the assembly's decisions, the *boulē* and the *archontes*, one can find no trace of any doctrine that individuals were in office in order to speak and act on behalf of their "constituents," that is, the subdivision of the state from which they had been drawn. The duty incumbent upon, say,

[38] Note that the *boulē* should be classified as a (collective) *archē* in the technical sense: see M. H. Hansen, *GRBS* 22, 1981, pp. 347-351; but for convenience's sake I shall adhere to the familiar distinction between the *boulē* and the (other) magistrates.

[39] J.A.O. Larsen, *Representative Government in Greek and Roman History*, Berkeley, 1955, p. 1. (His distinction between "true representatives" and mere message-bearing delegates has its origin, I believe, in Edmund Burke's *Speech to the Electors of Bristol*, 3 November 1774.) The criticism by M. I. Finley, *Politics in the Ancient World*, Cambridge, 1983, p. 74 with n. 16, of the concept of representation employed by Larsen (and Traill, *Organization*) should be noted, though it is tangential to my argument here.

the four fourth-century *bouleutai* from Teithras honored in SEG 21.520 was to do their best not for Teithras but for Athens.[40] And if the demesmen of Epieikidai crowned one of their number who had served as *archōn thesmothetēs*, there is no reason to suspect that he had used his year in high office directly to further the cause of his own deme—rather than simply, and indirectly, to bring it the kudos of his prominence.[41] Yet however much one can and should emphasize the importance which the Athenians clearly attached to magisterial independence, and thus the absence from their constitution of the type of representative government with which we are most familiar in the modern world, an equally important fact remains: to an extent and in ways modified from time to time, the *appointment* of the personnel of central government was a task for the subdivisions of the citizen-body, the demes and the tribes.

1. THE BOULĒ

Here the basic facts are not in dispute. A link between the *boulē* and the demes was fundamental to the Kleisthenic constitution from its outset, and remained so throughout the classical period and far beyond. In the Aristotelian *Ath. Pol.* the *boulē* is regarded as being drawn from (ἐξ or ἀπό) the tribes (21.3, 43.2) and divisible into trittyes (44.1); yet the abundant epigraphic evidence of the prytany catalogs both from the time of the *Ath. Pol.* and from other periods before and after it shows the names of the councillors listed by demes within the tribes, and listed with such a degree of consistency that the normal quota of the five hundred places to be filled annually by each deme can readily be established in all but a handful of instances.[42] What is more, in the only passage of the *Ath. Pol.* concerned with the actual appointment of the *bouleutai* (62.1) the impression is given that it was *in* the demes where this happened.[43]

---

[40] It was obviously another matter altogether if, as in SEG 21.520, the *bouleutai* were required by their own deme assembly to undertake duties within the deme; see lines 7-12 (quoted in Chap. 2, n. 97). Nor is my point affected by instances (e.g. [Demosth.] 50.6-8) where *all* the councillors had a task, from central government, to perform in their own demes.

[41] Again I choose an actual example, IG II²2837: amongst those who have crowned Kleonymos of Epieikidai (174), one of the *thesmothetai* of 329/8, are his fellow demesmen. It is of course entirely possible—but again another matter—that he had been of service to *individual* Epieikidai: note Themistokles' alleged attitude to the opportunities for, indeed effectively the right of, an archon to favor his *philoi* (Plut. *Moralia* 807B, cf. *Aristeides* 2; Connor, *Politicians*, pp. 44-45). For one way, sanctioned by the constitution itself, in which an archon could do this, see Chap. 10B, sec. 1.

[42] For the quotas, see Appendix 2.

[43] ?Aristot. *Ath. Pol.* 62.1: αἱ δὲ κληρωταὶ ἀρχαὶ πρότερον μὲν ἦσαν αἱ μὲν μετ᾽

Thus scholars have tended to assume, without discussing the matter directly, that it was the demes themselves which chose the members of the *boulē*.[44] If this is correct, it must have entailed a regular, yearly meeting of all the deme assemblies (or at least a regular item of business at such meetings), where the demesmen of Phaleron picked their nine "representatives," the demesmen of Leukonoion their three, and so forth. The original method of appointment was perhaps direct election, but the sortition attested by *Ath. Pol.* 43.2 (and 62.1) is likely to go back to the mid fifth century at least.[45] Whether the sortition process extended to every member of the deme who was not positively disqualified from serving[46] or simply discriminated by lot amongst a body of willing *prokritoi* is a matter of dispute; but if service on the *boulē* (rather like modern British jury-service) was for some demesmen a thing to be stoically endured rather than actively sought, there is nonetheless evidence that the politically ambitious might, if not ineligible, secure a place at will.[47]

This scenario may well correspond to the truth in most or even all respects. Yet residual problems should be noticed. For instance "there is evidence from the late fifth and the fourth centuries that, at the same time as the bouleutae were appointed, ἐπιλαχόντες, or deputies, were appointed also, so that a man would be available to take the place of a

---

ἐννέα ἀρχόντων ἐκ τῆς φυλῆς ὅλης κληρούμεναι, αἱ δ' ἐν Θησείῳ κληρούμεναι ⟨αἵ, Gertz⟩ διῃροῦντο εἰς τοὺς δήμους· ἐπειδὴ δ' ἐπώλουν οἱ δῆμοι, καὶ ταύτας ἐκ τῆς φυλῆς ὅλης κληροῦσι πλὴν βουλευτῶν καὶ φρουρῶν· τούτους δ' εἰς τοὺς δήμους ἀποδιδόασι. (Gertz' αἵ has not found favor with many editors but seems to me needed.) The numerous problems which this passage presents will be considered later, for most of them relate to the appointment of *archai* other than the council, and changes therein; the writer seems to affirm, however, that no such changes affected the appointment of councillors.

[44] This is, for example, the implication (though admittedly no more than that) conveyed by Rhodes, *Boule*, pp. 6-12. Compare (more directly): Hignett, *Constitution*, p. 227, ". . . each deme selected by lot as many candidates as its quota on the boule"; A.H.M. Jones, *Athenian Democracy*, Oxford, 1957, p. 105," . . . the allotment took place in the demes"; and the hypothetical picture confidently painted by Bicknell, *Studies*, p. 5.

[45] Rhodes, *Boule*, p. 7, cf. *Commentary*, pp. 517-518.

[46] For the disqualifications, see Rhodes, *Boule*, pp. 1-3.

[47] For bouleutic celebrities in key years, see Rhodes, *Boule*, pp. 3-4; Aeschin. 3.62 (cf. 3.3) alleges that Demosthenes had circumvented the lot by bribery to gain a seat in 347/6. Rhodes, *Boule*, p. 2, dismisses the "evidence that men were invited to volunteer as candidates" (chiefly Lysias 31.33 and Harpoc., ἐπιλαχών; cf. Isoc. 15.150 and [Lysias] 6.4 on other *archai* as "slight and less than cogent"; for a different view see (e.g.) Lang, "Allotment," pp. 83, 88, and Staveley, *Elections*, p. 51. Two issues should perhaps be distinguished here. One may agree with Rhodes that the basis of the whole system is unlikely to have been an *invitation* to volunteer, if that is what he is specifically disputing; however, the *option* to do so seems well enough attested. The difficult task, it would appear, was evading bouleutic service, not undertaking it from choice.

member who died or was rejected in the δοκιμασία [scrutiny]."[48] A fragment of dialogue from the comic poet Plato's *Hyperbolos* suggests that each of the five hundred councillors had his particular deputy ready and waiting to step in (and that the one understudying the wretched Hyperbolos would be sure to be needed);[49] and this is indeed directly stated by Harpocration and other lexicographers.[50] If they are correct, it is obvious that, say, the men of Phaleron had to produce not nine but eighteen potential councillors, the Leukonoeis not three but six, and so forth, with the grand total being not five hundred but a thousand each year. However, scholars have been understandably reluctant to accept so high a figure[51]—and an inscription recently published and interpreted by John Traill, *Agora 15*, no. 492, lends them some support in this. What the inscription appears to be is a list, from some year between ca. 380 and ca. 360, of councillors *and deputies*; and the conclusion that there were only half as many of the latter as of the former seems warranted by the likelihood that together their aggregate was only about seventy-five men, not a hundred, per tribe.[52] If this is indeed the true figure, even for a possibly limited period in the fourth century, it creates a certain difficulty for the idea of bouleutic appointments at deme level. More than a quarter of all demes had a bouleutic quota of only one—or less than one.[53] Such demes obviously cannot have been asked to nominate half a deputy. So were they not asked for any at all (and thus left potentially "unrepresented")? Or were they grouped into pairs and asked for one in alternate years? And how, and by whom, was it determined whether a deme with *any* odd-numbered quota should round the number of deputies up or down?[54]

Whatever the administrative solutions to such questions, it is worth canvassing the notion that they might have been more naturally and conveniently adopted (and the arithmetic rationalized) at *tribe* rather

[48] Rhodes, *Boule*, p. 7, citing the evidence in n. 9.

[49] Plato frs. 166-167, *apud* schol. Aristoph. *Thesm.*, line 808.

[50] Harpoc. (cf. Suda and *Etym. Magn.*), ἐπιλαχών; *Lex Seguer*. V, *Lexeis Rhetorikai*, ἐπιλαχών [= Bekker, *Anecd. Gr.* 1.256.3].

[51] E.g. Larsen, *Representative Government* (see above, n. 39), pp. 10-11, 194-195; Rhodes, *Boule*, pp. 7-8. Amongst those who have accepted the figure are Hignett, *Constitution*, p. 150, and Lang, "Allotment," p. 83, cf. 89.

[52] J. S. Traill, "Athenian bouleutic alternates," in *Classical Contributions: studies . . . M. F. McGregor*, Locust Valley, New York, 1981, pp. 161-169 (an expansion of *Organization*, p. 2 with n. 5); he determines the date by prosopography.

[53] See Chap. 1, n. 79, on Pambotadai and Sybridai.

[54] In *Agora 15*, no. 492 itself, the figures are haphazard, to say the least, and show both under- and over-"representation"; see Traill, "Athenian bouleutic alternates" (above, n. 52), pp. 165-166.

than deme level. Other considerations too may point to the tribes rather than the demes, if we look again at ?Aristot. *Ath. Pol.* 62.1. Once, says the writer there, there were two kinds of sortitive offices in the constitution, "those allotted, with the nine archons, from whole tribes" and "those allotted in the Theseion ⟨which⟩ were distributed to the demes"; however, once the demes became prey to corruption,[55] the sortition of offices of the second kind also was made from whole tribes, with the exception of councillors and guards (*phrouroi*),[56] whose appointment was (still) "assigned to the demes." Evidently, then, the procedural change which affected other offices did not apply to the *boulē*, which both before and after it came under the heading of appointments "allotted in the Theseion" and there "distributed to the demes." Insofar as these enigmatic formulations enable us to visualize a clear picture at all, it is not, I would suggest, a picture of individual deme assemblies at work; and in any case it would seem administratively inconceivable that the composition of the *boulē* should have taken shape piecemeal over many months, as one hundred and thirty-nine deme assemblies all met separately and individually in the city Theseion. Rather, surely, the meetings there were meetings of the ten *tribal* assemblies. We noted in Chapter 4 the deme decree of Eleusis which alludes to the demesmen assembling in the Theseion for the election of officials (*archairesiai*), and it is tempting to think that this may be an actual example of what *Ath. Pol.* 62.1 describes.[57] Too little is positively known of the workings of the tribal assemblies for this hypothesis to be tested from the other side of the fence, so to speak; but at any rate the idea that for some purposes— appointments made "from whole tribes"—the deme affiliation of the tribesmen was constitutionally irrelevant while on other occasions the procedure called for intra-tribal divisions by demes (*kata dēmous*)[58] encounters no objection in principle.

My suggestion is, then, that the actual process of sortition which re-

---

[55] What this means and when it happened will be considered below, in sec. 2.

[56] "The φρουροί may be the five hundred φρουροὶ νεωρίων [guards of the dockyards] of 24.3: it would be easy to use bouleutic quotas for five hundred, or for any multiple of five hundred" (Rhodes, *Commentary*, p. 691).

[57] SEG 28.103, lines 27-28, εἰς τὸν Μεταγειτνιῶνα μῆνα ταῖς ἀρχαι|ρεσίαις, ὅταν οἱ δημόται ἀγοράζωσιν ἐν τῶι Θησείωι; see Chap. 4, pp. 89-90. The Theseion (cf. Thuc. 6.61.2, Paus. 1.17.2, etc.) lay probably just outside the Agora, to its east or southeast (H. A. Thompson and R. E. Wycherley, *Agora 14*, pp. 124-126), and it had a large precinct which could easily have accommodated a tribal assembly: lexicographers speak of lawsuits being tried there (Phot. and *Etym. Magn.*, Θησεῖον); and an ephebic inscription of the first century (IG II² 1039 = SEG 22.110, lines 2-3) mentions a meeting there of the *boulē*—a body of six hundred men in that period.

[58] Cf. Chap. 4B, sec. 2, for the oath of 410 (Andoc. 1.97).

sulted, after necessary adjustments, in the final tribal complements of fifty councillors and an appropriate number of deputies was conducted at tribal level by special meetings (or at least special deliberations) of the tribal assemblies.[59] But, if so, the tribes were simply completing and rationalizing a process which the demes had begun, at meetings of their own—meetings which saw the compilation of provisional lists of candidates to be taken by the deme officials, accompanied by those candidates and by as many of their fellow demesmen as may be, to the Theseion.[60] What I am proposing, if it is felt to have any validity, thus does nothing to diminish the importance of the role commonly presupposed for the demes in this recurrent contribution to the operation of central government.[61]

2. THE MAGISTRATES

From the *boulē* we may now proceed to consider the appointment of the smaller boards of city magistrates. Here it will be seen that until at any

[59] According to Demosth. 39.10, by ca. 348 bronze *pinakia* which, as we know from other sources, represented the division of each tribe into ten sections were playing some part in the allotment not only of magistracies (on which see below, sec. 2) but also of the *boulē*; however, it is not at all clear how if at all this related to the tribes considered as groups of demes. See Kroll, *Allotment Plates*, pp. 2-5, 51-56, and esp. 91-94 (though he ignores—there—*Ath. Pol.* 62.1). Perhaps, despite the absence of differentiation in Demosth. 39.10, the function of the *pinakia* as regards bouleutic allotments was simply that of personal identification (cf. Kroll, *Allotment Plates*, p. 93)? Kroll has shown that the issuing of the non-dikastic *pinakia* (and hence the assignment of each individual to his section) was "on a long-term or permanent basis" (*Allotment Plates*, p. 75 and passim), but he does not directly consider how if at all a tribe's sections related to its constituent demes. Even if an initial attempt was made—and there is no reason to think that it was—to give (e.g.) all Eleusinians the letter *gamma* (like *Allotment Plates*, no. 28), the subsequent need to maintain the sections at equal strength (cf. *Allotment Plates*, p. 95) must have been more important than keeping this up (see *Allotment Plates*, nos. 62a, 96a, and 145b for other Eleusinians); it is thus hard to see any role for the sections as such in the mechanics of appointing the *bouleutai*.

[60] From SEG 28.103, lines 27-28 (quoted above, n. 57), we learn that the Eleusinians attended such a meeting—of their tribe Hippothontis, on my hypothesis—in the month Metageitnion. Possibly some festival of importance to the tribe brought its members to the city then anyway, but in any event it is interesting to note how early in the administrative year the meeting was fixed. (Mention of Metageitnion induced Coumanoudis and Gofas in the *editio princeps*—REG 91, 1978, pp. 298ff., at 298—to cite for comparison IG II² 1174, but this decree of Halai Aixonides is trebly irrelevant: the Halaieis are dealing with their *own* officials, the demarch and treasurer(s), who must render account *before*, not in, Metageitnion, in the year *after* they have held office.)

[61] Cf. Staveley, *Elections*, pp. 52-54, with a reconstruction not unlike my own (though he does not make it clear whether he regards the Theseion meetings as meetings of the tribal assemblies as such).

rate the second quarter of the fourth century the demes were made to play scarcely less prominent a part. The evidence, however, is more than usually lacunose and problematical; and we shall find ourselves obliged to devote at least as much discussion—as perhaps the Athenians themselves did—to minor offices as to major ones.

Posts filled by direct election,[62] with which there is nothing to suggest that the demes as such were ever involved, may first be set aside; the evidence as we have it concerns only sortitive offices. The greatest of such offices, even by the time of the Aristotelian *Ath. Pol.*, were the nine archonships, and we are told by the writer that they were filled in his own day (the 330s and 320s)[63] "from whole tribes," that is, without regard for their constituent demes. In the passage where this appears at its plainest (62.1)[64]—through a contrast drawn with other offices "distributed to the demes"—mention is also made of other sortitive magistracies similarly allotted "with the nine archons" (μετ' ἐννέα ἀρχόντων). From a phrase in the heliastic oath, as cited in Demosth. 24.150, it would appear that we are entitled to construe *with* as meaning "on the same day as";[65] but nowhere are these other offices actually identified and named for us. It has been supposed that they "should cover all the various boards of ten (and multiples of ten like the Forty),"[66] but we shall see solid grounds later for putting these in the writer's second category, that of offices filled through the demes; and indeed it is difficult to know what else to put in it.[67] More probably, then, what the offices

---

[62] See ?Aristot. *Ath. Pol.* 43.1 (civilian posts) and 61.1-7, cf. 44.4 (military posts; cf. Aeschin. 3.13 and 30).

[63] On the date of the *Ath. Pol.*, see Rhodes, *Commentary*, pp. 51-58.

[64] Quoted above, n. 43. The other two relevant passages are 8.1 (τὰς δ' ἀρχὰς ἐποίησε κληρωτὰς ἐκ προκρίτων, οὓς ἑκάστη προκρίνειε τῶν φυλῶν. προύκρινεν δ' εἰς τοὺς ἐννέα ἄρχοντας ἑκάστη δέκα, καὶ (ἐκ) τούτων ἐκλήρουν· ὅθεν ἔτι διαμένει ταῖς φυλαῖς τὸ δέκα κληροῦν ἑκάστην, εἶτ' ἐκ τούτων κυαμεύειν) and 55.1 (οἱ δὲ καλούμενοι ἐννέα ἄρχοντες τὸ μὲν ἐξ ἀρχῆς ὃν τρόπον καθίσταντο εἴρ[ηται]· [νῦν] δὲ κληροῦσιν θεσμοθέτας μὲν ἓξ καὶ γραμματέα τούτοις, ἔτι δ' ἄρχοντα καὶ βασιλέα καὶ πολέμαρχον κατὰ μέρος ἐξ ἑκάστης φυλῆς). Some of the problems in these two passages are pursued below; for the rest see Rhodes, *Commentary*, pp. 146-149, 613-614.

[65] Demosth. 24.150: οὐδ' ἀρχὴν καταστήσω ὥστ' ἄρχειν ὑπεύθυνον ὄντα ἑτέρας ἀρχῆς, καὶ τῶν ἐννέα ἀρχόντων καὶ τοῦ ἱερομνήμονος καὶ ὅσαι μετὰ τῶν ἐννέα ἀρχόντων κυαμεύονται τῇ αὐτῇ (Blass: ταύτῃ τῇ MSS) ἡμέρᾳ κτλ.

[66] Kroll, *Allotment Plates*, pp. 85-86, at 85, following the originator of this view, Wilamowitz (*Aristoteles*, vol. I, pp. 200-201); cf. F. G. Kenyon, *Aristotle on the Constitution of Athens*, 3d ed., Oxford, 1892, *ad loc.*

[67] The scholars cited in the preceding note (and others, e.g., Schoeffer, "Demoi," col. 29; Busolt/Swoboda, *Staatskunde*, p. 971; K. von Fritz and E. Kapp, *Aristotle's Constitution of Athens and related texts*, New York, 1950, p. 139, note *b*) have been obliged to resort to the supposition that this second category of appointments refers to jurors (and officials

of the first category shared in common with the archonships was a property qualification.[68]

The evidence so far considered mentions no role for the demes in such appointments. Two other passages of the *Ath. Pol.* (22.5 and 26.2) appear to do so, however. According to 22.5 "in the archonship of Telesinos [487/6] they cast lots for the nine archons, by tribes, from amongst the five hundred men previously selected by the demesmen, this for the first time since the tyranny; the earlier ones had all been elected."[69] Naturally I have translated here the text, Kenyon's OCT, which I regard as the correct one, but there are well-known alternatives at various points which combine to make the passage a most elusive one to comprehend and exploit. The least important of them, substantively speaking, is the variant "by the demesmen" (ὑπὸ τῶν δημοτῶν, in the London papyrus) or "by the demes" (ὑπὸ τῶν δήμων, in the Berlin papyrus, and favored by many German editors);[70] δημοτῶν is perhaps preferable as the *lectio difficilior*,[71] and also because it does not restrict us, as δήμων would, to the conclusion that the pre-selection process necessarily took place *in* the individual demes.

Such a conclusion would in any case be ruled out by the necessity, as many scholars since Kenyon have conceived it to be, to regard the figure of five hundred *prokritoi* as erroneous, either because the writer became confused between the appointment of the archons and of the council or else by textual corruption of the figure *one* hundred (ρ') to five hundred

---

appointed from their ranks). This is rejected, in my view rightly, by Rhodes, *Commentary*, p. 689.

[68] E.g. the Treasurers of Athena (?Aristot. *Ath. Pol.* 47.1, cf. 8.1) and—during the periods when they had a separate existence (see Rhodes, *Commentary*, pp. 391, 549-550)—the Treasurers of the Other Gods. (On the first appointment of the latter, note IG I³ 52, lines 13-15: ταμίας δὲ ἀποκυαμεύε|[ν το]ύτον τὸν χρεμάτον hόταμπερ τὰς ἄλλας ἀρχάς, καθάπερ τὸς τὸν hι|[ερὸ]ν τὸν τὲς ᾿Αθεναίας.) For this view see Lang, "Allotment," p. 83; Staveley, *Elections*, pp. 48-49; Rhodes, *Commentary*, p. 689.

[69] ?Aristot. *Ath. Pol.* 22.5: ἐπὶ Τελεσίνου ἄρχοντος ἐκυάμευσαν τοὺς ἐννέα ἄρχοντας κατὰ φυλὰς ἐκ τῶν προκριθέντων ὑπὸ τῶν δημοτῶν πεντακοσίων τότε μετὰ τὴν τυραννίδα πρῶτον· οἱ δὲ πρότεροι πάντες ἦσαν αἱρετοί. I cannot enter here into the vexed question of the apparent contradiction between the latter part of this passage and the claim in 8.1 (quoted above, n. 64) that *klērōsis ek prokritōn* went back to Solon; for a defence of that claim, see Rhodes, *Commentary*, pp. 146-148, 272-273.

[70] A more radical (conjectural) alternative is ὑπὸ τοῦ δήμου (J. W. Headlam, CR 5, 1891, p. 112; J. van Leeuwen in his edition of the *Ath. Pol.* with H. van Herwerden, Leiden, 1891, *ad loc.*), in association with an emendation of πεντακοσίων to πεντακοσιομεδίμνων (cf. P. J. Bicknell, *RFIC* 50, 1972, pp. 168-169). Rhodes' comment that the latter "is not likely to be right" (*Commentary*, p. 274; cf. below, n. 75) is equally applicable to the former.

[71] Cf. Rhodes, *Commentary*, p. 274.

(φ').[72] *One* hundred men is plainly too small a number to have emerged from the demes acting as separate entities.[73] The most powerful formal argument for believing in a total of only one hundred *prokritoi*, ten (not fifty) from each tribe, is the fact that this was the figure in the writer's own day;[74] and by that time more men were eligible. Conversely, as Badian has caustically emphasized, there can only in 487/6 have been something between five and eight hundred men *in toto* who met the high property qualification for an archonship, so that the group of *prokritoi*— if five hundred—would have been virtually, and nonsensically, self-selecting. Thus, Badian insists, Kenyon's footnoted emendation of the figure *five* hundred to *one* hundred in *Ath. Pol.* 22.5 is self-evidently correct, and "we can assert with fair confidence . . . that under the system of Telesinos ten men were elected by each tribe, and one of them became archon, by lot."[75]

A stubborn minority of scholars have nonetheless found it possible to accept the figure of *five* hundred as both textually and factually sound;[76] and despite Badian's strictures I am inclined to think that they are right to do so, if not necessarily for the right reasons.

We may begin with two general points. In the first place it may be a mistake to seek, for economy's sake, to harmonize the 487/6 procedure described in *Ath. Pol.* 22.5 with that which obtained in the writer's own time; and this point applies, in fact, equally well to reconstructions which attempt to reconcile the received text of 22.5 with that of 8.1 (and 55.1 and 62.1)[77] as to those which suppose only ten *prokritoi* from each tribe in all periods. In addition to the reform in the rules of eligibility (?Aristot.

[72] See Rhodes, *Commentary*, pp. 273-274; also Hignett, *Constitution*, p. 174. The deletion of δημοτῶν, to leave ἐκ τῶν προκριθέντων (of unspecified number) ὑπὸ τῶν πεντακοσίων (i.e., the *boulē*) is proposed by K. H. Kinzl in *Greece and the Eastern Mediterranean in Ancient History and Prehistory: studies . . . F. Schachermeyr*, Berlin and New York, 1977, pp. 199-223, at 216-217; I agree with Rhodes, *Commentary*, p. 274, that this has nothing to recommend it.

[73] Cf. Staveley, *Elections*, p. 38.

[74] See ?Aristot. *Ath. Pol.* 8.1 (quoted above, n. 64).

[75] Badian, "Archons," pp. 17-19 (quotation from p. 19); cf. Hignett, *Constitution*, p. 174, assuming a rather larger pool of eligible men. The calculation takes in *hippeis* as well as *pentakosiomedimnoi*; cf. Rhodes, *Commentary*, pp. 148, 273. In "Archons," p. 19, n. 49, Badian assumes, reasonably enough (cf. Rhodes, *Commentary*, pp. 274, 613-614), that it was now that the post of secretary to the *thesmothetai* was created, making the nine archons in fact a more administratively convenient college of ten (cf. ?Aristot. *Ath. Pol.* 55.1).

[76] See for instance Lang, "Allotment," pp. 87-89; Staveley, *Elections*, p. 38; Kroll, *Allotment Plates*, p. 94, n. 6.

[77] See for instance von Fritz and Kapp (above, n. 67), pp. 166-167, n. 58; Lang, "Allotment," pp. 87-89.

Ath. Pol. 26.2, discussed below) we know that at least two procedural changes occurred between the second half of the fifth century and the second half of the fourth: the substitution of pre-allotment (*proklērōsis*) for pre-selection (*prokrisis*) and, especially, the creation and use of internal tribal divisions other than the demes.[78] So there is no inherent difficulty in believing in a third such change, whether or not one can fully understand its causes or purpose. Secondly, for Badian "the demes as electoral units can be accepted only with grave suspicion," and to him the idea "sounds much more like a fourth-century construction . . . than like genuine tradition."[79] This suspicion is misplaced: the early decades of the Kleisthenic constitution represent exactly the period when it may have been thought desirable to develop a role for the demes in the administration of the polis. Badian finds incredible "an elaborate mechanism for picking a short list of 500 out of a number that quite possibly was not much over 500 itself."[80] Yet the principal object of the *prokrisis* may well have been to identify, as potential officeholders, those who laid claim to membership of the two highest income classes,[81] and nobody could do that more easily or appropriately than their fellow demesmen.

In the context of these general considerations, and in the light of others still to be mentioned, I would suggest that close attention to the phraseology of the unemended text of *Ath. Pol.* 22.5 can be made to yield up a picture of the 487/6 procedure—or at any rate its preliminary stages, our only concern here—which we can both accept and understand. It is a picture of an annual series of *tribal* assemblies which produced the body of five hundred men, their qualifications and status already checked in a scrutiny at deme level, who would draw lots *not only for the archonships but for all sortitive magistracies.*

To take the last point first: why did the writer speak of "*the* five hundred men previously selected by the demesmen"? As he had not already mentioned such a group, to which cross-reference would naturally be made in this way, the only valid explanation must surely be that the archons were not the only officials who were to be drawn from it. Rather, it must have represented the single pool of candidates which, at this time, furnished not only the archons (the only magistrates, as a rule, in whom the writer was interested) but also, for example, the *tamiai*, the *kōlakretai*,

---

[78] Cf. Kroll, *Allotment Plates*, p. 94, n. 6. On the tribal sections, see above, n. 59, and further below.

[79] Badian, "Archons," p. 19.

[80] Badian, "Archons," p. 19.

[81] Cf. on this point Staveley, *Elections*, p. 38; it is supported, as we shall see, by ?Aristot. *Ath. Pol.* 26.2.

the *pōlētai*, and the Eleven[82]—indeed, as I have suggested, all the boards of magistrates appointed by lot rather than by election.[83] How many such boards were in existence in 487/6, and therefore how many of the five hundred could realistically expect to hold office of some sort, are questions without answers, but we do know that at least two levels of income-qualification were of relevance—the archons being drawn from *hippeis* and *pentakosiomedimnoi*, the *tamiai* from the latter only.[84] It will have been in determining which particular individuals were eligible for which particular categories of office that the *prokrisis* "by the demesmen" was so crucial.

We may turn next to that very phrase: *prokrisis* "by the demesmen." What did this mean? Are we to visualize decisions in the individual demes and (by extension from that) in accordance with the bouleutic quotas? Five hundred, unlike one hundred, is certainly a number which could, theoretically, have resulted from operations conducted entirely at deme level. Yet even with the *boulē* we saw grounds for supposing that it was necessary for the tribes to coordinate and rationalize the process which the demes had begun; and there are even stronger arguments (albeit rather different ones) for the same conclusion in respect of this magisterial pre-selection. Although the number five hundred, fifty per tribe,[85] does bring the *boulē* irresistibly to mind, the analogies which it offers are more apparent than real. When, for example, the demesmen of Acherdous put up their single "candidate" for the *boulē*, they could be virtually certain that he would actually serve his term on that body. But as regards the magistracies, the five hundred individuals were indeed merely and genuinely candidates for office, and the man from Acherdous might very well not secure one. Moreover it must frequently have been the case that such a small deme could not bring forward a *pentakosiomedimnos* (or even, conceivably, a *hippeus*) at all, and so forfeited even the theoretical possibility of "representation" on boards which required that status in members.[86] These considerations strongly suggest that the bouleutic quotas can have served as only a general guide to the tribes in their deter-

[82] These are the four boards listed, with the archons, in ?Aristot. *Ath. Pol.* 7.3.

[83] Compare the proposal of Lang, "Allotment," pp. 88-89. I cannot, however, agree with her that such a unified system can have been feasible beyond, say, the third quarter of the fifth century; for we shall see later that there came a time when more than five hundred posts needed to be filled, and other procedures (representing, indeed, the division attested by *Ath. Pol.* 62.1) were therefore required.

[84] Archons: see above, n. 75. *Tamiai*: ?Aristot. *Ath. Pol.* 47.1, cf. 8.1.

[85] Strictly speaking we are not told (in ?Aristot. *Ath. Pol.* 22.5) that it *was* fifty *per* tribe, but that is surely beyond doubt.

[86] Cf. Badian, "Archons," p. 19; and see in general W. E. Thompson, "The regional distribution of the Athenian pentakosiomedimnoi," *Klio* 52, 1970, pp. 437-451.

mination of the actual complements of fifty names.[87] The extent to which
the quotas had to be treated with pragmatic, empirical flexibility may
also be judged by the phrase "from whole tribes" in ?Aristot. *Ath. Pol.*
62.1—though, conversely, if the quotas had been of no account at all
(which is in any case unlikely *a priori*) we might have expected "by the
tribesmen" rather than "by the demesmen" in 22.5. The wording of 22.5
is thus, I would maintain, precise: it was indeed "the demesmen" upon
whom the procedure relied. Whether or not they chose, as individuals,
to attend what might be termed the mechanical stage of the *prokrisis*, at
tribe level,[88] the really important part of their work had already been
done; for the basic eligibility of the individuals in each deme's group of
candidates, large or small, must normally have been taken for granted
by the tribe and its officials as something which the deme had already
verified and was now guaranteeing.

The importance of the demes' role in such verification is underlined
by another passage of the Aristotelian *Ath. Pol.*, 26.2. There we learn
that in 457/6[89] a change was made not in the method of filling the
archonships but in eligibility for them. "They made no change in the
appointment of the nine archons, but . . . they decided that the *zeugitai*
should be included in the preliminary selection of candidates who would
draw lots to become the nine archons; and the first of the *zeugitai* to be
archon was Mnesitheides. His predecessors had all come from the *hippeis*
and *pentakosiomedimnoi*, while the *zeugitai* had held only the lower
offices—except on occasions when the legal requirements may have been
disregarded."[90] Such at least is a translation of the standard texts (OCT
and Teubner) of the passage. However, in the London papyrus the final
clause actually reads: ". . . except on occasions when the legal requirements may have been disregarded *by the demes*" (εἰ μή τι παρεωρᾶτο
ὑπὸ τῶν δήμων τῶν ἐν τοῖς νόμοις). Most editors have followed Kenyon in omitting the words ὑπὸ τῶν δήμων on the grounds that they were
purposely deleted in the papyrus by the first of the four scribal hands;
some, though, have retained them in the belief that the supposed deletion

[87] Cf. Lang, "Allotment," p. 83, ". . . a property qualification would make proportional
representation of the demes very difficult" (but cf. ibid., p. 89).

[88] Attendance by the demarchs at least may be assumed; they will have come prepared
with their own lists of names and eager to see that justice was done with them as far as
was practicable.

[89] Or 458/7: consult Rhodes, *Commentary*, p. 330.

[90] ?Aristot. *Ath. Pol.* 26.2: τὴν δὲ τῶν ἐννέα ἀρχόντων αἵρεσιν οὐκ ἐκίνουν, ἀλλ᾽
. . . ἔγνωσαν καὶ ἐκ ζευγιτῶν προκρίνεσθαι τοὺς κληρωσομένους τῶν ἐννέα ἀρχόντων, καὶ πρῶτος ἦρξεν ἐξ αὐτῶν Μνησιθείδης. οἱ δὲ πρὸ τούτου πάντες ἐξ
ἱππέων καὶ πεντακοσιομεδίμνων ἦσαν, οἱ ⟨δὲ⟩ ζευγῖται τὰς ἐγκυκλίους ἦρχον, εἰ
μή τι παρεωρᾶτο τῶν ἐν τοῖς νόμοις.

is nothing more than an accidental blot.[91] No papyrologist, my opinion on the technical issue is valueless, but by general reasoning I cannot at all agree with Rhodes when he asserts that "the text is clearly better without these words."[92] On the contrary, the words suitably convey what must in fact have been the case, namely, that at deme level it was possible—before this extension of eligibility—for *zeugitai* to pretend, with or without official connivance, that they were members of a higher income group and thus eligible for the major as well as the minor magistracies.[93] Evidently the incidence of this was not high enough to necessitate a procedural change to counteract local abuse of the system; but we shall shortly see that in the fourth century the extent of dishonesty and malpractice in the demes did result in (or at least substantially contribute towards) a major procedural reform, and that the demes did not come well out of it.

✳

My contention is, then, that from 487/6[94] the procedure for the preselection of all sortitive city magistracies took the form of the provision by each tribe of fifty candidates whose qualifications for office had been examined and validated by their demes. To believe that the candidates for *all* sortitive positions, not merely the archonships, were pre-selected in this way in this period obviously frees us from the necessity of postulating some other, entirely imaginary system of appointment for the other officials. It also makes more sense, in itself, of the figure of five hundred *prokritoi*; we no longer have to suppose that four hundred and ninety of them were wasted, so to speak, every year. And one may go further. Discussion of the 487/6 system which reduces the body of candidates from five hundred to one hundred has often been founded on the idea that five hundred is too large a figure, yet it is in fact more appropriate to consider reasons why, over the course of time, it may have become too small. The procedure, as we are explicitly told in *Ath. Pol.* 26.2 (above), was unaffected by the relaxation in eligibility for archonships in the 450s, and indeed that is understandable enough; the reform simply opened the same magistracy to a wider circle of the citizen-body, in accordance with the developing ethos of the democratic constitution.

---

[91] See the editions of H. van Herwerden and J. van Leeuwen (Leiden, 1891), F. Blass (Leipzig, 1892), and T. Thalheim (Leipzig, 1st ed. 1909, 2d ed. 1914), *ad loc.*

[92] Rhodes, *Commentary*, p. 330. He does not give the references cited in the preceding note, and his response here is, for once, less than adequate.

[93] Compare ?Aristot. *Ath. Pol.* 7.4 (with Rhodes, *Commentary*, pp. 145-146): in the writer's own day candidates for office were reluctant to admit to being thetes.

[94] Of the period before that date we can say precisely nothing.

Another facet of that ethos, however, and one which necessarily did have a direct bearing upon appointment procedures, was *the multiplication of the magistracies themselves.*

Here yet another controversial passage of the *Ath. Pol.* comes into play: 24.3. There the writer asserts that in the second half of the fifth century the Athenians possessed, in addition to the five hundred *bouleutai,* "up to seven hundred domestic magistracies."[95] It has been orthodox practice to reject this figure, on the basis that it is fully twice as high as the aggregate which results from a count of all the offices listed in the second and (supposedly) systematic part of the *Ath. Pol.* (chaps. 47-62).[96] However, Mogens Herman Hansen has recently demonstrated that a figure of between six and seven hundred may be almost exactly right, both for the time when *Ath. Pol.* 24.3 was written and also for the time to which it refers.[97] Obviously we can only imagine rather than actually plot the process of growth in the number of offices toward this figure, but it seems reasonable to assume that the great majority of them were sortitive offices. More important, it is plain that as soon as the figure exceeded five hundred the 487/6 system with its five hundred *prokritoi* was no longer able to meet it. This occurred, we may suppose, at some time between the constitutional revolution of 462 and the beginning of the Peloponnesian War;[98] and once it had done so—or, conceivably, once it was clear that it was going to do so—a new appointment procedure was needed. What was this procedure? Surely the bipartite one attested, as we have seen, in *Ath. Pol.* 62.1: a distinction between offices which were "allotted, with the nine archons, from whole tribes" and those "allotted in the Theseion ⟨which⟩ were distributed to the demes." For the first of these categories (probably comprising, as we saw reason to believe earlier, offices which carried a property qualification) the 487/6 system of ten tribal fifties, representing the demes of their tribes as far as was consistent with putting up candidates of the required status, may have been retained. Alternatively, it was perhaps at this juncture that the special and separate pool of one hundred candidates, ten per tribe, for

[95] ?Aristot. *Ath. Pol.* 24.3: ἀρχαὶ δ᾽ ἔνδημοι μὲν εἰς ἑπτακοσίους ἄνδρας, ὑπερόριοι δ᾽ εἰς ἑπτακοσίους. The *second* "seven hundred" here has been universally regarded as an erroneous repetition of the first; see Rhodes, *Commentary,* p. 305.

[96] See, for instance, A.H.M. Jones, *Athenian Democracy,* Oxford, 1957, p. 6 with n. 9.

[97] Hansen, *"Archai";* he agrees (ibid., p. 166) with Jones that known cases of old offices abolished and new ones created roughly cancel each other out. The only previous attempt to justify the figure in *Ath. Pol.* 24.3 was that of Wilamowitz, *Aristoteles,* pp. 202-204, but Hansen's criteria are the more rigorous.

[98] Cf. Hignett, *Constitution,* p. 215, on this formative period for the institutions of radical democracy.

the archonships was introduced,[99] with some analogous arrangement, involving candidates in indeterminable numbers, for the other associated magistracies. But in any event one is bound to conclude, I believe, that the major innovation made at the time of which we are speaking was the creation of a quite separate mode of appointment, again involving five hundred candidates, for the *Ath. Pol.*'s second (and surely larger) category of offices.

The justification for this claim will emerge from a consideration of the two main questions which *Ath. Pol.* 62.1 raises in respect of this second category. What exactly did the writer mean by offices "distributed to the demes" (διηροῦντο εἰς τοὺς δήμους)? And what exactly did the demes "begin to sell" (ἐπώλουν) under this system which led to its abandonment?

Two procedural reconstructions have been offered, by Mabel Lang and E. S. Staveley.[100] Both believe in ten tribal fifties, made up from the demes in the same proportions as the bouleutic quotas,[101] but beyond that the differences between their schemes are more significant than the similarities. The scene which Miss Lang envisaged in the Theseion—"tribal headquarters," as she terms it—is not unlike that which we visualized earlier for the appointment of the council: a centralized act of tribal sortition on the basis of pre-selection of candidates, according to quota, at deme level. Staveley, however, found three "severe disadvantages" in this scenario and offered an "alternative and eminently more sensible" one of his own, as follows:

> ". . . the allotment conducted in the Theseion to which Aristotle refers constituted not the final stage, but a preliminary one, in the appointment procedure. It did not determine the identity of the various magistrates for the following year; it merely marked out the particular demes within each tribe to which the responsibility for appointing each magistrate should be assigned . . . Once this allocation of offices was over, it presumably fell to the deme organizations to invite applications for the office or offices which they were empowered to fill, and, if necessary, to conduct a sortition at deme

[99] I.e., the system of the writer's own day (?Aristot. *Ath. Pol.* 8.1; the replacement of *klērōsis* from *prokritoi* by a double *klērōsis* may have occurred independently, however). But I shall suggest below that this system was not in fact created until the second quarter of the fourth century.

[100] Lang, "Allotment," pp. 84ff.; Staveley, *Elections*, pp. 48-51, 69-72.

[101] Lang, "Allotment," pp. 83, 84, 89; Staveley, *Elections*, p. 70, cf. 50. (Miss Lang, it will be recalled, postulated five hundred candidates, in tribal fifties, for *all* magistracies, including the archonships. This can surely no longer have been the case in the second half of the fifth century; cf. above, n. 83.)

level to determine the successful candidates. It should be noted that this procedure would not only have been fairer and more simple to operate than the other; it would also have led naturally to the bargaining to which Aristotle refers. Both because the individual offices which were at the disposal of a deme were identified and because the final selection of the magistrate was made at local level, it is very credible that a wealthy demesman who aspired to the office in question should have attempted to buy his deme's good services in procuring it for himself."[102]

This scheme[103] claims as its foundation not only "Aristotle" (that is, *Ath. Pol.* 62.1, as Staveley construes it) but also, and equally, a tiny group of painted terracotta allotment-tokens (also discussed by Miss Lang) which seem to bear on the problem. The purpose and significance of the one specimen long known, IG I² 916, remained quite unsuspected until 1951, when Homer Thompson announced the discovery of three more in "a rubbish pit immediately behind the Stoa [of Attalos] . . . along with a mass of broken pottery of the second half of the fifth century B.C."; he went on to note that "the evidence of context and of letter forms indicates a date near the middle of the fifth century B.C."[104] These four small plaques, three centimeters square, are all halves of official *symbola*, two of them (including IG I² 916) top halves and two bottom. Each has one deliberately irregularly cut edge, where an originally rectangular plaque was divided in half by a cut unique, or so intended, to itself. On one side—we may call it the obverse—the two top halves each have painted a *dēmotikon*: "Xypetaion" on IG I² 916, "Halimos(ios)" on one of Thompson's. The two bottom halves each have painted, also on the obverse side, the letters ΠΟΛ, which can be nothing but an abbreviation for *pōl(ētēs)*.[105] On the reverse side of the plaques was painted an abbreviated version of the name of the tribe to which the deme in question belonged;[106] and it was painted in such a position, in the center of the plaque, that the jagged cut passed through it, leaving it equally decipherable on both (what had now become) the top and bottom halves.

---

[102] Staveley, *Elections*, p. 50.

[103] Accepted by Rhodes, *Commentary*, p. 690.

[104] H. A. Thompson, *Hesp.* 20, 1951, pp. 51-52, with plate 25*c* (reproduced here). Cf. [M. L. Lang,] *The Athenian Citizen*, Agora Picture Book no. 4, Princeton, 1960, fig. 8; and Staveley, *Elections*, p. 71, fig. II.

[105] Or, theoretically, *pol(emarchos)*; but see Lang, "Allotment," p. 86, pointing out that the appointment of archons took no account of demes. (The polemarch alternative is not even contemplated by Staveley, *Elections*, p. 70, or Rhodes, *Commentary*, pp. 689-690.)

[106] It does not actually survive on IG I² 916 (which was apparently recycled as a toy or souvenir), but, as Thompson noted, KEK(ROPIS) can be legitimately "restored."

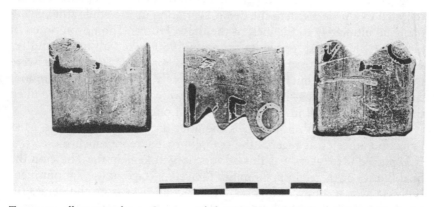

Terracotta allotment-tokens. Courtesy of the American School of Classical Studies at Athens.

This of course is the feature which shows that the plaques were indeed *symbola*, cut in half only to be reunited for some official purpose.[107] Mismatching, whether by accident or design, would be effectively ruled out by the need to rejoin both the haphazard cuts and the two halves of the tribe's name.[108]

The basic mechanics of using these tokens for the allotment of minor magistracies can thus be deduced from a scrutiny of their form and

[107] That they were for official rather than private use is clear, as Thompson observed, not only from the tribe and deme names but also from the fine terracotta fabric itself, which shows close similarities with that used for official measures in the same period. Professor Thompson tells me that the *writing*, besides, is of the "professional" character to be found on the measures, as opposed to that on (e.g.) most ostraka.

[108] Firing the plaques (*after* painting; cf. Lang, "Allotment," p. 81) was doubtless also designed, as Professor Thompson has suggested to me, to make them harder to tamper with.

manufacture; and here Miss Lang and Staveley are fundamentally in accord with each other.[109] For each tribe fifty tokens would be prepared, by painting the tribe's name in the center of what we have called the reverse and then cutting the plaques irregularly across it. Top and bottom halves would be taken away separately, for demotics (on the basis of the bouleutic quotas) to be painted on the obverse side of the former and offices to be filled on the reverse side of the latter. Firing would then take place; and not until the *symbola* were fitted together again on allotment-day in the Theseion would it emerge which deme had secured the opportunity to fill which office.[110] The object of the exercise, clearly, was that each tribe's representative(s) on all the various boards of magistrates should come from the constituent demes of that tribe by a process which reflected to a proper extent the demes' variation in size while still leaving the issue ultimately to the luck of the draw. Homer Thompson noted in his report that the three halves found in 1950 were "all intact and remarkably fresh." Possibly, therefore, these particular specimens were never actually used; but there is no real necessity for any such assumption, since clearly their use—if the same demes were not always to have filled the same posts—will in any case have been once-for-all.[111]

Still to be resolved, however, is the utter disagreement between Miss Lang and Staveley as regards the overall procedure in which these *symbola* played their part. Was this allotment by tokens in the Theseion the final (Lang) or merely a preliminary (Staveley) stage of the appointment process? Was it an event involving fifty actual men from the demes of, say, Pandionis—fifty candidates of flesh and blood, already designated as such and now waiting to know what if any would be their particular post—or simply fifty potential opportunities to hold office, with actual appointment to them separate, subsequent, and local? Staveley, as mentioned earlier, insists that Lang's procedure would have entailed "severe disadvantages," and these must now be examined. Yet his own alternative (quoted above) is more vulnerable than he supposes, on the grounds not so much of individual "disadvantages" as of overall and intrinsic implausibility, as a system purportedly devised and employed by the Athenian democracy of the second half of the fifth century (and indeed, insofar as offices were still "distributed to the demes" [*Ath. Pol.* 62.1] then, the first half of the fourth). No other aspect of magisterial appointments

[109] Lang, "Allotment," pp. 85-86; Staveley, *Elections*, pp. 70-72.

[110] For the appointment of an actual individual within a deme's quota of candidates (if it was more than one), see the suggestion of Lang, "Allotment," p. 86. (For Staveley, of course, this was an internal matter for the deme itself, at a later date; see on this theory below.)

[111] Cf. Lang, "Allotment," p. 86.

in classical Athens warrants the belief that the Athenians ever made the sort of conceptual distinction between offices and the persons filling them that Staveley's scheme demands[112]—let alone that they did so to the extent that their prime concern was to distribute the former, and leave open the choice of the latter to be determined (as Staveley himself visualizes) by readily corruptible means at parochial level.[113] It may be suggested, then, that if Staveley's objections to the procedure as set out by Miss Lang can be answered—as I would maintain they can—it is Lang's own scheme which remains the best that we have.[114]

Staveley's three criticisms,[115] and the responses which they invite, are as follows:

(a) In the first place, [the Lang procedure] would have involved a double process of selection—at deme level by vote, and at tribe level by lot—and it would possibly have necessitated the attendance of some five hundred persons, fifty from each tribe, at the final allotment. This might not have meant any great hardship, but it would have been unnecessarily troublesome when a simpler method could have been devised to achieve the same end.

This argument from convenience, as we may call it, actually makes many points in one, but they can all be answered. First, a double selection of *candidates* is no more problematical in itself than Staveley's own two-stage procedure, namely, distribution of offices followed by (single) selection of men to fill them. In any case the Athenian constitutional and judicial system teemed with procedures and mechanisms—the *klērōtēria*, to cite only the most obvious example—which strike us as complex and cumbersome; that is because their purpose was not simplicity for its own sake but rather equity and fairness in the result. (On the criterion of fairness see below, argument *b*.) As to what needed to be done first (Lang) or finally (Staveley) in the demes, there is no basis for Staveley's insinuation that the Lang procedure required a vote there and his own merely sortition—which is anyway no simpler *per se* than a vote. And as regards the supposedly unlikely attendance, at the final (on Lang's view) stage, of all five hundred candidates, this begs two questions in one. First, the matter of numbers is strictly irrelevant, for the attendance in person of all the candidates may not have been mandatory; and in any case *any*

---

[112] One is reminded, rather, of the *Roman* mentality in these matters, at least insofar as it is illustrated by C. Gracchus' *lex de provinciis consularibus* (Cicero *de domo* 9.24, etc.). (I owe this point to Professor Christian Habicht.)

[113] The precise nature of the corruption will be considered below.

[114] Miss Lang has been kind enough to tell me that her views are unchanged.

[115] Staveley, *Elections*, pp. 49-50.

number of people with a sufficiently strong incentive to attend a meeting will do so if they can.[116] The Theseion, as we have seen, could accommodate more than five hundred men with ease. But did it have to, in this instance? Here is the second question begged: Staveley should not have taken it for granted that the Theseion allotments dealt with all the ten tribes together, at a single meeting, when it is equally likely (to say the least) that what took place was a succession of ten separate tribal assemblies.[117]

(b) Secondly, the equitable operation of the lot and the arrangements designed to give each deme a chance of representation proportionate to its size would have been badly upset when the lot for a particular office fell upon someone in the pool of candidates who had already held the office and who, because of the ban on holding the same office twice, was therefore ineligible to take up his appointment. Ways could, of course, have been found of avoiding such a complication, the simplest perhaps being to exclude from the lot for any particular office all those who had previously held it; but such methods would have made nonsense of the proportionate chances of the various demes, the achievement of which would presumably have been the whole purpose of such a complex procedure.

This, the argument from fairness, is equally misconceived. Lang's scheme takes adequate account of the possibility of a certain number of the candidates proving ineligible for particular offices: they would not be excluded "from the lot" but discounted, if need be, once their deme had already drawn the right to fill a place on a particular board of magistrates which they themselves happened to have occupied.[118] And in no way did this make "nonsense" of the whole system. It was only right and proper that the larger demes should have the larger share of the possibilities not only of drawing an office but also of discovering that one of their own candidates had already held it.

(c) According to our information, the scheme was scrapped because the demes sold their quotas; and on [Lang's] view the trade

---

[116] Staveley's own scenario (*Elections*, pp. 70-71), by contrast, might seem to lead to hardly anyone's attending the Theseion meeting at all, so little of the process at that impersonal stage being of interest to anyone in particular! But in fact on *either* scheme the only men whose attendance was absolutely necessary were the officials.

[117] This in fact is what Lang *appears* to assume at "Allotment," pp. 85-86. The only obvious consideration which might lend support to the idea of a single meeting is the use of the tribe names on the tokens, which might seem otiose if only one tribe was meeting at a time; but all the plaques may well have been *prepared* at the same time, and what else (if so) would have served as the word to be divided by the cut?

[118] Cf. above, n. 110.

would have been not in the quotas of offices, but simply in the quotas of candidates which each deme was entitled to present at the tribal allotment. But, as it would have been impossible for any individual candidate to profit by such a transaction (his chances would always have been approximately 14 in 50), it is difficult to see who would have been the buyers. It is just possible that some demes had such corporate pride in being well represented on the magisterial boards that they were willing to use their funds to this end; but, against that, if deme pride did run so strong among the Athenians, it is unlikely that there would have been many sellers.

Here at least we reach an important and serious point, tendentiously presented though it is. Miss Lang's picture[119] of what, according to ?Aristot. *Ath. Pol.* 62.1, the demes "began to sell" (ἐπώλουν) does indeed envisage chicanery *between* demes, with the smaller ones "selling" their representation-quotas in the tribal fifties to larger ones. But this idea, while not wholly implausible as such (for the reason indicated by Staveley), is formally unsatisfactory in two respects in its context within the argument as a whole. First, it aims, oddly, to describe a possible abuse *before* the introduction of allotment by tokens—thereby obviously failing to explain what was amiss with the system under which the demes were doing their "selling." And thus, secondly, it effectively rules out the possibility of *inter*-deme malpractice once the token system was in use. To be sure, the abuse to which *Ath. Pol.* 62.1 refers very probably outlasted—or indeed may not even have arisen until after—the period of the token system, which seems to have been short-lived (see below). Nevertheless there is more to be said for Staveley's view of bribery and corruption *within* demes—that is, men immoderately desirous of holding office inducing their deme's officials to ignore or discourage rival applicants.[120]

To believe this, however, we are not obliged to accept the whole, unlikely procedural hypothesis under which the deme had already by this stage been "empowered" to supply its tribe's member of a specified magisterial college. Staveley sees no point in any particular individual's bribing his way into his deme's quota (and thus into the tribal pool of candidates) at a stage when, before the allocation of known offices to known demes, his chances of actually holding office at all were "approximately 14 in 50." This figure of fourteen is a version of Miss Lang's

---

[119] Lang, "Allotment," p. 85.

[120] Staveley, *Elections*, pp. 50, 111. Rhodes, *Commentary*, p. 690, while generally endorsing Staveley's scheme, in fact suggests, on this specific point, a modified version of Miss Lang's idea: "a man who wanted to become πωλητής might . . . be tempted to 'buy' the office from the deme to which it had fallen."

rudimentary calculation that "perhaps fifteen men were required from each tribe" to fill the offices allotted in the Theseion.[121] Yet, as we have seen, the number of magistracies in existence in the fifth and fourth centuries has been grossly underestimated (except in ?Aristot *Ath. Pol.* 24.3!);[122] and in proceeding on the assumption that no more than one hundred and fifty men would emerge from the Theseion allotments as officeholders, both Lang and Staveley palpably share the error which Hansen has now corrected. Simply by their place in the tribal fifties, we must suppose, either the great majority or even conceivably *all* of the five hundred candidates were assured of a post *of some sort*; the allotment was to determine what sort it was to be.[123] (Miss Lang and Staveley both naturally declare that the lower halves of the obverse side of about thirty-five of each tribe's fifty tokens were left blank,[124] but this is merely an inevitable product of their underestimation of the number of magistracies at stake.) That either all or nearly all of a tribal fifty secured office under this system need cause us no disquiet, for their colleagues the fifty councillors all did.[125] At all events the crucial stage of the process—and the opportunity for dishonesty and malpractice—did come at deme level, where each deme's component of both of the fifties took shape, and where ambitious men could decide whether a year as *bouleutēs* or as magistrate would bring them the greater advantage.[126]

✳

After so lengthy an attempt to grasp the character and significance of the token system of allotment to minor sortitive office it is only proper to extract and emphasize a point which might otherwise pass unheeded amid the welter of detail: the system was a short-lived one. "It cannot be said when, or for how long, this was the standard procedure, and indeed it is possible that it was only a temporary experiment. Certainly other methods are likely to have been used."[127] The tiny number of *symbola* so far discovered, in an area so extensively and intensively excavated as the environs of the Agora, does indeed point to a very short period of use—perhaps even a single year; and our only dating guide is Homer Thompson's observation that both the archaeological context

[121] Lang, "Allotment," p. 84.
[122] See above, p. 278.
[123] As Miss Lang notes ("Allotment," p. 84, n. 18), a phrase used by Harpoc., ἐπιλαχών—"those wishing to be councillors or magistrates were allotted" (ἐκληροῦντο οἱ βουλεύειν ἢ ἄρχειν ἐφιέμενοι)—could perhaps be taken to indicate that it was not possible to offer one's self initially as a candidate for any office (thus filled) in particular.
[124] Lang, "Allotment," p. 85; Staveley, *Elections*, p. 71.
[125] The parallel is not exact, to be sure, but suggestive.
[126] See above, nn. 123 and (on the *boulē*) 47.
[127] Staveley, *Elections*, p. 72. See further below.

and the letter forms of the three *symbola* found in 1950 suggest a date near the middle of the fifth century. Such a dating might warrant the conjecture that the token system was introduced at the same time as and (thus) as the first manifestation of the Theseion allotments themselves, but clearly it is equally possible that the latter were already in operation when the token experiment was tried out.[128] In either case it seems plain that the Theseion allotments, embodying the basic principle of deme "representation" in minor city magistracies, were retained long after the token system had come and gone.[129]

But for *how* long? Here we must return—for the last time—to ?Aristot. *Ath. Pol.* 62.1, where everything that we have discussed so far is described by the writer as the "previous" system (πρότερον μέν). He goes on to say that because of the corruption at deme level it was decided that "the offices allotted in the Theseion ⟨which⟩ were distributed to the demes" should also—that is, just as those "allotted, with the nine archons, from whole tribes"—be allotted "from whole tribes," save only for the *bouleutai* and the *phrouroi*, whose appointment was (still in his own day) "assigned to the demes."[130] According to Miss Lang, "there is no way of determining the date of the change, but if we may judge from the other cases in the *Constitution of the Athenians* where a former practice is contrasted with that of the present, πρότερον seems roughly to include the fifth century. The innovations, that is, seem to belong to 403 B.C. and the first half of the fourth century, although definite dates cannot always be assigned."[131] This is fair comment as far as the internal usage of the *Ath. Pol.* is concerned; for whereas there seem to be isolated instances of changes, reported in this fashion, which occurred only shortly before the time of writing,[132] it is doubtful whether any such changes are to be dated before 403/2,[133] the great watershed in Athenian constitutional development in the classical period.[134] We may therefore agree

---

[128] Lang, "Allotment," p. 85, seems to assume this.

[129] Both Lang ("Allotment," p. 85) and more briefly Staveley (*Elections*, p. 72) outline simple procedures of bean-allotment which could have been used before and/or after the period of the token system, with the same results.

[130] ?Aristot. *Ath. Pol.* 62.1 (quoted above, n. 43).

[131] Lang, "Allotment," pp. 82-83, citing for comparison *Ath. Pol.* 45.1 and 3, 49.3, 53.1, 54.5, 55.2 and 4, 56.3 and 4, 60.2, and 61.1 (on the last of which, see below, n. 133); on these and other such passages, see also J. J. Keaney, *Historia*, 19, 1970, pp. 326-336.

[132] See (e.g.) 51.3 and 53.4; Rhodes, *Commentary*, pp. 55-56.

[133] For a possible exception, see C. W. Fornara, *The Athenian Board of Generals from 501 to 404*, *Historia* Einzelschrift 16, Wiesbaden, 1971, pp. 19-27, on the *stratēgia* reform of 61.1.

[134] See in general P. J. Rhodes, "Athenian democracy after 403 B.C.," *CJ* 75, 1980, pp. 305-323.

with Lang in regarding this date as the *terminus post quem* for the procedural reform attested by *Ath. Pol.* 62.1.

For a *terminus ante quem*, however, one must look to external evidence—and what it suggests appears at first sight to pull in two rather different directions:

1. At some time between ca. 370 and ca. 362, as J. H. Kroll has shown, what he himself has termed the "Class III" bronze *pinakia* were introduced. These were individual nameplates designed to extend allotment by *klērōtēria* (allotment machines) from the allocation of jurors to jury-courts—a system inaugurated soon after 388—to the appointment of magistrates; and Demosthenes refers (in ca. 348) to the importance of such *pinakia* in sortition for the *boulē*, the archonships, and "the other magistracies."[135] The magisterial as well as the dikastic *pinakia* show each of the ten tribes divided into ten sections (μέρη or γράμματα), numbered A through K, to one of which every citizen was permanently assigned. Kroll very reasonably perceived a connection between these tribal sections and the appointment procedure for the archons attested by *Ath. Pol.* 8.1, that is, a two-stage sortition in which the first stage produced ten candidates from each tribe. And his further suggestion (on the basis of Demosth. 39.10 as well as on general grounds) that the sections were used in the process of appointment to other sortitive magistracies also, at any rate those organized in boards of ten, seems equally cogent.[136] Here, then, we would appear to have at worst a satisfactory *terminus ante quem* and at best an absolute date[137] for the discontinuation of the system under which the offices allotted in the Theseion were "distributed to the demes"; it was now the ten new subdivisions of a tribe which were electorally significant and not its constituent demes.

2. On the other hand there are certain items of evidence which seem at first examination to suggest that the "previous" procedure of *Ath. Pol.* 62.1, with the demes at its heart, was still in existence as late as 328/7. SEG 28.103, the pair of deme decrees of Eleusis from 332/1, refers in lines 27-28 to "the *archairesiai* [elections of officials] in the month Metageitnion, when the demesmen meet in assembly in the Theseion." Soon

---

135 Demosth. 39.10; see above, n. 59.

136 Kroll, *Allotment Plates*, pp. 91-94; cf. Rhodes, *Commentary*, pp. 149, 690-691, 704.

137 See on this point Rhodes, *Commentary*, pp. 690-691, and esp. Kroll, *Allotment Plates* p. 94 with n. 6, pointing out (as regards the archonships) that three procedural changes in pre-selection—its removal from the hands of the demes, the substitution of *klērōsis* for *prokrisis*, and the creation of the system of ten candidates per tribe—occurred between 457/6 and the 360s. His suggestion is that the first and second of these "are intimately related and were doubtless put into effect together"; in truth the same could be said of all three, and there seems no good reason not to imagine a single package of reforms at some time in Kroll's ca. 370 to ca. 362 period.

after that, in 330, Aeschines in his speech *Against Ktesiphon* was drawing a distinction between military posts filled by election and "magistracies which the *thesmothetai* allot in the Theseion"—a category regarded by the scholiast on the passage (surely with *Ath. Pol.* 62.1 in mind) as "certain petty administrative posts."[138] And from 327/6 we have a tribal decree of Aiantis in honor of a Rhamnousian who, as *thesmothetēs* (presumably in the preceding year), is said to have fulfilled duties which included the sortition "of the magistracies" (τῶν ἀρχῶν).[139]

Plainly this contradiction can only be apparent, not real,[140] and to resolve it one need do no more than pose the question: do any or all of the testimonia grouped under the second heading absolutely presuppose the continuing existence of the system under which offices were "distributed to the demes," or would they in fact be equally compatible with the operation of the tribal sections? The answer, surely, is the latter. No reference to the demes is made either by Aeschines (or—whether or not he had them in mind—his scholiast) or in the tribal decree. From Aeschines and the *deme* decree we see that the Theseion was still the venue for the sortition of offices, which might in any case have been a justifiable deduction from *Ath. Pol.* 62.1 as regards those formerly "distributed to the demes." What we are not entitled to conclude, however, is that it was to this and only this category of appointments that either Aeschines or the Eleusinians (or indeed the Aiantidai) were alluding. Aeschines appears to place *all* sortitive appointments in the Theseion; and the phraseology of *Ath. Pol.* 62.1 is not necessarily precise enough to weigh against this.[141]

Thus it is perfectly legitimate for us to assume that all three of our sources—Aeschines, the Aiantid tribal decree, and the Eleusinian deme decree—are referring to the unified, post-reform system of pre-selecting

---

[138] Aeschin. 3.13: ἀρχὰς ... ἃς οἱ θεσμοθέται κληροῦσιν ἐν τῷ Θησείῳ. Scholiast *ad loc.*: ... ἴσως τῶν θεσμοθετῶν ἐκεῖ ἀεὶ χειροτονούντων εὐτελεῖς τινας διοικήσεις.

[139] *Hesp.* 7, 1938, pp. 94-96, no. 15, esp. lines 5-7.

[140] Cf. Busolt/Swoboda, *Staatskunde*, p. 971, n. 3.

[141] That is, the writer may not have *intended* to imply, as he does imply, that his first category of appointments, those "allotted, with the nine archons, from whole tribes," were dealt with elsewhere; and if so we could readily accept (with Rhodes, *Commentary*, pp. 689-690) that *all* sortitions were made in the Theseion. Rhodes rejects the idea of Wilamowitz, *Aristoteles*, vol. I, pp. 203-204—based on *Lex Seguer.* V. *Lexeis Rhetorikai*, ἐν ποίοις δικαστηρίοις τίνες λαγχάνονται δίκαι; Ἡλιαία ... ἐν τούτοις ἀρχαιρεσίαι γίνονται [= Bekker, *Anecd. Gr.* 1.310.28-30]—that the *Ath. Pol.*'s first category of sortitions was held in the Heliaia, but a compromise position would be to see their transference from the Heliaia to the Theseion at the very time of the procedural reforms that we are considering (cf. Busolt/Swoboda, *Staatskunde*, p. 971, n. 3).

all sortitive officials (except the councillors) by means of the tribal sections. The testimonium least amenable, on the face of it, to this interpretation is the deme decree, in that it might naturally be taken as implying that the Eleusinians would attend the Theseion in 331/0 (and beyond) as a body of demesmen. But perhaps that appearance is deceptive, and they would actually go there as members not of the deme Eleusis but of the tribe Hippothontis (and its sections).[142] Alternatively, as I have suggested earlier, the meeting in question may have been the one which appointed the *bouleutai* (and the *phrouroi*)—a task still, as *Ath. Pol.* 62.1 states, "assigned to the demes."[143] An obstacle in the way of this interpretation, it might be felt, is the word *archairesiai*, which might not seem entirely appropriate to the appointment of councillors. However, they were regarded as holders of an *arche* in the technical sense,[144] and in any case the term *archairesiai* was a relic from the days when officials were indeed directly elected[145] or at least chosen by sortition from *prokritoi*.[146]

In view of this multiplicity of possibilities it would be foolish to insist that the *Ath. Pol.*'s "previous" procedure was still in use in the 330s and 320s; we should instead accept the implication, outlined above, of Kroll's non-dikastic *pinakia* that its abolition had been part of the procedural reforms to be dated within the period ca. 370 to ca. 362. Thenceforward the councillors continued to be appointed as before, but the rest of the sortitive *archai* were filled by the mechanics of tribes acting not as groupings of demes but as whole units with new internal subdivisions. That the corruptibility of the demes had been the sole cause of this, as ?Aristot. *Ath. Pol.* seeks to suggest, may be open to doubt. The effect of the change, nevertheless, was quite clearly to remove all vestiges of deme "representation" in city *archai* and, in the process, to realign one of the major boundaries between local and central government.

[142] Cf. above, n. 59.

[143] See above, p. 269.

[144] See above, n. 38.

[145] Compare the case of the demes' own officials: the word *archairesiai* was apparently still in use (Isaeus 7.28; [Demosth.] 44.39) long after *hairesis* had given way to *klerosis* as the actual method employed, at least for the demarchs.

[146] According to P. A. Rahe, "The selection of ephors at Sparta,"*Historia* 29, 1980, pp. 385-401, at 392-397, in the usage of Isocrates, Plato, and Aristotle, *klerosis* from *prokritoi* is a form of *hairesis*, not *klerosis*; but this is disputed by P. J. Rhodes, *Historia* 30, 1981, pp. 498-502.

CHAPTER 10

✳

LOCAL POLITICS AND
CITY POLITICS

In his dual capacity as demesman and citizen[1] an Athenian of the classical period was expected to take an active part in public life in both the microcosm of his own deme and the macrocosm of the polis as a whole. Employing the term "politics" in this simplest of its many senses—the business of government and the participation of individuals therein—this chapter will attempt to determine what can usefully be said about the politics of the deme and their relationship with the politics of the city.

A. The Character of Local Politics

As we saw in Chapter 9, the Athenians felt it necessary to introduce a not insignificant reform of their constitutional machinery (probably in the second quarter of the fourth century) on at least partial account of the fact that the demes were abusing the procedural responsibilities which had been assigned to them. They had begun, we are told, to "sell" opportunities to hold sortitive city office; and in consequence their part in the pre-selection of such officials, save only the councillors, was brought to an end.

That we hear of so few individual instances of malpractice of this kind is interesting but not, in a sense, surprising. Obviously the successful candidates would not have chosen to bring it to light, and those who had stepped aside for them would not normally have had any reason to do so either.[2] Thus the public revelation (or allegation) of this particular manifestation of local corruption must in general have occurred not in the demes themselves but in the wider arena of the city and its political

---

[1] Again (cf. Chap. 9, n. 1) for practical purposes we may ignore the intermediate groupings, notably the tribes.

[2] Cf. Staveley, *Elections*, pp. 110-111.

life.[3] The price of countermeasures was a drastic diminution in the demes' contribution to the operation of central government—a price, evidently, which the Athenians as a citizen-body did not consider too high to pay. And the result of the reform was therefore not only a decidedly more distinct cleavage between the spheres of central and local government but also the virtual extinction of what had thitherto been one of the most obvious foci of deme politics.

In the case, however, of the aspect of deme malpractice which our sources do attest, both as a general phenomenon and in particular instances, such results were far less easy to achieve and indeed were never wholeheartedly sought. On the contrary, the principles and procedures devised for the vital matter of the control of membership of the citizen-body itself represented, as we saw in Chapter 9A, a deliberate interlocking of the responsibilities of deme and polis; and it is instructive, in the light of this, to compare the reform of ca. 370 – ca. 362 in respect of magisterial pre-selection with the non-reform (as one might term it) of 346/5 in the regulation of access to citizenship. Dissatisfaction with the demes' standard of conduct on the former count resulted in the abolition of the greater part of their *locus standi* in the whole process. Yet the outcome of a presumably analogous disquiet as to the reliability of deme registration[4] was merely a requirement that the demes do their work again, more thoroughly.[5] Thus, whatever their salutary effect in the short term (and even that is disputable), the *diapsēphiseis* of 346/5 are indicative less of a genuine desire to solve the problems of inefficiency and impropriety in deme enrolments than of an unwillingness to reform the basis of the system itself, for all its manifest imperfections.

Deservedly or otherwise, particular demes seem to have acquired a reputation for corruptibility. "Today a slave, tomorrow a Sounian," ran a joke of the Middle Comic poet Anaxandrides, active in the second quarter of the fourth century.[6] The lexicographers report that the men of Potamos were ridiculed in the *Didymai* of Menander and by other comic poets for their tolerance of illegal registration.[7] And the unedify-

---

[3] Note Aeschin. 1.106-112 on Timarchos of Sphettos.

[4] "The whole polis was provoked to anger at those who had outrageously forced their way into the demes" (Demosth. 57.49).

[5] On the 346/5 episode, see Chap. 4B, sec. 1(b).

[6] Anaxandrides fr.4 (from the *Anchises*), lines 3-4: πολλοὶ δὲ νῦν μέν εἰσιν οὐκ ἐλεύθεροι,| εἰς αὔριον δὲ Σουνιεῖς. See Chap. 9, n. 15.

[7] Harpoc., Ποταμός· . . . ἐκωμῳδοῦντο δὲ ὡς ῥαδίως δεχόμενοι τοὺς παρεγγράπτους, ὡς ἄλλοι τε δηλοῦσι καὶ Μένανδρος ἐν Διδύμαις. (It is likely, though not at all demonstrable, that the "others" included the Old Comic poet Strattis, one of whose plays was called Ποτάμιοι.) Cf. Suda, Ποταμοί; *Etym. Magn.* 288.15 (Δρυαχαρνεῦ), cf. 738.44 (Σφήττιοι); *Lex Rhet. Cantabr.*, Σφήττιοι. No distinction is drawn here between the three Potamos demes.

ing record of the deme Halimous which came to light in or soon after
346/5 with Demosthenes 57—scandals not only in admission (57.59) but
also in exclusion (57.26, 58, and 60-61, quite apart from Euxitheos' case
itself)—will doubtless have been recalled some years later by the notorious episode of the ex-slave metic Agasikles, impeached for his attempt
to bribe his way into the citizen-body through illegal registration in that
selfsame deme.[8] Obviously neither comic poets nor forensic *logographoi*
are the most trustworthy of guides to literal fact. In the case of comedy,
especially, caricature and exaggeration can often retain only the lightest
of footholds in reality. Here, for example, the men of Sounion may well
have laid themselves open to Anaxandrides' scorn not because of any
long-standing laxity in their scrutiny procedures but rather through a
single *cause célèbre*. Nor in general can one readily suppose that even
the Athenians could have remained wedded as they were to the principle
of citizenship registration in the demes if corruption there had been the
rule and not the exception, however frequent and/or widespread.[9] On
the other hand, to brush aside the evidence of comedy and oratory is no
wiser than to afford it excessive credence; and in this instance the inescapable fact of the action taken, across the board, in 346/5 offers some
kind of guarantee that the problem had an existence outside the realms
of individual malice and fantasy. There is little profit to be gained in even
attempting to establish the true facts behind the apparently long-running
joke at the expense of the Potamioi or the cases of Euxitheos and Agasikles, and no such attempt will be made here. Instead we shall take this
and other testimony very largely at its face value—not as a series of
glimpses into what actually happened in particular demes on particular
occasions, but rather as the elements in a general model of the *type* of
political behavior in the demes to which their major role in controlling
the membership of the citizen-body gave rise. This is in fact our only

---

[8] Dinarchus wrote the speech for the prosecution (fr. 16; see Harpoc., Ἀγασικλῆς and
σκαφηφόροι), and the case is mentioned, as very recent, by Hyper. 4 (*Eux.*). 3; cf. Suda,
Ἁλιμούσιος. It is to be dated somewhere between 336 and 324 (M. H. Hansen, *Eisangelia*,
Odense, 1975, p. 105, no. 115). We do not know the outcome.

[9] Halimous, Potamos, and Sounion are all, it will be noted, small rural demes, where it
might be imagined that improper registration was at its easiest; and of course some 75%
of demes fell into this category! (In Demosth. 57.56-57 Euxitheos observes how just it is
that he has enjoyed the right of appeal to a jury-court against the vote of his fellow
Halimousioi; and he asks those of the jurymen who belonged to "the large demes"—ὅσοι
τῶν μεγάλων δήμων ἐστέ—to remember that they have been denying nobody an opportunity for accusation and defence, i.e., not to take it for granted in this case that the
Halimousioi have voted fairly. If one then asks why men from large demes should be
especially prone to such an assumption, the answer might be either that this is what they
would envisage for a small deme where everyone knew each other or else that this is what
they were used to in their own, larger demes.)

real opportunity to assess the character of local politics in any degree of detail, and it is unfortunate that in taking it we shall inevitably see only the unpleasant and unattractive aspects of the picture. To retain a balanced view it will be necessary to bear in mind the general remarks made in this paragraph, together with the fact that at least some of the detectable modes of behavior were equally suited to proper as to improper objectives.

Our first requirement is to penetrate, if we can, beneath the impersonal language in which the evidence is mainly (and understandably) couched. When any deme took the serious step of either enlisting a man in or, if appropriate, expelling him from its roll of members, the burden of responsibility for doing so fell necessarily upon the undivided collectivity of the demesmen. To that extent, no individual demesman of Sounion or Potamos could properly have claimed exemption from the ridicule directed at their demes by Anaxandrides and Menander, and no Halimousian could legitimately have evaded his small share of the adverse comment (if no worse) which must have accompanied the restoration, after appeal, of all but one of the ten men struck off in the affair of the reconstructed register (Demosth. 57.26 and 60-61). All the same, theoretical or legalistic responsibility is one thing, actual responsibility another. For our purposes here the latter may be simply defined as the responsibility borne by those acting illegally *in the unashamed knowledge that they are doing so*, and on that basis it is highly improbable that the entire body of the demesmen was in many or even any such cases actually to blame for the deme's decision. We are told, for example, that Agasikles "bribed the Halimousioi"; and in the sense, described above, that "the Halimousioi" then proceeded to enrol him, this is unexceptionable. Yet what does it really mean? Surely not that Agasikles had taken the absurd risk of approaching and attempting to bribe each and every one of the eighty or ninety demesmen of Halimous (cf. Demosth. 57.9-10 and 15), or even a numerical majority of them. What he must have done instead was to use his money to best advantage, by giving it either to the demarch (and other officials if necessary) and to those willing to lie about his ancestry or else to others within the deme who could bring influence to bear upon these two groups.[10] The general body of the demesmen will then have reached its decision either in ignorance of the true facts (or

---

[10] Harpocration's use (s.v. Ἀγασικλῆς) of the phrase Ἁλιμουσίους συνεδέκασε (Suda, Ἁλιμούσιος, has συνδίκασαι, wrongly; note the general comment in LSJ, under συνδεκάζω) is no proof that the entire deme was involved; from other instances of συνδεκάζειν, such as Aeschin. 1.86, it is clear that the word did not convey the idea of bribing absolutely every member of the body in question but simply enough of them to bring about the desired result.

after assurances that they were *not* true) or in fear of reprisals if they were disclosed; and to make matters certain a corrupt official may have been on hand to manipulate the actual balloting. The opposite manoeuvre, that of having someone *removed* from the register, must usually have been more difficult to contrive, as the demesmen had to be induced to reverse their original vote in the victim's favor.[11] But again, one may visualize their doing so either under duress, or after hearing new (perjured) testimony, or in a rigged ballot, or through any combination thereof.

In terms of what they can tell us about the workings of deme politics, it is obvious that improper registration is less significant than improper exclusion from the register. The former was, so to speak, a unilateral act—the introduction of an outsider—which, if successfully camouflaged, need not have occasioned any intra-deme controversy. The latter, by contrast, must always have been highly contentious. What one might call the prosecution (those seeking to bring about the vote for disfranchisement) and the defence (the intended victim himself, together with those—if any—still prepared to bear witness on his behalf) had to engage in claim and counterclaim. Our most vivid and disturbing insight into such a contest, and much else besides, is of course to be found in Demosthenes 57.[12] But it is in fact the totality of the surviving data, relating to all aspects of lexiarchical malpractice, which matches the inherent probabilities of our model of the mechanics of local corruption with a modicum of supporting evidence.

The question of bribery offers a suitable starting-point. Besides the case of Agasikles we hear of it explicitly on three occasions. Aeschines alleges in 1.114-115 that, during the *diapsēphiseis* of 346/5, the prominent politician Timarchos of Sphettos claimed that a certain Philotades of Kydathenaion was his freedman (*apeleutheros*)[13] and so persuaded the Kydathenaieis to vote his disfranchisement. Philotades naturally lodged an appeal, and Timarchos repeated his accusation under oath before the jury-court, but abandoned the case once it had come to light that he had accepted through an intermediary a bribe of two thousand drachmas from Leukonides, a relative of Philotades' by marriage. The size of the sum is rather surprising, though hardly more so than the existence of copies of a written agreement by which "the sale of the case"—Aeschines' own phrase—was effected.[14] Obviously the high political stakes in Aes-

---

[11] I use the language appropriate to cases of *unjust* expulsion.

[12] See the admirable summary and discussion in Haussoullier, *Vie*, pp. 41-45.

[13] And hence a metic: see in general Whitehead, *Metic*, pp. 16-17.

[14] Aeschin. 1.115: τῶν συνθηκῶν ἀνάγνωθι τὰ ἀντίγραφα, καθ᾿ ἃς τὴν πρᾶσιν ἐποιήσατο τοῦ ἀγῶνος.

chines' prosecution of Timarchos place some strain, to say the least, upon our credence of the details of such an episode. However, the importance of this sort of evidence lies less in its literal truth or falsehood than in its plausibility to the jury;[15] and in this instance it is indeed plausible enough that, in a large city deme like Kydathenaion, the hired appearance of a Timarchos was thought necessary to add conviction to what might otherwise have been summarily dismissed as a case of internal family feuding. Aeschines implies that the demesmen, including their officials, acted in good faith throughout the affair. It is obviously possible that he does so in order to highlight the culpability of Timarchos, the outsider, but it is equally true that the stratagem as he describes it *need* not have been in any sense an "inside job."

One may suspect, nonetheless, that what Euxitheos depicts in Demosth. 57.58-61 were more typical occurrences. In 57.59 he recounts how Euboulides and his associates had illegally enrolled as Halimousioi two foreigners, Anaximenes and Nikostratos, and had then seen to it that they were not exposed and expelled in the 346/5 *diapsēphiseis*—the occasion, of course, of the vote against Euxitheos himself. We are told that the bribe offered by Anaximenes and Nikostratos, when divided amongst "the conspirators" (οἱ συνεστηκότες), amounted to five drachmas apiece.[16] As this episode had taken place prior to the *diapsēphiseis*, held in the year of Euboulides' own demarchy (57.8), we are left to guess whether or not it had involved the corruption of any officials.[17] Euxitheos then proceeds, in 57.60, to claim that the clique "both destroyed and saved many men for the sake of money" (πολλοὺς . . . οἱ μετ' Εὐβουλίδου συνεστῶτες καὶ ἀπολωλέκασιν καὶ σεσώκασιν ἕνεκ' ἀργυρίου). This presumably takes up the allegation in 57.58 that "of brothers born of the same mother and the same father they have voted out some but not others, and have voted out elderly men with no means while leaving in their sons" (ἀδελφῶν ὁμομητρίων καὶ ὁμοπατρίων τῶν μέν εἰσιν ἀπεψηφισμένοι, τῶν δ' οὔ, καὶ πρεσβυτέρων ἀνθρώπων ἀπόρων, ὧν τοὺς υἱεῖς ἐγκαταλελοίπασιν). Unlike the affair of An-

---

[15] Cf. Dover, *Morality*, p. 13: "it is particularly important that a rhetorical case should not be mistaken for a case-history . . . it is only evidence for what the speaker (a) wished the jury to believe and (b) judged that they would not find it hard to believe."

[16] This sum seems as paltry as Timarchos' two thousand drachmas (above) sounds excessive. Might there be textual corruption here? If not, perhaps Euxitheos was seeking to imply not that his enemies were a very large group (for it was hardly in his interests to have done so) but rather that their threshold of corruptibility was so low.

[17] No indication of date is given, save the phrase καὶ νῦν in connection with the *diapsēphisis* itself. One cannot rule out the possibility that everything described in 57.59 took place within the year 346/5, with Euboulides as demarch, though there is nothing positively in favor of this.

aximenes and Nikostratos, who could have been registered in any year prior to 346/5,[18] what is described in 57.58 and 60 can have taken place only at a general *diapsēphisis*. By his use of the phrase "Euboulides and his fellow conspirators" (οἱ μετ' Εὐβουλίδου συνεστῶτες) in 57.60 Euxitheos was possibly seeking to create a context, as it were, for his own treatment in the *diapsēphisis* of 346/5—that is, the suggestion that others besides himself had been improperly expelled at the same time (if not necessarily for the same reasons; see below). We have no certain means of telling, for he never makes a plain statement on the point. But his alarming account of the balloting in 346/5 (57.9-16), which we must examine later, is presented as a drama in which there was only one victim, and it is noteworthy that he backs up his "protection-racket" allegations not with claims of further improprieties in 346/5 but with a fuller version, in 57.60-61, of the bizarre episode briefly introduced in 57.26: the purported loss of the *lēxiarchikon grammateion* by Euboulides' father Antiphilos and the extraordinary *diapsēphiseis* which Antiphilos, as demarch, had held to reconstitute it.[19] Again the blackmail motive is alleged;[20] and the scandalous nature of the affair is a certainty unless Euxitheos' assertion that nine of the ten *apepsēphismenoi* won their appeal was a simple (and readily disprovable) lie.

Even without explicit testimony of this kind it would be plain enough that illegal manipulation of the register was far easier if its official custodian, the demarch, was either eager or at least willing to betray his trust. When the younger Leostratos of Eleusis sought re-registration in Otryne[21] he "got together a few of the Otrynians and the demarch and persuaded them, when the *grammateion* was opened, to enrol him."[22] (The attempt failed, we are told, when Leostratos subsequently overplayed his hand by going openly to claim a *theōrikon* for the Great Panathenaia.) One would like to have heard more about these "few" Otrynians, and whether the demarch had been their ringleader or merely their reluctant accomplice. Since the operation of the lot elevated into

[18] See preceding note.

[19] The date is indeterminable, though Euxitheos asserts that all the "seniors" (πρεσβύτεροι) could recall the episode. In 57.62 he seems to imply that he as well as his father underwent this extraordinary *diapsēphisis*, but his phraseology there may be loose, and in any case we do not know his age (cf. Davies, *Families*, p. 95).

[20] Demosth. 57.60: δημαρχῶν ὁ Εὐβουλίδου πατήρ, ὥσπερ εἶπον, Ἀντίφιλος, τεχνάζει βουλόμενος παρά τινων λαβεῖν ἀργύριον κτλ.

[21] For the background, see Haussoullier, *Vie*, pp. 25-28, and Davies, *Families*, pp. 194-196.

[22] [Demosth.] 44.37: συναγωγῶν τινας τῶν Ὀτρυνέων ὀλίγους καὶ τὸν δήμαρχον πείθει, ἐπειδὰν ἀνοιχθῇ τὸ γραμματεῖον, ἐγγράψαι αὐτόν.

the demarchy many men who were otherwise obscure,[23] it is not difficult
to imagine the pressures—for good or ill—that may have been imposed
upon them by the prominent individuals and families of their demes. But
in the case of Antiphilos and Euboulides of Halimous there seems no
good reason to postulate any influence beyond their own, brought to
bear upon others.

Even if we discount a hefty proportion of what Euxitheos says about
him, Euboulides especially comes across as a forceful and domineering
figure—seemingly not of the highest social and economic status, but,
perhaps for that very reason, entertaining hopes of influence at city level
as well as power within the deme.[24] It was Euxitheos, as he tells us himself
(Demosth. 57.8), who had been at least partially responsible for a major
setback to Euboulides' political ambitions in the city arena, by testifying
for the defence when Euboulides had brought a *graphē asebeias* against
"the sister of Lakedaimonios" (see **19**). Having failed to obtain one-fifth
of the jury's votes, Euboulides will have suffered not merely a fine of a
thousand drachmas but also a ban from bringing in *graphai* in future;[25]
so we can readily accept Euxitheos' observation that this was the reason
for the demarch's enmity towards him. As there is no indication of the
date of the trial we cannot say whether Euxitheos' description of Euboulides as his "*old* enemy" (παλαιὸς ἐχθρός: 57.48) is in reference
to this same episode or to an earlier period. However, in connection with
the affair of the lost register Euxitheos mentions (57.61) that Antiphilos
was an enemy—for unexplained reasons—of his own father, Thoukritos,[26] so we know that to some extent the seeds of hostility between the
two combatants in 346/5 had been sown in the preceding generation.

Furthermore, since the dice are so heavily loaded against the Antiphilos/
Euboulides side in the presentation of the issues in Demosthenes 57, it
might be fair to surmise that Euxitheos himself had not been wholly
averse to continuing, even intensifying, the feud. Very late in his speech
(57.63-65) he reveals the fact that he too had served a term as demarch
of Halimous. His purpose in doing so is transparent: having given two
examples of how scandalously a "bad" demarch behaves he wants to
present a picture of a "good" one, himself, bent not on avarice and

[23] See Chap. 4, n. 153, expanded in Chap. 8, pp. 236-237.

[24] See **19**. One cannot but be somewhat suspicious of the coincidence of his being demarch
and *bouleutēs* in the same year (cf. Chap. 5, n. 100), even if he can hardly have foreseen
what a special year the *diapsēphiseis* were to make it.

[25] See, on this penalty, MacDowell, *Law*, p. 64. That payment of the fine ended the ban
was suggested by Harrison, *Law* II, p. 83.

[26] Not named here but in 57.41 and 67. In 57.61 the subject of ὧν ἐχθρὸς τῷ ἐμῷ πατρί
is left unstated, and A. T. Murray in the Loeb edition took it to be Euboulides; however,
the sentence next but one (καὶ τί δεῖ περὶ τῶν πατέρων λέγειν;) as well as the general
context make it plain that we are being told about Antiphilos.

corruption but, on the contrary, on a crusade against it. As demarch, he avers, he incurred the anger of the many men whom he compelled to pay rents owing on deme temple-lands and from whom he retrieved common funds which they had embezzled.[27] This sounds like an admirable record of devotion to duty, unquestionably. Equally, though, it is an indication either of how ingenuous he was in believing that his actions would not be bitterly resented or else of how unconcerned he was by the thought of the personal risks he was running. Whichever is the case, it is the reaction to the steps he had taken which he cites as the proof of a sworn conspiracy against him:[28] the refusal to vote on him "without favor or malice,"[29] the sacrilegious theft of arms which he had dedicated to Athena, the erasure of a decree which the demesmen had passed in his honor (*qua* demarch, one supposes), and, as culmination, a nocturnal raid on his "little house in the country" (τὸ οἰκίδιον . . . τὸ ἐν ἀγρῷ). Euxitheos does not name the men responsible for all this, those whose financial machinations at the deme's expense he claims to have thwarted; and this must make it rather unlikely that Euboulides had been amongst them. They may nonetheless very well have included some of the latter's friends and associates, to whom he would naturally have turned once, as we have seen, he had his own powerful reasons for contriving Euxitheos' downfall; and the unforeseeable episode of the 346/5 *diapsēphiseis*, produced by and conducted in an atmosphere more appropriate to a witch hunt, was obviously the golden opportunity for all whom Euxitheos had fairly or unfairly antagonized to come together and hatch their plot (57.49).

Its success palpably revolved around Euboulides himself and his handling of the crucial vote against his enemy (57.9-16). The demarch's first task, we gather, was to pace the proceedings in such a way that the case of Euxitheos came up as late in the day as possible.[30] This ensured that

---

[27] Demosth. 57.63: εἰ δὲ δεῖ τὴν δημαρχίαν λέγειν, δι' ἣν ὠργίζοντό μοί τινες, ἐν ᾗ διάφορος ἐγενόμην εἰσπράττων ὀφείλοντας πολλοὺς αὐτῶν μισθώσεις τεμενῶν καὶ ἕτερ' ἃ τῶν κοινῶν διηρπάκεσαν, ἐγὼ μὲν ἂν βουλοίμην ὑμᾶς ἀκούειν κτλ.

[28] 57.63, τεκμήριον ὡς συνέστησαν; 57.64, συνώμνυον οὗτοι ἐπ' ἐμὲ οἱ ὑπ' ἐμοῦ τὰ κοινὰ εἰσπραχθέντες. See further below, with n. 32.

[29] It is not altogether clear whether this oath was the one taken at the *diapsēphisis* or at his demarch's *euthynai*; see Chap. 4 with n. 29.

[30] 57.9: πρῶτον μέν, ἐπειδὴ συνελέγησαν οἱ δημόται, κατέτριψεν τὴν ἡμέραν δημηγορῶν καὶ ψηφίσματα γράφων. τοῦτο δ' ἦν οὐκ ἀπὸ τοῦ αὐτομάτου, ἀλλ' ἐπιβουλεύων ἐμοί, ὅπως ὡς ὀψιαίταθ' ἡ διαψήφισις ἡ περὶ ἐμοῦ γένοιτο· καὶ διεπράξατο τοῦτο. This would seem to suggest that the order in which the demesmen were to be scrutinized—Euxitheos says that his case was about the sixtieth (57.10) out of more than eighty cases in all (57.15)—had been decided separately and without manipulation; the fact, however, that Euxitheos claims that the vote on his case took him by surprise (57.12) perhaps indicates that it was an order known only to the presiding officials.

more than half of the seventy-three demesmen who had taken the oath at the outset of the voting (57.9) had by then left the meeting, held in the city, for their country homes and farms. These included the senior members of the deme (οἱ πρεσβύτεροι τῶν δημοτῶν), who might, perhaps, have been especially resistant to overt victimization; and those who remained, numbering no more than thirty, included "all those suborned by Euboulides (ἅπαντες οἱ τούτῳ παρεσκευασμένοι: 57.10). The precise purpose for which he had suborned them should be noticed. It was not, as we might have expected, to bear false witness against Euxitheos, for one of the oddest aspects of the whole affair is that no testimony, save a long vilifying harangue by Euboulides himself (57.11), was heard on *either* side.[31] Instead, the conspirators' role was to falsify the outcome of the voting itself, by casting "two or three" ballots apiece (57.13); and thus was Euxitheos' fate sealed.

No doubt it is (and was) only to be expected that men striving desperately to have a vote of disfranchisement against them quashed would cry "Conspiracy!" and sketch a picture of honest bodies of demesmen duped or terrorized into catastrophic errors of judgment and travesties of justice by cunning and unscrupulous cabals of those who occupied the key positions to control the presentation of the evidence—if any— and the casting of the votes.[32] Yet the predictability of this is insufficient reason in itself for us to believe that it was not, in the majority of instances, essentially the true explanation. What other mechanism of corruption could there have been? Wholesale bribery is frankly inconceivable. Wholesale intimidation is (just) credible; but on the only occasion when we catch a scent of it in any deme the issue is the understandable reluctance of *individuals* voluntarily to testify in court against a member of a powerful local family,[33] not the coercion of the whole deme into a corrupt vote on citizenship. Both evidence and probability surely make it safe to say that when a body of demesmen reached a decision about a man's right to citizen registration, and indeed about other matters too, it did so under normal circumstances on the basis of as much collective wisdom and rectitude as one may reasonably expect from human beings

[31] It is particularly curious that Euxitheos, on his own admission (57.14), had not even arranged for any of his own supporters to be present.

[32] The conspiracy "motif" is naturally ubiquitous in Demosth. 57: note especially the powerful verb καταστασιάζεσθαι ("to be overcome by faction") in the opening chapters (2, 7, 17) and the frequent use of συνίστασθαι (13, 16, 59, 60, 61, 63). See also Isaeus 12.12: Euphiletos of Erchia, the speaker's half-brother, had been ἀδίκως ὑβρίσθη [cf. Demosth. 57.5] ὑπὸ τῶν ἐν τῷ δήμῳ συστάντων.

[33] Isaeus 9.18, on the family of Thoudippos in Araphen; see Chap. 8, where this text is quoted in n. 21.

fulfilling a task which they knew to be a grave and serious one. It was when the "normal circumstances" were distorted by perjured testimony and/or fraudulent balloting that they found themselves, all unwittingly, engaged less in the exercise of their constitutional duty as demesmen and citizens than in the interplay of local politics.

Naturally the political element, if we may so describe it, in the many varieties of collective decision reached by a deme will often have been more obvious to all concerned, and often too less malign in its objectives. Individuals such as Euboulides—and for that matter Euxitheos—who sought, in or out of office, to shape those decisions bore a weighty responsibility for the political climate created thereby. In Demosthenes 57 (and the other evidence we have examined) we have a paradigm, as clear as can be, of what could happen when that responsibility was abused and the character of local politics disfigured and disgraced. Other evidence, literary and (especially) epigraphic, which has been presented in earlier chapters, and which reveals some of the more edifying byproducts of political life in the demes, tells a different but equally significant story.

B. The Relationship between Local and City Politics

Broadly interpreted, the relationship between local politics and city politics[34] in classical Athens is a theme with so many possible variations as to make it not so much a topic for discrete enquiry as a conceptual framework for a study of Athenian political life *tout court*. Many, even most, of these variations we are left to imagine. As far as evidence goes—and it is, as always, distressingly lacunose—three particular issues would seem to merit investigation. They are the extent to which those prominent in city politics and government could (and would) favor fellow demesmen, depended upon fellow demesmen for support, and had first cut their political teeth, as one might say, at deme level.

1. "COMPANIONABLE ASSOCIATES"

The phrase is taken from the title of a recent paper by Sterling Dow, in which he has drawn attention to an unjustly neglected facet of the Athenian democratic constitution.[35] That constitution, as he observes, "contained hardly any provision—only scholars very well informed would say it contained any provision at all—to make it likely that any official

[34] In both spheres I continue here to use the term "politics" in the simple sense adumbrated in the introduction to this chapter.
[35] Dow, "Associates."

should have easy, comfortable, companionable associates. The Democracy was certainly not intended to be a government by groups of cronies—politicians or others. Far from it. . . . If however in some few instances—so few that they have never been studied as such—the constitution did make some concessions to Gemütlichkeit, those instances might be interesting. They would necessarily contradict the democratic spirit, and there would be hazards of corruption."[36]

Dow claims two such instances above all, both of them reported in the Aristotelian *Ath. Pol.* In 44.1 the writer speaks of the *epistatēs* of the *prytaneis*, who for the night and day during which he served in that capacity was obliged to remain in the Tholos, together with "a trittys of the *prytaneis* which he bids (remain)" (καὶ μένειν ἀναγκαῖον ἐν τῇ θόλῳ τοῦτόν ἐστιν καὶ τριττὺν τῶν πρυτανέων ἣν ἂν οὗτος κελεύῃ). Here, as Dow explains, "the problem is whether the Epistates chose among Trittyes of fixed membership, already made up . . . or whether he selected one third (i.e., ca. 16) of the Prytaneis, picking whom he wished out of the whole 49."[37] Dow himself argues for the second of these alternatives—which in point of fact he is the first even to consider—partly by eliminating (to his satisfaction) the various versions of the first alternative and partly by asserting that the phraseology of *Ath. Pol.* 44.1 is more naturally to be construed as support for the second. On both counts, however, his case falls very far short of proof;[38] and since, even if he were right, it would not represent even notionally a significant opportunity for fellow demesmen to favor each other at the expense of others,[39] no more need be said of it here.

But Dow's other illustration of how the constitution permitted, indeed invited, the choice of companionable associates is one which is not only

[36] Dow, "Associates," p. 70.

[37] Dow, "Associates," pp. 72-80, at 73.

[38] The argument from phraseology (Dow, "Associates," p. 77) seems particularly two-edged. Admittedly the key phrase begins "*a* [not "one"] trittys of the *prytaneis*," but it is then amplified as "whichever *trittys* (ἣν) he bids," not "whichever of the *prytaneis*." This surely suggests a choice between trittyes "of fixed membership" (to use Dow's phrase), even if one still cannot perceive exactly how the fixing was accomplished. See the bibliography cited by Dow; also Rhodes, *Commentary*, p. 533, who declares Dow's thesis unlikely.

[39] On Dow's thesis (though he himself does not reduce it to these crude terms) an *epistatēs* from, say, Euonymon could, if he liked, pick his nine fellow councillors from that deme to share his sojourn in the Tholos, or at least as many of them as were congenial to him. If on the other hand his choice was merely between which of the three regular subdivisions of the Erechtheid *prytaneis* should be his companions (cf. Rhodes, *Commentary*, p. 533) it would be equally natural for him to choose the one which included Euonymon. What Dow's scheme would, obviously, have made possible is the frequent choice of particularly influential or clubbable individuals by men from demes—and indeed trittyes—*other than* their own.

attested beyond dispute (in both principle and practice) but also does disclose an important sphere of political activity where individuals were regularly the beneficiaries of appointments falling to other members of their demes.[40] In ?Aristot. *Ath. Pol.* 56.1 we learn that the three senior archons—the (eponymous) archon himself, the *basileus*, and the pole-march—each appointed two assessors, *paredroi*, of their own choice (λαμβάνουσι δὲ καὶ παρέδρους ὁ τ' ἄρχων καὶ ὁ βασιλεὺς καὶ ὁ πολέμαρχος δύο ἕκαστος οὓς ἂν βούληται). The singularity of this, in a constitution in which all other officials were either elected by the people or chosen by lot, is self-evident. Scholars have plausibly conjectured that it is a survival from the pre-democratic state.[41] Yet even the fact that under the developed democratic constitution these *paredroi* were subject to a preliminary *dokimasia* and final *euthynai* (?Aristot. *Ath. Pol.* 56.1) does not entirely eliminate the constitutional anomaly they represent; if anything it rather compounds it, for besides appointing their *paredroi* as an act of personal patronage the archons could apparently, if they saw fit, dismiss them.[42] Of their actual duties the author of the *Ath. Pol.* says nothing. We hear elsewhere, however, of a *paredros* of the *basileus* who assisted in the administration of the Eleusinian Mysteries (IG II²1230) and of an eponymous archon who, it would seem, allowed one of his *paredroi* formally to accept an indictment for maltreatment of an orphan ([Demosth.] 58.32). Two or three honorific decrees for archons in conjunction with their *paredroi* should also be noted.[43] Clearly the position of *paredros* must have been a coveted one, and the six appointments to it each year easy to fill.

Who then were the *paredroi*? Few of their names have been recorded; fewer still with a demotic or other means of identification; and fewest of all where such identification is matched by something comparable for the associated archon. A fresh study of the epigraphic evidence is promised by Dow.[44] Meanwhile, though, he has ventured the observation that "there are enough instances of fellow-Demesmen, and of close family

[40] Dow, "Associates," pp. 80-84.

[41] Thus e.g. J. M. Moore, *Aristotle and Xenophon on Democracy and Oligarchy*, London, 1975, p. 293; Rhodes, *Commentary*, p. 622.

[42] See [Demosth.] 59.83-84, cf. 72 (a *basileus* dismisses his *paredros*, apparently on the advice of the Areiopagos); see further below, n. 46. Hansen, "*Archai*," p. 171, argues that, despite the *dokimasia* and the *euthynai*, the archon's *paredroi* were not considered *archai* in the technical sense.

[43] IG II²668 (year 282/1); *Hesp.* 7, 1938, pp. 100-109, no. 18 [= SEG 25.89] (year 283/2); and perhaps (see Dow, "Associates," pp. 81-83) the first decree of O. W. Reinmuth, *The Ephebic Inscriptions of the Fourth Century B.C.*, Mnemosyne Suppl. 14, 1971, no. 1 [= SEG 23.78] (year 361/0).

[44] Dow, "Associates," p. 81 (cf. 83 on IG II²1696, which on the basis of Dow's new readings is no longer to be regarded as including *paredroi*).

relatives, to prove that the constitution . . . was, and was meant to be, an open invitation to appoint companionable associates." One can only concur. The archons were invited, in effect, to choose their *philoi*, their relatives and friends.[45] This may be taken to embrace not only those who were already in that category (on the basis of either or both of the criteria) but also those who aspired to be,[46] and indeed those whom the archon himself wished to be.[47] Sometimes the reason for his selection is beyond our fathoming,[48] but more often it is crystal clear. For instance, the eponymous archon of 394/3, Euboulides of Eleusis, gave one of the posts to his brother,[49] as did a *basileus* of the mid second century.[50] Charikleides, the eponymous archon of 363/2, chose his father,[51] and a *basileus* in the late fourth century either his father or his son.[52] And Nikias of Otryne, the eponymous archon of 282/1, singled out another Otrynian.[53] A relative, it might be argued, was a relative first and a fellow demesman only second—and the toleration of simple nepotism is certainly very striking in itself; but one way or another the spectacle of any or all of

[45] On *philoi*, see Connor, *Politicians*, pp. 3-32, esp. 30-31.

[46] For example, Stephanos of Eroiadai allegedly "bought" the position of *paredros* to the *basileus* Theogenes of Erchia and then became, for a time, his father-in-law ([Demosth.] 59.72-84). Even if Theogenes was less gullible than Apollodorus makes out, this is nonetheless a clear illustration of Dow's "hazards of corruption" ("Associates," p. 70).

[47] It is tempting to put this construction upon Aeschin. 1.158, where an anecdote omits the name of a presumably unmemorable archon but gives that of one of his *paredroi*—the prominent and long-lived politician Aristophon of Azenia. For such a celebrity to have served as *paredros* had evidently become something of a talking-point, and one would like to know whether the archon who had brought this about was a fellow demesman.

[48] E.g. the choice by Euthios of Teithras, eponymous archon in 283/2, of Meidogenes of Athmonon and Sokrates of Paiania (*Hesp.* 7, 1938, pp. 100-109, no. 18 = SEG 25.89). They are not even from his tribe (or from the same tribe as each other), though the case of Stephanos and Theogenes (above, n. 46) robs this fact of much intrinsic significance.

[49] IG II²2811: archon, Euboulides Epikleido(u) [of Eleusis]; *paredros*, Diktys Epikleido(u) of Ele[usis]. In the *editio princeps* (*Hesp.* 2, 1933, pp. 149-150, no. 1) B. D. Meritt suggested that we have here an indication that at this time only a single *paredros* was appointed; "but it is possible that this archon had two πάρεδροι, but only one shared in the dedication" (Rhodes, *Commentary*, p. 621). For other instances where we know only one *paredros*, see nn. 46, 47, and 51 (and [Demosth.] 58.32).

[50] *Hesp.* 40, 1971, pp. 257-258, no. 6: *basileus*, the well-known Miltiades of Marathon; *paredroi*, his brother Dionysios and Nikomachos of Perithoidai.

[51] Demosth. 21.178-179; the deme is unknown.

[52] *Hesp.* 40, 1971, p. 257, no. 5: *basileus*, [E]xekestides [Nikokr]atous of Alopeke; *paredroi*, Nikokrates Exekes[tidou of Alopeke] and Kleainetos Meno[nos – – – –]. The editor, T. L. Shear, Jr., assumes that Nikokrates is the son, but he might equally well be the father; cf. above, n. 51, and Dow, "Associates," p. 81 ("some at least of the Paredroi were senior persons; none can be proved to be juniors").

[53] IG II²668: archon, Nikias of Otryne; *paredroi*, Alkimachos of Myrrhinous and Antiphanes of Otryne.

the three senior archons discharging their duties in collaboration with at least one man picked by them from their own demes[54] was, it is plain, a commonplace one.

If the constitution itself offered other, regular opportunities for officials to grant preferment to their *philoi*, fellow demesmen included, we do not hear of them.[55] Noninstitutionalized ways (both proper and improper) in which this might occur are another matter, but from their very nature they are difficult to pin down in the evidence. To pursue the question of the relationship between local and city politics we need, then, to direct our attention to another issue: the place of the deme and demesmen in the mobilization of political support.

2. The Deme as Political Power-base

"(Kimon) removed the fences from his fields, in order that both strangers and the needy amongst the citizens might have the opportunity to help themselves freely to the produce. Also he gave a dinner at his home every day—a simple one, but sufficient for many—to which any poor man who wished came in, and so received sustenance which cost him no effort and which left him free to devote himself solely to public affairs. But Aristotle says that those for whom, if they wanted it, he provided the dinner were not the Athenians as a whole but his demesmen the Lakiadai. Also he was constantly attended by youths in fine clothing, each of whom, if Kimon was approached by one of the elderly citizens in need of clothes, would exchange garments with him—something which made a noble impression. These youths also carried a generous sum of money with them, and in the Agora would go up to those who were poor but respectable and silently press small change into their hands."[56]

[54] For another *possible* case of this, see 10: Euthydemos of Eleusis was apparently the only one of the two *paredroi* of the *basileus* to be honored by the Kerykes in IG II²1230; my guess would be that an Eleusinian *basileus* had picked him. See further below, n. 95.

[55] The uniqueness, as attested, of the senior archons' power to choose their own *paredroi* is rightly stressed by Dow, "Associates," p. 80 and passim, though at p. 84 he raises the possibility that the *paredroi* of the Hellenotamiai (ML no. 77, line 4; etc.) may also have been personal choices; and the same might be suspected of the *paredroi* of the generals (ML no. 77, line 50). On the other hand we know that the two *paredroi* for each of the ten *euthynoi* were allotted, like the *euthynoi* themselves, from the ranks of the *boulē* (?Aristot. *Ath. Pol.* 48.3).

[56] Plut. *Kim.* 10.1-3: τῶν τε γὰρ ἀγρῶν τοὺς φραγμοὺς ἀφεῖλεν, ἵνα καὶ τοῖς ξένοις καὶ τῶν πολιτῶν τοῖς δεομένοις ἀδεῶς ὑπάρχῃ λαμβάνειν τῆς ὀπώρας, καὶ δεῖπνον οἴκοι παρ' αὐτῷ λιτὸν μέν, ἀρκοῦν δὲ πολλοῖς, ἐποιεῖτο καθ' ἡμέραν, ἐφ' ὃ τῶν πενήτων ὁ βουλόμενος εἰσῄει καὶ διατροφὴν εἶχεν ἀπράγμονα, μόνοις τοῖς δημοσίοις σχολάζων. ὡς δ' Ἀριστοτέλης φησίν, οὐχ ἁπάντων Ἀθηναίων, ἀλλὰ τῶν δημοτῶν αὐτοῦ Λακιαδῶν παρεσκευάζετο τῷ βουλομένῳ τὸ δεῖπνον. αὐτῷ δὲ νεα-

Both the stated and the unstated sources of Plutarch's picture of Kimon's liberality have survived. The stated source, "Aristotle," is ?Aristot. *Ath. Pol.* 27.3. "The possesser of property on the scale of a tyrant," it reads, "Kimon not only performed the public liturgies with splendor but also maintained many of his demesmen; for any of the Lakiadai who wished· could come to him every day and receive reasonable means of subsistence, and in addition all his estates were unfenced, in order that anyone who wished could enjoy the produce."[57] The unstated (and major) source is Theopompus, in a long fragment of the tenth book of his *Philippika* preserved by Athenaeus. "Kimon the Athenian," Theopompus wrote, "stationed no guard over the crops in his fields and gardens, in order that those citizens who wished might go in and help themselves to whatever produce of the estates they needed. Furthermore he kept open house for all; and he always provided an inexpensive dinner for many men, and the poor amongst the Athenians came and went in to eat it. He also tended to those who, each day, asked something of him; and they say that he always took around with him two or three youths who had small change with them and whom he ordered to give it away whenever someone approached him and asked him for something. Also, they say, he made contributions to burial expenses. And often, besides, he did this: whenever he saw one of the citizens poorly clothed he would order one of the youths who were accompanying him to change clothes with the man. All this naturally won him high repute and first place amongst the citizens."[58]

νίσκοι παρείποντο συνήθεις ἀμπεχόμενοι καλῶς, ὧν ἕκαστος, εἴ τις συντύχοι τῷ Κίμωνι τῶν ἀστῶν πρεσβύτερος ἠμφιεσμένος ἐνδεῶς, διημείβετο πρὸς αὐτὸν τὰ ἱμάτια· καὶ τὸ γινόμενον ἐφαίνετο σεμνόν. οἱ δ' αὐτοὶ καὶ νόμισμα κομίζοντες ἄφθονον παριστάμενοι τοῖς κομψοῖς τῶν πενήτων ἐν ἀγορᾷ σιωπῇ τῶν κερματίων ἐνέβαλλον εἰς τὰς χεῖρας.

[57] ?Aristot. *Ath. Pol.* 27.3: ὁ γὰρ Κίμων, ἅτε τυραννικὴν ἔχων οὐσίαν, πρῶτον μὲν τὰς κοινὰς λητουργίας ἐλητούργει λαμπρῶς, ἔπειτα τῶν δημοτῶν ἔτρεφε πολλούς [τοὺς πολλούς in the London papyrus; but τούς is apparently scratched out and, accordingly, ignored by all editors except Blass] · ἐξῆν γὰρ τῷ βουλομένῳ Λακιαδῶν καθ' ἑκάστην τὴν ἡμέραν ἐλθόντι παρ' αὐτὸν ἔχειν τὰ μέτρια, ἔτι δὲ τὰ χωρία πάντα ἄφρακτα ἦν, ὅπως ἐξῇ τῷ βουλομένῳ τῆς ὀπώρας ἀπολαύειν. Besides Plut. *Kim.* 10.2 this version also appears, *via* Theophrastus (explicitly named), in Cicero *de officiis* 2.64, and in the second scholion to Aelius Aristides 46, *On the Four* (vol. 3, p. 517, Dindorf).

[58] Theopompus, *FGrH* 115 F89: Κίμων ὁ Ἀθηναῖος ἐν τοῖς ἀγροῖς καὶ τοῖς κήποις οὐδένα τοῦ καρποῦ καθίστα φύλακα, ὅπως οἱ βουλόμενοι τῶν πολιτῶν εἰσιόντες ὀπωρίζωνται καὶ λαμβάνωσιν εἴ τινος δέοιντο τῶν ἐν τοῖς χωρίοις. ἔπειτα τὴν οἰκίαν παρεῖχε κοινὴν ἅπασι· καὶ δεῖπνον αἰεὶ εὐτελὲς παρασκευάζεσθαι πολλοῖς ἀνθρώποις, καὶ τοὺς ἀπόρους [προσιόντας] τῶν Ἀθηναίων εἰσιόντας δειπνεῖν· ἐθεράπευεν δὲ καὶ τοὺς καθ' ἑκάστην ἡμέραν αὐτοῦ τι δεομένους, καὶ λέγουσιν ὡς περιήγετο μὲν αἰεὶ νεανίσκους δύ' ἢ τρεῖς ἔχοντας κέρματα τούτοις

The principal discrepancy between the *Ath. Pol.* and Theopompus here would be obvious enough even if Plutarch had not expressly drawn attention to it. Theopompus' Kimon is generous to all (poor) Athenians, indiscriminately; in the *Ath. Pol.* some, at least, of his munificence is restricted to his fellow demesmen.[59] To judge not only from chapter 10 of the *Kimon* but also from his shorter versions of the same material elsewhere, Plutarch believed that Theopompus' more general view of the matter was the true one.[60] It is noteworthy, indeed, that Plutarch himself actually set the scope of Kimon's liberality even wider than had Theopompus, with the claim—reflecting no more, surely, than his own stylistic elaboration—that foreigners as well as citizens were its beneficiaries. And this serves to underline the limitations of Plutarch's grasp of the finer nuances of the fifth- and fourth-century source material to which he had such enviable access. Most scholars have argued that, in favoring Theopompus' version, Plutarch made the wrong choice;[61] and if they are correct, this means that Theopompus himself must presumably be held responsible not merely for following a false trail, like Plutarch, but for laying it himself. Wade-Gery's thesis that, for this material, the *Ath. Pol.* and Theopompus shared a common late fifth- or early fourth-century source, possibly Critias, has won general acceptance.[62] On this assumption it is difficult to see why the author of the *Ath. Pol.* should have taken over a generalized view of Kimon's liberality and made it more specific and precise.[63] It is not very difficult at all, on the other hand, to see why Theopompus should have taken over a specific and precise one and made it more generalized. Such exaggeration would be more understandable in any event, but in this instance we have an important clue as to how it came about. Before quoting the long fragment of Theopom-

---

τε διδόναι προσέταττεν, ὁπότε τις προσέλθοι αὐτοῦ δεόμενος. καί φασι μὲν αὐτὸν καὶ εἰς ταφὴν εἰσφέρειν. ποιεῖν δὲ καὶ τοῦτο πολλάκις, ὁπότε τῶν πολιτῶν τινα ἴδοι κακῶς ἠμφιεσμένον, κελεύειν αὐτῷ μεταμφιέννυσθαι τῶν νεανίσκων τινα τῶν συνακολουθούντων αὐτῷ. ἐκ δὴ τούτων ἁπάντων ηὐδοκίμει καὶ πρῶτος ἦν τῶν πολιτῶν.

[59] It is not certain, but it is certainly likely, that Λακιαδῶν is to be understood with the *second* τῷ βουλομένῳ (see above, n. 57); that is, the open fields as well as the open house for demesmen only. See further below, n. 68.

[60] See *Perikles* 9.2, and the distant echo in *Moralia* 667D (πολλοὺς καὶ παντοδαποὺς ἑστιῶν ἡδέως); cf. Cornelius Nepos, *Cimon* 4.

[61] E.g., most recently, Davies, *Families*, p. 311, and *Wealth*, p. 97; Rhodes, *Commentary*, p. 340.

[62] H. T. Wade-Gery, *AJPh* 59, 1938, pp. 131-134 (= *Essays in Greek History*, Oxford, 1958, pp. 235-238). Cf. W. R. Connor, *Theopompus and Fifth-Century Athens*, Washington D.C., 1968, pp. 30-37, at 33 (cautious); Rhodes, *Commentary*, pp. 338-339.

[63] Cf. Connor, *Theopompus* (see preceding note), p. 110. Note, however, that in *Politicians*, pp. 19-20, he implicitly endorses Theopompus' version; see further below, n. 72.

pus which, as we have seen, was Plutarch's source, Athenaeus writes of the self-indulgence of the sons of the tyrant Peisistratos, Hippias and Hipparchos. "And yet their father Peisistratos," he goes on, "took his pleasures moderately; at any rate he did not station guards on his estates or in his gardens, as Theopompus relates in his twenty-first book, but allowed anyone who wished to go in and enjoy and take what he needed; and later Kimon too did just the same, in imitation of him."[64] Despite the fact that this citation (F135) and the quotation (F89) come from different books of Theopompus' *Philippika*, "it is as likely that Athenaeus found the comparison [between Kimon and Peisistratos] in Theopompus as that he made it himself, and we may guess that it was made by the common source of Theopompus and *A(th). P(ol).*"[65] The responsibility, however, for allowing it to distort and displace the precise picture of Kimon as a benefactor, first and foremost, of his fellow demesmen—and for either not seeing or not caring how this exaggeration "blurs the political point of the distinction between Kimon and Perikles as that between local dynast and national politician"—would seem to be Theopompus' own.[66]

We may surely take it as proven, then, that a writer (perhaps Critias) of the late fifth or early fourth century, reproduced accurately in the Aristotelian *Ath. Pol.* but inaccurately by Theopompus, represented Kimon as having provided a species of poor relief for his fellow demesmen of Lakiadai.

And although it is certainly not the same thing, there seems no good reason to disbelieve that Kimon actually did so. The author of the *Ath. Pol.* goes on to characterize Kimon's largess as a *chorēgia* (27.4)—an interesting extension of the word even beyond its not uncommon application to liturgies in general.[67] Exactly what this "choregy" entailed is not altogether clear,[68] but the political support which Kimon expected

---

[64] Theopompus, *FGrH* 115 F135: καίτοι ὁ πατὴρ αὐτῶν Πεισίστρατος μετρίως ἐχρῆτο ταῖς ἡδοναῖς· ὅς γε οὐδ' ἐν τοῖς χωρίοις οὐδ' ἐν τοῖς κήποις φύλακας καθίστα, ὡς Θεόπομπος ἱστορεῖ ἐν τῇ πρώτῃ καὶ εἰκοστῇ, ἀλλ' εἴα τὸν βουλόμενον εἰσιόντα ἀπολαύειν καὶ λαμβάνειν ὧν δεηθείη, ὅπερ ὕστερον ἐποίησε καὶ Κίμων μιμησάμενος ἐκεῖνον.

[65] Rhodes, *Commentary*, p. 340. In the *Ath. Pol.* version it is reduced to the general phrase τυραννικὴν ἔχων οὐσίαν (see above, n. 57).

[66] Davies, *Families*, p. 311; cf. Rhodes, *Commentary*, p. 340.

[67] See Rhodes, *Commentary*, pp. 340-341 on this.

[68] As regards what the *Ath. Pol.* itself says, we may take as certain the free meals, though the free access to crops is not explicitly limited to the Lakiadai (see above, n. 59). As to the elements which appear only in Theopompus—the changes of clothing, handouts of money, and burial expenses—there is no obvious way of determining (a) whether the *Ath. Pol.* could have mentioned them but did not or whether they are Theopompan inventions,

from it is plain enough.[69] Scholars have been reluctant to deploy the term *clientela* with reference to archaic and early classical Greece, where we know of no precise and proper equivalent of the legally regulated relationship between a *patronus* and his *clientes* which was characteristic of Roman society.[70] All the same, John Davies has recently observed that Kimon's use of some of his enormous property-power within his own deme was "of a kind startlingly similar to the Roman clientela," and this is fair comment in every way.[71] Perhaps some of those who came to eat in Kimon's kitchen or to pick his fruit were too proud to accept any suggestion that they were putting themselves in the position of being *obliged* to pledge him their political support—voting for his proposals in the *ekklēsia*, reelecting him as general, shielding him from the risk of ostracism, and so forth—and whether they accepted such a notion or not there is no sense in which his fellow demesmen offered Kimon an organized body of support, day in and day out.[72] Nevertheless, Lakiadai was a small deme, with no other (known) families of the stature of the Kimonids. They had lived and owned property there since at least the 540s;[73] and the fact that the Kleisthenic constitution—introduced just within Kimon's own lifetime[74]—set all the Lakiadai on a notionally equal footing as citizens and demesmen naturally made scant difference initially

---

and (b) whether, if these were indeed real practices, they benefited the Lakiadai only or a wider sector of the political support group which the likes of Kimon needed to sustain. See further below, n. 72.

[69] Cf. Davies, *Families*, pp. 311-312; Rhodes, *Commentary*, p. 339.

[70] See e.g. Connor, *Politicians*, p. 18. On the *patronus/cliens* relationship, see: J. A. Crook, *Law and Life of Rome*, London, 1967, chap. 3; P. A. Brunt, *Social Conflicts in the Roman Republic*, London, 1971, pp. 47-50.

[71] Davies, *Wealth*, p. 97; cf. M. I. Finley, *Politics in the Ancient World*, Cambridge, pp. 39-49, esp. 40-41. On the level of the family's resources, see above all Herod. 6.136.3 (the young Kimon pays the fifty-talent fine imposed on his father, Miltiades) and other evidence discussed by Davies, *Families*, pp. 310-312; cf. Rhodes, *Commentary*, p. 339.

[72] Connor, *Politicians*, p. 22. As noted above (n. 63), Connor seems here to endorse the generalized, Theopompan version of Kimon's liberality, and as a consequence his whole discussion of "the politics of largess" (*Politicians*, pp. 18-22) perhaps lacks the focus which it would have gained from a consideration of both ?Aristot. *Ath. Pol.* 27.3 and other evidence for the use of such methods *within demes*; cf. Chap. 8, n. 38. Connor speaks of Kimon's "skill in winning [through largess] the support of citizens too numerous, too poor, and too ill-born to be tied to him in other ways" (*Politicians*, p. 20), and there can be no dispute that a major public figure like Kimon needed the support of large numbers of such men; the point, though, is that *some* of them *were* "tied to him in other ways," through membership of the Lakiadai.

[73] This is deducible from Herodotus' story (6.34-35.2) of Miltiades and the Dolonkoi: see C. T. Seltman, *Athens: its history and coinage*, Cambridge, 1924, p. 136; Lewis, "Cleisthenes," p. 25; Davies, *Families*, p. 310.

[74] Born ca. 510: see Davies, *Families*, p. 302.

to the inherent inequalities of economic, social, and (thus) political status between them. In the 470s and 460s the position of Kimon in Lakiadai will still have been little less than that of lord of the manor, a position bringing him all the honor, deference, and allegiance (and, no doubt, all the subliminal fear of their ultimate withdrawal) as have fallen to the lot of such figures throughout the ages. Had he chosen it, a life of purely local predominance could have been his for the taking, as a particularly big fish in a particularly small pool. He opted instead for the large pool: a military and political career in the service of the city as a whole, a career in which a man only prospered if and for as long as he stood at the apex of a pyramid of support as wide as it was deep. Even a member of one of the largest demes—an Acharnian, say—would have had to look far beyond its limits for the mobilization of such support. In Kimon's case we know something of his attempts to build on his own assets of wealth and background by forging links with powerful *philoi* from other demes (who might be expected to speak, in general terms, for their own bodies of adherents); and this knowledge has been properly exploited in the best attempt so far to construct a model of Athenian political group-ings in the mid fifth century.[75] On the basis of ?Aristot. *Ath. Pol.* 27.3 it would not seem too much to claim that a place should be found within this model for some degree of "natural" political loyalty and allegiance on the part of those who (both before and after 508/7) dominated the life of their localities from whose who (from 508/7 onwards) were their fellow demesmen.

Having taken such care, however, to establish the validity of the deme-centered version of Kimon's liberality, it is only proper to admit at this point what an isolated datum it is and, accordingly, to attempt to discover the significance of that fact. Why is it that only this once do we hear *explicitly* of a man such as Kimon eliciting political goodwill by means of largess within his own deme? Could it be that this was no normal resort, and that Kimon was not driven to it until he found himself fighting for his political life in the second half of the 460s? Something of the kind has been conjectured, not implausibly, by Davies for the generality of Kimon's outlay, and notably his "numerous public buildings and works."[76] Yet as regards largess within Lakiadai we have already taken

[75] See Connor, *Politicians*, pp. 58-64.

[76] Davies, *Families*, pp. 311-312 (". . . substantial inroads into his capital resources for political purposes: not so much . . . to buy a political position inside and outside Athens as to protect his existing political position from the challenge of the Ephialtic Left"). For a list of projects financed either out of Kimon's private resources or from booty, see W. Judeich, *Topographie von Athen*, 2d ed., Munich, 1931, pp. 73-74. As well as Kimon's own needs in this period, note the more general argument of Davies, *Wealth*, pp. 105-114,

Davies' own point that the distinction drawn in ?Aristot. *Ath. Pol.* 27 (but blurred by Theopompus and hence also by Plutarch) is a distinction between Kimon the "local dynast" and Perikles the (would-be) "national politician";[77] and for all the schematism of its presentation one can accept as not only plain but also, broadly speaking, true the implication of this contrast—that the man compelled to generate his political support by means then novel was not Kimon but his younger rival.[78] Kimon's means, as I have argued above, were the traditional ones, albeit deployed in this case perhaps more systematically and with greater calculation than usual. However far it extended into the polis at large, and however much its composition shifted as one issue or link-up gave way to another, his entourage retained its local nucleus in the quasi-client group which the Kleisthenic constitution had redefined as his deme. And if we possessed the depth of source material for the first half of the fifth century that we do for later periods it would surely reveal no shortage of parallels for the type of political behavior described in *Ath. Pol.* 27.3.

The lack of good parallels *after* the 460s is another matter. Once the volume of literary and epigraphic evidence begins to grow to its fourth-century peak we could legitimately expect to find signs that the exercise of property-power within a man's deme was a necessity for a significant degree of prominence at city level *if indeed it was*. What the evidence suggests instead is that the burgeoning political consciousness of the common people and the correspondingly new approaches to the creation and maintenance of mass political support which evolved during the second half of the fifth century[79] found the old-fashioned, Kimonian methods of aristocratic local patronage at least inadequate and perhaps even (for those seeking a genuinely "national" appeal) postively disadvantageous. For a time public careers could still be fuelled principally by conspicuous consumption. The rather different but equally well-documented cases of Nikias—a man at least as rich as Kimon—and Alkibiades show this clearly enough.[80] But the former spent not a penny, as far as we know, for the special benefit of the Kydantidai; the latter's *megalo-*

---

esp. 113-114, that the Kimonids (like the Alkmaionids) employed their great wealth in both the fifth and the fourth centuries to combat the prestige of cult-power, from which they were excluded.

[77] See above, p. 308.

[78] Cf. Rhodes, *Commentary*, p. 339.

[79] On the significance of Perikles and (especially) Kleon here, see Connor, *Politicians*, pp. 87-136, esp. 119-128.

[80] For their wealth and expenditure, see Davies, *Families*, pp. 20-21 (Alkibiades) and 403-404 (Nikias). For criticism aroused by expenditure on this scale, see for instance Plut. *Nik.* 3-4.1 (with D. M. Lewis, *CR* 25, 1975, p. 89) on Nikias, and Thuc. 6.12.2 (attributed to Nikias!) on Alkibiades.

prepeia will likewise have made no greater impact in Skambonidai than anywhere else; and, at their level of celebrity at least, there is nothing to suggest that from now on this was at all unusual.

In any case, within the lifetime of these two men the ever-increasing democratization of Athenian politics and society was already calling into being what Davies has termed "the democratic power-base," in which for roughly a century, between the 420s and the 320s, the political value of great wealth and its expenditure *in any way* was largely superseded by "political skills more appropriate to democratic pressures and democratic institutions."[81] The change not only in the behavior but also in the actual composition of the politically active class brought forward individuals who built their careers on their own oratorical, forensic, and administrative abilities, and whose position in relation to their fellow demesmen was not and never had been akin to that of the Kimonids in Lakiadai. The only hint from the fourth century that a family politically prominent at city level might still exercise a "Kimonian" degree of dominance over its own deme is the claim by the speaker in Isaeus 9 that no Araphenian could be found to testify against Thoudippos.[82] Even pressed to the utmost, this hardly seems to reflect the basis for any sort of reliable locally oriented support deployable outside the deme. There is also a single fourth-century instance, in Lysias 16, of poor relief for fellow demesmen of a kind (if not on a scale) which can bear general comparison with that of Kimon in *Ath. Pol.* 27.3. However, although young Mantitheos cites both a family tradition of involvement in the city's affairs (16.20) and also his own eagerness to continue it (16.21), there is naturally no indication that he was proposing to launch a public career with sixty drachmas' worth of *ephodia* (16.14).[83]

More to the point, there is little likelihood that he *could* have done so even by increasing his outlay a hundredfold. This was not only because expenditure *per se* had (temporarily) stopped paying its major political dividends but also and especially because, once the locally or regionally based client-groups had broken down, the notion that political support needed to rest upon a local foundation seems to have become far less obvious than one might have supposed. In Chapter 8A we probed the

[81] Davies, *Wealth*, pp. 114-131 (quotations from 115 and 130), cf. 91-92 on the "renaissance" of privately financed public works in the 320s after a century during which it had been more usual to finance them by public means.

[82] Isaeus 9.18 (quoted in Chap. 8, n. 21); cf. above, p. 300.

[83] Lysias 16.14 (quoted in Chap. 8, n. 111); no such career for him, incidentally, is attested by other sources. In political terms the benefit to Mantitheos of his generosity was of course precisely the forensic *charis* which he sought by mentioning it; cf. Davies, *Families*, pp. 92-95.

nature of deme society sufficiently to discover that there was frequently an overlap, both semantic and pragmatic, between *dēmotai* and *philoi*; and it would be perverse to resist the assumption, purely on the grounds of how facile it might appear, that the average *rhētōr* or *politeuomenos* achieved his political goals in the city of Athens more often with than without the backing of men from his deme. In Chapter 8B we then saw how the concept of *dēmosia philotimia* in its local form positively encouraged both personal service and financial outlay on the deme's behalf: Leukios and his *agora* in Sounion (IG II²1180), Phro—— and his recreational facilities in Kephisia (*AD* 24, 1969, pp. 6-7), and the many liturgists, demarchs, and other honorands great and small. What one must be wary of doing is conflating these two sets of findings into the single hypothesis that those who did achieve prominence at city level were necessarily those who had won local prominence first. Both positive and negative evidence, as we shall now see, suggest otherwise.

3. The Demesman as Political Apprentice

The hypothesis mentioned at the end of the last paragraph—that an individual's road to success in Athenian democratic politics and government would begin at "grass roots" level, in his deme—is no abstract consideration devised for argumentative purposes by the author of this book. On the contrary, it was explicitly formulated by Bernard Haussoullier, and has been either explicitly restated or (more often) implicitly assumed in work on the subject ever since *La Vie Municipale*.

A relatively recent version of it is that of R. J. Hopper, in the quotation given at the very opening of this book. Hopper sees both the demes and the tribes as important here, in providing the scope for an Athenian's "practical wisdom [to be] developed and brought out by experience, so that he was not at a loss in state affairs"; the tribes constituted "an essential transition from local affairs to state affairs," while "a man who knew his deme business would not be lost in state business."[84] The notion is that of a graduated political and governmental apprenticeship, to be served in the microcosms of deme and tribe before progressing on to the macrocosm of the city itself. This is expressed most plainly in the phrase "training ground"—the deme, in Hopper's contention, fulfilling this function "for service in Council and Assembly," the tribe "for the major executive offices."[85]

The essence of these ideas, as we shall shortly see, is Haussoullier's,

[84] Hopper, *Basis*, pp. 13, 15, 17.
[85] Hopper, *Basis*, p. 16.

but with one interesting exception. Haussoullier had said very little about the tribes;[86] and certainly the refinement which postulates different roles for deme and for tribe—the former providing a schooling in collective deliberation, the latter one in individual administrative competence—is, to the best of my knowledge, Hopper's own. Since he himself mentions (and documents) the fact that the demes as well as the tribes appointed officials and that the tribes as well as the demes held assemblies, his reasons for the distinction which he claims are rather mystifying. Moreover, his model begs several difficult questions, such as whether the Athenians themselves would normally have classified participation in tribal affairs as being naturally an adjunct of deme activity or of city activity.[87] For these and other reasons it will be best, here, to leave the tribes out of account. But we may nonetheless salvage the form if not the content of Hopper's dichotomy by bearing in mind, as we turn to the source of his ideas, the need to distinguish between the general political *savoir faire* to be derived from the collective aspects of deme membership as such and the particular expertise and reputation which individuals might hope to gain as holders of local office and/or protagonists in deme politics.

The concept of the demesman as political apprentice—serving his time in Hopper's "training ground"—is forcefully expounded by Haussoullier at the very outset of *La Vie Municipale*, in its preface. "La vie municipale," he declared, "est une école de la vie publique, de la vie politique: tout à côté de l'État, association suprême qui comprend tous les citoyens, il est d'autres associations, civiles et politiques, fondées sur les mêmes principes; tout à côté de l'assemblée du peuple, il est d'autres assemblées qui mènent en quelque sort la même vie, l'assemblée du dème et l'assemblée de la tribu. Sans doute l'Athénien n'est pas tenu d'y faire un stage avant de paraître à l'assemblée du peuple, [. . .] mais, par la force même des choses, comme il vit le plus souvent sur le territoire de son dème, près de l'agora où se réunissent ses *démotes*, il est, même avant l'âge où il pourra faire partie d'une assemblée, préparé à la vie publique: il est dans un milieu politique pour ainsi dire, et de bonne heure il commence son éducation. Il y a plus: bien qu'il en ait le droit, ce n'est guère à vingt ans qu'il fréquentera l'assemblée du peuple, où il ferait triste figure et ne serait pas écouté; il se formera dans l'assemblée du dème, au milieu de ceux qu'il connaît depuis longtemps, et dans l'assemblée plus nombreuse de la tribu où il rencontre des citoyens venus de toutes les parties de l'Attique. C'est là qu'il acquiert cette experience et cette intelligence des

[86] See below, n. 89.

[87] Cases such as **299** (with the comments of Davies, *Families*, p. 103) or the demarch **11** offer a degree of support for the first of these alternatives, but my point is that generalization may be quite inappropriate.

affaires sans lesquelles une assemblée nombreuse comme l'Assemblée du peuple ou le Conseil aurait été impuissante à rien produire; c'est là qu'il devient auditeur et orateur."[88]

The emphasis here, clearly, is upon the politically educative role of the deme (and, to a much lesser extent, the tribe)[89] in the first and more general of the two senses which we have defined: the acquisition of political self-confidence and maturity by the young demesman in the friendly intimacy of his own deme's assembly before venturing even to attend, let alone to address, the city *ekklēsia*. We need not quarrel with this in the generalized terms in which it is stated. There is no cogent evidence, either programmatic or *ad hominem*, to cite either way, and no significant qualifications to be made in the probabilities of the matter aside from the one made by Haussoullier himself—that such preliminaries to political activity in the city arena were merely normal and natural, not obligatory. Some young men were doubtless too impatiently ambitious to bother with them.[90] Others might more profitably, as they saw it, develop their political skills by conversation with and observation of fathers, uncles, and other relatives and friends with big-city experience, rather than by studiously emulating a (possibly) incompetent demarch or absorbing the parochial concerns of local debate. Attendance at the *ekklēsia* and other means of gaining familiarity with the complex processes of city government and politics were necessarily more of a practical possibility for a demesman of, say, Koile or Alopeke than for a Dekeleian or a Marathonian—unless of course the latter took up residence in or nearer to Athens. These (and other) individual variants must be allowed for, and they are neither uninteresting nor unimportant. But even in sum they do not impair the general validity of Haussoullier's visualization of what the structure, the logic, and the practicalities of the political system itself all presented to most young Athenians as their obvious path to experience.

The related but distinct thesis that *individual political careers* likewise regularly began at deme level and progressed to the city from there was also advanced by Haussoullier, though in this instance he cannot strictly be called its originator. "Le dème a ses magistratures et ses sacerdoces, ses fêtes et ses assemblées, ses affaires à gérer; [. . .] c'est dans son sein, en s'occupant de ses intérêts et en rendant service à ses *démotes* ou

---

[88] Haussoullier, *Vie*, pp. i-ii.

[89] In fact Haussoullier dismissed the tribe shortly afterwards as being no more than "le réunion de plusieurs dèmes" (*Vie*, p. ii). This seems to me an oversimplification, but I cannot pursue the issue here.

[90] For a paradigm, see Glaukon, Plato's brother, in Xen. *Mem.* 3.6; cf. Chap. 4, nn. 95 and 97.

concitoyens et voisins du même dème, que l'on devait, le plus souvent, acquérir cette première notoriété qui, par degrés, devenait de la réputation et conduisait aux honneurs de la cité." These are the words not of Haussoullier himself but, as quoted by him, of the dedicatee of *La Vie Municipale*, Georges Perrot;[91] and Haussoullier's own, more extensive formulation (quoted above) is presented as an expansion of them. In point of fact, as we have seen, this is not really true, but Haussoullier does in effect expound the Perrot thesis when he comes, later in his book, to discuss deme magistracies. Why, he asks first, should men have wished to hold them? One reason (he answers) was that after doing so they could expect praise and recompense from their grateful fellow demesmen and bask in the reputation of being zealous servants of their local community. "Mais ils ont une ambition plus haute: ils veulent acquérir dans le dème l'influence qui leur est nécessaire pour parvenir aux charges de la cité. L'assemblée du dème est le premier et le plus petit des cercles où l'Athénien doive se faire connaître: c'est là que, simple administrateur, démarque, trésorier ou σύνδικος, il commence sa fortune politique."[92] And the same theme reappears with particular reference to demarchs. To be a demarch was "un moyen de se désigner, de s'imposer à l'attention de ses concitoyens, et de se préparer aux magistratures de la cité"; "le démarchat est une excellente école; le démarque fait, une année durant, son apprentissage de magistrat"; "rechercher le démarchat, c'est ordinairement entrer dans le cercle des hommes politiques; c'est y prendre place à côté des magistrats ou des orateurs qui, tout-puissants dans l'assemblée de peuple, gouvernent vraiment la cité."[93]

Nothing as mundane as documentation is offered in support of these ideas. Rather, they are (again) presented as self-evident truths; simple corollaries both of human nature, collective and individual, and of the nature of the Athenian political system. Yet whereas one felt able to accept, in these terms, the notion of an individual's general understanding of that system and his confidence that he could meet its demands as developing most naturally in his deme, the model embodied in Haussoullier's words quoted at the end of the last paragraph is something altogether more specific—and more problematical. It is little less, in fact, than the theory of an Athenian *cursus honorum*: a political career structure not, as Haussoullier rightly explains, prescribed in law, but quasi-formalized nonetheless by the individuals who sought, in his phrase, their political fortunes. What we are required to visualize is a graduated and

---

[91] G. Perrot, *Rapport de la Commission des Écoles d'Athènes et de Rome sur les travaux de ces deux Écoles pendant l'année 1875*, Paris, 1876, as quoted by Haussoullier, *Vie*, p. i.
[92] Haussoullier, *Vie*, p. 62.
[93] Haussoullier, *Vie*, pp. 132-133.

calculated progression from petty local office successfully discharged to the lofty circles of those who, in or out of office, formed the governing élite of the polis itself.

Is such a thing indeed a self-evident corollary of the Athenian democratic *politeia*? And is there in fact, irrespective of that, any means of weighing it against evidence? The first of these rhetorical questions can be answered, I believe, in the negative, and the second in the affirmative. What is more, as far as the evidence is concerned, what emerges is not merely a very significant lack of support for the Haussoullier model from tests which, were it valid, should have provided support but also, more positively, an indication that if any "normal" career pattern is to be identified it was a quite different one.

The evidence to which I refer is that of individual prosopography. The extent of its survival even in the fourth century arguably limits the questions which, for our purposes here, one may usefully ask of it to a distressingly low level of sophistication. However, the advantage of genuinely simple questions is that they usually have simple answers, and in this instance our basic question can properly be very simple indeed. What extent of prosopographical overlap is there between those attested as active (*a*) at deme level and (*b*) at city level? On Haussoullier's thesis such overlap ought obviously to be a considerable one, as individuals pursued the centripetal political careers which he had in mind. Those who did so successfully ought to be attested in group *b* as well as group *a*. Yet in fact the overlap is strikingly small. Let us first take, in turn, the three most readily definable components of group *a*: demarchs, other deme officials, and the proposers of deme decrees. Of the forty *demarchs* to whom we can give a name,[94] only two are known for certain to have held an appointment at city level; and in neither case can an "apprentissage de magistrat" as demarch be held to have paved the way for this.[95] Approximately the same number of *other deme officials* is known by name,[96] and here there is only one possible identification with a (later)

[94] That is, all (of 1-50) but 2, 23-28, 32, 33, and 48. In four other cases (1, 9, 31, and 50) the name is only partially preserved.

[95] The choice of Euthydemos of Eleusis (10) as one of the *paredroi* of the *basileus* (cf. above, n. 54) could just as well be before as after his demarchy, and in any case is possibly to be explained by the celebrity of his family in general and his father (163) in particular. Likewise Euboulides of Halimous (19) sought city prominence probably before, or (if not) certainly simultaneously with, his year as demarch. For another demarch *perhaps* as a city official, see 34.

[96] Here the definition must be somewhat arbitrary, but see (on a fairly generous interpretation) 51, 71, 72, 76, 79, 82, 89, 91, 94, 99, 100, 101, 102, 110, 112, 116, 131, 133, 144, 235, 236, 237, 238, 239, 240, 241, 242, 295, 296, 310, 311, 312, 313, 321, 330, 354, 355, 356, 357, 358, 359, 360.

holder of city office.[97] The *prosposers of deme decrees* make up admittedly a different kind of sample—wholly self-selected, one may assume—but for that very reason it is significant how few of them are also attested, in or out of office, at city level. Fifty-nine names are known (all but twelve of them in full),[98] but only eight of their bearers are identifiable participants in central government and/or city politics—five merely as city councillors; and again no regular progression from deme to city can legitimately be detected.[99]

Of course, even if such a progression had been the normal *ideal* pattern one could hardly expect to find it in all cases, but only on the part of a successful minority; thus, it might be objected, the figures given in the preceding paragraph simply show how small that minority was. The point is a valid one; the base of any pyramid (representing here the aggregate of the sort of career structures claimed by Haussoullier) will always be broader than its apex. Yet if we turn the enquiry round to contemplate the apex itself, those who demonstrably did achieve prominence at city level, there can be no argument with the fact that scarcely any of them are also attested in deme office or as active in any way in a local context. There is only one (likely) eponymous archon, for example, out of the two hundred and fifty or so who held that position during the period covered by this book.[100] There is not a single *stratēgos*, out of (again) some two hundred and fifty known by name in the fifth and fourth centuries.[101] And there are only three or four of the one hundred and fifty-seven known proposers of city laws or decrees (or amendments thereto) between 403 and 322.[102]

To disregard the figures presented in the last two paragraphs on the grounds that the prosopographical basis upon which they rest is inadequate would be an abuse of proper scepticism. Obviously one would wish that the totality of the data were far larger, in both the city and the

[97] See 321.

[98] See the list at the end of the Prosopography. The lost or incomplete names are those of **64, 159, 172, 173, 229, 294, 307, 335, 336, 337, 351,** and **368.**

[99] See **58, 120, 163, 171, 184, 216, 303,** and **344.**

[100] See **321.** We know the names of far fewer of the holders of the other eight archonships (for the fortuitous preservation of all nine from 370/69, see *Hesp.* 29, 1960, pp. 25-29, no. 33 = SEG 19.113), but it may still be noted that none of those whom we do know were demonstrably active in their demes.

[101] For the latest list, see Davies, *Wealth*, pp. 156-166; see also his lists (ibid., pp. 151-155) of the known taxiarchs, phylarchs, and hipparchs, of whom the same is true. We shall return to these military officials below.

[102] See **19, 163** (the doubtful case), **184,** and **262.** I have drawn the figure of one hundred and fifty-seven from the inventory of politically active citizens between 403 and 322 recently compiled by M. H. Hansen, *GRBS* 24, 1983, pp. 151-180.

deme domain. In the former, a simple increase in the overall volume of evidence would be invaluable, especially in increasing the known proportion of the hundreds of Athenians who held city office every year. And in the latter there is a grossly uneven *spread* of documentation, with the active personnel in a handful of demes comparatively well known (at any rate in the fourth century) while those elsewhere have gone largely or even entirely unrecorded. As evidence from both spheres grows, the overlap between those known to have been active in both may be expected to grow with it. But it would have to do so on a truly astonishing scale to undermine what comes across as the clear message of the evidence as it currently stands: first of all, that those active at deme level and at city level were, broadly speaking, different people; and secondly, that, where they are found in both, the Haussoullier pattern of centripetal progression from local beginnings was no more common than its obverse, and neither of them more common than an *apparently* random mix of local and "national" political activity.

The importance of this second point can be judged in the light of the character of the Athenian constitutional and political system, of which, as we have seen, the Haussoullier model is implicitly claimed as a natural corollary. The model hinges upon the assumption (again, tacit rather than overt) that individuals could determine the course and rate of their own public careers, if any. While this could not be called an outright fallacy it is indubitably an oversimplification; for it takes no account of the extent to which, especially in the fourth century, *sortition* was the preferred mode of magisterial appointment *in the city and the demes alike*.[103] Every year both the council of five hundred and also perhaps as many as seven hundred other sortitive offices in central government had to be filled.[104] All citizens over the age of thirty were eligible, unless

[103] Perhaps it is only fair to Haussoullier to recall how much of our information about the *city's* sortitive offices has come from two sources unavailable to him, the Aristotelian *Ath. Pol.* and, particularly, the wealth of epigraphic evidence which has accrued since the 1880s. As regards the *demes'* officials, he himself justifiably pointed out how rarely we know for certain which were appointed by lot and which by election (*Vie*, pp. 57-58), and he declared this to be true of the demarchs themselves. However, his clear but unstated leaning towards *elected* demarchs (made explicit in his later discussion of the issue: Daremberg/Saglio/Pottier, *Dictionnaire des antiquités grecques et romaines d'après les textes et les monuments*, vol. 2.1, Paris, 1892, p. 86 with n. 233) stems largely, as we have noted (Chap. 4, n. 153), from prosopographical observations which fail to distinguish deme officials in general and demarchs in particular from (e.g.) honorands in deme decrees, who broadly speaking were men of significantly higher status.

[104] For the figure of seven hundred officials, over and above the *bouleutai*, see Hansen, "*Archai*"; cf. Chap. 9, p. 278. How many of these posts were filled by sortition rather than by election can only be a rough estimate, but mine would be somewhere between six hundred and six hundred and fifty.

debarred for particular reasons *ad hominem*, for appointment both to the former and to (virtually all) the latter.[105] The age-limit for deme officials—the demarch, at least—was very probably the same.[106] The prospect of deme and/or city office will have been contemplated with resignation or even distaste by some, with relish by others; but how could either group foretell what the lot would actually bring? Perhaps an archonship for a man in his thirties (and unlikely, as such, to have held any other office first);[107] perhaps, conversely, a year as demarch or councillor for an elderly political nonentity.[108] On the face of it, the prevalence of sortition and the safeguards devised to preserve its random effects should have made impossible anyone's plans for a smooth and graduated progress from local to "national" officialdom, or indeed a calculated political career (based on office) of any kind whatever. Instead of a *cursus honorum*, even in effect only, one would have to think in terms simply of a multiplicity of local and central *honores* which fell to those who did not welcome them as freely as to those who did and which occurred, from the point of view of any particular individual, in an entirely adventitious manner. And as a result the Haussoullier thesis would not even be worth discussing any further.

But inevitably there are complicating factors, not the least of which is the issue of candidature. In itself, a system of sortition would produce such a wholly random pattern of officeholding as I have just described only if all those eligible to serve were indeed actually obliged to participate in the sortition process. If, on the contrary, lots were drawn only amongst those who had voluntarily presented themselves as candidates (whether for deme or city office), "then of course by constantly coming forward, any single individual would be able to ensure a considerable probability

[105] For the age-limit, see Rhodes, *Boule*, p. 1 with n. 7, and *Commentary*, pp. 510, 703; Hansen, "*Archai*," pp. 167-169.

[106] A lower limit for deme office would obviously lend some tenability to the idea of local magistracies as training for those of the city, but the many ways in which the demes were either eager or else obliged to follow the city's lead in constitutional matters invites the assumption—there is no evidence either way—that thirty was the minimum age for a formal role in local as well as central government. This must at least have been true of the demarchy, for reasons sufficiently stressed in earlier chapters.

[107] Amongst the archons of 370/69 (see above, n. 100) we find a certain Euboulos of Probalinthos as one of the *thesmothetai* (line 4); and only a churl would challenge the identification, by the editor, B. D. Meritt, with PA 5369, one of the leading figures in Athenian politics in the 350s and 340s, who was born ca. 405.

[108] For elderly demarchs, see 30 and, possibly, 6. (One cannot of course state for certain that they held no earlier offices, only that none are known.) The best-known elderly *bouleutēs* has to be the philosopher Sokrates, who "represented" Alopeke at the age of sixty-three (cf. Rhodes, *Boule*, p. 1, n. 8), and who in Plato's *Apology* (32A-B) is made to claim that he had never before this held city office; see further below, n. 113.

that he would be not infrequently among those chosen." These are the words of J. W. Headlam, who in his *Election by lot at Athens* discussed this candidature-or-conscription issue in respect of both the *boulē* and the other city magistracies, and argued that there was regular conscription for the former and at least the possibility of it (if volunteers were lacking) for the latter.[109] In his annotated revision of Headlam's monograph, D. C. Macgregor endorsed the view that officeholding was essentially compulsory, but claimed that Headlam had done less than justice to the evidence for voluntary candidature.[110] Certainly that evidence cannot and should not be ignored.[111] But nor can, or should, general considerations which suggest the necessity for (powers of) compulsion[112]—and there is perhaps a shred of evidence for this also.[113] It therefore seems that we must envisage some combination of volition and coercion.[114] But what remains indeterminable is the norm, that is, whether the compulsion was exercised only if and when there were insufficient volunteers or whether those who positively aspired to office had to take special steps, proper or improper, to stand alongside voluntary draftees.

Our inability to settle this issue is naturally regrettable in itself; yet from the point of view of its relevance to Haussoullier's assumption that individuals could control their own public careers—and in doing so would normally seek to prepare themselves for city offices by first discharging local ones—it is not a question which absolutely must be decided one way or the other. As we have seen, the individual prosopographical evidence does not bear out the predominance of any such career pattern. That is the central fact to which we must cling, and we now have two theoretical explanations for it:

[109] Headlam, *Election*, pp. 53-55, on the *boulē* (quotation from 53), and 94-95 on the other *archai*.

[110] D. C. Macgregor *apud* Headlam, *Election*, pp. 196-197.

[111] For references, see Chap. 9, n. 47 (and add Isaeus 7.39). Evidence of frequent terms in office by particular individuals (e.g. [Lysias] 20.5; Lysias 21.18; Andoc. 1.147; Aeschin. 1.106-107; cf. Hansen, "*Archai*," p. 167, n. 34) tends to point in the same direction.

[112] Chiefly the political hazards of major office and the humdrum aspects of minor ones; the great number of offices to be filled (above, n. 104); and the low level—often the complete absence—of salaries (see on this M. H. Hansen, *SO* 54, 1979, pp. 5-22; D. M. Lewis, *JHS* 102, 1982, p. 269) and other perquisites (see on this M. H. Hansen, *C&M* 32, 1971-1980, pp. 105-125).

[113] Namely, the bouleutic service of Sokrates: see above, n. 108. I agree with Headlam, *Election*, p. 53, n. 1 (against D. C. Macgregor, ibid., p. 197, citing A. E. Taylor, *Socrates*, London, 1932, p. 98, amongst others) that both Sokrates' advanced age and the opposition of his *daimonion* to τὰ πολιτικὰ πράττειν (Plato *Apol.* 31D) make it highly unlikely that he had volunteered as one of the ten councillors from Alopeke for 406/5.

[114] Cf. Lang, "Allotment," p. 83.

1. If emphasis is laid upon the degree of compulsion and conscription in magisterial appointments, at both city and deme level,[115] one must conclude, as stated earlier, that Haussoullier-style centripetal progression—or indeed any other form of individual initiative—was simply not a practical possibility.

2. If on the other hand the maximum scope is allowed, in both realms, for voluntary candidacy, and also for manipulation and corruption of the electoral processes themselves, our conclusion will be that the practical possibility did arise *but was not taken up on a significant scale.*

Although for clarity's sake I present these two scenarios as alternatives, the true situation, as explained, is likely to represent some combination of them, its exact constituent proportions indeterminable by appeal to the candidacy-or-conscription issue alone. However, since the second scenario is the more intrinsically interesting of the two we may perhaps permit ourselves a search for other grounds on which those engaged in political activity, local or urban, may legitimately be seen as a largely self-selecting and (to the extent that they sustained a political career over a period of years) self-determining group.

And indeed such grounds are not far to seek. First, as regards officeholding itself it would seem natural to suppose that such scope for voluntary candidacy and other ways, licit or illicit, of forcing the issue as did exist were exploited to the full—or in other words repeatedly—by those ambitious for a public career. If so, men who are attested as habitual officeholders[116] will, as a very general rule, be those whose careers were to the greatest extent possible the product of personal calculation and initiative. (It may incidentally be remarked that such initiative, whatever the impediments set in its way as regards *sortitive* office, on which we have rightly concentrated, doubtless played a major part in the securing of positions filled by direct *election.* A small number of civilian posts fell into this category,[117] but it comprised above all else the military offices [?Aristot. *Ath. Pol.* 61, cf. 43.1]; and there is some evidence to support what would anyway have been the likelihood that the most powerful of these, the ten annual generalships, were indeed attained normally, if again not statutorily, as the culmination of something akin to a *cursus hono-*

---

[115] The arguments rehearsed in the last two paragraphs may naturally be applied, *mutatis mutandis,* to deme as well as to city officials.

[116] See above, n. 111.

[117] In the second half of the fifth century they seem to have been *ad hoc* or technical appointments, such as envoys or architects (cf. Hignett, *Constitution,* p. 227); by the time of the *Ath. Pol.,* however, new and in some instances powerful civilian offices were filled by election—see ?Aristot. *Ath. Pol.* 43.1 (with Rhodes, *Commentary,* pp. 513-517) and 54.3-5. On the total number of elective posts, see above, n. 104.

rum.[118] Yet in part, no doubt, for that very reason, a military and a civilian career in the city's service had become by the fourth century almost mutually exclusive of each other, with the former pursued by "a largely dynastic military caste, closely tied to property" and the latter by "a much more fluid and open, largely non-dynastic political class."[119] Thus, while the career patterns of the former group are distinct and informative in themselves, they add up to a specialized phenomenon which can only distort our appreciation of the factors which shaped a normal—that is, civilian—public career in this period.)[120]

A second and far weightier justification for regarding the politically active as a predominantly self-selecting group, or at least a group with a large self-selecting nucleus, is the fact that holding magistracies was neither the only nor even necessarily the most important index of political "activity" or "prominence" in democratic Athens. Haussoullier, as we saw, envisaged ex-demarchs aspiring to take their place "à côté des magistrats ou des orateurs qui . . . gouvernent vraiment la cité." This shows that he himself was clearly (and *in principle* justifiably) postulating local experience as a prerequisite for city politics in the sense not only of filling city magistracies but also, more generally, of becoming one of the city's *rhētores*. The *rhētores* (or *politeuomenoi*) were the minority of Athenians, quasi-defined as a group in the fourth century and partially discernible earlier, who actively exercised their political rights of addressing the *ekklēsia* or a court, proposing city decrees, and so forth.[121] Insofar as

---

[118] See for instance Connor, *Politicians*, p. 10, and (explicitly) Davies, *Wealth*, p. 122, citing the evidence in n. 56: Aristoph. *Birds*, line 799 (Dietrephes of Skambonidai elected phylarch first, hipparch second; cf. Davies, ibid., pp. 152-154); Xen. *Mem.* 3.4.1 (Nikomachides regards service as *lochagos*—on which see below—and taxiarch as meriting election as general; cf. Davies, ibid., p. 152); and Theophrastus, *Fragmentum Vaticanum de eligendis magistratibus*, B, lines 172-183 (the absurdity of electing as generals men who have not first been taxiarchs or even phylarchs; see on this Rhodes, *Commentary*, pp. 676-677). The four groups of posts which made up the upper part of the *cursus*—phylarchs, taxiarchs, hipparchs, generals—are listed (out of order) in ?Aristot. *Ath. Pol.* 61; see also Davies, ibid., pp. 151-166, for known holders of them in the fifth and fourth centuries. The junior appointments are less well known, but note ?Aristot. *Ath. Pol.* 61.3 (with Rhodes, *Commentary*, p. 685) on *lochagoi*.

[119] See Davies, *Wealth*, pp. 122-130 (quotation from 124).

[120] As far as the demes are concerned it may be supposed that taxiarchs and phylarchs had some opportunity to make a favorable impression upon fellow demesmen under their command (cf. Connor, *Politicians*, p. 10), but no known holders of these posts are attested in a deme context, as stated above (at n. 101).

[121] On the fourth-century *rhētores*, see two articles by S. Perlman (*Athenaeum* 41, 1963, pp. 327-355; *PP* 22, 1967, pp. 161-176) and, especially, three by M. H. Hansen: *GRBS* 22, 1981, pp. 345-370, at 346-347 and 368-370; *GRBS* 24, 1983, pp. 33-55; and *GRBS* 24, 1983, pp. 151-180.

the individual skills[122] which characterized the members of this group—
Davies' "fluid and open, largely non-dynastic political class"—could be
displayed and developed to best effect in an official capacity, many of
the *rhētores* will have sought to hold formal magistracies from time to
time or at least welcomed them when they came.[123] But the real and
continuing basis of their position was informal: the extent to which they
could command the attention and support of their fellow citizens. Inevitably a great deal of their political activity has thus passed unrecorded,
but we can at least take account of several important indexes of it. In
two recent articles Mogens Herman Hansen has isolated a set of definite
criteria which can be used to define, as far as the evidence allows this,
the fourth-century Athenian *rhētores*. The criteria are the following: proposal of a decree in the *boulē* or *ekklēsia* (or an amendment thereto),
proposal of a law (*nomos*), delivery of a speech in the *boulē* or *ekklēsia*,
prosecution or defence in a political public action (or *synēgoria* for either),
mission as an ambassador, and administration of public money as an
elected treasurer. And on this basis Hansen has drawn up an inventory
of three hundred and eighteen individuals who, in the period from 403
to 322, are attested in one or more of these activities or capacities, and
may thus be accounted the *rhētores* of that period.[124] Very little of what
they did under these headings had an equivalent at deme level, but in the
proposers of deme decrees we catch a glimpse, at least, of the local
"political class"—or rather multiplicity of classes, each active within its
own small domain. And it was rare indeed, as we have seen, for a man
to be a *rhētōr* both there and in the city besides.[125]

✳

Was the demesman then a political apprentice? Only, it would seem, in
the more general of the two senses in which Haussoullier and others have
conceived him to be, namely, inasmuch as the demes offered a fairly
gentle introduction, for those who wished to avail themselves of it, to
the workings of a democratic assembly and the duties of its officials. For

---

[122] See Davies, *Wealth*, pp. 114-131.

[123] Note for example Demosthenes' offices in the years when he was already a well-
known political figure: *bouleutēs* in 347/6 (and possibly again in 337/6, though see Rhodes,
Boule, p. 4, n. 8); *sitōnēs* and τειχῶν ἐπιμελητής—the latter an elective post—after
Chaironeia (and possibly *sitōnēs* again in the early 320s, though see Davies, *Families*, p.
137); and cf. his *architheōria* to Olympia in August 324 (references in Davies, *loc. cit.*).

[124] See the second and third of Hansen's articles cited above (n. 121). His inventory (in
the latter) actually comprises three hundred and sixty-eight individuals, but for reasons
given above I leave aside the fifty whose sole attestation is as *stratēgos* (or as defendant in
an *eisangelia* arising directly from that office).

[125] See **19, 163, 184, 262**.

those who did not so wish, other opportunities and channels of acquiring basic political *savoir faire* were usually available.

That minority of demesmen who sought an active public career in city politics and government were also faced, theoretically, with a plurality of possible routes to their goal. Haussoullier's thesis was that the one which most naturally suggested itself was to pursue such a career in the deme first—in particular, to serve as its demarch—and only then to progress to the city, as a man already tried and tested in microcosm. But the individuals themselves appear to have thought (and acted) otherwise; and there is no more hint of any political doctrine than of any constitutional stipulation on the matter which might have given them pause before doing so. As far as such general considerations go, a more relevant one was the geographical factor: the need, for a public career (in or out of office) at city level, actually to be *in Athens*. Here, as pointed out earlier, the members of city demes had an enormous advantage, if they chose to take it. But how much time could, say, a politically ambitious Anaphlystian or Phegaian afford to spend amongst his fellow demesmen, whether he was engaged in building a city career in the first place or, equally vital, sustaining it thereafter?[126] One would give a lot to know how often Euboulos attended his deme assembly in Probalinthos, and whether Demosthenes ever evaded the demarchy of Paiania.

The likelihood that what currently appears as an almost negligible degree of overlap between those recorded as active at deme level and at city level will increase as further prosopographical data accrue has been conceded above. Certainly it would be far too schematic (and too tempting of fate) to assert that the two groups were mutually exclusive of each other. Yet, for all that, one's impression is that most of those Athenians whom family tradition and/or personal inclination persuaded to devote a significant amount of time and effort to public affairs had to decide— for purely practical purposes—whether to do this primarily (or even entirely) in the microcosm of their own demes, or primarily (or even entirely) at the seat of real power and influence, the city of Athens itself. For many the former course was both desirable and, in terms of their ambitions, sufficient. Resident, still, in their ancestral deme, they attended its assembly, perhaps discharging sortitive or elective office on its behalf and, according to their resources, enriching its communal life. City office—most obviously a year on the council—might draw them away from

---

[126] The case of the fifth-century general Phormion is instructive: it was, as we learn from Paus. 1.23.10, only during a hiatus in his political career that he "withdrew" (ἀναχωρήσας) to Paiania—surely, therefore, his ancestral deme (cf. C. W. Fornara, *The Athenian Board of Generals from 501 to 404*, Historia Einzelschrift 16, Wiesbaden, 1971, pp. 77-78).

time to time, but not for long.[127] For others, the satisfactions which the small pool could offer were inadequate, and they left the company of their fellow demesmen (if indeed they had ever known it) for the political allure of the city. Perhaps their careers had begun, modestly enough, at local level, perhaps not. In either case they spent their lives, in the main, as demesmen in the merely technical sense of the word, though a few saw fit—*after* they had achieved their larger reputations—to "return" to their demes as V.I.P. benefactors.[128]

Very occasionally, though, one does find an individual who displays a combination of both these career patterns. The two prime examples are an Eleusinian and a man from Halai Aixonides. Moirokles of Eleusis (163), the proposer of one deme decree and the honorand in two others, has been plausibly identified with the Moirokles who was a leading city politician in the third quarter of the fourth century;[129] and somewhat earlier Astyphilos of Halai (184) likewise seems to have divided his political energies, to equally good effect, between deme and polis. If comparable cases of this come to light in future we shall hope to learn more of the political aims and methods of men for whom their dual capacity as demesman and citizen carried an invitation, perhaps even an obligation, to seek responsibilities and rewards not in the one role or the other but in both.

[127] See 58, 120, 216, 303, 344.

[128] See, most obviously, Neoptolemos of Melite (292; Chap. 8, p. 247)—a most convenient deme, of course, for anyone seeking to combine "national" with "local" interests. Both Derkylos of Hagnous (179; Chap. 8, p. 247) and Xenokles of Sphettos (340; Chap. 8, p. 247) were benefactors of demes other than their own, but the principle is much the same; and see also 62. What one might call the impact of city celebrity upon deme life is otherwise to be seen most strikingly in Aixone, where it was doubtless the eponymous city archonship of Chremes (326/5) which impelled his two sons to the proposal of deme decrees (see Chap. 8, n. 66).

[129] For the identification, see 163, with references there. It is interesting to note that one of Moirokles' sons is attested only locally, the other only at city level (see under 10).

CHAPTER 11

———— ✳ ————

THE DEME IN COMEDY

In Part III so far we have pursued the theme of "deme and polis" by investigating on a factual level some aspects of the relationships between local and central government and local and city politics. This final chapter takes a different but, in its way, equally valid and instructive approach to that same theme. The Athenian polis in the classical and early Hellenistic periods existed and functioned as the consummation of its individual demes in both a real and also a psychological sense; and one can best appreciate the latter by examining the image of the demes, collectively and individually, which is projected in such genres of contemporary Athenian literature as were conceived for a large audience and thus mirror most closely—though not necessarily on that account most straightforwardly—the communal mentality of its members. Three genres above all, it will be agreed, may be so described: tragedy, comedy, and oratory.[1] Of these it is comedy which has the most to offer us here, not merely because it extends over the longest span of time[2] but also and more particularly because of the uniqueness of its blend of fantasy and reality.[3]

   That comedy preserves a wealth of information about and insight into

---

[1] For illuminating remarks on all three genres and their significance for the study of social psychology, see Dover, *Morality*, pp. 5-45 and passim.

[2] See below, n. 7. For our practical purposes here the period runs, in round figures, from the 470s to the 280s.

[3] Both tragedy and oratory share the blend, but in dissimilar proportions. One might say (very crudely) that in tragedy the "facts"—in the sense of allusions to political and social institutions contemporary not with the setting of the play but with the time of writing—are both fairly rare and usually peripheral to the main substance of plot and action (cf. Whitehead, *Metic*, pp. 34-38, for metics in tragedy), while in oratory the "fantasy" element is more properly to be described as political or forensic distortion of the facts. For the one passage in tragedy which reflects the Kleisthenic deme system, Sophocles *OC*, lines 77-80, see Chap. 2, p. 47. As to the evidence of oratory (on which see Edwards, *Demesman*, chap. 6), I have preferred to disperse it throughout this book, as appropriate, rather than to collect it in one place, but some of it is cited or re-cited for comparative purposes in what follows here.

the demes and their activities has of course long been recognized;[4] yet for this very reason much of it is easy to overlook. When large nuggets of gold lie plainly visible for the taking, why labor to pan for dust? Those scholars who do not sustain their interest in the search beyond a broad and token obeisance to Aristophanes' *Acharnians*[5] have indubitably seized upon the biggest and best nugget of them all, and in conjunction with other evidence the play evokes an unusually vivid picture of the men of this large and vigorous community.[6] Yet it is equally necessary to make what use we can of the totality of the comic data.

Of the hundreds of plays written and staged in each of the three periods into which Attic Comedy is conventionally divided—Old, Middle, and New[7]—all but a handful are now lost as entireties. But the losses, as is well known, are unequal; and since the only one of the three periods from which neither a complete play nor even a lengthy scene survives to us is the transitional Middle one,[8] there is a tendency both natural and (for all but true experts in the field) justifiable to be struck by the disparities, in content and in ethos, between the Old and the New manifestations of the genre. To this extent, following a particular topic and observing what we can of its treatment through the period of comedy as a whole take on especial interest and significance. In the case of the demes it will be seen that certain of the ways in which they were exploited for comic purposes by Aristophanes and his contemporaries seem to have found no place in the changed style of the later fourth and the third centuries; but in other respects we shall discover a notable degree of continuity.

A. Old Comedy

Represented as it is by the survival of eleven complete plays of Aristophanes[9] as well as by copious fragments of the plays of his elders

---

[4] See especially Haussoullier, *Vie*, pp. 196-200; Edwards, *Demesman*, chap. 5; Ehrenberg, *People*, pp. 155-158 (Old Comedy only).

[5] E.g. Schoeffer, "Demoi," col. 30; Lacey, *Family*, p. 278, n. 42.

[6] See Appendix 5.

[7] Old: the fifth century, especially its second half. Middle: ca. 400 to ca. 320. New: ca. 320 until roughly the end of the period covered by this book (or, by some definitions, beyond). Here we shall take Middle and New Comedy together; but see below, n. 9.

[8] The Greek original of the *Persa* of Plautus, however, probably belongs to this phase of the genre: see K. J. Dover in the (U.K.) Classical Association's *Fifty Years (and Twelve) of Classical Scholarship*, Oxford, 1968, p. 145.

[9] His *Ekklesiazousai* of 392 or 391 and *Ploutos* of 388 are now customarily classified

(chiefly Cratinus) and contemporaries (chiefly Eupolis), Old Comedy is and will probably always remain the best attested of the three phases of the genre. What survives is nonetheless a lamentably small proportion of what once existed; and anyone who aims to ransack Old Comedy for information about this or that particular subject has little option but to begin by reciting a litany of little-known authors and lost plays which, in some instances at least, should have added substantially to his knowledge.[10] As far as the demes are concerned we would wish to have had in front of us, above all, the *Demesmen* (Δημόται) of Hermippus, the *Demes* (Δῆμοι) of Eupolis, and three plays which, like Aristophanes' *Acharnians*, took as their title the name or demotic of one deme in particular: the *Man of Titakidai* (Τιτακίδης) of Magnes, our earliest known example;[11] the *Prospaltians* (Προσπάλτιοι) of Eupolis; and the *Potamians* (Ποτάμιοι) of Strattis.[12]

What can be made of such titles (and others like them which, as we shall see in section B, were chosen by poets of Middle and New Comedy)? Not much, the sceptic might wish to insist. Aristophanes' *Clouds*, after all, is noticeably short on meteorology, and entomology is less prominent, to say the least, in his *Wasps* than its title alone might have led us to imagine.[13] "Le titre était pourtant justifié par quelque scène, par quelque allusion plus ou moins longue à des moeurs locales, connues de tous."[14] Haussoullier's opinion does not seem too incautious. Perhaps it is as likely that the eponymous *Man of Titakidai* was a generalized representation of a country bumpkin[15] as a real and recognizable inhabitant of that obscure little community. On the other hand the plurality of *Prospaltians* and *Potamians* presumably indicates the composition of the chorus of those two plays, and an extent of characterization or caricature akin to that provided for the demesmen of Acharnai by Aristophanes.[16]

in Middle Comedy (cf. above, n. 7), but in their treatment of the demes they are really no different from the fifth-century plays; so we shall take all eleven together.

[10] Cf. Whitehead, *Metic*, pp. 39-40, on metics.

[11] Titakidai was not, however, one of the Kleisthenic demes but merely an identifiable hamlet within the large deme of Aphidna: see Chap. 1, n. 83.

[12] Note also the lost *Anagyros* (the deme eponym) of Aristophanes.

[13] Cf. Haussoullier, *Vie*, p. 199, making this point with reference to Plautus' *Poenulus* and Carthage.

[14] Haussoullier, *Vie*, p. 199.

[15] Note the numerous plays called *Agroikos* (e.g. by the Middle poet Antiphanes); Haussoullier, *Vie*, p. 200.

[16] According to *Etym. Magn.* 288.15 the men of Prospalta (and also of Thymaitadai) were ridiculed in comedy ὡς δικαστικοί—which might mean either personal litigiousness or else a fondness for sitting on juries (cf. the chorus of Aristophanes' *Wasps*). In either

To visualize even this much of the content of a play like Hermippus' *Demesmen* is more difficult; and what we know of Eupolis' *Demes* is a warning against the assumption that such plays were necessarily in any simple sense "about" the demes or their members.[17] However, a perusal of all the fragments of Old Comedy indicates—and the surviving plays of Aristophanes, as we shall see, confirm[18]—that a play did not in fact have to be "about" either the demes in general or any deme in particular for it to be set against the backcloth of the deme system and perhaps, at some point, to generate incidental humor from either a generally familiar aspect of deme life or else a well-known feature of a specific locality.

At the simplest level this amounted to nothing more than mentions of a particular deme by name[19] or allusions to real individuals with their demotics.[20] But much more interesting—both intrinsically and in the

case Eupolis' play may well be the only basis for this statement. On the other hand the (supposed) corruptibility of the Potamioi in matters of deme registration was apparently represented in several plays, that of Strattis *perhaps* amongst them; cf. Chap. 10, n. 7.

[17] Eupolis' *Demes*, staged probably in 412 (P. Geissler, *Chronologie der altattischen Komödie*, 2d ed., Berlin, 1969, pp. 54-55), depicted great Athenians of the past, from Solon to (apparently) Nikias, brought up from the underworld to give advice to the present; see e.g. Plut. *Per.* 3.4. Papyrus finds have produced fairly extensive fragments (for a conservative text, see C. Austin, *Comicorum graecorum fragmenta in papyris reperta*, Berlin, 1973, nos. 92-94, and add to his full general bibliography F. Sartori, *Una pagina di storia ateniese in un frammento dei Demi eupolidei*, Rome, 1975); the older ones are Kock, *CAF*, vol. 1, nos. 90-135. Evidently "the demes" formed, in some sense, the chorus, but the conjectural plot reconstruction by Edmonds in *FAC*, vol. 1, pp. 978-994, has generally been discounted as fanciful (an exception was Ehrenberg, *People*, pp. 60-61); and the import of the title remains obscure. Edmonds, *FAC*, vol. 1, p. 359, note *e*, and p. 993, conjured up an *agōn* between "the chief demes of Attika," some "living" (the chorus), some "dead" (represented by the dead leaders), and each arguing that it had done the city the most good. Even if this were not simply unintelligible (even to him: see *FAC*, p. 979, "the dead demes, whoever they were") and intrinsically silly, it is based upon restorations to his fr. 128D which are rightly ignored by Austin at *CGFPR* (see above), no. 94.

[18] I treat Aristophanes separately for convenience's sake, not to suggest any particular chronological or developmental relationship between him and the other poets of Old Comedy.

[19] E.g. Pherecrates fr. 134 (from the *Petale* of ?424): εἰς Κολωνὸν ἱέμην,| οὐ τὸν ἀγοραῖον ἀλλὰ τὸν τῶν ἱππέων. On Kolonos Agoraios—not a deme—see A. Fuks, *Eranos* 49, 1951, pp. 171-173; on the deme Kolonos, D. M. Lewis, *ABSA* 5, 1955, pp. 12-17.

[20] E.g. (*a*) Hagnon (PA 171) in Cratinus fr. 123 Edmonds (from the *Ploutoi*), lines 11-12: τοῦ Στειρίως γὰρ εὐκτὰ τοῦ[δ᾽ εἶναι κρίσιν],| ὃν καλοῦσ᾽ Ἅγνωνα νῦν καὶ δῆμον ἠ[γνόουν ὅτου]. For a more cautious text, see Austin *CGFPR* (above, n. 17), no. 73, lines 67-68, reporting alternative restorations for line 67 (= 11 Edmonds). In line 68 (= 12) Edmonds' idea is nonsense, as the demotic has already been given; I suspect δῆμον here may not mean "deme." (*b*) Meton (PA 10093) in Phrynichus fr. 21 (from the *Monotropos* of 414): Μέτων| ὁ Λευκονοιεύς. (*c*) Philonides (PA 14907) in Plato fr. 64 (from the *Laios*), lines 5-6: Φιλωνίδην| . . . τὸν Μελιτέα; cf. Nicochares fr. 3 and Theopompus frs. 4-5.

extent to which they are paralleled in Aristophanes (and elsewhere)—are the following three features:

1. References to natural produce, often fish or fruit, which was associated with particular demes:[21] nuts (perhaps acorns) from Pithos,[22] red mullet from Aixone,[23] Anagyrasian sea-perch[24] and tub-fish,[25] the figs of Teithras.[26] Sometimes there is good reason for suspecting that an ulterior meaning may have been intended in ostensibly innocent material of this kind—that is, either an allusion to some specific individual or group within the deme in question[27] or even to the supposed character of the demesmen as a whole; but it may be wrong to assume this in every instance.

2. Punning demotics. A fragment of Hermippus preserves the phrase Διαγόρου τοῦ Τερθρέως.[28] The verb *terthreuesthai* means "to split hairs," "to be excessively subtle or pedantic." As the whole phrase is in the genitive case one cannot unfortunately, say for certain whether the name of which this pun is presumably a distortion was a patronymic or a demotic. J. M. Edmonds (*ad loc.*) took it to be the former, and so it well might be; Aristophanes, as we shall see, punned freely on patronymics. The key facts—which we do not know—are what the *real* patronymic and demotic of this Diagoras were.[29] If his father's name was

---

[21] Since it is Athenaeus in the *Deipnosophistai* who more than any other single writer has preserved such comic extracts as we have, a disproportionate number of them—from all periods of the genre—are concerned with the pleasures of the table.

[22] Cratinus fr. 86 (from the *Kleoboulinai*): ἐπέδωκε βαλάνων ἄβακα τῶν ἐκ Φιττέως. For the connotation of βάλανοι, see Kock *ad loc.* Edmonds' recognition of the deme name Pithos here (*FAC*, vol. 1, p. 51, note *b*) seems preferable to either Meineke's Φηγέως or Kock's Εἰτέας, but his further suggestion that this is an allusion to the demagogue Androkles of Pithos is quite gratuitous—and possibly results from a subconscious connection of βαλάνων with the description of Androkles as βαλλαντιοτόμος, "cut-purse," in Ecphantides fr. 4.

[23] Cratinus fr. 221 (from the *Trophonios*), line 1: οὐδ' Αἰξωνίδ' ἐρυθρόχρων ἐσθίειν ἔτι τρίγλην.

[24] Plato fr. 160 (from the *Syrphax*): ὁδὶ μὲν Ἀναγυράσιος Ὀρφῶς ἐστί σοι (introduced as the friend of a glutton).

[25] Archippus fr. 27 (from the *Fishes*): a treaty between the Athenians and the fishes, the latter including Ἀναγυρουντόθεν τοὺς Κορακίωνας. Edmonds (*FAC*, vol. 1, p. 803, note *h*) sees here—surely, again, unnecessarily—"the pupils of some teacher of rhetoric of the deme Anagyrus nicknamed Corax 'Crow or Tub-fish' after the great Syracusan who wrote the first handbook of rhetoric c. 460."

[26] Theopompus fr. 11 (from the *Peace*): μάζαι, πλακοῦντες, ἰσχάδες Τειθράσιαι.

[27] Note Plut. *Moralia* 712A on the difficulty of understanding personal allusions in Old Comedy!

[28] Hermippus fr. 42 (from the *Moirai*), line 3.

[29] There is no reason to suppose that this is Diagoras "the atheist" (see W.K.C. Guthrie, *The Sophists*, Cambridge, 1971, pp. 236-237), who as a Melian would have had no demotic.

something even remotely like Terthreus, therein lay the pun; but if his deme was Teithras we have here a punning demotic to set beside the many in Aristophanes.

3. References to deme institutions. Again, outside Aristophanes a single example only has recognizably survived: the line, from an indeterminable play of Pherecrates, which runs ὑπέλυσε δήμαρχός τις ἐλθὼν εἰς χορόν.[30] The commonest meaning of the verb *hypolyein* is "to undo (shoes or sandals)," but that hardly seems to fit here.[31] Emendation is tempting;[32] explanation, however, is not impossible without it. Perhaps we should indeed visualize an amiable demarch letting down his official hair, so to speak, and joining in the fun of a dance (*choros*). On the other hand, the only other surviving appearance of "some demarch" in comedy (Aristoph. *Clouds*, line 37: δάκνει μὲ δήμαρχός τις ἐκ τῶν στρωμάτων) represents him, albeit good-humoredly, as a figure more likely to diminish than to increase the pleasure of his feckless fellow demesmen; so it may be that what Pherecrates' demarch has "undone" here is the dance itself.[33]

When we turn from these tantalizing vignettes (which, out of context, it is all too easy to misinterpret) to the rich oeuvre of Aristophanes, the setting of Old Comedy in a deme milieu becomes inescapably clear on a variety of different levels. With the sole exception of *Birds*, the action of every surviving Aristophanic play takes place in contemporary Attica. None is explicitly located within a particular, named deme.[34] However, many of the protagonists and other invented characters are given an appropriate (that is, rural) *dēmotikon*: Dikaiopolis of Cholleidai,[35] Stre-

[30] Pherecrates fr. 171 (*apud* Suda, δήμαρχοι).

[31] Cf. Kock, *CAF ad loc.*: "sententia prorsus obscura. nam de calceis exeundis cogitari non potest."

[32] Edmonds (*FAC*, vol. 1, p. 274) succumbed, emending to ὑπέδυ σε: "some demarch's joined the chorus and got under you." This has little to recommend it.

[33] For the demarch's "fonctions de police" (Haussoullier, *Vie*, p. 141) in a religious context, see Chap. 5A, sec. 2(d).

[34] Contrast, in this, Menander; see below, sec. B.

[35] *Ach.* line 406: Δικαιόπολις καλεῖ σε Χολλείδης, ἐγώ. But for this line, one would naturally take Dikaiopolis himself to be one of the Acharnians (see lines 33-34, with scholiast on the latter); and a scholiast on line 406 suggests that Χολλείδης is a humorous demotic whose purpose is to introduce the old joke in line 411 about Euripides' lame (χωλούς) characters. However, while a reference to lameness might well *precede* the comic designation of someone as a demesman of Cholleidai (and so make it clear that it *is* comic), I cannot see that in the reverse situation, as here, the audience could be expected to take the demotic at anything other than face value; and it is worth noting that Dikaiopolis and the Acharnians never address each other as fellow demesmen. For (inconclusive) topographic considerations, see J. S. Traill, *Hesp.* 47, 1978, p. 99 with n. 26.

psiades of Kikynna,[36] Strymodoros of Konthyle,[37] Chabes of Phlya,[38] Trygaios of Athmonon,[39] Euelpides of Krioa,[40] Antitheos of Gargettos,[41] and others.[42] And as both they and also the real-life characters whom the plays depict or mention[43] go about their business they make the sort of incidental, nonhumorous allusions to particular demes or their members which would have been natural to anyone in the audience.[44]

No group of demesmen is portrayed as fully as the Acharnians, but there are passing swipes at, for instance, the bragging Diomeians[45] and the fearsome women of Teithras,[46] and references to natural features or

---

[36] Clouds, line 134, cf. 210.

[37] Wasps, line 233.

[38] Wasps, line 234.

[39] Peace, lines 190 and 919.

[40] Birds, line 645; for his deme of residence, see below, n. 44, under c. Peisthetairos is given no demotic, in line 643 or anywhere else.

[41] Thesm., line 898.

[42] E.g. the character in fr. 27 (from the Amphiaraos of 414) who declares Λαμπτρεὺς ἔγωγε τῶν κάτω; and cf. Thesm., lines 619-622.

[43] Some, at least, of these are given their demotic (cf. above, n. 20) or otherwise identified by their deme: (a) Lysistratos of Cholargos (PA 9630) in Ach., line 855, Λυσίστρατος . . . Χολαργέων ὄνειδος; (b) Derketes of Phyle (see PA 3245) in Ach., line 1028, Δερκέτου Φυλασίου; (c) Chairephon of Sphettos (PA 15203) in Clouds, line 156, Χαιρεφῶν ὁ Σφήττιος (note, however, that K. J. Dover, Aristophanes: Clouds, Oxford, 1968, ad loc., suspects here "a weak pun on σφήξ, wasp, to suit the entomological context"); (d) Nikostratos of Skambonidai (PA 11011 + 11051) in Wasps, line 81, Νικόστρατος . . . ὁ Σκαμβωνίδης; and cf. Wasps, lines 894-895, ἐγράψατο | κύων (= Kleon) Κυδαθηναιεὺς Λάβητ' (= Laches) Αἰξωνέα.

[44] Here are five examples. (a) Pergase in Knights, line 321, πρὶν γὰρ εἶναι Περγασῆσιν ἔνεον ἐν ταῖς ἐμβάσιν (Demosthenes' deme was Aphidna, to which Pergase lay en route). (b) Peiraieus in Peace, line 165: Trygaios looks down from his beetle-ride to see someone defecating ἐν Πειραιεῖ παρὰ ταῖς πόρναις. (c) Halimous in Birds, line 496, κἀγὼ νομίσας ὄρθρον ἐχώρουν Ἁλιμουντάδε (although a demesman of Krioa—see above, at n. 40—Euelpides is evidently depicted as a resident of Halimous). (d) Diomeia in Frogs, lines 650-651, ἐφρόντισα | ὁπόθ' Ἡράκλεια τὰν Διομείοις γίγνεται. (e) Kerameis in Frogs, lines 1089-1098: an anecdote involves οἱ Κεραμῆς (cf., for Kerameikos, Knights, line 772; Birds, line 395; Frogs, line 129).

[45] Ach., line 605: amongst those despised by Dikaiopolis as misthophorountes are Διομειαλαζόνας. This may well refer to specific individuals, or even one individual, known to the audience; but a longer-term connection between Diomeia and alazoneia is suggested by the curious fourth-century phenomenon of the sixty jesters (Athen. 260A-B and 614D-E).

[46] Frogs, lines 475-477: τὼ νεφρὼ δέ σου | αὐτοῖσιν ἐντέροισιν ἡματωμένω | διασπάσονται Γοργόνες Τειθράσιαι. After the Tartesian lamprey (line 475), "Teithrasian gorgons" is presumably a surprising substitute for some more exotic adjective. The lexicographers offer the glosses we would expect (Hesych., Τιθράσια· χαλεπά, τραχέα; Suda, Τίθρασος· τόπος τῆς Λιβύης. καὶ Ἀριστοφάνης Γοργόνες Τιθράσιαι.'

products of other demes, at least some of which seem to have conveyed an element of collective or individual characterization of the demesmen in question:[47] the sprats of Phaleron,[48] a cloak from Thymaitadai,[49] a Trikorysian gnat,[50] Sphettian vinegar.[51] Such throwaway lines will have been guaranteed their quota of usually innocent laughter for the very simplest of reasons—the mere fact that the audience watching the play contained only a tiny minority of the members of any deme in particular, if indeed any of them at all. The average Athenian in this period may or may not have relished humor at the expense of his own deme, but almost always the joke was on someone else.

Was any deme reckoned *intrinsically* humorous? The prime candidate to be so described must obviously be Kopros, a small coastal deme which lay between Thria and Eleusis.[52] The very idea of a community called Shit (or even Excrement) has so many comic possibilties—or, to be exact, so much scope for reiteration of the same ones—that it must have been a godsend to comic poets whose powers of invention were running short, and a constant source of potential embarrassment and discomfiture to those who had to admit to its demotic. In Aristophanes the expected jokes duly make their appearance: Demos in *Knights* recalls being told by "a man of Kopros" of Kleon's plan that the jurors should fart themselves to death after a surfeit of cheap silphium,[53] while Blepyros' way, in *Ekklesiazousai*, of conveying the urgency of his need to defecate is to speak of a knock on the door by the same figure in allegorical form.[54]

ἔνθα αἱ Γοργόνες διέτριβον. ἀπὸ δήμου τῆς Ἀττικῆς πονηροῦ· διαβάλλουσι γὰρ τὸν δῆμον τοῦτον ὡς κακοπράγμονα), but the reference may well be to some recent *cause célèbre*; cf. *Thesm.*, lines 562-563, an Acharnian murderess.

[47] Cf. above, p. 331.

[48] *Ach.*, line 901: ἀφύας . . . Φαληρικάς; also in *Birds*, line 76, and fr. 507.

[49] *Wasps*, line 1138: ἐγὼ δὲ σισύραν ᾠόμην Θυμαιτίδα (instead of what it actually is, a Persian gown). Is this a colorful way of saying "rustic"?

[50] *Lysistr.* line 1032 (quoted by St. Byz., Τρικόρυνθον): οὐκ ἐμπίς ἐστιν ἥδε Τρικορυσία; As the scholiast suggests, either gnats abounded in swampy Trikorynthos or else πονηροί εἰσιν οἱ Τρικορύσιοι. (Compare Hesychius' gloss Συπαληττίους· κακούργους, which one may guess derives from comedy.)

[51] *Ploutos*, lines 720-721: εἶτ' ὄξει διέμενος Σφηττίῳ | κατέπλασεν αὐτοῦ τὰ βλέφαρ' ἐκστρέψας. Athen. 67C-D quotes line 720 and adds that Didymus, in explaining it, said ἴσως διότι οἱ Σφήττιοι ὀξεῖς. The scholiasts *ad loc.* consider alternatives to this, but Didymus' view is uniform in the lexicographers: Hesych., ὄξος Σφήττιον; Phot., Σφήττιοι; *Etym. Magn.* 738.44; *Lex Rhet. Cantabr.*, Σφήττιοι; cf. *Corpus Paroemiographorum Graecorum*, vol. I, p. 440, no. 29, cf. vol. II, p. 213, no. 93.

[52] For the location, see E. Vanderpool, *Hesp.* 22, 1953, pp. 176-177; cf. Traill, *Organization*, p. 52.

[53] *Knights*, line 899: νὴ τὸν Ποσειδῶ καὶ πρὸς ἐμὲ τοῦτ' εἶπ' ἀνὴρ Κόπρειος.

[54] *Ekkles.* lines 316-317: ὁ δ' ἤδη τὴν θύραν | ἐπεῖχε κρούων ὁ Κοπρεαῖος.

No doubt the demesmen of Anaphlystos and Paionidai laughed as heartily as anyone at such simple wit, but in fact they themselves were little better placed to evade witticisms on account of their deme-name alone. The verb *anaphlan* signified masturbation, and vigorous copulation was one of the several meanings of *paiein* (compare the modern vernacular "bang"). Nowhere—in what survives—does Aristophanes go to the lengths of suggesting, as he might well have done, that *all* Anaphlystians were dedicated onanists or *all* Paionidai in a chronically priapic state. He does, however, use the demotic of these two demes to impute such characteristics to particular, real individuals.[55] As to the men of Anagyrous, their deme derived its name from the malodorous *anagyris foetida*, or stinking bean-trefoil, so naturally they had to put up with jokes about smells.[56]

In cases like these the humor stood ready-made in the very name of the deme itself; and elsewhere too no change in the name was needed in order for it to be, in an appropriately prepared context, a source of amusement.[57] But if change was needed Aristophanes was quite happy to make it, to satisfy his (and presumably his audience's) sheer zest for wordplay. The deme-name and the personal demotic served equally well. In search of Dikaiopolis, whom they intend to pelt (*ballein*) with stones, the chorus of *Acharnians* declare that they must seek him out in Ballene— a jocular version, one assumes, of the deme Pallene;[58] and Demosthenes

[55] (a) Anaphlystios: see *Frogs*, line 431 (the homosexual Kleisthenes mourns Σεβῖνον ὅστις ἐστὶν Ἀναφλύστιος), and *Ekkles.*, lines 979-980 (Ἀναφλύστιον ζητῶν τιν' ἄνθρωπον – τίνα;| – οὐ τὸν Σεβῖνον, ὃν σὺ προσδοκᾷς ἴσως); Sebinos is itself a pseudonym implying another obscenity, βίνειν. (b) Paionides: see *Lysistr.*, line 852, ἀνὴρ ἐκείνης (sc. Μυρρίνης), Παιονίδης Κινησίας. The priapic scene which follows justifies the view of the scholiast *ad loc.* that the demotic is used for its sexual innuendo—but only if Kinesias was a real person known to the audience (as Myrrhine herself was: see J. Papademetriou, *AE* 1948-1949, pp. 146ff., developed by D. M. Lewis, *ABSA*, 50, 1955, pp. 1-7). I take him to be real, though not necessarily Myrrhine's real husband, if any; Aristophanes might well have "paired Myrrhine with an old antagonist" (Lewis, *loc. cit.*, p. 2) or simply with a young stud whose passion for the priestess, by now well past her prime, would seem comical.

[56] *Lysistr.*, lines 67-68: πόθεν εἰσίν; – Ἀναγυρουντόθεν – νὴ τὸν Δία | ὁ γοῦν ἀνάγυρός μοι κεκινῆσθαι δοκεῖ. See Hesych., Ἀναγυράσιος; Suda, Ἀνάγυρος; *Lex Seguer.* V, *Lexeis Rhetorikai*, Ἀναγυράσιος [= Bekker, *Anecd. Gr.* 1.210.3]; *Corpus Paroemiographorum Graecorum*, vol. I, p. 46, no. 55 (and p. 184, no. 25), vol. II, p. 479, no. 79.

[57] See e.g. the Kephale joke in *Birds*, lines 475-476: τὸν πατέρ' αὐτῆς ἐν τῇ κεφαλῇ κατορύξαι| – ὁ πατὴρ ἄρα τῆς κορυδοῦ νυνὶ κεῖται τεθνεὼς Κεφαλῆσιν.

[58] *Ach.*, line 234: ἀλλὰ δεῖ ζητεῖν τὸν ἄνδρα καὶ βλέπειν Βαλληνάδε. It would be a pity if Παλληνάδε, given in some manuscripts, is the correct reading; I prefer to believe in the joke. Note that the *ballein* word comes after (line 236, taken up by lines 281-283),

in *Knights*, marking by a whole string of untranslatable puns Kleon's stranglehold over both domestic and foreign affairs, speaks of his mind being in Klopidai—probably a distortion of the real deme name Kropidai, to carry implications of robbery or embezzlement (*klopeuein, kleptein*).[59] As regards demotics, those of real individuals could be modified so as to express something of their personality or other attributes—Proxenides the Bragsman and the like.[60] Also a punning demotic might be used allegorically. Shortly after describing his need to defecate as a knock on the door from a man of Kopros (above), Blepyros in *Ekklesiazousai* recollects having eaten a wild pear (*achras*) which, as he sees it, is what is thwarting this need; now, he says, the door has been bolted—by an Achradousian (i.e., Acherdousian).[61] And on occasion a demotic could be pure invention, as with the introduction of the old man Demos in *Knights*: "Mr Demos of the Pnyx."[62]

Individual demes, then, provided a virtually inexhaustible fund of simple humor as well as of neutral background material for Aristophanic comedy. But in addition many of the protagonists (and others) in the plays are made to act out a generic role as demesmen which would have been perceived by their real-life counterparts in the audience as corresponding to their own experience. For example, Dikaiopolis in *Acharnians*, the man who hates the city-center and longs for his own deme (line 33), is to be imagined as returning to it (lines 266-267) for his private celebration of the rural Dionysia.[63] It is not difficult to imagine

---

not before, the deme-name, but Βαλληνάδε has already warned the audience that a pun may be on its way; contrast the case discussed above, in n. 35.

[59] *Knights*, lines 78-79: ὁ πρωκτός ἐστιν αὐτόχρημ᾽ ἐν Χάοσιν, | τὼ χεῖρ᾽ ἐν Αἰτωλοῖς, ὁ νοῦς δ᾽ ἐν Κλωπιδῶν. There is something to be said for this traditional explanation—see the scholiast *ad loc.*—despite the fact that a real Klopidai seems to have existed (probably as one of the tiny communities subsumed under Aphidna: Traill, *Organization*, pp. 90-91).

[60] *Birds*, line 1126, Προξενίδης (PA 12257) ὁ Κομπασεύς; a conflation of *kompazein* with (presumably) Konthyleus. In *Lysistr.*, line 397, the Bouzyges Demostratos (PA 3611) is described as ὁ θεοῖσιν ἐχθρὸς καὶ μιαρὸς Χολοζύγης; the Chol- is explained by a scholiast *ad loc.* as διὰ τὸ μελαγχολᾶν, but this "need not be more than a guess and does not allow us to exclude the possibility of a pun on a demotic Χολαργεύς" (Davies, *Families*, pp. 105-106).

[61] *Ekkles.*, lines 361-362: νῦν μὲν γὰρ οὗτος βεβαλάνωκε τὴν θύραν, | ὅστις ποτ᾽ ἔσθ᾽ ἄνθρωπος ἀχραδούσιος (the ἀχράς had appeared in lines 354-355). Compare fr. 933, Ἀχραδοῦς, which is conceivably a reference to this same passage. A deme Achradous was taken seriously by St. Byz. (s.v.), but never existed; to add to the confusion, however, ἄχερδος was another name for the wild pear (cf. *Com. adesp.* fr. 1277, μοχθηρὸς ὢν καὶ τὴν γνώμην Ἀχερδούσιος).

[62] *Knights*, line 42: Δῆμος Πυκνίτης, δύσκολον γερόντιον. The mock demotic was appreciated by the scholiast *ad loc.* (. . . τὸν δῆμον δὲ ὥσπερ πολίτην τῆς Πυκνὸς εἶπε).

[63] *Ach.*, lines 201-202 and 237-279; see Chap. 7, pp. 213-214.

how much, as they watched this at the Lenaia of 425, the displaced rural demesmen of Attica yearned to do the same. In lighter vein—or so one assumes—depiction of or reference to the duties of a demarch, while perhaps less than entertaining for anyone who had ever seriously fallen foul of this universal figure of local authority, must have been a delight to those who had known only the *Schadenfreude* of watching him take action against their delinquent fellow demesmen. Harpocration reports that "Aristophanes in *Skenas Katalambanousai* shows that demarchs used to seize the property of debtors."[64] Whether this (lost) play actually portrayed such a thing in action or merely contained an allusion to it is not clear from Harpocration's words, but the latter would have sufficed for an amusing "one-liner" like the one in *Clouds*: tossing and turning on his bed in anguish at his son's debts, Strepsiades cries out that something is biting him in the bedclothes—a demarch![65]

It would not have been surprising if this joke had paved the way for the actual appearance on stage of the demarch of Kikynna at some point in the action of *Clouds*, but in fact Strepsiades' two creditors, when they are eventually introduced, attempt to recover their money from him by their own efforts. The first of them, at any rate, is also a Kikynneus; and despite his justifiable exasperation at Strepsiades' behavior he is made to remark how painful it will be to deliver a summons to a fellow demesman and so incur his hostility.[66] As we saw in Chapter 8, the sentiment can be paralleled in forensic oratory,[67] and reflects a view—common to both genres—that ideally a man's fellow demesmen either fell within the definition of, or at least were effectively inseparable from, his *philoi*.[68] Needless to say, the operative word here is "ideally." Aristophanes' own feud with his fellow Kydathenaieus Kleon is as good a reminder as any that in particular circumstances the ideal could find itself savagely mocked by the reality.[69] More to the point, though, is the fact that the ideal itself owed less to abstract morality than to the simple practicalities of everyday life. Strepsiades' creditor, as Sir Kenneth Dover has remarked, "is not obeying an absolute command 'Thou shalt not quarrel with a fellow-demesman,' but thinking of the embarrassment occasioned by ill-feeling

[64] Harpoc., δήμαρχος· . . . ὅτι δὲ ἠνεχυρίαζον οἱ δήμαρχοι δηλοῖ Ἀριστοφάνης ἐν Σκηνὰς Καταλαμβανούσαις (= Aristoph. fr. 484).
[65] *Clouds*, line 37: δάκνει μὲ δήμαρχός τις ἐκ τῶν στρωμάτων. Translators have naturally found the old "bumbailiff" (Shakespeare et al.) irresistible here.
[66] *Clouds*, lines 1218-1219: γενήσομαι | ἐχθρὸς ἔτι πρὸς τούτοισιν ἀνδρὶ δημότῃ.
[67] [Lysias] 20.13; Isaeus fr. 4 Thalheim; [Demosth.] 52.28—see Chap. 8, pp. 229-231.
[68] *Ach.*, lines 325ff.; *Knights*, lines 319-320; *Clouds*, lines 1206-1210; *Ekkles.*, lines 1023-1024; *Ploutos*, lines 253-254; [Lysias] 6.53; Lysias 27.12—see Chap. 8, p. 232.
[69] Cf. Edwards, *Demesman*, p. 51, with (in n. 41) other examples of intra-deme hostility.

between people who are thrown into frequent contact."[70] Aristophanes depicted in his plays an Attica where a man *was* thrown into frequent contact with his fellow demesmen—because they were his neighbors as well as his friends[71]—and where just about the worst thing they might do to him was to laugh at him.[72] What Aristophanes was creating, in doing so, could not properly be called fantasy as opposed to reality. It was, however, a reality with the untidy edges trimmed away and a considerable degree of stylization and wishful thinking in what remained.

B. Middle and New Comedy

The introductory remarks to our survey of Old Comedy may be taken, *mutatis mutandis*, to apply equally well here. Lost plays tantalize with their titles. It would have been fascinating to read, from the Middle period, Antiphanes' *Thorikians or The Mine-Driller* (Θορίκιοι ἢ Διορύττων)[73] and *Man of Phrearrhioi* (Φρεάρριος), and Timocles' *Ikarian Satyrs* (Ἰκάριοι Σάτυροι)[74] and *Marathonians* (Μαραθώνιοι); likewise, from the era of New Comedy, Diphilus' *Anagyros* (Ἀνάγυρος),[75] Menander's *Hala(i)eis* (Ἁλαεῖς),[76] Philippides' *Lakiadai* (Λακιάδαι), Posidippus' *Demesmen* (Δημόται), and the *Erchians* (Ἐρχιεῖς) written by an unknown author of the late third or early second century.[77] That none of these plays will necessarily have lived up, in terms of characterization, to the promise suggested by their titles is a possibility which must again be borne in mind.[78] Yet with Old Comedy we found reason to conclude that a play did not by any means have to be "about" a particular deme or the demes in general for it to be set in a deme context and/or to make play on various levels with deme life and terminology. Is this also true of comedy of the Middle and New periods?

[70] Dover, *Morality*, p. 277.

[71] For passages, see Chap. 8, nn. 37 and 48.

[72] See *Knights*, lines 319-321 (cf. above, n. 44, under *a*).

[73] On the subtitle, see Labarbe, *Thorikos*, p. 30, n. 2.

[74] I take this, with Kock, to refer to the deme Ikarion rather than to the Aegean island Ikaria.

[75] Aristophanes too, as noted above (n. 12), had written a play of this name, now lost.

[76] Halai Araphenides, not Aixonides: St. Byz., Ἁλαὶ Ἀραφηνίδες καὶ Ἁλαὶ Αἰξωνίδες. See further below, n. 81.

[77] IG II²2323, line 98 = SEG 25.194, line 81.

[78] A possible exception is Philippides' *Lakiadai*, if this either originated or at least exploited the proverbial connection between that deme and the use of radishes to humiliate those caught in adultery. See on this Hesych., Λακιάδαι; Suda, ὦ Λακιάδαι (and Πλακιάδαι!); *Corpus Paroemiographorum Graecorum*, vol. I, p. 467, no. 43.

Menander apart,[79] the fragments of New Comedy are unrevelatory; but those of the Middle period bear comparison in at least some respects with the comedy of the age of Aristophanes. Demotics are still given both to real individuals[80] and apparently to invented characters,[81] though there is no trace now of Aristophanes' exuberant demotic puns. Individual demes are still casually mentioned.[82] So too are natural products—notably fish—particularly associated with them.[83] As with such things in Old Comedy these allusions seem often to be innocuous enough,[84] but occasionally a whiff of characterization or caricature may be in the air;[85]

[79] I treat Menander separately, below; again (cf. above, n. 18, on Aristophanes) this is for convenience's sake, not to imply any particular chronological or developmental relationship between him and the other poets of New Comedy.

[80] Anaxandrides, *Protesilaus* fr. 41, line 18, Κηφισόδοτον τὸν 'Αχαρνῆθεν (PA 8326); Timocles, *Dionysos* fr. 7, line 1, ὁ δ' 'Αχαρνικὸς Τηλέμαχος (PA 13562, and R. G. Osborne, *LCM* 8.7, July 1983, p. 111), cf. *Ikarian Satyrs* fr. 16 (= 17 Edmonds), line 6, Τηλέμαχον 'Αχαρνέα. No doubt it is mere coincidence that both these men were Acharnians. For variant versions of the Acharnian demotic—properly 'Αχαρνεύς—cf. Aristoph. *Ach.*, lines 180, 324, 329 ('Αχαρνικοί) and 322 ('Αχαρνῇδαι); the regular one is used in lines 177, 200, 203, 224, 286. Also a real person, evidently, is Thearion the baker (see Plato *Gorgias* 518B and Athen. 112C-E), said in Antiphanes' *Omphale*, fr. 176, to have taught his "*dēmotai*" the craft of producing loaves in (?) animal shapes; but this surely means no more than his "fellow *citizens*" (cf. Chap. 1, n. 28).

[81] Antiphanes, *Tyrrhenos* fr. 211, line 1: δήμου δ' 'Αλαιεύς ἐστιν. Note that the scrap of dialogue which follows suggests that this demotic (irrespective of whether it refers to Halai Aixonides or Araphenides; as so often, we cannot tell) would naturally open the way for piscine jokes at the characters'—and indirectly the deme's—expense. Perhaps it did so in Menander's *Hala(i)eis*.

[82] E.g. Peiraieus in Philiscus fr. 2 (ὁ Πειραιεὺς κάρυον μέγ' ἐστὶ καὶ κενόν; this remark seems to suggest the very early years of the fourth century—Edmonds, *FAC*, vol. 2, p. 11, note f) and Alexis fr. 245, line 1. Compare Alexis fr. 203 on the "soft life" of the Kerameikos (not, one would surmise, an aspersion upon the deme Kerameis as such).

[83] Cf. above, n. 21.

[84] E.g., Nausicrates, *Naukleroi* frs. 1-2, lines 7-11, on the red mullet of Aixone (see above, p. 331, for the same in Cratinus); Eubulus, *Orthannes* fr. 75, line 4, and Sotades, *Enkleiomenai* fr. 1, line 30, on the sprats of Phaleron (see above, p. 334, for the same in Aristophanes; also Athen. 135A and 285E-F). On the κωβιοί of Otryne (and Phaleron), see next note.

[85] (a) Dekeleian vinegar: Alexis fr. 285 (play unknown), κοτύλας τέτταρας | ἀναγκάσας μεστὰς ἔμ' αὐτίτου σπάσαι | ὄξους Δεκελεικοῦ δι' ἀγορᾶς μέσης ἄγεις. This, it would seem, is a different kind of joke from Aristophanes' Sphettian vinegar (above, p. 334); Kock was surely right to suggest that ὄξους comes unexpectedly for οἴνου. (b) Otrynian gobies: Antiphanes, *Timon* fr. 206, lines 4-8, ἡμῖν δὲ τοῖς θνητοῖς ἐπριάμην κωβιούς. | ὡς προσβαλεῖν δ' ἐκέλευσα τὸν τοιχωρύχον, | τὸν ἰχθυοπώλην, "προστίθημι," φησί, "σοὶ | τὸν δῆμον αὐτῶν· εἰσὶ γὰρ Φαληρικοί." | ἄλλοι δ' ἐπώλουν, ὡς ἔοικ', 'Οτρυνικούς. For the pun on δημός (fat) and δῆμος, cf. Aristoph. *Wasps*, lines 40-41, where δῆμος = *populus*. (In attempting to locate the deme Otryne it has been disputed whether the κωβιός was a species living in fresh water

and the most direct reference to a particular group of demesmen—Anaxandrides' hit at the laxity of deme registration in Sounion[86]—embodies, albeit in humorous form, a more serious allegation of its kind than anything in Aristophanes. The latter (and his contemporaries) freely cast aspersions upon the citizen status of prominent *individuals*,[87] apparently without parallel condemnation of what must have been, had the charges been sound, the corruptibility or gullibility of the demes which had admitted them.[88] In Middle Comedy and, as we shall shortly see, in Menander there may be glimpses of a shift of emphasis, from individual to collective culpability, and of a more marked interest in the mechanics and the terminology of deme enrolment. But our evidence is too slight to make very much of this, and in any case the joke must have been, as often as not, the thing. This is certainly true of a fragment of the younger Cratinus in which (it would seem) a mercenary soldier, returning home after many years of foreign campaigning, declares that he had solved the difficulty of tracking down his fellow demesmen by becoming enrolled in the ... drinks-cupboard (*kylikeion*: punning, of course, on *grammateion*).[89]

What survives of the oeuvre of Menander is incomparably our best guide to the Athenians' taste in comedy during the last quarter of the fourth century and the first decade of the third;[90] and it is the extent of this survival, as much as the more subjective consideration of Menander's intrinsic stature within his genre, which invites one to compare his treatment of the demes (or any other subject) with that of Aristophanes. And such a comparison reveals continuity and change in approximately equal measure.

We may deal first with the physical setting of Menander's plays. Aristophanes, as noted earlier, had not felt the need to locate his plays within particular, named demes; it was enough that they were all, save only

---

or sea water; the former is argued by W. E. Thompson, *Mnemosyne* 22, 1969, p. 144, n. 13, the latter by Traill, *Organization*, p. 40, n. 11; but the citations in Athen. 309B-E actually suggest both habitats.)

[86] Anaxandrides, *Anchises* fr. 4, lines 3-4; see Chap. 9, n. 15. Compare Theophr. *Char.* 28 (κακολογίας).2: the son of Sosias the slave becomes, according to the Slanderer, Sosidemos the demesman.

[87] See Connor, *Politicians*, pp. 168-171; Davies, "Descent group," p. 112. On the same phenomenon in fourth-century oratory, see Dover, *Morality*, pp. 30-33.

[88] For a possible exception, Potamos, see above, n. 16.

[89] Cratinus Junior, *Cheiron* fr. 9: πολλοστῷ δ' ἔτει | ἐκ τῶν πολεμίων οἴκαδ' ἥκων, ξυγγενεῖς | καὶ φράτερας καὶ δημότας εὑρὼν μόλις, | εἰς τὸ κυλικεῖον ἐνεγράφην· Ζεύς ἐστί μοι | ἑρκεῖος, ἔστι φράτριος, τὰ τέλη τελῶ.

[90] This is true despite his relative lack of popular success during his lifetime (on which see Gomme/Sandbach, *Menander*, p. 2 with n. 1: only eight recorded victories). Yet the social historian if not the literary critic might be forgiven for wishing to read less of Menander and more of Philemon, who frequently defeated him.

Birds, set in contemporary Attica. In Menander, by contrast—and indeed, it would appear, in New Comedy as a whole—non-Attic settings were seemingly commonplace enough to make necessary some explicit statement, early in the play, on the matter of its locale.[91] Moreover it is indicative of the more literal-minded character of New Comedy that a general setting in Attica should mean, in point of fact, a specific one in this or that deme. One of the plainest examples of this is the very opening of *Dyskolos*, where Pan's prologue begins: "Imagine that the scene is Attica—Phyle—and the Nymphs' sanctuary from which I come belongs to the Phylasians and those who can farm the rocks here."[92] Further references either to the deme Phyle or to its members occur during the course of the play.[93] Likewise *Heros* is set in the small and, as far as we know, unremarkable deme of Ptelea,[94] *Sikyonios* probably in Eleusis,[95] *Epitrepontes* in an unidentifiable deme,[96] and doubtless the lost *Hala(i)eis* in Halai (Araphenides).[97] In addition, normal conversational allusions are made to particular demes—as, for instance, when Pan in *Dyskolos* declares that the misanthropic Knemon detests everyone for miles around, from his wife and his neighbors "as far as Cholargos, down there."[98] And the characters, where appropriate, are given a demotic: Blepes of Eleusis,[99] Phanias of Euonymon,[100] Kinesias of Skambonidai[101]—none of them obviously chosen for the sake of the sort of pun or other joke which Aristophanes and his audience would have relished.[102]

[91] Cf. Gomme/Sandbach, *Menander*, p. 135, on *Dyskolos*, line 1 (quoted in next note).

[92] *Dyskolos*, lines 1-4: τῆς 'Αττικῆς νομίζετ' εἶναι τὸν τόπον, | Φυλήν, τὸ νυμφαῖον δ' ὅθεν προέρχομαι | Φυλασίων καὶ τῶν δυναμένων τὰς πέτρας | ἐνθάδε γεωργεῖν. In line 3 the καί implies no distinction between the two groups: Gomme/Sandbach, *Menander*, p. 136.

[93] Φυλή, lines 522-523; Φυλάσιοι, lines 520-521; δῆμος, lines 260-263; τόπος (cf. line 1), lines 330-331, 507-508, 608-609.

[94] *Heros*, lines 21-22: ποιμὴν γὰρ ἦν Τίβειος οἰκῶν ἐνθαδὶ | Πτελέασι.

[95] Eleusis is mentioned in line 57 of the play, and Blepes has the Eleusinian demotic (lines 187-188). For the problem consult Gomme/Sandbach, *Menander*, p. 290.

[96] *Possibly* either Acharnai (see line 257) or Halai Araphenides (see line 451); see Gomme/Sandbach, *Menander*, p. 290.

[97] See above, n. 76.

[98] *Dyskolos*, lines 32-34: ἀπὸ τούτων ἀρξάμενος τῶν γειτόνων | καὶ τῆς γυναικὸς μέχρι Χολαργέων κάτω | μισῶν ἐφεξῆς πάντας. See also *Dyskolos*, lines 407-409 (ἐὰν ἴδῃ γὰρ ἐνύπνιον τὸν Πᾶνα τὸν | Παιανιοῖ, τούτῳ βαδιούμεθ᾽, οἶδ᾽ ὅτι, | θύσοντες εὐθύς); *Sikyonios*, lines 354-355 (πρόσθες θυγάτριον | 'Αλῆθεν ἀπολέσας ἑαυτοῦ τετραετές); and *Heauton Timoroumenos* fr. 140, Edmonds lines 3-4 (τῶν 'Αλῆσι χωρίον | κεκτημένος κάλλιστον).

[99] *Sikyonios*, lines 187-188.

[100] *Kitharistes*, lines 96-97.

[101] *Sikyonios*, lines 346-350.

[102] (a) The dialogue in *Sikyonios*, lines 346-354, is not easy to grasp (cf. Gomme/Sandbach, *Menander*, pp. 664-665), but I am not at all persuaded by the suggestion of P. H.

As far as the characterization of individual demes is concerned, it looks as though we have lost the best that Menander could contrive. According to Harpocration, the demesmen of Potamos were ridiculed in his *Twin Sisters* (Δίδυμαι) for their easygoing acceptance of illicit deme registration.[103] A line from the *Kanephoros* refers to "some abusive old woman" (γραῦς τις κακολόγος) as "Aixonian through both parents" (ἐκ δυοῖν Αἰξωνέοιν).[104] And the phrase "Trikorysian queen" (Τρικορυσία βασίλιννα) occurs in another fragment, from an unknown play.[105] Extensive commentary is possible in none of these cases, but it may at least be suggested that Menander was not, in any of them, truly originating a humorous point but rather exploiting one which was already in existence. The procedural shortcomings of the Potamioi, as Harpocration reports, provided material for other comic poets besides Menander—the fifth-century Strattis *perhaps* amongst them;[106] the implications of calling someone an "Aixonian" are recognized, by a member of that deme, in Plato's *Laches*;[107] and it is conceivable that the "Trikorysian queen"— presumably, as Kock surmised, a woman of irritatingly regal demeanor— owes something to Aristophanes' gnat from the same deme.[108]

It is a pity, all the same, that we cannot now read *Didymai* and discover for ourselves whether the hapless men of Potamos were taken to task at length for their conduct or simply allowed to escape, like Anaxandrides' Sounians, with a glancing blow. Perhaps the latter is more probable, given the general absence of savagery and caricature from Menander's

Vellacott, *Menander: plays and fragments*, Harmondsworth (Penguin Books), 1967, p. 221, that the demotic Skambonides is chosen for the sake of wordplay on *skambos* (bow-legged: but LSJ give no instances from this period) and the *simos* (snub-nosed) of line 352. (*b*) In *Kitharistes*, lines 96-99, the exchange runs as follows: εἶδον κόρην ἐνταῦθα Φανίου [τινὸς] | Εὐωνυμέως.— Εὐωνυμεῖς κἀ[κεῖ τινές] | εἰσ' ἐν Ἐφέσῳ;— χρέα μὲν οὖν [πρᾶξων παρῆν] | ἐντεῦθεν. This is hardly a joke, but rather an allusion—its point obscure—to the tradition that settlers from Euonymon had gone to Ephesos, where one of the five tribes in the fourth century was that of the Euonymoi (Gomme/Sandbach, *Menander* p. 416; cf. *RE* 5, 1905, col. 2798). (For a demotic pun in Menander's one-time teacher, Theophrastus, see *Char.* 21 (μικροφιλοτιμίας).9; cf. Lucian, Συμπόσιον ἢ Λαπίθαι 19.)

[103] Harpoc., Ποταμός.

[104] *Kanephoros* fr. 256.

[105] Fr. 907.

[106] See Chap. 10, n. 7, and above, n. 16.

[107] Plato *Laches* 197C: οὐδὲν ἐρῶ πρὸς ταῦτα, ἔχων εἰπεῖν, ἵνα μή με φῇς ὡς ἀληθῶς Αἰξωνέα εἶναι; the speaker is Laches himself, for whom see above, n. 43. Note also Harpoc., Αἰξωνῆσιν; Hesych., αἰξωνεύεσθαι; St. Byz., Αἰξώνεια; Suda, αἰξωνεύεσθαι and Αἰξωνῆς; *Etym. Magn.* 36.57 (αἰξωνεύεσθαι); *Lex Seguer.* VI, *Synagoge Lexeon Chresimon*, αἰξωνεύεσθαι and Αἰξωνῆσιν [= Bekker, *Anecd. Gr.* 1.353.31 and 358.23].

[108] For the gnat, see above, p. 334.

arsenal of humor. Even so, the point *may* have had a not unimportant bearing upon the plot of the play—at any rate if, like so many of the plots of New Comedy, it turned at some stage upon the need to establish that someone was (or, possibly, was not) of legitimate citizen birth. Such an issue arose in Menander's *Carthaginian* (Καρχηδόνιος), if one may judge from the mere ten lines or so which have been well preserved. The dialogue in lines 32-39 runs as follows:

—Tell me, who is your mother?
—Mine?
—Yes; and say who your father is too. Imagine the demesmen are making registrations.
—My mother is the daughter of Hamilcar, general of the Carthaginians, you runaway slave! Why that look?
—Ha! You come to us as the maternal grandson of Hamilcar and expect to get a citizen girl?
—Yes, once I'm registered according to the laws.[109]

It is probable that the action of this play took place in Athens,[110] and possible, as Sandbach has noted, "that the person involved was mistaken about his parentage and proved to be a full Athenian,"[111] for another fragment refers to the impossibility of really knowing, as distinct from merely assuming or suspecting, who one's father is.[112] But there is not even a basis for conjecture as to whether such a recognition scene was set in, or led into, a *real* deme assembly meeting, at which the "Carthaginian" secured the registration he desired,[113] or whether an already existing registration came to light.

---

[109] *Karchedonios*, lines 32-39: καὶ τίς ἐστί σοι, φράσον, | μήτηρ; – ἐμοί; – νή· καὶ τίνος πατρὸς λέγε. | τοὺς δημότας νόμιζε ποιεῖν ἐγγραφάς. | – θυγάτηρ 'Αμίλκου τοῦ στρατηγοῦ, δραπέτα, | Καρχηδονίων ἐμή 'στι μήτηρ. τί βλέπεις; | – ἔπειτ' 'Αμίλκου θυγατριδοῦς ὢν πράγματα | ἡμῖν παρέχεις οἴει τε λήψεσθαι κόρην | ἀστήν; – ἐπειδ[άν γ' ἐγ]γραφῶ κατὰ τοὺς νόμους. For an alternative attribution and interpretation of line 39, see Gomme/Sandbach, *Menander*, p. 409.

[110] See Gomme/Sandbach, *Menander*, p. 408.

[111] Gomme/Sandbach, *Menander*, p. 408.

[112] *Karchedonios* fr. 261: αὐτὸν γὰρ οὐθεὶς οἶδε τοῦ ποτ' ἐγένετο, | ἀλλ' ὑπονοοῦμεν πάντες ἢ πιστεύομεν.

[113] The "imagine" (νόμιζε) of line 34 calls to mind the νομίζετ' of *Dyskolos*, line 1 (quoted above, n. 92); cf. Gomme/Sandbach, *Menander*, p. 409; but in fact the difference between the two passages is more significant than the similarity. In *Dyskolos* the *audience* is being asked to "imagine" that the whole play is set in Phyle—which thus becomes its actual setting. In *Karchedonios* a *character* is being asked, momentarily, to "imagine" that he is at a deme registration meeting—which, despite the *kēryx* of line 40, remains imaginary. For another (possible) fleeting reference to deme registration in Menander, see *Samia*, line 10, with Gomme/Sandbach, *Menander*, pp. 545-546.

It is again the state of the text which impairs our understanding of a passage in *Sikyonios* where, it has been ,suggested, a deme assembly meeting is involved. The relevant section (lines 183-191) of Blepes' "messenger-speech" runs thus:

Having come back from town in order to meet my fellow demesman, whoever he was, who would be sharing out a skinny little ox, and being suitably reviled by everyone as they took their portions—I was one of them: for I'm Blepes the Eleusinian, named after the goddess' deme—I stopped when I saw a mob by the propylaia, said "Excuse me," and saw a girl sitting there; so I joined the ring of people surrounding her.[114]

Then, in the remainder of line 191 and what survives of line 192 come first, the phrase εὐθὺς δῆμος ἦν ("there was at once a deme"), second, the word κύριος (guardian), and third, the phrase τ]ῆς καθημένης κόρης ("of the seated girl"). The second and the third of these elements seem naturally to cohere together; and one may agree with Sandbach's suggestion that "an inquiry was made to discover who the girl's κύριος was."[115] But it is less easy to agree with the commentators that this amounted to a formal meeting of the Eleusinian deme assembly.[116] An "assembly" of one sort or another may certainly be envisaged—and no doubt demesmen of Eleusis, whether resident there or, like Blepes, come from town for the *hestiasis*, formed its major constituent. Nevertheless the word δῆμος here is unlikely, in my view, to mean anything more than it does in an earlier passage of this same play—a "crowd" or "gathering."[117]

As a portrayal of a fragment of deme life, then, the interest of lines 183ff. of *Sikyonios* is probably confined to Blepes' remarks, quite incidental to the burden of his narrative, about the *hestiasis* which had drawn him from the city to his ancestral deme of Eleusis. Yet that interest is

---

[114] *Sikyonios*, lines 183-191: ἐξ] ἄστεως δ᾽ ἥκων ἵν᾽ ἐντύχοιμί τωι | τῶν δημοτῶν μέλλοντι λεπτὸν βοΐδιον | νέμειν ἀκούειν θ᾽ ὅσα προσέστ᾽ αὐτῷ κακὰ | ὑπὸ τῶν λαβόντων μερίδα—τούτων δ᾽ αὐτὸς ἦν· | τοῦ τῆς θεοῦ δήμου γὰρ εἰμ᾽ ἐπώνυμος, | Βλέπης Ἐλευσίνιος—ἐπέστην ὄχλον ἰδὼν | πρὸς τοῖς προπυλαίοις, καὶ "πάρες μ᾽" εἰπὼν ὁρῶ | καθημένην παῖδ᾽ εἷς τε τούτων τῶν κύκλῳ | γενόμενος. E. W. Handley, *BICS* 12, 1965, p. 49, reads τῶι (not τωι) in line 183 and takes this to refer to the demarch; such an odd periphrasis seems unlikely, and in any case this picture of a deme *hestiasis* is paralleled in other sources (see below).

[115] Gomme/Sandbach, *Menander*, p. 652.

[116] Thus E. W. Handley, *BICS* 12, 1965, p. 50; Gomme/Sandbach, *Menander*, p. 652.

[117] I refer to *Sikyonios*, lines 59-60, [εἰ συνδρα]μεῖται δῆμος, εἷς τις οὐ ταχὺ | [τὴν παῖδ᾽] ἀφελκύσαιτ᾽ ἄν—"if a crowd gathers, no one (*sc.* her present owner) will be able to snatch the girl away"; cf. Gomme/Sandbach, *Menander*, p. 639.

still considerable. The idea of stinginess at a deme *hestiasis* occurs also in one of Theophrastus' *Characters*, that of the Skinflint (*mikrologos*), who carves the meat very small before serving it to his fellow demes-men;[118] and it is hard to resist the supposition that one of these passages served as the model for the other. What is more, an oddly detailed re-flection of one passage or the other—Menander's, more probably—recurs in one of the *Idylls* of Theocritus.[119] But it is Menander's *hestiasis* which stays longest in the mind, and the verbal economy with which a whole sequence of cartoon-like pictures is conjured up: first the dismay of the prosperous but penny-pinching Eleusinian when called on to discharge his *hestiasis*; then his malicious determination to observe only the letter, not the spirit, of his duty; and finally the mixture of rage and glee with which his fellow Eleusinians, served paltry helpings from a mangy beast, told him what they thought of such behavior. It is a vignette which we should not have been surprised to find in Aristophanes. The fact that we find it instead in Menander tells us something not only about Menander—his gift for the evocative detail[120]—but also about the durability of deme life, fully three centuries after Kleisthenes, as material for the comic stage.

[118] Theophr. *Char.* 10 (μικρολογίας).11: καὶ ἑστιῶν τοὺς δημότας μικρὰ τὰ κρέα κόψας παραθεῖναι.

[119] Theocritus *Idyll* 4, lines 20-22 (λεπτὸς μὰν χὠ ταῦρος ὁ πυρρίχος· αἴθε λά-χοιεν | τοὶ τῶ Λαμπριάδα τοὶ δαμόται ὅκκα θύωντι | τᾷ Ἥρᾳ τοιόνδε), cited by Gomme/Sandbach, *Menander*, p. 651. Consult the note in A.S.F. Gow, *Theocritus*, 2d ed., Cambridge, 1952, vol. 2, pp. 80-81.

[120] Cf. W. G. Arnott in vol. 1 of the Loeb Menander (1979), pp. xxxi-xxxii.

IV

---　✳　---

CONSPECTUS: THE DEMES
AND HISTORY

CONSPECTUS

THE DEMES AND HISTORY

At this point in a book it would not be unreasonable for readers to expect a convenient summary of the conclusions which have emerged, readily or laboriously, from the author's investigation of the various parts of his subject. I must therefore make it plain at the outset of these final pages that such a précis has been eschewed here, at least as a primary aim. In so far as the chapters of this book or their constituent sections have given rise to anything as recognizable as "conclusions," those which are to be reckoned either certain or at least highly probable have been sufficiently emphasized already, while those of a speculative character would not become any the less so for reiteration here. All the same, a review of *some* kind is called for, as—if nothing else—an indication by the author of what in his own estimation his efforts have amounted to.

In my Preface I referred to my intention of devoting to the Kleisthenic demes a combination of monograph and manual. The connotation of these two terms, if not self-evident, has, it is to be hoped, become apparent during the course of the study. As an intensive treatment of a single subject—pursued, indeed, to the virtually total exclusion of related topics into which others might have found it attractive or advantageous to stray[1]—the book is patently a monograph, written at the margins of the latest specialized evidence and considered opinion, and aiming amongst other things to clarify where the former ends and the latter (including the author's own) begins. Yet my contention was that to yoke such an objective with that of providing, besides, a handbook of first resort for anyone seeking to grasp the totality of our present knowledge of the internal organization and activities of the Kleisthenic demes would be not merely possible but positively desirable. The particular exigencies of individual aspects of the subject have brought now the one, now the other of these twin purposes to the fore. My aim has been, though, to keep them in broad equilibrium overall, with the single proviso that

---

[1] Especially the higher tiers of the Kleisthenic political organization (trittyes and tribes) and the kinship-groups to which most of those so organized also owed allegiance (phratries, and in some instances *genē*); cf. Chap. 8, n. 31.

irritating the expert by "introducing" him to items of evidence or general background with which he is perfectly familiar[2] has seemed to me a more venial fault than failing to make clear to nonspecialists the significance of any datum, old or new, within two concentric contexts—the sum of the documentation in both an actual and an ideal sense.[3]

For this concentration upon the evidence, and upon the methodological problems which it poses, no apology is necessary; and any inclination on the reader's part to return at this point to a more reflective consideration of Chapter 2 would be a profitable one to follow. The principal methodological difficulties adumbrated there have been illustrated all too clearly in Part II (and to a lesser extent Part III). Ancient historians must always resign themselves to working with a body of evidence which their counterparts in other fields will declare derisory.[4] The problems of understanding any single institution or phenomenon on the basis of inadequate documentation, however, are multiplied almost beyond measure when there is not one object of study but one hundred and thirty-nine of them. And what it is imperative to recognize is that even massive increases in our data—such that, evenly spread, we would know as much about every deme as we currently do about Eleusis or Aixone (itself not nearly enough!)—would in no way diminish the crucial and constant necessity of evaluating each item of evidence in the light of the same question: does it support any generalization? Are we learning merely about *a* deme or, more valuably, *the* deme? Throughout this book I have tried to bear in mind the need to pose this question (explicitly or implicitly) at every turn and to classify the data accordingly; whatever errors may have been made in classifying and using any specific item of evidence, the evaluation process itself remains paramount.

The other major difficulty posed by the source material itself stems from its grossly uneven chronological distribution. With certain excep-

---

[2] The professional scholar may betray his embarrassment at thus (seemingly) condescending to his peers by over-frequent resort to the words *naturally, obviously, of course,* and the like. I have deleted much of this verbiage, and can only crave indulgence for what remains.

[3] By the "ideal" documentation I mean not such actual data as have not yet come to light (but will one day do so) but rather, and abstractly, the totality of data to which the very existence of the deme system *could* have given rise (but in fact did not)—for example, the preservation on stone of all decrees of all demes.

[4] Note, for instance, the 1961 G. M. Trevelyan Lecturer E. H. Carr (*What is History?*, Harmondsworth, Penguin Books, 1964, p. 14): "When I am tempted, as I sometimes am, to envy the extreme competence of colleagues engaged in writing ancient or medieval history, I find consolation in the reflexion that they are so competent mainly because they are so ignorant of their subject. The modern historian enjoys none of the advantages of this built-in ignorance."

tions—the passages from the first half of the Aristotelian *Ath. Pol.* discussed at length in Chapter 9, for example—the Kleisthenic demes' first century of existence has left little trace in the record; and the documentation grows thin again after ca. 300. As regards deme decrees, our single most important category of evidence (albeit of the type from which generalization is only rarely permissible), it is worth reiterating that of the total number currently known two-thirds come from the fourth century, and indeed over half from the second half of that century.[5]

The obstacles which are thus set up in the path of any *diachronic* study of the demes are plain. One solution, adopted by Bernard Haussoullier, is not even to attempt such a thing. His *essai sur l'organisation des dèmes au quatrième siècle* ostensibly treated the demes within the period during which they are best known. In fact, however, what he did was to take the fourth century not so much as a *period*, within which change and development or their absence were to be plotted, but rather as a synchronic *Zeitpunkt* best suited, in documentary terms, to static analysis of deme life and organization. By doing this Haussoullier obviously spared himself the irksome necessity of surmising whether, for example, different procedures for deme enrolment or for appointing demarchs preceded (or succeeded) the system attested in the fourth century; and within that century itself he had, as he saw it, no occasion to raise such broader issues as the reestablishment of life in the rural demes after the upheavals of the Peloponnesian War and its immediate aftermath.[6] To recognize the attractions of Haussoullier's policy it would be supererogatory to count the number of times such phrases as "in the fourth

---

[5] We shall return later to the significance of these figures.

[6] Thucydides' remark that in 431 the rural Athenians "had only recently reestablished themselves after the Persian Wars" (2.16.1, ἄρτι ἀνειληφότες τὰς κατασκευὰς μετὰ τὰ Μηδικά; for the 480 evacuation, see Herod. 8.40-41 and ML no. 23) offers some indication of how long, in the fourth century, it must have taken them to recover from the two Peloponnesian War evacuations, of 431 (Thuc. 2.13.2, 14-17, 52.1-2; cf. ?Aristot. *Ath. Pol.* 27.2, Aristoph. *Ach.*, lines 32-33, etc.) and 413 (Thuc. 7.27.2-28), compounded by the postwar regime of the Thirty Tyrants (on which see for instance Lysias 31.18, where the speaker depicts Philon περιιὼν κατὰ τοὺς ἀγροὺς καὶ ἐντυγχάνων τῶν πολιτῶν τοῖς πρεσβυτάτοις, οἳ κατέμειναν ἐν τοῖς δήμοις ὀλίγα μὲν τῶν ἐπιτηδείων ἔχοντες, ἀναγκαῖα δέ). J.A.O. Larsen has called the 431 evacuation "one of the most momentous decisions in Greek history" and has pointed out the inverse proportion between the city dwellers voting for it and the countrymen primarily affected by it (*CPh* 44, 1949, p. 175 with n. 28). He also suggests, surely rightly, that Xenophon must have had this episode in mind when suggesting that separate votes by *geōrgoi* and *technitai* on the issue of whether to defend or to abandon the *chōra* at a time of enemy invasion would result in only the latter voting for evacuation (*Oec.* 6.6-7). It is perhaps surprising that we do not find this sort of thing being said more strongly and more often in the first half of the fourth century; cf. in general G. Murray, *JHS* 64, 1944, pp. 1-9.

century at least" have appeared in this book, in which synchronic analysis has inevitably—and rightly—loomed large. Yet the diachronic dimension too has not infrequently come into play, as regards both the internal doings of the demes (Part II) and their relationship with the state (Part III). The fact of the matter is that the evidence *is* distributed, however disproportionately, over two and a half centuries—to take only the period to which this book has limited itself—and that is too long a period within which to close our eyes to the processes of change.

What then can usefully be said on the subject of "the demes and history"?[7] Unless and until the documentation increases very dramatically indeed there can be no real argument with von Schoeffer's blunt observation: "von einer eigentlichen Geschichte der D(emoi) kann wegen Mangels an Documenten nicht die Rede sein."[8] But if indeed no question can arise of a continuous history of the demes (as opposed, merely, to isolated episodes such as the constitutional reforms of the 360s or the *diapsēphiseis* of 346/5), there are long-term historical questions at issue nonetheless. And with regard to what is arguably the most complex and elusive of them—the extent to which, over time, the deme system either retained or lost its essential internal vitality—I believe that the usual picture requires a degree of correction.

Although the Kleisthenic deme system changed the political organization of Attica from a basis of kinship to one of territoriality, it has not gone unremarked that, in making deme membership hereditary, the system embodied the potentiality for demes to become over the course of time more and more like the nonterritorial kinship-groups which they had been designed to supplant.[9] As well as being significant in itself—as a testimony to the conservatism which would have prevented Kleisthenes, had it even occurred to him to do so, from tying deme membership to actual residence[10]—this fact has far-reaching consequences of several kinds for our study of Athenian history and society in the classical period and beyond. In prosopography it is the most mixed of blessings. Its redeeming feature (as one might say) is that we can always tell, of any individual whose demotic is known, the deme where his ancestor of

---

[7] Since the phrase is ambiguous I must explain that I do not mean by it the impact of the course of Greek history itself (in the classical and early Hellenistic periods) upon the Athenian polis, and thus necessarily upon the demes of which it was constituted, but rather the history of the demes and the deme system *per se*.

[8] Schoeffer, "Demoi," col. 8.

[9] See e.g. Lacey, *Family*, pp. 90-91; Murray, *Early Greece*, p. 255; Hansen, "Political activity," p. 227.

[10] Cf. Schoeffer, "Demoi," col. 8: "das Geschlechtsprincip war den Hellenen zu stark eingeimpft und durfte nicht durch freie Association oder mechanische Gliederung ersetzt werden, ohne die Festigkeit der Organisation in Frage zu stellen."

508/7 had chosen to be registered; what we cannot, without additional evidence, determine is the (usually more material) question of whether he himself still lived there. And transferred from the individual to the collective level this state of affairs necessarily creates a fundamental dilemma: how far *did* Athenian families in fact remain in their ancestral demes, and how far did they move elsewhere? Clearly an answer to this, even in very general terms, will be intimately related to the issue of the viability (or otherwise) of the demes as political and social entities at a time far removed from their origins, with such viability being doubted most by those who place the greatest emphasis upon migration from ancestral demes.[11]

The standard assemblage of evidence, of various kinds, which illustrates such migration is to be found in the second chapter of Gomme's *Population*; and it falls far short, as he himself repeatedly insisted, of anything which could be described as statistical proof.[12] The migration was of course mainly—though not, it should be noted, exclusively—from the countryside of Attica into the city or Peiraieus, and for reasons which may readily be divined: the clear attractions of an urban life for aspiring politicians; an economic and/or cultural allure for others; in any case the disruption, willy-nilly, of the Peloponnesian War, after which a proportion of the country folk will have seen a better future for themselves in town.[13] And it is the work of a moment to find a dozen good examples of individual migrators.[14] Yet individual examples of men and families

---

[11] One may cite von Schoeffer and Busolt/Swoboda as spokesmen for this dual view. The former wrote (*a*) of a significant country-to-city migration from the second half of the fifth century onwards and a consequent split between the "städtische" members of a deme, devoting themselves primarily to the political life of the city and leaving to the "ländliche" members the business of the deme itŝelf (Schoeffer, "Demoi," col. 7; cf. Busolt/Swoboda, *Staatskunde*, pp. 878-879), and also (*b*) of "das allmähliche Sinken des Gemeingeistes in den D(emen) im Verlauf des vierten und wohl noch mehr der folgenden Jahrhunderte" (Schoeffer, "Demoi," col. 8; cf. Busolt/Swoboda, *Staatskunde*, p. 875). Without begging either question at this stage it may be noted that von Schoeffer's assertion that there are *no* deme documents later than the fourth century ("sehr bezeichnend fehlen nach dem 4. Jhdt. die D.-Urkunden vollständig") was not even true when he wrote it.

[12] Gomme, *Population*, pp. 37-48.

[13] For the Peloponnesian War as a watershed in this respect, see Thuc. 2.14-17 (cf. above, n. 6), preferable to the "urban proletariat" picture of ?Aristot. *Ath. Pol.* 24.1. (How we lack an equally good witness from the first quarter of the fourth century!) However, that country-to-city migration was heavy *before* 431—as Schoeffer, "Demoi," col. 7 (see above, n. 11), and Gomme, *Population*, p. 46, both imply—is hard to sustain in the face of Thucydides' testimony; and the rapid return to viability of the Attic countryside after 404, with a smaller *permanent* loss of population to the city than is often supposed, is convincingly argued by V. D. Hanson, *Warfare and Agriculture in Classical Greece*, Pisa, 1983, pp. 111-143, esp. 137ff.

[14] Family of Hyperanthes Acharneus, buried in the Kerameikos (IG II²5652, 5676, 5677,

still living in their ancestral demes in the fourth century are equally easy to come by.[15] To multiply such evidence—on either side—would in fact be otiose. The scales would never tilt of their own accord, so to speak, and the problem is impervious to an objective, quantifiable solution pitched at the individual level. If a solution of this kind is ever to be attained, its source will probably be a statistical count of grave monuments, but such an operation encounters at least two serious obstacles: first, one learns only about the residence of men of sufficient means to have a grave monument at all;[16] and second, the provenance of the stones, in IG at least, is too rarely recorded. Where provenance is known, what emerges is that "tombstones found in the Mesogaios or the Paralia commemorate almost invariably citizens buried in their ancestral deme, whereas tombstones found in or near Athens record more citizens belonging to the Paralia and the Mesogaios than to the Asty itself."[17] Yet,

---

5678, 5685; see Davies, *Families*, p. 516); Philokedes Acharneus, resident of Coastal Lamptrai (IG II²1204; see **62**); Meidias Anagyrasios, house in Eleusis (Demosth. 21.158); Timotheos Anaphlystios, house in Peiraieus ([Demosth.] 49.22); Kallidamas Cholleides, resident of Peiraieus (IG II²1214; see **150**); Dorotheos Eleusinios, house in Athens ([Demosth.] 59.59); various Leukonoeis related by marriage to the family of Alkibiades, buried in the Kerameikos (IG II²5434, 6719, 6722, 6723, 6746, 7400; see Davies, *Families*, pp. 21-22); Stratokles ex Oiou, house in Melite (Isaeus 11.42); Theopompos ex Oiou, house "in town" (Isaeus 11.44); Demosthenes Paianieus, house in Peiraieus (Dinarch. 1.69, Aeschin. 3.209); Themistokles Phrearrhios, house in Melite (Plut. *Them.* 22.1-2); Timarchos Sphettios, house "behind the (akro)polis" (Aeschin. 1.97).

[15] To cite, again, only a round dozen: Demeas Acharneus (IG II²5788), Kallias Aixoneus (**85**), Philotheros Aixoneus (**6**), family of Euboios Anagyrasios (IG II²5639; Davies, *Families*, p. 188), family of Nikodemos Dekeleieus (IG II²5980 and 5983, cf. 10607 and 12865), Aichmeas Eleusinios (IG II²6022), family of Astyphilos of Halai Aixonides (see **184**), family of Nikon Kephalethen (IG II²6370; Davies, *Families*, p. 413), family of Demainetos Paianieus (see Davies, *Families*, pp. 103-104), family of Kirrhias Prasieus (see **319**), family of Hierokles Rhamnousios (see **323**), Aristophanes Rhamnousios (see under **324**). Note in general Traill, *Organization*, p. 74, n. 8: "that many Athenians in the fourth century still lived in the demes of their forefathers is attested time and again in the orators . . ." He is right, I believe, to point to the conservative mentality which would see staying in one's own deme as desirable *per se*, though his appeal to W. S. Ferguson's observations (*Hellenistic Athens*, London, 1911, p. 375, n. 1) on the *enktētikon* tax as a reinforcing "deterrent to the ownership of *property* in another deme" (my italics) has no necessary relevance to changing *residence*; besides, as we know nothing of the level(s) of the tax, nor how widespread it was beyond the single deme, Peiraieus, in which it is attested, we cannot in fact assume that it had any deterrent effect whatever upon the sort of Athenians who were in a position to acquire estates in different parts of Attica (cf. Davies, *Wealth*, pp. 52-54; Osborne, *Demos*, chap. 3) and/or a town house near the civic center.

[16] After ca. 317, however, it would admittedly have been easier to afford the only types permitted: see J. Kirchner, "Das Gesetz des Demetrios von Phaleron zur Einschränkung des Gräberluxus," *Die Antike* 15, 1939, pp. 93-97; H. Möbius, *Die Ornamente der griechischen Grabstelen*, 2d ed., Munich, 1968, pp. 39, and 44, n. 50.

[17] Hansen, "Political activity," pp. 234-235, drawing on an unpublished compilation by

interesting though this is, it does not provide a more reliable or exact indicator of the overall pattern of residence than those offered by evidence of other kinds. The same can be said (if for different reasons) of the approach taken in a recent article by Mogens Herman Hansen.[18] Hansen draws attention to the fact that only about a quarter of politically active Athenians—defined as such by attestation as *stratēgoi, rhētores*, or *dikastai*[19]—in the fourth century were members of the demes of the Asty region. He suggests (rightly, no doubt) that fourth-century Athenians were more accustomed to walking long distances than we effete moderns are, and that a journey of as much as four hours to the city center would have seemed nothing out of the ordinary. On this basis some two-thirds of the "politically active" were members of demes near enough to Athens (i.e., within about eighteen kilometers) to make repeated journeys there— if they did not live there already—a practical proposition; but even so one-third of them remain, for whom there can have been little option, Hansen contends, but to leave their ancestral demes and take up residence in or near the city. The argument seems irreproachable as it stands. Yet how far, if at all, can we extrapolate from the behavior and priorities of this (as Hansen himself has shown) tiny minority of the "politically active" to those of the population in general?[20]

It may then be, paradoxically, that quantifiable data of this kind produce a distorted picture overall, while a more authentic set of clues to behavior patterns is to be found in evidence of a far vaguer sort. Certainly such evidence suggests that remaining in one's ancestral deme was the normal thing in the *fifth* century. For example, Aristophanes' comic creation Strepsiades of Kikynna lives in the country and thus surely in his own deme. When shown a map of Attica his question, "And where are the men of Kikynna, my *dēmotai*?" is immediate; and the clear implication that most of them lived there too is confirmed later in the play when he appeals, for protection against assault, to "neighbors and kinsmen and *dēmotai*."[21] In [Lysias] 20 the jury is expected to approve of the elderly Polystratos of Deiradiotai—unlike his fellow demesman Phrynichos—for having returned, after his education in the city, to farm

---

Aksel Damsgaard-Madsen (which doubles the figures given by Gomme, *Population*, pp. 44-45).

[18] Hansen, "Political activity," esp. pp. 233ff.

[19] Cf. Chap. 1, n. 73.

[20] *Bouleutai*, arguably, were a more representative sample of ordinary Athenians than were *stratēgoi, rhētores*, or even *dikastai*, and Hansen reasonably postulates a high level of absenteeism by members from (and resident in) outlying demes, save in the crucial days of their tribe's *prytaneia*.

[21] Aristoph. *Clouds*, lines 134 (demotic), 138 (country residence; cf. lines 47, 68-72, etc.), 210 (map), 1322 (assault; cf. *Lysistr.*, lines 684-685, and *Ekkles.*, line 1115).

in (presumably) his own deme.[22] Given his age, this must refer to the late 460s or early 450s, but its main interest lies in what it reveals of attitudes at the time of the case itself, in 410/09.[23] By then the second wartime evacuation of Attica, in 413, had once again driven the farmers into the city (cf. [Lysias] 20.33), yet no suggestion arises of anything more than a temporary interruption to normal rural life; and it is noteworthy that within a year of the end of the war "large numbers at least" of the members of two important demes, Eleusis and Aixone, had apparently resumed residence there.[24]

As regards the *fourth* century, where the question becomes one of even greater moment, the *locus classicus* is Demosthenes 57.10. There Euxitheos explains that "most" (οἱ πλεῖστοι) of his fellow Halimousioi still lived in Halimous in 346/5, and had thus left the meeting, held in the city, without witnessing his victimization. Was this a lie? Although there is no obvious forensic reason why it should have been, one is obliged to ask why, if such a pattern of residence had been usual, it needed to be mentioned; and the answer which suggests itself is that a predominance of city dwellers on the jury[25] made the explanatory point necessary.

The dangerous notion of a "typical" deme has been avoided throughout this book, so it would be self-defeating to resort to it now. Yet if there is at least no good reason for regarding Halimous as positively *un*typical of its time, the value of Euxitheos' statement becomes plain enough; indeed it is a statement which, in the light of a general line of argument which scholars have occasionally perceived, one would have been surprised *not* to find in some context or other. The argument is briefly presented by R. J. Hopper as follows. "It is difficult to believe, as is sometimes suggested, that the country population declined permanently in the fourth century; if the demes lost importance in relation to state affairs, it is clear that they had a good deal of local business."[26] And John Moore has argued, more fully and forcibly, in the same vein. "Membership of a deme was hereditary from the date of the [Kleisthenic] reform and original registration. To us in our highly mobile society, this might suggest that political units would shortly be totally divorced from the geographical areas in which people lived; that this is not so is shown by the fact that local government remained in the hands of the deme assembly and its officers—nothing could be more absurd than local government

---

[22] [Lysias] 20.11-12 (cited by Gomme, *Population*, p. 39, n. 4).

[23] For the date of the case, see T. Lenschau, *RE* 21, 1952, col. 1832; Polystratos was aged seventy or more at the time ([Lysias] 20.10, cf. 35).

[24] Gomme, *Population*, p. 46, citing Xen. *Hell.* 2.4.8-9 (Eleusis) and 26 (Aixone).

[25] See Hansen, "Political activity," p. 234.

[26] Hopper, *Basis*, p. 23, n. 87.

by people who do not live in the area. No doubt some families moved, particularly into the city, but it cannot have been a large proportion of the population."[27] In the very strictest terms this reasoning is fallacious, for quite obviously the Athenians did not think it essential for "local government" to be, by definition, the concern of local residents only. Had they thought so, either deme membership would have changed with deme residence or at least a deme's members would have been periodically redefined. Nevertheless, Moore has found the best general argument available in favor of the proposition that even in the second half of the fourth century "a large proportion" of Athenians still lived in their ancestral demes: the argument that *otherwise the internal organization of the demes themselves would have broken down.*

The significance of this conclusion is manifest even if we acknowledge, as we must, the limits of inference which it allows. What should actually be visualized as "a large proportion" of resident demesmen? The same, perhaps, as Euxitheos meant when he spoke of "most" Halimousioi? If so the point is important, for "most" must surely mean what it says— the majority, more than half. But even if what we are told of Halimous was indeed generally true, there is a world of difference between 51 percent and 99 percent, and no sufficiently detailed means, in this case, of determining which figure is nearer the mark. Were it the former (or something in the vicinity of it), deme self-government would have been difficult, no doubt, but hardly impossible, at least as regards business to which a low attendance-quorum[28] was attached. Yet how practicable would, for instance, theoric distributions in the demes ([Demosth.] 44.37) have been if large numbers of those eligible to receive them had moved elsewhere? As Moore points out, we stand at risk of anachronism if we assume without question that the mere potentiality for migration and mobility is proof that it actually occurred on a large scale or at a rapid rate during the first two centuries after Kleisthenes. The signs are, rather, that in that period the rate was slow,[29] and that the (supposedly conse-

---

[27] J. M. Moore, *Aristotle and Xenophon on Democracy and Oligarchy*, London, 1975, p. 238; cf. Osborne, *Demos*, p. 225, n. 90.

[28] See next note.

[29] The only two recorded quorum figures for deme assemblies (cf. Chap. 4, n. 45) *perhaps* offer slight evidence for lower anticipated attendance in the fourth century than in the fifth: IG I^{3}250, lines 11-14, Lower Paiania (date 450-430), bouleutic representation eleven, quorum one hundred; IG II^{2}1183, lines 21-22, Myrrhinous (date after 340), bouleutic representation six, quorum thirty. Busolt/Swoboda, *Staatskunde*, p. 965, n. 2, take the latter figure as clear proof that "many" Myrrhinousioi were living in the city by then, yet they themselves make the necessary comparison—relevant to both figures—with the city *ekklēsia* and its (occasional) quorum of only six thousand (cf. M. H. Hansen, *GRBS* 17, 1976, pp. 115-134). As to the disparate anticipated attendance, it is possible that the

quent) "gradual decline of *Gemeingeist* in the demes"[30] was a very gradual one indeed. To suppose otherwise might be not only anachronistic in itself but also unjustifiably dismissive of much "valuable evidence for the continuing strength of *campanilismo*";[31] and here we must return to the matter of the overall chronological distribution of the demes' documents. Unless those which survive are a thoroughly treacherous guide, with regard to their chronological spread, to the totality of those which once existed,[32] that spread creates a pattern so pronounced, so graphic, that some attempt at comment and, if possible, explanation is mandatory.

Both the presence and the absence of documents at any given time is— or may be—significant. That there is no simple correlation between their presence and von Schoeffer's *Gemeingeist* (or Davies' *campanilismo*) is immediately evident when one considers the fifth century. The communal vitality of the demes then has never been doubted, and yet the documentation is sparse. The demes seem to have been rather slow to grasp their right to immortalize their decisions (and their initiative in taking them) on stone. By degrees the example of the polis itself showed the way, though before the advent of the honorific decree—and without, of course, affairs of foreign policy to concern them—it was the regulation of cult and religion which the demes found appropriate for the medium.[33] However, any great increase even in documents of that solemn kind was abruptly forestalled by the Peloponnesian War, throughout much of which the regular institutions of the rural demes must have been in abeyance;[34] and the necessarily adverse effects of the war upon deme life and activity[35] may go at least some of the way toward explaining the

---

religious business of the Paianians' decree was such as to stimulate wider interest than the *euthynai* procedure in Myrrhinous.

[30] Schoeffer, "Demoi," col. 8 (see above, n. 11).

[31] Davies, *Families*, p. 576, with reference to IG II²3101; see introduction to Chap. 8B.

[32] That more—perhaps many more—remain to be discovered cannot be doubted: excavation (indeed, location) of many of the city demes is rendered impossible by the urban sprawl of modern Athens, while in rural Attica archaeological work has been haphazard, to say the least. One may venture to suppose nevertheless that the *chronological* distribution of our present "sample" of documents would not be radically altered by future finds.

[33] See for instance IG I³242 (Peiraieus), 243 fr. 10 (Melite), 244 (Skambonidai), 245 (Sypalettos), 248 (Rhamnous), 251 (Eleusis), 253-254 (Ikarion), 256 (Lamptrai), 258 (Plotheia).

[34] D. M. Lewis has dated IG I³258, the financial accounts and decree of Plotheia, to the years 425-413, i.e., between the two periods of evacuation. No other deme documents from the time of the Peloponnesian War (with the possible exception of IG I³253-254, Ikarion) are extant. See further, next note.

[35] See above, nn. 6 and 13. We are entirely uninformed as to how, during the two periods of evacuation, those rural demesmen who were displaced (see V. D. Hanson, *Warfare and Agriculture in Classical Greece*, Pisa, 1983, pp. 134-137 with map on 138, for those who

surprisingly slow reappearance of deme documentation in the fourth century. In the immediate aftermath of the war it is likely enough that many demes were faced with work of physical reconstruction and repair,[36] while in the longer term a different kind of reorganization is revealed by the clutch of sacrificial *fasti*.[37] But it is not until the 360s and 350s that deme decrees on "secular" subjects are found,[38] as the prelude to what one can only call, by comparison both with what preceded it and with what followed it, a spate of decrees and other documents committed to stone throughout the rest of the fourth century.

Why this spate occurred when it did is a simple question without an obviously simple answer. Were the demes encouraged, explicitly or implicitly, by the state to place more of their transactions and proceedings on public display? Were some demes emulating others? One cannot tell. The documents themselves yield up no such underlying secrets when prodded and probed, and no external considerations are self-evidently relevant. But it is at least plain that, with great and small demes alike now setting masons to work, talk of a "gradual decline of *Gemeingeist*"[39] in the deme system carries scant conviction. A better case could be made for speaking of its *Blütezeit*, given both the sheer quantity and also the character of recorded activity. The Sounians might be ridiculed for their standards of deme enrolment,[40] but they still had the collective pride to be glad of a new *agora*, the gift of a wealthy demesman.[41] In even smaller demes, benefactors were honored,[42] members thanked for community service honestly discharged.[43] *Philotimia* toward the deme was everywhere called for, displayed, and rewarded.[44] No doubt the very concept

---

arguably were not) carried on their business and sustained their corporate identity. The *possible* relaxation of the Periklean citizenship law during the war (on which see now Patterson, *Citizenship Law*, pp. 140-147) may be partly accounted for by problems of ensuring proper deme registration.

[36] Such work perhaps formed the background to SEG 24.197, where a group of Athmoneis (see Chap. 8, nn. 74-75) apparently made payments to their deme at the beginning of the fourth century; cf.—a century later—IG II²1215 (?Erikeia).

[37] SEG 21.541 (Erchia); IG II²1358 (the Marathonian Tetrapolis and its demes); SEG 21.542 (Teithras); AC 52, 1983, pp. 150-174 (Thorikos)—see Chap. 7B. Cf. IG II²1356 (*lex sacra* on the *hiereōsyna* for various priestesses, Halai Aixonides).

[38] Note especially the cluster from Halai Aixonides: IG II²1174 and 1175; AD 11, 1927-1928, pp. 40-41, no. 4. Cf. IG II²1178 (Ikarion) and 1173 (deme unknown).

[39] Schoeffer, "Demoi," col. 8 (see above, n. 11).

[40] Anaxandrides fr. 4; see Chap. 9, n. 15.

[41] See IG II²1180 and 338.

[42] E.g. Antiochid Eitea (SEG 28.102). On a *possible* decline, at this time, in the population of Eitea, see Traill, *Organization*, p. 22.

[43] E.g. Epikephisia (IG II²1205) and Halimous (SEG 2.7).

[44] See Chap. 8B.

will tempt the cynical to be cynical: why this need (it might be asked) so to stimulate public spirit unless it was palpably flagging, in demoralized and depopulated villages which were outliving their original definition and purpose as each decade passed? Does not a call for any public virtue ring out when the need for that virtue is most urgent? Indeed it may; yet the ideology will soon lapse—as that of *philotimia* did not—if it elicits no response. Besides, in this case, the proponents of deme "decline" cannot be allowed to win the argument both ways, by claiming as proof of the phenomenon *both* the paucity of deme documents in the third century and beyond (see below) *and* their abundance in the fourth. In the second half of the fourth century the Kleisthenic demes were demonstrably alive and well: that is the clear message which the evidence, literary as well as epigraphic,[45] transmits, and neither misplaced sophistication nor its academic counterpart, intrusive hindsight, can gainsay it.

Resisting the use of hindsight, all the same, is not easy when one tries to understand the situation *after* ca. 300 and the extent to which little less than a transformation seems to have taken place. A gradual fall in the level of documentation would have been understandable. Instead we find a steep one, made all the more so by the absence of inscriptions from demes such as Aixone and Halai Aixonides with an established tradition of erecting them. It is always possible that future discoveries will blunt the present sharpness of the contrast, while hindsight may raise the suspicion that the relative abundance of the fourth-century material might actually conceal the fact that some demes which had once "published" their documents were no longer doing so in that period. But on the face of it the *third* century is the time when we can, at last, entertain the idea that the accumulated and accumulating effects of political, social, and demographic change, in the context of often unstable conditions at large, were making a serious impact upon the communal vitality and viability of the demes.

On the political level the reorganization of 307/6 did not, to be sure, affect the demes directly, yet the creation of the two new tribes Antigonis and Demetrias may well have been unsettling in an indirect way, at least for the thirty demes which found themselves unceremoniously hoisted out of the tribes of which they had formed part for two hundred years and allocated afresh.[46] Social and demographic change is easier to imagine

---

[45] See Chap. 11B for the evidence of Middle and New Comedy, especially Menander. The possibility that the depiction of the demes here is a nostalgic one, reflecting circumstances which no longer obtained, does not (I believe) arise.

[46] See on this Traill, *Organization*, pp. 26-27 and 31-33 (and 58-61 on the changes in bouleutic quotas, for nearly fifty demes, which accompanied it).

than to illustrate, but it is likely that both were accelerated by and during the Athenians' intermittent struggles against their Macedonian overlords in the first half of the third century.[47] One should not overlook evidence that links with ancestral demes might still be strong in the *second* half of that century,[48] but such "links" fall short of proof either that the rural demes were by then as well populated as they had been in earlier times or, even if they were, that their communal life and activities continued unchanged. It is noteworthy that, with only a few exceptions,[49] the demes which we know to have put up public inscriptions in the third century can be regarded for one reason or another as special cases: Peiraieus,[50] always an anomaly,[51] and the two garrison-demes of Eleusis and Rhamnous.[52] Although the interaction between deme and garrison, both in these two demes and in certain others, was complex in its manifestations, overall there is apparently something of a paradox to be observed: while the participation of garrison troops (or others) in the political decisions

[47] See in general E. Will, *Histoire politique du monde hellénistique*, 2d ed., Nancy, 1979, pp. 85ff.; and esp. Habicht, *Untersuchungen*, chaps. 1-8.

[48] IG II²791 (re-edited with two new fragments by B. D. Meritt, *Hesp.* 11, 1942, pp. 287-292, no. 56) is the record of a decree of the year of the archon Diomedon—long taken to be 232/1 but in fact either 247/6 or, in the latest study (by Habicht; see below), 244/3—which invites *epidoseis* of between fifty and two hundred drachmas εἰς τὴν σωτηρία|ν τῆς πόλεως καὶ τὴν φυλακὴν τῆς χώρας (lines 16-17, cf. 30-31) and appends a list of names of those who came forward with them. There are a few foreigners, but most of the eighty names are those of citizens, with their demotics; and most of the demotics are those of demes in the *mesogeios*, the agricultural "midlands" of Attica, as W. S. Ferguson was the first to notice and emphasize (*The Priests of Asklepios*, Berkeley, 1907, pp. 159-161, and *Hellenistic Athens*, London, 1911, pp. 203-207, 231-232; cf. A. Jardé, *Les céréales dans l'antiquité grecque*, Paris, 1925, p. 163, and S. Dow, *HSPh* 48, 1937, p. 107 with nn. 2-3). In *Population*, p. 40, n. 4, Gomme objected to the idea of drawing any conclusions from this, on the grounds that "families may have been long divorced from their demes by that time," but for once his salutary scepticism in such matters seems excessive. The specific object of the appeal is announced in lines 10-12 as the safe harvesting of crops, which not only makes it perfectly understandable why men with the demotics Erchieus, Paianicus, Sphettius, and the like figure so prominently in the list (while men of city demes are for the most part conspicuous by their absence) but also warrants the inference that these individuals retained land if not necessarily residence in their ancestral demes more than two and a half centuries after the original registration there. For a full discussion of the document, see C. Habicht, *Studien zur Geschichte Athens in hellenistischer Zeit*, Hypomnemata 73, Göttingen, 1982, pp. 26-33.

[49] See IG II²1215 (?Erikeia); *Hesp.* 39, 1970, pp. 47-53 (Phrearrhioi); cf. IG II²1216 and SEG 14.81 (demes unknown).

[50] IG II²1214; *Hesp.* 3, 1934, pp. 44-46, no. 33.

[51] See Appendix 4.

[52] For the documents, see Appendix 6; and note also the Eleusinian *fasti* (SEG 23.80), which fall within the period ca. 330-270.

of the demesmen represented a breakdown in what might be termed the integrity of the demes concerned, it also—especially in Rhamnous—seems to have at least prolonged and perhaps even increased the vigor of public life in these strangely mixed communities.

Of our only two deme decrees from the *second* century, one is (again) from Eleusis,[53] the other from a city-center deme, Melite,[54] where both a good level of resident demesmen and also a reasonably secure life for them may be visualized. By the time that these two decrees—the last ones that we have—had been enacted, in the first half of the second century, there had been two more reorganizations of the Athenian tribal system, in 224/3 and 201/0, each involving for the first time since Kleisthenes the creation of a new deme,[55] and the latter hastening the "complete collapse" of the quota-system for bouleutic representation.[56] Quite what *la vie municipale* amounted to generally in the age of the demarch Pamphilos and the priestess Satyra lies beyond prudent conjecture. From an even later period, however, we perhaps have a hint that the demes which responded best to the many internal and external changes of the Hellenistic age were those which, like third-century Rhamnous, were open to change themselves. IG II²2953 is a thank-offering (*charistērion*) to "Ares and Augustus" which has been plausibly connected with the latter's reconstruction in the Athenian Agora of the Ares temple from Acharnai.[57] The body responsible for the offering describes itself as "the *koinon* of the Acharnians." What does this mean? "Sinon le dème d'Acharnes, tout au moins . . . une société en rapport avec le dème," ventured Graindor;[58] "l'ensemble des démotes d'Acharnai," insisted Louis Robert.[59] It is very hard to say. The various officials listed, including the priest of Ares, do not seem to have demotics (and thus may not be Acharnians), though the maker of the offering was proud enough to record his own membership of the deme: ──ος Διογνήτου Ἀχαρνεὺς ἐποίει. Our only real clue is the phrase "*koinon* of the Acharnians" itself, where we might have expected simply "the Acharnians." It looks like a phrase appropriate to a rather wider, less exclusive group than the collective demotic alone

[53] IG II²949, lines 30ff., in honor of the demarch Pamphilos (14).

[54] *Hesp.* 11, 1942, pp. 265-274, no. 51, in honor of the priestess Satyra (293).

[55] See Chap. 1, n. 66.

[56] Traill, *Organization*, pp. 61-64 (quotation from 61).

[57] See H. A. Thompson, "Itinerant temples of Attica," *AJA* 66, 1962, p. 200, and esp. H. A. Thompson and R. E. Wycherley, *Agora* 14, pp. 162-165; cf. also H. A. Thompson, *Hesp.* 50, 1981, pp. 352-353.

[58] P. Graindor, *Athènes sous Auguste*, Cairo, 1927, p. 97, n. 4.

[59] L. Robert, *Études épigraphiques et philologiques*, Paris, 1938, p. 295 with n. 2.

would have embraced.[60] Be that as it may, it was manifestly a body of men with gratitude to express for the emperor's interest in their bellicose deity, and with an institutional means of expressing it. In these respects, if in no others, their descent from the Acharnian demesmen whom Thucydides and Aristophanes knew is surely a lineal one.

[60] Compare the various "*koinon*" formulas in SEG 25.155 (Rhamnous), lines 3-4, 34-35, and 39-40 (see Appendix 6), the last of which, at any rate, includes the Rhamnousioi themselves.

APPENDIX 1

— ✳ —

DĒMOS AND *DĒMOI* BEFORE
KLEISTHENES

Students of the demes of Attica (or indeed of anywhere else) have rarely
paused to ask two preliminary questions: when, and why, did this meaning of the multi-purpose word *dēmos* come about? It is worth attempting
to answer both of these questions if we can; and to answer the first will
take us most of the way toward answering the second.

In a note on the meaning of the term *dēmokratia*, J.A.O. Larsen made
such an attempt in *CPh* 68, 1973, pp. 45-46. He writes there (p. 45) as
follows. "Probably the use of the same word [*dēmos*] for the sovereign
people and for a small country district seems so inexplicable that most
of us have simply accepted it without attempting to explain it. [But] the
examples and treatment in LSJ enable a student to trace the development
of the meaning. The earliest known meaning seems to be 'country' or
'land.' If the term is then applied to small districts, the use for the demes
of Attica becomes natural and it is not surprising to find it later applied
also to wards within the city. The first crucial step in the change of
meaning came when *demos* was applied to the people of the countryside,
and, since the people of the countryside were largely poor, the word came
to mean the people of the lower classes." In point of fact, however, all
the meanings which Larsen presents here in a chronological and causal
sequence are found *together* in our earliest literary source, Homer; and
it is by no means obvious that Larsen's is the most cogent semantic
hierarchy that can or should be constructed from them. We may compare
that of LSJ itself, upon which he clearly depends: (*a*) "district, country,
land"; (*b*) "the people, inhabitants of such a district"; (*c*) "*hence* (since
the common people lived in the country, the chiefs in the city), the
commons, common people." (The emphasis here is mine.) LSJ, however,
declined to extend this explanatory framework to the two remaining
principal meanings of the word *dēmos*, namely, "in a political sense, the
sovereign people, the free citizens" (though as a historico-political de-

velopment its emergence from usage *c* is plain enough), and—our concern here—"township, commune."

It would be otiose to cite the Homeric evidence *in extenso* here; a summary can reveal its salient features. In terms of the LSJ *a/b/c* meanings, a breakdown of the instances of the word *dēmos* runs as follows: for the *Iliad*, *a* – 21, *b* – 21, *c* – 2; for the *Odyssey*, *a* – 62, *b* – 16, *c* – 0. Admittedly, to present these (or any such) figures summarily may make the business of categorization appear a simpler matter than in some cases it is. By and large the *Odyssey* presents the more difficulties in this respect, so that, for example, 13.186 (δήμου Φαιήκων ἡγήτορες) could be argued to fall under category *b* rather than *a*, while consideration of the broad context might lead to a reclassification of, say, 13.14 as type *c* rather than *b*. Nonetheless, within an acceptable margin of error the main conclusions to be drawn are manifest. In Homer, LSJ's "district, country, land" is the normal meaning of *dēmos*, though "the people, inhabitants of such a district" are naturally closely associated with it and may sometimes move to the semantic center. When it is indeed the people rather than the place which is meant, there is normally no social differentiation explicit, nor even, except in the most general sense, implicit. Very occasionally, however, the meaning is certainly "the commons, common people," as distinct from their betters. (See *Iliad* 2.198, which introduces the Thersites episode, and 12.213, the curious δῆμον ἐόντα. As my figures imply, I can find nothing in the *Odyssey* as clearcut as this, though 2.239 and 13.14 come quite near it; but in view of the prominence of this connotation later—see below—it is arguably latent in some of the passages that I have classified as type *b*.)

The palpable rarity, here revealed, of usage *c* is important, and may indeed support Larsen's assertion that this was a later extension (". . . came to mean . . .") of the word's original and basic meaning; a usage which took on a clear definition, we may surmise, in the eighth century and gathered increasing momentum thereafter as a concept of significance in the evolution of the polis and its social and political structure. In the *Works and Days* of Hesiod (ca. 700) the single allusion to a "new" *dēmos*, in contradistinction to *basileis* (line 261), is balanced by the "old" Homeric δῆμόν τε πόλιν τε (land and city, line 527). By a century later, however, the poems of Solon were either developing or at least reflecting the politicization of the word once and for all (see the fragments in ?Aristot. *Ath.Pol.* 12 and Plu. *Sol.* 16 and 18), at any rate as far as Athens is concerned; and all over the Greek world, during the latter part of the seventh century and on through the sixth century, the *dēmos/dāmos* was defining its grasp upon constitutional power and expressing that fact in public inscriptions (see for instance ML nos. 4, 5, 8, 13, 14, 17).

What this led to, both historically and semantically speaking, in the fifth century and beyond is common knowledge and irrelevant to our inquiry here, except inasmuch as we may perhaps have in this fact—that is, the most important and interesting connotation of the word *in the classical period*—the main reason why scholars have attempted (with plainly unsatisfactory results) to invoke it in an explanation of why the Attic demes were called *dēmoi*. Larsen's reasoning we have already seen. His proposed sequence, whether offered as a logical or a chronological one, is not entirely clear, though the final phase at least specifies a role for the LSJ usage *c*. But A. E. Raubitschek was altogether plainer, in *Dedications*, p. 469. "It may be tentatively suggested," he states there, "that the designation *demos* for the rural communities of Attika came into existence at a time when the agricultural population was oppressed by the big landowners; it may be a name derived from *demos* in the meaning of 'common men.' " On this view, the application of the word *dēmos* to the towns and villages of Attica did not extend back much if at all beyond the sixth century; it was essentially a development of the post-Solonic period, before which, according to Raubitschek, the old names of these local communities was *polis*.

If this theory could be accepted it would substantially answer both of the questions with which we are concerned here. At least, in giving this answer to the question of *when* the Attic demes were first so called it would locate the issue in a period where the "common men" explanation of *why* they were so called seems at first sight readiest to hand. And although, strictly speaking, we cannot *demonstrate* that the Attic demes were called demes until Kleisthenes (and even then on retrospective testimony only!), it is indeed likely enough that this was their name earlier in the sixth century also. The Peisistratid *dikastai kata dēmous* would be adequate proof of this, unless there were reason to suspect (as there is not) that their original title was something different. Besides, as has regularly been observed, when Herodotus recounts the events of Athenian history before Kleisthenes he alludes frequently to the *dēmoi*, both individually (e.g. 1.60.4, the Phye story) and also collectively in contradistinction to the *asty* (e.g. 1.60.5, 1.62.1). Thus it would be perverse to deny that the rural communities of Attica were called demes as *early* as the first half of the sixth century; instead the real question becomes whether we should suppose—with Raubitschek and, by implication, Larsen—that they were not called demes until as *late* as that period.

In my opinion there are serious obstacles in the way of any such supposition. First, as already suggested, a more or less unavoidable corollary of this answer to the matter of dating is the "common men" explanation of *why* this usage came about; and that explanation is simply unacceptable in factual terms for this period. It is demonstrably untrue of sixth-century Attica that (as LSJ put it) "the common people lived in the country, the chiefs in the city"; and once we begin to track backwards in time from then in search of a period for which this statement would, arguably, hold good, the evidence of Homer comes into play again, with its clear indication that the older and, one might say, deeper meaning of the word *dēmos* is simply an area of land and the people who live on it. The figures given above for the distribution of the different Homeric usages would be sufficient proof of this in themselves, but in fact the great antiquity of this connotation of the word is attested in a source far earlier still: the Linear B tablets. The word *da-mo* is found on tablets from both Knossos and Pylos, and it appears to mean "an entity which can allocate holdings of land, probably a village community" (thus the Glossary definition in M.G.F. Ventris and J. Chadwick, *Documents in Mycenaean Greek*, 2d ed., Cambridge, 1973, p. 538; cf. L. R. Palmer, *The Interpretation of Mycenaean Greek Texts*, Oxford, 1963, pp. 186ff., esp. 188-189). Nor has the connection between this and the problem which we have been considering here passed unnoticed in the most recent general survey of Mycenaean society. "At Pylos we also have references to the *damos*, the word which in its later Greek form is the ordinary term for the people collectively (hence our *democracy*). But in Attica it has also the special sense of a local administrative unit of the same sort of size as the English parish. Since we know that the Pylian kingdom was divided for administrative purposes into sixteen districts, it is tempting to suppose that these were already called 'demes' and that the term could thus be used for the people of the district collectively" (J. Chadwick, *The Mycenaean World*, Cambridge, 1976, p. 76, with elaboration extending on to p. 77, cf. pp. 113-117; for further detail see D. M. Jones, "Land tenure at *Pakijane*: some doubts and questions," in *Proceedings of the [1965] Cambridge Colloquium on Mycenaean Studies*, Cambridge, 1966, pp. 245-249, at 245-246, and M. Lejeune, "Le récapitulatif du cadastre Ep de Pylos," ibid., pp. 260-264).

So this investigation has taken a somewhat surprising turn. Instead of attempting—fruitlessly—to explain how the word *dēmos* as village, a rural community on its own land, could have developed in the seventh or sixth century out of a connotation of the word as "common men" (which can itself be shown to be a late development), we have found that no explanation is necessary: *this is what the word had always meant.* The "common men" strand should never have been brought into the discussion, for it is a semantic side-growth which leads on to nothing beyond itself.

We thus have a likely picture of development, semantic and historical, which runs as follows. *If* what has been revealed of Pylos was also true of the other Mycenaean kingdoms, including Athens/Attica, a "deme" was a local subdivision of the land and, by extension, the people living on it. Etymologically, indeed, the word appears to signify a division or part (cf. Palmer, *Interpretation*, p. 188; see above), and it may well be an older word than *p(t)olis*, which is not found in the Linear B texts but first occurs, as far as we are concerned, in the *Iliad*. Whether this permits us to say that the word *polis* was unknown in Mycenaean times is another question; there is no other word so obviously suited to describing the citadel-strongholds, such as the Athenian *(akro)polis*, from which the kings of that age maintained their rule over the surrounding countryside and its towns (though if there was indeed another word, *wa-tu*, i.e., *asty*, seems to have the best credentials; see F. Gschnitzer in *Actes du Sixième Colloque International sur les textes mycéniens et égéens*, Neuchâtel, 1979, pp. 109-132, at 126-127). At all events, upon the dissolution of Mycenaean society into that of the Dark Age, the old geopolitical terminology will doubtless have been temporarily swept away along with everything else; but as far as Athens and Attica are concerned a modest renaissance was under way, as we saw in Chapter 1A, by the second half of the ninth century, and it may be supposed that much of the old terminology was found to be still (*mutatis mutandis*) applicable then. To be sure, venerable towns with long histories—Eleusis, Aphidna, Thorikos, and the like—seem now to have laid claim to the title of *polis*, with all the implications of self-determination that that word was now taking on; and some of them evidently clung to it unofficially long after their incorporation into the single all-embracing polis of "the Athenians." On the other hand, for the numerous villages newly settled in the Geometric and archaic periods the natural and obvious term now was the one it had always been: *dēmos*, a local community living on its own land.

THE KLEISTHENIC DEMES

(with their tribal affiliation and bouleutic representation)

The figures for bouleutic representation (given here in brackets following the deme names), which give a fair indication of the relative sizes of the demes, are those of Traill, *Organization*—with his own addenda in some instances; see the notes below. As explained in Chapter 1A, these are figures attested, or in some cases estimated, for the fourth century (until 307/6), but it is generally held that they had remained unchanged since being originally fixed by Kleisthenes.

Tribe I Erechtheis: fourteen demes
  Agryle, Upper (2)
  Agryle, Lower (3)
  Anagyrous (6)
  Euonymon (10)
  Kedoi (2)
  Kephisia (6)
  Lamptrai, Upper (5)
  Lamptrai, Lower or Coastal (9)
  Pambotadai (1, apparently alternating with Sybridai)
  Pergase, Upper (2)
  Pergase, Lower (2)
  Phegous (1)
  Sybridai (1, apparently alternating with Pambotadai)
  Themakos (1)

Tribe II Aigeis: twenty-one demes
  Ankyle, Upper (1)
  Ankyle, Lower (1)
  Araphen (2)

Bate (1 or 2, variably)
Diomeia (1)
Erchia (7 or 6, variably)
Erikeia (1)
Gargettos (4)
Halai Araphenides (5)
Hestiaia (1)
Ikarion (5 or 4, variably)
Ionidai (2 or 1, variably)
Kollytos (3)
Kolonos (2)
Kydantidai (1 or 2, variably)
Myrrhinoutta (1)
Otryne (1)
Phegaia (3 or 4, variably)
Philaidai (3)
Plotheia (1)
Teithras (4)

Tribe III Pandionis: eleven demes
Angele (2 or 3, variably)
Konthyle (1)
Kydathenaion (12 or 11, variably)
Kytheros (2 or 1, variably)
Myrrhinous (6)
Oa (4)
Paiania, Upper (1)
Paiania, Lower (11)
Prasiai (3)
Probalinthos (5)
Steiria (3)

Tribe IV Leontis: twenty demes
Aithalidai (2)
Cholleidai (2)
Deiradiotai (2)
Eupyridai (2)
Halimous (3)
Hekale (1)
Hybadai (2)
Kettos (3)
Kolonai (2)

Kropidai (1)
Leukonoion (3)
Oion Kerameikon (1)
Paionidai (3)
Pelekes (2)
Phrearrhioi (9)
Potamos, Upper (2)
Potamos, Lower (1)
Potamos Deiradiotes (2)
Skambonidai (3)
Sounion (4)

Tribe V Akamantis: thirteen demes
Cholargos (4)
Eiresidai (1)
Eitea (2)
Hagnous (5)
Hermos (2)
Iphistiadai (1)
Kephale (9)
Kerameis (6)
Kikynna (2)
Poros (3)
Prospalta (5)
Sphettos (5)
Thorikos (5 or 6, variably)[1]

Tribe VI Oineis: thirteen demes
Acharnai (22)
Boutadai (1)
Epikephisia (1 or 2, variably)
Hippotomadai (1)
Kothokidai (2 or 1, variably)
Lakiadai (2)
Lousia (1)
Oe (6 or 7, variably)
Perithoidai (3)
Phyle (2)
Ptelea (1)

[1] It is not known which other Akamantid deme compensated for this variation.

Thria (7)
Tyrmeidai (1 or 0, variably)[2]

Tribe VII Kekropis:[3] eleven demes
Aixone (?8)
Athmonon (5)[4]
Daidalidai (1)
Epieikidai (1)
Halai Aixonides (6)
Melite (7)
Phlya (7)
Pithos (3 or 2, variably)
Sypalettos (2)
Trinemeia (?2)[5]
Xypete (7)

Tribe VIII Hippothontis: seventeen demes
Acherdous (1)
Anakaia (3)
Auridai (1)
Azenia (2)
Dekeleia (4)
Elaious (1)
Eleusis (11)
Eroiadai (1)
Hamaxanteia (1)[6]
Keiriadai (2)
Koile (3)
Kopros (2)
Korydallos (?1)

[2] That is, possibly, one shared with another small Oineid deme (cf. above, Erechtheis); Traill suggests Epikephisia or Hippotomadai.

[3] This is the worst-documented tribe for quotas, despite additional evidence since *Organization* was written (see next two notes); a total of exactly fifty *bouleutai* can be attained only by multiple conjecture, which I eschew.

[4] See Traill, *Hesp.* 47, 1978, pp. 270-272, no. 2; this replaces his earlier, estimated figure of six. On what it means for other estimated Kekropid quotas he does not comment.

[5] But apparently only one in the new fragment (cited in the preceding note).

[6] See Traill, *Hesp.* 47, 1978, pp. 272-273, no. 4; this replaces his *Organization* figure of two, which turns out to have been based on an incorrect restoration in IG II²2377, B, line 27 (= *Agora 15*, no. 20, line 42). Again Traill does not venture an opinion as to which other Hippothontid quota must now be correspondingly raised by one; the obvious candidates would seem to be Korydallos or Oinoe.

Oinoe (?2)
Oion Dekeleikon (3)
Peiraieus (9)
Thymaitadai (2)

Tribe IX Aiantis: six demes
Aphidna (16)
Marathon (10)
Oinoe (4)
Phaleron (9)
Rhamnous (8)
Trikorynthos (3)

Tribe X Antiochis: thirteen demes
Aigilia (6)
Alopeke (10)
Amphitrope (2)
Anaphlystos (10)
Atene (3)
Besa (2)
Eitea (2 or 1, variably)
Eroiadai (1)
Kolonai (2)
Krioa (1)
Pallene (6 or 7, variably)
Semachidai (1)
Thorai (4)

APPENDIX 3

---- ✳ ----

DEME DOCUMENTS

The purpose of this Appendix is simply to list, with summary descriptions, all the epigraphic documents recording activity by demes which have been mentioned and used in this book. The first reference in each case is the one that I have found most convenient for repeated citation (and the date is the one given there unless otherwise indicated). The *editio princeps* is regularly noted only for post-IG documents. Cross-references and additional bibliography are supplied where appropriate. The arrangement is alphabetical by demes, chronological within each deme's entry.

ACHARNAI

1. SEG 21.519 (G. Daux, Χαριστήριον εἰς ᾿Αναστάσιον Κ. ᾿Ορλάνδον I, Athens, 1964, pp. 87-90). Decree of the Acharneis (line 1), "paullo post med.s.IV" (in fact 340-335 on the basis of its sculptured relief: B. Holtzmann, *BCH* 96, 1972, pp. 73-79), concerning the construction of altars for Ares and Athena Areia; first eighteen lines only. *Editio princeps*: L. Robert, *Études épigraphiques et philologiques*, Paris, 1938, pp. 293-296. See also Tod, p. 304.

2. IG II²1206. Acephalous decree of demesmen (lines 11-12, 14, 19), "fin.s.IV," prescribing annual financial duties for the demarch and treasurer in connection with the leasing of the theater. The identification of the deme as Acharnai was made by Köhler (*apud* IG II 5, 587b) on the basis of a heavily restored reference to Athena Hippia (cf. IG II²1207 [= no. 3, below], line 4, and Paus. 1.31.5) in lines 15-16; weak as this is, no alternative has been suggested.

3. IG II²1207. The opening of a decree of the Acharneis ("demesmen" and proposer's demotic in line 2; and found at Menidi), "fin.s.IV?," apparently granting honors to a priestess; six fragmentary lines only.

4. IG II²2953. Thank-offering to Ares and Augustus, "aetate Augusti," by τὸ κοινὸν τῶν ᾿Αχαρνέων (line 4). See *Agora 14*, pp. 162-165.

AIXONE

5. IG II²2492. Land lease (lines 1-31) and associated decree (lines 31-47) of the Aixoneis (passim), internally dated by the Athenian eponymous archon of 345/4 (line 19). *Syll.* 966; R. Dareste, B. Haussoullier, and T. Reinach, *Recueil des inscriptions juridiques grecques* I, Paris, 1891, XIII *bis*; H. W. Pleket, *Epigraphica I: texts on the economic history of the Greek world, Textus Minores* 31, Leiden, 1964, no. 42; *Pachturkunden* no. 25; S. Isager, *Forpagtning af jord og bygninger i Athen,* Copenhagen, 1983, no. 1.

6. IG II²1197. Acephalous decree of the Aixoneis (thus from its provenance; see Eliot, *Coastal Demes,* pp. 7-21, esp. 7-8), "c.a. 330," granting honors to a group of named individuals, apparently *syndikoi* (see lines 12-15).

7. IG II²1198. Decree of the Aixoneis (lines 7-8, 24-26) granting honors to two deme *chorēgoi*; internally dated by the Athenian eponymous archon of 326/5 (lines 3-4).

8. IG II²1196. Large fragment, inscribed both on the front and on the right side, of a decree of the Aixoneis (thus from its provenance; see Eliot, *Coastal Demes,* pp. 7-21, esp. 7-8) concerning the leasing of pasturage-rights and the procedure for arbitration in disputes about them. *Syll.* 914. Dated "c. 335-330" by Kirchner in IG but more probably to be put in 326/5; see Whitehead, "Demarchs," pp. 38-39.

9. IG II²1199. Two decrees of the Aixoneis (thus from their provenance; see Eliot, *Coastal Demes,* pp. 7-21, esp. 9-10) granting honors to *hieropoioi* and others connected with the *hieron* of Hebe; internally dated by the Athenian eponymous archon of 320/19 (lines 15-16; see on this Whitehead, "Demarchs," pp. 37-38).

10. IG II²1200. Decree of the Aixoneis (line 7) granting honors to two deme *chorēgoi*; internally dated by the Athenian eponymous archon of 317/6 (lines 3-4); first ten lines only.

11. IG II²1201. Decree of the Aixoneis (line 5) granting honors to Demetrios of Phaleron; surely datable, therefore, to the period 317-307; first thirteen lines only. *Syll.* 318. In line 11 the IG restoration [ἐπιμελητὴς αἱ]ρεθείς is one letter too long for the *stoichēdon* line of 33 letters: the title must instead be either νομοθέτης (S. Dow and A. H. Travis, *Hesp.* 12, 1943, pp. 148-159) or στρατηγός (H.-J. Gehrke, *Chiron* 8, 1978, pp. 173-175, after de Sanctis); see SEG 28.101. On lines 8-11, see SEG 29.130.

12. IG II²1202. Decree of the Aixoneis (line 2 and passim) granting honors to two men who are perhaps deme *chorēgoi* (cf. above, nos. 7 and 10, and below, no. 13); internally dated (line 1) by Theophrastos

the Athenian eponymous archon of 313/2 (rather than his namesake of 340/39: see Pickard-Cambridge, *Festivals*, p. 49 with n. 3, and SEG 26.133).

13. (N. Kyparissis and W. Peek) *AM* 66, 1941, pp. 218-219, no. 1. Decree of the Aixoneis (line 12) granting honors to two deme *chorēgoi*; internally dated (line 6) by Theophrastos the Athenian eponymous archon of 313/2 (rather than his namesake of 340/39: see Pickard-Cambridge, *Festivals*, p. 49 with n. 3).

?ANAGYROUS

14. IG II²1210. Fragment from a decree of demesmen (demarch in lines 5-6), "fin.s.IV," granting honors to an individual. Its discovery at Vari suggests that the deme is Anagyrous (Kirchner *ad loc.*; cf. Traill, *Organization*, p. 74, n. 10).

ATHMONON

15. SEG 24.197 (S. N. Koumanoudes, *AD* 21A, 1966, pp. 134-140). Acephalous catalog of names (thirty-six surviving), nearly all with patronymics, and an internal rubric (line 4) οἵδε ὑπὲρ αὐτõ ἐτάξαντο; early fourth century. Evidently a list of those who have made payments of some sort to their deme, which the discovery of the stone at Amarousi identifies as Athmonon.

16. IG II²1156, lines 52-63 (with 64). Decree of the Athmoneis (line 64) granting honors to the Kekropid ephebes of the year 334/3 (line 53) and their *sōphronistēs* Adeistos of Athmonon (105). Not an independent stele, but appended to the *monumentum ephebicum* and tribal decree of Kekropis (cf. below, no. 26). *Syll.* 957, lines 77-88.

17. IG II²1203. Decree of the Athmoneis (thus from the discovery of fr. *a* at Amarousi, and its mention of the Amarousia festival; cf. Paus. 1.31.4-5 and IG I²865) granting honors to the six deme *merarchai* of the year 325/4 (lines 3-4, 7-8).

CHOLARGOS

18. IG II²1184. Acephalous decree of the Cholargeis (lines 19-20, 25) concerning their Thesmophoria festival; internally dated by the Athenian eponymous archon of 334/3 (lines 23-24). *Lois, Suppl.* no. 124 (with bibliography).

EITEA

19. SEG 28.102 (A. G. Kaloyeropoulou, *AD* 25, 1970, pp. 204-214; cf. E. Vanderpool, ibid., pp. 215-216). Decree of the Eitaioi ("demesmen" in line 7 and passim, with demotics of proposer and honorand) granting

honors to Hippokles (**151**); internally dated by the Athenian eponymous archon of 332/1 (lines 17-18). This deme, modern Grammatiko, seems— *pace* P. J. Bicknell, *Historia* 17, 1978, pp. 369-374—to be the Eitea of tribe X Antiochis, not its homonym in V Akamantis: see Vanderpool, *loc. cit.*, and J. S. Traill, *Hesp.* Suppl. 19, 1982, p. 170 with n. 25.

ELEUSIS

20. IG I³251 (I²183). Fragmentary *lex sacra*; ca. 445. *Lois*, no. 6. Not demonstrably a deme document *stricto sensu*.

21. IG II²1185. Acephalous decree of the Eleusinioi (lines 5 and 8), "med.s.IV," granting honors to a Theban (cf. next entry).

22. IG II²1186. Two decrees of the Eleusinioi (line 3 and passim), "med.s.IV," granting honors to Thebans (lines 2-3, 37-38). *Syll.* 1094. Only the first three lines (36-38 in the continuous numbering) of the second decree are preserved.

23. IG II²1188. Decree of the Eleusinioi (lines 5-6 and passim), "med.s.IV," granting honors to the hierophant Hierokleides of Paiania (**300**).

24. IG II²1190. First two lines of a decree of the Eleusinioi (line 1), "post med.s.IV"; subject unknown.

25. IG II²2845. Statue base, "post med.s.IV," inscribed with the names of four Eleusinioi (**155, 156, 163, 170**) who dedicated to Dionysos after being crowned by their fellow demesmen.

26. IG II²1156, lines 45-51 (with 64). Decree of the Eleusinioi (line 64) granting honors to the Kekropid ephebes of the year 334/3 (lines 50-51). Not an independent stele, but appended to the *monumentum ephebicum* and tribal decree of Kekropis (cf. above, no. 16; and see also next entry). *Syll.* 957, lines 70-76.

27. IG II²1189. Decree of the Eleusinioi (line 8) inscribed below a dedication by the Hippothontid ephebes of the year 334/3 (line 2) and granting honors to them and their [*sōphronistēs*].

28. SEG 28.103 (S. N. Coumanoudis [= Koumanoudes] and D. C. Gofas, *REG* 91, 1978, pp. 289-306, at 290-291). Two decrees of the Eleusinioi (line 9 and passim) concerned with the leasing of stone-quarrying rights to produce revenue for the cult of Herakles-in-Akris; internally dated by the Athenian eponymous archon of 332/1 (lines 25-28, 49, 52). See J. and L. Robert, *Bull. Epig.* 1979, no. 185, for comments on the *editio princeps*; and SEG 29.131.

29. Pouilloux, *Forteresse*, no. 2 (W. Peek, *AM* 67, 1942, p. 21, no. 24). Fragment of a (?)series of decrees, ca. 330, recording honors for the officers of Pandionid ephebes (and perhaps also the ephebes themselves)

from various bodies including the Eleusinioi (lines 9-10). See also below, nos. 95 and 102.

30. IG II²1191. Decree of the Eleusinioi and other Athenians in garrison in Eleusis (lines 3-5) granting honors to Xenokles (of Sphettos: see **340**) for religious services; internally dated by the Athenian eponymous archon Archipp[os], i.e., either 321/0 or 318/7 (see C. Ampolo, *PP* 34, 1979, pp. 170-171), in line 2. *Syll.* 1048. Only the first twenty-eight lines survive.

31. IG II²1187. Decree of the Eleusinioi (line 3 and passim) granting honors to the *stratēgos* Derkylos of Hagnous (**179**) for services which include his "education" of the deme's young men (lines 4-5). *Syll.* 956. A date of 319/8 is established in the comprehensive study by F. W. Mitchel, *Hesp.* 33, 1964, pp. 337-351, esp. 341-348; cf. Davies, *Families*, pp. 97-98.

32. IG II²2971. Statue base of Demetrios of Phaleron, ca. 315/4, in commemoration of his crowning by various bodies including the Eleusinioi (crown *k*). *Syll.* 319.

33. IG II²1192. Decree of the Eleusinioi (lines 3-4, 9, 12), "fin.s.IV," granting honors to a demesman of Phyle. First thirteen lines only.

34. IG II²1193. Decree of the Eleusinioi (line 11 and passim), "fin.s.IV," granting honors to the peripolarch Smikythion of Kephale (**230**). *Syll.* 356.

35. IG II²2500. Extremely fragmentary record of an agreement between the Eleusinioi and the Thriasioi whereby the former appear to pay rent to the latter for use of an *agora*; "fin.s.IV."

36. (J. C. Threpsiades) *Hesp.* 8, 1939, pp. 177-180 (= IG II²1194 + 1274 + new fragment). Decree of the Eleusinioi (line 2 and passim), ca. 300, granting honors to the demarch Euthydemos (**10**). First twenty-five lines only.

37. SEG 23.80 (Dow/Healey, *Calendar*). Sacrificial *fasti*, ca. 330-270. A re-edition of IG II²1363 (*Syll.* 1038). *Lois*, no. 7. See also Dow, "Six calendars," pp. 175, 178-179.

38. IG II²1280. Decree of the Eleusinioi and other Athenians stationed at Eleusis (lines 2-4), "ante 266/5," apparently granting honors to Antigonos Gonatas. First six lines only.

39. IG II²1218. Fragmentary decree of demesmen (lines 13 and 17), "med.s.III." The deme is identifiable as Eleusis from the provenance, but the subject (not honorific) is indeterminable.

40. SEG 22.127 (Y. Garlan, *BCH* 89, 1965, pp. 344-348, joining IG II²1219 and 1288). Part of a decree of the Eleusinioi and other Athenians living in Eleusis (lines 21-22) granting honors; mid third century or

(Garlan) 213/2. SEG 22.127 gives a slightly more cautious text than Garlan's.

41. IG II²1299, lines 51-80. Decree of the Eleusinioi (line 63 and passim) granting honors to the *stratēgos* Aristophanes of Leukonoion (**280**); internally dated by three Athenian eponymous archonships, the last that of Ekphantos (236/5). Inscribed on the same stele as a soldiers' decree. F. G. Maier, *Griechische Mauerbauinschriften* I, Heidelberg, 1959, no. 22.

42. IG II²949, lines 30ff. Decree of the Eleusinioi (line 34) granting honors to the demarch Pamphilos (**14**); internally dated (line 31) by the Athenian eponymous archonship of Pelops (165/4: Meritt, "Archons," p. 182). Inscribed below a decree of the *boulē* and *ekklēsia*, which have also honored him. First nine lines only.

N.B. Decrees enacted solely by *troops stationed in* Eleusis are not listed here; for these see Appendix 6.

EPIEIKIDAI

43. IG II²2837. Statue base dedicated by Kleonymos of Epieikidai (**174**), one of the *thesmothetai* of 329/8 (lines 2-3), who has been crowned by various bodies including "the demesmen" (right side).

EPIKEPHISIA

44. IG II²1205. Decree of the Epikephisioi ("demesmen" in line 1 and passim, proposer's demotic in lines 2-3), "fin.s.IV" (but see under **176**), granting honors to "those elected by the demesmen to prosecute Neokles" (lines 3-5). First ten lines only.

ERCHIA

45. SEG 21.541 (Daux, "Démarchie," with addenda and corrigenda in *BCH* 88, 1964, pp. 676-677). Sacrificial *fasti* of a deme (demarch in E, lines 57-58), identifiable as Erchia by locatives (passim) and by the discovery at Spata, 375-350. *Lois*, no. 18. See also Jameson, "Calendar," and Dow, "Demarkhia" and "Six calendars;" SEG 22.131.

46. IG II²1213. Fragment of a decree or *lex sacra* of a deme (τὸν δῆμον in line 7), identifiable as Erchia by the discovery at Spata; "s.IV." On the character of the document, see P. J. Bicknell, *REG* 89, 1976, pp. 599-603 (SEG 27.4).

?ERIKEIA

47. IG II²1215. Central part of a decree of demesmen (line 4 and passim), "init.s.III," granting honors to someone in connection with a financial levy on deme officials for the reconstruction of *hiera* and *ana-*

thēmata. The deme may perhaps be identifiable as Erikeia from the discovery at Kypseli; see Traill, *Organization*, p. 39, cf. 74, n. 10.

?EUPYRIDAI

48. IG II²1362. Edict of the priest of Apollo Erithaseos "on behalf of himself and of the demesmen" (lines 3-4) to prohibit the removal of wood from the *hieron*; "fin.s.IV." The deme may perhaps be identifiable as Eupyridai from the discovery at Kamatero; cf. Traill, *Organization*, p. 46. *Syll.* 984. *Lois*, no. 37.

GARGETTOS

49. (W. Peek) *AM* 67, 1942, pp. 7-8, no. 5. Acephalous decree of the Gargettioi (locative in line 5, "demesmen" in line 10) granting honors to Epikydes (of Acharnai: see 56); second half of the fourth century. N. C. Kotzias, *Polemon* 4, 1949, pp. 10-16.

HALAI AIXONIDES

50. SEG 12.52 (P. D. Stavropoullos, *AE* 1938, pp. 23-25). Twenty fragmentary lines of religious accounts found at Zoster (on which see Eliot, *Coastal Demes*, pp. 25-34); late fifth century. Not demonstrably a deme document *stricto sensu* (unless line 3 is − − δήμ]αρχον − − ?).

51. IG II²1356. Acephalous *lex sacra* on the *hiereōsyna* for various priestesses; "init.s.IV." On the place of discovery, see Eliot, *Coastal Demes*, pp. 27-28. *Lois*, no. 28.

52. IG II²1174. Decree of demesmen (line 2 and passim) prescribing a *euthynai* procedure for the deme's chief officials; internally dated by the Athenian eponymous archon of 368/7 (line 8). First twenty lines only. The deme is identifiable as Halai Aixonides from prosopographical links with IG II²2820 (below, no. 54) as well as from provenance; see A. Wilhelm, *BCH* 25, 1901, pp. 93-104 (and *Attische Urkunden* 5, 1942, pp. 135-147); W. K. Pritchett, *Hesp.* 15, 1946, p. 162; Eliot, *Coastal Demes*, pp. 27-28.

53. IG II²1175. Decree of demesmen (lines 2-3) requiring oaths to be taken by deme officials and others after a (?)religious scandal. For the identification of the deme as Halai Aixonides (and the date as ca. 360), see the references under the preceding entry. The stone itself does not survive, and Fourmont's transcript of lines 3-18 is unintelligible: see IG.

54. IG II²2820. Statue base recording a dedication to Aphrodite by twenty-four named individuals "elected by the Halaieis to make the *agalma* for Aphrodite (and) crowned by the demesmen" (lines 1-3). For the identification of the deme as Halai Aixonides (and the date as ca. 360), see the references above, under no. 52.

55. (K. Kourionotes) *AD* 11, 1927-1928, pp. 40-41, no. 4. Decree of

the Halaieis (line 1 and passim) granting honors to the priest of Apollo Zoster and his four elected assistants; provenance identifies the deme as Halai Aixonides, not Araphenides (cf. Eliot, *Coastal Demes*, p. 29). Re-edited by W. Peek, *AM* 67, 1942, pp. 9-10, no. 7, correcting the name in line 11 from Lischeas to Aischeas (see **180**) and thus raising Kourio-notes' date of the late fourth century to ca. 360 (since Aischeas is also in IG II²2820; above, no. **54**).

56. (W. Peek) *AM* 67, 1942, pp. 8-9, no. 6. Two fragments from the middle of honorific decrees connected with the cult of Apollo Zoster (cf. above, no. **55**); provenance identifies the deme as Halai Aixonides (cf. Eliot, *Coastal Demes*, p. 29); second half of the fourth century. *Editio princeps*: K. Kourionotes, *AD* 11, 1927-1928, pp. 42-43, nos. 6-7; but Peek both reads more and restores more.

57. (W. Peek) *AM* 67, 1942, p. 10, no. 8. Six fragmentary lines from the end of a decree of demesmen (line 6), apparently connected with the cult of Apollo Zoster (cf. above, nos. **55** and **56**); provenance identifies the deme as Halai Aixonides (cf. Eliot, *Coastal Demes*, p. 29); late fourth century. *Editio princeps*: K. Kourionotes, *AD* 11, 1927-1928, pp. 41-42, no. 5; but Peek's restorations, with a longer line, are better justified.

58. IG II²2761B. *Horos* of a house pledged to the Halaieis for two hundred drachmas; found between the Pnyx and the Areiopagos; un-dated. (Finley, *Land and Credit*, p. 95, takes the deme to be Halai Aix-onides, not Araphenides, on no stated basis.) *Syll.* 1195, II. Finley, *Land and Credit*, no. 5.

HALAI ARAPHENIDES

59. (N. C. Kotzias) *AE* 1925-1926, pp. 168-177. Acephalous decree of the Halaieis (line 5) granting honors; provenance identifies the deme as Halai Araphenides, not Aixonides (cf. Traill, *Organization*, p. 40); mid fourth century. J. Papademetriou, *PAAH* 1956, pp. 87-89.

60. (P. D. Stavropoullos) *AE* 1932, *Chronika*, pp. 30-32. Decree of the Halaicis (line 8 and passim) granting honors to a deme liturgist; provenance identifies the deme as Halai Araphenides, not Aixonides (cf. Traill, *Organization*, p. 40); mid fourth century. J. Papademetriou, *PAAH* 1956, pp. 87-89.

61. Report in *Ergon* 1957, pp. 24-25 (= *PAAH* 1957, pp. 45-47) of a decree of Halai Araphenides from the year of the Athenian eponymous archon Nikomachos (341/0); cf. G. Daux, *BCH* 82, 1958, pp. 678-679. No text yet published.

HALIMOUS

62. SEG 2.7 (J.J.E. Hondius, *ABSA* 24, 1919-1921, pp. 151-160). Decree of the Halimousioi (lines 10-11) granting honors to Charisandros

(215) for religious services, some of them *vice* the demarch; between 330 and 325. Hondius' reconsidered text for SEG reproduces the *editio princeps* but reads "sacrifices" (ΘΥΣΙΩΝ) for "properties" (ΟΥΣΙΩΝ) in line 5.

IKARION

63. IG I³253 (I²186). Accounts of sacred monies including those of Dionysos and Ikarios handed over, for six (presumably consecutive) years, by demarchs; between 450 and 425. A deme decree of the Ikarieis is on the reverse; see next entry.

64. IG I³254 (I²187). Acephalous decree of the Ikarieis (line 2) concerning deme *chorēgia* and *antidosis*; ?between 440 and 415. Lapses into unintelligibility after the first fifteen lines.

65. IG II²1178. Decree of the Ikarieis (lines 1-2) granting honors to a demarch (29) and two *chorēgoi* (219, 226); "ante med.s.IV." On the apparent distinction in lines 4-5 between Ἰκαριεῖς and ὁ δῆμος ὁ Ἰκαριέων, see the note in IG, and Lewis, "Cleisthenes," p. 32 with n. 93.

66. IG II²1179. Fragmentary opening (seven lines) of a decree of the Ikarieis (lines 1-2) granting honors to a demarch; "med.s.IV."

67. SEG 22.117 (E. Mastrokostas, *AE* 1961, *Chronika*, pp. 23-24, no. 2). Decree of the Ikarieis (line 1) granting honors to the demarch [– –]aios (31); datable to ca. 330 by the mention (lines 6-7) of his successor Thoukydides (see 30). An improved re-edition of the *editio princeps* by D. M. Robinson, *Hesp.* 17, 1948, pp. 142-143, no. 3.

KEPHISIA

68. (E. Vanderpool) *AD* 24, 1969, pp. 6-7. Decree of the Kephisieis (line 9) granting honors to Phro[– –] (232); second half of the fourth century. *Editio princeps* (in brief): *AD* 21, 1966, *Chronika*, p. 106. J. and L. Robert, *Bull. Epig.* 1971, no. 286, suggest restorations for lines 7 and 8.

KERAMEIS

69. (J.V.A. Fine) *Hesp.* Suppl. 9, 1951, pp. 12-13, no. 23. *Horos* of a house sold subject to redemption to the deme of the Kerameis for three thousand drachmas. Finley, *Land and Credit*, no. 67A.

KOLLYTOS

70. IG II²1195, lines 6ff. Decree of the Kollyteis (line 10) concerning sacrifices; "post med.s.IV." Left-hand edge of thirteen lines only. (Lines 1-5 on the stele are the end of a city decree.) *Lois*, no. 38.

KYDATHENAION

71. *Agora 16*, no. 54 (= Agora Inventory I 5212; not yet published). The bottom of an opisthographic stele inscribed with two decrees of the Kydathenaieis (side A, line 6, Κυδ; side B, line 6, "demesmen") granting honors, apparently to individuals or groups who have been crowned by the *boulē* and *ekklēsia* and also by the Athenian cleruchs in Samos and Hephaistia (Lemnos); between 365 and 322 (i.e., the period of the Samian cleruchy: Diod. 18.18.1).

KYTHEROS

72. IG II²2496. Lease of three buildings in Peiraieus to Eukrates of Aphidna (103) by eight men described as "the *meritai* of (the) Kytherioi" (Κυθηρίων οἱ μερῖται, lines 8 and 22-23); "post med.s.IV." R. Dareste, B. Haussoullier, and T. Reinach, *Recueil des inscriptions juridiques grecques* I, Paris, 1891, XIII *ter; Syll.* 1216; *Pachturkunden*, no. 35; S. Isager, *Forpagtning af jord og bygninger i Athen*, Copenhagen, 1983, no. 8. Some scholars have connected this document not with the deme of Kytheros but with the island of Kythera: thus e.g. Köhler *apud* IG II 1058; Wilamowitz, *Hermes* 22, 1887, p. 244; Schoeffer, "Demoi," col. 17. For the contrary view, see e.g. Haussoullier, *Vie*, pp. 72-74; Kirchner *apud* IG II²2496; Jameson, "Leasing," pp. 72-73.

LAMPTRAI

73. IG I³256. Acephalous *lex sacra* on cult for the Nymphs; provenance suggests a link with Lamptrai, though not demonstrably a deme document *stricto sensu*; dated between 440 and 430 by the IG editor, D. M. Lewis (though initially put in the fourth century: see the *editio princeps* by M. T. Mitsos, *AD* 20A, 1965, pp. 80-83). *Lois*, no. 178. J. Bousquet, *BCH* 91, 1967, pp. 92-95 (SEG 23.76).

74. IG II²2967. Dedication to Apollo by at least thirty-six named |Lamp]treis; "med.s.IV" (in fact before 342/1; see Davies, *Families*, p. 537). Prosopography makes the restoration of the demotic certain (see the notes in IG), and the discovery of the stone at Lambrika indicates that the deme is *Upper* Lamptrai (Eliot, *Coastal Demes*, pp. 47-61, esp. 51-52; cf. Traill, *Organization*, p. 38, and *Hesp.* Suppl. 19, 1982, p. 165).

75. IG II²1204. Decree of the Lamptreis (lines 2-3, 15-17) granting honors to Philokedes of Acharnai (62); "fin.s.IV." The discovery of the stone at Kitsi indicates that the deme is *Lower* (or Coastal) Lamptrai: Eliot, *Coastal Demes*, pp. 47-61, esp. 52-53; cf. Traill, *Organization*, p. 38, and *Hesp.* Suppl. 19, 1982, p. 165.

MARATHON

76. IG II²1358. Sacrificial *fasti* of the Marathonian Tetrapolis and its constituent demes; first half of the fourth century. In col. II (of face A), lines 1-53, the entry for the deme of Marathon is virtually complete; for Trikorynthos, see below, no. 128. Face B is read by W. Peek, *AM* 67, 1942, pp. 12-13, no. 10. *Lois*, no. 20. S. Dow, *Historia* 9, 1960, pp. 282-283, and "Six calendars," pp. 174-175, 178-179. (I have not seen G. M. Quinn, *The Sacrificial Calendar of the Marathonian Tetrapolis*, diss. Harvard, 1971, summarized in *HSPh* 76, 1972, p. 299.)

MELITE

77. IG I³243, fr.10. Five fragmentary lines from the opening of a decree of the Meliteis (line 72); between 480 and 450. For the document as a whole, which seems to originate from the Athenian state (and includes a decree of the *"boulē"*, i.e., perhaps the Areiopagos), see the *editio princeps* of B. D. Meritt, *Hesp.* 36, 1967, pp. 72-84, no. 15 (SEG 24.1); cf. Ostwald, *Nomos*, p. 4, n. 4.

78. IG II²2394. The beginning of a list of names with patronymics, dated by the Athenian eponymous archon Theophrastos and the demarch **34** (lines 1-2); *pace* Boeckh (*apud* CIG 94), surely not the prescript of a decree but some sort of catalog. The prosopographical link with Melite comes in line 3 with Euthydemos Euthydomou, who is a [*diaitē?*]*tēs* in IG II²1927, lines 3-5; however, given both the problems surrounding the character and date of IG II²1927 (see B. D. Meritt, *Hesp.* 16, 1947, p. 151, no. 43; D. M. Lewis, *ABSA* 50, 1955, p. 29; Davies, *Families*, p. 205; E. Ruschenbusch, *ZPE* 49, 1982, pp. 267-281) and also the confusing homonymity within IG II²2394 (see under **34**), it is impossible to assign the latter with certainty either to the earlier (340/39) or the later (313/2) archonship of Theophrastos. The stone itself does not survive, and Fourmont's transcript is problematical from line 7 onwards: see IG.

79. SEG 22.116 (J. Threpsiades and E. Vanderpool, *AD* 19, 1964, pp. 31-33, no. 1). Decree of the Meliteis (lines 8-9 and passim) granting honors to their fellow demesman Neoptolemos (**292**); ca. 330.

80. (O. Broneer) *Hesp.* 11, 1942, pp. 265-274, no. 51. Decree of the Meliteis (line 2 and passim) granting honors to Satyra, priestess of the Thesmophoroi (**293**); first half of the second century (from letter forms).

MYRRHINOUS

81. IG II²1182. Acephalous decree of the Myrrhinousioi (line 4) granting honors to a financial official of the deme (see under **296**); "med.s.IV."

82. IG II²1183. Central section of a long decree of demesmen (line 15

and passim) detailing a procedure for the *euthynai* of deme officials, and other matters; "post a.340." The deme is identifiable as Myrrhinous by association with IG II²1182 (see preceding entry); cf. Traill, *Organization*, p. 42.

PAIANIA

83. IG I³250. Acephalous decree (side A, lines 1-14) on religious matters and *lex sacra* (lines 15-36) of the Paianieis ("demesmen" in line 14, and discovery at Liopesi, on which see Traill, *Organization*, p. 43); between 450 and 430. *Editio princeps*: W. Peek, *AM* 66, 1941, pp. 171-181 (SEG 10.38). *Lois, Suppl.* no. 18. The quorum of one hundred demesmen in the decree (line 11-14) identifies the deme as *Lower* Paiania (bouleutic representation 11) rather than Upper (bouleutic representation 1).

PEIRAIEUS

84. IG I³242. Fragment of a *lex sacra*; between 490 and 480. *Editio princeps*: A. Papagiannopoulos-Palaios, *Polemon* 3, 1947-1948, pp. 17-19 (SEG 12.4). Not demonstrably a deme document *stricto sensu*.

85. IG II²1177. Acephalous decree of the Peiraieis (lines 12-13) concerning their Thesmophorion, etc.; "med.s.IV." *Lois*, no. 36.

86. IG II²1176 + . Acephalous leasing agreement for the theater, and associated honorific decree, of the Peiraieis (passim). *Pachturkunden*, nos. 30 and 31; S. Isager, *Forpagtning af jord og bygninger i Athen*, Copenhagen, 1983, no. 3. Fragments, found in the Agora, additional to the IG text: B. D. Meritt, *Hesp.* 29, 1960, p. 1, no. 1 (SEG 19.117) and *Hesp.* 32, 1963, p. 12, no. 10 (SEG 21.521); and see now, above all, R. S. Stroud, *CSCA* 7, 1974, pp. 290-298, with the new internal date from the Athenian eponymous archon of 324/3 (line 9). I cite line numbers in accordance with Stroud's new text of lines 1-20; this entails adding seven to all line numbers in the IG text.

87. IG II²2498. Procedures governing land leases of the Peiraieis (line 2); internally dated by the Athenian eponymous archon of 321/0 (line 1). R. Dareste, B. Haussoullier, and T. Reinach, *Recueil des inscriptions juridiques grecques* I, Paris, 1891, XIII; *Syll.* 965; *Pachturkunden*, no. 29; S. Isager, *Forpagtning af jord og bygninger i Athen*, Copenhagen, 1983, no. 2.

88. (B. D. Meritt) *Hesp.* 3, 1934, pp. 44-46, no. 33. Fragmentary decree of the Peiraieis (lines 5 and 9) "to do apparently with the financing of some public work of construction" (Meritt); found in the Agora; early third century.

89. IG II²1214. Decree of the Peiraieis (line 4 and passim) granting honors to Kallidamas of Cholleidai (**150**); first half of the third century

(ca. 280 according to P. Gauthier, *REG* 92, 1979, pp. 394-396). *Syll.* 912.

90. IG II²2623. "*Horos* of (the) territory of (the) Peiraieis" (ὅϱος Π[ει]ϱαέων [χώ]|[ϱ]ας); fourth century or later (from letter forms).

PHALERON

91. IG II²3102. Dedication by the Phalereis (line 1) to mark their victory in the festival of the Tetrakomoi; "med.s.IV."

PHEGAIA

92. (S. G. Miller) *Hesp.* 41, 1972, pp. 279-280, no. 5. *Horos* of a house sold subject to redemption to the Phegaieis for either three hundred or seven hundred drachmas.

PHLYA

93. IG II²2670. *Horos* of an estate put up as *apotimēma* for the dowry of Hippokleia, daughter of Demochares of Leukonoion (**281**), to the value of one talent, and hypothecated by whatever its worth exceeded that to the (tribe) Kekropidai, the (*genos*) Lykomidai, and the Phlyeis; "probably in the 360s" (Davies, *Families*, p. 347, cf. 141-142). *Syll.* 1188; Finley, *Land and Credit*, no. 146; see also J.V.A. Fine, *Hesp.* Suppl. 9, 1951, p. 141, n. 100.

PHREARRHIOI

94. (E. Vanderpool) *Hesp.* 39, 1970, pp. 47-53. Fragmentary *lex sacra* of the Phrearrhioi (line 12) concerning the cult of Demeter and Kore, etc.; mid third century.

PHYLE

95. Pouilloux, *Forteresse*, no. 2 (W. Peek, *AM* 67, 1942, p. 21, no. 24). Fragment of a (?)series of decrees, ca. 330, recording honors for the officers of Pandionid ephebes (and perhaps also the ephebes themselves) from various bodies including the Phylasioi (lines 9-10). See also above, no. 29, and below, no. 102.

PLOTHEIA

96. IG I³258 (II²1172). Financial decree of the Plotheieis (line 11), preceded by a list of funds on loan from which the income is allocated to cult expenses; dated 425-413 by the IG I³ editor, D. M. Lewis (to the fourth century in IG II²). *Pachturkunden*, no. 21.

97. (E. Tsophopoulou-Gkini) *AE* 1980, pp. 94-95. Small fragment of a decree, or other document, of demesmen (line 1); second half of the

fourth century. Built into the early Christian church at Mygdaleza, it is assigned by its editor to the deme Hekale (cf. Traill, *Organization*, p. 46); however, as both the phrase ἐς Ἀπολλώνια (line 2) and the mention of the Ἐπακρέες (line 1) occur also in no. 96 (lines 8 and 30), and since Plotheia has generally been located nearby (cf. Traill, *Organization*, p. 41), there seem good grounds for ascribing this document to—if not necessarily for identifying its precise find-spot with—Plotheia.

PRASIAI

98. IG II²2497. Land lease of the Prasieis (lines 1-2); "post med.s.IV." *Pachturkunden*, no. 27. The name of the demesman lessee, Kirrhias (lines 3, 10, 15), is supplied by E. Vanderpool, J. R. McCredie, and A. Steinberg, *Hesp.* 31, 1962, p. 56 (SEG 21.645).

99. SEG 21.644 (E. Vanderpool, J. R. McCredie, and A. Steinberg, *Hesp.* 31, 1962, pp. 54-56, no. 138). Fragmentary land lease of the Prasieis (lines 3-4 and passim); second half of the fourth century. *Pachturkunden*, no. 28; for other bibliography, see SEG *ad loc.*

RHAMNOUS

100. IG I³248. Accounts of the financial resources, in reserve or on loan, of the cult of Nemesis (lines 3-4) of Rhamnous, for five (probably consecutive) years between ca. 450 and 440. *Editio princeps*: P. D. Stavropoullos, *AE* 1934-1935, pp. 128-132 (SEG 10.210). Pouilloux, *Forteresse*, no. 35; ML, no. 53; see also Finley, *Land and Credit*, p. 285, n. 43.

101. IG II²2493. Lease of a *temenos* by "the demesmen from the *meros* of Archippos and Stesias" (lines 3-4); internally dated by the Athenian eponymous archon of 339/8 (lines 12-13). *Pachturkunden*, no. 26. For the attribution to Rhamnous and other matters, Jameson, "Leasing," is now fundamental.

102. Pouilloux, *Forteresse*, no. 2 (W. Peek, *AM* 67, 1942, p. 21, no. 24). Fragment of a (?)series of decrees, ca. 330, recording honors for the officers of Pandionid ephebes (and perhaps also the ephebes themselves) from various bodies including the Rhamnousioi (lines 9-10). See also above, nos. 29 and 95.

103. IG II²2849. Dedication of five marble thrones (four of which survive) to Dionysos by the "priest of the founder-hero" (ἱερεὺς ἥρω ἀρχηγέτου), who has been crowned by various bodies including "the demesmen" (crown *d*); provenance shows the deme to be Rhamnous; "s.IV." Pouilloux, *Forteresse*, no. 25 (specifying the last quarter of the century); cf. *Forteresse*, nos. 26 for the "founder-hero" and 27 (see **334**) for the possible name of the priest.

104. IG II²3109. Dedication to Themis by a deme liturgist, Megakles Megakleous Rhamnousios (**328**), who has been crowned by his fellow demesmen; "init.s.III." Pouilloux, *Forteresse*, no. 39.

105. SEG 24.154 (B. C. Petrakos, *AD* 22A, 1967, pp. 38-52). Decree of the Rhamnousioi (proposer's demotic in line 2, and provenance) granting honors to the *stratēgos* Epichares (**362**); internal *terminus post quem* (line 5) from the Athenian eponymous archonship of Peithidemos, i.e., either 268/7 (H. Heinen, *Historia* Einzelschrift 20, Wiesbaden, 1972, pp. 102-117, cf. 213; Habicht, *Untersuchungen* p. 116 with n. 11) or 265/4 (Meritt, "Archons," pp. 174, 191, reiterated in *Hesp.* 50, 1981, pp. 78-84, cf. 94). J. and L. Robert, *Bull. Epig.* 1968, no. 247; Heinen, *loc. cit.*, pp. 152-154 (a re-edition).

106. SEG 31.110 (B. C. Petrakos, *AE* 1979 [1981], pp. 72-73, no. 29). Fragmentary opening of a decree of the Rhamnousioi (known Rhamnousian proposer in line 1—see **329**—and provenance), and conceivably others, apparently in honor of one or more Eretrian military officials; ?mid third century (within the adult lifetime of **329**).

107. IG II²1217. Fragmentary decree of the Rhamnousioi ("demesmen" in lines 3 and 8, and provenance) granting honors to a man who has possibly been demarch (see **42**); internally dated (line 3) by the Athenian eponymous archonship of Antipatros (263/2 or 262/1). Pouilloux, *Forteresse*, no. 6 (with doubts about much of the IG restoration).

108. IG II²3467. Summary formula of a decree of "Rhamnousioi and those of the citizens living in Rhamnous" in honor of the *epimelētēs* Endios of Aithalidai (**69**). Pouilloux, *Forteresse*, no. 8. Perhaps ca. 256/5: see Pouilloux, *Forteresse*, p. 120, on his no. 7.

109. SEG 22.120 (E. Mastrokostas, *PAAH* 1958, p. 32). Decree of the Rhamnousioi (line 1) granting honors to Kallippos of Melite (**290**) for his command of the garrison; "med.s.III."

110. SEG 25.155 (S. Dow and P. Traywick, *Glotta* 45, 1967, pp. 195-202). Decree of the Rhamnousioi (line 1) and "the *koinon* of those stationed at Rhamnous" (lines 3-4, with other formulations passim) granting honors to Dikaiarchos of Thria (**352**); internally dated by the Athenian eponymous archonship of Ekphantos (236/5). *Editio princeps*: P. D. Stavropoullos, *Hellenika* 3, 1930, pp. 153-162; for other editions and bibliography, see SEG *ad loc.*

111. SEG 15.112 (S. B. Kougeas, *AE* 1953-1954, pp. 130-136, no. 3). Decree of the Rhamnousioi "and those of the citizens living in Rhamnous" (lines 1-2, but cf. 21-22 and 33-34) in honor of the trierarch Menandros of Eitea (**153**); internally dated by the Athenian eponymous archonship of Niketes (225/4: Meritt, "Archons," p. 177). Pouilloux,

Forteresse, no. 17 and *BCH* 80, 1956, pp. 64-69, no. 2; L. Moretti, *Iscrizione Storiche Ellenistiche*, Florence, 1965, no. 29.

112. IG II²1313. Opening of a decree of the Rhamnousioi (and others?) in honor of a *xenagos* and his men. Late third century: see Pouilloux, *Forteresse*, no. 22.

113. SEG 31.112 (B. C. Petrakos, *AE* 1979 [1981], p. 72, no. 28). Acephalous decree of the Rhamnousioi "and the soldiers stationed in the garrison" (lines 1-4) in honor of a Phokian *xenagos* and his men; late third century (from letter forms).

114. SEG 31.111 (B. C. Petrakos, *AE* 1979 [1981], p. 73, no. 31). Apparently the opening line of a decree of the Rhamnousioi (proposer's demotic, and provenance), and conceivably others; third century.

115. SEG 31.115 (B. C. Petrakos, *AE* 1979 [1981], p. 73, no. 32). Fragmentary opening of an honorific decree, apparently of the Rhamnousioi (τῶι δήμ[ωι in line 3, δήμω[ι in line 4, either or both of which might, however, be the Athenian *dēmos*; and provenance), and conceivably others; ?third century.

N.B. Decrees enacted solely by *troops stationed* in Rhamnous are not listed here; for these see Appendix 6. Note also SEG 31.114, the exact nature of which is indeterminable.

SKAMBONIDAI

116. IG I³244 (I²188). *Lex sacra* of the Skambonidai (named passim); ca. 460. *Lois*, no. 10.

SOUNION

117. IG II²1180. Decree of the Sounieis (lines 3 and 13-14) concerning the new deme *agora* provided by Leukios (338); "med.s.IV." For the *agora*, see E. Kakavoyiannis, *AD* 32A, 1977, pp. 182-217, at 189; Osborne, *Demos*, p. 35 with n. 60.

118. IG II²1181. Fragmentary (?)opening of a decree, possibly granting honors to the man named in line 2, Tharrhias Tharrhiadou (of Erchia: see 177); internally dated by the Athenian eponymous archon of 331/0 (lines 1-2). Although discovered in Sounion, this is a deme decree only by presumption (in line 4, τ]οῦ δήμου could be the deme, or equally well the Athenian *dēmos*). Compare SEG 10.10 (*AM* 59, 1934, pp. 35-39), listed as a deme decree of Sounion by Traill, *Organization*, p. 74, n. 10, but actually a city decree *from* Sounion concerned with the cults of Sounion and their financing: see now IG I³8.

119. IG II²1260. Central section of a decree classified in the Corpus as "Atheniensium qui Sunii in statione erant"; "307-304." But the re-

mains are equally consistent with its being a deme decree of Sounion (mentioned in lines 8 and 22).

N.B. Decrees enacted solely by *troops stationed in* Sounion are not listed here; for these see Appendix 6.

SPHETTOS

120. SEG 25.206 (A. G. Kaloyeropoulou, *BCH* 93, 1969, pp. 56-71). Statue base of Demetrios of Phaleron set up by the Sphettioi; ca. 315/4.

SYPALETTOS

121. IG I³245 (I²189). Possibly acephalous (and certainly obscure) *lex (sacra)* of the Sypalettioi (lines 4-5 and 10-11); between 470 and 460. On the "entrenchment-clause" in lines 5-12 (i.e., the bulk of what survives) see D. M. Lewis in *PHOROS: tribute to B. D. Meritt*, Locust Valley, New York, 1974, pp. 81-89, at 81.

TEITHRAS

122. SEG 21.542 (J. J. Pollitt, *Hesp.* 30, 1961, pp. 293-297, no. 1). Fragment of an opisthographic stele preserving approximately one month of the sacrificial *fasti* of a deme, identifiable as Teithras from the discovery at Pikermi (cf. Traill, *Organization*, p. 41); first half of the fourth century. *Lois, Suppl.* no. 132; see also Dow, "Six calendars," pp. 176, 178-179.

123. SEG 24.151 (H. Möbius, *AM* 49, 1924, pp. 1-13, no. 1, with improved texts by A. Wilhelm, *APF* 11, 1933-1935, pp. 189-200). Two decrees—the second and longer setting out a land lease—of the Teithrasioi (line 2 and passim); "ca.med.s.IV." H. W. Pleket, *Epigraphica I: texts on the economic history of the Greek world, Textus Minores* 31, Leiden, 1964, no. 41; *Pachturkunden*, no. 24. On the phrase ἐ[π]' ἀμφότερα in line 14, see J. Tréheux, *BCH* 77, 1953, pp. 155-165.

124. SEG 24.152 (H. Möbius, *AM* 49, 1924, pp. 1-13, no. 2). Summary record of land leases in Teithras (passim); "ca.med.s.IV."

125. SEG 24.153 (H. Möbius, *AM* 49, 1924, pp. 1-13, no. 3). Decree of the Teithrasioi (line 4) granting honors to Euthippos (**49**) for expenditure on an *agalma*; "ca.med.s.IV."

126. SEG 21.520 (E. Vanderpool, *Hesp.* 31, 1962, pp. 401-403, no. 3). Decree of the Teithrasioi (lines 1-2) granting honors to the deme's four members on the *boulē* in either 331/0 or 330/29 (lines 4-5). *Agora 15*, no. 45.

THORIKOS

127. (G. Daux) *AC* 52, 1983, pp. 150-174. Sacrificial *fasti*, virtually complete for months 2-12, with oath of the *euthynos* and *paredroi*; first

half of the fourth century. *Editiones principes*: E. Vanderpool in H. F. Mussche et al., eds., *Thorikos and the Laurion in archaic and classical times*, MIGRA 1, Ghent, 1975, pp. 33-42 (from a copy by D. F. Ogden of a copy made from the stone; twenty-eight lines only); and Dunst, "Opferkalender" (from an independent and more complete copy; reproduced as SEG 26.136). Re-edited by Labarbe, *Thorikos*, no. 50. But Daux's edition, foreshadowed in *CRAI* 1980, pp. 463-470, supersedes all others by being the first based upon autopsy of the stone itself. For a more summary version, see Daux in *GettyMusJ* 12, 1984, pp. 145-152.

TRIKORYNTHOS

128. IG II²1358. Sacrificial *fasti* of the Marathonian Tetrapolis and its constituent demes; first half of the fourth century. In col. II (of face A), lines 54-56, the entry for the deme of Trikorynthos begins. For general references see above, no. 76 (Marathon).

XYPETE

129. IG II²3103. Dedication by the Xypetaiones (line 1) to mark their victory in the festival of the Tetrakomoi; internally dated by the Athenian eponymous archon of 330/29 (line 2).

DEME UNIDENTIFIABLE

130. IG II²1173. Fragmentary opening (fourteen lines) of a decree of demesmen (τὸν δήμαρ]|χον in lines 12-13) granting honors to (?)a demarch and (?)*chorēgoi*; "ante med.s.IV." The proposer's name, Leonteus, offers some slight grounds for thinking that the deme may be Acharnai; cf. Davies, *Families*, p. 36.

131. IG II²2829. Dedication by [Ch]arinos Charon[idou], who has been crowned (*qua* councillor, apparently) by various bodies including οἱ δ[ημόται]; "med.s.IV" (from his appearance in IG II²1642, line 36; see on this document A. M. Woodward, *ABSA* 57, 1962, pp. 7-13). D. M. Lewis, *ABSA* 50, 1955, p. 30, suggests that the deme is Euonymon, *if* the honorand's brother is [Cha]rias Charonidou Euonymeus (PA 15343); this is doubted by Woodward, *loc. cit.*, p. 12, but accepted in *Agora 15*, no. 24, and index.

132. IG II²3202. Record of crowns awarded by various bodies including "the demesmen" (no. 11); internally dated by the Athenian eponymous archon of 334/3. The honors are usually assumed to have been granted to a plurality of honorands, the *prytaneis* of a tribe (thus IG, followed in *Agora 15*, no. 33); but a single honorand is at least as likely.

133. IG II²1209. Decree of demesmen (lines 1-2) granting honors to

τῶν δημο[τ]‖[ῶν οἱ ταχθέντε]ς ἐν τοῖς ἐπιλέ‖[κτοις (lines 2-4); "post a.319" (thus Köhler, relating it to the events after the death of Antipatros—for a likely connection with events in 317, see J. H. Oliver, *Hesp.* 4, 1935, pp. 35-37, no. 5; P. Roussel, *RA* 18, 1941, pp. 220-222; S. Dušanić, *BCH* 89, 1965, pp. 128-141).

134. IG II²1211. Fragment of an opisthographic stele recording two decrees or *leges sacrae* of demesmen (side A, line 7); side A "fin.s.IV," side B "s.III, ut videtur."

135. IG II²1212. (?)Acephalous and fragmentary decree granting honors; "fin.s.IV." Taken since Köhler to be a deme decree because of the reference to treasurers (τοὺς] ταμία[ς) in line 12. The provenance is disputed: Vari, according to Eliot, *Coastal Demes*, p. 36, which would identify the deme as Anagyrous; but "in vico Kara" according to IG; and Traill, *Organization*, p. 38 (cf. 74, n. 10), suggests that Kara may be the site of the deme Themakos. Yet could a tiny deme like Themakos afford crowns of a thousand drachmas (lines 7-10)? Perhaps Euonymon?

136. IG II²1216. Two fragments of a (?)decree; "s.III." Taken to be a deme document because of the *euthynos* in A, line 7, cf. 10.

137. SEG 14.81 (B. D. Meritt, *Hesp.* 23, 1954, pp. 242-243, no. 15). Fragment from the end of a decree of demesmen (lines 6-7) granting honors; internally dated (line 8) by the Athenian eponymous archonship of Diognetos (264/3).

138. IG II²3214. *In corona*: Μνησίθεον οἱ δημόται; "s.III."

DUBIA

139. IG I²845. Thirteen lines from some sacrificial *fasti*. Taken to be those of "un dème en relations cultuelles avec Oinoe" by Sokolowski, *Lois*, no. 16, with reference to lines 5 and 11. *If* this is Aiantid, not Hippothontid, Oinoe, the obvious choice would be one of the other demes of the Marathonian Tetrapolis (Marathon, Probalinthos, Trikorynthos). But in fact the document does not demonstrably stem from a deme at all and has been claimed by S. Dow (*Hesp.* 30, 1961, p. 67) as part of Nikomachos' city law code of 411-401.

140. IG II²1208. Fragment of a decree granting honors; "post med.s.IV." It is suggested as a deme decree in IG but could have originated from any corporate body; as the length of line is unknown, the IG restorations are far from secure.

141. IG II²598. Fragment of a decree; "fin.s.IV." It is suggested as the product of a deme or tribe by A. S. Henry, *The Prescripts of Athenian Decrees*, *Mnemosyne* Suppl. 49, 1977, p. 61, because its proposer has neither demotic nor patronymic.

142. IG II²1221. Fragmentary opening of a decree, apparently granting

honors; "ca. 200" (with *terminus post quem* of 224/3, as the proposer is a Berenikides). Classified as a deme decree in IG; and Traill, *Organization*, p. 29, n. 12 (cf. 74, n. 10), suggests that the deme is indeed Berenikidai. However, there is no internal indication that this is a deme decree, and some indication (the *astynomoi* in line 8) that it was not. (Thus there is probably no support here for Traill's further argument for the location of Berenikidai near Eleusis, where this stone was found.)

143. IG II²1220. Fragment of a decree, apparently granting honors; first half of the second century. It is suggested as a deme decree of the Eleusinioi (from its provenance) in IG, but it could have originated from any corporate body.

APPENDIX 4

PEIRAIEUS

With a bouleutic quota of nine (see Appendix 2), it is clear that the citizen population of Peiraieus in the late sixth century was already considerable, yet there is no reason to suppose that at the outset the *deme* of Peiraieus either was or was expected to become in any way extraordinary in itself. It was simply one of the two largest demes assigned to tribe VIII Hippothontis (the other being Eleusis), internally organized in the same way as the rest of the demes in the deme system. What made Peiraieus out of the ordinary, during the course of the fifth century, was its development, pioneered by Themistokles, as the Athenians' principal harbor and port (Thuc. 1.93.3, etc.; for a recent discussion, see R. J. Lenardon, *The Saga of Themistokles*, London, 1978, pp. 87-97) and the accelerated physical growth and elaboration which accompanied and reflected this new military and economic significance. Linked to the upper city by the Long Walls, internally replanned by the visionary skills of Hippodamos (see J. R. McCredie in *Studies presented to G.M.A. Hanfmann*, Mainz, 1971, pp. 95-100; Wycherley, *Stones*, pp. 262-266), and housing a large and proverbially cosmopolitan population of both citizens and foreigners, Peiraieus in the second half of the fifth century had in most important respects patently outgrown its origins and status as a mere deme among demes.

The first formal acknowledgment of this, in institutional terms, seems to have come not under the fifth-century democracy but from the oligarchical Thirty in 404-403, who set up ten of their adherents as "governors of the Peiraieus" (τοῦ Πειραιέως ἄρχοντες: ?Aristot. *Ath. Pol.* 35.1 and 39.6, with other sources cited by Rhodes, *Commentary*, p. 438). No doubt this sprang from a well-founded apprehension that Peiraieus would be the focal point for radical opposition to their regime, and called for special controls as such. Nonetheless, as a recognition, besides, that Peiraieus presented unique administrative problems, it was apparently a step which the restored democracy saw reason to follow and to extend. In the second section of the Aristotelian *Ath. Pol.* we are told of several features of the fourth-century Athenian constitution which reflected the separate and special status of Peiraieus. Five of the ten *astynomoi* held office there (*Ath. Pol.* 50.2), as did five of the ten *agoranomoi* (51.1), five of the ten *metronomoi* (51.2), and fifteen (formerly five) of the thirty-five (formerly ten) *sitophylakes* (51.3). In addition, two (perhaps formerly one: see Rhodes, *Commentary*, p. 679) of the ten *stratēgoi* were posted to Peiraieus (61.1); and the currency law of 375/4 (*Hesp.* 43, 1974, pp. 157-188) provided *inter alia* for the appointment of a (slave) *dokimastēs* of silver coins "in Peiraieus" besides the one already functioning "in the *asty*."

What did this multiplication of city officials with special responsibility for Peiraieus mean for the *deme* of Peiraieus, and in particular for its own officials? To some extent the situation in Peiraieus need not be seen as significantly different from that of any of the other demes in what had now become the urban *Doppelstadt*, whose demarchs and other personnel must have been quite well accustomed to discharging their duties in close conjunction with the *astynomoi*, the *agoranomoi*, and other city officials. (See on this Kahrstedt, *Staatsgebiet*, pp. 44-45.) Yet no other urban deme was as large or as important as Peiraieus had now become, and the normal principle of self-determination by individual demes through the medium of their assemblies of members was therefore not necessarily applicable to the full in this unique case. Such at any rate must have been the rationale behind the fact that, at some time before the *Ath. Pol.* was written, the demarchy of Peiraieus had become a state appointment: κληροῦσι . . . εἰς Πειραιέα δήμαρχον (54.8). The date of this is indeterminable, though IG II²1177, as we shall see below, sets the middle of the fourth century as *terminus ante quem*.

We are told neither how nor where this sortition was conducted. (I know of no basis for Osborne's assertion, *Demos*, p. 77, that it was the responsibility of the *boulē*.) Nor, more important, is it made clear whether candidacy was restricted to the demesmen of Peiraieus or open to all. Most scholars have roundly declared the latter to be the case (see for instance Wilamowitz, *Aristoteles*, vol. I, p. 232; Schoeffer, "Demarchoi," col. 2707; Busolt/Swoboda, *Staatskunde*, p. 966; M. Amit, *Athens and the Sea: a study in Athenian seapower*, Collection Latomus 74, Brussels, 1965, p. 82); yet this would have been a major departure from, indeed violation of, traditional practice, and the arguments which have been cited in support of it are not cogent. For example, the archon-plus-demarch dating of the leasing regulations IG II²2498 (line 1) can be matched in two other demes, Eleusis (IG II²1191, lines 1-2) and Melite (IG II²2394, lines 1-2); and the supposed parallel, for an outsider as demarch, afforded by the Sounian "demarch of Oropos" is a chimera (see Whitehead, "Demarchs," pp. 40-42). The only known demarch of Peiraieus, Phrynion, appears in IG II²2498 with no demotic, so he at least was surely a *dēmotēs* himself. Obviously we would require more evidence to decide the question conclusively (cf. Rhodes, *Commentary*, p. 611). But it would be perfectly understandable if the object of the system was not to impose upon the demesmen of Peiraieus demarchs who belonged to other demes but simply to choose from the usual internal candidates in a more open forum than the deme assembly.

As regards the functions of the demarch of Peiraieus, the only ones mentioned in *Ath. Pol.* 54.8 fall in the religious domain—the organization of the (rural) Dionysia and the appointment of *chorēgoi* for it. In these respects his responsibilities seem merely those of all demarchs (cf. Pickard-Cambridge, *Festivals*, p. 46). But a crucially important indication of the essential difference in standing between the demarch of Peiraieus and all other demarchs comes in a provision of a Peiraieus deme decree of the middle of the fourth century, IG II²1177, lines 13-17: "if anyone contravenes any of this [i.e., violates the conventions of the Thesmophorion], the demarch is to impose a fine on him and take the matter to the jury-court under the terms of the laws which are laid down about these things" (εἰάν τίς τι τούτων παρὰ τα|ῦτα ποιεῖ, ἐπιβολὴν ἐπ[ι]βαλόντα τ|ὸν δήμαρχον εἰσάγει[ν] εἰσστὸ δι|καστήριον χρώμενον τοῖς νό-μοι|ς οἱ κεῖνται περὶ τούτων). The key phrase here is not εἰσάγειν εἰς τὸ δικαστήριον, which is not used here in the technical sense of presiding over the court but means simply bringing the prosecution (see Chap. 5, n. 52). Rather, what is significant is that the demarch can impose a summary fine on his own initiative (ἐπιβολὴν ἐπιβαλόντα). Haussoullier, *Vie*, p. 103, declared that all demarchs could do so, and that this was a sign that all demarchs were genuine *archontes* (cf. Aeschin. 3.27 for this criterion). However, the argument can be turned on its head—and has been, by Hansen, "*Archai*," pp. 154 and esp. 173: demarchs other than the demarch of Peiraieus were *not*, properly speaking, holders of an *archē*, for two *archai* could not be held simultaneously, and yet we know that Euboulides of Halimous was *bouleutēs* and demarch in the same year (Chap. 4, n. 11; for the *boulē* as an *archē*, see Hansen, *GRBS* 22, 1981, pp. 347-351). Thus Haussoullier was mistaken in believing that all demarchs could impose *epibolai*. The demarch of Peiraieus demonstrably could, however, do so; and he is thus revealed as the only demarch who was not merely appointed by the state but considered to be one of its own magistrates, with enhanced powers accordingly.

No other peculiarities in the internal administration of the deme of Peiraieus can be similarly attributed to action by the Athenian state. Amongst its other known officials, only the *horistai* of IG II²1177, lines 21-24, are unattested elsewhere, and there is nothing to suggest that they were anything other than the normal *type* of deme appointment, that is, devised by each deme on its own initiative to meet its own needs.

APPENDIX 5

———— ✳ ————

ACHARNAI

Whereas Peiraieus grew from a medium-sized deme into a very large and administratively atypical one *after* the creation of the Kleisthenic deme system (see Appendix 4), Acharnai was evidently enormous even in the late sixth century. Its remarkable bouleutic quota of twenty-two (*Agora* 15, no. 17, lines 42-64) was by far the highest of any deme, taking up almost half of the representation of its tribe, VI Oineis, and, by thus exceeding sixteen or seventeen, creating a unique anomaly at the level of the trittyes. (For the likely solution to this, see J. S. Traill, *Hesp.* Suppl. 19, 1982, p. 169.) What is more, the mechanical implications of the quota, namely, that the Acharneis made up 44 percent of their tribe and thus 4.4 percent of the citizen-body as a whole, can be corroborated with surprising accuracy by other means. Gomme's figure (*Population*, p. 61) of 452 prosopographically attested individual Acharnians represents much the largest figure for any deme, and 3.68 percent of his total of 12,279 Athenians in all (cf. S. Dow, *TAPhA* 92, 1961, pp. 66-80, at 73; see further below). And in a list of Oineid ephebes of ca. 330 (W. K. Pritchett, *Hesp.* Suppl. 8, 1949, pp. 273-278) there are 24-26 Acharneis out of a possible total of 57. This is especially valuable and striking for its indication that the population of Acharnai was still closely in line with its bouleutic quota even in the second half of the fourth century.

A further index of the great size of Acharnai is to be found in Thucydides 2.19-20; but it involves a notorious crux of interpretation. In 2.19.2, Acharnai, where the invading Spartan army has just arrived, is described as "the largest place of the so-called demes of Attica" (χωρίον μέγιστον τῆς ᾿Αττικῆς τῶν δήμων καλουμένων). This is expanded in 2.20.4 as "being a great part of the polis—for there were three thousand (Acharnian) hoplites" (μέγα μέρος ὄντες τῆς πόλεως, τρισχίλιοι γὰρ ὁπλῖται ἐγένοντο); and it is the notion that the Acharnians could have provided three thousand hoplites out of fewer than twenty-nine thousand in all (Thuc. 2.13.6-7, discounting the metics) which most scholars have found incredible. An important exception is W. E. Thompson, *Historia* 13, 1964, pp. 400-413, who argued that there are enough margins of error in scholars' calculations of what they think the figure ought to be—notably A. W. Gomme, *A Historical Commentary on Thucydides*, vol. 2, Oxford, 1956, pp. 73-74 (see further below)—to make three thousand not necessarily correct but not impossible. However, the difficulty with Thompson's reasoning is the fact that all these margins of error—for example, in the relative sizes of the tribes—have to be stretched in the same direction, so that the sequence of calculations involved is actually more vulnerable than the one to which he objects. As to the observation of A. R. Burn, *Historia* 15, 1966, p. 376, that the population of Acharnai in 431 will have included many Athenians who had migrated there from other demes to swell the ranks of the Acharnian charcoal-burners, this is very probably true, but surely irrelevant. Thucydides will not have been thinking of such men when he wrote of "the Acharneis" (2.20.4 and 21.3); nor would he have included them in a hoplite figure given to justify (γάρ) his description of "the Acharneis" as "a great part of the polis." In any event it is hard to see on what basis the number of hoplites *living in* Acharnai could have been easily discovered.

If then the figure of three thousand Acharnian hoplites cannot be correct, what is to be done with it? Possible solutions were usefully reviewed by Sterling Dow, "Thucydides and the number of Acharnian hoplites," *TAPhA* 92, 1961, pp. 66-80 (page references to this hereinafter), but he rejected them all in favor of the idea that Thucydides had been "carried by enthusiasm into gross overstatement." Dow maintains, in other words, that Thucydides did write "three thousand," as a piece of rhetorical exaggeration which he did not expect his readers, particularly those outside Athens, to be in any position to question (Dow, pp. 78-79). Most scholars, he insists, have resorted to the "arbitrary" solution of textual emendation far too readily; and his objections to some of this are well founded. For example, F. Polle's elegant conjecture of "citizens" (πολῖται) for "hoplites" (ὁπλῖται)—*Neue Jahrbucher* 135, 1887, pp. 109-111—cannot be the answer. Taken to refer to adult males only, it still leaves the figure of three thousand too high; if on the other hand it embraces all persons of citizen status—men, women, and children—it results in three thousand being too *low* a figure; in any case Thucydides was not in the habit of giving such all-embracing figures even if he knew them (Dow, pp. 69-70). Also too low are some of the suggested emendations of the figure "three thousand," such as Müller-Strübing's "three hundred," i.e., Τ′ becoming ͵Γ (*Aristophanes und die historische Kritik*, Leipzig, 1873, p. 649; cf. on this Müller, *de demis*, pp. 9-10); for Dow follows Gomme in believing that the actual number of Acharnian hoplites at this time must have been approximately twelve hundred. Gomme himself had tentatively suggested a palaeographic means whereby "twelve hundred" could have been corrupted into "three thousand" (by XHH becoming XXX); and Dow (p. 68) offered a variant of his own (acrophonic χ, one thousand, becoming alphabetic ͵γ, three thousand), designed to show up this whole approach to the problem as too facile.

Dow's argument is thus revealed as an oddly perverse one: if, he seems to be saying, there are several relatively simple solutions to a problem (as distinct from a single complicated one), none of them can be correct. Yet *one* of them surely *is* correct. It may be agreed that we shall never know for certain what figure Thucydides wrote, except that it must have been much lower than three thousand. (Human as Thucydides was, Dow's notion of his "gross overstatement" on this point is a cure worse than the disease.) And *if* it was twelve hundred, that would be in satisfactory accordance both with the facts as we know them (see Dow's version, pp. 70-71, of Gomme's calculations) and also—*pace* Dow, pp. 76-78—with Thucydides' overall presentation of the significance of Acharnai, and the attitude of the Acharnians, in 431.

Thuc. 2.19ff. is indeed noteworthy for several reasons. It is the only occasion in Thucydides' work when any individual Athenian deme *qua* deme is prominent in events (cf. Edwards, *Demesman*, p. 55), and the vignette is a vivid one. The Acharnians are represented as fully aware of their numerical and psychological influence in the polis (2.21.3: οἵ τε Ἀχαρνῆς οἰόμενοι παρὰ σφίσιν αὐτοῖς οὐκ ἐλαχίστην μοῖραν εἶναι Ἀθηναίων), and, as the Spartan king Archidamos is made to anticipate in 2.20.4, they are foremost in the call for active resistance to the invaders. This characterization of the Acharnians as proud and belligerent—as befitted demesmen who gave cult to Ares and Athena Areia (SEG 21.519, cf. Tod, no. 204)—can be set in a context of other fifth-century sources which in sum, as Dover has remarked, constitute a "notable exception" to the general absence, otherwise, of martial traditions attaching to individual demes (K. J. Dover in Gomme, *Historical Commentary* [see above], vol. 4, Oxford, 1970, p. 446). A striking early example (ca. 485) occurs in Pindar's *Second Nemean* ode, composed to celebrate the victory of Timodemos of Acharnai in the pankration: Ἀχάρναι δὲ παλαίφατον | εὐάνορες (lines 16-17; on Timodemos, see ML, pp. 26-27). However, famous *individual* Acharnians (as Dow noted, p. 74 with n. 8) are rare; what one finds instead is a collective, impersonal stereotype of the Acharnian character. We do not know the name of the fifth-century comic poet who coined the word δρυαχαρνεύς (Kock, *CAF*, vol. III, p. 413, *adespota* no. 75), but we can believe the lexicographers who commented on it (Hesych., δρυαχαρνεῦ; *Etym. Magn.* 288.15) that, in the caricature world of Old Comedy, the Acharnians were the proverbial wild men, as tough and unyielding as old oak. (Note also the adage Ἀχαρνικοὶ ὄνοι, Acharnian asses: *Corpus Paroemiographorum Graecorum*, vol. II, p. 16, no. 90.) The fullest version of this picture, in Aristophanes' *Acharnians* (see esp. lines 178-185, 204-236, 280-365, 665-675), surely exploited rather than created the stereotype, though the generally affectionate tone of the portrayal may well not have been universally relished; contrast Andoc. fr. 5 Sauppe (*apud* Suda, σκάνδιξ), where the wish never to see again "the charcoal-makers coming into the *asty* from out of the mountains" (ἐκ τῶν ὀρῶν τοὺς ἀνθρακευτὰς ἥκοντας εἰς τὸ ἄστυ) looks like a clear reference to the Acharnians (cf. Aristoph. *Ach.*, lines 211-218 and passim). For the equally formidable Acharnian *women*, see Aristoph. *Lysistr.*, lines 61-63, and *Thesm.*, lines 562-563.

APPENDIX 6

———— ✳ ————

THE GARRISON DEMES

Any traveller through classical or early Hellenistic Attica would have come upon a great variety of fortresses, fortified camps, refuges (*Fluchtburgen*), watchtowers, and so forth (cf. Y. Garlan, *Recherches de poliorcétique grecque*, Paris, 1974, pp. 78-82). The archaeological remains of many of these sites, as is clear from J. R. McCredie's judicious *Fortified Military Camps in Attica* (*Hesp.* Suppl. 11, 1966—hereinafter McCredie), makes them difficult to fit into any simple typology, but in theory at least certain distinctions are obviously called for (cf. McCredie, pp. 88-100); and for our purposes here we need above all to isolate those garrisoned fortifications which made some significant, long-term impact on the life of the demes upon which they were superimposed.

By emphasizing, first, the factor of "long-term" impact we may exclude, for example: (*a*) *Dekeleia*, in which the Peloponnesians occupied a fortified military camp between 413 and 404 (Thuc. 7.19.1-2, cf. 27-28; Xen. *Hell.* 2.3.3)—though there may have been a permanent (Athenian) fortification elsewhere in the deme (see McCredie, pp. 56-58); and (*b*) *Koroni*, briefly occupied by Ptolemaic forces during the Chremonidean War and in any case unconnected with the deme center of Prasiai (see McCredie, pp. 1-16, drawing on *Hesp.* 31, 1962, pp. 26-61).

Some twenty-five other sites may also be set aside, as being—to judge from the remains—what McCredie terms (mere) "fortifications or camps" as opposed to "established forts or garrisons" (see his Plate 1). Those which fell within the territory of identifiable demes include the following six:

1. *Anagyrous (Vari)*. Perhaps part of an Athenian signalling network between Sounion and Peiraieus (Eliot, *Coastal Demes*, pp. 41-42; McCredie, pp. 28-29); cf. below, Atene. (Yet there was *possibly* a garrison there in the late fourth century: IG II²1210, lines 0-1, ἐπεμελήθη δὲ κ]|αὶ τῆς φυλακ[ῆς – – –].) See further H. Lauter-Bufe, *AM* 94, 1979, pp. 161-192.

2. *Anaphlystos*. A *teichos* there is attested by both Xen. *Poroi* 4.43 and [Scylax] *Periplous* 57; but "there are no recognizable remains" (McCredie, p. 77, n. 156).

3. *Aphidna*. Listed, together with Eleusis, Phyle, Rhamnous, and Sounion, in the forged (?third-century) decree of Kallisthenes inserted into Demosth. 18.38 (on which see McCredie, pp. 92-93) as one of the great fourth-century *Fluchtburgen*. This is probably mistaken, but the character and purpose of the Aphidna fortifications remain obscure (McCredie, pp. 81-83).

4. *Atene*. Perhaps part of an Athenian signalling network between Sounion and Peiraieus (Eliot, *Coastal Demes*, pp. 131-135; McCredie, pp. 25-28); cf. above, Anagyrous.

5. *Besa*. The establishment of a "defence" (ἔϱυμα) there, to serve (with Anaphlystos and Thorikos) as a *Fluchtburg* for the mining district, is recommended by Xen. *Poroi* 4.43-44. The remains do not positively confirm that this was the function of the fortifications there (McCredie, pp. 75-77).

6. *Trikorynthos*. There are remains of a fortified akropolis, which may or may not date back to Mycenaean times and may or may not be identical with the deme center (McCredie, pp. 37-41).

In the category of "established forts or garrisons" McCredie places the following nine sites: Eleusis, Mounichia, the Mouseion, Oinoe (Myoupolis), Panakton (?Gyphtokastro), Phyle, Rhamnous, Sounion, and Thorikos. (In his Plate 1 a classification-symbol for Thorikos is actually missing, but his description of the masonry, pp. 33-34, cf. 90, leaves little doubt that he puts Thorikos in this category.) However, Panakton—a source of contention between the Athenians and the Boiotians during the Archidamian War (Thuc. 5.3.5, cf. 18.7 and 35-46), garrisoned in the mid fourth century (Demosth. 54.3-6, cf. 19.326), and on a strategic par with Eleusis and Phyle in the late fourth and the third centuries (IG II²1299, 1303-1307, 2971)—was neither a deme itself nor even near enough to any known deme-center to be relevant here. And of the remaining eight we lack information about any impact upon deme life as such in five instances:

1. *Mounichia* (in Peiraieus). Its strategic potential (cf. Plut. *Sol.* 12, Diog. Laert. 1.144) was universally appreciated, from the tyrant Hippias (?Aristot. *Ath. Pol.* 19.2) through the Four Hundred in 411 (Thuc. 8.92.5, with Rhodes, *Commentary*, p. 456) and the democratic counterrevolutionaries of 403 (Xen. *Hell.* 2.4.11ff.; ?Aristot. *Ath. Pol.* 38.1-3; etc.) to

the occupying Macedonian powers from 322 onwards (see in brief McCredie, pp. 103-105). In the time of the *Ath. Pol.* it was garrisoned by ephebes (42.3) and in the special care of one of the board of *stratēgoi* (61.1, with Rhodes, *Commentary*, p. 679). But none of the deme documents of Peiraieus betray the slightest reflection of any of this.

2. *The Mouseion* (presumably in Koile). Apparently first fortified and garrisoned by Demetrios Poliorketes in 294 (Plut. *Demetr.* 34, Paus. 1.25.8; H. A. Thompson and R. L. Scranton, *Hesp.* 12, 1943, pp. 331-332, 337-338), and similarly exploited thereafter (e.g. by Antigonos Gonatas: Paus. 3.6.6).

3. *Oinoe* (of tribe VIII Hippothontis). Fortified, if not already in the late sixth century (see Herod. 5.74.2), at any rate before the Peloponnesian War (see Thuc. 2.18-19.1 and 8.98). But *apparently* little used from the fourth century onwards; cf. *RE* Suppl. 8, 1956, col. 372.

4. *Phyle.* Already a "stronghold" (χωρίον ἰσχυρόν) by the time of its exploitation in the democratic counterrevolution of 403 (Xen. *Hell.* 2.4.2ff., with this phrase in 2.4.2; ?Aristot. *Ath. Pol.* 37-38; etc.). For its strategic importance in the late fourth and the third centuries, see IG II²1299, 1303-1307, and 2971; for the occupation by Kassandros, Plut. *Demetr.* 23 (with McCredie, p. 104). In Pouilloux, *Forteresse*, no. 2, the Phylasioi are one of three bodies of demesmen to honor the officers of Pandionid ephebes (and perhaps also the ephebes themselves) in ca. 330; but we are entirely ignorant as to how deme and garrison interacted thereafter.

5. *Thorikos.* The *teichos* there mentioned by both Xen. *Poroi* 4.43 and [Scylax] *Periplous* 57 was built, according to Xen. *Hell.* 1.2.1, in 410/09. The Belgian excavators of Thorikos have preferred a date of 412, to coincide with the fortification of Sounion (Thuc. 8.4) and also, possibly, Rhamnous (but see Pouilloux, *Forteresse*, pp. 58-60); see for instance Labarbe, *Thorikos*, no. 24, n. 1; but note on this McCredie, p. 34. At all events the absence of other, later references to it is puzzling.

Of these five fortresses it is only Phyle which (for the reason given above) can definitely be numbered among the *phylaktēria* that, according to ?Aristot. *Ath. Pol.* 42.4, housed the ephebes during their year as *peripoloi.* Panakton was doubtless another (see above). And so were the three demes of Eleusis, Rhamnous, and Sounion, which experienced for over a century "une vie complexe où les soldats coudoient les civils" (Pouilloux, *Forteresse*, p. 79, writing of Rhamnous)—"les soldats" being at first the Athenian ephebes, serving their period of full-time national service under the reform of ca. 335/4 (on which see Rhodes, *Commentary*, pp. 494-495), and subsequently, in the later fourth century and through the third, miscellaneous garrisons of Athenian and/or foreign troops. But the evidence for the "vie complexe" of these three communities, and especially for the impact of garrison upon deme, is complex in itself, and raises many more questions than it solves.

1. *Eleusis*. (A *teichos* there: [Scylax] *Periplous* 57; *castellum* in Livy 31.25.2; cf. Xen. *Hell*. 2.4.8, ?Aristot. *Ath. Pol*. 39-40, Plut. *Demetr*. 33. For the site, see in brief G. E. Mylonas in R. Stillwell et al., eds., *The Princeton Encyclopedia of Classical Sites*, Princeton, 1976, pp. 296-298.) We have early evidence of the presence of ephebes in Eleusis (IG II²1156, lines 45-51; IG II²1189; Pouilloux, *Forteresse*, no. 2), but nothing to prepare us for the surprise of IG II²1191. In what appears otherwise to be a normal deme decree (archon-dated to 321/0 or 318/7)—for example, the proposer is an Eleusinian—the resolution formula reads thus: "resolved by the deme of the Eleusinioi and the Athenians in the garrison" ([ἔδ]οξεν Ἐλευσ[ινί]ων [τῶι δήμωι] | [κα]ὶ Ἀθηναίο[ι]ς [τοῖς ἐν τῆι φυλ]|[α]κῆ[ι], lines 3-5). There is no means of telling whether the demesmen had taken their own decision to associate the garrison in the enactment of this honorific decree or whether they had somehow been directed from Athens to do so. And subsequently the juridical picture grows more, not less, confusing, with (apparently) three different categories of decree being passed:

(i) "Normal" decrees of the demesmen alone, with Eleusinian proposers, continue through the remainder of the fourth century (IG II²1187, 1192, 1193; *Hesp*. 8, 1939, pp. 177-180), with an example as late as the third quarter of the third century (IG II²1299, lines 51-80).

(ii) Further instances of deme-plus-garrison decrees occur in the second half of the third century: IG II²1280; SEG 22.127 (= IG II² 1218 + 1288; the reference to the demesmen in line 21 is restored but there is no good alternative); and note also SEG 25.155 (Rhamnous), lines 12-14, referring to Eleusis. The status of the proposer is preserved only in IG II²1280, where he is a Kydathenaieus.

(iii) Between the 260s and the end of the third century, troops alone (of various kinds) seem to have enacted numerous decrees: IG II²1272, 1279 (cf. Y. Garlan, *BCH* 89, 1965, pp. 339-344, no. 3), 1285, 1287, 1299 (lines 1-50), 1303, 1304, 1304b, 1305, 1306, 1307. It should be noted, however, that where the resolution formula or any comparable phrase has not been preserved (e.g. 1279,

1285, 1287) this Corpus classification *may* be arbitrary. The proposer of 1272 is an Eleusinian; of 1279, a Sounian.

Whatever determined the constituency, so to speak, for enacting any particular decree, it does *not* seem to have been the type of honorand in question; compare, for example, IG II²1193 (a *peripolarchos* honored by the demesmen alone) and 1272 (a *grammateus* honored by troops alone).

2. *Rhamnous.* (A *teichos* there: [Scylax] *Periplous* 57; cf. Plut. *Demetr.* 33. For the site, see in brief C.W.J. Eliot in *Princeton Encyclopedia*, p. 753.) Despite the fact that this is the best known of the garrison demes in both archaeological and epigraphical terms (see Pouilloux, *Forteresse*, pp. 79-92, 106-167) the juridical complexities revealed in Eleusis are here increased rather than diminished. Again the presence of ephebes is attested early (*Forteresse*, nos. 1, 2, 2 *bis*), and an instance of a joint decree of "demesmen" and "soldiers" (στρατιῶται) *may* occur before the end of the fourth century (IG II²2849 = *Forteresse*, no. 25; it is possible, though, that the crowns for this priest were awarded separately). Thereafter we are ill served for documents as regards the first third of the third century, but from the 260s onwards one may distinguish—at least in theory—between the same three categories of decree as at Eleusis:

(i) The demesmen of Rhamnous alone were apparently responsible for IG II²1217 (*Forteresse*, no. 6) and SEG 24.154, and certainly for SEG 22.120. The proposers are Rhamnousioi in all cases.

(ii) Demesmen and troops combined to enact *Forteresse*, nos. 8 (IG II²3467) and 17 (cf. *BCH* 80, 1956, pp. 64-69, no. 2; SEG 15.112)—the latter proposed by a demesman of Oe; also SEG 31.112.

(iii) Troops alone, variously designated, took it upon themselves to enact *Forteresse*, nos. 7, 10 (IG II²2977), 11 (IG II²1286), 14 with addendum (cf. *BCH* 80, 1956, pp. 57-63, no. 1), 16 (IG II²1310), 18, 19 (cf. *BCH* 80, 1956, pp. 69-75, no. 3), and 21 (IG II²1312, where δήμωι in line 3 is expanded in line 5 as δ]ήμωι τῶι Ἀθηναίων τῶι Ῥαμνοῦντι); also SEG 22.128.

Such classification is not always a simple matter, however. Sometimes this is because of the imperfect preservation of the documents. In *Forteresse*, no. 13 (IG II²1311), for example, the summary formula "those Athenians serving as soldiers in Rhamnous" (Ἀθηναίων οἱ στρατευόμενοι Ῥαμνοῦντι, lines 13-15) does not of itself exclude association with the deme; compare *Forteresse*, no. 17 (below). Conversely, in *Forteresse*, no. 22 (IG II²1313) the Rhamnousian demotic of the proposer, while admittedly (as Pouilloux noted *ad loc.*) a sign that the deme is involved, does not make it certain that troops were not. Yet in addition, and more important, some decrees show an *intrinsic* confusion in their voting constituency. In *Forteresse*, no. 17—classified above as type ii—the opening formula "resolved by the Rhamnousioi and those of the citizens living in Rhamnous" (ἔδοξεν Ῥαμνουσίοις καὶ τοῖς οἰκοῦσιν τῶν πολιτῶν Ῥαμνοῦντι, lines 1-2) later becomes δεδόχθαι Ἀθηναίων τοῖς συνπλεύσασιν ἐν τῶι ἀφράκτωι (lines 21-22, cf. 33-34; see on this *BCH* 80, 1956, pp. 65-69). And, as Pouilloux observed *ad loc.*, an unparalleled degree of "confusion juridique," even "incoherence," is to be seen in *Forteresse*, no. 15 (SEG 25.155). The decree opens "resolved by the Rhamnousioi" (ἔδοξεν Ῥαμνουσίοις), with a Rhamnousian proposer; the deme assumes the expenses of the document (lines 41-43); and the five-man commission charged with its implementation is made up entirely of demesmen (lines 43-47; contrast *Forteresse*, no. 17, just discussed, lines 28-32). A deme document, then? The honorand is said to have benefitted "the *koinon* of those stationed in Rhamnous" (τὸ | [κ]οινὸν τῶν Ῥαμνοῦντι ταττομένων, lines 3-4, cf. 34-35 and 39-40); the resolution formula is "resolved by the Rhamnousioi and the other Athenians and all those living in Rhamnous" (δεδόχθαι Ῥαμνου|σίοις καὶ τοῖς [ἄλ]λοις Ἀθηναίοις καὶ τ[οῖ]ς οἰκοῦσιν ἐν Ῥαμνοῦν|τι πᾶσιν, lines 30-32; on the second καί here, see Pouilloux, *Forteresse*, p. 131); the summary formula is "those of the citizens living in Rhamnous" ([οἱ οἰ]κοῦντες | τῶν πολιτῶν | Ῥαμνοῦντι, lines 48-50); and the inscription of the two stelai—a provision unique in itself, for Rhamnous (though cf. the Aixonian lease IG II²2492, lines 20ff.)—is charged jointly to the (military) *epimelētai* and the Rhamnousian demarch (lines 36-38).

As with Eleusis, any general principles which may at the time have been seen to govern which body enacted which decree are now unfathomable. For example, why the demesmen alone honored a demarch (*if* that is what the honorand in IG II²1217 had been; see Pouilloux's commentary to *Forteresse*, no. 6) may be understandable, but it is far less clear why they alone should honor a garrison commander (SEG 22.120).

3. *Sounion*. (A *teichos* there: [Scylax] *Periplous* 57. Fortification in 412: Thuc. 8.4. For the site, see in brief I. M. Shear in *Princeton Encyclopedia*, pp. 854-855.) On present evidence—which is admittedly less than that for Eleusis and, especially, Rhamnous—it would seem that the relationship between the demesmen of Sounion and the troops stationed there from time to time was one of symbiosis, not (even partial) coalescence. A possible reason for this is the fact that, whereas at Eleusis and Rhamnous the deme center lay within part of the fortifications themselves, at Sounion the two were near but distinct (cf. McCredie, pp. 91-92). It

may also be relevant to note that Sounion itself was a far smaller deme than either Rhamnous or, particularly, Eleusis. At all events, from third-century Sounion we have neither "pure" deme decrees (to follow IG II²1180) nor deme-plus-garrison decrees, but simply decrees of troops: IG II²1270 (SEG 25.151), 1281 (SEG 25.152), 1300, 1302, and 1308. (Kirchner's restoration of τὸν δήμαρ]χον in line 12 of 1300 is dubious; see Pouilloux, *Forteresse*, p. 132.) Where the status of the proposers is known (1270 and 1281), they are not Sounieis. (The fragmentary IG II²1260, from the late *fourth* century, is similarly classified in the Corpus; however, what remains of it is equally consistent with its being a deme decree, and I have included it as such in Appendix 3.)

PROSOPOGRAPHY

———————— ✳ ————————

A list of all known *dēmotai* would amount to little less than one of all known Athenians. My purpose here is simply to provide a prosopographical resource for the investigations pursued throughout this book (but chiefly in Chapters 8 and 10) by cataloguing men—and a few women—who are named in the demes' documents or otherwise attested as active in a deme context. Demarchs (**1-50**) and others (**51-368**) are listed separately; and honorands in deme decrees are honored in their own deme unless otherwise indicated.

A departure from the normal practice in such prosopographies (e.g. Davies, *Families*) is the presentation of the featured names in English transliteration rather than in Greek; this is so as not to deter the Greekless reader from venturing into this part of the book. Square brackets within these and other names given in English serve the usual purpose of indicating letters no longer preserved; but the epigraphists' underdot for a letter imperfectly preserved (e.g. ε̣) has been represented by a preceding question mark (?e).

I. Demarchs

?ACHARNAI (**1**)

1   [. .⁴. .]*menes*. IG II²1206, line 18; late fourth century.

AGRYLE (**2**)

2   [. . . ? . . .]. Walbank, "Confiscation," p. 80; 402/1.

AIXONE (**3-6**)

3   *Demosthenes* (PA 3583). IG II²2492, lines 21-22; 345/4.
4   *Dorotheos* (PA 4601). IG II²1198, lines 15-16 and 20; 326/5.
           Surely to be identified with Dor[– –] in IG II²1196, line 4: see
           Whitehead, "Demarchs," pp. 38-39.
5   *Hegesileos* (PA 6285 *and* 6337, with different spellings). IG
           II²1202, lines 13-14 and 20, and *AM* 66, 1941, pp. 218-219,
           no. 1, line 9; 313/2.

6 *Philotheros* (PA 14502). IG II²1197, line 20; ca. 330. As the name is relatively rare, he is doubtless also the Φιλοθή[ρου of line 5, that is, father of 100, one of the honorands (apparently *syndikoi*). Probably also to be identified with the Philotheros of the epitaph IG II²13042-3 (mid fourth century, from Aixone/Glyphada), who is depicted holding hands with Chairippe, presumably his wife.

— (PA 10620, Neaichmos the supposed demarch of Aixone in IG II²1199, line 16, is actually PA 10619, the Athenian eponymous archon of 320/19: see Whitehead, "Demarchs," pp. 37-38.)

?ANAGYROUS (7)

7 *Theophilos* O[– – –] (PA 7111). IG II²2852, a dedication after serving as demarch (δημαρχήσας ἀνέθηκεν); late fourth or early third century. Its discovery at Vari would indicate that the deme is Anagyrous; and if so he is perhaps to be identified with PA 7127, Theophilos ʼΑ⟨να⟩γυρά(σιος), one of the *lampadēphoroi*-ephebes of tribe I Erechtheis in IG II²3105 (Pouilloux, *Forteresse*, no. 2 *bis*), line 44.

APHIDNA (8)

8 *Platon*. Walbank, "Confiscation," p. 85; 402/1.

ATHMONON (9)

9 *Po*[– –]. IG II²1203, line 20; 325/4.

ELEUSIS (10-14)

10 *Euthydemos* (II) *Moirokleous* (PA 5534, cf. 5535). Honorand (*qua* demarch) in *Hesp.* 8, 1939, pp. 177-180; ca. 300. Also honored by the dedication *AE* 1971, pp. 126-127, no. 21, of the same date. Identified by J. C. Threpsiades (*Hesp. loc. cit.*) with PA 5518, the Euthydemos who is *paredros* of the *basileus* in IG II²1230, lines 3-4, from the end of the fourth century. Threpsiades' stemma developed Kirchner's notes to IG II²2845 and is in turn followed, with modifications, by K. Clinton, *AE loc. cit.*; see also S. N. Coumanoudis and D. C. Gofas, *REG* 91, 1978, p. 295. The demarch's grandfather, Euthydemos (I), is the priest of Asklepios PA 5533 (IG II²47, lines 23-32; IG II²4962, lines 11-13, dated 355/4 by W. K. Pritchett and B. D. Meritt, *The Chronology of Hellenistic Athens*, Cambridge, Mass., 1940, pp. 74-75). For the demarch's father,

Moirokles Euthydemou (I), see **163**; for his younger brother
Kallippos Moirokleous (PA 8059)—ambassador, general, and
synedros in the first half of the third century—see Threpsiades
loc. cit.

11   *Gnathis* (II) *Timokedous* (II) (PA 3048, cf. 3049 with
stemma). IG II²1186, line 19; mid fourth century. His grandfather Gnathis (I) Timokedous (I) recorded a choregic victory
at the rural Dionysia of 402/1: see **160**. His father Timokedes
(II) Gnathidos (I), postulated by Kirchner's stemma, is one of
three crowned taxiarchs of 356/5: *Hesp*. 32, 1963, pp. 36-
37, no. 33. His son Timokedes (III) Gnathidos (II) proposed
a deme decree in the late fourth century: see **169**. Timokedes
Timasiou (**170**) is perhaps a relative.

12   *Isarchos* (PA 7686). IG II²1193, lines 14-15 and 29; late fourth
century.

13   *Onetor* (*Aiso[nos]*) (PA 11467). IG II²1191, line 1; 321/0 or
318/7 (see Appendix 3, no. 30). Restored by Kirchner as the
proposer of the deme decree IG II²1192 (line 1), late fourth
century: Ὀνήτ]ωϱ Αἴσω[νος. (1191 gives the *nomen* only.)

14   *Pamphilos Archontos* (PA 11542). Honorand (*qua* demarch)
in both the city decree and the deme decree on IG II²949;
165/4.

HALAI AIXONIDES (**15-16**)

15   *[N]ikostr[a]tos.* IG II²1175, line 22; ca. 360. (Not in PA, since
IG II 572 did not read a proper name here.) Wrongly identified
in *Agora 15*, index, with Nikostratos Nikom[– –] (Halaieus),
bouleutēs or deputy in ca. 370, who is from Halai Araphenides; see Whitehead, "Demarchs," pp. 39-40 (and
J. S. Traill in *Classical Contributions: studies . . . M. F.
McGregor*, Locust Valley, New York, 1981, p. 168, n. 32).
He might still, however, be Nikostratos Nikeratou Halaieus
(IG II²5509, grave monument from Spata, mid fourth century)
and/or the twice syntrierarch Nikostratos Halaieus (PA
11019: IG II²1605, lines 38-39, and 1622, line 266), whose
assignation to Halai Araphenides by Davies, *Families*, pp.
410-411, is based on a misconception (see Whitehead, *loc.
cit.*). PA 11082, Nikochares Nikostratou in the Kekropid catalog IG II²2385, line 48, from the mid fourth century, is
perhaps the demarch's son.

16   *Phi[leriphos A]ische[o]u.* IG II²1598, lines 37-38 (*rationes
centesimarum*); ?320s. Restored by Kirchner as Phi[lippos] on

the strength of lines 40-41, i.e. demarch and purchaser the same man. This is quite possible—see Davies, *Families*, pp. 537-538—but Phi[leriphos] was the very attractive suggestion of W. Peek, *AM* 67, 1942, pp. 19-20 (= SEG 21.573, lines 37-38), to make the demarch the son of **180**. For a possible relative and homonym from the same period (though a different tribe), see Davies, *Families*, p. 535, on IG II²3047.

HALAI ARAPHENIDES (17)

17   A[rchi]as. AE 1925-1926, pp. 168-177, lines 11-12 and 18; mid fourth century. The name is a common one, but he is surely PA 2459, that is, father of PA 1404, Apollodoros Archiou, *bouleutēs* for Halai Araphenides in 341/0 (*Agora 15*, no. 38, line 51). See also PA 6852.

HALIMOUS (18-22)

18   *Antiphilos* (PA 1266). Demosth. 57.26 and 60; held office before 346/5. His son is **19** (q.v.).

19   *Euboulides Antiphilou* (PA 5323). Demosth. 57.8 and passim; demarch (and *bouleutēs*) in 346/5. His father is **18**—our only example of father and son serving as demarch. A "best-born" family: Demosth. 57.46-48, esp. 48 (pre-selected for a priesthood of Herakles; but on the "best-born" criterion, see Chap. 7, n. 25). Proposed the city honorific decree IG II²218 (line 6) in 345. In the same year or earlier, brought an abortive *graphē asebeias* against "the sister of Lakedaimonios" (Demosth. 57.8), i.e., Plangon, daughter of Promachos of Alopeke, on whom see J. C. Threpsiades, *Polemon 5*, 1952-1953, pp. 59-63 (SEG 12.193).

20   *Euxitheos Thoukritou* (PA 5902; stemma in Davies, *Families*, between pp. 94 and 95; corrections to it proposed by W. K. Lacey, *CQ* 30, 1980, pp. 57-58). Demosth. 57.63-64 (and passim); held office before 346/5. Honored, presumably *qua* demarch, by his deme: Demosth. 57.64. Also held other sortitive deme offices (Demosth. 57.48) and was pre-selected for a "best-born" priesthood of Herakles (Demosth. 57.46-48 and 62; but on the "best-born" criterion, see Chap. 7, n. 25; and note the argument of A. Andrewes, *JHS* 81, 1961, pp. 6-8, that the family did not belong to a *genos*). Elected phratriarch: Demosth. 57.23. His father Thoukritos likewise held sortitive deme offices (Demosth. 57.25-26), though apparently not the demarchy. Tho(u)kritos Kephisodoro(u), Halimousian

bouleutēs in ?370/69 (*Agora 15*, no. 13, lines 15-16) should
be a relative: Davies, *Families*, p. 95.

21   *Ischyrias.* SEG 2.7, line 6; between 330 and 325 (and pre-
            sumably immediately preceding **22**). As the name is relatively
            rare he might, as Hondius suggested, be PA 7730, the subject
            of Lycurgus' speech *Against Ischyrias*—and/or (it may be
            added) the Ischyrias who made a dedication in the mid fourth
            century (IG II²4382).

22   *Kybernis.* SEG 2.7, line 20; between 330 and 325 (and pre-
            sumably immediately following **21**). He had two noteworthy
            descendants (see under PA 8918): Kybernis K[yd]iou Hali-
            mousios proposed the city decree IG II²680 in the mid 240s;
            and the Athenian Kydias who died fighting the Gauls at Ther-
            mopylai in 279 (Paus. 10.21.5) was reasonably identified by
            S. A. Koumanoudes as his father.

IKARION (23-32)

23-28   (Six lost names): IG I³253, lines 1, 5, 8, 11, 15, 21; third
            quarter of the fifth century.

29   *Nikon* (PA 11110). Honorand (*qua* demarch) in IG II²1178,
            lines 2 and 5; before the middle of the fourth century.

30   *Thoukydides.* SEG 22.117, lines 6-7; ca. 330 (and the year
            after **31**, whom the decree honors). To be identified with PA
            7273, *diaitētēs* in ca. 330 (IG II²2409, lines 17-18; for the
            date, see D. M. Lewis, *ABSA 50*, 1955, pp. 27-30). It is plau-
            sibly suggested in *Agora 15*, index, that two of the Ikarian
            bouleutai of 304/3, Χ[αρ]ί[δ]ημος Θουκυδίδου (*Agora 15*,
            no. 61, line 47) and [Θου]κυδίδης Ἀντ[ι]δώρ[ο]υ (ibid., line
            44) were respectively son and nephew of the demarch.

31   [– –]*aios* [*Sos*]*igenous.* Honorand (*qua* demarch) in SEG
            22.117, lines 1 and 7; ca. 330 (and the year before **30**). A
            possible relative is Peithon Sosigenous (*sc.* Ikarieus), one of
            the four *pythaistai* in IG II²2816 (first half of the fourth
            century).

32   [. . . . .¹⁰ . . . .]. Honorand (*qua* demarch) in IG II²1179, line
            3; mid fourth century.

KERAMEIS (33)

33   [. . . .?. . . .]. Walbank, "Confiscation," p. 76; 402/1.

MELITE (34)

34   *Euthydomos* (PA 5566). IG II²2394, line 2; 340/39 or 313/2
            (see Appendix 3, no. 78). Three other Meliteis called Euthy-

domos are attested by this same document (see **286** and **287**) but there are no positive grounds for identifying the demarch with any of them. If he is indeed none of them—as Kirchner evidently assumed when allocating the PA numbers—he might then conceivably be PA 5573, Euthydomos Demetriou Meliteus, co-contractor in 347/6 with Philon of Eleusis to build the *skeuothēkē* (IG II²1668, line 3) and one of a board of ten magistrates who dedicated on IG II²2825 (line 7) in the mid fourth century; but as the name was so common in this deme (note also PA 5571, the *xylourgos* in IG I³475, line 247) all such links are quite uncertain.

OINOE (of Aiantis) (35)

35   *Mnesarchide*[s]. IG II²1594, line 51 (*rationes centesimarum*); ?320s.

OION (36)

36   *Nothippos*. Walbank, "Confiscation," p. 83; 402/1.

PEIRAIEUS (37)

37   *Phrynion* (PA 15022). IG II²2498, line 1; 321/0.

PHALERON (38)

38   [*M*]*enippos*. Walbank, "Confiscation," p. 75; 402/1.

RHAMNOUS (39-44)

39   *Autokleides*. IG I³248, lines 1-2; ca. 450-440.
40   *Demophanes*. IG I³248, line 32; ca. 450-440. A likely descendant and homonym was syntrierarch between 356 and 346/5 (IG II²1622, line 676): Davies, *Families*, p. 140.
41   *Euainetos*. IG I³248, line 27; ca. 450-440. A possible descendant is Αἰσχρ⟨ί⟩ων Εὐαινέτου Ῥα[μνούσιος, *grammateus* in 196/5 (*Agora 15*, no. 166, line 2).
42   *Kleochares Kleodoridou*. Honorand in IG II²1217, *qua* demarch *if* Pouilloux (*Forteresse*, no. 6) is right to restore the word in the lost second half of line 2; 263/2 or 262/1 (Athenian eponymous archonship of Antipatros). A member of a family prominent in third-century Rhamnous, the main stemma of which can be reconstructed from identifications proposed in *Agora 15*, index: the father of **42** is Kleodorides Strombichidous, *bouleutēs* in 281/0 (*Agora 15*, no. 72, line 199); his younger brother Strombichos Kleodoridou is on a deme commission in 236/5 (see **331**); and his son Kleodorides Kleo-

charou(s) has a grave monument of the mid third century (SEG 21.918). Note also [Kl]eochares Teisonid[ou] (325), who proposed this decree in honor of his relative the (?)demarch; and Antiphilos Kleocharous, *bouleutēs* in 303/2 (*Agora 15*, no. 62, line 282; and cf. the statue base *AE* 1979, p. 71, no. 27), reasonably suggested in *Agora 15*, index, as an ancestor of them both.

43   *Mnesiptolemos.* IG I³248, lines 15-16; ca. 450-440.

44   *Nausimenes.* IG I³248, line 20; ca. 450-440.

SKAMBONIDAI (45)

45   *Archedemo[s].* Walbank, "Confiscation," p. 85 (with 87-88 on the attribution to this deme); 402/1.

?SOUNION (46)

46   *Prokles* (PA 12237). IG II²1672, line 273; 329/8. On Prokles as demarch of Sounion, not Oropos, see Whitehead, "Demarchs," pp. 40-42. A descendant, [. . . .]ikles Prokleous, was *bouleutēs* after 255 (*Agora 15*, no. 88, line 8); this seems too long a gap for them to be father and son.

SPHETTOS (47-48)

47   *A[nt]ipa[tros].* IG II²1601, line 17 (*rationes centesimarum*), as restored by D. M. Lewis in M. I. Finley, ed., *Problèmes de la terre en Grèce ancienne*, Paris and The Hague, 1973, p. 192, n. 2; ?320s. Lewis suggests a link ("cf.") with PA 1178, Antipatros the father of the Sphettian *bouleutēs* of 281/0, Phoxias (PA 14944: *Agora 15*, no. 72, line 17). Note also Ἀντίπατ⟨ρ⟩ος Κτησ⟨ι⟩βί⟨ο⟩υ of Sphettos, a third-century addition to the mid fourth-century funerary *lekythos* IG II²7504, which makes the demarch a likely collateral relative of the well-known Xenokles (340); see Davies, *Families*, pp. 414-415.

48   [. . . . ? . . . .]. Walbank, "Confiscation," p. 76; 402/1.

TEITHRAS (49)

49   *Euthippos.* SEG 24.151, line 1; mid fourth century. Surely to be identified with Euthippos the honorand (though not explicitly *qua* demarch) in SEG 24.153, lines 1 and 4, from the same period.

DEME UNKNOWN (*perhaps* Acharnai: see Appendix 3, no. 130) (50)

50   [. . . .]*kles Kalli*[– –]. IG II²1173, lines 4-5; before the middle of the fourth century. But the certainty that he is the honorand in this decree is greater than that of the restoration of [δήμαρχο]|ς in lines 2-3.

II. Others

ACHARNAI (51-65)

51   *Antiphanes E?p*[– –]. IG II²3104, line 3; victorious *kōmarchos* in either 340/39 or 313/2 (Athenian eponymous archonship of Theophrastos). The earlier date is perhaps preferable in view of the grave monument (IG II²5783) of PA 976, the boy Antias Antiphanous Acharneus, depicted in the arms of his mother Aristolea; Möbius dated the stele 340-317, so Antiphanes *floruit* in the mid fourth century (W. K. Pritchett, *Hesp.* Suppl. 8, 1949, p. 278).

52   [*Dem*]*os*[*t*]*rato*[*s*]. IG II²3106; father of victorious *chorēgos* in dithyramb and tragedy at the rural Dionysia; fourth century.

53   *Dion Dionos.* Tod, no. 204, lines 1-2; priest of Ares and Athena Areia, who dedicated the stele bearing the ephebic oath; fourth century.

54   *Diopeithes Diodoro(u)* IG II²3092, line 2; *chorēgos* (with **61**) at the rural Dionysia; early fourth century. Linked ("cf.") by Kirchner *ad loc.* with PA 4316, the Acharnian S[– – –] Diopeithous who was one of a group of Athenian (?)soldiers in Euboia in (?)323: *BCH* 15, 1891, pp. 406-408, no. 7.

55   *Diotimos* (PA 4381, cf. 4382-4383). Lysias 31.16; one of a group of men elected (in 404/3) "to arm the demesmen from the funds contributed." His son is **63**. Two homonyms may be related: Diotimos Diomnestou Acha[rneus], epitaph of the second half of the fourth century (IG II²5792); Diotimos Achar(neus), *symproedros* in a decree of Athenian cleruchs on Samos, 346/5 (C. Michel, *Recueil d'inscriptions grecques*, Brussels, 1900, no. 832). The latter is identified by M. Crosby, *Hesp.* 19, 1950, p. 218, as Diotimos Mnesistrato(u) Achar[in a mining lease of the mid fourth century (ibid., pp. 210-218, no. 5); this, as she noted, creates a link with another prominent Acharnian family (see **61**).

56   *Epikydes Philokydou(s)* (PA 4921). *AM* 67, 1942, pp. 7-8,
            no. 5, lines 11-12; honored by Gargettos; second half of the
            fourth century. He has his demotic in IG II²1588 (lines 3, 4,
            8), a mining lease datable to 320/19 (M. Crosby, *Hesp.* 19,
            1950, p. 281). His father Philokydes is PA 14646, *bouleutēs*
            in 360/59 (*Agora 15*, no. 17, line 59). Osborne, *Demos*, pp.
            123-124.

57   *Hippotherides.* IG I³971 (altar of Herakles, Menidi) and *Hesp.*
            4, 1935, p. 148, no. 1 (= *Dedications*, no. 246); dedicated
            twice, ca. 500.

58   *Kalliteles Stesiou.* Proposer of SEG 21.519 (line 2); shortly
            after the middle of the fourth century. Reasonably identified
            by L. Robert in the *editio princeps* as PA 8206, Kalliteles the
            Acharnian *bouleutēs* of 360/59 (*Agora 15*, no. 17, line 56).

59   *Leon.* SEG 21.519, line 1; priest (of Ares and Athena Areia)
            used as dating formula; shortly after the middle of the fourth
            century.

60   *Mnesimachos Mnesistrato(u)* (PA 10337). IG II²3092, line 4;
            chorēgos (with **63**) at the rural Dionysia; early fourth century.
            Evidently the son of **61**, q.v.

61   *Mnesistratos Misgonos* (PA 10368). IG II²3092, line 1; *cho-
            rēgos* (with **54**) at the rural Dionysia; early fourth century.
            Evidently the father of **60**. In notes *apud* IG II²2825 and 3092
            Kirchner himself corrected the simple four-generation stemma
            which he had given at PA 10337 (= **60**), i.e., Misgon/Mne-
            sistratos (I)/Mnesimachos/Mnesistratos (II): the four genera-
            tions should remain, ending with Mnesistratos (II)
            Mnesimachou the member of a board of magistrates in the
            mid fourth century (IG II²2825, line 6); however, two Mne-
            simachoi must be differentiated, (*a*) **60** and (*b*) *anepsiadous*
            of the magistrate, *diaitētēs* in 325/4 (IG II²1926, line 96), and
            dedicator to Asklepios on IG II²4402. Another son of **61**
            appears on a mining lease of the mid fourth century; see under
            55.

62   *Philokedes Aristarchou* (PA 14508). IG II²1204, lines 3-4 and
            8-10; honored by Coastal Lamptrai (and evidently resident
            there); late fourth century. Areiopagite—thus ex-archon—in
            a city decree of 305/4 (IG II²1492, line 128). A possible relative
            is Aristarchos Demokleous Achar(neus), a member of the
            genos of the Salaminioi in 363/2: *Hesp.* 7, 1938, p. 4, line
            77, with W. S. Ferguson's note *ad loc.* (p. 14).

63   *Theotimos Diotimo(u)* (PA 7058). IG II²3092, line 5; *chorēgos* (with 60) at the rural Dionysia; early fourth century. His father is 55.

64   [– – – –]*okleous* (i.e., end of patronymic only). Proposer of IG II²1207 (line 1); ?late fourth century.

65   [. . . ? . . .]. IG II²1207, lines 3-4; honored as priestess of Athena Hippia; ?late fourth century.

AIGILIA (66-68)

66   *Kleostratos Timostheno(u)s* (PA 8623). IG II²3096, line 3; dedicated to Dionysos as victorious *chorēgos* (with his father 68 and elder brother 67) at the rural Dionysia; before the middle of the fourth century. To be identified with the *grammateus* κατὰ πρυτανείαν of 343/2: IG II²223C (= *Agora 15*, no. 34), lines 1-2; 224, line 2; 225, line 4.

67   *Meixonides Timostheno(u)s* (PA 9761). IG II²3096, line 2; dedicated to Dionysos as victorious *chorēgos* (with his father 68 and younger brother 66) at the rural Dionysia; before the middle of the fourth century.

68   [*Timo*]*sthenes Meixonido(u)* (PA 13810). IG II²3096, line 1; dedicated to Dionysos as victorious *chorēgos* (with his sons 66 and 67) at the rural Dionysia; before the middle of the fourth century. Friend and partner of Phormion in [Demosth.] 49.31-32, which gives the demotic.

AITHALIDAI (69)

69   *Endios Aischeou.* IG II²3467, lines 5-6; honored as (military) *epimelētēs* by "Rhamnousioi and those of the citizens living in Rhamnous;" ?ca.256/5. (For the date, see Pouilloux, *Forteresse*, p. 120, on his no. 7, where Endios is one of two men honored by the *isoteleis* stationed in Rhamnous.)

AIXONE (70-102)

70   *Anthias* (PA 954). IG II²2492, line 42; mentioned in a decree concerning a land lease; 345/4.

71   *Anticharmos Nausonos* (PA 1318). IG II²1199, lines 8-9; honored as one of four *hieropoioi* (with 72, 94, and 99); 320/19. His father is 93, his brother 87; and for a possible son see 101.

72   *Aristokles Kalliphontos* (PA 1857). IG II²1199, lines 10-11; honored as one of four *hieropoioi* (with 71, 94, and 99); 320/19. His father Kalliphon and uncle Aristokles were

crowned by Athenian cleruchs on Imbros in 352/1: *BCH* 18, 1894, pp. 505-507, no. 1.

73   *Aristokrates Aristophanou(s)* (PA 1909). Proposer of IG II²1201 (line 2), in honor of Demetrios of Phaleron (see **309**); and himself honored as *?chorēgos* (with **86**) in IG II²1202 (line 6), of 313/2.

74   *Auteas Autokleous* (PA 2699). IG II²2492, lines 2 and 33; leased land from the deme, with his father **75**, in 345/4. Also honored as *chorēgos* (with **97**) in 313/2: *AM* 66, 1941, pp. 218-219, no. 1, lines 1-2.

75   *Autokles Auteou* (PA 2721). IG II²2492, lines 2 and 33; leased land from the deme, with his son **74**, in 345/4. A likely relative is Autokles Timeou Aixone(us), Treasurer of the Goddess in 350/49 (IG II²1436, line 2).

76   *Charikles* (PA 15408). IG II²1199, lines 20-21; honored as herald; 320/19.

77   *Demokrates Euphiletou* (PA 3518). IG II²1198, lines 4-5; honored as *chorēgos* (with **84**); 326/5. Also named on a curse-tablet in the late 320s: see Davies, *Families*, p. 360, with full discussion (359-360) of the various branches of this well-known (e.g. from Plato's *Lysis*) and affluent family; see also **85**.

78   *Eteokles Skaonos* (PA 5218). Proposer of IG II²2492, lines 31-47 (at 31-32); 345/4. Also chosen by it (line 47) as one of an *ad hoc* committee of three (with **83** and **93**). As the name is relatively rare he might be the Eteokle[s – –] who manumits a slave in IG II²1553, lines 2-4.

79   *Euxenides Kallippou* (PA 5882). IG II²1197, lines 3-4; honored as *?syndikos*; ca. 330. His name is restored there by M. Mitsos from the fuller version in the catalog IG II²1927, lines 48-49: see SEG 25.144.

80   *Glaukides Sosippou* (PA 2973). Proposer of two deme decrees in 313/2: IG II²1202 (lines 2-3) and *AM* 66, 1941, pp. 218-219, no. 1 (line 1). The grave monument of his father S?osipp[o]s Glaukid[ou] Aixoneus, from the second half of the fourth century, was found at Aixone/Glyphada itself (SEG 18.97); and his (presumably younger) brother Smikythos Sosippou is attested as a *hippeus* in ca. 323 (IG II²1955, line 18).

81   *Glaukon Kallikratous* (PA 3021). IG II²1200, lines 5-6; honored as *chorēgos* (with **90**); 317/6. His father is **86**.

82   *Go[rg. . . . .[11]. . . . .]* (including patronymic). IG II²1197, line 8; honored as *?syndikos*; ca. 330.

83   *Hagnotheos* (PA 149). IG II²2492, lines 46-47; chosen as one of an *ad hoc* committee of three (with **78** and **93**); 345/4.

84   *Hegesias Lysistratou* (PA 6316). IG II²1198, lines 5-6; honored as *chorēgos* (with **77**); 326/5. Kirchner cited Nakion Ἡγησίο Αἰξω(νέως), on a grave monument of the first half of the fourth century (IG II²5452) found in Peiraieus; she is perhaps the aunt of **84**.

85   *Kallias Kalliadou* (PA 7848). IG II²1199, lines 23-24; honored as priest of the Herakleidai; 320/19. The patronymic comes from his grave monument, IG II²5430. Probably a member of the same rich and active family as **77**; see Davies, *Families*, pp. 360-361, with comments on several certain or possible relatives, including **102**.

86   *Kallikrates Glaukonos* (PA 7952). IG II²1202, lines 5-6; honored as *?chorēgos* (with **73**); 313/2. Also proposer of the Kekropid tribal decree in praise of the ephebes of 334/3 (IG II²1156, lines 26-35). His son is **81**.

87   *Kallisthenes Nausonos* (PA 8096). IG II²1199, lines 25-26; honored as cult archon; 320/19. His father is **93**, his brother **71**; and for a possible nephew, see **101**.

88   *Kimon* (PA 8427). IG II²1199, line 19; honored as cult *sōphronistēs*; 320/19. See further under **92**.

89   *Laches Melanopou* (PA 9020, cf. 9019 with stemma). IG II²1197, line 14; the named member of a group of *syndikoi*-honorands mentioned in a deme decree of ca. 330. The patronymic is given by Demosth. *Ep.* 3.24-26. He is possibly the Lach[es] who made a dedication in ca. 330: see B. D. Meritt, *Hesp.* 16, 1947, p. 152, no. 44. An important and interesting family which includes the fifth-century *stratēgos*; see PA 9017-9020.

90   *Leontios Dionos* (PA 9033). IG II²1200, lines 4-5; honored as *chorēgos* (with **81**); 317/6. Diodoros Dionos Aix(oneus), whose grave monument IG II²5418 was dated 340-317 by Möbius, is presumably his brother.

91   *Leophilos Eudikou* (PA 9163). IG II²1197, lines 8-9; honored as *?syndikos*; ca. 330. He also appears in the catalog of [*diaitē?*]*tai* IG II²1927 (on which see under Appendix 3, no. 78), lines 50-51.

92   *Megalexis* (PA 9704). IG II²1199, lines 19-20; honored as cult *sōphronistēs*; 320/19. Perhaps in fact an error for Metalexis:

thus S. N. Koumanoudes, *REG* 73, 1960, p. 92, comparing
Στρατοκλέης (Μ)εταλήξιδος of Steiria in the bouleutic list
(from the first half of the fourth century) which he publishes
there, pp. 88-89, at 89, line 37 (= *Agora 15*, no. 10). But in
either case one may suspect here a faulty patronymic attaching
to the preceding name, Kimon (**88**); note that **98** has one.

93   *Nauson* (PA 10607 with stemma). IG II²2492, lines 46-47;
chosen as one of an *ad hoc* committee of three (with **78** and
83); 345/4. His sons are **71** and **87**; and for a possible grandson see **101**.

94   *Nearchos Chairigenous.* IG II²1199, line 9; honored as one
of four *hieropoioi* (with **71, 72,** and **99**); 320/19. (Not in PA
because the name was read differently for IG II: see PA 7804.)
His father Chairigenes was *bouleutēs* before the middle of the
fourth century: *Agora 15*, no. 16, line 11.

95   *Philaios Chremetos* (PA 14218). Proposer of IG II²1199 (line
1); 320/19. His brother is **96**. As the name Chremes is rare,
their father has been correctly identified as PA 15568, the
Athenian eponymous archon of 326/5.

96   *Philoktemon Chremetos* (PA 14640). Proposer of two deme
decrees: IG II²1198 (line 1), of 326/5, and IG II²1200 (line
1), of 317/6. His brother is **95**. As the name Chremes is rare,
their father has been correctly identified as PA 15568, the
Athenian eponymous archon of 326/5.

97   *Philoxenides Philippou.* AM 66, 1941, pp. 218-219, no. 1,
line 2; honored as *chorēgos* (with **74**); 313/2. His father was
plausibly identified by G. A. Stamires with PA 14384, the
Philippos of Aixone whose daughter Kallistomache married
Lykophron, youngest son of the statesman Lykourgos ([Plut.]
Vit. X Or. 843A; see Davies, *Families*, pp. 351-353), and who
also appears on the *horos* IG II²2752 (= Finley, *Land and
Credit*, no. 87) as creditor for a debt of one talent on a house,
stonemason's workshop, and yard.

98   *Pythodoros Pytheou* (PA 12409). IG II²1199, line 20; honored
as cult *sōphronistēs*; 320/19. Kirchner suggested an identification with PA 12408, the Pythodoros of Aixone mentioned
by Athen. 554E-F and Aelian *VH* 4.25, whose sons were
Kriton (PA 8822) and Thrasyllos (PA 7339, a madman who
imagined that all ships sailing into Peiraieus were his own).
Be that as it may, a likely brother for **98** is Euthykles
Py[theou?] Ai[xoneus], whose grave monument of the late

fourth century (SEG 12.169A) was found near Aixone/Gly-phada itself.

99   *Theodotos Aischronos* (PA 6787). IG II²1199, line 10; honored as one of four *hieropoioi* (with **71**, **72**, and **94**); 320/19. Also attested as ephebe in 334/3 (IG II²1156, line 18). His grandfather, as Kirchner saw, is PA 6786, Theo[d]otos of Aixone, curator of the dockyards in 362/1 (IG II²1622, lines 501-504).

100   [– – –]*s Philothe*[*rou*]. IG II²1197, lines 4-5; honored as ?*syndikos*; ca. 330. Doubtless son of the demarch **6**.

101   [– – –]*tes Antich*[*a* – –] (PA 1317). IG II²1197, lines 6-7; honored as ?*syndikos*; ca. 330. Claimed by Kirchner as the son of **71** (and grandson of **93**); the chronological fit is very tight, however.

102   [– – –] *Kalliou*. IG II²1197, lines 7-8; honored as ?*syndikos*; ca. 330. Perhaps the son, or else another relative, of **85**.

APHIDNA (**103-104**)

103   *Eukrates Exekiou* (PA 5752). IG II²2496, line 12 and passim; leased three buildings in Peiraieus from the Kytherioi; after the middle of the fourth century. His father is **104**.

104   *Exekias* (PA 4733). IG II²2496, lines 20-22; stood surety for his son **103**, for a lease of three buildings in Peiraieus from the Kytherioi; after the middle of the fourth century.

ATHMONON (**105-149**)

105   *Adeistos Antimachou* (PA 205). IG II²1156, lines 31-32, 41-42, 47-48, 58-59; Kekropid *sōphronistēs* of ephebes in 334/3, and honored for it not only by his tribe (lines 26-35) and the *boulē* (lines 36-44) but also by the demes of Eleusis (lines 45-51) and Athmonon itself (lines 52-63). He is perhaps unlikely to be the Adeistos who appears on a cavalry tablet of ca. 360-340 (*Hesp.* 46, 1977, p. 111, no. 16); but there is a possible uncle, of at least moderate wealth, in **111**.

106   *Agatharchides Euphorbo(u)*. SEG 24.197, line 11; financial contributor; early fourth century.

107   *Ameinias Theodoro(u)*. SEG 24.197, line 34; financial contributor; early fourth century. For a possible brother and, perhaps, grandfather, see **147-148**; and note also **146**.

108   *Andron Aischylo(u)*. SEG 24.197, line 31; financial contributor; early fourth century. A likely descendant is PA 918, Andron Andreou Athmoneus, who died in the early third

century (IG II²5323). A more speculative connection is suggested by IG II²417, line 25, recording the *eutaxia* liturgy of fifty drachmas contributed in ca. 330 by Charidemos Aischylou A[. . . .]εύς; *if* this Kekropid demotic is Ἀ[θμον]εύς rather than Α[ἰξων]εύς (see Davies, *Families*, pp. 6-7), Aischylos the adoptive father of Charidemos (see [Demosth.] 58.30-31) might well be a son of 108.

109   [*A*]*ntidoros Ergotelo(us)*. SEG 24.197, line 12; financial contributor; early fourth century.

110   *Antiphon Aristomachou* (PA 1289). IG II²1203, line 11; honored as one of the six *merarchai* of 325/4.

111   *Ariston Adeisto(u)*. SEG 24.197, line 33; financial contributor; early fourth century. As the name Adeistos is uncommon he may well be the uncle of 105; and his own father was perhaps either Adeistos Mi[. . .]k[− −] (IG II²10577, grave monument of the early fourth century) or PA 204, Adeistos Po[− −], of (?)liturgical census in ca. 380 (IG II²1928, line 21; see Davies, *Families*, p. 5, and, on this whole group of documents, *Wealth*, Appendix 1). In any event, note also the (late?) grave monument IG II²5357, with the name of Chariessa Ἀρίστωνος ἐξ Ἀθμονέων.

112   *Chairephanes Chariadou* (PA 15177). IG II²1203, lines 8-9; honored as one of the six *merarchai* of 325/4. An *eschatia* of his was sold in the *rationes centesimarum* accounts of the ?320s (*Hesp.* 9, 1940, pp. 330-332, no. 38, face A, line 1); and a grave monument with the names of his parents, himself, and his brother has been found at Porto Raphti (see G. Daux, *BCH* 87, 1963, p. 718).

113   *Chairias Pyrrhio(u)*. SEG 24.197, line 17; financial contributor; early fourth century.

114   *Derkylides Derkylo(u)* SEG 24.197, line 26; financial contributor; early fourth century.

115   *Diodotos Dionos*. SEG 24.197, line 36; financial contributor; early fourth century.

116   *Dionysophanes Dionysodorou* (PA 4305). IG II²1203, lines 9-10; honored as one of the six *merarchai* of 325/4. A possible late descendant is Dionysodoros, *bouleutēs* from Athmonon in 173/2 (*Agora* 15, no. 206, line 111); and note also Polykrateia, daughter of Dionysodoros of Athmonon, who commemorated her son's service as *basileus* in the third or second century (IG II²3863).

117　　*Eudemides Eudemo(u)*. SEG 24.197, line 7; financial contributor; early fourth century.

118　　⟨*E*⟩*udramon Parmonido(u)*. SEG 24.197, line 19; financial contributor; early fourth century.

119　　*Eukleides Eukleido(u)*. SEG 24.197, line 32; financial contributor; early fourth century.

120　　*Euphronios* (PA 6109). Proposer of IG II²1156, lines 52-63 (at 52), of 334/3; and *bouleutēs*, apparently, in ca. 300 (*Hesp.* 47, 1978, pp. 278-280, no. 7, line 18).

121　　⟨*E*⟩*uthydemos A*⟨*k*⟩*esandro(u)*. SEG 24.197, line 16; financial contributor; early fourth century. Presumably brother of **122**.

122　　*Euthydikos Akesandr*[o](*u*). SEG 24.197, line 4; financial contributor; early fourth century. Presumably brother of **121**.

123　　*Eutropos Koloio(u)*. SEG 24.197, line 5; financial contributor; early fourth century. As the name Koloios is otherwise attested only once in Attica, Dionysios Koloiou who dedicated to Athena in the late sixth century (IG I³617; *Dedications*, no. 148) is surely an ancestor.

124　　*Euxitheos Kallio(u)*. SEG 24.197, line 25; financial contributor; early fourth century.

125　　*Hierokles Archestrato(u)*. SEG 24.197, line 30; financial contributor; early fourth century. Soundly identified in the *editio princeps* (S. N. Koumanoudes) with PA 7485, *paredros* of the Hellenotamiai in 418/7 (IG I³370).

126　　[*I*]*sokles*. SEG 24.197, line 15; financial contributor; early fourth century.

127　　*Isotimides Smikrio(u)*. SEG 24.197, line 13; financial contributor; early fourth century. As the name Isotimides is otherwise attested only once in Attica, he is sure to be PA 7721, proposer of the *asebeia* decree of Andoc. 1.8 and 71-91; and PA 12741, Smikrias Athmoneus, *epistatēs* of the *proedroi* in 369/8 (*Inscr. Délos*, no. 88, line 4) is doubtless his son.

128　　*Kallias Apollodoro(u)*. SEG 24.197, line 22; financial contributor; early fourth century.

129　　*Kollytides Medimacho(u)*. SEG 24.197, line 18; financial contributor; early fourth century.

130　　*Kteson Eutycho(u)*. SEG 24.197, line 28; financial contributor; early fourth century.

131　　*Lykophron Lykiskou* (PA 9257). IG II²1203, lines 10-11; honored as one of the six *merarchai* of 325/4. His father must be at least a relative of and perhaps actually identical with Lykiskos Smikylionos of Athmonon, manumittor of three slaves in IG II²1564, lines 4-13; and he *might* also, as Sundwall thought (*Beiträge*, p. 57), be PA 9214, Lykiskos the Athenian eponymous archon of 344/3.

132   *Lysimachides Kallio(u)*. SEG 24.197, line 29; financial contributor; early fourth century. Identified in the *editio princeps* (S. N. Koumanoudes) as the son of PA 7828, the Kallias Lysimachidou who dedicated at Delphi—as a very young man, presumably—a horse from Persian War spoils.

133   *Lysip[po]s Lysiou* (PA 9557). IG II²1203, line 12; honored as one of the six *merarchai* of 325/4. Also in a Kekropid catalog of the mid fourth century or slightly later (IG II²2385, line 61). Probably a member of the wealthy family which includes PA 9430, the syntrierarch Lysikles Lysippou; see Davies, *Families*, pp. 355-356.

134   *Mnesimachos Salaiponos*. SEG 24.197, line 20; financial contributor; early fourth century.

135   *Nausistratos Strombonos*. SEG 24.197, line 23; financial contributor; early fourth century.

136   *Onesippos Onasantos*. SEG 24.197, line 8; financial contributor; early fourth century.

137   *Phalanthos Demetrio(u)*. SEG 24.197, line 10; financial contributor; early fourth century. Perhaps the father of **144**.

138   *Phileas Aichmokleido(u)*. SEG 24.197, line 9; financial contributor; early fourth century.

139   *Philistides*. SEG 24.197, line 15; financial contributor; early fourth century.

140   *Pistias Kothonos*. SEG 24.197, line 27; financial contributor; early fourth century. Probably a relative (?son; ?father) of **141**.

141   *Pistokles Pistio(u)*. SEG 24.197, line 21; financial contributor; early fourth century. Probably a relative (?son; ?father) of **140**, and of PA 11829, Pistokles Pisthetairo(u) Athmoneus, whose fourth-century grave monument (IG II²5347) was found near Amarousi itself.

142   *Protomachos Protio(u)*. SEG 24.197, line 18; financial contributor; early fourth century.

143   *Smikrion*. SEG 24.197, line 15; financial contributor; early fourth century.

144   *Smikythion Phalanthou* (PA 12767). IG II²1203, lines 12-13; honored as one of the six *merarchai* of 325/4. Perhaps the son of **137**. A homonymous descendant, PA 12768, is attested as ephebe in 237/6 (IG II²787, line 17).

145   *Sosibios Sosimeno(u)s*. SEG 24.197, line 37; financial con-
        tributor; early fourth century. His father Sosimenes is possibly
        one of the two (?)brothers whose grave monument (of between
        390 and 365) is IG II²5352.

146   *Theodorides Theodorou* (PA 6816-6817). Proposer of IG
        II²1203 (line 2), in or immediately after 325/4; also in a Ke-
        kropid catalog of the mid fourth century or slightly later (IG
        II²2385, line 25). From a wealthy family: see Davies, *Families*,
        pp. 488-489, on PA 12699. For the name Theodoros, cf. **107**
        and **147-148**; but it is too common to be certain that there
        is a connection.

147-148 *Thougeiton Theodoro(u)*. SEG 24.197, lines 6 and 35; finan-
        cial contributor; early fourth century. Since this is the only
        name appearing twice in this document, it is plausibly sug-
        gested in the *editio princeps* (S. N. Koumanoudes) that we
        have two homonyms here, the elder Thougeiton Theodoro(u)
        in line 6 and his grandsons Ameinias (**107**) and Thougeiton
        Theodoro(u) in lines 34-35. For the name Theodoros, cf. **146**;
        but it is too common to be certain that there is a connection.

149   *Thrasykles Thrasyllo(u)*. SEG 24.197, line 3; financial con-
        tributor; early fourth century.

CHOLLEIDAI (150)

150   *Kallidamas Kallimedontos* (PA 7902). IG II²1214, lines 1-2
        and passim; honored by Peiraieus (and evidently resident
        there); ?ca. 280 (see Appendix 3, no. 89). His father is surely
        Kallimedon Choll[eides], one of a board of ten officials hon-
        ored by the city in ca. 325: *Hesp.* 15, 1946, pp. 177-178, no.
        25 (SEG 14.112), line 8.

EITEA (of Antiochis) (151-152)

151   *Hippokles Demokleous*. SEG 28.102, lines 3-4 and 11-12;
        honored in 332/1. Doubtless to be identified with PA 7622,
        the father of the woman Samakion, whose grave monument
        of the second half of the fourth century (IG II²6007) was found
        in the Kerameikos.

152   *Timokrates Timokleous*. Proposer of SEG 28.102, line 2;
        332/1. A likely ancestor has been seen in PA 13733, Timokles
        Eiteaios, Treasurer of the Goddess in 423/2 (IG I³302, line
        30; 303, line 1; 369, line 36); but there are complications.
        A. E. Raubitschek restored [. . . .kr]ates Timo[kleo(u)s Ei-
        teai]os as one of the "Heroes of Phyle" (*Hesp.* 10, 1941, p.

288, line 37), and it has been found tempting to see him as
[Timokr]ates, son of the Treasurer and (?)grandfather of 152:
thus A. G. Kaloyeropoulou in the *editio princeps*, followed
by P. J. Bicknell, *Historia* 17, 1978, pp. 370-371 (SEG 28.45,
cf. 102). However, while the "Hero" is from Akamantid Eitea,
the deme decree stems almost certainly from Eitea in Antiochis
(references at Appendix 3, no. 19); so the Treasurer may be
either father of the "Hero" *or* an ancestor of 152, but not
both. Similarly, there is no means of assigning to the one Eitea
or the other PA 13727, Timokles Ei[teaios] the third-century
priest of Asklepios (IG II²1534, line 202; Sundwall, *Beiträge*,
p. 78 with n. 1).

EITEA (of Akamantis *or* Antiochis) (153)

153   *Menandros Teisandrou.* SEG 15.112, lines 3, 23, 35-37; hon-
           ored as trierarch by the Rhamnousioi "and those of the citi-
           zens living in Rhamnous"; 225/4.

ELEUSIS (154-173)

154   *Anaxandrides Timagoro(u)* (PA 802). IG II²3090, line 1; vic-
           torious *chorēgos* (with 160) at the rural Dionysia; 402/1.
           Kirchner reasonably surmised that his grandson is PA 801,
           [Anaxandr]ides [A]naxandrou Eleusi(nios) who manumitted
           a slave in ca. 330 (IG II²1571, line 3).

155   *Antiphanes Euxenidou.* SEG 28.103, lines 48-49; priest of
           Herakles-in-Akris; (mentioned in) 332/1. The patronymic re-
           sults from an identification, proposed in the *editio princeps*
           (*REG* 91, 1978, pp. 295-296), with one of four Eleusinioi
           crowned by their deme after the middle of the fourth century
           (IG II²2845, line 4; see also 156, 163, and 170). A further
           identification is suggested there with PA 1231, father of a man
           who served as [*diaitē?*]*tēs* (IG II²1927, lines 70-72: PA 5884,
           Euxenides Antiphanou(s) of Eleusis); however, the chrono-
           logical problems posed by that document—see under Appen-
           dix 3, no. 78—make PA 5884 just as probably the father as
           the son of 155.

156   *Antitheos Kall[i]kleous.* IG II²2845, line 2; one of four Eleu-
           sinioi crowned by their deme after the middle of the fourth
           century (see also 155, 163, and 170).

157   *Athenodoros Go[– – –].* IG II²3100; victorious *chorēgos* (in
           comedy) at the rural Dionysia; mid fourth century. A possible

homonymous descendant was *grammateus* in 125/4: *Agora 15*, nos. 249 (line 2) and 250 (lines 1-2).

158   *Epigenes*. Proposer of SEG 28.103, decree I (line 2); 332/1. In the *editio princeps*, identifications are prudently eschewed, but two homonyms noted (*REG* 91, 1978, p. 295, n. 6): Epigenes the Keryx in a city decree of 367 (Tod, no. 137, lines 11-13); and Epigenes Lysaniou Eleusinios (PA 4794), whose (?)fourth-century grave monument is IG II²6031.

159   *E[. . . . Gna]thonos* (PA 3050). Proposer of IG II²1188 (line 2); mid fourth century. His mother is perhaps PA 14755, Philoumene Γνάθωνος Ἐλευσινίο(υ), whose grave monument IG II²6054 was set up between 365 and 340.

160   *Gnathis* (I) *Timokedous* (I) (PA 3049, with stemma). IG II²3090, line 1; victorious *chorēgos* (with **154**) at the rural Dionysia; 402/1. Grandfather of the homonymous demarch **11**; see also **169** and **170**.

161   *Hieron A[– – –]*. IG II²3107; victorious *chorēgos*, presumably at the rural Dionysia; fourth century.

162   *Kallimachos Kallikratous* (PA 8013). Proposer of two honorific decrees for Thebans in the mid fourth century: IG II²1186, lines 1 and 36. His son or father, Kallikrates Ka[l]lima(chou), is named in a Hippothontid catalog after the middle of the fourth century (IG II²2393, lines 5-6).

163   *Moirokles Euthydemou* (I) (PA 10401). Proposer of IG II²1191 (lines 5-6) in 321/0 or 318/7 (see Appendix 3, no. 30); also one of four Eleusinioi crowned by their deme after the middle of the fourth century (IG II²2845, line 1; see also **155, 156**, and **170**); and honored again by the deme in 332/1 (SEG 28.103, lines 6-17). A member of an active Eleusinian family including his son the demarch **10** (q.v.); and note also Euthystratos Euthydemou, *bouleutēs* in 335/4, who, *if* he is an Eleusinios, may well be Moirokles' brother (*Agora 15*, no. 43, lines 182-183, with index). C. Ampolo, *PP* 34, 1979, pp. 176-178 (cf. *RFIC* 109, 1981, pp. 187-204) argues that to construe "Salaminios" in Harpoc., Μοιροκλῆς, as meaning "of the *genos* of the Salaminioi" removes the only obstacle in the way of identifying this Eleusinian Moirokles with PA 10400, the Moirokles active in city politics in the third quarter of the fourth century (Demosth. 19.293 and *Ep.* 3.16; Plut. *Demosth.* 23; Arrian *Anab.* 1.10.4; etc.). The economy of this has obvious attractions, though note the comments of K. Clinton, *AE* 1971, pp. 126-217, on Moirokles the tilemaker at-

tested in 330/29 (IG II²1672, lines 209-210), who may not even be an Athenian citizen.

164   *Philippos* (PA 14391). Proposer of IG II²1187 (line 1); 319/8.

165   *Philokomos Phalanthidou*. Proposer of SEG 28.103, decree II (line 18), and honored in decree I (lines 3, 10, 13); 332/1.

166   *Protias*. Proposer of IG II²1156, lines 45-51 (at 45); 334/3.

167   *Theoboulos [Theeboul]ou*. Proposer of *Hesp*. 8, 1939, pp. 177-180 (line 1); ca. 300. A homonymous descendant is *kosmētēs* of ephebes in 185/4: IG II²900, line 19, with *Hesp*. 15, 1946, p. 197.

168   *Theodotos Demokratou(s)* (PA 6791). Proposer of IG II²1299, lines 51-80 (at 51); after 236/5. Demokra[tes – –] the *bouleutēs* of 281/0, if an Eleusinios, is perhaps his father: *Agora 15*, no. 72, line 128, with index.

169   *Timokedes (III) Gnathidos (II)* (PA 13719). Proposer of IG II²1193 (line 1); late fourth century. Son of the demarch **11**, great-grandson of **160**; see also **170**.

170   *Timokedes Timasiou*. IG II²2845, line 3; one of four Eleusinioi crowned by their deme after the middle of the fourth century (see also **155**, **156**, and **163**). Probably related to the Timokedes/Gnathis family (**11**, **160**, **169**).

171   *Xenokrates Xenokratou(s)* (PA 11248). Proposer of IG II²949, lines 30ff. (at 30); 165/4. Previously the proposer of two city decrees in honor of *prytaneis: Agora 15*, nos. 180 (line 6) and 212 (line 6). The homonym who is *tamias* of the *prytaneis* in 135/4 is probably his son: *Agora 15*, no. 243, lines 24-25 and passim, with index.

172   *[– –]thes Nausi[st]ratou* (PA 10590). Proposer of IG II²1190 (line 2); after the middle of the fourth century. A possible descendant, Nausistratos of Eleusis, appears on a *horos* from Eleusis, archon-dated to 289/8, as creditor for a debt of two hundred drachmas on a house: *AD* 14, 1931-1932, p. 31, no. 4 (J.V.A. Fine, *Hesp*. Suppl. 9, 1951, no. 26; Finley, *Land and Credit*, no. 6).

173   [. . . . . . . .¹⁷. . . . .] (presumably name with patronymic). Proposer of IG II²1189 (line 4); 334/3.

EPIEIKIDAI (**174**)

174   *Kleonymos Kleemporou* (PA 8683). IG II²2837; honored (as city *thesmothetēs*) by various bodies including his deme; 329/8. Also in a Kekropid catalog of the mid fourth century or slightly later (IG II²2385, lines 80-81).

EPIKEPHISIA (175-176)

175 *Neokles*. IG II²1205, line 5; prosecuted by elected representatives of his deme; late fourth century (but see next entry).

176 *Pythodoros Philokleous* (PA 12419). Proposer of IG II²1205
(lines 1-2); late fourth century—but perhaps not *very* late, if
(as seems reasonable) he is to be identified with the homonym
from the same deme who in 343/2 stood surety for the lease
of sacred property of Zeus Olympios, apparently by his son
[.....]os: see M. B. Walbank, *Hesp.* 52, 1983, p. 106, fr. *d*,
lines 4-8, with commentary, ibid., pp. 128-129. There is no
good reason, *pace* Haussoullier, *Vie*, p. 101 with n. 2, to
identify or even connect him with 367.

ERCHIA (177)

177 *Tharrhias Tharrhiadou*. IG II²1181, line 2; (?)honored by Sounion; 331/0. (It is not certain, however, that the document is
a deme decree: see Appendix 3, no. 118.) His demotic results
from an identification with PA 6590, *bouleutēs* in 341/0
(*Agora 15*, no. 38, lines 5, 74, 82, 83).

?EUONYMON (178)

178 *Charinos Charonidou* (PA 15440). IG II²2829; honored, apparently as *bouleutēs*, not only by his fellow *prytaneis* but
also by his deme; mid fourth century. Also a dedicating *theō-
ros* in IG II²1642, line 36. For references to discussion, especially on the establishment of the demotic, see Appendix 3,
no. 131.

HAGNOUS (179)

179 *Derkylos Autokleous* (PA 3248-3249). IG II²1187, lines 1-2,
7-8, 13-14; honored by Eleusis; 319/8. For the date, and the
career of this politician and general, see F. W. Mitchel, *Hesp.*
33, 1964, pp. 337-351; Davies, *Families*, pp. 97-98.

HALAI AIXONIDES (180-212)

180 *Aischeas Phileriphou*. IG II²2820, line 14; dedicated as member of a deme commission concerned with (and honored for)
the erection of a statue of Aphrodite; ca. 360. Also (at about
the same time) honored as a member of another religious
commission of the deme: *AD* 11, 1927-1928, pp. 40-41, no.
4, line 11, as read by W. Peek, *AM* 67, 1942, pp. 9-10, no.
7. For his son, restored as demarch in the ?320s, see 16.

181   [Ar]geios Democharou[s] (PA 1583). IG II²2820, line 9; ded-
        icated as member of a deme commission concerned with (and
        honored for) the erection of a statue of Aphrodite; ca. 360.
        Restored by Kirchner at IG II²1743, line 9, as bouleutēs be-
        tween 390 and 360, but this is not followed in Agora 15, no.
        7, line 9: [− −ᶜᵃ¹²− −]αρος ('Αλ.).

182   [Ar]istomachos Astyana[ktos] (PA 1968). IG II²2820, line 10;
        dedicated as member of a deme commission concerned with
        (and honored for) the erection of a statue of Aphrodite; ca.
        360. Both he and his father appear on IG II²1593 (lines 2-5),
        land sales of the mid fourth century. His brother is doubtless
        183; and his (?)son Ast[yanax] Aristoma(chou) has been re-
        stored as a bouleutēs of 303/2 (Agora 15, no. 61, line 210).

183   [As]tydamas Astyanak[tos] (PA 2651). IG II²2820, line 12;
        dedicated as member of a deme commission concerned with
        (and honored for) the erection of a statue of Aphrodite; ca.
        360. His brother is doubtless 182 (q.v.).

184   Astyphilos Philagrou (I) (PA 2664, cf. 2662-2663). Proposer
        of IG II²1175 (line 1), ca. 360; and dedicated as (first-named)
        member of a deme commission concerned with (and honored
        for) the erection of a statue of Aphrodite (IG II²2820, line 5),
        also ca. 360. A well-attested individual in any case: bouleutēs
        between 390 and 360 (Agora 15, no. 7, line 7); proposer of
        city decrees in 377 (Tod, no. 122, line 3) and 373/2 (Hesp.
        3, 1934, pp. 2-3, no. 3, line 4); named on a curse-tablet
        (Wünsch 49) and in funerary inscriptions on marble lekythoi
        (IG II²5497-5499, second half of the fourth century). D. Pep-
        pas Delmousou, AAA 10, 1977, pp. 226-241 (SEG 27.25)
        discusses his prosperous and active family and their peribolos
        at Voula (cf. also R.S.J. Garland, ABSA 77, 1982, pp. 171-
        172), and gives a stemma beginning with Diokles (I) Halaieus
        "Kekropias" (graffito on a red-figure bell-krater of ca. 430:
        D. M. Robinson, AJA 35, 1931, p. 159) and reconstructible
        as far as Leon (II) Autokratous, grandson of Astyphilos'
        brother Leon (I) Philagrou; Leon (I), PA 9110, was bouleutēs
        in the same year as Astyphilos (Agora 15, no. 7, line 6) but
        predeceased him (IG II²11961-11962, funerary inscriptions
        on marble lekythoi, first half of the fourth century). Two
        possible sons of Leon (I) may be added to the stemma: Kleo-
        medon Leontos A[− − −] in IG II²1594 (rationes centesima-
        rum; ?320s), A, line 15; and now Philagros Le[ontos? Ha-
        lai(eus)?], guarantor for a lease of sacred property in 343/2

(M. B. Walbank, *Hesp*. 52, 1983, p. 108, fr. *a*, lines 4-5, with commentary at p. 132—where an additional but impossible identification is proposed with the Philagros of IG II²2824, lines 4-5 (see under **198**); Walbank retracts this, at my suggestion, ibid., pp. 427-428). For Astyphilos' son and nephew, see respectively **195** and **198**.

185   *Chaireas Chairiou* (PA 15098). IG II²2820, line 8; dedicated as member of a deme commission concerned with (and honored for) the erection of a statue of Aphrodite; ca. 360. The grave monument IG II²5525 reveals that his daughter Chairelea married **189**, eldest son of **190**; cf. Davies, *Families*, pp. 197-198.

186   *[Eu]klees Eukleidou* (PA 5715). IG II²2820, line 15; dedicated as member of a deme commission concerned with (and honored for) the erection of a statue of Aphrodite; ca. 360. Suggested by Kirchner as Euk[– –] Euk[– –] Halai[eus] (IG II²5481, grave monument of the mid fourth century; cf. SEG 13.79). A possible relative is Eukles Lakleous of Halai: IG II²1594 (*rationes centesimarum*; ?320s), lines 20-21; IG II²4653, dedication from a cave near Vari.

187   *[Eu]ktemo[n E]uthemon[os]* (PA 5791). IG II²2820, line 19; dedicated as member of a deme commission concerned with (and honored for) the erection of a statue of Aphrodite; ca. 360. Syntrierarch in 322 (IG II²1632, lines 180-181); Davies, *Families*, pp. 197-198. His father is **190**, his brothers **189** and **207**. (Which of the three brothers is named in IG II²1175, lines 5-6, is indeterminable.)

188   *[Eu]philetos Hagnotheou* (PA 6058). IG II²2820, line 13; dedicated as member of a deme commission concerned with (and honored for) the erection of a statue of Aphrodite; ca. 360. His brother is presumably **203**, and their father **192** (q.v.).

189   *[Eu]polis* (II) *Euthemonos* (PA 5940). IG II²2820, line 18; dedicated as member of a deme commission concerned with (and honored for) the erection of a statue of Aphrodite; ca. 360. He may have served as *pōlētēs* in the last third of the fourth century (though see Davies, *Families*, p. 198). Son-in-law of **185**, son of **190**, and brother of **187** and **207**. (Which of the three brothers is named in IG II²1175, lines 5-6, is indeterminable.)

190   *Euthemon Eupolidos* (I) (PA 5474-5475). Proposer of IG II²1174 (line 1); 368/7. Also dedicated as member of a deme commission concerned with (and honored for) the erection of a statue of Aphrodite, ca. 360 (IG II²2820, line 7); and named on a curse-tablet (Wünsch 24b). His sons are **187, 189,** and **207;** see Davies, *Families,* pp. 197-198.

191   *Hagnias Melesiou. AD* 11, 1927-1928, pp. 40-41, no. 4, lines 11-12; honored as member of a religious commission of the deme; ca. 360.

192   *Hagnotheos Ekphantidou.* Proposer of *AD* 11, 1927-1928, pp. 40-41, no. 4 (line 1); ca. 360. Presumably the father of **188** and **203;** and reasonably identified by B. D. Meritt with the Hagnotheos Ἁλαι[εύς] on a grave monument of the mid fourth century (*Hesp.* 37, 1968, pp. 294-295, no. 39 = *Agora 17,* no. 52).

193   [*Hie*]*ron Nautou* (PA 7533). IG II²2820, line 21; dedicated as member of a deme commission concerned with (and honored for) the erection of a statue of Aphrodite; ca. 360. As Kirchner observed, a likely relative—I would suppose nephew—of **196.**

194   [*Men*]*andr*[*os?*] *Hegesiou* (PA 9867). IG II²2820, line 26; dedicated as member of a deme commission concerned with (and honored for) the erection of a statue of Aphrodite; ca. 360.

195   *Menyllos Astyphilou* (PA 10062). IG II²2820, line 22; dedicated as member of a deme commission concerned with (and honored for) the erection of a statue of Aphrodite; ca. 360. The son of **184** (q.v.), and well attested in his own right: plausibly restored as *bouleutēs* of the second half of the fourth century (*Agora 15,* no. 31, line 33); named on a curse-tablet (Wünsch 50, cf. 47 and 48); and died in the decade 340 to 330 (five grave monuments: see SEG 27.25).

196   *Nikomenes Hieronos* (PA 10970). IG II²2820, line 6; dedicated as member of a deme commission concerned with (and honored for) the erection of a statue of Aphrodite; ca. 360. (See W. K. Pritchett, *Hesp.* 15, 1946, p. 162, n. 62.) Also made a report to his deme assembly in ca. 360 (IG II²1175, lines 1-2); named on a curse-tablet (Wünsch 24b); and a member of the board of Delian Amphiktyones, 375/4-374/3 (IG II²1635, line 61; this identification by W. S. Ferguson, *CR* 15, 1901, pp. 38-40). Erroneously linked in *Agora 15,* index, with two *bouleutai* of Halai Araphenides; see Whitehead, "Demarchs," p. 39. As Kirchner observed, a likely relative—I would suppose uncle—of **193.**

197   *Pantakles Sokratous. AD* 11, 1927-1928, pp. 40-41, no. 4, line 11; honored as member of a religious commission of the deme; ca. 360. Sokrates is a common name, but there might nonetheless be a link with **201** and/or **208**; and note also Sokrates ?E[– – –], *bouleutēs* in 304/3 (*Agora* 15, no. 61, line 197).

198   [*Phil*]*agros* (II) *D*[*iok*]*leous* (PA 14208). IG II²2820, line 24; dedicated as member of a deme commission concerned with (and honored for) the erection of a statue of Aphrodite; ca. 360. Nephew of **184** (q.v.), hence cousin of **195**. As Davies notes (*Families*, pp. 534-535), there is no means of determining whether PA 14208 *bis*, Philagros [Ha]lai(eus) the syntricrarch of 322 (IG II²1632, line 192) is this man or the Philagros who was one of the [*epimelēt*]*ai* of Aigeis in either 340/39 or 313/2 (IG II²2824, lines 4-5); and the same may be said, despite Kirchner's note *ad loc.*, of the Phil[a]g[ros Ha]laieus mentioned in IG II²1593, line 3 (land sales of the mid fourth century). For Philagros Le[ontos? Halai(eus)?], cousin of **198**, see under **184**.

199   [*Phil*]*ippos Athe*[*n*]*ippou* (PA 234). IG II²2820, line 20; dedicated as member of a deme commission concerned with (and honored for) the erection of a statue of Aphrodite; ca. 360. His father was *possibly* PA 233, the Athenip[pos] who was syntrierarch before 356 (IG II²1612, line 379; see Davies, *Families*, p. 5); and he himself is perhaps the Philippos of Halai who bought two estates in his deme, for four talents, in the third quarter of the fourth century (IG II²1598, lines 37ff., as read by W. Peek, *AM* 67, 1942, pp. 19-20 = SEG 21.573; cf. **16**, and Davies, *Families*, pp. 537-538, for a suggested identification with PA 14376 and/or 14377; see also **210**).

200   *Polystratos Charmantidou. AD* 11, 1927-1928, pp. 40-41, no. 4, lines 1-2, 7-8, 15; honored as priest of Apollo Zoster; ca. 360. Reasonably identified by Kroll, *Allotment Plates*, pp. 242-243, no. 155, with the Polystratos of Halai whose nondikastic *pinakion* is IG II²1879.

201   [*Sok*]*rates ?T?h?eothei*⟨*d*⟩*ou* (PA 13100). IG II²2820, line 28; dedicated as member of a deme commission concerned with (and honored for) the erection of a statue of Aphrodite; ca. 360. Presumably the son of **208**; and **197** is a possible relative.

202   [*Theo*]*boulo*[*s Th*]*eodotou* (PA 6677). IG II²2820, line 27; dedicated as member of a deme commission concerned with (and honored for) the erection of a statue of Aphrodite; ca. 360. Perhaps the son of either **204** or **205**; and Theodotos

The[– – –] the *bouleutēs* of 281/0 (*Agora 15*, no. 72, line 95), if from this deme, is a possible descendant.

203   [*Theo*]*doros Hagnotheou* (PA 6851). IG II²2820, line 16; dedicated as member of a deme commission concerned with (and honored for) the erection of a statue of Aphrodite; ca. 360. His brother is presumably **188**, and their father **192** (q.v.).

204   [*Theo*]*dotos Theaitetou* (PA 6788). IG II²2820, line 23; dedicated as member of a deme commission concerned with (and honored for) the erection of a statue of Aphrodite; ca. 360. Perhaps the father of **202** (though **205** might equally well be).

205   *Theodotos Theodotou*. AD 11, 1927-1928, pp. 40-41, no. 4, lines 10-11; honored as member of a religious commission of the deme; ca. 360. Perhaps the father of **202** (though **204** might equally well be), or at least somehow connected with **202** and/or **204**.

206   *Theod*[– – –]. SEG 12.52, line 4; mentioned in religious accounts; fifth century.

207   [*Theo*]*philo*[*s Eu*]*themonos* (PA 7123). IG II²2820, line 25; dedicated as member of a deme commission concerned with (and honored for) the erection of a statue of Aphrodite; ca. 360. His father is **190**, his brothers **187** and **189**. (Which of the three brothers is named in IG II²1175, lines 5-6, is indeterminable.) Possibly to be identified with Theophilos E[– –], *bouleutēs* in 304/3 (*Agora 15*, no. 61, line 196), though, as Davies notes (*Families*, p. 597), the chronological stretch is arguably too long.

208   [*The*]*otheides Sokratous* (PA 6916). IG II²2820, line 11; dedicated as member of a deme commission concerned with (and honored for) the erection of a statue of Aphrodite; ca. 360. Presumably the father of **201**; and **197** is a possible relative.

209   *Timarchos*. SEG 12.52, line 17; mentioned in religious accounts; fifth century.

210   [. . .]*ippos A*[*is*]*chinou* (PA 343). IG II²2820, line 17; dedicated as member of a deme commission concerned with (and honored for) the erection of a statue of Aphrodite; ca. 360. His father is Aischines Polyzelou, of (?)liturgical census in 381/0 (*Hesp.* 15, 1946, p. 160, no. 17, line 4; see Davies, *Families*, p. 6, and, on this whole group of documents, *Wealth*, Appendix 1). The restoration [Phil]ippos would permit an identification with the Philippos of Halai who bought two estates in his deme, for four talents, in the third quarter of the fourth century; see under **199**.

211   [– – –]s. SEG 12.52, line 12; *grammateus* in religious accounts; fifth century.

212   [– – –]*stratos*. SEG 12.52, line 19; *grammateus* in religious accounts; fifth century.

HALAI ARAPHENIDES (213-214)

213   *Peithias*. Proposer of *AE* 1932, *Chronika*, pp. 30-32 (line 1); mid fourth century.

214   *Philoxenos Phrasikleous. AE* 1932, *Chronika*, pp. 30-32, lines 1-2, 9-10, 16-17; honored as deme liturgist; mid fourth century.

HALIMOUS (215-216)

215   *Charisandros Charisiadou*. SEG 2.7, lines 3, 11-13; honored for religious duties, some of them *vice* a demarch; between 330 and 325. His father is conceivably the Charisiades who gave evidence in court in 346/5 on behalf of his cousin Euxitheos (**20**): see Demosth. 57.20. A likely descendant is PA 15474, Charisandros Halimousios, *hoplomachos* of the ephebes in the 240s (IG II²766, lines 10 and 41-42, with *Hesp.* 17, 1948, pp. 5-7).

216   *Theophilos*. Proposer of SEG 2.7 (line 2); between 330 and 325. Reasonably identified by Hondius in the *editio princeps* with PA 7125, *epistatēs* of the *proedroi* in 346: Tod, nos. 167 (lines 6-7) and 168 (line 4).

IKARION (217-229)

217   [*A*]*rchippos Archede*[*kto*(*u*)] (PA 2555, cf. 2554). IG II²3094; dedicated as victorious *chorēgos* at the rural Dionysia; early fourth century. His daughter, as Kirchner saw, is surely PA 8543, Kleitopolis (IG II²6282, grave monument of the second half of the fourth century).

218   *Diognetos Ergaso*(*u*) (PA 3861). IG II²3095, line 3; dedicated as victorious *chorēgos* (with his brother **225** and their father **220**, q.v.) at the rural Dionysia; mid fourth century.

219   *Epikrates* (PA 4893). IG II²1178, lines 8-9; honored as *chorēgos* (with **226**); before the middle of the fourth century. His daughter, as Kirchner saw, is surely PA 4858, Epikrateia (IG II²6279, grave monument of the second half of the fourth century).

220   *Ergasos Phanomacho*(*u*) (PA 5048). IG II²3095, line 1; dedicated as victorious *chorēgos* (with his sons **218** and **225**) at

the rural Dionysia; mid fourth century. A likely grandson, as Kirchner noted (*apud* IG II²3095), is the Ergasos of Ikarion mentioned as a supplier of reeds in the Eleusinian accounts of 329/8 (IG II²1672, lines 189 and 194).

221   *Hagnias* (PA 131). IG II²3098; dedicated as victorious *chorēgos* (with **227** and **228**, presumably his sons) at the rural Dionysia; mid fourth century. Syntrierarch in 356 (IG II²1612, line 141) and principal trierarch before 323/2 (IG II²1631, lines 637-638); probably also to be identified with the Hagnias who was syntrierarch before 362/1 ([Demosth.] 50.41-42); see Davies, *Families*, pp. 3-4.

222   *Kallippos* (PA 8071). Proposer of IG II²1178 (line 1); before the middle of the fourth century.

223   *Menest[ratos]* (PA 10009). Proposer of IG I³254 (line 2); perhaps between 440 and 415. Menestratos the Ikarian *bouleutēs* in the last decade of the third century (*Agora 15*, no. 138, line 64) is a likely descendant.

224   *Mnesilochos Mnesiphilou* (PA 10326). IG II²3099; victorious *chorēgos* at the rural Dionysia; probably mid fourth century.

225   *Phanomachos Ergaso(u)* (PA 14074). IG II²3095, line 2; dedicated as victorious *chorēgos* (with his brother **218** and their father **220**, q.v.) at the rural Dionysia; mid fourth century.

226   *Praxias* (PA 12159). IG II²1178, line 9; honored as *chorēgos* (with **219**); before the middle of the fourth century.

227   *Xanthides* (PA 11154). IG II²3098; dedicated as victorious *chorēgos* (with **221**, q.v., presumably his father, and **228**, presumably his brother) at the rural Dionysia; mid fourth century.

228   *Xanthippos* (PA 11166). IG II²3098; dedicated as victorious *chorēgos* (with **221**, q.v., presumably his father, and **227**, presumably his brother) at the rural Dionysia; mid fourth century.

229   [. . . .⁸. . . .]. Proposer of IG II²1179 (line 1); mid fourth century.

KEPHALE (**230**)

230   *Smikythion* (PA 12771). IG II²1193, lines 2, 11-12, 17-18; honored as peripolarch by Eleusis; end of the fourth century. His patronymic occupies eight letter spaces in line 12 but only seven in line 18.

KEPHISIA (231-232)

231   [E]pikles. Proposer of AD 24, 1969, pp. 6-7 (line 1); second half of the fourth century.

232   Phro[– – –]. AD 24, 1969, pp. 6-7, lines 1 and 10; honored for various benefactions; second half of the fourth century. (It is only an assumption, however, that he belonged to this deme.)

KOLLYTOS (233)

233   Eukadmides (PA 5667). Proposer of IG II²1195, lines 6ff. (at 6); after the middle of the fourth century.

KYDATHENAION (234)

234   [Amei]nokles Tachyllou. Proposer of IG II²1280 (lines 1-2), a decree of the Eleusinioi "and the Athenians stationed in Eleusis"; before 266/5. Depending upon how much "before," he is either the grandson of a *bouleutēs* of 304/3 (*Agora 15*, no. 61, line 64)—thus Kirchner *ad loc.*—or even the same man (PA 697; *Agora 15*, index). His father Tachyllos was perhaps a ?*bouleutēs* in 343/2 (*Agora 15*, no. 493, line 14). Pyrrhos Tachyllou Kydathenaieus, on a grave monument of the mid fourth century (IG II²6592) looks like a brother, but note J. S. Traill, *Hesp.* 35, 1966, p. 232.

KYTHEROS (235-243)

235   Antimachos Amphimachou (PA 1127). IG II²2496, lines 2-3; one of eight "*meritai* of (the) Kytherioi"; after the middle of the fourth century.

236   Chaireas Mnesicharou(s) (PA 15104). IG II²2496, lines 7-8; one of eight "*meritai* of (the) Kytherioi"; after the middle of the fourth century. Presumably brother of 242.

237   Demaretos Leosthenou(s) (PA 3297). IG II²2496, lines 4-5; one of eight "*meritai* of (the) Kytherioi"; after the middle of the fourth century.

238   Ktesias Ktesiphontos (PA 8845). IG II²2496, line 5; one of eight "*meritai* of (the) Kytherioi"; after the middle of the fourth century. Presumably brother of 240 and/or 241, and relative of 239 (q.v.); see Davies, *Families*, p. 338.

239   Ktesias Timokratou(s) (PA 8889). IG II²2496, line 7; one of eight "*meritai* of (the) Kytherioi"; after the middle of the fourth century. Presumably related to the sons of Ktesiphon (238, 240, 241), as well as to Timon Timokratous, *tamias* of

Athena in 377/6 (PA 13846; IG II²1410, lines 4-5); see Davies, *Families*, p. 338.

240   *Ktesichares Ktesiphontos* (PA 8902). IG II²2496, lines 6-7; one of eight *"meritai* of (the) Kytherioi"; after the middle of the fourth century. Presumably brother of **238** and/or **241**, and relative of **239** (q.v.); see Davies, *Families*, p. 338.

241   *Ktesippos Ktesiphontos* (PA 8888). IG II²2496, lines 5-6; one of eight *"meritai* of (the) Kytherioi"; after the middle of the fourth century. Presumably brother of **238** and/or **240**, and relative of **239** (q.v.); see Davies, *Families*, p. 338. An earlier homonym and likely relative is PA 8889, Ktesippos Simylous, of (?) liturgical census in ca. 380 (IG II²1929, line 20; see Davies, *Families*, p. 338, and, on this whole group of documents, *Wealth*, Appendix 1).

242   *Pheidostratos Mnesicharou(s)* (PA 14171). IG II²2496, lines 3-4; one of eight *"meritai* of (the) Kytherioi"; after the middle of the fourth century. Presumably brother of **236**.

243   *Philippides* (PA 14350). IG II²2496, lines 1-2; priest, used as dating formula; after the middle of the fourth century.

LAMPTRAI, UPPER (**244-277**)

244   *Antiphilos* (PA 1271). IG II²2967, line 18; one of the named [Lamp]treis who dedicated to Apollo; mid fourth century.

245   *Archestratos* (PA 2429). IG II²2967, line 34; one of the named [Lamp]treis who dedicated to Apollo; mid fourth century. Perhaps to be identified with [. . .]estratos L[amptreus], *epistatēs* in a city decree of 353/2 (IG II²139, lines 4-5).

246   *Aristophanes* (PA 2091). IG II²2967, line 20; one of the named [Lamp]treis who dedicated to Apollo; mid fourth century.

247   *Aristophilos* (PA 2101). IG II²2967, line 19; one of the named [Lamp]treis who dedicated to Apollo; mid fourth century.

248   A[. . ⁵ . .]os. IG II²2967, line 28; one of the named [Lamp]treis who dedicated to Apollo; mid fourth century.

249   *Epikrates* (PA 4900). IG II²2967, line 7; one of the named [Lamp]treis who dedicated to Apollo; mid fourth century. With so common a name there can be no certainty that he is related to either of the homonyms noted by Kirchner *ad loc.* (the *epibatēs* of IG II²1951, line 85; and PA 4901, Epikrates Phileou, *epistatēs* of the *proedroi* in 303/2, IG II²495-497).

250   [E]*pi*[– – –]. IG II²2967, line 2; one of the named [Lamp]treis who dedicated to Apollo; mid fourth century.

251   *Eualkos* (PA 5263). IG II²2967, line 17; one of the named [Lamp]treis who dedicated to Apollo; mid fourth century.

252   *Eudemos Epi*(– – –) (PA 5403). IG II²2967, line 5; one of the named [Lamp]treis who dedicated to Apollo; mid fourth century. Either he or **253** is doubtless Eud?e[m]o[s], *bouleutēs* in 336/5 (*Agora 15*, no. 42, line 61).

253   *Eudemos* [. .]o(– – –) (PA 5402). IG II²2967, line 4; one of the named [Lamp]treis who dedicated to Apollo; mid fourth century. Either he or **252** is doubtless Eud?e[m]o[s], *bouleutēs* in 336/5 (*Agora 15*, no. 42, line 61).

254   *Euphiletos* (PA 6072). IG II²2967, line 12; one of the named [Lamp]treis who dedicated to Apollo; mid fourth century.

255   *Euthetos* (PA 5472). IG II²2967, line 10; one of the named [Lamp]treis who dedicated to Apollo; mid fourth century. As Kirchner saw, his son is surely PA 5637, the *praktōr* Euthymachos Euthetou Lamptreus: C. Michel, *Recueil d'inscriptions grecques*, Brussels, 1900, no. 831 (Imbros, late fourth century).

256   *Euthynos* (PA 5657). IG II²2967, line 8; one of the named [Lamp]treis who dedicated to Apollo; mid fourth century. Attested also as trieropoiic *tamias* in 346/5 (IG II²1622, lines 387-390) and as father of the woman Theano (IG II²6671, grave monument of the second half of the fourth century).

257   *E[uxithe]os* (PA 5908). IG II²2967, line 29; one of the named [Lamp]treis who dedicated to Apollo; mid fourth century.

258   *G[. . . .]mos.* IG II²2967, line 30; one of the named [Lamp]treis who dedicated to Apollo; mid fourth century.

259   *Hagnon* (PA 170). IG II²2967, line 15; one of the named [Lamp]treis who dedicated to Apollo; mid fourth century.

260   *Hieronymos* (PA 7566). IG II²2967, line 3; one of the named [Lamp]treis who dedicated to Apollo; mid fourth century. Syntrierarch between 355 and 346/5 (IG II²1622, lines 587-588), with two known sons: Philokrates (PA 14619), who paid the debt on his father's ship between 345/4 and 342/1 (IG II²1622, line 589); and Hieron, who was of ephebic age in ca. 350 (*lampadēphoros* in IG II²3105, line 24) and whose grave monument of the late fourth century is *Hesp.* 22, 1953, p. 181, no. 7. See Davies, *Families*, p. 536-537.

261   *I[– – –].* IG II²2967, line 25; one of the named [Lamp]treis who dedicated to Apollo; mid fourth century.

262   *Kallikrates (Charopidou)* (PA 7946 + 7953). IG II²2967, line 6; one of the named [Lamp]treis who dedicated to Apollo; mid fourth century. The patronymic results from Kirchner's

identification of him with the proposer of city decrees in 345
(IG II²215, lines 5-6) and 339 (IG II²233 = Tod, no. 175,
line 5).

263   *Kallistratos* (PA 8173). IG II²2967, line 9; one of the named
        [Lamp]treis who dedicated to Apollo; mid fourth century.

264   *Kineas (Stephanou)* (PA 8434 + 8436). IG II²2967, line 33;
        one of the named [Lamp]treis who dedicated to Apollo; mid
        fourth century. Syntrierarch before 356 (IG II²1612, line 370),
        and member of a rich and active family; see Davies, *Families*,
        pp. 491-493, with "possible stemma."

265   *Kleitekton* (PA 8533). IG II²2967, line 13; one of the named
        [Lamp]treis who dedicated to Apollo; mid fourth century.

266   [K]*leo*[. . . .]*s*. IG II²2967, line 26; one of the named
        [Lamp]treis who dedicated to Apollo; mid fourth century.

267   *Kletippos* (PA 8535, as Kleitippos). IG II²2967, line 14; one
        of the named [Lamp]treis who dedicated to Apollo; mid fourth
        century.

268   *Kydimachos* (PA 8932). IG II²2967, line 11; one of the named
        [Lamp]treis who dedicated to Apollo; mid fourth century.

269   *Lysanias* (PA 9316). IG II²2967, line 21; one of the named
        [Lamp]treis who dedicated to Apollo; mid fourth century. In
        Agora 15, index, a twofold identification is suggested: with
        Lysanias Lysan[iou?], *bouleutēs* in 367/6 (*Agora 15*, no. 14,
        line 41); and with the father of Demetrios Lysaniou Lamptreus
        (IG II²6654, grave monument of the mid fourth century; pre-
        viously noted by Kirchner). The *bouleutēs*, however, came
        from Lower/Coastal Lamptrai; thus, unless Eliot (*Coastal
        Demes*, chap. 5) was wrong to locate Upper Lamptrai at Lam-
        brika (where IG II²2967 was found) rather than at Kitsi Pigadi
        (where IG II²6654 was found, apparently), these two men can
        be linked with each other but neither of them with **269.**

270   *Lysimachos* (PA 9519). IG II²2967, line 23; one of the named
        [Lamp]treis who dedicated to Apollo; mid fourth century.

271   *Nikeratos* (PA 10743). IG II²2967, line 16; one of the named
        [Lamp]treis who dedicated to Apollo; mid fourth century.

272   *Phrynion* (PA 15017). IG II²2967, line 22; one of the named
        [Lamp]treis who dedicated to Apollo; mid fourth century.

273   S[. . . .⁸. . . .]*o*[*s*]. IG II²2967, line 24; one of the named
        [Lamp]treis who dedicated to Apollo; mid fourth century.

274   *Teisia*[*s*] (PA 13480). IG II²2967, line 35; one of the named
        [Lamp]treis who dedicated to Apollo; mid fourth century. (In

fact the name is possibly Geisias: see J. and L. Robert, *Bull. Epig.* 1950, no. 100.)

275 [. . .⁶. . .]*mides.* IG II²2967, line 32; one of the named [Lamp]treis who dedicated to Apollo; mid fourth century.

276 [. . .⁶. . .]?*mides.* IG II²2967, line 27; one of the named [Lamp]treis who dedicated to Apollo; mid fourth century.

277 [.]*us*[. .]*es.* IG II²2967, line 31; one of the named [Lamp]treis who dedicated to Apollo; mid fourth century.

LAMPTRAI, LOWER (278)

278 [*K*]*ephi*[*s*]*o*[*d*]*oros* (PA 8374). Proposer of IG II²1204 (line 1); late fourth century. Kirchner's suggestion that his son might be PA 6348, Hegesippos Kephisodorou Lamptreus, was based on the dating of the latter's grave monument IG II 2275 to the late fourth century; as IG II²6669, however, it has been set in the *mid* fourth century; thus, if they are related at all, PA 6348 will be the father, not the son, of 278.

LAMPTRAI, UPPER or LOWER (279)

279 *Melesias Aristokrato(us)* (PA 9814). IG II²1176+, lines 29 and 39; honored by Peiraieus as one of the four lessees of the Peiraieus theater (with 302, 305, and 308); 324/3. His father, PA 1916+1917, was syntrierarch between 356 and 346/5 (IG II²1622, lines 627 and 634): see Davies, *Families*, p. 59 (and note that the new archon-dating of IG II²1176+ eases the chronological problem mentioned there), including references to other relatives.

LEUKONOION (280-281)

280 *Aristophanes* (II) *Aristomenous* (II) (PA 2092 *bis*). IG II²1299, lines 51-80; honored (as *stratēgos*) by Eleusis; after 236/5. His grandfather Aristophanes (I) Aristomenous (I) was trierarch in 322 (IG II²1632, line 93): see Davies, *Families*, pp. 63-64, on the family as a whole.

281 *Demochares* (PA 3715). IG II²2670 is the *horos* of an estate put up as *apotimēma* ("probably in the 360s": Davies, *Families*, p. 347) for the dowry of his daughter Hippokleia, to the value of one talent, and hypothecated by whatever its worth exceeded that to the (tribe) Kekropidai, the (*genos*) Lykomidai, and the (deme of the) Phlyeis. Of liturgical census (Demosth. 28.3): see Davies, *Families*, pp. 141-142, cf. 347, on the family as a whole.

MELITE (282-294)

282   *Antias Euphiletou* (PA 974). IG II²2394, line 8; in catalog of
        names; 340/39 or 313/2.

283   *Antikleides Antiphan(– –)* (PA 1044). IG II²2394, lines 9-10
        (as reconstructed from Fourmont's faulty copy); in catalog of
        names; 340/39 or 313/2.

284   *Chairylle.* SEG 22.116, line 5; priestess (of Artemis Aristo-
        boule) used as dating formula; ca. 330. As the name is very
        rare—indeed unique, apparently, in this *eta*-form—she is very
        probably the Chairylle who is cursed on Wünsch 89b (dated
        by him to the fourth century).

285   *Demosthene[s De]mopha[nous]* (PA 3581). IG II²2394, line
        6; in catalog of names; 340/39 or 313/2.

286   *Euthydemos Euthydo[mou]* (PA 5540). IG II²2394, line 3; in
        catalog of names; 340/39 or 313/2. His father *might* be the
        demarch **34** (q.v.), but see also **287**.

287   *Euthydo[mos Eu]thydo[mou]*. IG II²2394, line 5; in catalog
        of names; 340/39 or 313/2. Either his father or even, con-
        ceivably, he himself *might* be the demarch **34** (q.v.), but see
        also **286**.

288   *Hagniades Kaliou (sic)* (PA 123a, superseding 306: the reading
        is Wilhelm's version, *BPhW* 1902, p. 1097, of Fourmont's
        Ainiades). IG II²2394, line 7; in catalog of names; 340/39 or
        313/2.

289   *Hegesippos* (II) *Hegesiou*. Proposer of SEG 22.116 (line 7);
        ca. 330. Reasonably taken by Threpsiades and Vanderpool in
        the *editio princeps* to be the son of PA 6327 (IG II²2383, line
        18, Kekropid catalog of between 360 and 350; IG II²1926,
        lines 121-122, *diaitētēs* in 325/4) and grandson of PA 6349,
        Hegesippos (I) Meliteus, curator of the dockyards in 366/5
        (IG II²1622, lines 506-512). Payment for the latter was made
        by Thallos Meliteus and Aristomachos Meliteus, who were
        presumably his sons, and for each of them also a likely son
        is known: Hegesippos (III) Thallou, in a catalog of ca. 321
        (*Agora 15*, no. 494, line 20, with index); and PA 6350, He-
        gesippos (IV) Aristomachou, *bouleutēs* in 281/0 (*Agora 15*,
        no. 72, line 41) and *grammateus* κατὰ πρυτανείαν in 276/5
        (IG II²684-685). (This last involves a long chronological
        stretch, however, and Hegesippos (IV) may simply have been
        a collateral relative.)

290   *Kallippos Theodotou.* SEG 22.120, line 2; honored by Rhamnous for garrison duties; mid third century.

291   *Klearis[tos Hie]rokl[e – –]* (PA 8472). IG II²2394, line 4; in catalog of names; 340/39 or 313/2.

292   *Neoptolemos Antikleous* (PA 10652). SEG 22.116, lines 1-3, 8-9, 20; honored for benefactions to the deme's cult of Artemis (Aristoboule); ca. 330. The most notable member of a notable (and rich) fourth-century family; see Davies, *Families*, pp. 399-400 (and add the new *horos* recording moneylending by N. and his *eranos*: C. Conophagos, *Le Laurium antique*, Athens, 1980, p. 389, no. 2, as cited by Osborne, *Demos*, p. 237, n. 50).

293   *Satyra,* "wife of Krateas of Melite." *Hesp.* 11, 1942, pp. 265-274, no. 51, lines 2 and 8-9; honored as priestess of the Thesmophoroi; first half of the second century. Her husband was identified by Broneer *ad loc.* with Krateas Nikolaou, whose second-century grave monument is IG II²6860.

294   [– – –ᶜᵃ· ¹⁸ – – k]*leous* (i.e., end of patronymic only). Proposer of *Hesp.* 11, 1942, pp. 265-274, no. 51 (line 1); first half of the second century.

MYRRHINOUS (295-296)

295   *Meix[i]as* (PA 9753). IG II²1182, lines 23-24; deme *antigrapheus*; mid fourth century. A possible relative is the Meixidemos of Myrrhinous whose *synoikia* in Peiraieus was "denounced"—by a fellow demesman—in 341 as a result of his debts to the state (*Hesp.* 5, 1936, pp. 393-413, no. 10, lines 115ff.); for prosopographical links and other implications, see Osborne, *Demos*, pp. 1-10.

296   *Pheidippos* (II) (*Apemonos*) (PA 14159). IG II²1182, line 23; disburses money (with **295**) for the inscription of the decree, in which he is probably the honorand; mid fourth century. His father is PA 1350, Apemon Pheidippou (I), victorious *chorēgos* in boys' dithyramb at the Thargelia, early fourth century (IG II²1138, lines 17-19); and he himself contributed to the cost of a bouleutic dedication at the Amphiareion in 328/7 (*Agora 15*, no. 49, line 37). Davies, *Families*, p. 42.

OA (297)

297   *Euthyno[s].* SEG 24.152, lines 3-4; lessee of a deme estate in Teithras; around the middle of the fourth century.

OE (298)

298   *Timokrates Epigenou(s)*. Proposer of SEG 15.112 (lines 2 and
            30-31), a decree of the Rhamnousioi et al.; after 225/4. A
            possible ancestor is PA 4816, Epigenes of Oe, syntrierarch in
            322 (IG II²1632, lines 68-69), plausible descendants of whom,
            as ephebes in the last quarter of the second century, are noted
            by Davies, *Families*, p. 180.

PAIANIA, UPPER or LOWER (299-300)

299   *Demosthenes* (III) *Demainetou* (I) (PA 3596). IG II²3097;
            victorious *choregos* at the rural Dionysia; mid fourth century.
            He, his elder brother Demeas (IV) Demainetou (I), and their
            father Demainetos (I) Demeou (III), PA 3276, all recorded
            anthippasia victories as phylarchs of Pandionis in or before
            the middle of the fourth century: IG II²3130. On this family
            "active in deme and tribal affairs in the middle of the fourth
            century," see Davies, *Families*, pp. 103-106, esp. 103-104.

300   *Hiero[k]l[eides Tei]samenou* (PA 7470). IG II²1188, lines 3-
            5, 16-18; honored (as hierophant) by Eleusis; mid fourth cen-
            tury. To be identified, as Kirchner noted *ad loc.*, with the
            Hierokleides P[aia]nieus of IG II²7057 (grave monument of
            the mid fourth century).

?PAIONIDAI (301)

301   [.....¹².....]*eious* (i.e., end of patronymic only). IG
            II²1212, lines 1-2; co-honorand (with 361) in a decree of an
            unidentifiable deme (see Appendix 3, no. 135); end of the
            fourth century. His demotic is P[....⁸....], and
            Π[αιονίδην] is preferable to the only other match, the rare
            form Π[λωθέαθεν].

PEIRAIEUS (302-307)

302   *Aristophanes Smikytho(u)* (PA 2094). IG II²1176+, lines 28-
            29, 38-39; honored as one of the four lessees of the deme's
            theater (with 279, 305, and 308); 324/3. Kirchner's identifi-
            cation of him *ad loc.* with the Aristophanes Peiraie(us) who
            was one of the contributors to a public or private project in
            Peiraieus in ca. 350 or soon after (IG II²2329, line 4) can
            survive the new archon-dating of IG II²1176+; and it is tempt-
            ing to see the Smikythos of line 10 of IG II²2329 as his father.

303   *Diodoros* (PA 3955). Proposer of IG II²1214 (line 1); perhaps
            ca. 280 (see Appendix 3, no. 89). Identified by Kirchner with

the *symproedros* in a city decree of 318/7 (IG II²449, line 10), but a better chronological match would be [Di]odoros[– – –], *bouleutēs* from Peiraieus in 281/0 (*Agora 15*, no. 72, line 140); cf. P. Gauthier, *REG* 92, 1979, p. 396.

304   *Kalliades (Philinou)* (PA 7798). Proposer of IG II²1176+, lines 32-40 (at 32); 324/3. The patronymic results from the identification of him by Köhler and Kirchner with the co-honorand (with his brother Lysimachides) in IG II²1252, a decree of *orgeōnes* from the second half of the fourth century. A likely relative, as Kirchner saw, is Kalliades Kallikratous Peiraieus, who died in the first half of the fourth century (IG II²7170, grave monument).

305   *Oinophon Euphiletou* (PA 11368). IG II²1176+, lines 30-31, 39-40; honored as one of the four lessees of the deme's theater (with **279**, **302**, and **308**); 324/3.

306   *Theaios* (PA 6622). IG II²1176+, line 32; honored in connection with the leasing of the deme's theater; 324/3.

307   [. . . .¹⁰. . . .]s *Philistidou*. Proposer of *Hesp.* 3, 1934, pp. 44-46, no. 33 (line 1); early third century. The patronymic offers several possible links: Philistides Lamprokl(eous), *bouleutēs* in 303/2 (*Agora 15*, no. 62, line 249); Philistides Sostratou and Sostratos Philistidou, on a grave monument after the middle of the fourth century (IG II²7195); Theodotos Philistidou and Philistides Theodotou, on a grave monument of the early third century (SEG 18.109). Given the evident frequency of the name in this deme, PA 14440, Philistide[s] the Hippothontid *bouleutēs* of 410/09 (IG I³102, lines 4-5), is a likely ancestor.

PELEKES (308)

308   *Arethousios Aristoleo* (PA 1588). IG II²1176+, lines 30, 40; honored by Peiraieus as one of the four lessees of the Peiraieus theater (with **279**, **302**, and **305**); 324/3. Soundly identified by Kirchner with the only known homonym, PA 1587, the Arethousios of [Demosth.] 53, in dispute with his brother Nikostratos (PA 11007) over slaves; cf. Davies, *Families*, p. 481, n. 1.

PHALERON (309-313)

309   *Demetrios (I) Phanostratou* (PA 3455). Honored by Aixone (IG II²1201), Eleusis (IG II²2971), and Sphettos (SEG 25.206) during his ten-year (317-307) rule in Athens. See Davies, *Fam-*

ilies, pp. 107-110 for the family and its property; and in general H.-J. Gehrke, *Chiron* 8, 1978, pp. 149-193.

310   *Philostra[tos– – – –]*. IG II²3102, line 3; one of four *[kōmarchoi]* for the deme's victory in the festival of the Tetrakomoi; mid fourth century.

311   *Pl[– – – – – – –]* (including patronymic). IG II²3102, line 2; one of four *[kōmarchoi]* for the deme's victory in the festival of the Tetrakomoi; mid fourth century.

312   *[– – –]machos Satyrou*. IG II²3102, line 2; one of four *[kōmarchoi]* for the deme's victory in the festival of the Tetrakomoi; mid fourth century.

313   *[– – –]n Theophilou*. IG II²3102, line 3; one of four *[kōmarchoi]* for the deme's victory in the festival of the Tetrakomoi; mid fourth century.

PHYLE (314)

314   [. . . .]. IG II²1192, line 2; honored by Eleusis; end of the fourth century.

PITHOS (315)

315   *Diokles ([Diocha]rous* (I)) (PA 4048). Isaeus 8.19-20; his wife was chosen by the wives of the demesmen as one of the *hieropoioi* for the deme's Thesmophoria; between 383 and 363. On Diokles himself and the rich mining family of which he was a member, see Davies, *Families*, pp. 158-159.

PLOTHEIA (316-318)

316   *Aristotimos* (PA 2076). Proposer of IG I³258 (line 11); between 425 and 413.

317   *[K]allias Kallio(u)* (PA 7882). IG II²4885; dedicated on a statue base in his deme; first half of the fourth century. With so common a name there can be no certainty about Kirchner's identification of him *ad loc.* with PA 7881, dedicator of a *phialē chalkē* in the mid fourth century (IG II²1412, line 6; 1421, lines 102-103; etc.).

318   *Kallippos* (PA 8081). IG II²4607; dedicated an altar to Aphrodite in his deme; end of the fourth century.

PRASIAI (319-320)

319   *[K]irrhias* (II) *Poseidippou*. IG II²2497, lines 3, 10, 15 (with the *nomen* restored by E. Vanderpool, J. R. McCredie, and A. Steinberg, *Hesp.* 31, 1962, p. 56); lessee of land from his

deme; after the middle of the fourth century. IG II²7286 is
the grave monument (found at Markopoulo/Prasiai itself) of
both Kirrhias and his father Poseidippos Kirrhiou (I), PA
12132 (syntrierarch between 356 and 346/5: IG II²1622, line
711), together with (presumably) their wives. On the family,
see Davies, *Families*, p. 469; note, however, that Poseidippos'
ownership of the dikastic *pinakion* IG II²1989 is doubted by
Kroll, *Allotment Plates*, p. 200, no. 100b, and that the name
of Poseidippos' brother, involved in the leasing of temple property on Delos in the middle of the fourth century, is now read
as [– – –]phos, not[– – –]ros (*Inscr. Délos* no. 104-8, face B,
line 33).

320 *Polyssthenes (sic).* SEG 21.644, lines 8, 15, 18; lessee of land
from his deme (though as no demotic is used in what survives
of the stele it is a likelihood rather than a certainty that he
was a Prasieus); second half of the fourth century. The consistent erasure of his name perhaps indicates that he defaulted
on the agreement. As noted in the *editio princeps* (*Hesp.* 31,
1962, p. 56), no connection can be established with either of
the contemporary (and morphologically orthodox) homonyms (Demosth. 23.202; IG II²414c, line 6, with *Hesp.* 9,
1940, p. 336, no. 42, line 11).

RHAMNOUS (321-337)

321 *A[r]chippos.* IG II²2493, lines 3-4; named (with 330) as head
of a *meros* (of the demesmen) leasing out land; 339/8. (See
in general Jameson, "Leasing.") Either identical with or at
least related to PA 2562, Archippos the Athenian eponymous
archon of 318/7; cf. Jameson, ibid., pp. 68 and 72, n. 20.

322 *Elpinikos Mnesippou.* Proposer of SEG 25.155 (lines 1-2), of
236/5; and one of the five men chosen by it (line 45) from
the demesmen to put their decree into immediate effect.

323 *Hierok[les].* IG II²2493, line 5; named as former tenant in a
deme land-lease; 339/8. (See in general Jameson, "Leasing.")
Almost certainly a member of a family prominent in the deme
through several generations in the fourth and third centuries
(cf. Jameson, ibid., p. 71 with n. 19); see for instance IG
II²3462 (cf. under 324) and 4452, and especially the funerary
peribolos published by B. C. Petrakos, *PAAH* 1977 [1980],
pp. 3-18 (SEG 30.215-219, 221, and 231). For stemmata, see
Petrakos in ΣΤΗΛΗ, τόμος εἰς μνήμην Νικολάου Κοντο-
λέοντος, Athens, 1978-1979, pp. 402-407, at 406; S. C.

Humphreys, *JHS* 100, 1980, p. 119 with table 2; R.S.J. Garland, *ABSA* 77, 1982, pp. 165-166. See also **324** and **326**.

324   *Hieropoios* (PA 7510). Proposer of SEG 22.120 (line 1); mid third century. Two sons are known: PA 7497, Hierokles Hieropoiou (IG II²3462, statue to Nemesis and Themis on behalf of his mother Aristonoe, priestess of Nemesis; end of the third century); and Aristophanes Hieropoiou (SEG 21.914, grave monument of the late third century). A collateral branch, it would seem, of the family of **323** and **326**.

325   [*Kl*]*eochares Teisonid*[*ou*]. Proposer of IG II²1217 (line 1), of 263/2 or 262/1, in honor of his relative the (?)demarch **42**. See also **331**.

326   *Lykeas Hierokleou(s)*. SEG 25.155 (Pouilloux, *Forteresse*, no. 15), lines 45-46; one of the five men chosen from the demesmen to put their decree into immediate effect; 236/5. Identified by Pouilloux *ad loc.* with PA 9192, Lykeas Rhamno(sios) the priest of Asklepios in the mid 240s (IG II²1534B, line 213). The brothers Kephisios and Hierokles Lykeou, who were buried (SEG 21.916) in the third century in the family *peribolos* (see references under **323**), were perhaps this man's uncle and father, respectively. Note also Lykeas Kephisiou, Rhamnousian *bouleutēs* of 281/0 (*Agora* 15, no. 72, line 195), who was buried in the mid third century in another family's *peribolos* (B. C. Petrakos, *PAAH* 1975 [1977], pp. 15-25; S. C. Humphreys, *JHS* 100, 1980, pp. 118-119; R.S.J. Garland, *ABSA* 77, 1982, p. 164).

327   *Lysitheos Diokleou(s)*. SEG 25.155, line 47; one of the five men chosen from the demesmen to put their decree into immediate effect; 236/5.

328   *Megakles Megakl*[*eou*]*s* (PA 9703). IG II²3109; dedicated to Themis after being crowned by his deme for liturgies; beginning of the third century.

329   *Nikostratos Epitelou(s)*. Proposer of SEG 24.154 (line 2), after 268/7, and of SEG 31.110 (line 1). His grave monument has recently been discovered at Rhamnous: see *AE* 1979 [1981], p. 27, no. 7 (SEG 30.225). Perhaps a descendant of PA 11050, the Nikostratos of Rhamnous who was syntrierarch between 356 and 346/5 (IG II²1622, line 692; Davies, *Families*, p. 412); in any case probably the brother of Epikouros Epitelou[s], *anagrapheus* in 293/2 (IG II²389 and 649; *Hesp.* 7, 1938, pp. 97-100, no. 17; cf. *Hesp.* 18, 1949, p. 8).

330   *Stesias*. IG II²2493, line 4; named (with **321**) as head of a *meros* (of the demesmen) leasing out land; 339/8. (See in general Jameson, "Leasing.")

331   *Strombichos Kleodoridou*. SEG 25.155, line 46; one of the five men chosen from the demesmen to put their decree into immediate effect; 236/5. Brother of the (?)demarch **42**. See also **325**.

332   *Thrasykles Thrasymachou*. Proposer of IG II²1313, a decree of the Rhamnousioi (et al.?) datable to the late third century on the assumption (made by Pouilloux, *Forteresse*, p. 138) that this man is the son of **333** (q.v.).

333   *Thrasymachos Antimachou*. SEG 25.155 (Pouilloux, *Forteresse*, no. 15), line 46; one of the five men chosen from the demesmen to put their decree into immediate effect; 236/5. A son is identified by Pouilloux *ad loc.* as **332**; and another son, presumably the elder, is known from a columnar grave stele of the second century (*AE* 1979, pp. 27-28, no. 8: Antimachos Thrasymachou).

334   *Xenokra[tes (II) Phan?]okratous* (PA 11250). Pouilloux, *Forteresse*, no. 27; taken since the *editio princeps* (Lolling, *AM* 4, 1879, pp. 285-286) to be the name of the priest of the founder-hero missing from IG II²2849 (*Forteresse*, no. 25), a series of marble thrones whereon the priest, crowned by various bodies including his deme, dedicated to Dionysos in the (?late) fourth century. (See however Pouilloux *ad loc.* on this.) As PA 11250 his patronymic was restored as [Xeno]kratous, but in fact he should probably be identified with [Xeno?]krates Phanokratou[s], Rhamnousian *bouleutēs* in 281/0 (*Agora 15*, no. 72, line 198)—thus J. S. Traill, *Hesp.* 38, 1969, p. 491 (note on line 223), with other likely matches: the father, Phanokrates, is probably the Phanokrates Xenokratous (I) of Pouilloux, *Forteresse*, no. 29 (funerary *naiskos* of the late fourth century; cf. SEG 30.227-230); and a possible uncle, Niko?k[rate]s Xenokrato(u)s (I) of Rhamnous, acquired property in Aphidna in the mid fourth century (*Hesp.* 5, 1936, p. 402, no. 10, line 184, with Meritt's comment at p. 413). Note also the cornice-fragment *Forteresse*, no. 28; with the first two letters missing the name could be either that of **334** or his father.

335   [– – – –]*I. [D]orotheou*. Proposer of SEG 31.111 (sole surviving line); third century. PA 3357, Demetrios Dorotheou,

a possibly Rhamnousian and certainly Aiantid ephebe in 107/6 (IG II²1011, line 112), is conceivably his descendant.

336   [– – – –]. Proposer of SEG 31.112 (line 1); late third century.

337   [– – – –]. Proposer of SEG 31.115 (line 1); ?third century.

SOUNION (338-339)

338   *Leukios* (II) (*Theokleous*) (PA 9057). IG II²1180, lines 4-5, 10, 24; presented a new *agora* to his deme; mid fourth century. His father has been plausibly restored as one of the "Heroes of Phyle," [Theokles Leu]kio(u) (I) So(u)ni[eus] (B. D. Meritt, *Hesp.* 2, 1933, pp. 154-155; cf. A. E. Raubitschek, *Hesp.* 10, 1941, p. 287, no. 78, line 33); and he himself is well attested for mining activity (*Hesp.* 10, 1941, p. 14, no. 1, lines 46 and 80; *Hesp.* 19, 1950, p. 210, no. 5, lines 5-6; ibid., p. 244, no. 16, face A, col. 2, lines 70-71; ibid., p. 263, no. 20, lines 5-6) as well as for contributing fifty drachmas to the *eutaxia* liturgy in ca. 330 (IG II²417, line 16). Davies, *Families*, p. 341.

339   *Theodelos* (PA 6745). Proposer of IG II²1180 (line 2); mid fourth century.

SPHETTOS (340)

340   *Xenokles* ((I) *Xeinidos* (I)) (PA 11234). IG II²1191, line 10; honored for religious services by the Eleusinioi et al.; 321/0 or 318/7. A likely collateral relative of the demarch **47** (q.v.). On his well-documented public and liturgical career, see: Davies, *Families*, pp. 414-415; C. Ampolo, *PP* 34, 1979, pp. 167-175.

TEITHRAS (341-351)

341   *Andra⟨r⟩e[s] P[ythe]o⟨u⟩*. SEG 24.152, lines 1-2; lessee of a deme estate; around the middle of the fourth century.

342   *Antias*. SEG 24.152, line 3; lessee of a deme estate; around the middle of the fourth century.

343   *Apollodoros One(siphontos?)*. SEG 24.152, line 5; lessee of a deme estate; around the middle of the fourth century. This expansion of his abbreviated patronymic was A. G. Woodhead's editorial suggestion in SEG *ad loc.*, citing PA 1201, Antisthenes Onesiphontos Teithrasios, secretary of *prytaneis* in 256/5 (*Agora* 15, no. 85, lines 5-6, 22, 93-94); but obviously other names, such as the common Onesimos, cannot be ruled out.

344   *Blepyr[os Phyleidou].* SEG 21.520, lines 13-14; honored as
        bouleutēs; 331/0 or 330/29. The restoration soundly assumes
        that he is PA 2882, curator of the dockyards in 349/8 (IG
        II²1620, lines 45-46). He is doubtless also the Blepyros who
        proposed the Teithrasian deme decree SEG 24.153 (line 1)
        around the middle of the fourth century; and his father [Phy-
        lei]des Ble[pyrou Teithras]ios appears, as Kirchner noted, in
        the accounts of the *pōlētai* before the middle of the fourth
        century (IG II²1580, lines 19-20).

345   *Eudikos.* Proposer of SEG 24.151, lines 1-5 (at 2); around
        the middle of the fourth century.

346   *Mantik[les . . .²⁶ . .].* SEG 21.520, lines 14-15; honored as
        bouleutēs; 331/0 or or 330/29.

347   *Pandios.* Proposer of SEG 24.151 lines 6ff. (at 6); around the
        middle of the fourth century.

348   *Xanthippos.* SEG 24.151, lines 8-9 and passim; lessee of a
        deme estate; around the middle of the fourth century.

349   *[–]anes An[– – –].* SEG 21.520, lines 15-16; honored as *bou-
        leutēs*; 331/0 or 330/29. To allow for the patronymic of Man-
        tikles (**346**) the *nomen* must be very short, and Vanderpool
        in the *editio princeps* suggested [M]anes or [Ph]anes; for the
        name of an Athenian citizen the latter is surely preferable.

350   *[– –i]niade[s . . . . ? . . . . o]u.* SEG 21.520, lines 16-17; hon-
        ored as *bouleutēs*; 331/0 or 330/29.

351   *[. . . .⁸. . . .].* Proposer of SEG 21.520 (line 2); 331/0 or
        330/29.

THRIA (352)

352   *Dikaiarchos Apolloniou.* SEG 25.155, line 2 and passim; hon-
        ored by the Rhamnousioi et al. for garrison duties; 236/5.
        Compare IG II²1311 (Pouilloux, *Forteresse*, no. 13) where
        those honoring him are "the Athenians stationed in Rha-
        mnous." The undated funerary columella of Dikaiarchos
        Apolloniou Thriasios (IG II²6250) will be either his or that
        of a homonymous ancestor or descendant; and note also
        Apollonios Threiasios (*sic*) in a catalog of the *genos* of the
        Amynandridai from the last quarter of the first century (IG
        II²2338, line 56).

XYPETE (353-360)

353   *Isarchos Philonos.* SEG 12.100, lines 25-30; buried his fellow
        demesman Theophilos (and his wife), for which the *pōlētai*

of 367/6 adjudicated in his favor a claim for thirty drachmas on Theophilos' house, later "denounced" by Theomnestos of Ionidai. For his brother, and the family as a whole, see **358**.

354   *Kephisios Kephi[s]iou.* IG II²3103, line 10; one of the *kō-mastai* for the deme's victory in the festival of the Tetrakomoi; 330/29.

355   *Lykinos Lykonos.* IG II²3103, line 7; one of the four *kōmar-choi* for the deme's victory in the festival of the Tetrakomoi; 330/29.

356   *Pamphilos* (I) *Aischyto(u).* IG II²3103, lines 5 and 8; both one of the four *kōmarchoi* (line 5) and one of the *kōmastai* (line 8) for the deme's victory in the festival of the Tetrakomoi; 330/29. (His brother **359** also held both posts, the distinction between which is opaque.) Honored by the city of Argos, as *proxenos* and *euergetēs* of the Argives, between ca. 330 and 300: M. Piérart and J.-P. Thalmann, *BCH* Suppl. 6, 1980, pp. 261-269, no. 3 (SEG 30.355). A likely cousin, as Davies noted (*Families*, p. 555), is Pamphilos (II) Melesippou of Xypete, whose name was added to a grave monument in the late fourth century (IG II²7045, lines 13-14); and Prokleides Pamphilou of Xypete, secretary to the *boulē* and *dēmos* in 303/2 (*Agora 15*, no. 62, line 350) will be the son of either Pamphilos (I) or Pamphilos (II): Davies, *Families*, p. 600. See also under **359**.

357   *Peisidamas Peisido(u).* IG II²3103, line 6; one of the four *kōmarchoi* for the deme's victory in the festival of the Te-trakomoi; 330/29.

358   *[Ph]ilai[o]s Philo?n?os* (I) (PA 14219 + 14858). IG II²3103, line 11; one of the *kōmastai* for the deme's victory in the festival of the Tetrakomoi; 330/29. Also attested as *sōphro-nistēs* of Kekropid ephebes in 305/4 (IG II²478, line 33). His father Philon (I) Kleiniou (I), PA 14814 + 14815 + 14857, was *bouleutēs* around the middle of the fourth century (*Agora 15*, no. 18, line 4, with index) and manumittor of a slave in ca. 330 (IG II²1570, line 64); his elder brother Kleinias (II) Phi-lonos (I), PA 8509, was *[diaitē?]tēs* in IG II²1927 (see under Appendix 3, no. 78), lines 17-18; another brother is **353**; and his son Philon (II) Philaiou, PA 14859, was commemorated on a funerary columella of the late fourth century (IG II²6941).

359   *Philton Aischyto(u).* IG II²3103, lines 4 and 9; both one of the four *kōmarchoi* (line 4) and one of the *kōmastai* (line 9) for the deme's victory in the festival of the Tetrakomoi;

330/29. (His brother **356** also held both posts, the distinction between which is opaque.) From the rarity of the name-root Philt- a relationship may be inferred (cf. Davies, *Families*, p. 555) with PA 14785, Philtades Ktesiou (or Ktesikleous) of Xypete, principal trierarch in 322 (IG II²1632, line 243; cf. [Demosth.] 35.20 and 34). See also under **356**.

360   *Pythe*[*as* – – –]. IG II²3103, line 12; one of the *kōmastai* for the deme's victory in the festival of the Tetrakomoi; 330/29.

DEME UNKNOWN (361-368)

361   [*A*]*thenokle*[*s*]. IG II²1212, line 3; co-honorand (with **301**) in a decree of an unidentifiable deme (see Appendix 3, no. 135); end of the fourth century. His demotic ends in -ios (line 4)

362   *Epichares*. SEG 24.154, line 2; honored (as *stratēgos*) by the Rhamnousioi; after 268/7.

363   *Leonteus* (PA 9032). Proposer of IG II²1173 (line 2); before the middle of the fourth century. *If* the deme is Acharnai (cf. Davies, *Families*, p. 36), an Acharnian *bouleutēs* of ca. 321, [Th]rasyll[os] [Λ]εοντέω[ς] (*Agora* 15, no. 54, lines 3-4, the man to whom Davies refers) might be the son of **363**.

364   [*L*]*ykomedes* (PA 9228). IG II²1173, lines 7-8; associate honorand (with **50**); before the middle of the fourth century.

365   *Mantitheos*. The speaker in Lysias 16 (from the period 392-390), where we learn (16.14) of his voluntary *ephodia* to poor fellow demesmen. Of hippic census, he claims a family background of public service (16.20). Davies, *Families*, pp. 364-365 demonstrates that the usual (e.g. under PA 9674) identification of him with Mantitheos of Thorikos (Demosth. 39.27) "is unsafe prosopographically and near to impossible chronologically"; hence his deme is unknown.

366   *Mnesitheos* (PA 10284). IG II²3214; crowned by his (unidentifiable) deme; third century.

367   *Pythodoro*[*s*]. IG II²1211, A, line 9; context (and deme) indeterminable; end of the fourth century. See under **176**.

368   [. . . . ? . . . .]. Proposer of IG II²1209 (line 1); deme unidentifiable; after 319 (see Appendix 3, no. 133).

Proposers of deme decrees: 13, 58, 64, 73, 78, 80, 95, 96, 120, 146, 152, 158, 159, 162, 163, 164, 165, 166, 167, 168, 169, 171, 172, 173, 176, 184, 190, 192, 213, 216, 222, 223, 229, 231, 233, 234,

278, 289, 294, 298, 303, 304, 307, 316, 322, 324, 325, 329, 332, 335, 336, 337, 339, 344, 345, 347, 351, 363, 368. (Total 59)

Honorands in deme decrees: 11, 14, 20, 29, 31, 32, 42, 49, 50, 56, 62, 65, 69, 71, 72, 73, 74, 76, 77, 79, 81, 82, 84, 85, 86, 87, 88, 89, 90, 91, (?)92, 94, 97, 98, 99, 100, 101, 102, 105, 110, 112, 116, 131, 133, 144, 150, 151, 153, 155, 156, 163, 165, 170, 174, (?)177, 178, 179, 180, 181, 182, 183, 184, 185, 186, 187, 188, 189, 190, 191, 193, 194, 195, 196, 197, 198, 199, 200, 201, 202, 203, 204, 205, 207, 208, 210, 214, 215, 219, 226, 230, 232, 279, 280, 290, 292, 293, (?)296, 300, 301, 302, 305, 306, 308, 309, 314, 334, 340, 344, 346, 349, 350, 352, 361, 362, 364, 366. (Total 113-116)

SELECT BIBLIOGRAPHY

———— ✳ ————

To keep this bibliography within reasonable bounds I have excluded from it works to which reference is made only once or twice within any one chapter. Such works are cited fully in footnotes as they occur; the remainder are listed here, under author and short title. See also "Conventions and Abbreviations."

Andrewes, "Reform bill"   A. Andrewes. "Kleisthenes' reform bill." *CQ* 27, 1977, pp. 241-248.

Andreyev, "Agrarian conditions"   V. N. Andreyev. "Some aspects of agrarian conditions in Attica in the fifth to third centuries B.C." *Eirene* 12, 1974, pp. 5-46.

Badian, "Archons"   E. Badian. "Archons and *strategoi*." *Antichthon* 5, 1971, pp. 1-34.

Behrend, *Pachturkunden*   D. Behrend. *Attische Pachturkunden: ein Beitrag zur Beschreibung der μίσθωσις nach der griechischen Inschriften. Vestigia* 12. Munich, 1970.

Bicknell, *Studies*   P. J. Bicknell, *Studies in Athenian Politics and Genealogy. Historia* Einzelschrift 19. Wiesbaden, 1972.

Bicknell, "Pendants"   P. J. Bicknell. "Athenian politics and genealogy: some pendants." *Historia* 23, 1974, pp. 146-163.

Busolt/Swoboda, *Staatskunde*   G. Busolt and H. Swoboda. *Griechische Staatskunde*, vol. 2. Munich, 1926.

Coldstream, *Geometric Pottery*   J. N. Coldstream. *Greek Geometric Pottery*. London, 1968.

Coldstream, *Geometric Greece*   J. N. Coldstream. *Geometric Greece*. London and New York, 1977.

Connor, *Politicians*   W. R. Connor. *The New Politicians of Fifth-Century Athens*. Princeton, 1971.

Damsgaard-Madsen, "Démarques"   A. Damsgaard-Madsen. "Le mode de désignation des démarques attiques au IVᵉ s.av.J.C." In O. S. Due et al., eds., *Classica et Mediaevalia F. Blatt septuagenario dedicata. C&M* diss. 9. Copenhagen, 1973, pp. 92-118.

Daux, "Démarchie"   G. Daux. "La Grande Démarchie: un nouveau calendrier sacrificiel d'Attique." *BCH* 87, 1963, pp. 603-634.

Daux, "Calendrier"   G. Daux. "Le calendrier de Thorikos au Musée J. Paul Getty." *AC* 52, 1983, pp. 150-174.

Davies, *Families*   J. K. Davies. *Athenian Propertied Families 600-300 B.C.* Oxford, 1971.

Davies, "Descent group"   J. K. Davies. "Athenian citizenship: the descent group and the alternatives." *CJ* 73, 1977, pp. 105-121.

Davies, *Wealth*   J. K. Davies. *Wealth and the Power of Wealth in Classical Athens.* New York, 1981.

Deubner, *Feste*   L. Deubner. *Attische Feste.* 2d ed. Revised and enlarged by B. Doer. Berlin, 1966.

Diller, *Race Mixture*   A. Diller. *Race Mixture among the Greeks before Alexander.* Urbana, 1937.

Dover, *Morality*   K. J. Dover. *Greek Popular Morality in the time of Plato and Aristotle.* Oxford, 1974.

Dow, "Demarkhia"   S. Dow. "The Greater Demarkhia of Erkhia." *BCH* 89, 1965, pp. 180-213.

Dow, "Six calendars"   S. Dow, "Six Athenian sacrificial calendars." *BCH* 92, 1968, pp. 170-186.

Dow, "Associates"   S. Dow. "Companionable associates in the Athenian government." In L. Bonfante and H. von Heintze, eds., *In Memoriam Otto J. Brendel: essays in archaeology and the humanities.* Mainz, 1976, pp. 69-84.

Dow/Healey, *Calendar*   S. Dow and R. F. Healey. *A Sacred Calendar of Eleusis. Harvard Theological Studies* 21, 1965.

Dunst, "Opferkalender"   G. Dunst. "Der Opferkalender des attischen Demos Thorikos." *ZPE* 25, 1977, pp. 243-264.

Edwards, *Demesman*   J. B. Edwards. *The Demesman in Attic Life.* Diss. Johns Hopkins, 1914 [1916].

Effenterre, "Mobilisation"   H. van Effenterre. "Clisthène et les mesures de mobilisation." *REG* 89, 1976, pp. 1-17.

Ehrenberg, *People*   V. Ehrenberg. *The People of Aristophanes: a sociology of Old Attic Comedy.* 2d ed. Oxford, 1951.

Eliot, *Coastal Demes*   C.W.J. Eliot. *Coastal Demes of Attika: a study in the policy of Kleisthenes. Phoenix* Supplement 5. Toronto, 1962.

Feaver, "Priesthoods"   D. D. Feaver. "Historical development in the priesthoods of Athens." *YClS* 15, 1957, pp. 123-158.

Finley, *Land and Credit*   M. I. Finley. *Studies in Land and Credit in ancient Athens 500-200 B.C.: the horos-inscriptions.* New Brunswick, 1952.

Gomme, *Population*   A. W. Gomme. *The Population of Athens in the fifth and fourth centuries B.C.* Oxford, 1933.

Gomme, "Problems"   A. W. Gomme. "Two problems of Athenian citizenship law." *CPh* 29, 1934, pp. 123-140.

Gomme/Sandbach, *Menander*   A. W. Gomme and F. H. Sandbach. *Menander: a commentary*. Oxford, 1973.

Habicht, *Untersuchungen*   C. Habicht. *Untersuchungen zur politischen Geschichte Athens im 3 Jahrhundert v. Chr. Vestigia* 30. Munich, 1979.

Hansen, "*Archai*"   M. H. Hansen. "Seven hundred *archai* in classical Athens." *GRBS* 21, 1980, pp. 151-173.

Hansen, "Political activity"   M. H. Hansen. "Political activity and the organization of Attica in the fourth century B.C." *GRBS* 24, 1983, pp. 227-238.

Harrison, *Law* I and II   A.R.W. Harrison. *The Law of Athens*. Volumes 1 (*The Family and Property*) and 2 (*Procedure*, ed. D. M. MacDowell). Oxford, 1968 and 1971.

Haussoullier, *Vie*   B. Haussoullier. *La Vie Municipale en Attique: essai sur l'organisation des dèmes au quatrième siècle*. Paris, 1884.

Headlam, *Election*   J. W. Headlam. *Election by Lot at Athens*. 2d ed. Revised with notes by D. C. Macgregor. Cambridge, 1933.

Hignett, *Constitution*   C. Hignett. *A History of the Athenian Constitution to the end of the fifth century B.C.* Oxford, 1952.

Hopper, *Basis*   R. J. Hopper. *The Basis of the Athenian Democracy*. Sheffield University Inaugural Lecture. Sheffield, 1957.

Jameson, "Calendar"   M. H. Jameson. "Notes on the sacrificial calendar from Erchia." *BCH* 89, 1965, pp. 154-172.

Jameson, "Leasing"   M. H. Jameson. "The leasing of land in Rhamnous." *Hesp.* Supplement 19, Princeton, 1982, pp. 66-74.

Jeffery, *Archaic Greece*   L. H. Jeffery. *Archaic Greece: the city-states c.700-500 B.C.* London and New York, 1976.

Kahrstedt, *Staatsgebiet*   U. Kahrstedt. *Staatsgebiet und Staatsangehörige in Athen*. Stuttgart and Berlin, 1934.

Kroll, *Allotment Plates*   J. H. Kroll. *Athenian Bronze Allotment Plates*. Cambridge, Mass., 1972.

Kussmaul, *Synthekai*   P. Kussmaul. *Synthekai: Beiträge zur Geschichte des attischen Obligationenrechtes*. Diss. Basel, 1969.

Labarbe, *Thorikos*   J. Labarbe. *Thorikos: les testimonia*. Comité des fouilles belges en Grèce. Fouilles de Thorikos 1. Ghent, 1977.

Lacey, *Family*   W. K. Lacey. *The Family in Classical Greece*. London, 1968.

Lang, "Allotment"   M. L. Lang. "Allotment by tokens." *Historia* 8, 1959, pp. 80-89.

Latte, *"Askoliasmos"*   K. Latte. *"Askoliasmos."* Hermes 85, 1957, pp. 385-391.

Lewis, "Cleisthenes"   D. M. Lewis. "Cleisthenes and Attica." *Historia* 12, 1963, pp. 22-40.

MacDowell, *Law*   D. M. MacDowell. *The Law in Classical Athens.* London, 1978.

Meritt, "Archons"   B. D. Meritt. "Athenian archons 347/6-48/7 B.C." *Historia* 22, 1977, pp. 161-191.

Mikalson, *Calendar*   J. D. Mikalson. *The Sacred and Civil Calendar of the Athenian Year.* Princeton, 1975.

Mikalson, "Religion"   J. D. Mikalson. "Religion in the Attic demes." *AJPh* 98, 1977, pp. 424-435.

Müller, *de demis*   H.A.O. Müller, *de demis atticis.* Diss. Göttingen (but published Nordhausen), 1880.

Murray, *Early Greece*   O. Murray. *Early Greece,* Brighton (Sussex) and Atlantic Highlands, N.J., 1980.

Nemes, "Public property"   Z. Nemes. "The public property of demes in Attica." *ACD* 16, 1980, pp. 3-8.

Osborne, *Demos*   R. G. Osborne. *Demos: the discovery of classical Attika.* Cambridge, 1985.

Ostwald, *Nomos*   M. Ostwald. *Nomos and the Beginnings of the Athenian Democracy.* Oxford, 1969.

Parke, *Festivals*   H. W. Parke. *Festivals of the Athenians.* London, 1977.

Patterson, *Citizenship Law*   C. Patterson. *Pericles' Citizenship Law of 451-50 B.C.* New York, 1981.

Pickard-Cambridge, *Festivals*   A. W. Pickard-Cambridge. *The Dramatic Festivals of Athens.* 2d ed. Revised by J.P.A. Gould and D. M. Lewis. Oxford, 1968.

Pouilloux, *Forteresse*   J. Pouilloux. *La Forteresse de Rhamnonte: étude de topographie et d'histoire.* Paris, 1954.

Raubitschek, *Dedications*   A. E. Raubitschek (with L. H. Jeffery). *Dedications from the Athenian Akropolis.* Cambridge, Mass., 1949.

Rhodes, *Boule*   P. J. Rhodes. *The Athenian Boule.* Oxford, 1972.

Rhodes, *Commentary*   P. J. Rhodes. *A Commentary on the Aristotelian Athenaion Politeia.* Oxford, 1981.

Richardson, "Epakria"   R. B. Richardson. "A sacrificial calendar from the Epakria." *AJA* 10, 1895, pp. 209-226.

Schoeffer, "Demarchoi"   V. von Schoeffer. "Demarchoi (1)." *RE* 4.2, 1901, cols. 2706-2711.

Schoeffer, "Demoi"   V. von Schoeffer. "Demoi." *RE* 5.1, 1903, cols. 1-131.

Snodgrass, *Archaic Greece*   A. M. Snodgrass. *Archaic Greece: the age of experiment*. London, 1980.

Solders, *Kulte*   S. Solders. *Die ausserstädtischen Kulte und die Einigung Attikas*. Lund, 1931.

Staveley, *Elections*   E. S. Staveley. *Greek and Roman Voting and Elections*. London, 1972.

Sundwall, *Beiträge*   J. Sundwall. *Epigraphische Beiträge zur sozial-politischen Geschichte Athens im Zeitalter des Demosthenes*. *Klio* Beiheft 4, 1906.

Thompson, "Deme"   W. E. Thompson. "The deme in Kleisthenes' reforms." *SO* 46, 1971, pp. 72-79.

Traill, *Organization*   J. S. Traill. *The Political Organization of Attica: a study of the demes, trittyes, and phylai, and their representation in the Athenian council*. *Hesp.* Supplement 14, Princeton, 1975.

Walbank, "Confiscation"   M. B. Walbank. "The confiscation and sale by the poletai in 402/1 B.C. of the property of the Thirty Tyrants." *Hesp.* 51, 1982, pp. 74-98.

Whitehead, *Metic*   D. Whitehead. *The Ideology of the Athenian Metic*. *PCPhS* Supplementary volume 4. Cambridge, 1977.

Whitehead, "Demarchs"   D. Whitehead. "Notes on Athenian demarchs." *ZPE* 47, 1982, pp. 37-42.

Whitehead, "*Philotimia*"   D. Whitehead. "Competitive outlay and community profit: *philotimia* in democratic Athens." *C&M* 34, 1983, pp. 55-74.

Wilamowitz, *Aristoteles*   U. von Wilamowitz-Moellendorff. *Aristoteles und Athen*. Berlin, 1893. References to the second of the two vols. unless otherwise stated.

Wycherley, *Stones*   R. E. Wycherley. *The Stones of Athens*. Princeton, 1978.

INDEX OF PASSAGES CITED

An all-embracing *index locorum* for this book would be elephantine, and of questionable value. This one accordingly restricts itself to what may be reckoned a (substantial) central core of literary and epigraphic documentation.

LITERARY TEXTS

Aeschines

1.63: 233
1.77-78: 106
1.86: 106, 294
1.114: 106
1.114-115: 107, 295-296
1.157: 152, 212, 213, 216
2.150: 227
2.182: 106
3.30: 110, 271
3.41-45: 222, 257
scholia to 1.43: 212
scholia to 1.77: 106

Alexis

fr. 203: 339
fr. 285: 339

Anaxandrides (Comicus)

fr. 4: 259, 292, 293, 294, 340, 342, 359
fr. 41: 339

Andocides

1.83-84: 40, 49, 110
1.97: 40, 49, 109, 269
fr. 5 Sauppe: 49, 400

Antiphanes (Comicus)

fr. 176: 339
fr. 206: 339

Antiphon

6.12: 49, 229
fr. 67: 49, 68

Archippus

fr. 27: 331

Aristophanes

Acharnians
  lines 32-34: 332, 336, 351
  lines 201-202: 336
  line 234: 335
  lines 237-279: 213-214, 336
  lines 266-267: 336
  lines 325-349: 232, 337
  line 406: 332
  line 605: 333
  line 855: 229, 333
  line 901: 334
  line 1028: 333
  scholia to line 406: 332

Birds
  line 76: 334
  lines 475-476: 335
  line 496: 333
  line 645: 333
  line 1126: 336
  scholia to line 645: 51, 208, 210
  scholia to line 997: 28, 87

Clouds
  line 37: 126, 332, 337
  line 134: 74, 127, 333, 355

EPIGRAPHIC TEXTS

INDEX OF DEMES

———————— ✳ ————————

GENERAL INDEX

Library of Congress Cataloging-in-Publication Data

Whitehead, David, Ph.D.
The demes of Attica, 508/7-ca. 250 B.C.

Bibliography: p.   Includes indexes.
1. Greece—Politics and government—To 146 B.C.
2. Attikí (Greece)—Politics and government.
3. Attikí (Greece)—Social conditions.   4. Local
government—Greece—Attikí.   I. Title.
DF82.W47 1985   938   85-42709
ISBN 0-691-09412-8 (alk. paper)